Japanese Capitals in Historical Perspective

Place, Power and Memory in Kyoto, Edo and Tokyo

Edited by
Nicolas Fiévé and Paul Waley

First Published in 2003
by RoutledgeCurzon
11 New Fetter Lane, London EC4P 4EE

Simultaneously published in the USA and Canada
by RoutledgeCurzon
29 West 35th Street, New York, NY 10001

RoutledgeCurzon is an imprint of the Taylor & Francis Group

Editorial Matter © 2003 Nicolas Fiévé and Paul Waley

Typeset in Sabon by LaserScript Ltd, Mitcham, Surrey

Printed and bound in Great Britain by
Antony Rowe Ltd, Chippenham, Wiltshire

All rights reserved. No part of this book may be reprinted or reproduced or utilised in any form or by any electronic, mechanical, or other means, now known or hereafter invented, including photocopying and recording, or in any information storage or retrieval system, without permission in writing from the publishers.

British Library Cataloguing in Publication Data
A catalogue record of this book is available from the British Library

Library of Congress Cataloging in Publication Data
A catalog record for this book has been requested

ISBN 0–7007–1409–X

Contents

List of illustrations vii
List of contributors xi

Introduction: Kyoto and Edo-Tokyo: Urban Histories in Parallels
  and Tangents 1
  Paul Waley and Nicolas Fiévé

PART ONE: Power and the Spatial Imprints of Authority

 1 Castles in Kyoto at the Close of the Age of Warring States:
    The Urban Fortresses of the Ashikaga Shoguns Yoshiteru and
    Yoshiaki 41
    Takahashi Yasuo, with Matthew Stavros

 2 Social Discrimination and Architectural Freedom in the Pleasure
    District of Kyoto in Early Modern Japan 67
    Nicolas Fiévé

 3 Urbanisation and the Nature of the Tokugawa Hegemony 100
    Beatrice M. Bodart-Bailey

 4 Metaphors of the Metropolis: Architectural and Artistic
    Representations of the Identity of Edo 129
    William H. Coaldrake

PART TWO: Memory and the Changing Passage of Space

 5 Kyoto's Famous Places: Collective Memory and 'Monuments'
    in the Tokugawa Period 153
    Nicolas Fiévé

Contents

<table>
<tr><td>6</td><td>Representing Mobility in Tokugawa and Meiji Japan
Jilly Traganou</td><td>172</td></tr>
<tr><td>7</td><td>By Ferry to Factory: Crossing Tokyo's Great River into a New World
Paul Waley</td><td>208</td></tr>
<tr><td>8</td><td>From a Shogunal City to a Life City: Tokyo between Two Fin-de-siècles
Mikako Iwatake</td><td>233</td></tr>
<tr><td>9</td><td>Time Perception, or the Ineluctable Aging of Material in Architecture
Murielle Hladik</td><td>257</td></tr>
</table>

PART THREE: Place Between Future and Past

<table>
<tr><td>10</td><td>The Past in Tokyo's Future: Kōda Rohan's Thoughts on Urban Reform and the New Citizen in *Ikkoku no shuto* (One nation's capital)
Evelyn Schulz</td><td>283</td></tr>
<tr><td>11</td><td>Visionary Plans and Planners: Japanese Traditions and Western Influences
Carola Hein</td><td>309</td></tr>
<tr><td>12</td><td>Kyoto and the Preservation of Urban Landscapes
Yamasaki Masafumi, with Paul Waley</td><td>347</td></tr>
<tr><td>13</td><td>Preservation and Revitalization of *machiya* in Kyoto
Kinoshita Ryōichi</td><td>367</td></tr>
<tr><td>14</td><td>Conclusion: Power, Memory, and Place
Paul Waley</td><td>385</td></tr>
</table>

Glossary   392
Index   405

List of illustrations

1 '*Rakuyō narabini rakugai no zu*' (Map of the streetcapes of the capital and its surroundings), showing Kyoto in 1653.   13
2 Edo, early to mid nineteenth century.   18
3 '*Genkon Kyōto shigai-zu*' (Map of the present streets in Kyoto), showing Kyoto in 1894.   24–25
4 Map of Yamashiro province in 1894.   27
5 The fifteen wards of Tokyo, approximately 1920, and main railways.   28
6 Late sixteenth century Kyoto (circa 1570).   48
7 Kyōto in the seventeenth century.   72–73
8 Inoue Shunjosai '*Shimabara shōkei: shiki no nagame*' (Picturesque landscape of Shimabara: contemplation of the four seasons), woodblock print, 1839.   78–79
9 Contemporary layout of the Sumiya *ageya*.   81
10 Outside view of the Wachigaiya *okiya* (built in 1857).   83
11 Outside view of the Wachigaiya *okiya* (built in 1857).   84
12 Inside garden of the Sumiya with the *garyō* pine tree.   87
13 Outside view of Sumiya *ageya* (Tokugawa period).   88
14 Outside view of Sumiya *ageya* (Tokugawa period).   89
15 Nishimura Chūwa, Sakuma Sōen, and Oku Bunmei, '*Shimabara*.' From Akizato Ritō's *Miyako rinsen meishō zue*, vol. 5 (1799).   90

List of illustrations

16 Inside view of the Sumiya. *Tokonoma* of the *Misu no ma*. 93
17 Inside view of the Sumiya. Windows of the *Aogai no ma*. 96
18 Map of Minaguchi, believed to be from after the Kyōhō era (1716–36). Note the castle in the lower left corner and temples at some distance from the town in the upper part of the map. 104
19 Section of a map of Edo from the Kyōhō era (1716–36) showing the Tokiwabashi gate at the outer moat in the lower part and the Ōtemon gate at the inner moat in the upper part of the map. 114
20 Simplified map showing the shogun's route on leaving Edo Castle for Ueno. 123
21 Nishi Honganji Karamon. Front and side elevations. 132
22 Karamon, Tōshōgū, Nikkō. 134
23 *Edozu byōbu*. Detail of the right two panels of the left screen showing Edo Castle and vicinity. 135
24 *Edo meishozu byōbu*. Detail of the right four panels of the right-hand screen. 136
25 *Aobyōshi*. Detail of *daimyō* gatehouse styles and regulations. 141
26 Ikedamon. Precincts of Tokyo National Museum. 142
27 Rōjūmon. Chiba Prefecture. 142
28 Hiroshige, '*Shichū han'ei Tanabata matsuri*' (The city flourishing, Tanabata festival), *Meisho Edo hyakkei* (One hundred famous views of Edo). 145
29 Hiroshige, '*Yamashita-chō Hibiya Soto-Sakurada*' (Hibiya and Soto-Sakurada from Yamashita-chō), *Meisho Edo hyakkei* (One hundred famous views of Edo). 147
30 Nishimura Chūwa, Sakuma Sōen, and Oku Bunmei '*Sumiya, yukigeshiki*' (Snow landscape at the Sumiya house). 160
31 Takehara Shinkei (Shunchōsai) '*Sumiya*' (the Sumiya house). 160
32 '*Shimabara*.' From Nakagawa Kiun's *Kyō warabe* (The child of the capital), 1658, vol. 2. 161
33 '*Shijō-gawara*.' From Nakagawa Kiun's *Kyō warabe* (The child of the capital), 1658, vol. 1. 161
34 '*Nijō no shiro*' (Nijō Castle). From Nakagawa Kiun's *Kyō warabe* (The child of the capital), 1658, vol. 2. 166
35 Ichikochi Dōin and Hishikawa Moronobu, '*Tōkaidō kōmoku bunken no zu*' (Proportional map of the Tōkaidō in detail), 1690. 179

List of illustrations

36 Ichikochi Dōin, '*Tōkaidō bunken ezu*' (Proportional map of the Tōkaidō), 1752. 179

37 Bakufu Dōchū Bugyōsho (Magistrate of the Bakufu), '*Tōkaidō bunken nobe ezu*' (Proportional linear map of the Tōkaidō), 1806. 182

38 Hokusai, '*Tōkaidō meisho ichiran*' (Famous places of the Tōkaidō at a glance), 1818. 186

39 Kuwagata Shōi, '*Tōkaidō saiken ōezu*', (Large picture map with detailed views of the Tōkaidō), mid nineteenth century. 186

40 Kuwagata Keisai, '*Nihon meisho no e*' (A picture of the famous places of Japan), early nineteenth century. 187

41 Tenshodō (Publisher), '*Tetsudō senro chinsen ritei hyō*' (Railway distances and fares chart), 1898. 190–191

42 Teishinshō Tetsudōkyoku (Communications Ministry, Railways Office) (Publisher), '*Dai Nihon tetsudō senro zenzu*' (General railway map of Japan), 1902. 193

43 Ferries and bridges across the Sumida from Senju bridge downstream, *ca.* 1860–1910. 211

44 The Sumida river and the entrance to Sanyabori canal showing the Takeya ferry landing stage and various types of river craft. Ogawa Isshin, *Scenes in the Eastern Capital of Japan* (1911). 212

45 The Oumaya quay, Komagata hall, and distant view of Kinryūzan temple. Hiroshige, *Ehon Edo miyage* (Illustrated books of Edo souvenirs). 219

46 30th Anniversary of Tokyo. Ueno on the day of the festival. *Fūzoku gahō*, 25 April 1898. 241

47 30th Anniversary of Tokyo. Nihonbashi on the day of the festival. *Fūzoku gahō*, 25 April 1898. 242

48 Ise Shrine. 260

49 Walls of Ryōanji. 265

50 Detail of a rafter. Manshū'in Kyōto. 266

51 Basement of pillar. Tōkōji temple in Hagi (built in 1698). 267

52 Utida Yosikazu, Utida Yosifumi, Takayama Eika, *et al.*, 'Urban Plan for Datong,' 1939. 318

53 'Reconstruction Plan of Nagoya,' 1946. 320

List of illustrations

54 Ishikawa Hideaki, 'Satellite Cities Concept,' 1946. 324
55 Utida Yosifumi, 'Proposal for the rebuilding of Shinjuku,' (*Teito fukkō keikaku Shinjuku-chiku*) 1946. 326
56 Takayama Eika, Tange Kenzō, Ikebe Kiyoshi, Asada Takashi, Ōtani Sachio, 'Proposal for the Hongō educational district,' 1946. 328
57 Tōge Sankichi, 'Hiroshima in 1965.' 329
58 Tange Kenzō *et al.*, 'Hiroshima City Reconstruction Plan and Land Use Plan,' 1947. 331
59 Tange Kenzō *et al.*, 'Model of the competition project for the peace park,' (1st prize) 1949. 332
60 Nishiyama Uzō, 'Monument for the Greater Asian Hemisphere,' 1942. 335
61 Nishiyama 'Cities on mountain slopes,' 1946. 336
62 Nishiyama Uzō, Neighborhood unit, 1946. 340
63 Nishiyama Uzō, Zoning of a metropolis, 1946. 341
64 Map showing Conservation Zones and Preservation of Suburban Green Districts in and around Kyoto. 349
65 Map of urban landscape zoning in Kyoto. 352
66 Map of Aesthetic Zones in Kyoto. 354
67 Adjustment models for Aesthetic Zones 1 and 2. 355
68 Adjustment models for Aesthetic Zones 3, 4, and 5. 356
69 Recently built, traditional *machiya*-style shop, Kyoto. 370
70 Destruction of a traditional *machiya*. 375
71 Disappearance of traditional urban landscape of the Kyoto *machiya*. 376
72 Layout of the Hata residence (first floor) (Shimogyō-ku, Kyoto). 380
73 Layout of a traditional Kyoto *machiya* (ground floor and first floor). 381
74 Section of a traditional Kyoto *machiya*. 382
75 Model for modernization of a traditional *machiya*. Momochitarukan, Kyoto. 382

Contributors

Beatrice M. Bodart-Bailey is professor of Japanese history in the Department of Comparative Culture of Ôtsuma Women's University, Tokyo. She has written extensively about the government of the fifth Tokugawa shogun, and has recently published a new annotated translation of Engelbert Kaempfer's seventeenth-century report on Japan.

William H. Coaldrake is foundation professor of Japanese at the University of Melbourne. He received his doctorate from Harvard University in the history of Japanese architecture. His publications include *The Way of the Carpenter: Tools and Japanese Architecture* (Weatherhill, 1990), based on his experiences as a member of the Kyoto Guild of Traditional Master Builders, and *Architecture and Authority in Japan* (Routledge, 1996).

Nicolas Fiévé is Researcher in Japanese civilization at C.N.R.S., Institut des Hautes Etudes Japonaises, in Paris, France. His work has focused largely on medieval and premodern architecture and urbanism in Kyoto. His major publication *L'architecture et la ville du Japon ancien. Espace architectural de la ville de Kyôto et des résidences shôgunales aux XIVe et XVe siècles* received in 1997 the Shibasawa-Claudel Prize and the Giles Prize from the French *Académie des Inscriptions et Belles Lettres*. He is currently coordinator of a project to compile a historical, urban and architectural atlas of Kyoto. He is also involved in research on the evolution of the urban landscape of modern Kyoto.

Carola Hein is assistant professor at Bryn Mawr College in the Program in Growth and Structure of Cities. She obtained her doctorate at the Hochschule für bildende Künste in 1995 on the topic of 'Hauptstadt

Europa.' She has published and lectured widely on topics of architectural and urban planning history and actuality. From 1995 to 1999 she was a Visiting Researcher at Tokyo Metropolitan University and Kogakuin University researching on the reconstruction of Japanese cities after World War II and the Western influence on Japanese urban planning. In October 2001, she organized a conference on the reconstruction of Japanese Cities at Bryn Mawr College with the support of the Japan Foundation and is working (together with Ishida Yorifusa and Jeffry Diefendorf) on the publication of an edited volume on the topic.

Murielle Hladik is an architect (D.P.L.G., Ecole d'Architecture de Paris-La-Villette, 1995). She was research fellow at Kyoto University (1995–97), where she conducted research into degradation and the conservation of traditional buildings leading her to an aesthetic and philosophical interpretation of 'patina' and the specificity of time perception in Japan. She coordinated a French-Japanese symposium on 'Crossed Views on Architecture and the City' (Paris, March 2000). She is currently a doctoral candidate in the Department of Philosophy, Université de Paris 8.

Mikako Iwatake obtained her Ph.D. from the University of Pennsylvania in 1993. She is a visiting associate professor at the Center for International Education, Waseda University in Tokyo, where she teaches anthropology courses. Her current research interests include historical and spatial aspects of Tokyo, folklore studies as intellectual history, and ethnography in Finnish Karelia.

Kinoshita Ryōichi is an architect specializing in the design and restoration of traditional Japanese wooden buildings. He is especially involved in the preservation of the wooden town-houses of Kyoto known as '*kyô-machiya*.' Kinoshita is a leading member of several Kyoto-based NGOs including the Kyoto Townhouse Revitalization Society, Kyoto Mitate, the Kyoto Architectural Craftsmen's Guild, and the Kyoto International Committee of Art and Cultural Exchange.

Evelyn Schulz is professor at Universität München and was formerly associate professor at the Institute of East Asian Studies, University of Zurich. She obtained her Ph.D. in 1995 at University of Heidelberg (title of her dissertation: 'Diary of One who Returned to Japan [*Kichōsha no nikki*] [1909] by Nagai Kafū: The Conception of Aesthetic Counterworlds as a Means of Criticising Japan's Modernization'). Specialized in modern Japanese literature, she is especially interested in the relationship between urban space and text as well as discourses on modernity and the city. She recently completed work on her habilitation thesis, 'Reports about the Prosperity of Tokyo' [*Tōkyō hanjō ki*]: A Genre of Japan's Topographical Literature and its Images of Tokyo' (2000).

Contributors

Matthew Stavros is a doctoral candidate in the Department of East Asian Studies, Princeton University. Specializing in premodern Japanese history, his research interests include medieval urban history, fortified architecture, castle-towns (*jōkamachi*), and the analysis of space as a function of power.

Takahashi Yasuo is professor of Engineering at Kyoto University. Specializing in Japanese urban and architectural history, his work has largely focused on medieval Kyoto with major publications including: *Kyōto chūsei toshi-shi kenkyū* (Research on the medieval history of Kyoto), and *Rakuchū rakugai: kankyō bunka no chūsei-shi* (The capital and its environs: environmental culture in medieval history). Among books edited are: *Nihon toshi-shi nyūmon* (Introduction to Japanese urban history) and *Zushū: Nihon toshi-shi* (Illustrated history of Japanese cities). His most recent publication is a book on traditional homes (*machiya*) in Kyoto.

Jilly Traganou is a lecturer at the University of Texas at Austin. She obtained her doctorate in Architecture in 1998, at the University of Westminster in London, UK. The title of her dissertation was 'The Transformations of the Tōkaidō from the Edo to the Meiji Period.' Her theoretical work focuses mainly on issues of spatial representation and the travelling culture of Japan. Currently she is working on a book about representation of the Tōkaidō in Tokugawa and Meiji Japan.

Paul Waley is a senior lecturer in Human Geography at the University of Leeds. He has a longstanding research interest in the historical geography of Edo-Tokyo, and has written copiously on the city for both a general as well as an academic readership. He is currently involved in research on river restoration and public participation in river basin networks, and he writes and researches more generally on landscape and on planning issues in contemporary Japan. He is co-editor of the *European Journal of East Asian Studies*.

Yamasaki Masafumi is currently a professor at Ritsumeikan University. He has worked for conservation of Japanese historic townscapes mainly in the Kansai region including Kyoto. He is the author of a number of reports and policy proposals on conservation plans of historical areas in Japanese cities. He has written a history of the urban landscape of Kyoto and is now engaged in research on urban design in *jōkamachi*, castle-towns.

Introduction

Kyoto and Edo-Tokyo: Urban Histories in Parallels and Tangents

Paul Waley and Nicolas Fiévé

A Divided History

For a number of years now, politicians in Japan have been discussing a relocation of the national capital away from Tokyo. Whether any such move will really resolve the problems caused by concentration at the centre is doubtful, and it is quite likely that if the politicians and bureaucrats ever pack their bags and prepare for a move, events will have rendered the relocation irrelevant. This will not be the first time, however, that the capital of Japan is moved from one place to another. On the contrary, Japan's capital has moved several times, as often, if not more so, than in any other country of comparable size. Having said that, there are only two cities whose historical weight and importance as capitals counts, Kyoto and Edo-Tokyo, and it is with these two cities, as well as the road that linked them, that this book is principally concerned.

In bringing together a number of contributions on the two great urban centres of Japan (forming with Osaka a triumvirate of cities), this book constitutes something of a rarity in the historiography of Japanese urbanism, both in Japanese and other languages. Books on Japanese urban history have tended to be segmentalised. Few individual writers have extended their purview beyond a scholarly base camp; this spatial retiscence has been matched by a hesitance to cross temporal dividing lines. If you write about *chūsei* (medieval) Kyoto, you leave *kinsei* (early modern) Kyoto well alone. Similarly with Edo-Tokyo. Few historians have been ambitious enough to attempt to tell a story that straddles the change of regime of 1868. This reluctance can be attributed in part to the different nature of the archival material concerned and in part to the staking of intellectual territory by communities of scholars based in national universities with local roots. No doubt there are additional reasons too. Among the few Japanese historians who have attempted a work of global synthesis, the names of Nishikawa Kōji and Yazaki Takeo stand out for the breadth of their vision, although both their works in question are now somewhat dated (Nishikawa 1972; Yazaki 1968).

This book has its origins in a session of the conference of the European Association of Japanese Studies held in Budapest in 1997, where nine of the contributors presented papers. It is this genesis in a conference that no doubt helps to explain our lack of temerity in treating the two great cities over such a long time span. The first chapter in this book, written by Takahashi Yasuo with Matthew Stavros, deals with change in the style of castle construction and its significance for evolving power structures in mid sixteenth century Kyoto. The final two chapters, by Yamasaki Masafumi and Kinoshita Ryōichi, discuss issues surrounding the preservation of landscape and conservation of wooden buildings in contemporary Kyoto. It is equally the wide disciplinary background of the contributors to this book that has allowed us to stray beyond the customary pathways of Japanese historiography. Architectural historians form the core (Fiévé, Takahashi, Coaldrake, Traganou, and Hladik fall into this category), but others are geographers (Waley), historians (Bodart-Bailey), literary historians (Schulz), anthropologists (Iwatake), historians of planning (Hein), and planners (Yamasaki). Kinoshita is the only practicing architect, but Takahashi, Yamasaki, Hladik, Hein, Traganou, and Fiévé are all trained as architects. Notwithstanding this diversity, however, the chapters of this book share an appreciation of the importance of the spatial composition of cities and the intricate interplay between power as the arbiter of spatial forms, between memory and the representation of spaces and their designation as place, and between places caught between a past preserved in their form and a future seeking to fix new forms. The following pages of the introduction are designed principally to serve as a background to the history of Kyoto and Edo-Tokyo and to connect and contextualize the various chapters. They conclude with a brief consideration of the relationship between these two capital cities.

Kyoto

For more than ten centuries, from 794, the city of Kyoto was the Japanese imperial capital, until 1869 when the Emperor transferred his permanent residence to Tokyo, which immediately became the *de facto* capital of Japan. Right up until the beginning of the seventeenth century, Kyoto had enjoyed a unique status, not just as the imperial city but also as the only major agglomeration in a country which was otherwise largely rural in character. It was only towards the end of the sixteenth century that urban agglomerations began to develop more widely throughout Japan. What would later become the basis for the infrastructure of today's towns and cities began as 'quarters under the castle' (*jōkamachi*), as 'harbour quarters' (*minatomachi*), and as 'quarters built within the temple precincts' (*jinaichō*) (Nishikawa 1972: 167–323; Nakai 1991: 519–37; McClain 1982).

For centuries, then, Kyoto was the seat of power in Japan – political, spiritual, cultural, and even economic power. This is why any historian who wants to explore the period between 794 and 1600 is obliged to study Kyoto in one way or another. There are only a limited numbers of works in Western languages that explore aspects of the history of the city. Among the best known of these are the studies by Ivan Morris (1964, 1980) and Francine Hérail (1991, 1995) on the cultural life of Heian, the ancient capital; Mary Elizabeth Berry's monograph on *The Culture of Civil War in Kyoto* (1994); and the numerous articles on medieval and early modern history by John W. Hall and Jeffery P. Mass – to quote the best known authors.

However, to find a Western study that attempts to give a comprehensive overview of all of Kyoto's eleven centuries of history, we have to turn to the four articles written in the 1920s by Richard Ponsonby-Fane (1878–1937), which were published together in 1956 under the title *Kyoto the Old Capital of Japan (794–1869)*. This peerless compilation offers the kind of detailed descriptions that could only have been written by someone with a passionate interest in the city. Ponsonby-Fane focuses on what for him was the essential question: what did this city look like? By way of answer he undertook a systematic study, era by era, of the capital's 'monuments,' the various government buildings, palaces, Buddhist temples, Shinto shrines, and even the bridges and schools which date from the early modern era. He established these descriptions on the basis of historical texts, such as the local gazetteers of Kyoto (see the chapter on the famous places of Kyoto by Fiévé) and the *Heian Tsūshi* (Complete annals of Heian; 1895), a compilation written under the auspices of the municipal authorities and published to celebrate the 1100th anniversary of Kyoto's existence. Rather than attempting to offer an explanation of the mechanics of urban evolution, Ponsonby-Fane adopted the Sino-Japanese tradition of 'listing,' and indeed to Western readers what he offers may seem to be no more than an inventory. However, because he complements this with a concise but comprehensive chronology of the principal events in Kyoto's history, he manages to offer Western readers an insight into the significance of the city's 'monuments.' Ponsonby-Fane's work is a veritable encyclopaedia of the various sites that were centres of power in Kyoto; nevertheless, it cannot be described as 'urban history' in the sense that Braudel intended, nor does he attempt to deal with urban change as a function of the economic, social, political, and cultural evolutions that the city underwent.

This is why John W. Hall's article 'Kyoto as historical background' (1974) can be said to fill a lacuna, offering for the first time a synthesis of the various studies of Kyoto's history. Building on what had become classic works, such as those of Yazaki (1962) on the development of Japanese towns, or the earlier volumes of *Kyōto no rekishi* (The History of Kyoto 10 vols; 1968 to 1976), Hall demonstrates how the various stages in urban development were the direct consequence of corresponding evolutions in political power, and how these in turn were a reflection of the profound changes that were taking place in the economic character of Japanese society. When Heian was founded, it was an imperial city; the very way in which the city took material form exemplifies aristocratic power (*kuge*) which was then at its zenith. When we reach the twelfth century and see how Heian evolved progressively into the medieval *miyako*, we find that a new city took shape, torn between the contradictory but complementary powers of the civil aristocracy, the military aristocracy, religious institutions, and the emerging merchant class. Later, during the Tokugawa period (1603–1867), when there was a flourishing merchant bourgeoisie in the major cities – Kyoto as well as Edo and Osaka – Hall underlines that, as far as Kyoto was concerned, it was the political authority of the shogunate as expressed in the decisions of the governor of Kyoto (*Kyōto shoshidai*) which regulated not only the life of the aristocrats but also of the commoners, who were now disenfranchised from all political activity.

While it is true that the various different expressions of power were to have unavoidable consequences for the development of urban planning and development, at the same time each new stage in this development found expression in different and specific forms of urban layout. It is these very differences, still visible today, which give contemporary Kyoto its rich architectural tapestry. As the only major Japanese city not to have suffered from bombing during the Second World War, Kyoto offers in microcosm an exceptional example of a whole range of styles of Japanese urbanism – from aristocratic, through medieval, to early modern and modern – all superimposed. Our knowledge of this heritage has been greatly enriched in the past decade, thanks to a number of Japanese-language studies on urban history, of which the volume by Nishikawa K. and Takahashi T. (1997) is pre-eminent and in particular some especially rich work on the medieval period (for example, Amino 1995; Gomi 1996; Takahashi Y. 1993).

Heian, The Great Aristocratic Capital of the Heian Period

Kyoto is situated in a basin-shaped plain, protected by forested mountains to east, north, and west. Mount Hiei (to the north-east) is 848 metres high, and Mount Atagoyama (to the north-west) is 924 metres high, whereas the average height of the plain is just 50 metres. Two rivers border the plain, both flowing to the south: the River Katsura (formerly known as River Kadono) and the River Kamo.

Originally, in 784 the nearby area of Nagaoka had been chosen as the site for a new capital and building work had begun, but after a series of events which were judged inauspicious the work was abandoned, and a new site at Uda in the Kadono district was designated instead. According to the *Onmyōdō*, based on the ancient rules of Chinese geomancy, the natural characteristics of this plain made it an ideal site in which to construct the Imperial Palace. However appropriate the natural space, it still needed to be invested with symbolic meaning, so that the both cosmogonic space for which it would become the physical symbol and the site of the Palace would be 'pleasing to the four gods' (*shijin sōō*) who inhabited each of the four quadrants. Four natural features were deemed to correspond to these cosmographic figures: the Kamo River to the east, the highways to the west, the Ogura Lake to the south, and Mount Funaoka to the north. The emperor himself was symbolically associated with the Pole Star.

Heian, the new capital (founded in 794), just like its predecessor Heijō (modern-day Nara, which was the capital city from 710 to 784), was based on the contemporary model of the city of Chang'an: that is, the great Chinese capital begun during the Sui dynasty (581–618) and developed throughout the Tang dynasty (618–907). The Forbidden City at Chang'an, although theoretically the centre of urban space, was in fact displaced to the north in order to privilege the east-west axis of the silk road. On the southern side of the great highway which bisected the city, a market was established in the western part of the city for the caravans which arrived from central Asia, while symmetrically placed in the east was the Chinese market. A capital city like Fujiwara (694–710), where the Imperial Palace was located in the centre of the city, was far closer to the ideal Chinese model. However, the aristocrats of Heijō and Heian preferred to look to Chang'an for their inspiration, with the Imperial Palace off centre to the north and with two markets, one to the east and the other to the west (Fiévé 2001).

Absolutely everything about the ancient capital was in the 'Chinese' monumental style and was clearly meant to symbolise the place of the emperor at the very centre of society. According to the *Engi shiki* (Procedures of the Engi era), the basic plan of Heian was rectangular, approximately 4.46 kilometres from east to west by approximately 5.18 kilometres from north to south. A series of avenues running at right angles to each other marked out the system of division into wards and districts (*jōbōsei*), like an immense chess-board. The city was divided into two parts, the 'capital to the right' (*ukyō*) and the 'capital to the left' (*sakyō*). This corresponded to the emperor's view of the city, looking to the south. The dividing line between the two halves was a large ceremonial avenue, known as *Suzaku-ōji* (literally, 'the great avenue of the Red Bird'). This avenue, lined with willow trees, was 84 metres wide and stretched 3.78 kilometres from the Rashōmon gate to the Imperial Palace. The two parts were divided by east-west avenues into wards (*jō*), each of which comprised four districts (*bō*). The districts were further divided into 16 blocks (*chō*), each about

120 metres from east to west. Four such blocks constituted a sub-district (*hō*). The way in which each plot was numbered also reflected the central place of the Imperial Palace, which was used as the point zero for such calculations. This right-angle system of planning was the basis for all the city's zones, whether blocks, sub-districts, or districts. The vast properties which belonged to aristocrats occupied at least 25 percent of a block, and the biggest were the size of four blocks, that is, a sub-district. In the middle of plots such as these stood a principal palatial building which opened southwards onto a courtyard and a large garden with a lake and even islands.

The grandiose, monumental and geometrical way in which Heian was laid out was specifically intended to create a symbolic space within which every element – the Imperial Palace, the abodes of the aristocracy, the avenues, the ornamental gates – were all designed to signify the place of the Emperor at the centre of the world (Fiévé 1996: 63–91). The various parts of the city were not all developed in the same way. Some were never built. According to a decree of 828, thirty-four years after the foundation of the capital, fewer than half its street blocks (520 out of 1,088) were occupied by buildings, either official constructions or the homes of commoners. In any case, those who planned and built the city had drafted a plan that was far too ambitious, at least in terms of population; Heian only had a maximum of 120,00 to 130,000 at the time of its greatest prosperity. In addition, it cost so much to lay out the city, an expense borne by the common people, that by 805, Emperor Kanmu (737–806) decided to call a halt to the works that he had initiated some ten years earlier. This was why certain districts were never built and retained the appearance of cultivated fields, as they were to remain for centuries to come. As with the earlier capitals of Heijō and Fujiwara, and to a certain extent Chang'an itself, the urban landscape of a city like Heian had nothing in common with European cities. There was no *agora*, no public space where the citizens could gather, and in the middle of large swathes of cultivated fields or fallow land were groups of mansions hemmed in by walls or huge monastic complexes, sometimes several kilometres from the next as at Heijō. Scattered among these vast compounds were blocks occupied by the common people, normally in the form of fields and vegetable gardens in the middle of which were modest wooden houses. The border between 'town' and country was not therefore as clearly delineated as the theoretical plan of the capital would lead the observer to expect.

Medieval *miyako*

From the eleventh and twelfth century onwards, the fragmentation and the militarisation of the classes who had until then held political power led to the emergence of a new form of society, and with it a change in the style of urban model. The pure lines of the old geometric plan, with the Imperial Palace at its hub and all the august solemnity that it symbolised, disappeared, as the old spiritual order gave way to the new secular one, one that no longer expressed itself in terms of architectural monuments. With the symbolic centre – that is, the old Palace – gone, all the various parts of the city (districts, roads, markets, housing, etc.) were all set free from their former symbolic restraints, and were gradually restructured according to the demands of change in medieval society (Fiévé 1996: 92–131). The evolution of urban and architectural forms was given a further impulse by the destruction and reconstruction that occurred as a consequence of the wars and natural disasters that were so characteristic of much of the city's history. It was in the thirteenth and fourteenth centuries that the organic growth of the city reached its completion, encouraged by men from varied backgrounds, classes, and occupations.

Whereas the old blocks (*chō*) of the Heian era, roughly square in shape, represented a compact ensemble, bounded by a wall and broad avenues, the new urban quarters (which were still sometimes referred to as *chō* but more commonly with the alternate reading of *machi*), were focussed on little roads which were lined by the modest establishments of traders and artisans. These lanes had become the animated centres of urban life. The quarters, which had been standardised in shape and size, were no longer designated by numbers but toponomically, with a name or title linked to an economic activity or to some past event firmly fixed in the collective memory. The whole concept of *machi* is something of a leitmotif in the history of urban Japan (as indeed it is in this book). Social as well physical units within the city, the *machi* dominate the imagination of historians of Kyoto in particular but are an important element in the history of Edo too.

During the thirteenth and fourteenth centuries the social composition of Kyoto changed, a change spurred in part at least by an expansion in arable land together with improvements in agriculture. This was followed by an increase in the demand for artisanal production in Kyoto and an influx of goods in the markets of the capital. The growing number of prosperous merchants and artisans inhabiting the city required a much larger social stratum of people to furnish their needs. More and more traders set up stalls to sell their wares on either side of the city's roads, eventually covering their full length. Gradually, the popular quarters of the medieval city took shape. The traders' shops can be understood in retrospect as the prototype for the town-houses (*machiya*) of the Tokugawa period (*Kyōto shi* 1968, vol. 3; Noguchi 1988).

For several extended periods from the twelfth to the fifteenth centuries, the development of craft work, trade, and travel all made the capital a dynamic place and encouraged the flourishing of a lively urban culture. Kyoto was characterized by the kind of community that could be found in each of the quarters. This meant it was structured both vertically according to a hierarchy of social origins and also horizontally according to community, usually grouped around the clan deity (*ujigami*). The way medieval Kyoto was composed was remarkably eclectic from the point of view of architecture and urban planning. Reflecting the social diversity of its inhabitants, the city contained Buddhist temples and Shinto shrines, the fortified compounds of leading members of the military class, the palaces of courtiers, modest town-houses (*machiya*), ateliers and shops (*mise*) and store-rooms (*kura*) – a whole variety of architectural forms, techniques, and materials in close proximity. Often, ordinary houses would be built over time within the grounds of a religious institution or a former palace, creating an imbrication of the new with the old.

The unrest that characterized so much of the Age of Warring States (1467–1573) led to various collective defence measures being taken (such as the arming of ordinary people and the building of enclosures and fences) and made the community spirit of the commoners' blocks even more tight-knit. In times of peace, on the other hand, the regular religious festivals (*matsuri*) and other popular celebrations brought the people together in great numbers, which led to a flourishing of all the arts of entertainment, notably dance, theatre, puppetry, and music. These festive occasions were also moments when it was possible to escape the rigorous hierarchy that structured human relations in everyday life (Takahashi Y. 1983: 291–488).

The eleven troubled years of the Ōnin era (1467–77) formed something of a watershed in the city's history. The fighting left the greater part of the city in ashes, Kyoto having served as battlefield for a succession of destructive and murderous clashes between rival armies (Berry 1994). Once peace was restored, the *bakufu* (shogunal government) did not reconstruct the old streets and cityscape. The populace preferred to take refuge in two fortified agglomerations, *Kamigyō no kamae* (the fortifications of the upper capital) to the north and *Shimogyō no kamae* (fortifications of the lower capital) to the south. Within these areas, roads, houses and new blocks were constructed according to need. The blocks of which the capital was now constituted and which bound the commoners together in mutual defense comprised the main street and the houses on either side of it. They were called *ryōgawa machi* ('both side' blocks, best translated perhaps as street-blocks). The new Kyoto was completely unlike the ancient capital. It had a far smaller population, probably fewer than 100,000 inhabitants. In the upper town, Kamigyō, the palace was sited at Tsuchimikado (as it still is today), near the houses of the leading members of the military class and the residences of the court nobles. These dwellings, considerably smaller than in previous times, now stood side by side with commoners' houses. The lower town, Shimogyō, became the economic hub of the new Kyoto; it was more densely populated, and it was here that the rich merchants settled.

Although more than a kilometre apart, the upper town and the lower town were linked by Muromachi Avenue. It was this part of the former city where the great palatial residences, the fine mansion houses, and the temples with their lofty pagodas and magnificent gardens had all given way to more modest buildings, as often as not built close to *machiya* houses, and rather rudimentary in architectural terms, with wooden or even thatch roofs. Takahashi Yasuo shows quite clearly, though, in his chapter on the residences built in Kyoto in the mid sixteenth century for the shoguns Yoshiteru (1536–65) and Yoshiaki (1537–97), that the linking of these two areas was already a priority from this time. Takahashi's chapter demonstrates in addition that fortresses were part of the capital long before it is generally assumed. The construction of an urban fortress by the shogun Yoshiteru in 1559 in the sparsely urbanized terrain between the upper and lower towns was a departure from the traditional custom of building only non-fortified residences within the town proper. On this same site, shortly after the destruction of its predecessor, Yoshiaki built a second fortress. Takahashi argues that these buildings launched a new style of urban development, especially in the way that they concentrated onto one site both the residences for the samurai and those of the *daimyō*. In the case of Kyoto, this restored a central focal point to an area which had lost its centrality because of war. The new complex, all the more monumental because the Yoshiaki fortress incorporated a dungeon, was a foretaste of a phenomenon that would flourish only a few decades later, the *jōkamachi*, literally, the 'quarters under the castle,' but generally referred to as 'castle towns.' These castle towns were distinctive urban settlements. They were built in all parts of the country by the *daimyō* to serve as an urban headquarters for themselves and their vassals. Edo became the ultimate example of this model of city building, but Kyoto was the first city to be transformed in accordance with the new ideas of urban planning. It is appropriate at this stage therefore to examine the emergent *jōkamachi* in a little more detail.

Castle Towns and *daimyō* Power

As the construction of Yoshiteru and Yoshiaki's castles suggests, the Kyoto of social and spatial communities formed in mutual defence was forced to give way before a new urban system which emerged in the latter part of the sixteenth century and reflected a rapidly evolving political situation. The contending forces of waning aristocratic patronage, prosperous regional market centres, and limited essays in urban self-government often with ecclesiastical support gave way before a contemporaneous coalescence of power among regional hegemons and their national exemplars and leaders. The actions of the first two national unifiers, Oda Nobunaga (1534–82) and Toyotomi Hideyoshi (1536–98), laid down a pattern which was replicated by the emergent regional hegemons, the *daimyō*. The policies of Hideyoshi in particular were to have a long-lasting effect on the social structure of the country and therefore on the physical composition of its cities. The cadastral survey he undertook became a model for *daimyō* throughout the country. That, together with other reforms, had the most profound effect on Japanese society, creating rigid social ranks and a framework of towns and villages that was the administrative equivalent. It made a distinct urban stipend-earning class of the warrior elements, who had previously tended to be land-holding and village-based, a class of people more akin to the European image of local feudal vassals.

Castles were the embodiment of *daimyō* power, while, in the words of John Whitney Hall, 'the morphology of the castle town was in essence a cross-section of the pattern of Japanese feudal society' (Hall 1968: 178). Wakita Osamu has since developed this idea in a comment that applies equally to Edo and to other early modern castle towns. 'One of Hideyoshi's most consequential initiatives,' he writes, 'was to decree that Osaka's geography articulate a correspondence between space, function, and status' (Wakita 1999: 263). The Japanese castle towns that appeared up and down the country bore a uniformity of pattern that can still be observed today in modern Japanese cities. The dominant consideration was control, but the imposition of this control in terms of the urban structure of the new castle towns was effected pragmatically, with new decrees drawn up and implemented according to the requirements of time and place.

The defensibility of the site had been the overriding consideration in the construction of castles built in the earlier sixteenth century and preceding period. These fortifications had often been built on hills and prominences overlooking, but at some distance removed from, an already existing marketing town (Yamori 1988: 18). The greater power that lay in the hands of the *daimyō* at the end of the sixteenth century, by making it possible for them to bring their markets with them, or in some cases coopt an existing market town into their new scheme, afforded them the opportunity to place a much higher priority in their choice of a site on the security of their whole domain rather than just the castle (Hall 1968). The new castle town was a more integrated urban space than its predecessor. The vassals and retainers of *daimyō* were moved within the walls of the town's enlarged fortifications, and the morphology of the town was thus changed as the castle ceased to be an isolated citadel. A similar process occurred under very different circumstances in China in the progression from the dual walled configuration of the ancient city to the single outer, perimeter walls of later Chinese regional administrative capitals (Nishikawa 1972: 19). The major difference in Japan is that, with the exception of Kyoto (which remained *sui generis* in many other ways), the commoners' districts tended to remain outside the fortifications of the early modern castle town, which retained the rationale of the military stronghold while soon tacitly acknowledging the primacy of the market, a dichotomy that would eventually conspire to bring about its decline.

Introduction

Early Modern Kyoto

The effects of these changes on the structure of Kyoto (or Keishi as it was known at least until the end of the eighteenth century) has tended to be underplayed by modern historians, and yet the process of unification led to a very noticeable centralisation of political authority over Kyoto's urban space. We have already alluded to the building of Yoshiaki's fortress. Subsequently, there was Nobunaga's project to make the city part of a plan for self defense. Similarly the major works undertaken under the aegis of Toyotomi Hideyoshi and the urban planning which was continued by his successors were to effect a profound change in the ties which linked Kyoto's inhabitants to the way the city's living space was laid out.

As soon as Maeda Gen'i (1539–1602) took up his functions as prefect (*bugyō*) of Kyoto in 1583, he took charge of all dealings with the court. He issued a great number of decrees in order to place shrines, temple precincts, and urban land belonging to court nobles under Hideyoshi's control. In 1586 (Tenshō 14), the building of a vast forterss and residence, known as Jurakudai, was planned, and around this central castle the military (*buke*) were instructed to build their residences. Thus the town became a *jōkamachi*, and a whole new urban topology was born.

In 1590–91, Kyoto as a city evolved in four key ways, developments which were to spell the end for the few extant remains of the ancient city. First, some of the old square blocks (*chō*), unchanged since the town had been the aristocratic capital Heian, were cut through by a new central thoroughfare running north-south. This meant that hitherto empty space within the clusters of buildings of the old blocks now became available for building. Street stalls and houses were soon constructed, thereby increasing the number of facades that opened onto the main street. Secondly, the various Buddhist institutions were moved to the eastern edge of town, and re-sited on the right bank of the River Kamo. Thirdly, in 1591, an earthen rampart (*odoi*) 22.5 kilometres in length was built around the city. The enclosure was trapezoidal in cross-section, with a base about nine metres wide and rising to a height of between three and six metres. The top was finished off with a wood and bamboo fence. A canal six to eighteen metres wide ran parallel to the enclosure or rampart along its outer side. Although its primary function was to protect the city against potential attacks, it also served to hold back the seasonal floods of the Kamo, for which purpose the western bank was later reinforced with stone walls and wooden fences. The building of the enclosure was accompanied by the demolition of all forms of fortification within and between quarters. In this way, the construction of the enclosure played a key role in the suppression of the old spatial divisions, replacing them with a homogeneous urban arrangement built around the castle. The final step (again in 1591) was the abolition of ground rent (*jishisen*) – a land tax on which the court, its nobles, the temples and the shrines had built their power. This decision concerned all *intra muros* buildings and the surrounding estates. The measures outlined above brought about nothing less than a complete transformation of the city, as well as making the habitation of hitherto unoccupied space possible (*Kyōto shi* 1969, vol. 4: 227–350).

When the Tokugawa won power at the beginning of the seventeenth century, they continued the policies that Hideyoshi had begun. From 1592 to 1605, Kyoto remained the centre of political life, even though, as early as 1603, the *bakufu* had been transferred to Edo. At that time, Ieyasu (1542–1616) took control of Fushimi Castle, restored it, and set up residence there. When Hidetada (1578–1632) succeeded him in 1605, he too stayed there for two years before settling definitively in Edo. During the 5th Month of the year 1602, Ieyasu commenced the construction of a fortified palace at Nijō-Horikawa, the Nijō castle, which still stands on its original site. Apart from one occasion at the time of the siege of Osaka castle, Nijō was used exclusively for those ceremonies that symbolised the relationship between the court and the *bakufu*. Local affairs were administered by a governor (*shoshidai*), Itakura Katsushige (1545–1624), succeeded by his elder son Itakura Shigemune (1585–1656), who held the post from 1619 to 1654. The governor's main task was to ensure that the court, its nobles and the citizenry remained quiescent under the authority of the Tokugawa.

As we have already seen, the transformation of the capital (as with other cities) was designed to make it an urban space whose organisation reflected the new social system. The residences for the military (*buke yashiki*) were established around Nijō Castle; the courtiers were grouped around the emperor's palace; the temples were confined to the periphery of the city. With the problem of urban space thus resolved for the military, the courtiers and the Buddhist clergy, attention now turned to arrangements for commoners. The homogenization of the town centre continued, and it became reserved for merchants and artisans. It is within this context of social control that entertainment was segregated and entertainers subject to discrimination, with the prime example being the brothel district of Shimabara, something that Fiévé discusses in Chapter Two.

During the Genna (1615–24) and Kan'ei (1624–30) eras, Kyoto enjoyed an unparalleled level of prosperity. The residential districts were expanding at a great rate. In a city that was bubbling over with life, places such as Gojō-ōhashi and Shijō-gawara were famous for their street-side shows, fairs, and other itinerant attractions. The tea houses with their permissive ambience were part of this landscape. Such places of popular entertainment are very clearly depicted on the *Rakuchū rakugai zu byōbu*, 'Screens of the Capital and its Surroundings' (Fiévé 1992b) (fig. 1).

Kyoto experienced a huge increase in its population towards the end of the seventeenth century. This was the great era of expansion for the textile merchants. The house of Echigoya, which later became Mitsui, for

Introduction

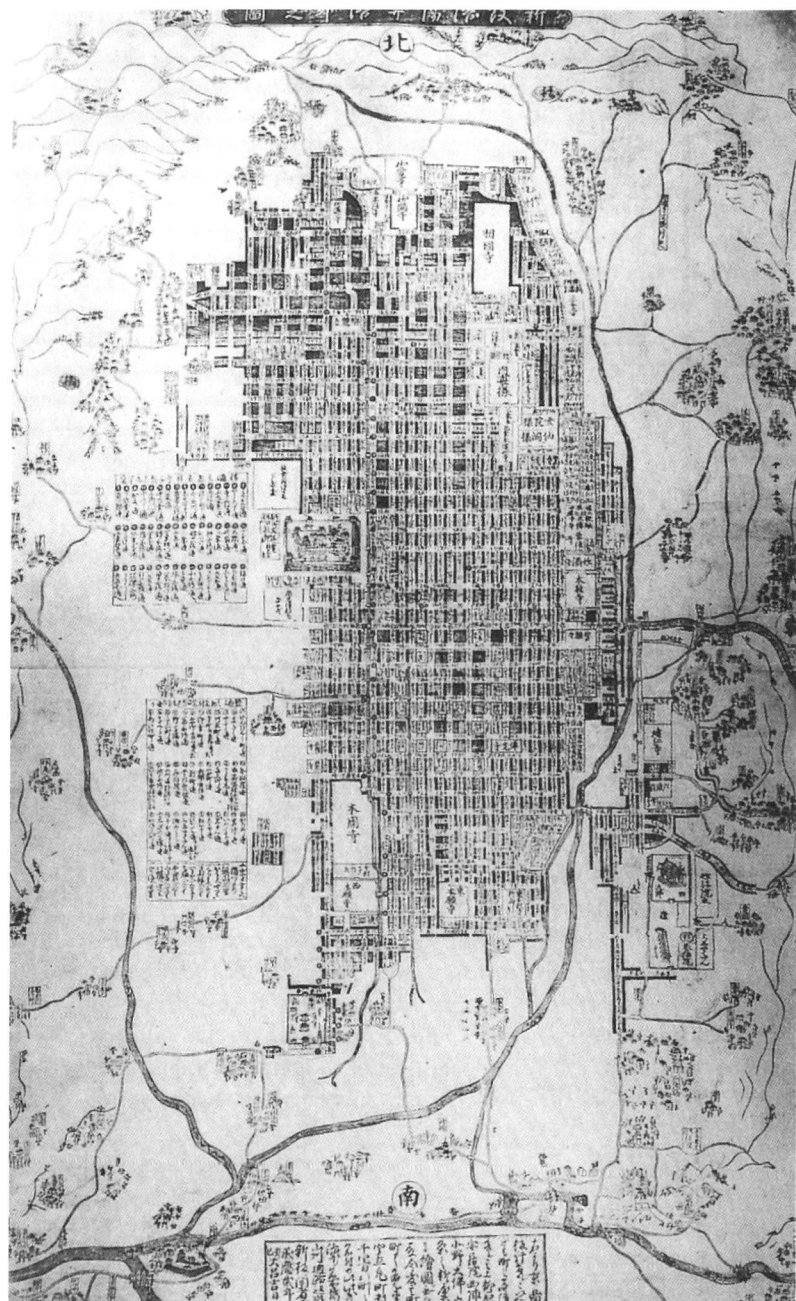

Figure 1 '*Rakuyō narabini rakugai no zu*' (Map of the streetcapes of the capital and its surroundings), showing Kyoto in 1653. Courtesy of Kyōto Shiyakusho (from *Kyōtoshi shi*, vol. 4, 1944).

example, began trading around this time. It was within this context of economic prosperity that the street blocks (*machi*) of the early modern city developed, and indeed, until quite recently gave shape to the historical centre of Kyoto. Along the public space of the street, the houses (*machiya*) with their shops were semi-public places, forming a sort of buffer zone between the street at the front of the house and the private space at the back, within whose grounds certain communal features – such as a well, a bath house and a vegetable garden – could be found.

The major building work undertaken by Toyotomi Hideyoshi and the policy of spatial segregation implemented by Hideyoshi and by his Tokugawa successors completely changed the urban organisation of the city because of the way it organized different social groups into spatially discrete areas. On a physical level, there were few examples of monumental architecture. The fortified palaces of Jurakudai and Nijō Castle were exceptional, as was the city's *enceinte*. During the entire Tokugawa period and on through the first twenty-five years of the Meiji era, the city at the scale of the street block was moulded by the people who lived there, the petty traders and craftsmen, their families, servants, and the like. We find absolutely nothing in Kyoto that corresponds to the symetrical axes, the majestic thoroughfares and avenues that we find from the seventeenth century in Europe.

However, even if in their material form, the city and its buildings cannot be said to be monumental, as Fiévé argues in his chapter on the famous places of Kyoto, the city was organised conceptually around certain key areas, or 'famous places' (*meisho*), which held a firm place in the people's collective memory. Looked at this way, Kyoto, like the other early modern Japanese cities, can be said to have been organized around the monumental in a very literal sense – the Latin word *monumentus* meaning 'something that brings something to mind.' It is, however, an immaterial monumentality, and therefore radically different from that of Western or indeed of Chinese cities. The fact that there is no culture of buildings themselves being the focus or repository of collective memory later became a determining factor in the shaping of the modern and contemporary city, allowing, if not actually encouraging, the disappearance of the built form of the old city (see also the chapter on the preservation and revitalization of *machiya* by Kinoshita).

Edo: Foundation and Early Configuration

The spectacular burst of townbuilding in the late sixteenth and early seventeenth centuries, one that surely knows no parallel in the world, found its consummation in Edo. The story of the construction of Edo, exemplar of the early modern castle town, and its subsequent expansion is one that has never lost its lustre for Japanese historians, although arguably the best account remains that of Naitō Akira (Naitō 1966). As with Kyoto, historical writing on Edo evolved out of a tradition of amateur scholarship (by people like Mitamura Engyo (1870–1952) and Yada Sōun (1882–1961) based on a nostalgic regard for a way of life that had disappeared. In the 1970s it was vastly enriched through a five volume work of scholarship, *Edo chōnin no kenkyū* (Research on Edo commoners), edited by Nishiyama Matsunosuke. Since then a new generation of scholars have been active, refining and elaborating the insights of Nishiyama and his colleagues, and a selection of Nishiyama's own work has been translated into English (1997). It is worth noting, in view of the multi-disciplinary nature of this book, that many of the leading contributions to Edo scholarship have been made by ethnographers like Miyata Noboru (1981) and architectural historians like Tamai Tetsurō (1986). An inevitable point of reference is the encyclopaedic *Tōkyō hyakunen shi* (The history of Tokyo's hundred years), which was written by leading scholars in the history and structure of Tokyo (and, in the first of its six volumes, Edo). In English, the work of Henry Smith remains the principal reference point, and in particular three seminal papers he wrote in the 1970s and 1980s (Smith 1978, 1979, 1986). In recent years, a number of monographs have appeared that have added sustained new insights into our understanding of Edo and other cities and the people who lived there; those by Leupp (1992) and Hur (2000) stand out in this regard. Broader in scope but all the more compelling for that is Hanley's study of *Everyday Things in Premodern Japan* (1997).

More generally, there is a copious literature in Japanese (within which the work of Yamori Kazuhiko is outstanding) on castle towns, their genesis, growth, and changing morphology. In English, however, the picture is somewhat different. McClain's study of the growth of Kanazawa remains the only notable monograph that tackles the nature and growth of early modern castle towns and their changing social and physical structure; it is of relevance to Edo in a number of ways. McClain has been involved in two more recent projects, both of which are rich stores of information and sources of new ideas. *Edo and Paris: Urban Life and the State in the Early Modern Era* is a bold and unusual essay in sustained comparison, but one which can nonetheless be read purely for what it has to say about Edo (McClain *et al.* 1994). *Osaka: The Merchants' Capital of Early Modern Japan* represents an introduction to urbanism during this period that constitutes much more than the portrait of one city (McClain and Wakita 1999).

Tokugawa Ieyasu, son of the lord of a small castle near Nagoya and a *daimyō* whose domain extended over the three provinces of Mikawa, Suruga, and Tōtōmi, is said by tradition to have entered the post town of Edo on the first day of the eighth month, 1590 (Mizue 1977: 82). He had had his domainal power base moved on Hideyoshi's orders from his strategic home territory along the Tōkaidō, the East Sea Road, to the more distant Kantō plains. Although at this time Ieyasu was under the overall dominion of Hideyoshi, there is no doubt that he aspired to national hegemony. In the light of this, his choice of Edo is very much in keeping with the enormous confidence shown by the *daimyō* of the period in their ability to mobilize large resources and to use construction technology to alter the physical environment to suit their town-planning needs.

To build headquarters commensurate with the extent of the Tokugawa land holdings would mean the construction of a sizable town. The terrain at the foot of the castle, however, was scarcely suited to such an endeavour. Much of it was marshy, and the waters of the bay almost reached the foot of the castle hill. The problems of building a castle town, a *jōkamachi*, on the reedy banks of the bay would surely have seemed formidable. But, as Beatrice Bodart-Bailey writes in her contribution to this volume, 'the very difficulties that had detracted from the site as an area for settlement, gave it exceptional strategic value.' Certain strategic considerations are obvious. The town was located at the junction of the Tōkaidō and roads to the north and inland to the west. It stood on the easternmost point of several ridges of diluvial high ground overlooking the mouth of one of the principal rivers in the Kantō plain. Its port at the head of the bay was protected from storms unlike those of Odawara and Kamakura, the two older settlements in the region. Indeed, there is much about the location of Edo that is reminiscent of another great castle town that was in the process of construction at this time, Hideyoshi's Osaka, a city that was soon after to be transformed 'from military redoubt to a bastion of commercial vitality and artisanal production' (McClain 1999: 75).

By the time Edo had been largely built in the 1620s and 30s, the Tokugawa had created within the city a spatial miniature of the political jigsaw puzzle into which they had turned the whole of the country. Dominating the fledgling city was the castle and the black walls and golden tiles of its mighty keep. With its several separate but adjacent enceintes (*maru*), it was certainly one of the largest integrated complexes of buildings that ever existed before the modern age. In its immediate environs were situated the residences of the various collateral branches of the Tokugawa family. Beyond these were the splendidly decorated residences of the senior Tokugawa retainers and of the most powerful *daimyō*. These were arranged in such a way as to hem in the compounds of the most powerful of potential rivals between those of loyal allies, much as had been done for *daimyō* land-holdings. Military considerations were paramount in the conception and planning of the city. All else followed on from this. The Tokugawa required all *daimyō* to spend some time (from 1636, every other year in most cases) in the city, where their wives were to remain on a permanent basis. This system, known as *sankin kōtai*, led to vast outlays on the part of the *daimyō* on travel and on maintenance of their residences in Edo, expenditure which had a stimulating effect on the economy of Edo and helped to bolster the incomes of merchants and artisans.

As in Kyoto and most of the new castle towns, temples were either moved to or built on the fringes of town. There were several reasons for this. Temples provided a cremation service, one that would have been much in demand with all the accidents that would inevitably have happened to construction workers (Tamai 1986: 35). But the cremations themselves were a source of danger, of fire, and this was an additional reason for siting the temples at the city limits. Temples also fulfilled a symbolic role, that of blocking the inauspicious northeast entrance to the city taken by evil spirits (*kimon*) and its obverse, the southwest entrance (*ura kimon*).

The commoners' districts, those parts of town that were settled by merchants and artisans, were built in approximately square blocks of housing. These were the *machi*, or *chō*. They were dominated by the massive presence of the castle and its keep. But they were centred around a bridge, Nihonbashi, which had been built in 1603 as part of the reclamation of land from the marshes along the bay. This bridge became the focal point of commoner activity in the city as well as the point from which all distances along the country's main highways were calculated. Cutting into the commoners' blocks were the arms of the canals, from which small boats disgorged the bundles and barrels delivered to the city by larger vessels which dropped anchor in the waters of the bay. The port was an essential component for Edo. The east of the country produced very few of the goods that were necessary to maintain a large population. The towns of the Kantō plain were rudimentary and few; the technology available for fishing, for sake-brewing, and for all forms of artisanal work was very limited. Goods had to be shipped in from the west, and people too had to be tempted to come to live in Edo. Originally, Ieyasu used the same sort of inducements as other *daimyō*. He granted land to designated merchants and artisans (*goyōtashi*) and exempted them from rent payments (*jishi menkyo*). The merchants came from Odawara, which had previously been the largest castle town in the east, as well as from various of the prosperous ports and market towns of the Kinai area. Considering the conditions that prevailed in the east of Japan in the early seventeenth century, the speed with which a city this size was built is nothing if not astounding (fig. 2).

Edo as the Mature Early-Modern Castle Town

By the time of the Great Meireki Fire of 1657, Edo had become one of the two largest cities in the country, larger probably than Kyoto and certainly Osaka. With its estimated population of 400,000, Edo contained most of the typical characteristics of the larger castle towns of the period. It was only after the fire that the mould of the castle town was broken and new elements were introduced into the layout of the city.

The Great Meireki Fire was really a concatenation of different fires that struck within a few fiercely cold and windblown winter days, destroying

Introduction

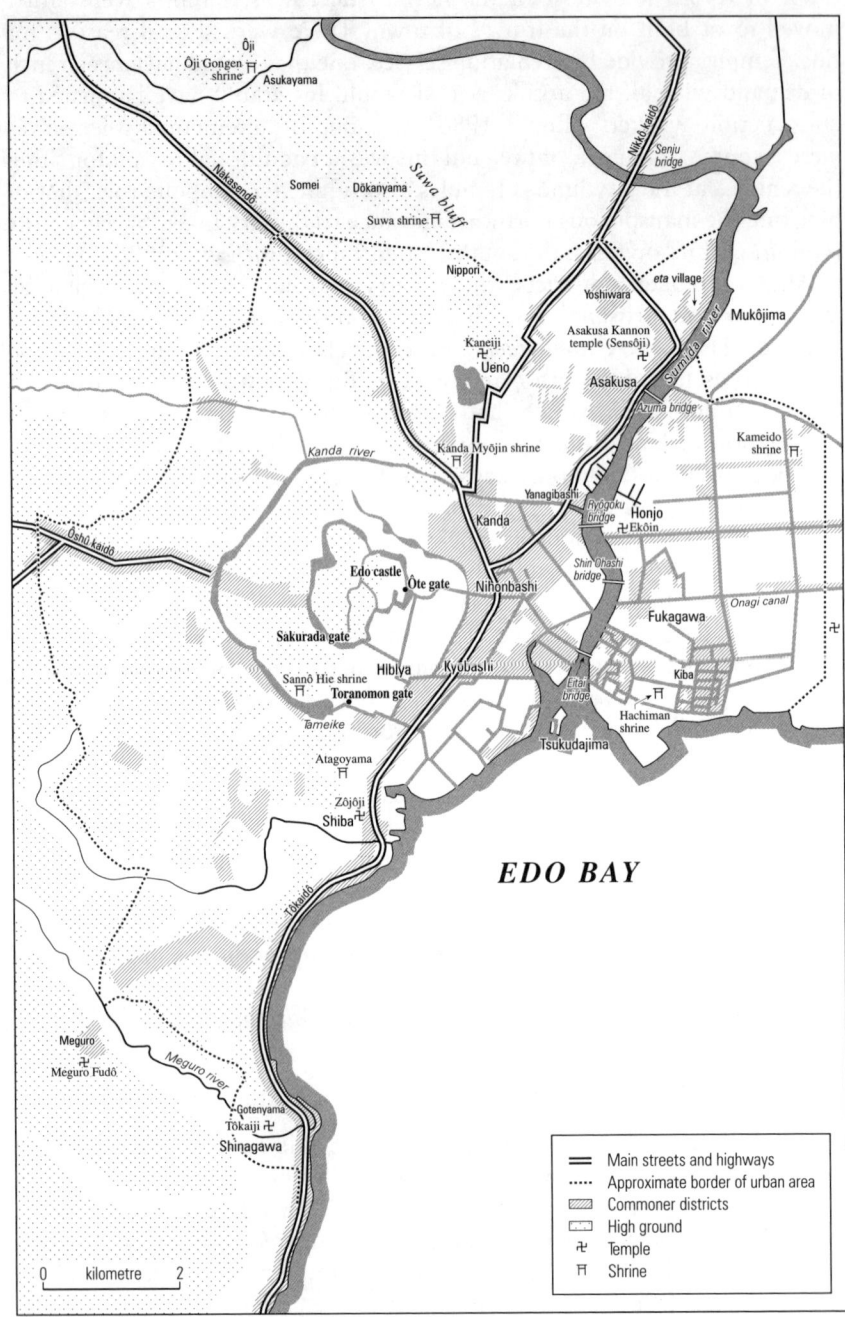

Figure 2 Edo, early to mid nineteenth century.

nearly all the city. There are thought to have been more than 100,000 fatalities during the two days and nights through which the fires burnt. Although various measures were introduced after the fire, this was by no means the last of the great Edo conflagrations, and it was not until the next century that a system of fire brigades was instituted among the townsmen. A number of measures were adopted after the fire to make the city less congested and the castle less prone to destruction by fire. The shogunate first of all commissioned the drawing of a map using trigonometric cartographic techniques learnt from the Dutch. On the basis of a more accurate appraisal, it was decided both to expand the size of the urban areas and create wider streets and firebreaks, especially in the districts inhabited by commoners. The first bridge was built across the Sumida River, and the land east of the river, still largely marsh, was developed. Temples were moved there, as well as many wharves, with the several timber quarters in the city concentrated in one district across the river. New commoners' blocks were built there, and *daimyō* were given land on the east bank for use as suburban residences or storehouses. The *daimyō* themselves were now allowed at least two estates in Edo, but their design was strictly controlled and architectural embellishment forbidden (with the partial exception of gatehouses).

Edo was a city that had been precisely organized, its physical layout reflecting political forces, social status, and economic pursuits. It is often claimed that as time passed the Tokugawa grew more secure in their hold on power and allowed this sense of security to reflect itself on the face of their city through more relaxed physical control. This is an argument that is contested in this book by Bodart-Bailey. Based on a reading of Kaempfer and of other historical sources, she challenges conventional arguments, according to which growing security led to a revision of urban policy. On the contrary, she argues, after the Great Meireki Fire, 'the residences of the most important families... were moved away from the castle.' Whatever the intent, however, the social and spatial delineations originally drawn up by the shogunate became blurred, and a shift occurred in the locus of power during the two and a half centuries of Tokugawa rule. This growing fluidity is traced in his contribution to this book by William Coaldrake through an examination of the changing metaphors of art and architecture. Coaldrake's argument is built around three different expressions of urban culture, monumental projects of the early period, a pictorial depiction dating from the middle period, and later *ukiyo-e* woodblock prints. The ceremonial manifestations of power and prestige slowly recede in this way before the assertion of an iconoclastic manifestation of an altered balance of power. The trappings of elite rule, incorporated for example in the gates of *daimyō* residences, is held up as an elaborate charade.

Life in Edo was characterised by movement, an idea developed by Nishiyama in his introductory chapter to *Edo chōnin no kenkyū*. Most samurai retainers of the *daimyō* travelled back and forth between Edo and their domainal headquarters, spending only one year in two, or shorter periods, in the city. The merchants and artisans too faced frequent moves. Whole street-blocks were transplanted to different parts of town if they stood in the way of a road to be widened or a *daimyō*'s compound to be enlarged. For them, the sense of impermanence was heightened by the regularity of the fires that made life in the commoner districts a very uncertain affair. Many traders and craftsmen had themselves migrated into the city. The Edo wholesale and retail system was dominated until well into the eighteenth century by the branches of organizations whose headquarters were in Kyoto or in the two commercially advanced provinces of Ise and Ōmi, their employees all being single men sent from the shops' home base. Even for those smaller establishments which were not part of a trading network, it was the custom that they should be named after the home province of the proprietor. Thus the streets of Edo bore the air of a geographical jigsaw puzzle, its pieces strewn across the board: Echigoya next to Kazusaya next to the omnipresent Ōmiya. A third group of inward migrants whose presence played an increasingly prominent part in the social constitution of the city were the hawkers, tinkers, porters, and other day labourers who inhabited the backstreets. People moved into and around Edo, but so too did goods, entertainments, information, and ideas. Edo was above all a city of consumption and of exchange of information. The flow of wealth from the fiefs of *daimyō* around the country to Edo was enormous, as we have already seen. The movement, however, occurred in both directions. Equally, as Bodart-Bailey indicates, 'the nature of the Tokugawa *bakufu* with its administrative capital away from the commercial hub of the country [Osaka] and strict control over the movement and settlement patterns of both samurai and commoners shaped urbanization throughout the country.'

This book concerns itself with Japan's two great capital cities, Kyoto and Edo. It would be wrong, however, to consider these two cities as being completely discrete urban entities, sharing nothing in their formation and history. It should become clear to readers as they make their way through this book that the two cities were linked in any number of ways. They were of course connected in a simple physical sense, by the great Tōkaidō highway. Throughout the Tokugawa period, travellers of whatever status were required to use certain highways (the nature of the terrain limits the choice of route in any case). Despite these constraints, however, there was a constant flow of people and goods making their way down the highways. In his study of travel in Tokugawa Japan, Vaporis claims by the start of the nineteenth century it had almost become 'a national obsession' (Vaporis 1994: 259). Engelbert Kaempfer, the physician whose descriptions of Tokugawa Japan are drawn on by Bodart-Bailey, was struck by the country's highways, 'as crowded as the streets of a populous European city.'

'On leaving one village,' he wrote, 'one enters the next, and in this fashion rows of houses built next to each other continue for many miles with merely a change in name.' With no city walls to form a physical block, Edo spread into Shinagawa and Kyoto into Fushimi. Urban sprawl was already a familiar phenomenon in Tokugawa Japan.

From Edo to Tokyo and Beyond

The conjoined nature of the settlements along the Tōkaidō is reflected in the maps of the route. In the words of Jilly Traganou, in her contribution to this book, landscape is represented 'as text, as narrative ... continuity.' Maps show a mythicized landscape, they show a 'topological space according to which the spatial qualities remain unaltered even if geometrical attributes change.' The maps emphasize continuity and legibility, linearity and the standpoint of the traveller. Traganou compares maps of the Tōkaidō in the Tokugawa period and Meiji era; they suggest a different route, different cities, a different country. The difference, however, was not quite so clearcut. Early Meiji maps were based largely on cartographic developments of the Tokugawa period. And much later still, so Traganou writes, 'in the early Shōwa era in the 1930s, popular road maps were still based on Tokugawa models.' The basic contrast remains, and nowhere is this more manifest than in maps of Edo and Tokyo. The old city of the shoguns was not destroyed by bombardment or pillaging. Rather, it withered away or perished in episodic fires.

The new leaders of the country, who were for the most part lower or middle ranking samurai from three powerful provinces in the far southwest of the country (Satsuma, Chōshū, and Tosa), formed a regime that aspired to legitimacy by its use of the emperor as symbol and head of state. Political supremacy was deftly acquired through, on the one hand, a rapid dismantling of the old social structures and swift incorporation of large segments of the former elite and, on the other, a strategic appropriation of parts of the old spatial structures. Some of the ground had already been lain when, in 1862, the rules of alternate attendance for *daimyō* were relaxed, leading to a sharp decrease in the size of the lordly establishments and a deleterious effect on the city's economy (Smith 1986: 350). The former *daimyō* returned, however, in 1871, when they were subsumed into a new aristocracy, whose members were obliged to keep their primary residences in the new capital. In the same year, 1871, the old system of feudal provinces was abolished and prefectures introduced. The following year, land certificates (*chiken*) were issued as a form of title deed and the separate categories of commoner, temple-and-shrine, and military land were abolished (Ishizuka 1977: 55).

The new organs of imperial government appropriated the space vacated by the shogunate and the leading *daimyō*. The site once occupied by the castle retained its symbolic significance, becoming the seat of imperial power. The compounds of the most powerful of the *daimyō*, which lay directly to the east and south of the castle, had been rased and ministries of the new government built on some of the sites. Others had been earmarked for use by the new armed forces. The army, indeed, was able to expropriate many of the prime sites around the palace, only to vacate them in the 1880s and 1890s once they had become too cramped. As former samurai and commoner residents who had left the city in the late 1860s returned, Tokyo's population started growing again and by the end of the 1880s it had returned to its former levels. For several decades, however, its growth was slower than that of Osaka, whose regional economy was considerably more sophisticated.

The choice of the shogun's city as the new imperial capital might seem a surprising one. Although the decision elicited some fairly lengthy deliberation, there were good reasons for choosing Edo in preference to Kyoto. The subject provoked several petitions to the emperor. Osaka had its champions, as did a division of the functions of capital between Edo and Kyoto (Smith 1984: 355). Among the reasons for favouring Edo were its greater proximity to the fractious provinces of the northeast, its greater distance from potential danger from European warships, and its natural situation in a protected bay (Ishizuka and Narita 1986: 16).

Questions relating to how to rebuild and replan Japan's new imperial capital of Tokyo ('the eastern capital') spurred debate at the time and have since been well covered in the contemporary historiography of Meiji Tokyo (Fujimori 1982; Ishizuka 1968). The central figure in Japanese-language writing on Meiji and Taishō Tokyo is probably Ishizuka Hiromichi. His studies of social and economic history are carefully grounded in an appreciation of the city's changing geography (Ishizuka 1977). Two other important contributions to the social history of the city are those written by Nakagawa Kiyoshi (1986) and Yoshimi Shunya (1987). Ishida Yorifusa has written widely on the history of planning in modern Tokyo. A number of architectural historians have contributed important works, in particular Fujimori Terunobu (1982) and Kawazoe Noboru (1979). The work of literary and cultural historians such as Maeda Ai (1982) and Unno Hiroshi (1983) has also illuminated aspects of Tokyo's history. The English language literature remains sparse. Smith's essay 'Tokyo as an idea: an exploration of Japanese urban thought until 1945' is still the principal exposition of ideas about urbanism (Smith 1978), while Edward Seidensticker's *Low City, High City* (1985) remains the most approachable point of entry into and avenue of peregrination through the city. Much of David Stewart's study of modern Japanese architecture (1987) is focused on Tokyo. Tokyo as national capital and centre of economic and political activity casts a strong presence over a number of other works, such as Sally Ann Hastings' *Neighborhood and Nation in Tokyo, 1905–1937* (1995).

Introduction

The question of what sort of city the nation's capital should become is the central issue addressed by Kōda Rohan (1867–1947) in his treatise *Ikkoku no shuto* (One nation's capital), written in 1899, which is examined by Evelyn Schulz in her chapter in this book. Rohan's vision was an essentially moral one. He describes the city in terms of community, Schulz writes, a community in which individuals have responsibility. He conceptualizes the city in terms that can be readily related to Western ideas, using the analogy of the human body. At the same time, however, his moralising vision is rooted in classical Chinese education, relating good to moral and physical cleanliness.

The Modern City of Kyoto (1869–2000)

Prosperous Kyoto may once have been, but its prestige and authority had been steadily eroded throughout the Tokugawa period. Screech discusses the craft and care with which Matsudaira Sadanobu allowed the emperor to diminish his already reduced stature in the period of rebuilding after the fire of 1788 (2000: 151). The loss of the emperor to the eastern capital engendered further decline and a long period of reassessment in Kyoto, some of it historically oriented (in a manner discussed in this book by Iwatake Mikako in connection with Tokyo) and some of it designed to place Kyoto at the forefront of a modernizing and Westernizing nation.

In 1894, to mark the 1100th anniversary of the foundation of Heian, the local authorities launched a major modernization scheme. Huge Western-style avenues were driven through the city and lighting was installed on the public highways. The construction of a canal not only provided a solution to the problem of water supply for the new districts but also established a waterway link with Lake Biwa and made the construction of a hydro-electric scheme possible, thereby providing a much needed source of power for the city and its industries. A system of public transport – a tramway system – was inaugurated (fig. 3).

Around the same time, the city council voted in favour of Kyoto hosting the Fourth National Industrial Exhibition. A park was created to serve as a site for the exhibition and a new shrine, Heian Jingū, was built there. Today these districts house Kyoto's national museums, following a pattern which replicates that of Ueno in Tokyo. The shrine was designed as a reduced-scale model of the old Throne Room (*Daigokuden*) of the imperial palace, and symbolically served since 1895 to house the spirit of Emperor Kanmu. This was the first such explicit monument constructed in Kyoto – in imitation of Western capitals – to the glory of the emperor and to the city's own past splendour as imperial capital. It is around this time that commemorative monuments, in Western style, were erected in Kyoto and other major cities of the Japanese archipelago to mark the authority of the nation's rulers. One way in which this was done in Japanese cities at this time was to site the

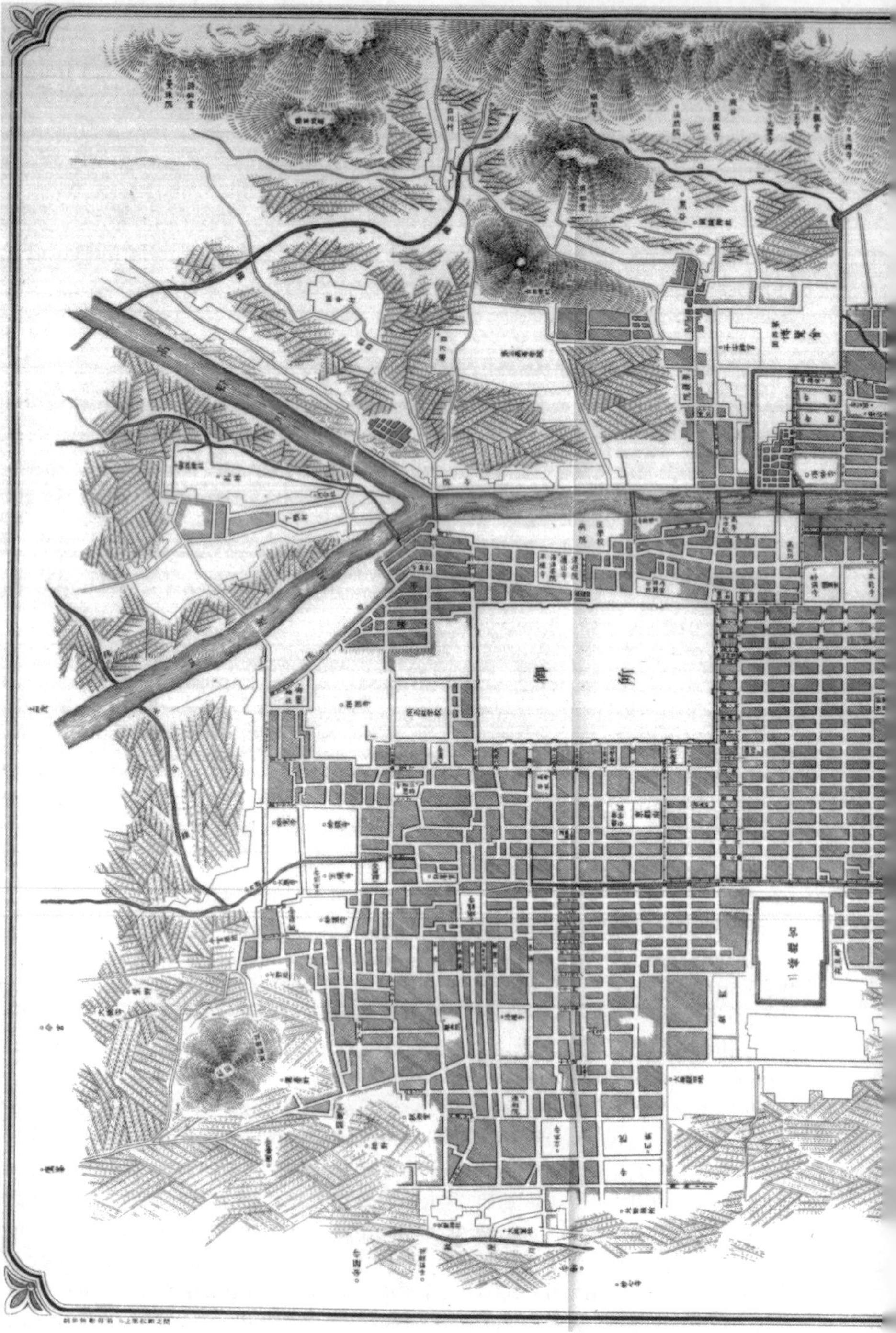

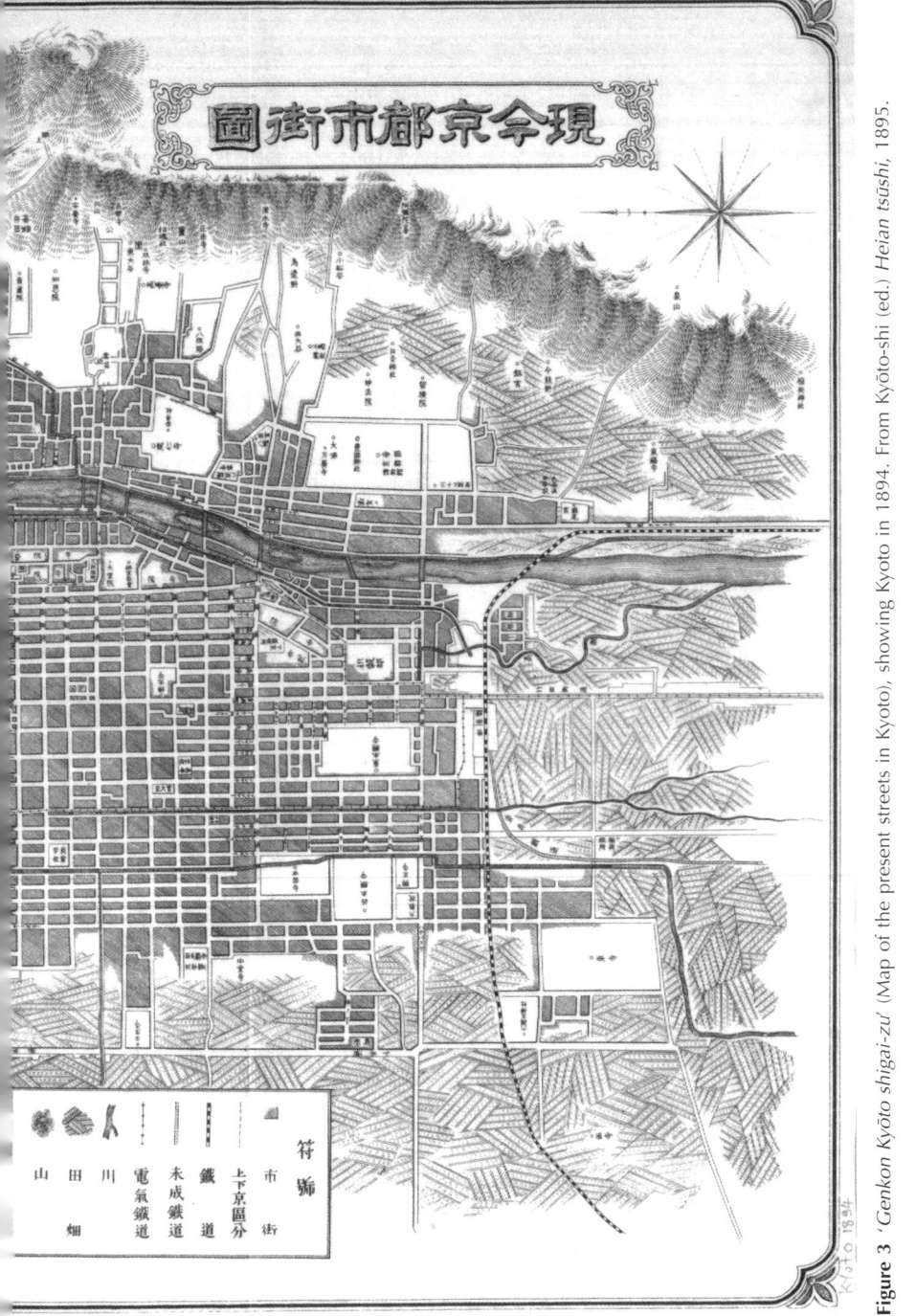

Figure 3 'Genkon Kyōto shigai-zu' (Map of the present streets in Kyoto), showing Kyoto in 1894. From Kyōto-shi (ed.) *Heian tsūshi*, 1895.

main government building, the seat of the prefecture, at the head of a major road axis. In Kyoto, the Heian Shrine occupied a similarly pivotal location. Equally, this is the period when numerous schools, hospitals, and institutes of learning were established, including the famous Imperial University of Kyoto (1887), forerunner of Kyoto University.

In 1889, the municipality of Kyoto sat within a plain of 30 square kilometres; today it stretches into the mountains and its surface area covers about 610 square kilometres. Since the Second World War, all of the basin, right up to the foot of the mountains, has been filled with housing. While this kind of urbanisation has certainly enlarged the city, it has not radically changed the nature of the city's old neighbourhoods. Right up until the 1980s, the historic centre of the town still retained the characteristic wooden *machiya*, all of which were reconstructions in the wake of the great fire of 1864 but which faithfully preserved the characteristics of the Tokuwaga period. Kyoto was a city that stretched horizontally, one whose only vertical features were the bordering mountains and the occasional pagoda. The city's neighbourhoods continued to consist of streets lined by shops and ateliers organised around a series of narrower streets, within which islands of space remained, reserved for private housing with courtyards and gardens (fig. 4).

Reshaping and Redefining the Nation's Capital

By the early years of the twentieth century, Tokyo had resumed its former position as the country's largest metropolis, a process that was to be confirmed over succeeding decades despite the devastation caused by the Great Kantō Earthquake of 1923. A national railway system was now in place, with Tokyo its hub. The industrialization of Tokyo, although not quite on the level experienced in Osaka, had further underlined Tokyo's preeminent position. The growing concentration of 'imperial-city' functions in Tokyo accelerated the same trends. During the 1910s, concern about social conditions in the city had contributed to a feeling that the Municipal Reform Act of 1888 was no longer a sufficient instrument – a modern tool for town planning was required. However, the Town Planning Act (*Toshi keikaku hō*) of 1919, while more generalized in its scope and intent than its predecessor, amounted to little more than an adjustment of the city's infrastructure, a revised and updated act of municipal improvement. Its principal innovation was the introduction of a system of zoning. Four years after the passing of the Town Planning Act, the Great Kantō Earthquake occurred, providing an occasion for sweeping revision of the act's powers. Gotō Shinpei (1857–1929), the home minister and former mayor of Tokyo, drew up a grandiose plan for reconstruction, but this too, perhaps overly ambitious in the first place, was considerably watered down. Its main achievement (one that should not however be underestimated) consisted of

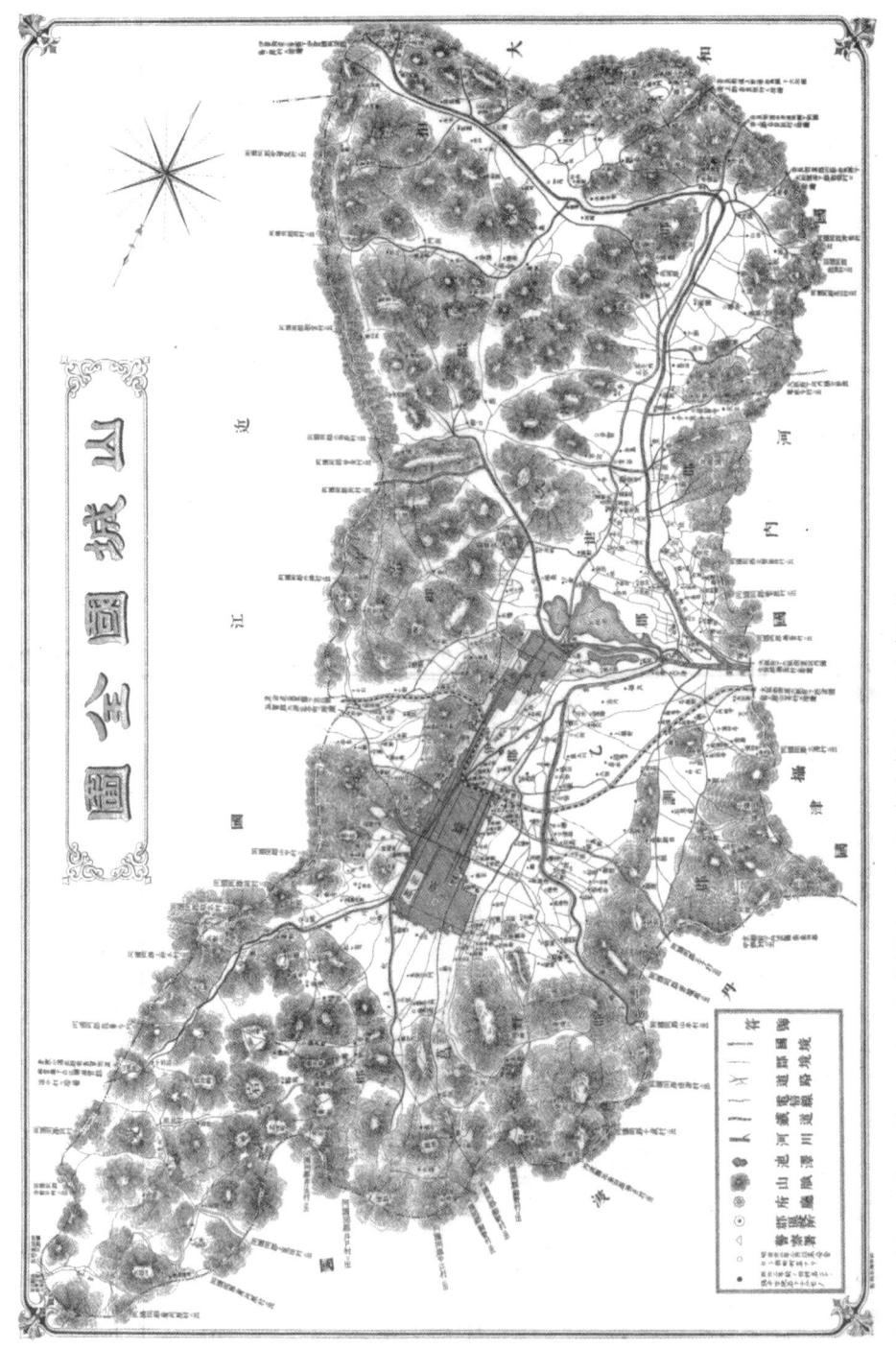

Figure 4 Map of Yamashiro province in 1894. From Kyōto-shi (ed.) *Heian tsūshi*, 1895.

Introduction

the building of a large number of steel bridges and the execution of a sizable land readjustment programme (fig. 5).

Despite the almost total destruction of the city twice in the space of twenty-two years, Tokyo was not rebuilt according to a grand plan. This is not to say that such plans were never drawn up. As Carola Hein argues in her chapter, grand designs disappeared before the growing absorption with the detail of planning techniques and engineering solutions. Reconstruction in Tokyo was too urgent and too many interests were at stake to allow for the dislocation that implementation of a grand plan would have necessitated. Instead, architects and engineers cast their gaze further

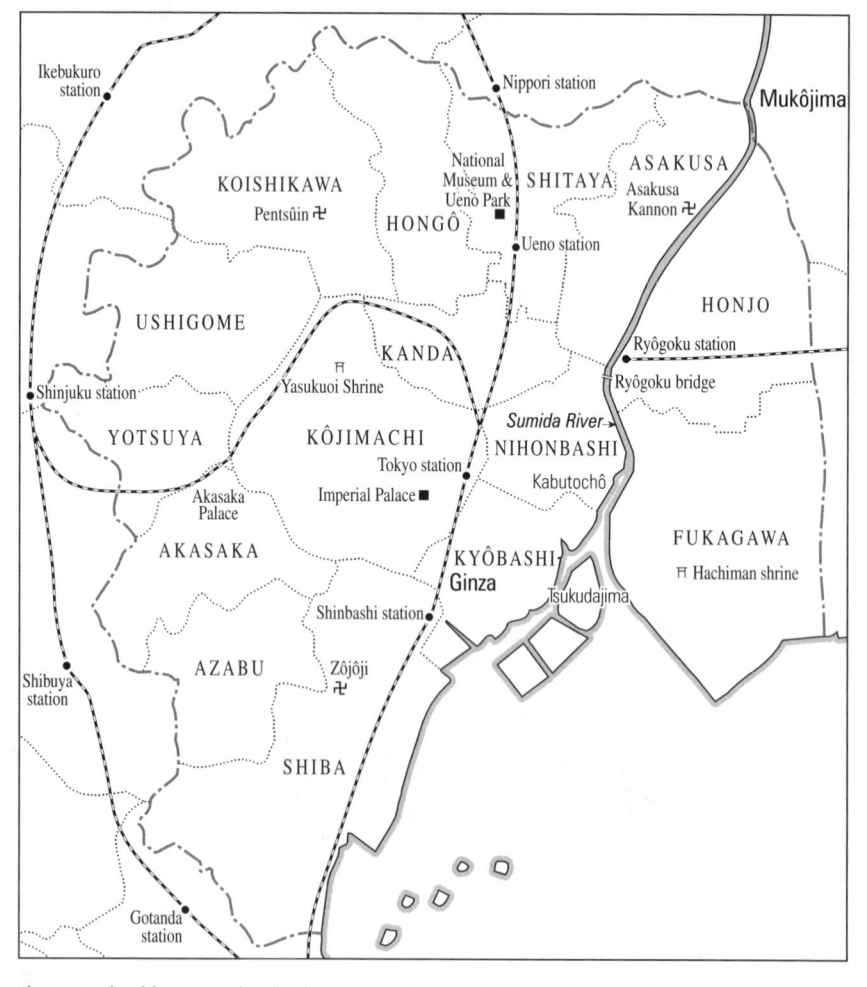

Figure 5 The fifteen wards of Tokyo, approximately 1920, and main railways.

afield, principally to the greater freedom offered by colonial territories such as Manchuria. Of Japanese cities, Hein writes, it was Nagoya which received the greatest attention from planners. She contrasts these planned interventions with the neighbourhood-oriented ideas of Nishiyama Uzō (1911–94) which she sees as having had the more long-lasting impact on the development of Tokyo, Kyoto, and other Japanese cities. This fits in well with the arguments advanced by other writers who have reflected on the development of Japanese urbanism and have drawn attention to such aspects as its cellular nature, with neighbourhood block replicated many times over, its lack of monumentality and grand views, its plasticity and fluidity (Waley 1997; Bognar 1990; Jinnai 1985; Ashihara 1989). In his chapter, Waley suggests that a prevailing nostalgic lyricism is one consequence of the lack of physical statement about urban power, prestige, and metropolitan and national ambition.

A capital city without monuments and other physical reminders of the past is likely to rely on different means of situating itself historically. Various chapters in this book reflect on the importance of the collective memory as a way of situating and giving significance to contemporary activities. Fiévé applies these ideas to Kyoto, while Murielle Hladik discusses the varying meanings given to the process of aging of material over time. Any individual act of recollection, and more so a collective one, is shaped and defined by ideological forces. In her contribution to this book, Iwatake examines the succession of anniversary celebrations that have marked Tokyo's history. These have been frequent events, and anything but politically neutral. As Iwatake points out, they are loaded with ideological intent. These celebrations are a political instrument for signifying current ideology through reference to the past. This periodic redefinition of the nation's capital played on its historical role in order to reinforce its position within empire and the wider world.

Tokyo has also defined itself through its name (not unlike Kyoto before it), and through the changes in its name we have an indication of the capital's development and growth (Machimura 1994). In the prewar and wartime years, the imperial capital (*teito*) was known bombastically as Greater Tokyo, *Dai Tōkyō*, and in 1943 it became the Tokyo Metropolis, *Tōkyō to*. Subsequently, various plans have added new terms that attempt to capture the growth of the conurbation into the surrounding prefectures of Saitama, Kanagawa, and Chiba. Some plans sought to disperse central functions out of Tokyo and into satellite cities in these three surrounding prefectures and in the west of the metropolis. In another plan, a number of sub-centres were designated to dissipate the pressures in the heart of Tokyo. As Ishida has pointed out, these plans, although they apply on very different scales, have tended to have the same result; they have exacerbated the central pull of the Tokyo conurbation and have contributed to the overall area of urban sprawl (Ishida 1994).

Introduction

In the 1980s a combination of factors conspired to underline Tokyo's standing as a world city (Machimura 1992 and 1998; Waley 1997). Pressure from Washington met a responsive cord among politicians in Tokyo, keen to see their capital projected onto the world stage. Huge capital flows and new investment patterns dictated a logic of speculation in property. The ideological banner declaring Tokyo a world city was unfurled proudly from the top of the new City Hall, completed just as the economic bubble was bursting, in 1991. As Tokyo was re-invented, the rest of the country was realigned. Despite plans and funding to decentralize and reinject vigour into the regions, they become dessicated as Tokyo's coffers filled. As busily as politicians hailed the age of the regions, they were involved in pursuing policies that reinforced Tokyo's primacy. Never have the comments of the author Kaikō Takeshi (1930–89) been more apposite: 'When foreigners say that Tokyo is not Japan, I answer, "No, Tokyo very definitely *is* Japan". All the elements that make up the country are gathered in the capital' (quoted in Ishizuka and Narita 1986: 2).

The Development of Contemporary Kyoto, the Protection of its Urban Landscape, and the Conservation of its Architectural Heritage

Many of the inhabitants of the great cities of the west of Japan would dispute this vision. Kyoto in particular manages to continue to represent a somewhat different version of Japanese urbanism. It still feels immediately different to anyone arriving in the city, whether for the first or the fiftieth time, however one might choose to define that difference. One could start with its historical heritage, which is such that its leaders and residents have to contend with a vastly different range of problems than those of most other Japanese cities, especially Tokyo. It is to some of these issues that we will now turn, as we examine ways in which a country that had never attempted to preserve its memories in physical monuments implemented a regime of preservation and protection, albeit a rather tepid one.

In the early years of the Meiji era, Japan was the first non-Western country to establish legislation to protect its ancient architectural and artistic heritage. Since then, between 1871 and 1975, no fewer than five laws have been passed, defining ever more inclusively what constituted this heritage and intensifying the various measures needed to ensure its protection. The first of these – the Ordinance concerning the Conservation of Antiquities (*Koki kyūbutsu hozon fukoku*) of 1871, and the Law Conserving Ancient Shrines and Temples (*Koshaji hozon hō*) of 1897 – had as their principal objective arresting the destruction of Buddhist buildings, statues, and artefacts. This was necessary because of the decree promulgated in 1868 establishing Shintoism as the state religion and separating Shinto and Buddhist places of worship. Buddhist temples had suffered a wave of iconoclastic vandalism in the wake of this measure. The laws of 1871 and 1897 represented, to some extent, a necessary historical correction. The subsequent laws of 1919 and 1929, however, showed a growing appreciation of what counted as national heritage. The Law Conserving Places of Historical, Picturesque, or Natural Memory (*Shiseki meishō tennen kinenbutsu hozon hō*) of 1919 defines what constitutes 'places of memory' (*kinenbutsu*), 'picturesque sites' (*meishō*), historical sites' (*shiseki*) and 'natural sites' (*tennen*). The 1929 Law for the Conservation of National Treasures (*Kokuhō hozon hō*) extends the limits of what counts as heritage beyond the religious to include the preservation of any kind of ancient building. Indeed, it makes 'national treasures' (*kokuhō*) the highest value in the cultural hierarchy. The legislation in force today, the Law for the Protection of Cultural Properties (*Bunkazai hogo hō*), dating from 1950 and revised in 1975, is a synthesis of all the preceeding legislation, and extends the state's oversight and control over a vast range of forms of heritage, now defined as 'cultural property' (*bunkazai*).

Over and above this national legislative apparatus protecting the cultural heritage, the Kyoto city authorities have produced a whole series of local ordinances and set up systems of urban conservation through zoning and the designation of preservation districts. Yet – as the chapters by Kinoshita Ryōichi on the preservation of *machiya* and Yamasaki Masafumi on the preservation of landscape suggest – the national legal provisions protecting the national heritage and the local systems for the preservation of the urban landscape have proved ineffective against the rapid destruction of the architectural heritage and against the definitive modification of Kyoto's centuries-old urban landscape, which had managed to survive the ravages of war and of economic development until the 1970s.

Ever since the 1980s – and paradoxically given that the population is falling and aging (current estimates put the population in 2025 at 1.18 million, with 29 percent over the age of 65) – land speculation has been the root cause of the destruction of this heritage. As in Tokyo or Osaka, narrow parcels of land are bought up and then combined to form large plots with frontage on the main thoroughfares, allowing the speculators to benefit from vastly increased ground occupancy ratios and build eight, ten, or even twelve-storey buildings. An exorbitant level of death duty means that small landowners have found it difficult if not impossible to retain their family homes (see the chapter by Kinoshita). The city's old patchwork of land parcels, the architectural rhythm of the city, and the traditional building concepts have all been radically changed, and Kyoto's former urban lanscape is disappearing slowly but surely. The system of zoning according to land use, whether residential, commercial, or industrial, which was established by the Town Planning Act of 1919, designated the historical centre of the city a commercial zone, leading to a complete transformation of the life-style of the inhabitants of this district, no longer able so easily to live and work in the same building. This tendency did not change as a result of the passage of new or revised Town Planning Acts in 1938, 1971, or 1991, despite a progressive reduction in the extent of the industrial zones and an increase in various detailed classifications for the residential zones.

Since the second half of the twentieth century, the very nature of the houses has changed radically. Wood has disappeared as a building material in favour of less fragile, more economic, and so-called 'non-degradable' materials. The outside gardens and their trees, which had been a feature of those residential quarters built between the Meiji era and the Second World War, are fast disappearing. Similarly, the mountains and forests, which traditionally formed a backdrop to the city, are less and less visible because of the increased height of the new buildings within the city. Not that these developments have gone without being contested: there are a good number of Kyoto citizens who are asking probing questions about what their city should look like in the future (see the chapter by Yamasaki).

Not only does the evolution in the relationship between people and their environment relate to a formal universe. As Murielle Hladik argues in her chapter, it also has a specific relationship with time, the passing of the seasons and with the aging of materials.

Despite the changes of recent years, Kyoto still has numerous reminders of its past. For example, it has nearly 2000 temples and shrines. It attracts 37 million visitors per year. Twenty percent of Japan's National Treasures and fifteen percent of its important cultural heritage is to be found here. In 1993, UNESCO listed several of Kyoto's historic sites as well as parts of nearby Uji and Ōtsu as part of Humanity's Cultural Heritage. The seventeen listed historic buildings and four historic gardens include some 160 items which are classified as 'important cultural heritage.' Unfortunately this cultural heritage fails to recognize the local vernacular architecture, which, because it is 'unofficial,' is rapidly disappearing.

Nowadays, Kyoto, with its one and a half million inhabitants, is no longer a prime city in terms of Japan's economic infrastructure. It remains Japan's premier university city, with 38 institutions of higher education, and nearly 10 percent of its population are students. Despite a considerable degree of diffusion throughout Japan, the traditional textile industry is still flourishing, thanks largely to new computer technology. This ancient capital has retained a special place in the Japanese collective memory because of a whole series of factors. It is the site of numerous art schools and workshops, for painting, music, ceramics, Noh, the tea ceremony, and flower arrangement – to mention just a few. It contains the imperial palace, *Kyōto gosho*, where the *daijōsai* (enthronement rituals) are celebrated. It is in Kyoto, with its hundreds of temples and shrines, that ancient religious feasts are still observed. Above all, perhaps, Kyoto retains its position at the centre of a rich natural site, its surrounding hills still covered with thick forest vegetation. The combination of these socio-cultural and environmental factors, with their balance of cultural heritage, local style, and natural site, give to Kyoto a thick layer of collective meaning. For all these reasons, Kyoto retains the aura of a capital city.

Kyoto and Edo-Tokyo: Japan's Two Capitals

Capital is a word with various meanings and associations. It is a monetary value that we place on assets real and to be realized, a definition that gives its name to an all-encompassing social, political, and economic system. It is a decorated top stone on a column. And it is the central city, the seat of government in a modern state or empire. The primal associations are with Rome and the Campidoglio. The derivation is from the Latin word meaning head. A capital city is an expression of centralized political power normally defined in reference to an exterior source of power. To be a capital, a city needs to be the centre of a political entity that claims authority over a territory. We think of a city as capital of a state or an empire, immobile, unlike the early capitals of seventh century Japan, moving around the Yamato basin on the death of a sovereign.

The original equivalents to the concept of capital in China and Japan are the words *jing* (*kyō* in Japanese) and *du* (*to* in Japanese). With its extensive territory, large bureaucracy, and ritualized ceremonial of government, the existence of a central urban site was crucial in China. In Japan, the functions of a capital city did not coalesce so easily. Indeed, for much of Japanese history, there were two power centres, and sometimes more. Both Kamakura in the thirteenth century and later and more importantly Edo were centres of military and political power, while Kyoto remained, in theory at least, the locus of ceremonial power. But, however much Kyoto's economy picked up again, Tokugawa control and Edo's primacy were such that Kyoto was cast irredeemably into a secondary role. As Schulz reminds us, the current Japanese word for a capital city, *shuto*, is a term that dates back only as far as the Meiji era. It expresses therefore the position of Tokyo within nation and empire.

The history of Japanese capitals can be seen as an interplay between centralizing impulses and the urge to pull away and form new centres far from established power. Such was the emperor Kanmu's motivation in founding Heian away from the tentacular control of the Buddhist clergy. Similar motives were probably held by Tokugawa Ieyasu when he established his headquarters in the far east of the country, an area where he felt safe enough to establish his own power base unmolested. At first sight, Kyoto and Edo-Tokyo would appear to have little in common, but there are at least some similarities. Both cities were founded in a conscious act of urban establishment. Both sites were problematical. Kyoto's needed drainage, so much so that it proved in part to be uninhabitable. There were problems in Edo assuring a regular supply of water, especially to the samurai residences in the hilly west of the city. Both cities came to derive their vibrancy and their prosperity from their mixture of social cultures. Tokugawa-period Kyoto was largely a city of merchant and artisans informed by an impoverished layer of courtiers and a residual samurai presence. Edo's huge population was approximately balanced between commoners and samurai, and increasingly a mingling occurred between these two populations as social dividing lines became increasingly blurred, just as the spatial ones did.

The differences were, however, considerable, and it is perhaps more fitting to end this introduction with an allusion to them. Kyoto evolved within its original plan. Indeed, the original enceinte soon proved to be quite unrealistic, and the city turned and twisted shape over the centuries with scant regard for its formal structure. Edo on the other hand soon grew beyond its intended size, sprawling down the main highways leading out of the city and spilling into the spaces in between. Edo was *primus inter pares* among the early modern castle towns that were built in such profusion in the last decades of the sixteenth and first of the seventeenth centuries. It was one, but by far the biggest one, of many *jōkamachi*. Kyoto was very much *sui generis* among Japanese cities. While it is true, as Takahashi points out in this book, that Oda Nobunaga and after him Toyotomi Hideyoshi both tried to turn it into a castle town, Kyoto remained an exception among Japanese cities, different in both social formation and spatial configuration.

References

Amino Y. (1995) '*Chūsei no Kyōto*' (Medieval Kyōto). *Kyōtoshi rekishi shiryōkan kiyō*, 12.

Ashihara Y. (1989) *The Hidden Order: Tokyo through the Twentieth Century*. Tokyo: Kodansha International.

Berry M. (1994) *The Culture of Civil War in Kyoto*. Berkeley: University of California Press.

Bognar, B. (1990) *The New Japanese Architecture*. New York: Rizzoli.

Fiévé N. (forthcoming, 2002) '*Réflexions sur le processus d'imitation d'un modèle dans l'urbanisme du Japon ancien: de Chang'an à Heiankyō*.' In R. Hagelstein et P. Servais (eds) *Perceptions et organisation de l'espace: une comparaison Orient-Occident*. Collection Rencontres Orient-Occident 4. Louvain-la-Neuve: Academia-Bruylant.

—— (1996) *L'architecture et la ville du Japon ancien. Espace architectural de la ville de Kyōto et des résidences shōgunales aux XIVe et XVe siècles*. Coll. Bibliothèque de l'Institut des Hautes Études Japonaises, Collège de France/Université de Paris VII. Paris: Maisonneuve et Larose.

—— (1992a) 'Urban Evolution of the City of Heiankyo: A Study of the Iconographic Sources, Part 1.' *Japan Forum*. 4(1): 91–107.

—— (1992b) 'Urban Evolution of the City of Heiankyo: A Study of the Iconographic Sources, Part 2.' *Japan Forum*. 4(2): 285–304.

Fujimori T. (1982) *Meiji no Tōkyō keikaku* (Meiji plans for Tokyo). Tokyo: Iwanami Shoten.
Gomi F. (ed.) (1996) *Chūsei o kangaeru: toshi no chūsei* (Reflections on the Middle Age: the medieval city). Tokyo: Yoshikawa Kōbunkan.
Hall J. W. (1974) 'Kyoto as historical background.' In J. W. Hall and J. Mass (eds) *Medieval Japan: Essay in Institutional History*. Stanford: Stanford University Press, pp. 3–38.
—— (1968) 'The Castle Town and Japan's Modern Urbanization.' In J. W. Hall and M. Jansen (eds). *Studies in the Institutional History of Early Modern Japan*. Princeton: Princeton University Press.
Hanley, S. (1997) *Everyday Things in Premodern Japan: The Hidden Legacy of Material Culture*. Berkeley: University of California Press.
Hastings. S. (1995) *Neighborhood and Nation in Tokyo, 1905–1937*. Pittsburgh: University of Pittsburgh Press.
Hayashiya T. (1964) *Machishū: Kyōto ni okeru 'shimin' keisei shi*. Tokyo: Chūō Kōronsha.
—— (1962) *Kyōto*. Tokyo: Iwanami shoten (Iwanami shinsho D 95).
Hayashiya T. (and G. Elison) (1977) 'Kyoto in the Muromachi Age.' In J. W. Hall and Toyoda T. (eds) *Japan in the Muromachi Age*. Berkeley: University of California Press, pp. 15–36.
Hérail F. (1995) *La cour du Japon à l'époque de Heian aux Xe et XIe siècles*. Paris: Hachette.
—— (1987, 1988 and 1991) *Notes journalières de Fujiwara no Michinaga (995–1018). Traduction du Midō kanpakuki*, 3 volumes. Genève: Droz.
Hur Nam-lin. (2000) *Prayer and play in late Tokugawa Japan: Asakusa Sensoji and Edo Society*. Cambridge: Harvard University Press.
Hyūga S. (1983) *Kinsei Kyōto machiya no keisei to tenkai no katei ni kansuru shiteki kenkyū* (Historical studies on the formation and development process of the Kyoto pre-modern *machiya*). Ph.D. dissertation. Kyoto: Kyoto University of Arts and Technology.
Ishida Y. (1994) 'The results fell far short or even the contrary: The dispersion policies of Tokyo from the 1860s to the 1990s and in the future.' Paper presented to the Seventh Conference of the European Association of Japanese Studies, Copenhagen, 22–26 August.
Ishizuka H. (1977) *Tōkyō no shakai keizai shi* (The social and economic history of Tokyo). Tokyo: Kinokuniya Shoten.
—— (1968) '*Meiji-ki ni okeru toshi keikaku: Tōkyō ni tsuite*' (Town planning in the Meiji Era: the case of Tokyo). In Tōkyō Toritsu Daigaku Toshi Kenkyūkai (ed.) *Toshi kōzō to toshi keikaku* (Urban structure and town planning). Tokyo: Tōkyō Daigaku Shuppankai.
Ishizuka H. and Narita R. (1986) *Tōkyōto no hyakunen* (The hundred years of Tokyo Metropolis). Tokyo: Yamakawa Shuppansha.
Jinnai H. (1985) *Tōkyō no kūkan jinruigaku* (The anthropology of space in Tokyo). Tokyo: Chikuma Shobō.
Kawazoe N. (1980) *Tōkyō no genfūkei: toshi to den'en to no kōryū* (The archetypal landscape of Tokyo: interchange between city and countryside) Tokyo: NHK Books.
Kyōto-shi (ed.) (1968 to 1976) *Kyōto no rekishi* (History of Kyoto), 10 volumes. Kyoto: Gakugei Shorin.
—— (1895) *Heian Tsūshi* (Complete history of Heian), 20 volumes. Kyoto: Kyoto shi sanjikai. Reprint (1977). Kyoto: Shin Jinbutsu Ōrai Sha.
Leupp, G. (1992) *Servants, Shophands, and Laborers in the Cities of Tokugawa Japan*. Princeton, NJ: Princeton University Press.

Machimura T. (1998) 'Symbolic use of globalization in urban politics in Tokyo.' *International Journal of Urban and Regional Research* 22 (2).

—— (1994) *'Sekai toshi' Tōkyō no kōzō tenkan: toshi risutorakucharingu no shakaigaku* (The structural transformation of 'world city' Tokyo: a sociology of urban restructuring). Tokyo: Tōkyō Daigaku Shuppankai.

—— (1992) 'The urban restructuring process in Tokyo in the 1980s: transforming Tokyo into a world city.' *International Journal of Urban and Regional Research* 16 (1): 114–128.

Maeda A. (1982) *Toshi kūkan no naka no bungaku* (Literature in urban space). Tokyo: Chikuma Shobō.

McClain J. (1982) *Kanazawa: A Seventeenth-Century Japanese Castle Town*. New Haven, Conn.: Yale University Press.

McClain, J., and Wakita O., eds. (1999) *Osaka: The Merchants' Capital of Early Modern Japan*. Ithaca: Cornell University Press.

McClain, J., et al, eds. (1994) *Edo and Paris: Urban Life and the State in the Early Modern Era*. Ithaca: Cornell University Press.

Miyata N. (1981) *Edo saijiki* (Calendar of Edo festivals). Tokyo: Yoshikawa Kōbunkan.

Mizue R. (1977) *Edo shichū keisei shi no kenkyū* (A study of the history of the formation of the city of Edo). Tokyo: Kōbundō.

Morris I. (1964) *The World of the Shining Prince: Court Life in Ancient Japan*. New York: Knopf.

Naito A. (1966) *Edo to Edo jō* (Edo and Edo castle). Tokyo: Kajima Shuppankai.

Nakagawa K. (1985) *Nihon no toshi kasō* (Japan's urban underclass). Tokyo: Keisō Shobō.

Nakai N. (1991) 'Commercial Change and urban growth in early modern Japan.' In J. W. Hall (ed.) *The Cambridge history of Japan, vol. 4: Early modern Japan*. Cambridge: Cambridge University Press, pp. 519–95.

Nishikawa K. (1972) *Nihon toshi shi kenkyū* (A study of Japanese urban history). Tokyo: Nihon Hōsō Kyōkai.

Nishikawa K. and Takahashi T. (1997) *Kyōto 1200 nen* (Kyōto one thousand and two hundred years' history). Tokyo: Sōshisha.

Nishikawa K. and Takahashi T. (1997). *Heian kara machishū no toshi e* (From Heian to a city of commoners). Tokyo: Sōshisha.

Nishiyama M. (1997). *Edo Culture: Daily Life and Diversions in Urban Japan, 1600–1868*. Hawaii: Univ of Hawaii Press.

—— (ed.) (1972–74) *Edo chōnin no kenkyū* (Research on Edo commoners). 5 vols. Tokyo: Yoshikawa Kōbunkan.

Noguchi T. (1991) *Chūsei Kyōto no machiya* (Machiya of Kyoto in the Middle Age). Tokyo: Tōkyō Daigaku Shuppankai.

Ponsonby-Fane R.A.B. (1956) *Kyoto, The Old Capital of Japan (794–1869)*. Kyoto: The Ponsonby Memorial Society.

Screech, T. (2000). *The Shogun's Painted Culture: Fear and Creativity in the Japanese States, 1760–1829*. London: Reaktion Books.

Seidensticker, E. (1985). *Low City, High City: Tokyo from Edo to the Earthquake*. New York: Knopf.

Smith, H.D. II (1986) 'The Edo-Tokyo transition: in search of common ground.' In M. Jansen and G. Rozman (eds.) *Japan in Transition*. Princeton: Princeton University Press.

—— (1979) 'Tokyo and London: comparative conceptions of the city.' In A. Craig (ed.) *Japan: A Comparative View*. Princeton: Princeton University Press.

—— (1978) 'Tokyo as an idea: an exploration of Japanese urban thought.' *Journal of Japanese Studies* 4(2): 45–80.

Steinhardt N. (1990) *Chinese Imperial City Planning*. Honolulu: University of Hawaii Press.
Stewart, D. (1987) *The Making of a Modern Japanese Architecture: 1868 to the Present Day*. Tokyo: Kodansha International.
Takahashi Y. (1983) *Kyōto chūsei toshishi kenkyū* (Studies in urban history of medieval Kyoto). Kyoto: Shibunkaku Shuppan.
Takahashi Y., Yoshida N., Miyamoto M. and Itō T. (eds) (1993) *Nihon toshi shi* (History of Japanese cities). Tokyo: Tōkyō Daigaku Shuppankai.
Tamai T. (1986) *Edo: ushinawareta toshi kūkan o yomu* (Edo: reading the lost city space). Tokyo: Heibonsha.
Tokyo Metropolitan Government (ed.) (1979–80) *Tokyo hyakunen shi* (The history of Tokyo's hundred years). 7 vols. Tokyo: Gyōsei.
Ueda A. (1976) *Kyō machiya: komyūnitei kenkyū* (Machiya of Kyoto: A collective research). Tokyo: Kajima Shuppankai.
Ueda A. and Tsuchiya A. (eds) (1975) *Machiya: kyōdō kenkyū* (Machiya: A collective research). Tokyo: Kajima Shuppankai.
Unno H. (1983) *Modan toshi Tōkyō: Nihon no 1920 nendai* (Tokyo the modern city: the 1920s in Japan). Tokyo: Chūō Kōron.
Vaporis, C. (1994) *Breaking Barriers: Travel and the State in Early Modern Japan*. Cambridge: Harvard University Press.
Wakita H. (1981) *Nihon chūsei toshi ron* (On the medieval cities of Japan). Tokyo: Tōkyō Daigaku Shuppankai.
—— (1981) 'Dimensions of Development: Cities in Fifteenth-Century Japan.' In J. W. Hall, Nagahara K., and Yamamura Y. (eds) *Japan Before Tokugawa: Political Consolidation and economic Growth, 1500–1650*. Princeton, N.J.: Princeton University Press, pp. 295–326.
Waley, P. (1997) 'Tokyo: Patterns of Familiarity and Partitions of Difference.' *American Behavioral Scientist* 41(3): pp. 396–429.
Xiong V. C. (2000). *Sui-Tang Chang'an: A Study in the Urban History of Late Medieval China*. Ann Arbor: University of Michigan.
Yamori K. (1988) *Jōkamachi no katachi* (The form of castle town). Tokyo: Chikuma Shobō.
Yazaki T. (1968) *Social Change and the City in Japan* (translated by David Swain). Tokyo: Japan Publications Inc.
—— (1962) *Nihon toshi no hatten katei* (Evolution process of the Japanese city). Tokyo: Kōbundō. Translated as *Social Change and the City in Japan*.
Yoshimi S. (1987) *Toshi no doramatourugii* (The urban drama). Tokyo: Kōbundō.

PART ONE

Power and the Spatial Imprints of Authority

CHAPTER 1

Castles in Kyoto at the Close of the Age of Warring States

The Urban Fortresses of the Ashikaga Shoguns Yoshiteru and Yoshiaki

Takahashi Yasuo, with Matthew Stavros

Introduction

One of the most enduring images of Japan during the fifteenth and sixteenth centuries is probably that of its prodigious castles. These forbidding stone fortresses with high ramparts and soaring towers, served as regional nerve centers where provincial warlords built their headquarters and based their armies. During this time of protracted civil strife, would-be rulers vied for power, capturing, destroying, and rebuilding various fortresses throughout the countryside. Castles were not merely a backdrop to events but indeed a component in the shaping of history. Without question, these architectural marvels command a significant profile in the history of Japan's long age of civil war.

In the study of fortified architecture in medieval Japan, it is important to keep in mind that the mighty castles we likely envision, with deep moats, high walls, and looming lookout towers, did not actually come into being until quite late in the period. In fact, the first wartime structure that exhibited significant martial potential was the headquarters of the thirteenth Muromachi shogun, Ashikaga Yoshiteru, who built a fortress in the center of Kyoto in 1559, a whole century after the onset of what became known as the Age of Warring States (*sengoku jidai*, 1467–1573). Until then, provincial warlords (and the shogun himself) often barricaded themselves within makeshift mountain forts which boasted neither formidable defenses nor favorable locations. These were rudimentary camps that capitulated easily to any determined aggressor.

During the Age of Warring States, nowhere were the signs of civil strife as visible as they were in the capital. Throughout this period, the townspeople of Kyoto hid their lives behind walls, barricaded their homes, and carved a system of moats throughout their city. The urbanized portion of the city itself shrunk into two main fortified islands known as Kamigyō and Shimogyō, situated in the north and south of the city respectively. Into these, the population densely compacted itself. In time, collaborative, self-governing 'block federations' (*machi-gumi*) were formed out of affiliations between townspeople who shared common hardships and together took on the task of defending their neighborhoods.

On an administrative level, the Muromachi shogunate, a military government that had first come to power in 1336, was in shambles as a vanquished shogun moved from shelter to shelter in search of allies. A lack of central authority gave rise to a national theater of civil war, animated by the profiles of numerous powerful provincial warlords who maintained castles and armies in disparate fiefdoms throughout the land.

After a century of general chaos following the Ōnin War (1467–77), endeavors toward peace began where the fighting had started, in the capital city of Kyoto. Here, the surviving members of the Ashikaga line of hereditary shogun were at work to reestablish their nearly defunct military administration. In 1559, the thirteenth Muromachi shogun, Ashikaga Yoshiteru (1536–65), constructed a castle-headquarters in the central section of Kyoto. Six years later, Yoshiteru was killed and his fortress destroyed. Later, Yoshiteru's younger brother, Yoshiaki (1537–97), became shogun and built the massive Nijō Castle at the same location.

With the construction of Yoshiteru's, then later, Yoshiaki's Nijō Castle, Kyoto underwent a significant wartime evolution, and, moreover, a major transformation was affected regarding the conceptualization of wartime martial architecture. Following the example of these structures, fortified bases throughout the country came to be places of far greater military potential and, furthermore, were no longer built outside urban settlements. The scale and military potential of fortified architecture changed and ushered in a period of castle construction that created the legacy that remains with us today (such as the grand structures in Matsumoto, Himeji, and Hikone).

In previous work, I have considered this shift in castle construction from outlying areas to the city, looking at the turning of political attention back to Kyoto during the years leading up to national unification at the end of the sixteenth century (Takahashi 1996). In this chapter, however, I intend to take a more focused look at the castle-fortresses of the shoguns Ashikaga Yoshiteru and Ashikaga Yoshiaki in an attempt to put to rest various arguments about their size, location, and architectural character. Also, and perhaps most significantly, I intend to discuss the effect each structure had on the urban landscape of Kyoto, the role each played within the context of the city's history, and the way both contributed to the transformation of Kyoto from a medieval, war-time city, into an early-modern castle-town.

The Castle of Yoshiteru: From Fort to Fortress

Throughout the early part of the Muromachi period (from 1336 to the outbreak of the Ōnin war in 1467), the shogun customarily took up residence in palatial estates within the capital. The opulent Muromachi dono and Sanjō bōmon dono, for example, were palaces of luxurious design and amenity. As the urban landscape of Kyoto was transformed by the destruction of the Age of Warring States, however, so too were the headquarters of the shogun. In fact, after 1527, due to the random violence and lawlessness characteristic of the age, Ashikaga Yoshiharu (1511–50), the twelfth Ashikaga shogun, kept himself largely removed from the capital. Even while in Kyoto between 1534 and 1542, Yoshiharu avoided official residences, opting to live in temples such as Nanzenji or Shōkokuji, located outside the urbanized city center. Several outlying, rudimentary forts were also used as residences after about 1547.

Yoshiteru's decision to move back to Kyoto in 1558 was therefore a bold statement of his intention to retake control of the capital, reassert the dominion of his office, and unify the country under a rejuvenated administration. Despite the eventual failure of his plan, Yoshiteru did, nevertheless, succeed in turning national attention back to the capital. It henceforth became clear to the numerous would-be rulers who vied for power mainly out in the provinces that national unification was not feasible without first securing control of Kyoto.

Yoshiteru's castle was the first significantly fortified shogunal headquarters to be built within an urban setting. By not avoiding the city, but rather utilizing the urban landscape as an element in the calculation of his own safety, Yoshiteru's example revolutionized the way shogunal and even *daimyō* bases were henceforth conceived and built. Furthermore, Yoshiteru's castle in Kyoto transformed the cityscape into the precursor of the early-modern urban phenomenon known as the *jōkamachi*, or 'castle-town.' Let us begin our study with an overview of the history of Yoshiteru's castle, from its construction in 1559, to its fall, six years later.[1]

Construction, Expansion, and the Fall of Yoshiteru's Castle

In the winter of 1558, having made peace with the warlord Miyoshi Nagayoshi (1522–64), Yoshiteru was able to return to Kyoto from Ōmi, where he had resided in exile for five years. Without appropriate quarters of his own in the city, the shogun took temporary lodging at Shōkokuji temple, then later in the sprawling Nichiren temple of Honkakuji (also known as Myōkakuji).

Before the autumn of 1559, sources tell of a grand ceremony marking the beginning of construction on a new shogunal headquarters within the city. The property of the former Buei residence (*Buei-tei*), was chosen for the site of the new castle (*Mokudai nikki* [Mokudai journal], 1559.8.1).² On that occasion, public officials were assigned various responsibilities while labor duties were distributed to townspeople (*Tokitsugu kyōki* [Noble journal of Yamashina Tokitsugu], 1560.2.24). Kitano Shrine, for example, was ordered to dispatch a number of workers from each home within its proprietary lands to work on the castle's construction (*Mokudai nikki*, 1559.8.1). In the 11th month, Yoshiteru specifically conscripted the townspeople from the block-federation of Roku-chō to begin digging the castle's moats, while at the same time issuing a citywide order requiring the donation of various garden trees to adorn the palace grounds (*Oyudononoueno nikki* [Oyudono courtly journal], 1559.11.3; *Genjoō nenki* [Genjoō annual], 1559.11). In a journal entry written six months after the beginning of construction, imperial treasurer Yamashina Tokitsugu (1507–1579), commented on the splendid condition of the shogun's inner residence, the moat, and the palace of Keijūin (Yoshiteru's mother) which stood on the grounds (*Tokitsugu kyōki*, 1560.2.24).³ Though the castle was not yet finished in its entirety, the shogun moved from Honkakuji into the completed main palace on the 19th day of the 6th month, 1560.⁴

Construction of castle fortifications continued long after Yoshiteru's move to the new residence (*Ise Sadasuke ki* [Journal of Ise Sadasuke]; *Oyudononoueno nikki*, 1559.11.3). In fact, records indicate that completion of the moat was delayed until the winter of 1561 due to a diversion of labor to a particular 'imperial project' (*Kanemigi kyōki* [Journal of Yoshida Kanesuke], 1565, date unknown).⁵ We also know of continuing progress on a so-called 'outer fortress' as late as 1564. Yamashina Tokitsugu makes reference in his diary to 'an enormous campaign organized to gather stones for a castle wall' at the end of the 10th month, 1564 (*Tokitsugu kyōki*, 1564.10.26).⁶ Within the shogun's palace, construction of a main audience chamber (*taimen-sho*) began in the middle of the 11th month, while the building of other official facilities and the designing of gardens continued through the end of the year (*Tokitsugu kyōki*, 1564.10.18 and 12.16).

The Portuguese missionary Luis Frois (1532–97) visited Yoshiteru at his new palace just after the new year, 1565. His glowing description of the grounds illustrates how successfully the project had progressed:

> The shogun's mansion is surrounded by an enormous moat, spanned by a beautiful, broad, bridge made of wood. At the entrance, as many as 400 high-ranking officials from all parts of the country were amassed to be received at the palace. There were also a great number of horses and beautiful palanquins assembled on a broad square outside the grounds. (Frois, *Nihon-shi*, Chapter 18)

It appears that efforts to fortify the castle's defenses continued without rest right up to the winter of 1565, when the forces of Miyoshi Yoshitsugu (d. 1573) and Matsunaga Hisahide (1510–77) launched a fierce and sudden campaign against the shogun. According to contemporary accounts, '[though it was a palace] surrounded on four sides by a deep moat, and impressive wall,' troops were able to charge the grounds through 'its still unfinished gateways.'[7]

When the dust had settled, the battle had claimed the lives of Yoshiteru and many of his closest advisors. Needless to say, the new castle was left largely in ruins, and in the words of a contemporary diarist, was 'burned to nothing, reduced to black earth,' and 'forever relegated to history.'[8]

Apparently, however, the palace of Yoshiteru's mother, which stood within the castle's outer walls, was spared the conflagration. Records indicate that the several remaining structures were dismantled and relocated to the grounds of various temples around the city. The main audience chamber, for example, was moved to the precincts of Shōkokuji. The small drawing room, along with the tea and bath houses, were moved to Rokuon'in at Saga, while the storehouse and utility rooms (buildings of far greater opulence than their names alone convey) were relocated to Honkokuji (*Tokitsugu kyōki*, 1565.7.9). In each case, the structures were converted into sub-temples dedicated to honor the shogun and his mother. In this way, the castle's former site was cleared, leaving nothing more than a trench and broken wall where the edifice once stood. Later, in the 2nd month of 1567, Shinnyodō temple was constructed on the ruins of the castle, and in the following 5th month, a prayer ceremony was held there in honor of the fallen shogun (*Tokitsugu kyōki*, 1567.2.10; 1567.5.17, 19, 20, and 21).

Having outlined the rise and fall of Yoshiteru's castle, let us now turn away from the chronology of events to examine the physical character of the castle, beginning with perhaps the most significant factor in any structure's viability as a martial headquarters, location. To be sure, location is of primary concern to the urban historian because of the way a structure has the potential to affect and be affected by its surroundings. In the case of Yoshiteru's castle, this is of particular relevance because of the sheer size and martial profile of the compound. Built right into the urban landscape of medieval Kyoto, the exact location of Yoshiteru's castle within that setting is of vital concern to an accurate telling of the city's history. As simplistic as such an examination may seem, numerous conflicting theories exist today. Because, however, an authoritative resolution is yet to be found, let us take on this task, beginning with a look at the findings of previous scholarship.

Location and Its Significance: The Urban Castle of Ashikaga Yoshiteru

The modern debate regarding the location of Yoshiteru's castle began with the research of Yumoto Fumihiko, who in 1895 published his findings in *Heian tsūshi* (The annals of Heian), where he explained that Yoshiteru's residence was 'between Karasuma, Muromachi, Kadeno-kōji, and Kasuga-kōji avenues.' According to this, the compound covered a land area one block wide and two blocks tall, located roughly in the center of the city. According to Yoshida Tōgo's *Nihon chimei dai jiten* (Great dictionary of Japanese place-names; 1900), the castle compound was situated south-west of the Konoe–Karasuma intersection. Yoshida claims that 'the location corresponds with the present-day Bueijin-chō neighborhood in central Kyoto.'

Usui Kōsaburō's *Kyōto bōmokushi* (Chronicle of Kyoto neighborhoods; 1915) largely agrees with Yoshida's findings, adding only that, in fact, it was Yoshiteru's residential 'palace' and not the entire castle compound which corresponds to the present-day Bueijin-chō neighborhood. Usui specifies that the greater castle grounds covered a land area of four square blocks, bordering on Kadeno-kōji in the north, Kasuga-kōji (Marutamachi avenue) in the south, Karasuma avenue in the east, and Machi-kōji avenue in the west. Therefore, if Usui's claim were correct, Yoshiteru's castle straddled Muromachi avenue, thus interrupting the main causeway between the city's two urban islands of Kamigyō and Shimogyō (see fig. 6).[9]

According to the more recent research of Suzuki Shin'ichi and Seta Katsuya, the residence in question stood at the intersection of Kadeno-kōji and Muromachi avenues but was built 'upon the remains of the Buei residence.'[10] The most precise theory to date is that of Yokota Fuyuhiko (1993) who explains, 'Yoshiteru's palace stood between Karasuma and Muromachi at Kadeno-kōji avenue. We may furthermore assume that the location corresponds with the land south of Kadeno-kōji, now named Bueijin-chō.'

Regardless of the accuracy of previous research, scholars have often failed to substantiate their findings with reference to reliable textual sources. This may have been due to a general lack of appreciation of the importance of location in the telling of Kyoto's urban history. Establishing clearly the location of Yoshiteru's castle is, however, not only important for what it tells us about the urban dynamics of the capital at this time, it is a key to any discussion of Yoshiaki's castle, which was later built upon the same site. Therefore, in an attempt to avoid the error of my predecessors, I will begin my own examination by clearly listing below the various sources used for this study. Finally, I will attempt to establish that Yoshiteru's *palace* (his shogunal residence) was built upon the remains of the powerful Shiba family headquarters (known as the *Buei-tei*) in central Kyoto and that the structure was bordered by Kadeno-kōji to the north, Nakamikado-kōji to the south, Muromachi-kōji to the west, and Karasuma-kōji to the east, covering a land area of a single street block.

Source 1, *Tokitsugu kyōki* (Noble journal of Yamashina Tokitsugu), 1567.5.17: 'The remains of the shogun Yoshiteru's residence are between Karasuma, and Muromachi, at Kadeno-kōji. The old castle stood at the intersection of Kadeno-kōji and Muromachi, at the location of the current Shinnyodō temple.'

Source 2, *Shinnyodō ibun* (Extant record of Shinnyodō temple), No. 8. An address from the Muromachi shogunate to Shinnyodō temple (1569.2.20): 'The remains of Kōgen-in palace – on the eastern side of Muromachi avenue, at the intersection of Kadeno-kōji...' (Akamatsu 1962).[11]

Source 3, *Mokudai nikki* (Mokudai journal), 1559.8.3: 'It is said that Yoshiteru's main shogunal palace stands at the former site of the Buei residence.'

Source 4, *Ashikaga kiseiki* (War record of the Ashikaga family): 'The Nijō Palace is the fort of the Buei encampment. The Nijō Palace is the former Buei encampment at Kadeno-kōji avenue.'

Source 5, *Hosokawa ryōke ki* (Record of the two houses of Hosokawa), 1565: 'The Nijō fort for the Buei encampment (the castle which stood there previous to the Nijō Buei encampment) ...'

Source 6, *Noritoki kyōki* (Noble journal of Yamashina Noritoki), 1408.11.6: 'The residence of Shiba Yoshimasa is at the intersection of Kadeno-kōji and Muromachi avenues.'

Source 7, *Kammon gyoki* (Noble journal of Gosukō-in), 1416.8.9: 'The Buei residence at Kadeno-kōji avenue ...'

Source 8, *Kennai ki* (Noble journal of Madeno-kōji), 1431.12.27: 'The Shiba Yoshiatsu residence is at the intersection of Nakamikado and Karasuma avenues.'

Source 9, *Ōnin ki* (Ōnin War record), 1467.7.25: 'The Shiba Yoshikado residence stands at the intersection of Kadeno-kōji and Muromachi avenues.' (fig. 6)

Taken together, the above sources appear overwhelming. Upon careful examination, however, we are able to use them to pinpoint the exact location of Yoshiteru's castle. Sources 1 and 2 indicate that the shogun's residence was located east of Muromachi avenue and west of Karasuma avenue. This leaves us with the question of whether the site stood north or south of Kadeno-kōji avenue. Sources 3, 4, and 5 indicate that the castle-palace was built upon the remains of the Shiba Buei-tei residence, which was apparently destroyed to accommodate the castle's construction. Therefore, by employing sources 6, 7, 8, and 9, we can pinpoint the location of the Shiba residence, and, correspondingly, the place where Yoshiteru's castle was later erected. A set of illustrated folding screens

Power and the Spatial Imprints of Authority

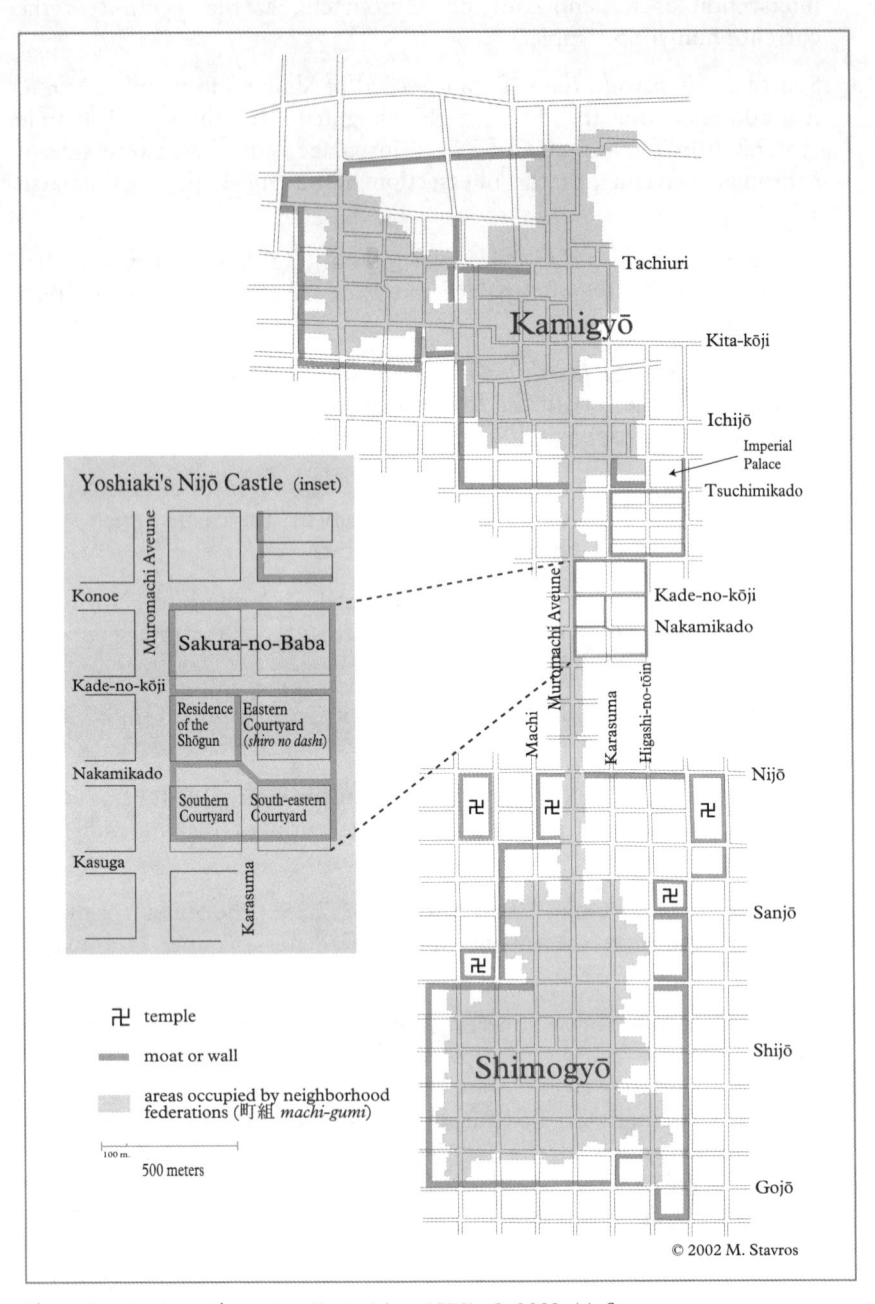

Figure 6 Late sixteenth century Kyoto (circa 1570). © 2002, M. Stavros.

depicting Kyoto at this time, known as the *Uesugi bon rakuchū rakugai zu byōbu* (Uesugi screens showing the capital and its surroundings), further augment the textual record, leading us to conclude that Yoshiteru's palace indeed covered one square street block, southeast of the Nakamikado–Muromachi intersection.[12]

When considering the various documents, we need to distinguish between the variant references to Yoshiteru's 'palace' (*goten* or *gosho*) and his 'castle' (*oshiro*). This is to say, sources make it clear that Yoshiteru's residential 'palace' (which covered one block) was surrounded by a broader fortified land area constituting his greater 'castle' grounds. Within the greater castle grounds stood not only the residential compound of the shogun, but also the residences of his mother and wife, grounds for running his horses, and numerous other structures. Archeological excavations have, in fact, uncovered the existence of a moat running east to west along Konoe-ōji, one block north of where the shogunal palace stood. Despite a lack of conclusive textual or archeological data clearly establishing the boundaries of the greater castle grounds, we can generally assume that the property covered a total land area of two city blocks, bordered by Konoe avenue in the north, Nakamikado in the south, Higashi-no-tōin in the east, and Muromachi in the west (see fig. 6).

Now that we have established the exact location of Yoshiteru's palace and castle, we will see how the edifice fits into the urban landscape of Kyoto during the Age of Warring States. First of all, despite the precedent set by all previous shoguns, who established their headquarters either in Kamigyō or Shimogyō, Yoshiteru chose not to build in either of these areas. To be sure, the land between Kamigyō and Shimogyō had remained largely 'deurbanized' throughout the fifteenth and sixteenth centuries. Why then did Yoshiteru, who had returned to Kyoto with the intent of gaining control of the city, build his headquarters in such an undeveloped area? Let us explore some of the possible explanations.

First of all, we must consider the social climate into which Yoshiteru was entering in 1558. Since the outbreak of civil war in 1467, Kyoto had suffered a relentless succession of raids and random attacks stemming from the successive emergence of would-be military leaders who sought to claim the capital for themselves.[13] Intermittent violence, compounded by the social malady inherent in a largely lawless society, transformed the city into a wartime posture of urban fortification. As a result, Yoshiteru may have recognized the liability inherent in forcefully procuring land within the densely populated areas of Kamigyō or Shimogyō. In this way, the shogun not only saved himself from the criticism of townspeople and nobility who would have been displaced, but also gained the trust of the city by not disrupting what meager threads of urban order did exist. In this way, the shogun was more able to affect development in a way that would not have been possible had he built in a more populated area.

Furthermore, Yoshiteru probably saw the strategic advantages of positioning his headquarters adjacent to the city's central pivot-point along Muromachi avenue, standing directly between the two populated urban islands of Kamigyō and Shimogyō. In addition to the strategic centrality of the location, the urban development related to his castle would complement the flow of people and goods along Muromachi avenue between the north and south sectors.

The Character of Yoshiteru's Castle

Let us now take a look within the walls of Yoshiteru's castle to examine the character of the property, the nature of its defenses, and the appearance of its architecture.

Despite the scarcity of sources describing the structures that stood within the castle grounds, we are able to confirm the existence of a main residence (*tsune gosho*), an audience chamber (*taimensho*), a drawing room (*kozashiki*), and a reception hall (*osue*), all located within the shogun's residential compound.[14] Yoshiteru apparently tended to entertain guests and conduct official business within his personal residence, rather than keeping with tradition and using the more formal audience chamber. This was the case, for example, when imperial treasurer Yamashina Tokitsugu, made several official visits to the shogun's palace in 1563. On the first occasion, the nobleman was received within the drawing room, then upon his second visit that year, within Yoshiteru's own residential quarters (*tsune gosho*). While we might be inclined to think the shogun chose to break with custom for the sake of engaging his visitors in more intimate settings, Yoshiteru's avoidance of the official audience chamber was more likely to be due to construction taking place at the site. This was the case in 1563 and 1564, when sources confirm that major repairs were underway there (*Tokitsugu kyōki*, 1563.1.1; 1564.5.22 and 10.18).

Records indicate that the residences of Yoshiteru's wife, his mother, the palace of Kasuga no tsubone, as well as the home of the shogun's consorts were all located outside Yoshiteru's residential compound (Frois, *Nihonshi*, Chapter 19). Furthermore, as previously mentioned, after the castle was destroyed in 1565, sources tell of the movement of various structures associated with Yoshiteru's mother, including a tea-house, a bath-house, a storage building, and a utility room.[15]

In addition to the various residences on the castle grounds, it appears that a large portion of the castle was used as horse riding and stabling grounds. *Tokitsugu kyōki*, for example, tells us, 'Today when 14 or 15 of the shogun's horses were mounted and displayed on the riding grounds, there was hardly enough room to see as so many people had flocked to the scene' (*Tokitsugu kyōki*, 1564.2.14; 1565.4.24).[16] Luis Frois' mention of a 'broad square outside the (palace) compound,' was likely referring to the same horse stabling area at the north end of the castle grounds. We might assume that the remaining part of the castle grounds were devoted to elaborate gardens such as the chrysanthemum garden Luis Frois took particular notice of upon one of his visits in the summer of 1564 (Frois, *Nihon-shi*, Chapter 19).

Despite the undoubted amenities of such a castle, first and foremost, the edifice was most prized for its potential as a martial fortress. The accounts of Luis Frois as well as the *Ashikaga kiseiki* (War Record of the Ashikaga Family), make reference to a deep moat and stone wall along the outer perimeter of the grounds. Recent archeological excavations at the intersection of Konoe and Karasuma avenues uncovered the remains of a pair of east-west running trenches that correspond to the castle's outer boundaries.[17] Apparently, textual sources indicate that three gates punctuated the castle walls: a western gate, an eastern gate, and a 'rear' gate (assumed to be on the northern side) (*Tokitsugu kyōki*, 1564.6.4 and 10.26). The gate facing Muromachi avenue was where Tokitsugu and other noble guests entered the grounds upon each official visit. We may therefore assume that this western gate was, in fact, the main entrance.

Despite the failure of Yoshiteru to restore the fortunes of the Muromachi shogunate, his castle in Kyoto came to be a remarkable reminder of the centrality of the capital during what otherwise was a decentralized age. To be sure, securing control of the capital was essential to a viable bid for national leadership. In 1565, Yoshiteru was captured and killed by the warlord Matsunaga Hisahide (1510–77) and his death was followed by scores of conflicts until Oda Nobunaga, a general from the province of Owari, began to piece together a semblance of unity through the creation of provincial alliances. It was Nobunaga's political cunning and overwhelming martial prowess which made it possible for Yoshiteru's younger brother, Yoshiaki, to enter the capital safely in the winter of 1568. As we will see in the coming discussion, again a mighty shogunal headquarters was erected in the capital. This time, however, under the planning and supervision of Nobunaga, Yoshiaki's castle came to be a fortress far grander in scale than any the country had seen before.

The Castle of Yoshiaki: The Making of the 'Shogun's Castle'

In 1568, Oda Nobunaga entered the capital supporting Ashikaga Yoshiaki as the legitimate fifteenth Muromachi shogun. With no immediate location to establish a base of power in the city (at this time, little remained of Yoshiteru's structure), Yoshiaki took up residence in the fortified Nichiren temple of Honkokuji in Shimogyō. Soon thereafter, however, due to an incident in which Honkokuji was suddenly surrounded by the forces of the Miyoshi clan, Oda Nobunaga decided to begin construction of a shogunal headquarters in the city. This decision led to the planning of Yoshiaki's castle-fortress, later known as Nijō-jō, or Nijō Castle.[18]

Despite the significance of Yoshiaki's castle to the urban history of medieval Kyoto, reliable data and research concerning its exact location, architectural character, and general appearance remain to a large extent unavailable.[19] Therefore, let us begin a thorough examination of Nijō Castle by looking at the remarkable events surrounding its construction in 1569.

The Pace of Construction

At the end of the first month, 1569, sources tell of Oda Nobunaga's decision to 'resurrect the castle of Yoshiteru' at the location where the Shinnyodō temple had since been built in honor of the former shogun.[20] A letter written by Frois at the time speaks of that decision, and explains plans 'to build [a new castle] larger and more grand than any the country has seen before.'[21] Before construction began, the land was prepared by razing the several structures belonging to Shinnyodō and confiscating the surrounding property.

Actual construction began on the 2nd day of the 2nd month with the stacking of a stone wall at the west end of the grounds, along Muromachi avenue. Five days later, a wall eight meters high had been built, and by the 19th day, the southern wall was also complete. Records further indicate the completion of a secondary inner stone wall by the 7th day of the 3rd month (*Bunmeibon setsuyō shū* [Bunmei encyclopedia of terms and words]). Three days later, a massive gate was erected in the south, on top of which a large turret (*yagura*) was built. Completion of a similar gate followed on the 28th day at the west end of the grounds. For decorative purposes, three to four hundred garden stones were procured from the residences of nobility in the city and dragged to the castle grounds. The grounds were later extended to the south and east of the shogun's residential compound to create broad courtyards, known as *shiro no dashi*. At this frenetic pace of construction, Yoshiaki was able to move into his new castle as early as the 14th day of the 4th month, 1569.

It was said that Oda Nobunaga himself, with hoe and bamboo cane in hand, commanded every aspect of the castle's construction. Yamashina Tokitsugu was astounded by the pace of progress, noting the collaborative effort of laborers conscripted from the eleven provinces of Owari, Mino, Ise, Ōmi, Iga, Wakasa, Yamashiro, Tanba, Settsu, Kawachi, and Izumi (*Tokitsugu kyōki*, 1569.2.14 and 3.7). Records indicate no fewer than 15,000 workers at the site at one time and sometimes as many as 25,000. Frois commented that it was because of the enormous availability of manpower that the castle's construction, which should have taken four or five years, was completed in a mere seventy days.[22] In order to hasten the move to Nijō, Yoshiaki had many of the structures he had been using at Honkokuji temple dismantled and transferred to the new site. A large number of the shogun's vassals followed suit, pillaging minor temple structures for raw materials to build their own residences in the vicinity of the shogun's new castle.[23] As a result, Honkokuji was virtually stripped of its primary structures. Furthermore, because stone was in such high demand for the building of the walls and moats, Nobunaga ordered the felling of numerous stone statues throughout the city. This pattern of destruction at one location for the sake of construction at another became characteristic of Nobunaga's building style throughout the period.

Palace Location and Castle Boundaries

Due to a lack of authoritative historical sources, various theories exist regarding the exact size and location of Yoshiaki's Nijō Castle. The simple table below represents the findings of various scholars and the boundaries they have derived for the site.

Boundaries of Nijō Castle (fig. 6)

Source	North	South	East	West	Size (square blocks)
Nihon chimei dai jiten[24]	Konoe	Kasuga	Karasuma	Machi	3 × 2
Kyōto no rekishi, vol. 4	Kadeno-kōji	Kasuga	Karasuma	Machi	2 × 2
Suzuki Shin'ichi	Takatsukasa	Nakamikado	Karasuma	Machi	3 × 2
Yokota Fuyuhiko	Konoe	Kasuga	east of Karasuma	west of Machi	3 × 3
Takahashi Yasuo	Konoe	north of Kasuga	Higashi-no-Tōin	Muromachi	3 × 2

Note the following street-name equivalents (16th c.= contemporary): Takatsukasa-kōji = Shimochōja-machi avenue; Konoe-ōji = Demizu avenue; Kadeno-kōji = Shimodachiuri avenue; Nakamikado-ōji = Sawaragichō avenue; Kasuga-kōji = Marutamachi avenue; Machi-no-kōji = Shinmachi avenue; Karasuma-kōji = Karasuma avenue; Higashi-no-tōin = Higashi-no-tōin avenue.

The boundaries of Yoshiaki's castle (fig. 6), as defined in volume four of *Kyōto no rekishi* have come to be those commonly accepted. Unfortunately, however, the assumptions of this widely used source are based wholly upon the accounts of Luis Frois, who, despite an enthusiastic mention of the castle's size ('two square blocks'), never precisely states the actual boundaries of the grounds (Frois, *Nihon-shi*, Chapter 18). We are therefore presented with the task of remedying this oversight.

While building the north-south subway line under Kyoto in 1975, the remains of what appear to have been moats and stone walls from Yoshiaki's castle were excavated at three locations along Karasuma avenue: at the intersections of Demizu avenue (Konoe), Shimodachiuri (Kadeno-kōji), Sawaragi-chō (Nakamikado-ōji), and a location about 30 meters north of Marutamachi avenue (Kasuga-kōji).[25] In recent years, these archeological findings have served as the foundations for the work of such scholars as Suzuki Shin'ichi and Yokota Fuyuhiko. As a result, it has come to be a fixed assumption that the castle grounds spanned three city blocks from north to south. Nevertheless, more recent surveys and archeological findings have given birth to a myriad of new suppositions. Therefore, by explicating the various textual sources and through an appreciation of the architectural data, it is my intention here to advance a new and authoritative theory regarding the precise location of Yoshiaki's palace and the boundaries of his greater castle grounds.

First of all, we know from numerous textual sources that the castle's construction commenced with the building of the shogun's residential compound (*goten*) at the intersection of Kadeno-kōji and Muromachi avenues, upon the remains of Yoshiteru's former palace compound. To accommodate the new project, the structures of Shinnyodō temple were razed and surrounding land was procured.

In a letter sent from Kyoto to his Jesuit brothers in India on the 17th day of the 5th month, 1569, Luis Frois describes the decision to build a new shogunal headquarters in the city:

> Two large structures [of Shinnyodō temple], now stand at the site of the palace where the former shogun (Yoshiteru) was killed. Nevertheless, it has been decided that a new castle is to be built, the likes of which this country has never seen before. Nobunaga is moving forward with the destruction of Shinnyodō temple buildings and the confiscation of four square blocks of land, upon which to begin work on the massive stone structure. (*Yasokaishi Nihon tsūshin* [Society of Jesus communiqué from Japan], 1569.6.1; Frois, 1569.5.17)

From this and other sources, we can be quite sure that the new shogunal palace was built at the same location as the previous edifice of the shogun Yoshiteru. Frois' reference to the confiscation of an enormous plot of land, covering 'four square blocks,' however, brings us to the question of just how much land area Yoshiaki's new compound actually covered (one block being equal to about 1.44 hectares).

Initially, we can surmise with a measure of confidence that Frois' mention of 'four square blocks' was actually a reference to land from four *different* city blocks confiscated in order to accommodate the castle grounds, as opposed to four *whole* city blocks. Later statements in his *Historia de Iapam* (History of Japan), in fact, confirm that the missionary was under the impression that the castle would eventually cover a land area of two ciy blocks (Frois, *Nihon-shi*, Chapter 32). Other sources, as well as archeological data, however, demonstrate that the final manifestation of Nijō Castle in fact covered a land area much broader than two city blocks. While Frois may have been misinformed, it is more likely that his judgement about the castle's final size was simply premature. This is to say, while the castle may initially have covered only two city blocks, its grounds quite probably expanded throughout the period of Yoshiaki's residence there, eventually covering a much greater land area. Frois' account is therefore not entirely reliable.

Let us therefore see what written records can tell us about the expansion of the castle grounds. In the *Hosokawa ryōke ki* [Record of the Two Houses of Hosokawa], the following entry makes clear reference to land expansion that accompanied the initial building of the castle:

> Digging a moat and laying a stone wall, a palace was built into which it is said the new shogun will soon move. From the second month of the same year [1569], the castle grounds of the shogunal [*Buei*] encampment were extended to the north and east.

This northern and eastern expansion was, in fact, recorded in various other sources, including *Sokenki* and *Ashikaga kiseiki*. Furthermore, the above record describes an expansion of the main palace by one whole block in all directions (*Dai Nihon shiryō*, vol. 10, part 2. 1560.2.2). The discrepancies in these various sources may be related to the way castle outcroppings and stone walkways around the edifice were perceived. Otherwise, the inconsistency might well be due simply to inaccuracy or error. Considering, therefore, the archeological data and the various reliable sources, let us review what we can confidently deduce about the boundaries of Yoshiaki's Nijō Castle.

First, we know with little doubt that the shogun's palace, his residential compound, was built on the one block of land southeast of the Kadenokōji–Muromachi intersection (the same location as Yoshiteru's former palace). From there, the grounds were expanded to cover the two city blocks south and southeast of the palace compound. Similarly, with the construction of walls and moats to fortify the site, the two blocks to the north and northeast of the palace, formerly land associated with Yoshiteru's castle, were likewise incorporated into the grounds. Finally, the castle bordered on Muromachi avenue in the west, Higashi-no-tōin in the east, Konoe in the north, and extended nearly to Marutamachi (Kasuga) avenue in the south.

Now that we have established its boundaries, let us turn to look at Nijō Castle's fortifications, its use of space, and the structures that existed within its walls.

The Layout of Yoshiaki's Castle

Luis Frois appears to have visited Nijō Castle shortly after its completion in 1569. Here, he describes the grounds:

> Around the outside, a deep moat has been dug, filled with water and graced with various types of ducks. A suspended bridge traverses the moat. Three large gates with mighty turrets punctuate a stone wall of 6 or 7 ells in height, and a width of 6, 7, or 8 ells. Inside, there is a smaller moat and an amusement area. The inner grounds are luxurious and beautiful beyond words. (*Yasokaishi Nihon tsūshin*, 1569; Frois, 1569.5.17)

Frois' account confirms the assumption that a double ring of moats in fact did exist around the shogun's palace. In addition, we learn from the *Genpon Shinchō-ki* (War record of Oda Nobunaga) that these moats were 'stone-lined to prevent erosion.'

As already mentioned, an archeological survey conducted along Karasuma avenue uncovered the remains of moats running east-west at four locations: where Karasuma avenue intersects Konoe, Kadeno-kōji, Nakamikado, and a location about 30 meters north of Kasuga (Marutamachi). According to the archeological report, the remains found along Kadeno-kōji and Nakamikado appear to be those of the inner moat, while those at Konoe and Kasuga were part of the outer moat (Kyōto-shi 1975; Tamamura 1996). Apparently, the inner moat tightly surrounded the block upon which the shogun's residential compound stood, while the outer moat surrounded the greater castle grounds.

The inner moat had a width of about 8.5 meters at its base and probably widened toward the top. A culvert that allowed for water to flow between the inner and outer moats cut across the grounds from east to west, apparently turning toward the south at its middle before connecting to the outer moat at the east end of the property (fig. 6). The outer moat around the castle grounds was over 8.5 meters wide in the north, where it was spanned by a large wooden bridge. It is likely that the outer moat was not as carefully constructed as the inner moat, the outer probably being, in fact, a rudimentary trench that existed previous to the castle's construction. Perhaps it was a remnant of Yoshiteru's castle, employed by Yoshiaki to augment his own fortifications.

Records make definitive mention of turrets (*yagura*) built above the outer castle gates facing south, west, and east.[26] Sources commonly recorded the shogun taking walks in the vicinity of a massive southern turret.[27] We might also assume that a gate accompanied the bridge that crossed the northern moat. However, we are unable to verify this.

Apparently, as part of the castle's expansion process, a three-storied castle tower, or *tenshu*, was erected in the south-west of the grounds. This was often used by Yoshiaki as a place to meet with members of the nobility or to watch dance performances by townspeople.[28] According to the *Genki ninenki*: 'The youths of our town held a dance concert in front of the southern turret, before the castle tower [*tenshu*]' (*Dai Nihon shiryō*, Vol. 10, part 2, 1571.7.25). This reference to a *tenshu* existing in the grounds of Nijō Castle in 1571 is the earliest known mention of such architecture in Japanese history. What makes this remarkable is that *tenshu* castle towers, or *tenshukaku*, came to be a standard architectural feature of virtually all castles built throughout Japan after this time. Let us therefore examine when the *tenshu* at Nijō Castle was constructed.

On the 22nd day of the 7th month, 1570, Yamashina Tokitsugu wrote, 'Not having visited for some time, I called upon the shogun and got to see the three-storied, south-west tower (*tenshu*)' (*Tokitsugu kyōki*). According to this, the tower had already been completed at the time of the visit. Because Tokitsugu called on Yoshiaki regularly, we can therefore assume that the *tenshu* was built just prior to this summer visit. In the early days of the construction of the castle, documents speak of the creation of an eight meters high stone base near the southwest corner of the grounds. This may have later served as the foundation of the *tenshu* castle tower.

Construction of shogunal quarters continued even after Yoshiaki's move to the castle. Upon its completion, however, the compound boasted both a main and rear residence (*tsune gosho* and *oku gosho* respectively). As already mentioned, Yoshiaki apparently used his residential quarters for hosting visitors, most probably because his palace was completed before official audience chambers were.[29] As a gift from the Hosokawa family, extravagant gardens were designed and created throughout the inner palace grounds.[30] Sources make it clear that at this time Nijō Castle was unique in that its grandeur and opulence contrasted sharply with its heavy fortifications. In time, however, Nijō Castle came to be regarded as the prototype of what historians now call the 'early-modern' castle fortress (*kinsei jōkaku*). Later examples include the castles built at Himeji, Hikone, and Matsumoto.

Evidence proving the existence of vassal residences on the grounds of Nijō Castle remains extremely scarce. Nevertheless, as we have already seen, at the time of the castle's construction, samurai disassembled structures at Honkokuji temple and moved them to Nijō for their own use. According to *Tokitsugu kyōki* (1571.1.25) and *Kanemi kyōki* (Journal of Yoshida Kanechika), upon returning home one day, a vassal by the name of Shōkōbō was surprised to find his wife in the throes of an affair with another man. Shōkōbō was finally struck down and killed by the unwelcome guest (*Tokitsugu kyōki* 1571.1.26). The phrasing in these sources describes Shōkōbō's residence as being 'within the shogun's castle' and 'on the palace grounds,' providing strong evidence that vassal residences did indeed exist within the castle walls. We can assume with some confidence, however, that such residences were located between the castle's inner and outer moats, outside of the shogun's residential compound.

As already mentioned, it is apparent from various sources that a large portion of the castle grounds were used as stabling and exercise grounds for horses. According to *Genpon shinchō-ki* (Original Nobunaga record), horse exercise grounds by the name of Sakura-no-Baba, the Cherry-blossom Riding Grounds, were created at Nijō castle when Nobunaga ordered the planting of numerous cherry trees at the site. In contrast, however, *Tokitsugu kyōki* mentions a sightseeing visit to 'Sakura-no-Baba and the moats of the shogun's palace' in 1566, actually prior to the construction of Nijō Castle (1571.12.28). We may therefore assume that the name Sakura-no-Baba, and perhaps the area itself, existed previous to the building of Yoshiaki's castle, perhaps going back to Yoshiteru's time. During the interlude between the existence of Yoshiteru's castle and Yoshiaki's Nijō Castle, Sakura-no-Baba was apparently used as an open area to run horses and hold banquets – an empty field for public use (*Tokitsugu kyōki*, 1571.2.28 and 12.6).

After Nijō Castle was built, Sakura-no-Baba served as parade and troop inspection grounds. Records indicate one occasion when men of the Tokugawa house paraded their horses there before as many as 20,000 spectators.[31] After battles as well, the area was used to display and inspect the heads of enemies claimed on the battle field.[32]

The imperial treasurer, Yamashina Tokitsugu and other members of the imperial court write of using Sakura-no-Baba for summertime walks and moon watching.[33] Townspeople also took advantage of the open space to hold their ever-popular *furyū* dance shows. For example, in the 7th month of 1571, sources indicate that as many as 100,000 performers and spectators, dancing in unrestrained celebration, converged upon Sakura-no-Baba (*Dai Nihon shiryō*, 1571.7.25). After the palace at Fushimi, south of the capital, and the stage in front of Yoshiaki's *tenshu* castle tower, Sakura-no-Baba was apparently the favored place for such dancing spectacles.

While the exact location of this open area within the castle grounds remains unknown, we may be able to make some estimations based upon place-names that remain in Kyoto to this day. For example, a neighborhood in the center of the city still bears the name Sakura-no-Baba. Assuming that the location of the former riding grounds at least roughly corresponds with this neighborhood, the grounds likely met Konoe avenue in the north, Kadeno-kōji in the south, Muromachi in the west, and Higashi-no-tōin in the east; comprising the northern one-third of the castle property.

Above, we discussed several reasons why Yoshiteru may have chosen to build his earlier castle in a relatively undeveloped part of the city. Yoshiaki, followed suit and built at the same location, but he did it perhaps for a different reason. To be sure, it seems clear that it was Nobunaga rather than Yoshiaki who chose the location, and in doing so was intending to revitalize that part of the city. To these ends, Nobunaga encouraged *daimyō* to construct residences in the vicinity of the castle in the hope of stimulating a degree of urban development there. *Genpon shinchōki* tells of construction: 'At the front and back, left and right of the palace, *daimyō* from all provinces built, of their own will, numerous homes in rows.'

Many historical documents record similar events. An entry in *Tokitsugu kyōki* from the 2nd day of the 4th month, 1569, speaks of the planning and building of homes for officials 'in the service of the shogun.' Furthermore, *Rōjin zatsuwa* (Miscellaneous talk of the elders) tells of samurai who, when ordered to find residences for themselves, confiscated structures from Honkokuji temple, reassembling them in the vicinity of the castle. *Tōdai-ki* (Historical chronicle of Matsudaira Tadaaki) records a similar case when Honkokuji structures were seized for use by shogunal guards. Despite this information, the extent of *daimyō* residential construction in central Kyōto is largely unclear. Furthermore, the scale and land area occupied by these residences is unknown. Nevertheless, because the most urbanized portions of the city stood some distance to the north and south (the fortified sections of Kamigyō and Shimogyō respectively), it is probably not inappropriate to assume that samurai residences radiated out from all four sides of the castle.

Tokitsugu kyōki confirms that samurai housing and urban development existed at the intersection of Kasuga and Machi-kōji. The entry, from the 10th month, 1570, tells of a shogunal vassal named Gonchūbō who, 'served *sake* at [his residence near] the Kasuga–Machi intersection.' According to a visual depiction of the capital at this time (*Rakuchū rakugai-zu byōbu*), it appears that the land around this intersection was not populated prior to the construction of Yoshiaki's palace. We might conclude therefore that samurai residences went up around the castle after its construction in 1569 – effecting significant stimulus at the city center.

The Fall of Nijō Castle

By 1573, Yoshiaki's relationship with Nobunaga, a man he had previously esteemed like a father, had deteriorated to the point of estrangement. Therefore, in anticipation of possible retribution, Yoshiaki ordered supplementary reinforcements on the castle's moats and the walls around the central compound.[34] Yoshiaki's preparations came too late, however, and Nobunaga's attack too soon. On the 23rd day of the 3rd month, 1573, Nijō Castle sustained a massive and sudden blitz from the forces of Nobunaga. Unable to hold off the swarms of Nobunaga's battle-hardened troops, Yoshiaki was eventually forced to leave his castle in disgrace the following, 7th month. The castle was subsequently overrun and its structures destroyed. What remained was pillaged by the townspeople of Kyōto.[35] Although the shogun survived the attack and was able to flee into exile, he remained largely impotent, with only a nominal following. Yoshiaki was the fifteenth and final shogun of the Ashikaga military administration. He died in 1597.

Because Nobunaga had no intention of using the place for himself, the site of Nijō Castle was largely abandoned. Several years after Yoshiaki's defeat (the 9th month of 1576), records indicate that only the western turret and the south and east gates remained intact. These, however, were eventually dismantled and transferred to Ōmi province where they were used in the construction of Nobunaga's own castle at Azuchi, about forty kilometers east of Kyoto.[36] In hindsight, by clearing the former castle site and by ordering the people of Kamigyō to fill in the outer moat, it seems that Nobunaga was not only trying to make way for urban development but also to prevent the site, with its favorable location and pre-dug trenches, from being used by an opposing warlord as a possible martial base in the capital.[37] *Rōjin zatsuwa* tells of a time, much later, when the former castle site had been redeveloped, explaining, 'all that remains of the warlord's [Yoshiaki's] former edifice is a stone wall to the east. Homes now spread out to the west.'

Street blocks that were initially incorporated into the castle grounds were re-zoned into residential land after which they were given neighborhood names reflecting their relationship to the former castle. This is evident in visual depictions of the capital painted at the dawn of the early-modern era, around 1600. For example, in both *Rakuchū rakugai-zu byōbu* and *Rakuchū e-zu*, the area south of the Kadeno-kōji–Muromachi intersection is indicated as Bueijin-chō (Warlord's Encampment block). South of this was Daimon-chō (great gate block). South of Konoe–Karasuma was Sakura-no-Baba block, and south of that, Hori-no-uchi-chō (block within the moat).

The Historical Significance of Yoshiaki's Nijō Castle

At the time of the castle's existence, Muromachi avenue was the main corridor connecting the capital's fortified urban islands of Kamigyō and Shimogyō. Until recently, it was thought that Nijō Castle bisected Muromachi avenue, thus dividing the city in half. This was also the author's assumption until a more thorough investigation revealed quite different facts (Takahashi 1993). As we have seen, the castle in fact stood at a tangent to Muromachi avenue, effectively complementing the city's north-south causeway.

This finding is important for a number of reasons. Yoshiaki's castle stood two blocks south of Kamigyō and three blocks north of Shimogyō. Centrally located between the city's two main urbanized areas, Nijō's main gate opened to Muromachi avenue in the west. During and after its construction, the building of *daimyō* and samurai residences adjacent to the castle came to stimulate urban development in the central part of the city which, by the 1570s, eventually led to the reconnection of Kamigyō and Shimogyō. Nobunaga's successor, Toyotomi Hideyoshi, took off from there, affecting even greater urban re-organization after 1590. By the advent of the Tokugawa period in 1600, Kyoto had shed its war-torn appearance and blossomed into a thriving city.

Nobunaga apparently had revolutionary ideas about castle construction. As already mentioned, up to about this time the headquarters of regional warlords were located in rudimentary forts, usually built outside densely populated areas and most definitely outside the capital itself. Nobunaga, however, saw this as an evasion of engagement and felt it more appropriate not to avoid the city, but rather to integrate the city into a plan of self-defense. This was accomplished, as we see in the case of Nijō, through the building of samurai and *daimyō* residences adjacent to the castle, effectively transforming the urban landscape into an extension of the fortress and a factor in the fortress' safety. The castles of Yoshiteru and Yoshiaki, characterized by their location within an urban setting, and use of the urban landscape, were precursors of the early-modern urban phenomenon known as the *jōkamachi*, or 'castle-town.' Provincial warlords who administered their fiefs from extra-urban hill-top barracks took notice of the new structures in the capital, seeing the advantages of their design and spatial arrangement. As a result, similar castles came to be planned and built throughout the provinces.

Nijō Castle did, then, have a number of unique characteristics. These consisted principally of a double ring of moats; the use of stone walls for both fortification and architectural integrity; a castle tower (*tenshu*); broad enclosed courtyards known as *shiro no dashi*; residences for vassals and their families within the castle grounds; and the main gate opening onto the side of the main street, thereby establishing a complementary relationship with the surrounding city.

A double ring of moats and stone walls were features of the earlier castle, built by Yoshiteru. In fact, it is clear that Yoshiteru's castle served as the kernel, both physically and ideologically, upon which was built Yoshiaki's succeeding edifice. The other features listed above were unique to Nijō Castle; adaptations made by Nobunaga himself. What is perhaps more remarkable about these various architectural characteristics, however, is not their existence at Nijō but rather that most of the castles built after this time, including those of Toyotomi Hideyoshi and Tokugawa Ieyasu (Jurakudai, Edo Castle, and the later Nijō Castle), all exhibited similar traits.

In Conclusion

No longer seeing the purpose of governing the capital through the guise of a puppet shogun, Oda Nobunaga deposed Ashikaga Yoshiaki in 1573 and effectively dissolved the Muromachi shogunate. Thereafter, the office of shogun remained vacant until Tokugawa Ieyasu was appointed in 1603. In the meantime, having secured a measure of control over the capital and its environs, Nobunaga set about building his own castle and military headquarters at Azuchi, in the province of Ōmi. After the main structures were erected, having learned the advantages of building within an urban setting, great resources were then expended on spurring urban development around the new castle.

Back in the capital, even after the destruction of Nijō, the city was well on its way toward regeneration. The construction of numerous samurai homes and the influx of people to serve the warrior class led to the rezoning of streets and blocks in the city center. Neighborhoods were born and block-federations took shape, as the city enjoyed its longest period of peace in over a century. The population was finally able to begin moving outside of the barricaded existence it had maintained throughout the Age of Warring States. The result was the eventual reconnection of the urban islands of Kamigyō and Shimogyō.

Right up to the end of the sixteenth century, regional warlords continued to fight it out in the provinces while constructing great castles. In each case, stylistic characteristics and locational attributes strongly reflected those of the earlier castles of Yoshiteru and Yoshiaki. Perhaps the climax of castle architecture in Japan, however, came with the completion of Ieyasu's massive fortress in Edo (the whole series of buildings was eventually completed, after much difficulty, in 1640). In this case as well, the strategic placement of vassal homes around the central fortress, and the technique for the stacking of stone ramparts mimicked the spatial ideology and architectural innovation introduced first at Yoshiaki's Nijō Castle.

While the main purpose of this chapter has been to explain the location and physical character of the castles of the Ashikaga shoguns Yoshiteru and Yoshiaki, we have also come to see the important contribution these structures made to the transformation of Kyoto from a medieval, wartime city into an early-modern castle-town. Furthermore, it is clear that these structures influenced the way castle architecture was thereafter contrived and built throughout the country. To be sure, these shogunal headquarters were in fact, the first such structures in Japan to fit the image most of us have of castle architecture in the early-modern period, with massive walls, wide trenches, and soaring stone towers – perhaps the first such structures worthy of their names as *castles*.

Notes

1 Important research on Yoshiteru's palace can be found in Suzuki M. (1965), Suzuki S. (1979), Seta (1994), and Yokota F. (1993).
2 *Genjoō nenki* tells of the ceremony. In this case, *Buei* residence (*Buei-tei*) refers to the residence of the Shiba military (Buei) family in Kyoto. This terminology can be ambiguous as *Buei-jin*, or *Buei-tei*, can also refer to the shogun or his residence.
3 Keijūin was the wife of former shogun Yoshiharu.

Castles in Kyoto at the Close of the Age of Warring States

4 According to the *Ashikaga kiseiki*, 'Construction [fortification] began on the shogunal mansion in the winter of 1564. A house tax of 2 gold pieces was collected from the people of Sesshū Kamishimo-gun ... The postwar construction project was so big that it became a nuisance to the six provinces surrounding Kyoto.' According to the *Shiryō sōran*, construction began at the site of the Muromachi-dono. This, however, is in error.

5 *Oyudononoue nikki* confirms that a 'giant trench,' *ōbori*, was completed around the castle (1561.8.19).

6 There is mention in the *Iwanami Nippon jisho* of, 'Moat walls made of stone in the same fashion as *ishigaki*-stone walls.' That is, moats were stone-lined.

7 Similarly quoted in both *Ashikaga kiseiki*, *Tokitsugu kyōki* (1567.2.10).

8 *Tokitsugu kyōki* tells of the fortress being left in ruins while the epic diary (various authors) of *Oyudononoue nikki* dramatically describes the site as being reduced to 'black earth.'

9 This theory was commonly accepted until quite recently, perhaps because of the fact that in so many other cases, *daimyō* of the early-modern period constructed urban castles in the center of towns, so that main streets radiated outward from their castle gates.

10 According to the explanation of Suzuki Shin'ichi and that in *Kyōto no rekishi*, vol. 4, the remains of the Buei residence are thought to have stood south of Kadeno-kōji and west of Muromachi. *Buei*, or 'martial officer,' refers to the shogun in this case.

11 Kōgen'in is Yoshiteru's *hōmyō* or *kaimyō*, the name given to him following his death.

12 *Uesugibon* depicts the *Buei-tei* as being southeast of the Nakamikado-Muromachi intersection.

13 The newest and perhaps most ambitious overview of this period's strife can be found in Berry (1994).

14 For accounts about the appearance of Yoshiteru's castle, see, Frois, *Nihon-shi*, Chapter 19, *Tokitsugu kyōki* (1564.6.4) and (1564.9.18), and *Ise Sadasuke ki* (1560.2.24).

15 The structure in which Keijū'in lived was actually on a different block than Yoshiteru's palace. According to a *Tokitsugu kyōki* entry from the 1st day, 3rd month of 1563, and the 9th day of the 7th month, 1565, the *tsune gosho*, main audience chamber, smaller *zashiki*, tea house, bath house, storage and utility houses, as well as a garden existed on the grounds.

16 On the 20th day of the 2nd month of 1567, the same record speaks of the 'Sakura-no-Baba,' most likely referring to the same riding grounds. The Sakura-no-Baba would later come to be used by Yoshiaki as well.

17 Kyoto City Karasuma High-Speed Railway Investigation Committee, *Heian-kyō kankei iseki chōsa gaihō*, 1975. And, *Kyōto-shi kōsokutetsudō Karasuma sennai iseki chōsa nenpō*, 1, 2, 3 (1979, 1980, 1981).

18 Yoshiaki's castle is often referred to as *kyū Nijō-jō* (the former Nijō Castle), or *Nijō-dai*. Neither name, however, was used at the time of the castle's existence. Important historical records from the 2nd day, 2nd month, 1569, about Yoshiaki's Nijō Castle are reproduced in part 2 of vol. 10, *Dainihon shiryō*. Yoshiaki's *Nijō-jō* should not be confused with the Nijō Castle that stands in Kyoto today, built almost half a century later by Tokugawa Ieyasu.

19 Suzuki Shin'ichi (1979) does investigate the location of Yoshiaki's Nijō Castle, yet leaves room for doubt in his conclusions. Upon examination of palace location, history and makeup, Yokota (1993) states, 'more consideration is necessary to investigate the development process that took place through temple

fortification and the transformation between Yoshiteru's castle and Yoshiaki's castle, eventually leading to the construction of Jurakudai castle.'
20 *Tokitsugu kyōki*, on the 27th day, 1st month, 1569, speaks of, 'the rebirth of the old castle of shogun Yoshiteru at the site of Shinnyodō temple at Kadeno-kōji and Muromachi Avenues.' A similar entry from the *Shinshō gokuraku-ji monjo*, dated the 26th day, 1st month, 1569, says, 'The shogun's palace will be built at the Shinnyodō temple site' (Okuno 1969). Akamatsu Toshihide in his 1962 *Kyōto jishi-kō*, quotes documents of the Shinnyodō temple written by officials of the shogun in 1569, explaining that the shogun's new castle will be built at the remains site of Kōgen-in's [Yoshiteru] castle, the present site of Shinnyodō temple, standing east of the Kadeno-kōji–Muromachi intersection.'
21 *Nihon Yasokai nenpō* [Annual record of the Society of Jesus in Japan] (in *Dai Nihon shiryō*).
22 According to the *Tamonin nikki* (Tamonin journal) of the 28th day, 2nd month of the same year, 'It has been said that construction is being done by tens of thousands of samurai.'
23 *Tōdai-ki* tells of samurai seizing temple buildings and moving them to the vicinity of the castle.
24 According to Yoshida Tōgo's *Dai Nihon chimei jisho* (under the heading, *Nijō joshi*), military and other records show that Yoshiteru's castle was expanded one block both to the northeast and southwest. The Buei residence remains are recorded as standing south of Kadeno-kōji and west of Karasuma. Assuming this, however, the eastern border of Yoshiaki's castle should be Higashi-no-tōin. Why it is recorded as Karasuma is unclear.
25 *Kyōto-shi kōsoku tetsudō Karasuma sennai iseki chōsa nenpō* (1975, 1979, 1980, 1981); Tamamura (1996).
26 Various entries from *Tokitsugu kyōki* speak of castle gates and turrets: 11th day, 3rd month, 1569, 'Yesterday, a south gate and turret were built.' Twenty-eighth day, 3rd month 1569, and the 24th day, 9th month, 1573, 'Yesterday it was the south gate, today it was the eastern gate that was disassembled and moved to Gōshū, Azuchi.' Though there is no historical record speaking of a turret over the eastern gate, we may assume that it resembled the west and south gates, which both had turrets.
27 Being a regular visitor to the castle grounds, Yamashina Tokitsugu recorded various facts regarding the site. Third day, intercalary 5th month, 1569, 'The shogun was at the southern turret.' Twenty-first day, leap month between the 5th and 6th month, 1569, 'We [the shogun and I] strolled past the southern turret and spoke of various things.' Twenty-fifth day, 7th month, 1571, 'Going with the shogun, we viewed dance shows at the southern turret.' Thirteenth day, 9th month, 1576, 'The western turret has been moved to Gōshū.'
28 *Tokitsugu kyōki*, 22nd day, 7th month, 1570, 'Not having visited for some time, I called upon the shogun and viewed the 3 storied southwest turret, accompanied by the shogun, discussing various things.' *Dai Nihon shiryō*, 25th day, 7th month, 1571, 'The youths of our town held a dance concert in front of the south turret, before the *tenshu*.' *Tokitsugu kyōki*, 29th day, 7th month, 1571, 'The people of Shimogyō performed 4 dances before the shogun as we watched from the turret. Later we had sake at the residential (*tsune*) palace.'
29 Two entries in *Tokitsugu kyōki*, dated the 1st day, 7th month, 1569, and the 25th day, 1st month, 1571, tell of meetings with the shogun at the new (*tsune*) palace. The *Kanemi kyōki* records, 'meeting with the shogun at the rear palace,' dated the 9th day of the 4th month, 1573.

30 *Tokitsugu kyōki* records a most humorous event on the 3rd day, 3rd month, 1569: 'By order of Oda Nobunaga, three to four thousand men dragged a giant stone from the garden of Hosokawa Uma no Kami's residence, accompanied by flutes and drums, to the intersection of Kadeno-kōji and Muromachi avenues. Because, upon arrival, the sun had already begun to set, they were unable to get the stone past the castle moat and were forced to leave it in the street. It was a most surprising site.'

31 It is reasonable to assume that Tokugawa Ieyasu himself was among those who participated in such parades.

32 According to *Tokitsugu kyōki* in an entry for the 17th day, 3rd month, 1570, 'I was there when the shogun inspected a parade of Mikawa Tokugawa's men on horseback with bristling saddles and reigns, at Sakura-no-Baba.' *Kanemi kyōki*, in an entry for the 15th day, 11th month, 1570, has it thus: 'The shogun mounted a horse at Sakura-no-Baba.' Tokitsugu speaks of the spoils of war and the stabling grounds in an entry for the 7th day, 8th month, of 1571, 'As a result of the battle of the previous 4th day, today the shogun inspected the 240 or so heads displayed at Sakura-no-Baba.'

33 'We took an evening stroll under the full moon at the Sakura-no-baba' *Tokitsugu kyōki* (1570.7.9).

34 The *Kanemi kyōki* speaks of the order by Yoshiaki to the head of Yoshida Town to dispatch men for work at the castle. Entries for the 17th day, 2nd month, and the 20th and 21st days of the 4th month speak of such requests for assistance. Finally, on the 28th day of that month, it became clear that the men were needed to construct supplemental castle fortifications.

35 *Kanemi kyōki*, on the 12th and 13th days of the 7th month, recounts the pillage of Yoshiaki's castle. *Tokitsune kyōki*, on the 14th day, 9th month, 1576, has the following: 'Going to visit the site of the old shogunal castle, it seems as if the townspeople have taken the stones from the previously standing wall'; and on the 18th day, 9th month, 1576: 'Wanting to see the garden of the old shogunal palace, I went along as well. It appears as though townspeople have carried away all the garden stones.'

36 'The western turret has been moved to Ōmi' (*Tokitsugu kyōki* 1576.7.12).

37 *Tokitsugu kyōki*, 25th day, 10th month, 1576, 'The secondary moat of the shogun's castle has been filled in by the people of Kamigyō.'

References

Akamatsu T. (1962) *Kyōto-fu ji-shi kō* (Interpreting temple history in Kyōto prefecture). Kyoto: Hōzōkan.

Berry, M.E. (1994) *The Culture of Civil War in Kyoto*. Berkeley: University of California Press.

Frois, L. (1978) *Nihon-shi* (History of Japan; original title, *Historia de Iapam*; trans by Matsuda K. and Kawasaki M.), *vol. 4*. Tokyo: Chūō Kōronsha.

Kyōto-shi (ed.) (1895) *Heian Tsūshi* (Complete annals of Heian), 20 vols. Kyoto: Kyōto-shi sanjikai. Reprint (1977), Kyoto: Shin Jinbutsu Ōrai Sha.

Kyōto-shi (ed.) (1968 to 1976) *Kyōto no rekishi* (History of Kyoto), 10 volumes. Kyoto: Gakugei Shorin.

Kyōto-shi Kōsoku Tetsudō Karasuma Sennai Iseki Chōsakai (Kyoto City, Karasuma High-Speed Railway Investigation Committee) (1975), *Heian-kyō kankei iseki chōsa gaihō* (Report on Heian-kyō Related Site Excavations). Kyoto: Kyōto-shi Kōsoku Tetsudō Karasuma Sennai Iseki Chōsakai.

Kyōto-shi Kōsoku Tetsudō Karasuma Sennai Iseki Chōsakai (Kyoto City Karasuma High-Speed Railway Investigation Committee) (1979, 1980, 1981), *Kyōto-shi kōsoku-tetsudō Karasuma sennai iseki chōsa nenpō*, 1, 2, 3 (1979, 1980, 1981). Kyoto: Kyōto-shi Kōsoku Tetsudō Karasuma Sennai Iseki Chōsakai.

Okuno T. (1969) *Oda Nobunaga monjo no kenkyū* (Research on historical document of Oda Nobunaga). Tokyo: Yoshikawa Kōbunkan.

Seta K. (1994) '*Kubō no kōsō* [Conception of the shogun].' In *Rakuchū rakugai no gunzō* (View of the Inner and Outer Capital). Tokyo: Heibonsha.

Suzuki M. (1965) *Nihon chūsei toshi kenchiku no kenkyū* (Research on Japanese medieval urban architecture). Published privately by author.

Suzuki S. (1979) *Nijō-jō to nijō gosho* (Nijō Castle and Nijō palace), in *Kokugaku-in zasshi*, vol. 80, January.

Takahashi Y. (1993) '*Chū-kinsei toshi no kūkan to kōzō*' (Space and structure of medieval and early modern cities). In *Kansai kinsei kōkogaku kenkyū*, vol. III (The Journal of Kansai Early-Modern Era Research Society of Archeology). Osaka: Kansai Kinsei Kōkogaku Kenkyūkai.

Takahashi Y. (1996) '*Kyō no shiro no rekishi: Nijō-jō*' (History of Kyōto castles: Nijō Castle). In *Nijō-jō* (Nijō Castle). Tokyo: Gakushū Kenkyūsha, pp. 18–21.

Tamamura T. (1996) '*Hakkutsu ga kataru Nobunaga Nijō-jō*' (What excavations tell us about Nobunaga's Nijō Castle). In *Nijō-jō* (Nijō Castle). Tokyo: Gakushū kenkyūsha, pp. 36–39.

Tōkyō teikoku daigaku shiryō hensanjo (1901–) *Dai Nihon shiryō*. Tokyo: Tōkyō Teikoku Daigaku Shuppan.

Usui K. (1915) *Kyōto bōmokushi* (Chronicle of Kyoto neighborhoods). Kyoto: Rinsen Shoten.

Yokota F. (1993) '*Jōkaku to ken'i*' (Castles and power). In *Iwanami kōza, Nihon tsūshi*, vol. 11. Tokyo: Iwanami Shoten.

Yoshida T. (1900) *Dai Nihon chimei jisho* (The great dictionary of Japanese place-names). Tokyo: Toyamabō.

CHAPTER 2

Social Discrimination and Architectural Freedom in the Pleasure District of Kyoto in Early Modern Japan

Nicolas Fiévé

Nagare o tatsuru kawatake no yūjo
'The courtesan is like the river bamboo standing in the current'

The adoption of neo-Confucianist thought as the norm, in which human order is understood as analogous to the natural order, and with the emphasis that it gives to morality rather than metaphysics, permitted the development of the theory whereby everything was ordered according to its place and function in society.

(Hérail 1986: 318)

As far back in urban history as we are able to trace, our towns and cities have always spawned certain anonymous areas, not part of the 'normal' town, most often to be found on the fringes. These are zones of transgression, by day as by night. The city limits, near the city walls, near the gates which gave access to the town, the edge of town, the districts around stations and markets – these are all areas which attracted 'non-conventional' trade and commerce. As conurbations grew, so too these spaces moved ever outwards, away from the traditional town centres: far enough away from the city centre to escape regular surveillance but not so far as to fall under the strictures of countryside traditions. The evolution of such areas is a constant feature of all cities, but the activities which used to be associated with a certain part of a town can persist long after the area itself may have evolved. So, for example, when a city expands to engulf what used to be its periphery, the activities that were practiced there – which originally may have been considered unlawful – can survive, not just in the short term but in the long term too. Such practices indeed often tend to be become more 'acceptable' within the now enlarged urban community. In Paris, for example, there is an area which, from being the *Cour des*

Miracles in medieval times, later became the site of the gallows and much later again in the Paris of Haussmann was the site of Les Halles (the food market); this area around the Saint-Denis and Bonne Nouvelle districts has always been a centre for prostitution and other illicit commerce. Even though the Paris of today has pushed its boundaries far beyond those of the old Saint-Denis gate, the phenomenon still persists. The various features that characterise the layout of a city are an expression of the multifarious rhythms – however contradictory – of daily life.

The Japanese city, and in particular the city of Kyoto, was – and still is – a parallel example of dynamic urban evolution. The bar districts of Gion, Ponto-chō, and Kitano, which have become centres of night life within the present-day city can all be traced back through history not only to early modern times but even further back to the very origins of the city. Nowadays, to find the 'love hotels,' the 'soap lands,' and the various other meeting places that are more or less socially unacceptable nowadays, however, one has to look further out toward the limits of the modern conurbation: beyond the Meishin Expressway interchange to the south; or to the east of Yamashina; to the areas which are not really part of the city, nor even its suburbs, and yet which cannot really be called 'out in the country.'

The point of this chapter is not to offer a historical inventory of Kyoto's various marginal zones. What concerns us is the period during which the early-modern city developed, in other words, throughout the seventeenth century, when the centralised government of the Tokugawa attempted to impose on the citizens of Kyoto – of whatever class – a town-planning system which was based on the social codes of society as established by the military class. In particular, we shall examine how this new segregational spatial arrangement affected the lowest classes most, especially in the way it tried to wipe out 'public' prostitution by confining it – on the basis of the Chinese model – within licensed 'public' districts, which were separate and purpose-built.

The fundamental question which concerns us here is not so much what happened historically speaking to the 'licensed district' of Kyoto but rather the attempt to ascertain, on the basis of this example, what were the models – in both urban and architectural terms – adopted to shape subsequent urban planning. Before the early modern period, the parts of Kyoto where prostitution took place were not defined by an *a priori* architectural or urban model peculiar to such districts. But when and wherever a new district was planned, this necessarily implied setting in place the means of its construction. From the person who made the initial demand, through the architect to the master of works, there was a chain of command which influenced the initial conception, the design, and the construction of the buildings. And – as so often in architecture and town planning – it was not so much current innovative thinking but rather the weight of existing models which proved decisive in shaping the 'new' architecture. So we find a whole series of pre-existing styles which served as models for the different phases of the construction of Kyoto's 'licensed district': the Chinese model of the 'licensed district,' the parcelling up of available space borrowed from existing popular usage in Kyoto, the interior layout of buildings copied from Kyoto's large town-houses but imitating some caracters of the upper-class style of architectural decoration.

The Terrain Beyond the Urbanised Limits of the City, the Places of Entertainment, and Prostitution in the Ancient Capital

In ancient Japanese society, and especially in Yamato era, the archetypal rural community was usually a grouping of dwellings at the foot of a mountain, at the edge of a forest – wherever the deities were believed to be. These deities descended among people during the regular festivals that gave a rhythm to the agrarian calendar before returning to the forest or the mountain. Kyoto's site, a basin surrounded by mountains, has always been strongly marked by this traditional way of understanding space, in spite of the principles of Chinese topomancy on which the old capital, Heian, had been established in 794.[1] The outermost parts of town were exactly the right kind of place for this contact with the other world, and it is no wonder that numerous sanctuaries were situated there. For the same reason it was here that executions and cremations took place, here that tombs and cemeteries were located. These peripheral zones carried a strong symbolic influence on the way that space for daily life came to be organised. As Amino Yoshihiko has written,

> Geographical margins, the borders between territories, places where the world of nature meets the world of humankind (beaches, river banks, sand banks in the middle of the river), all these were considered particularly appropriate for siting a shrine and sometimes a market as well. Sites such as these which had a link with a place that was considered as sacred – because they were a point of contact with the world of deities – permitted relations between humans themselves which were of a different nature from the relations which united them in non-sacred places. (Amino 1994: 148–49)

The same holds true for the areas around rivers, given that river banks symbolised – for the medieval mind – the gateway to the other world. In the Kyoto of the medieval period (1185–1573), it was those who belonged to the lowest and most discriminated classes, the 'non-humans' (*hinin*) as they were known, who used to come to the banks of the River Kamo, bring their dead there, and leave them, unburied, for the river to carry them off in one of its periodic floods. The river banks were also where executions were carried out. These were areas considered 'soiled' by the presence of death and of dead bodies, but the river waters cleansed this. In the course of the fourteenth and fifteenth centuries these areas also became meeting places, especially around the bridges, where hawkers, peddlers, and travelling merchants would gather. Direct and quick commercial transactions between people who did not know each other were possible in these places, precisely because they were without or beyond the areas regulated by conventional social connections.

In the Muromachi period (1336–1573), entertainers were at the same time both free and discriminated against (this was quite explicit for the status of some artists close to the Ashikaga shoguns). Alongside the relative freedom that these kinds of people received, women entertainers enjoyed an unusual degree of autonomy. It is these two elements, on which recent research in medieval history has shed light, that give us a better understanding of the status and the role of the courtesan-artists at the end of the Middle Ages. There were 'courtesans' (*asobime*, *yūjo*, or *ukareme*) and 'court dancers' (*shirabyōshi*), but also certain categories of 'itinerant nuns' (*bikuni*) and 'wandering shaman-priestesses' (*aruki miko*) too, part of an unofficial and non-established but nevertheless visible part of the urban population of Kyoto. The fact that most of these women engaged in prostitution was not the sole determining factor that led society to discriminate against them.

It must remembered that prostitution had previously existed in Kyoto. In the *Yūjōki* (Notes on women of pleasure, late eleventh century), Ōe no Masafusa (1041–1111) describes the women who were to be found on the boats plying between Heian and the sea. There are a few famous examples of courtesans in the Heian period (784–1185) who came from good families, such as the poetess Shirome (dates unknown), daughter of the Governor of Tango (Takigawa 1967). From early on, diverse forms of prostitution, from ordinary prostitutes to high class courtesans, coexisted. Some *shirabyōshi* dancers were kept by great families; an example is Shizuka Gozen (dates unknown), who became the spouse of Minamoto no Yoshitsune (1159–89). During the Kamakura shogunate (1185–1333), the development of trade encouraged the spread of prostitution across the whole country. The civil strife that marked the end of the Muromachi period, threw a great number of women, nuns, and temple and shrine maidens onto the streets, where they were often condemned to prostitution in order to survive. It is known that during the same period, the Ashikaga shoguns themselves kept courtesans who were practitioners of the arts of entertainment (music, dance, and singing) (Takigawa 1967). On the other hand, many records from the Muromachi period refer to prostitution in street blocks near Kujō avenue (Kujō no yūri), situated at the extreme south of the city (fig. 7).

A couple of famous anecdotes will help illustrate the differences between the way that courtesans were perceived by the common people and how they were considered by the authorities at the beginning of the Tokugawa

Social Discrimination and Architectural Freedom

period (1603–1867). It is clear from the adventure recounted in the *Saru Genji no sōshi* (Notes of Saru Genji) that in the fifteenth century some courtesans were able to move freely throughout the city, where they could be admired. The hero of the story, named Saru Genji, is a sardine-seller who falls in love with a beautiful woman as she passes by over Gojō bridge in her palanquin. In the face of such beauty and such apparent class, Saru Genji thought she must be the daughter of a noble family. However, he discovers from his employee that she is a 'companion for pleasure' (*yūkun*), one of the capital's famous courtesans. In order to seduce her, Saru Genji impersonates a *daimyō*, gathering round himself a retinue of two hundred people from among his friends.

In the city of Kyoto as transformed by Toyotomi Hideyoshi (1536–98) in the sixteenth century, an earthen rampart (*odoi*) drew a border between *rakuchū*, the inside, urbanised world, and *rakugai*, the outside world. During this period, the various trading and exchange activities which had long been a lively feature of the main thoroughfares continued to develop, right up to the gates of the city. Markets were set up in the empty spaces and the undefined zones on the urban fringes, and it was here, most notably to the east, on the banks of the River Kamo, that the 'people of the bank' (*kawaramono*) lived. Here, too, was where the itinerant populations of artists came and set themselves up: jugglers, acrobats, illusionists, people who practised folk-medecine, story-tellers, as well as itinerant begging monks and nuns. These people also went freely about the city and plied their trade when and where they thought best. 'Games on public thoroughfares' (*daidōgei*) were part of the landscape of everyday life.

Nevertheless, according to the newly defined social codes of the Tokugawa *bakufu*, prostitution soon became the subject of extremely rigorous control by the authorities. This is evident from another popular traditional story about Governor Itakura Shigemune (1585–1656), which has very close parallels to the beginning of Saru Genji's story. It is said that in 1640, Shigemune passed a very high ranking woman accompanied by her retinue, making her way through the streets of the capital. Not knowing who she was or if etiquette demanded that he should dismount his horse to bow to her, he went back home very embarrassed. When he learned sometime later that she was a *tayū*, a high ranking courtisan from Rokujō-misuji (fig. 7), Shigemune became very angry and, decided to lock all the city's prostitutes in a district away from the centre, at Suzaku (Takada 1993: 45). The fame and popularity of this legend – certainly apocryphal, but supposed to lie at the origin of the 'pleasure district' of Kyoto, known as Shimabara – indicates how strongly the people of Kyoto reacted against courtesans being excluded from urban life.

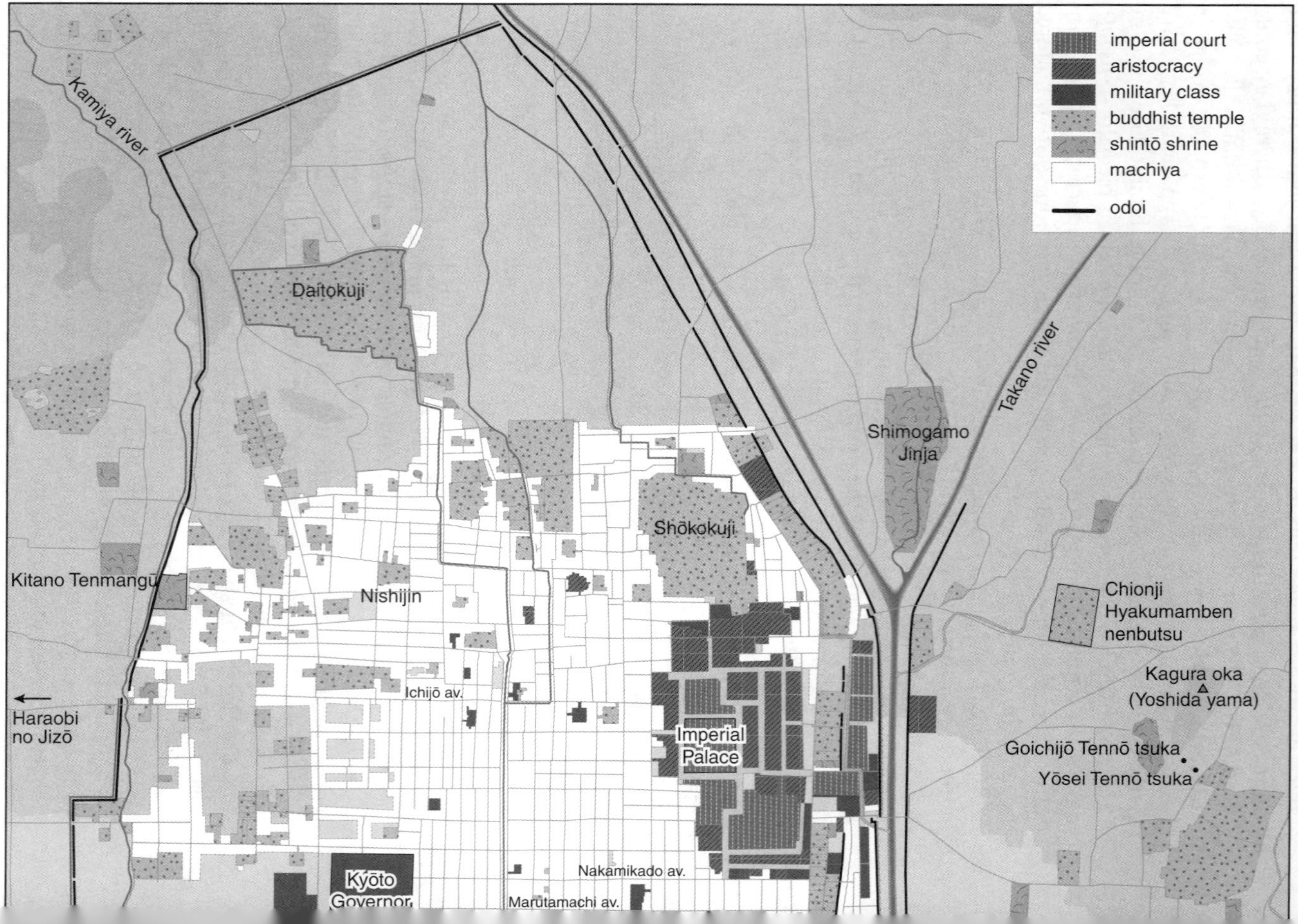
imperial court
aristocracy
military class
buddhist temple
shintō shrine
machiya
odoi
Kamiya river
Daitokuji
Takano river
Shimogamo Jinja
Shōkokuji
Kitano Tenmangū
Nishijin
Chionji Hyakumamben nenbutsu
Kagura oka
(Yoshida yama)
Ichijō av.
Haraobi no Jizō
Imperial Palace
Goichijō Tennō tsuka
Yōsei Tennō tsuka
Nakamikado av.
Kyōto Governor
Marutamachi av.

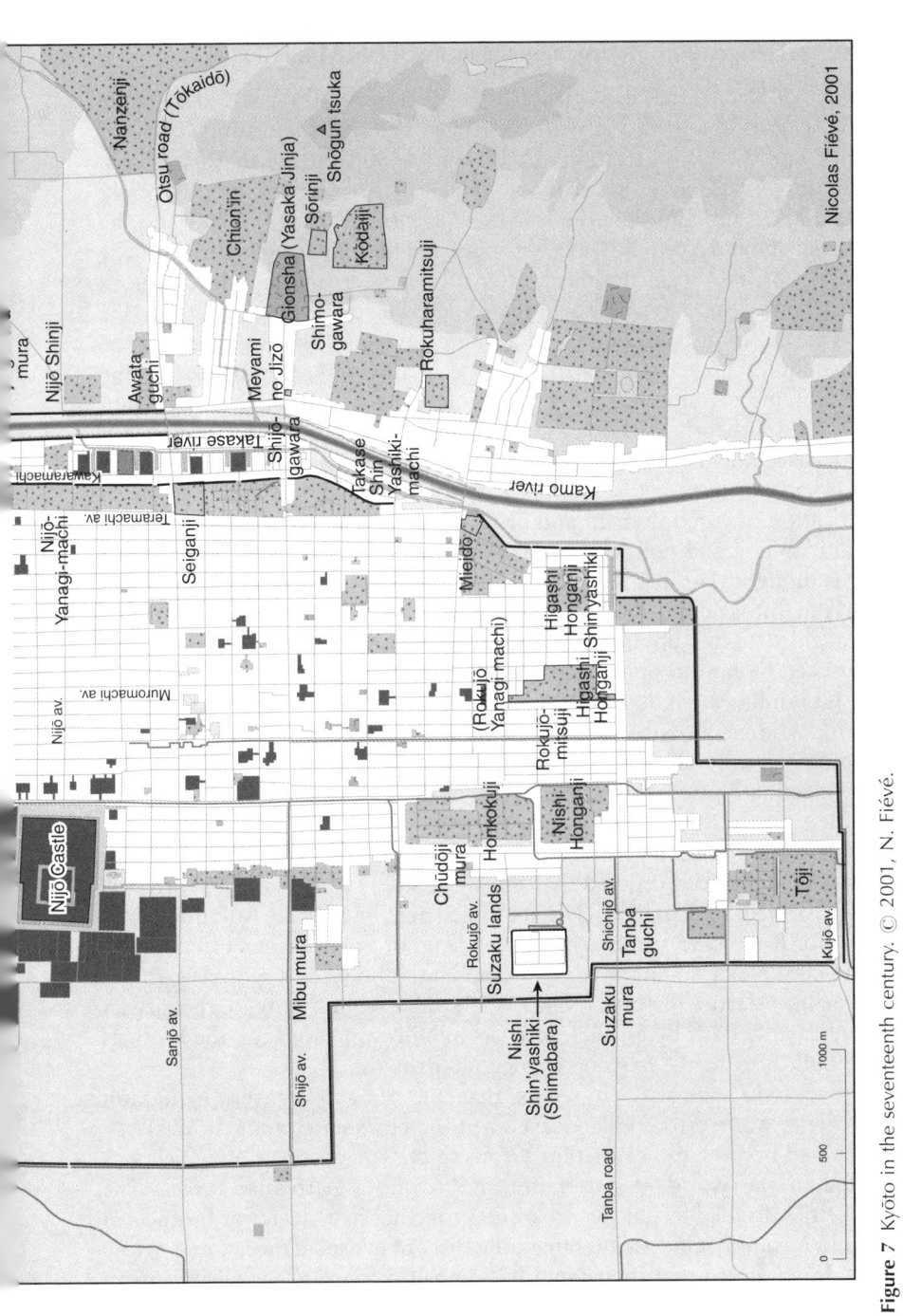

Figure 7 Kyōto in the seventeenth century. © 2001, N. Fiévé.

From the Multifunctional Space of the Medieval City to the Specific Designation of Urban Space in the Early Modern City

The city of Kyoto, rich in its profusion of architectural types and dynamic in the way its shape and structure changed through the century or so of conflict and confusion from about 1460 to 1560, became the object of a significant experiment in urban planning. In his chapter in this book, Takahashi Yasuo considers the role of Oda Nobunaga (1534–82) and the Ashikaga shogun Yoshiaki (1537–97) in beginning the restructuring of the city. This process was continued, after a brief interruption, and enhanced some twenty years later by Toyotomi Hideyoshi (see the Introduction). He had a castle, Jurakudai, built, and around it were set the residences of the main military power-holders of the day. In this way, Kyoto became the precursor and the first embodiment of an urban genre that was very soon to reach its apotheosis in Edo, the early-modern castle town (jōkamachi). Urban space now became an object of central control and planning in a way that it had not been before. It was a reflection of political power. As such the location of entertainment and prostitution districts became a subject of social planning and political decision-making.

It is thought that in 1589 – a little more than two years after Hideyoshi built the Jurakudai – Hara Sanzaemon (dates unknown) and Hayashi Mata'ichirō (dates unknown), who were both men of the people, were authorised by him to open licensed brothels on land one kilometre east of the Jurakudai at Nijō-yanagi-no-banba, on Nijō avenue.[2] The new quarter, known as Nijō-yanagi-machi, was integrated among the other buildings already clustered in that part of the city. It is rumoured that these meeting houses were at the origin of the Hayashi and Hara families' wealth.

When Tokugawa Ieyasu started building his Nijō Castle (Nijō-jō) in 1602, the authorities ordered that the Hara and Hayashi families' brothels be transferred to Rokujō.[3] This new quarter, known as Rokujō-misuji-machi, or Rokujō-yanagi-machi was made up of three clusters of buildings: Ue-no-chō, Naka-no-chō, and Shimo-no-chō, modelled, it would seem, on Changan's pleasure districts (Naitō 1983: 82), except that there the district was not marked off by an enclosure. As in Nijō-yanagi-machi, the brothels were built next to the existing residential areas (fig. 7).

From 1617 onwards, it seems that the shogun's governor Itakura Shigemune wanted to regulate several of the city's entertainment districts, which had become too exuberant for his taste. The prostitution which was related to the world of entertainment became a particular target. The authorities decided to put the prostitutes together in a cluster of brothels in Rokujō-misuji-machi. At the same time, lists of artists, dancers, and actors were drawn up so that they could be compelled to exercise their talents in strictly defined districts. Shigemune authorised them to settle in a limited number of places: in Shijō-gawara, on either bank of the River Kamo, at Yamato-ōji, and at Gojō.[4]

The official institutionalisation of the brothels and their consequent segregation within the world of entertainment and pleasure activities was decided by the authorities in 1640, when the licensed district of Nishi Shin'yashiki was built. In a decree dated the 7th Month of that year, the governor of Kyoto ordered the transfer of the brothels at Rokujō-misuji-machi to land at Suzaku and ordered the establishment of a district to be enclosed by a wall and licensed for prostitution. This was Nishi Shin'yashiki, to become better known under the name of Shimabara; its nickname has its origin in the 1637–38 *Shimabara no ran* rebellion, the insurrection by the Christians from the Shimabara peninsula in Kyushu.[5]

When Hideyoshi had the 'earth enclosure' (*odoi*) built (see the Introduction), vast areas of nonurbanised space were included, most notably to the north and to the west. When the ground rent or land tax was abolished, a good part of these now tax-exempt lands were very soon urbanised. They were called 'new lands' (*shinchi*). The building of the pleasure district of Nishi Shin'yashiki is just one example of this phenomenon of urbanisation, which was to last just over a century. Among the key stages in the occupancy of the 'new lands,' mention should be made of the development in 1614 of the River Takase districts, lying between the city walls, the River Kamo, and the Nijō and Shijō avenues; the urbanisation of the banks of the River Kamo from 1669 onwards; the building of the Takase Shin'yashiki blocks (1670) south of Shijō; and the transfer in 1708 after the fire of that year of several temples to the eastern bank of the river. The urbanisation of these 'new lands' allowed the authorities to establish unifunctional spaces, with temples on one side and places of entertainment on the other.

On maps from the late Tokugawa period, one can clearly see scattered around the periphery of the city the neat and precise boundaries marking out the hamlets allocated to the lowest social groups.[6] These lowest classes on the social ladder were now institutionalised as 'full of stains' (*eta*) and 'non-humans' (*hinin*). People involved in entertainment were often classified as *rōnin*, misfits who did not correspond exactly enough within the new system of social status. Among these people, women prostitutes suffered particular discrimination. They were separated from people involved in different entertainment activities and were shut away in Shimabara. The other places of entertainment were located around Shijō-gawara. A distinction was now made among the various kinds of entertainment. The 'spectacles' (*misemono*) and the 'games on public thoroughfares' (*daidōgei*), which until then had been part of urban activity, were now performed in temporary lean-tos (*kakegoya*) and installed on the sand bank in the middle of the River Kamo. All the theatrical arts (*kabuki*, *jōruri*, *kyōgen*) were grouped east of the river, in purpose-built theatres on either side of Shijō avenue (Gion Shinchi to the north, Gion-machi to the south).[7]

The creation of the enclosed district in the seventeenth century arose partly from a determination to control the population and its social groupings and partly as a result of a whole series of urban planning decisions which had been taken a century earlier.[8] The traces of the medieval town space where men and women of different social origins and of different professions had lived together were gradually erased by Hideyoshi's major works. They were replaced by a juxtaposition of different single-purpose spaces (based on one single activity for one single class of people). Under Hideyoshi, the 'zoning' of the city was determined with a view to consolidating power and control; under the Tokugawa, this was accomplished by allocating a specific zone according to newly established institutional social status.

Shimabara, Kyoto's Official Prostitution District

In the capital, the courtesans' district comprised the three clusters of buildings at Rokujō, at Nishi-no-Tōin, and at Chūdōji on the moor at Shichijō, west of Suzaku, to the north of the great road to the Tanba Sea. This district is called Shimabara. Like Shimabara castle, which fell during Amakusa's insurrection at Hizen, three of its sides are completely closed [by an enclosure]; only one of its side has a gate. That is how it came to get its name. (*Ukiyo monogatari*, 1660)

The Shimabara district was built in open countryside, inside the city ramparts but four hundred metres away from the nearest houses, outside the city like Yoshiwara in Edo or, later, Minatosaki-machi in Yokohama. The district was about two kilometres south of Nijō Castle, and as such, well away from the city's busiest districts (fig. 7).

The Suzaku lands were in the countryside, outside the built-up area, but within the enclosure (*odoi*). This district was on the same latitude as the Honganji temple but several hundred metres further away, very close to the city gate of Tanba (*Tanba-guchi*). This gate was on one of the principal roads to the west, the main road to the province of Tanba. This geographical situation made the licensed district an extremely convenient stopping place, as evidenced by its various inns. In their urban plans, the *bakufu* authorities were simply adapting the informal geographical organisation which already existed: a peripheral district not within the city limits, near to one of the city gates, and on a main thoroughfare (fig. 7).

The generic word used to designate the pleasure district is the 'beautiful women district' (*keisei-machi* or *keisei-chō*). *Keisei*, literally 'to ruin the fortress,' is a metaphor used first in China then in Japan to designate beautiful women.[9] The Shimabara was shut off by a great wall and surrounded by a moat – reminiscent of the fortified districts of the Middle Ages or of the 'quarters built within the precincts of the temple' (*jinaichō*). Though it borrowed this architectural form, its purpose was very different; this enclosure was not to keep outsiders out, but to keep those inside in.

The basic plan of the pleasure district was a rectangle, 106 *ken*, or 207 metres, wide (east-west) and 126 *ken*, 246 metres, long (north-south), which is the size it still has today. The moat was one and a half *ken* wide, and the cob enclosure was six *shaku* high and one *shaku* thick.[10] These dimensions are very close to those of the first Yoshiwara, the pleasure district of Edo, which was 117 *ken* wide and 147 *ken* long, according to Naitō Akira's reconstruction of the old maps of the district (Naitō 1983). Shin Yoshiwara – the second or 'new' Yoshiwara, relocated outside the city in a position not dissimilar to that of Shimabara in the 1660s – was a little wider (145 *ken* wide, 191 *ken* long) (Naitō 1983: 249–60). The only entrance gate (*daimon*) in Shimabara was dug on the eastern, city side of the enclosure. A main street (*michisuji*) two *ken* wide crossed through the middle of the district (east to west) and three secondary alleys (*michi*) one and a half *ken* wide divided it crossways (north-south). Along the *michisuji*, there were shops providing for the needs of everyday life. The entire district was divided by this street and these alleys into six areas. Six gates (three on the north side, three on the south side) gave access to the alleys and to the six different areas within the district (fig. 8).

> The prostitution district was transferred to Nishi Shin'yashiki [Shimabara]. The clusters of buildings inside the enclosure are organized in two symmetrical groups: [on the east side] Naka-no-chō [to the north] and Ue-no-chō [to the south]; [in the centre,] Chūdōji-chō [to the north] and Tayū-chō [to the south]; [on the west side] Shimo-no-chō [to the north] and Ageya-chō [to the south]. (Kyōto-fu, 1872)[11]

The brothels were aligned along the alleyways that crossed the district. The ordinary rank prostitutes were enclosed in the cluster of buildings nearest the entrance; the more one advanced westward, the higher was the social rank of the buildings' occupants. The meeting houses (*ageya*) – restaurants with private receptions rooms, where the great *geisha* and courtesans were invited by their customers – were situated at the very end (west part) of Shimabara.

The number of districts, of houses and of individuals in the pleasure district:

Blocks: 6, including 5 for brothels (*keiseiya*) and 1 for meeting houses (*ageya*).

Houses: 70 in Shōtoku 5 [1715], including 31 brothels (*keiseiya*), 21 meeting houses (*ageya*) and 18 tea-houses (*chaya*).

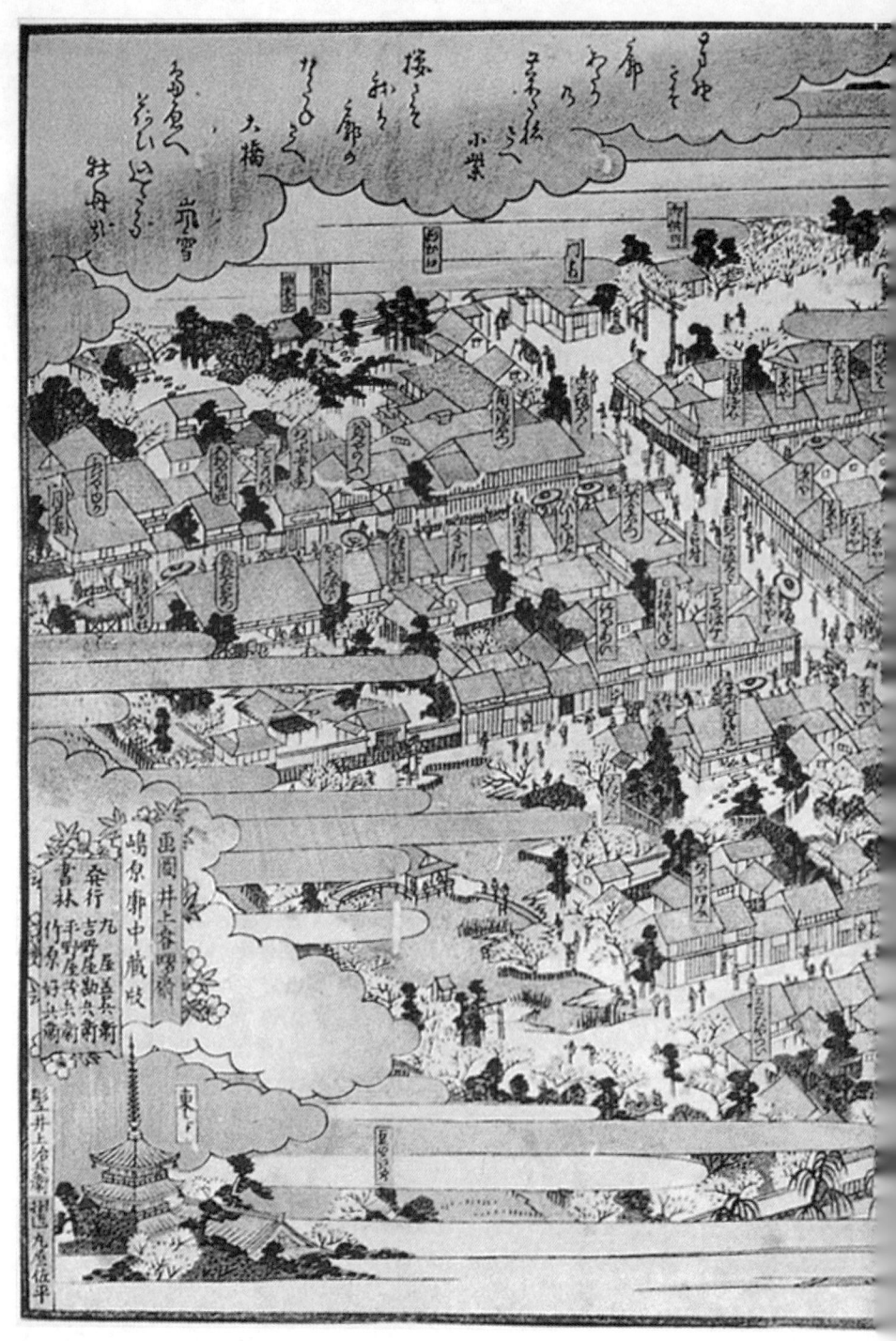

Figure 8 Inoue Shunjosai '*Shimabara shōkei: shiki no nagame*' (Picturesque landscape of Shimabara: contemplation of the four seasons), woodblock print, 1839. Courtesy of the Sumiya hozon-kai, Kyoto.

嶋原勝景
四季乃ながめ

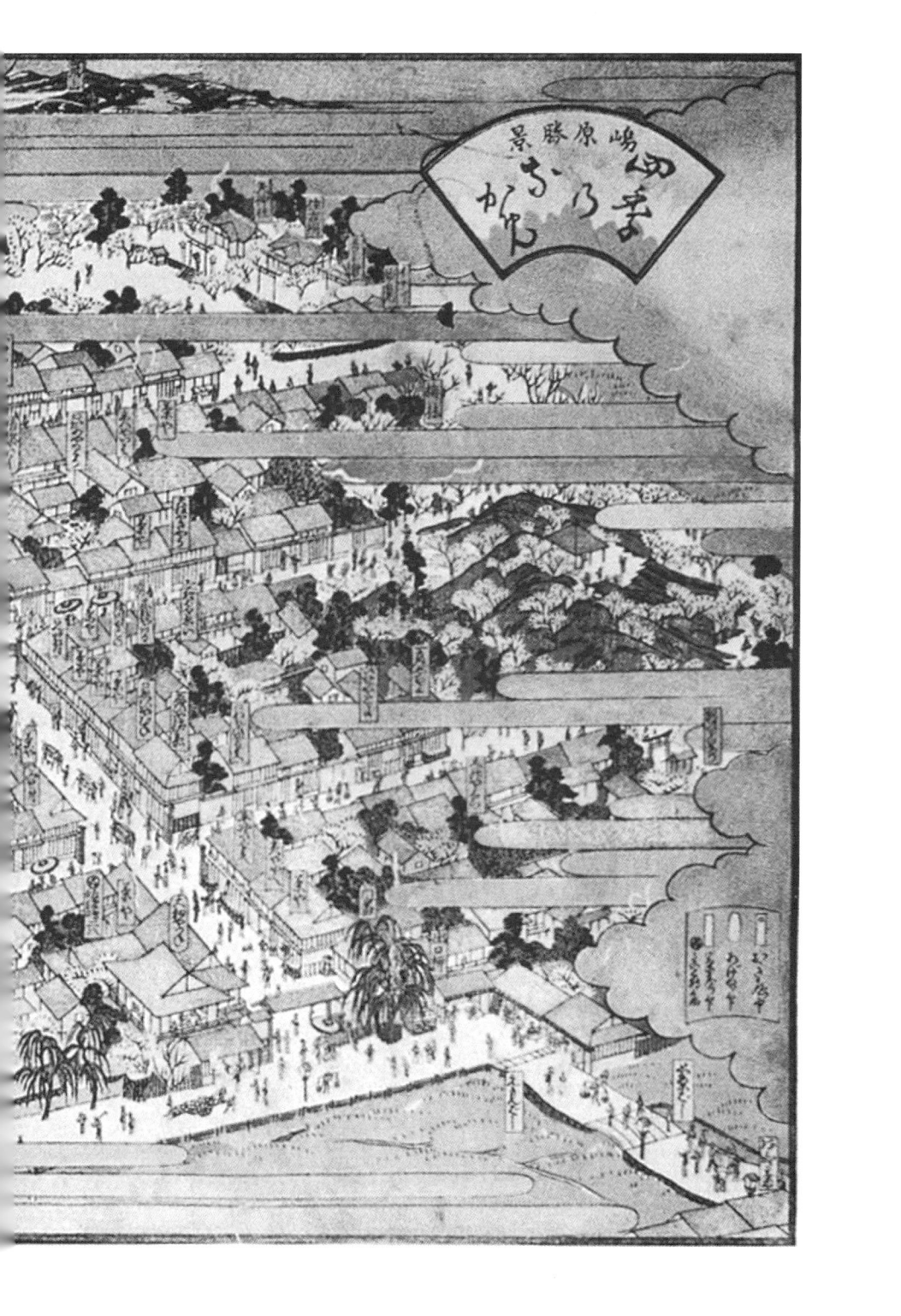

Individuals: 408 men and 1,175 women, including 549 prostitutes. This group comprises 18 *tayū*, 85 *tenjin*, 58 *kakoi*, 161 *hashi* and 227 *kamuro*. (*Kyōto oyakusho muki taigai oboe-gaki*)[12]

The *tayū* was a high ranking courtesan. A rendez-vous with her did not take place in a brothel, but she went about the quarter with her entourage (several young attendants, or *kamuro*, and an umbrella carrier) for meetings in an *ageya*. The *tenjin* was a second rank courtesan who was either invited into an *ageya* or entertained her customer in a *chaya* (tea-house). The *kakoi* (abbreviation for *kakoi jorō*) was, as the name suggests, a 'locked-up prostitute' in a brothel. She usually sat behind the wooden bars of the house facade, through which prospective customers could see her from the alley. The *hashi* was a lower ranking prostitute. The *kamuro* were young girls, attendants and apprentices in the service of the *tayū* and the *tenjin*; *kamuro* were aged between seven and fourteen, when they were considered old enough to take their place with their elders (Segawa Seigle 1993).

Shimabara was at its zenith in the Genroku era (1688–1703), when it had a total population of nearly 1,800. As well as several inns where passers-by could stay, the district had a theatre and a Shinto shrine. Subsequently, other quarters such as Gion Shinchi, nearer to the commercial centres, gained a reputation for their tea and tea-houses (*chaya*). This was to the detriment of Shimabara, situated, as it was, so far from the centre, and by the Meiwa era (1764–71), Shimabara was being described in the following terms: 'The cob wall circling Shimabara is quite dilapidated' (*Mita miyako monogatari* 1802). In 1801, Kyokutei Bakin (1767–1848) wrote in his *Kiryo manroku* (Notes taken while on a journey) that 'even the cob enclosure has collapsed in places and, except for the meeting houses [*ageya*], the buildings and the alleys are in pretty bad shape. [Moreover] the high ranking courtesan's [*tayū*] behaviour is not up to the standard of those from Gion! ... The people from Kyoto do not go to Shimabara. To go there, the road is long and the journey there and back is rather boring.'

The total decline of Shimabara was checked only by the authorities' determination not to let pleasure and prostitution activities freely develop throughout the city. In 1761, for example, the following decree was issued: 'Every tea-house [*chaya*] in the capital must have official authorisation, just as do those of the licensed district.' (Kyōto-fu, 1872).

As part of the reforms of the Kansei era (1789–1800), in 1790 all the city's 'street-girls' (*inbaita*) from Gion-machi, from Gion Shinchi, and from the city's various tea-houses were rounded up. Some 1,300 women were detained and sent as 'maids' (*hashita*) to Shimabara. For a time the tea-houses were closed for business, and when they did re-open, those which were not already under the control of the city had to make an official

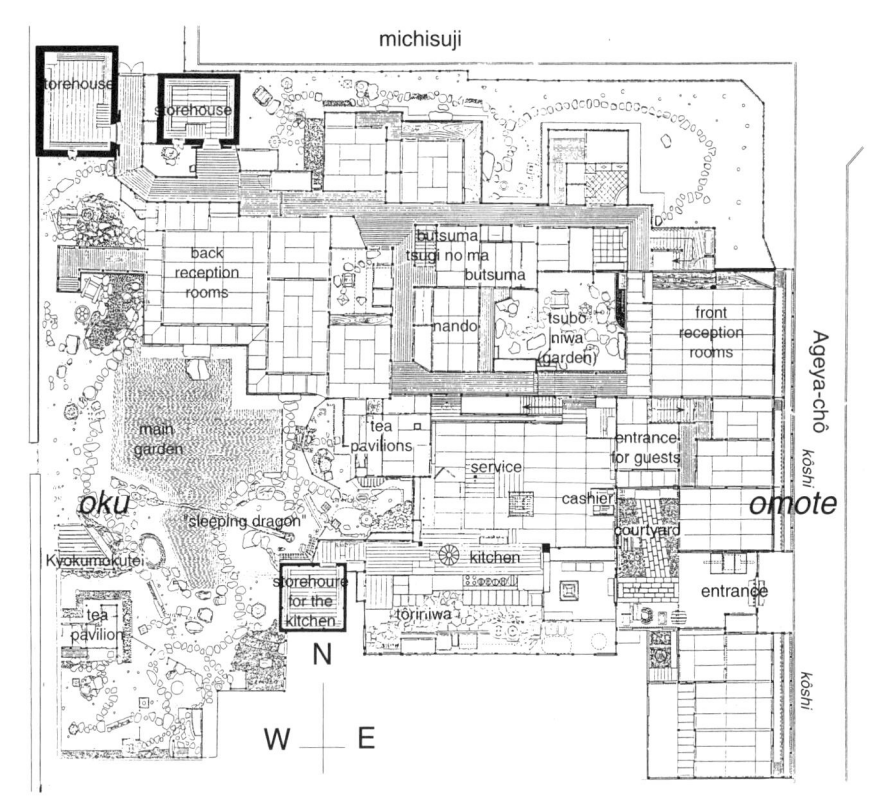

Social Discrimination and Architectural Freedom

Figure 9 Contemporary layout of the Sumiya *ageya*.

payment of fifteen silver *kanme*. The ban did not last long, however; at the end of the same year, official documents speak of authorising:

> For a period of five years, some twenty pleasure houses – for the whole city – located in the four districts of Gion-machi Gion Shinchi, Shichijō Shinchi, Nijō Shinchi, and Kitano Kami Shinchi are free of these measures. Each of these establishments is allowed a maximum of fifteen prostitutes. (Kyōto-fu, 1872)

Thanks to measures such as these, Shimabara maintained its status as the principal pleasure district. It had numerous houses and employees, and it fell to the district itself to supervise the other places of prostitution, which were put under its authority, either by administering them itself or by levying a commission on the revenues.

Within the framework of the reforms of the Tenpō era (1830–43), in 1842, we discover that 'The capital's only pleasure district is that of *keisei-chō*.' In 1851, however, permission was extended to the four districts of

Gion-machi Gion Shinchi, Shichijō Shinchi, Nijō Shinchi, and Kitano Kami Shinchi enabling them to carry on their trade for a limited period of ten years. However, some 'lands where one works outside' [of Shimabara] (*dekasegichi*) remained under the authority of the official district.

At the end of the *bakufu*, in 1867, prostitution was authorised throughout the whole city. After the Meiji restoration, as part of the new urban administration system, Shimabara lost its privileged status. The prostitution business continued because by now that part of the town had expanded. However, the changes brought about by the modernisation of rail and road were to have a negative influence on the district's economic activity.

In 1876, the Tōkaidō railway line was built, connecting Kyoto and Osaka and later Tokyo (see the chapter by Traganou). In 1897, the Kyoto line was constructed, linking Kyoto with the provinces to the west. It was during this same period that the lie of the road to Tanba was modified, so that it now reached the city some 800 metres further to the south, at Shichijō (Seventh Avenue). Despite the construction of a station at the Tanba Gate, these changes led to a falling off in the number of people who had to pass through Shimabara. Concurrently (figs. 10 and 11), prostitution began to flourish in other districts, most notably in those around the new main railway stations (fig. 3).

In 1958, the *keisei-chō*, that is, the official prostitution district of Kyoto, was outlawed by the Law Forbidding Prostitution (*Baishun bōshi hō*), the enclosure wall was completely destroyed and the walled licensed district was entirely suppressed.

The closure of the brothels led to the almost complete collapse of the district's economic activity. It was too far from the commercial centres around Shijō–Kawaramachi crossroads, and was not in the part of the city visited by tourists. In fact, it was now in one of Kyoto's industrial zones and well away from any of the main stations that link Kyoto to the Osaka-Kobe agglomeration. Unlike Gion, to the north of Shijō Avenue, Shimabara's reconversion into an area of restaurants, bars and night-clubs has not proved successful. Today, the district is completely integrated as part of the city, even though the division of the district in blocks has survived. The main gate has been rebuilt and several buildings dating from the eighteenth and early twentieth centuries are still standing.

A Case-study: the Layout of the Sumiya *ageya* as a Typical Example of Tokugawa Period Popular Architecture

The recent economic collapse of the Shimabara district together with its geographical situation within Kyoto had the serendipitous consequence of preserving the old district from property speculation and rebuilding. Some of the old blocks' 'houses' are clearly discernible, even from no more than a

Social Discrimination and Architectural Freedom

Figure 10 Outside view of the Wachigaiya *okiya* (built in 1857). Shimabara, Kyoto. © 2001, N. Fiévé.

stroll through the old streets. Among these houses, the Sumiya – the biggest and most elegant of the meeting houses' block – still survives and stands as a valuable witness to this block's former architectural style.

The Sumiya was situated in Ageya-chō, on the corner of the central avenue and the west gate (fig. 8). It was left untouched by the great fire of 1854, which destroyed more than half of Shimabara. Fortunately, it also escaped the modernisation that most of the houses in the district suffered as part of the reconstructions which occurred during the Meiji era (1868–1912). It is thought that the Sumiya was first built in the old Rokujō-misuji-machi district and so dates back to before 1641, when it was transferred to Shimabara at the time that this was constructed as the licensed district. The

Figure 11 Outside view of the Wachigaiya *okiya* (built in 1857). Shimabara, Kyoto. © 2001, N. Fiévé.

building's main door opens out onto the north-south alley, which originally was 1.5 *ken* wide (2.92 metres). In 1641 it sat on a parcel of land 5 *ken* wide by 22.75 *ken* deep (9.75 by 22.75 metres). As was customary in the layout of buildings in the Shimabara, it occupied the full extent of the plot. During the years 1673 to 1680, however, the Sumiya had annexed the greater part of the neighbouring plot to the north belonging to the Ōsakaya house, which tripled its depth to 15 *ken* (the Ōsakaya was an *okiya*, that is, a house where the *tayū* resided, as distinct from an *ageya*, where they met and entertained their customers). In 1787, by annexing the Nakamuraya house to the south, the Sumiya became the biggest *ageya* in Shimabara, with a total street facade of 16 *ken* (31.2 metres), a 22 *ken* garden (42.9 metres), and a total depth of 22.75 *ken* (44.4 metres). From 1641 onwards, the Sumiya belonged to the Nakagawa family, who were to administer it for thirteen generations. In 1998, part of the house became a museum, run by the Sumiya Preservation Society (*Sumiya hozon-kai*).[13]

The main structure of the building as it stands today dates back to the years from 1673 to 1680, in other words, the time when the neighbouring Ōsakaya house was purchased, although it is almost certain that parts of the building are much older. In subsequent years, right up to the end of the Tokugawa period, additional reception rooms were built at the bottom of the garden; three tea houses and a three clay barns were also built within its grounds. The total floor space amounts to 1,794 square metres.

Interior Space Organised as Kyoto machiya

Throughout the Middle Ages, houses and shops in Kyoto existed within the same building, known as *mise* (from the verb *miseru*, to show or be seen) and built right onto the roadway. Unbuilt land was situated behind the building, and served as a vegetable garden. As Hyūga Susumu has shown, it is not until the fifteenth century that we have textual and iconographic evidence of the apparition of garden pavilions (*an*) or of courtyard gardens (*niwa*) among the wealthy merchants' houses. The construction of a pavilion at the foot of the garden had become generalised by the sixteenth century, when we find it being called the 'room at the bottom' (*oku no zashiki*), the 'detached room' (*hanare zashiki*), or the 'tea-room' (*chanoyu zashiki*) (Hyūga 1983: 3–18). This building, which usually housed a hearth for boiling water for tea, gradually developed, to the extent that it became the second main feature of the house, serving as a reception room. This second structure led to an increasing differentiation between the parts adjacent to the road, which were linked to matters of business, and these spaces at the bottom of the garden, reserved for leisure and private activities. This evolution in the style of wealthy merchants' housing in Kyoto is also linked to the enormous growth in popularity of the custom of holding tea business meetings (*chaya*), which is why these rooms were so often referred to as 'tea-rooms' (*chanoyu zashiki*).

This contrast between front and back was facilitated by the traditional shape of land parcels in Kyoto, which were very deep with only a narrow facade onto the street. This system simply continued a tradition dating back to the way the districts were set out in the Heian period.[14] By the sixteenth century, it had become common to construct deeper with a new building at the back side of the main building (called *oku mune*, from *oku* meaning the inner part and *mune* meaning the main roof-timber), but this imposed an adjustment on the layout of the houses (see the chapter by Kinoshita). A passageway was created to permit access to open space at the back directly from the street (*roji*, or *sukiya tsūro* as it was then called), which very soon itself became a strip of decorative garden, so giving birth to the *tsubo niwa*. The building at the foot of the garden survived; but what had originally been the vegetable garden, rendered an economic anachronism in the wealthy commercial society of the Tokugawa period, now became a decorative garden. In the seventeenth century we find that this is the model being adopted for the houses of the upper classes. Even if the existence of garden pavilions can be shown to be an established feature of the houses of the nobility, the linear layout may have been inspired by the city's great *machiya* (Fiévé 1996: 139–90). Finally, a century later, the construction of reception rooms on the upper floor (called *nikai zashiki*) became a standard feature of Kyoto town-houses.

At the beginning of the Tokugawa period, just at the very moment that the Shimabara district was being built, the use of predefined architectural models was conditioned by etiquette and social norms. As William Coaldrake indicates in Chapter Four, each social class was expected to respect the form of architecture which gave visible expression to their standing and position in society. It would have been utterly unthinkable to use upper-class architectural styles in building a pleasure district. So in Shimabara, it is no surprise to find that the brothel-keepers and the other proprietors within the district used ordinary *machiya*-style town-houses of the sort described above as their architectural model.

This is why the basic plan of the Sumiya – and of other known surviving buildings – shares all the main characteristics we have just outlined (fig. 9). On the east side, the entire street facade is occupied by a first structure (*omote mune*). A second structure (*oku mune*) sits deeper in the lot. Both of these structures date from the years 1673 to 1680 and constitute the oldest part of the house. In 1952 they were classified as Important Cultural Properties (*jūyō bunkazai*).[15] Linking the two structures is a corridor with intermediate rooms on either side and an inner courtyard (*zentei*). In this way, the two parts, front and back, made one huge single building. Access from the street was by way of a sort of porch leading straight into the inner courtyard, which permitted a twofold entrance: for the guests to the reception rooms, and to the servants' quarters for all those concerned with the running of the house. There are indications on a number of old plans that some of the rooms may have been split up later on, but as far as essentials are concerned, the Sumiya house as it stands today is an exceptional example of the architecture of the world of entertainment in the middle of the Tokugawa period.

On the south side, a space made of beaten and later paved earth (*doma*) was used by the servants. This afforded direct access to the 'garden crossing' (*tōriniwa*) and the central courtyard of the garden without having to pass via the raised floorway of the house. Along this passageway was situated the floored kitchen space with its well and its fireplace. According to the Kyoto conventions, the *machiya* form of architecture has no ceiling over the kitchen space so as to allow the smoke from the fires to escape up into the open space under the rafters and out through the spaces between the tiles. A great work room which served as both kitchen and serving room stood alongside the *tōriniwa*. It is here that the meals were prepared, and so it served as the heart of the house for the servants and the courtesans. This is where the managers of the house and the cashier's office would have been. Invited guests, on the other hand, reached the back of the property via a central corridor located to the north and which ran alongside a small indoor garden (*tsubo niwa*). The buildings at the back gave on to a large landscaped garden, whose principal feature was a ten metre long 'sleeping dragon' (*garyō*); this was the nickname given to the huge branch of a

Figure 12 Inside garden of the Sumiya with the *garyō* pine tree. © 2001, N. Fiévé.

famous centenarian pine tree, which featured in drawings of famous places (figs. 12 and 30).[16] The most modern parts of the building are the reception rooms constructed in the north-eastern part of the garden.

The Function of the Layout of the Sumiya

The inside of the house was organised in terms of two opposing ways of structuring space. The principal of these was founded on a front-back (*omote/oku*) opposition, typical of houses of this period, in our case the front being the east (the street side) and the back being the west (the main garden side) (fig. 9). On the ground floor, this opposition traced out a half-open space along the facade which fulfilled the functions originally played by the medieval *mise*. All of the facades were constructed of removable elements, *kōshi*, a kind of screen of wooden bars which let those inside see outside without themselves being easily visible from the outside. However, these removable elements could be taken down for certain festivals. The rooms immediately behind these *kōshi* became a sort of lodge overlooking the street, ideal for watching a procession go by (figs. 13 and 14). In an illustration from *Miyako rinsen meishō zue* (Illustrated collection of the picturesque gardens of the capital) entitled 'Shimabara,' those in the street are observing a dance being performed in the front rooms of the building, which serves as a sort of stage (fig. 15). The first suite of rooms giving on to

Figure 13 Outside view of Sumiya *ageya* (Tokugawa period). Shimabara, Kyoto. © 2001, N. Fiévé.

the street was severely limited in expanse by the space accorded to the small interior garden (*tsubo niwa*), by the entrance for invited guests (*genkan*), by the entry porch, and by the interior courtyard (*zentei*), which formed a north-south component parallel to the street. Beyond, there was a buffer between the front and back, comprising secondary rooms (*butsuma, butsu tsugi no ma, nando*), a corridor, toilets, and the huge space allocated to the kitchen and to the *tōriniwa*.

The central axis (east-west) ran through the middle of the house and led via the long corridor into the interior garden. The rooms, situated on either side and behind, constituted the main part (*oku*) of the house (fig. 9). The northern half consisted of the working area for the *geisha* and courtesans, where they received their clients (the front reception room, the room for the

Social Discrimination and Architectural Freedom

Figure 14 Outside view of Sumiya *ageya* (Tokugawa period). Shimabara, Kyoto. © 2001, N. Fiévé.

geisha and courtesans themselves, changing rooms, the interior garden). This was also where the altar (*butsudan*) to the ancestors stood. The southern section was the business part of the house, reserved for the various service tasks and for meals, as well as the reception room and the cashier's room. The sitting rooms (*zashiki, oku no zashiki*), the separate pavilions (*hanare zashiki*), and the tea pavilions (*chashitsu*) were all arranged around a large garden. There was a secondary garden which belonged to the tea pavilion, sitting within the large garden. This space at the back, completely isolated from the outside, meant the invited guests could amuse themselves quite freely, without fear of being observed from the street.

'In the Snow at Sumiya,' another illustration from the *Miyako rinsen meishō zue*, shows the courtesans and their guests having a snowball fight

89

Figure 15 Nishimura Chūwa, Sakuma Sōen, and Oku Bunmei, 'Shimabara.' From Akizato Ritō's *Miyako rinsen meishō zue*, vol. 5 (1799).

(fig. 30). Conventionalised smiles are evident all round in a bucolic scene which masks the sordid destiny of the majority of these women who were effectively prisoners. The illustration shows that about a third of the garden was a lawn placed at the disposal of the guests, something which was extremely rare in Japan at this time.

There was a first floor over the oldest parts of the house (*omote mune* and *oku mune*), laid out as a series of individual rooms and reception rooms. Basically, these rooms were bordered by verandas which serve as a corridor; this gallery also overlooked the open areas of the ground floor, namely, the central courtyard, the interior garden, and the main garden at the back. The whole of this floor was preserved for rendez-vous between the prostitutes and their clients. There was a very clear distinction between what happened there on the one hand and the business and cooking confined to the floor below on the other.

The Style of Decoration of the Sumiya and Architectural Freedom in Shimabara

The main structure of the roof rafters of the Sumiya certainly matches that of the great *machiya* of Kyoto, in terms not only of matter and form but also in the construction techniques that were employed. However, it is well worthwhile stopping to note the various fixtures and fittings – the shelves and the alcoves – built to hold valuable objects of decoration such as floor vases, incense-burners, and paintings. As I have shown in earlier works, such decorative elements as the 'alcove' (*tokonoma*), shelves in the form of a 'writing alcove' (*shoin*), and 'staggered shelving' (*chigaidana*) were the fruit of a long evolution in the ornamentation of houses belonging to the military class (Fiévé 1996: 219–38). The ornamentations we find here at the Sumiya are classic examples of work from the late sixteenth century. They belong to the architectural style, known today as *shoin-zukuri* derived from the name of the pieces arranged as a 'writing alcove' (*shoin*). In the Sumiya we find typical examples attributed to this style. Fujioka Michio's various works on the Imperial Palace have clearly shown that at the end of the sixteenth and beginning of the seventeenth centuries, the use of *tokonoma* and asymmetrical shelving was rare among the aristocratic classes, rare even in the Imperial Palace (Fujioka 1956: 279–430). Theoretically, mere commoners were not allowed to build such ornamentation in their homes.[17] The richness of the interior decoration is enhanced by the painting of *fusuma* carried out by some of the greatest artists of the Tokugawa period such as Maruyama Ōkyo (1733–95) and Ganku (1756–1838), and by the '*Kōhakubai zu byōbu*' (Screen of the red and white plum blossoms), executed by Yosa Buson (1716–83).

The superb *shoin* and *tokonoma* alcoves and staggered shelving of the Sumiya house show how the architectural models formerly belonging to military class were being copied by people in ordinary houses as early as the end of the seventeenth century. We need to remember that well-off visitors – from every social group – frequented the *keisei-machi*, even *bushi*, as evidenced by the sabre holder installed in the entrance; such decorative elements were probably in place to assure high-ranking guests of the favourable standing of the establishment. And since it was also frequented by well-off merchants, it is highly probable that it led to these architectural styles trickling down throughout the commoner classes.

For precisely this reason, the Damask Room (*Donsu no ma*) and its contents are particularly interesting. The room has an alcove with a platform containing two *tatami* mats (which served as a seat usually reserved for people of high rank), an ensemble in the form of a writing alcove (*tsuke shoin*) which allows the light to fall on the *tokonoma* alcove, and long asymmetrical shelves. The model on which all of these elements were based is the residential architecture of the military and the private apartments of the superior of a monastery. However, they lack the austerity that was found in the original source. The craftsman adapted and transformed the basic model to suit the circumstances. The ornamental nails (*kugikakushi*) on the lintels were encrusted with enamels or with mother-of-pearl, giving a surprising coloured and luminous touch not usually found in such architecture. The exceptional length of the shelves helps to soften their form. The visual games provided by the undulating motifs on the uprights of the *shōji* adds a third dimension, which manages to be both hard and soft and which underlines the dominant beige of the cob walls.[18]

The fact that these are adaptations of models borrowed from the *shoin-zukuri* style is very evident from the way that completely foreign architectural elements were arranged together: some elements in the style of military mansions, others borrowed from the style of town-houses, others again from the architecture of tea-houses, which were very much in vogue in Kyoto society. The tea ceremony, which had developed since the sixteenth century, consisted – in its highest form – of an aesthetic quest to know the world better through experiencing material need. It took place within a city, yet the participants isolated themselves at the bottom of gardens, in humble pavilions reminiscent of the kind of hut to which a sage or a hermit might retire to get away from the world. Pieces of bamboo, straw, reeds, wood, both with and without bark and of great variety, and bare cob-walls – all of these became features of garden pavilions within the compounds belonging to leading nobles and military lords – and all of which was in marked contrast to the standards of noble architecture that adorned their reception rooms. The appearance of such materials and such forms, hitherto unthinkable in the great houses of the licensed district, constituted a veritable revolution, but was carefully confined to the limits of the garden pavilion, and it did not influence the architecture of any other part of the house.

In the pleasure district of Shimabara, inside the Sumiya house, far away from the conventions which regulated the lives of people in all social classes, the mixing of styles and of influences was possible. In a place which was 'outside the social norms,' there was room for experimentation in new combinations drawn from elements of architecture of the *shoin-zukuri* style, of the Kyoto *machiya*, and of the tea pavilions. The tea ceremony, very much in vogue at this time, was a standard city leisure activity, and we can reasonably surmise that the spatio-temporal and the work-leisure contrast which regulated everyday life encouraged a very rapid identification of the world of tea pavilions with that of houses of pleasure.

Today, the Sumiya has two other tea pavilions, but they are much later constructions (the *Kyokumoku-tei* or 'pavilion of the twisted tree' was already depicted in *Miyako rinsen meishō zue* published in 1799), and their location at the bottom of the garden is not at all unusual. On the upper floor of the oldest part of the house there is a tea-room (*kakoi no ma*). It looks like a straightforward *chashitsu*, and it has a twisted post, a bark *tokonoma*, a window (*shitaji mado*) through which the bamboo and reed of the cob wall can be seen, a roof which is lower than usual. It is made up of areas of different height to differentiate between the place of the host and the place of the guests. The combination of materials used gives the room an unfinished and peaceful atmosphere. Over and above these rooms designed for sharing tea, the originality of the Sumiya can be seen in the large reception rooms, where numerous decorative elements associated with tea are quite freely placed alongside those based on other models. For example, there is a ceiling of woven reeds. Elsewhere, there are openings in the form of the full moon, of a *calebasse*, or of a fan, built in the style of windows from rustic country houses. Elsewhere again, we find a lintel of *tokonoma* in bamboo or a twisted post. This stylistic eclecticism, to which historians of architecture assign the general term *sukiya-zukuri* style, inherited its conceptual freedom from the architecture related to tea, both in terms of materials and the forms employed (fig. 16).[19] But other models of architecture from town-houses are also mixed in, as well as the altogether more noble decoration from the great houses of the Tokugawa period.

In some ways, the architectural example of the Sumiya house might be considered reminiscent of the aristocratic detached villa of Katsura (Katsura Rikyū, built between 1615 and 1664), which itself is a free

Figure 16 Inside view of the Sumiya. *Tokonoma* of the *Misu no ma*. Courtesy of the Sumiya hozon-kai, Kyoto.

adaptation of the *shoin-zukuri* style. There, the uniqueness of the architecture is expressed, among other ways, in the formal richness of the alcoves, the asymmetric shelving and the verandas, as well as in the elements borrowed from tea-related architecture. The architectural solutions devised by the craftsmen of Katsura are not the same as those of the Sumiya house, but we can see the same quest to escape from excessively rigid models and to adapt wherever possible. When the villa at Katsura was planned, the aesthetic sensibility of the seventeenth century aristocracy could not find free expression in the archaic *shinden-zukuri* forms, neither in the rigidity of those of *shoin-zukuri* – a style whose most typical devices were reserved for the warrior classes. Faced with such a cultural impasse, Katsura represents an original response.

At Katsura, as with the Sumiya house, it was the freedom of expression derived from tea-related architecture which permitted these buildings to transcend the impasse of form and rigidity. Of course, it has to be said that the Sumiya has certain 'baroque' overtones which are quite foreign to the pure line of aristocratic buildings, but the quality of such detailed and sensual decoration offers an eloquent contrast to the austerity of the townhouses of the time. The architectural freedom that the Sumiya embodies is the material trace of space beyond social norms, the space that Shimabara represented. And it conveys, too, something of the dreams that it must have inspired in its occupants and visitors.

From the start of the nineteenth century, the influence of these styles known as *sukiya-zukuri* would touch all of urban architecture. The 'Japanese house' as perceived and imagined by westerners at the end of the nineteenth century is the fruit of these evolving developments. Nowadays, this is readily confused with what is called the 'Japanese style' (*wafū*), much used in tourist haunts such as inns and restaurants, creating a stereotyped image that claims to be 'traditional.'

Conclusion

This chapter has allowed us to underline a few aspects of the discrimination entertainers of various types had to suffer at the very beginning of the Tokugawa shogunate and to examine the consequences that this had both on the urban organisation of the capital and on architectural developments in buildings used by the common people.

In terms of urban planning, it is quite clear that the authorities simply fell back on existing models. Sometimes this simply meant segregating the 'licensed district,' choosing a nonurban site, away from the city centre, on a main thoroughfare, near to one of the city gates. Sometimes this meant borrowing from foreign models – such as copying the Chang'an 'licensed district.' Quite clearly it is difficult to avoid the attraction of existing models. All models have a very strong symbolic significance and all too

Social Discrimination and Architectural Freedom

conveniently become an easy and readily justifiable solution because they ensure that the building will immediately be recognised by all (for what it is supposed to be). This is why it is so difficult to avoid falling back on existing models. It is quite natural, then, that the choice of architectural style on the part of the private individuals who were responsible for the buildings within the district should be precisely those urban traditions which they, as men of the people, knew so well. In choosing their carpenters, it was this natural instinct which proved stronger than any political constraints.

Architecture stands like a petrifaction in time of the theatre in which men and women once played out their lives, a concrete expression of ways of life now long gone. So the boundary of the licensed district serves as a reminder of the enclosed space reserved for certain discriminated categories of people; the old *okiya* where the courtesans resided bear witness to their imprisonment; and *ageya* like the Sumiya bring alive the scenario in which *geisha* and courtesans had to exercise or endure their professional activity. The architecture of the district and its houses bear the marks of a public life organised around the alleys, which contrasted with the more intimate behaviour which took place within the precincts of the buildings. We find this same contrast in the layout of the interior space of the house, where there is a clear and distinct separation of those areas which were for service or work and those reserved for receiving customers. The basis for the architecture at Shimabara, then, is quite unambiguously modelled on the town-houses of Kyoto. However, the ornamental decoration of this Sumiya shows a liberty of style in its use of forms, colour, and materials borrowed from the architecture of the upper classes – somewhat surprisingly, given the rigorous contemporary social code and etiquette. This highly original mix of influences is a reflection here, without any doubt, of the rich variety of those who frequented the house: warriors, monks, aristocrats, and merchants. The existence of a room decorated in Chinese style, the 'Mother-of-pearls Room' (*Aogai no ma*) (fig. 17) with a Western-style balcony is worthy of note for the exotic touch that it adds to the building. But this diversity alone is not enough to explain the freely eclectic way in which elements have been borrowed. The Sumiya house shows that in a society where a respect for norms and rigorous architectural models prevailed, whenever possible a very free and varied architectural vernacular broke through. In terms of architectural expression, then, we must conclude that the licensed district of Shimabara represents a zone of freedom.

Figure 17 Inside view of the Sumiya. Windows of the *Aogai no ma*. Courtesy of the Sumiya hozon-kai, Kyoto.

Notes

Abbreviations
KSCM: *Kyōto-shi no chimei*. See references below Hayashiya T., Murai Y. and Moritani K. (1979).

1 In Kyoto, except for temples and shrines, the land at the foot of the hills was not urbanised until comparatively recently, after World War II. From the 1930s onwards, urban regulation tended to protect these areas, and even today, any development of the slopes around Kyoto is a considered a sensitive subject by many (see the chapter in this volume by Yamasaki).
2 Nijō-yanagi-machi lay west of Kyōgyoku avenue, east of Made-no-kōji, south of Reisen-no-kōji and north of Oshi-kōji. In other words, it covered the site of present-day Hoteiya-chō, Kajiya-chō, Seimei-chō, Tawaraya-chō, Owari-chō and parts of Roku-chōme, Tōjiji-chō, Yamamoto-chō, and Daruma-chō (KSCM 1979: 719).
3 This district was situated east of Nishi-no-tōin, west of Muromachi, south of Gojō, and north of Uo-no-tanae.
4 The exact site of the first rooms or places of entertainment is not certain. However, a possible reconstruction of the late seventeenth century theatre

Social Discrimination and Architectural Freedom

district is included in the exhibition catalogue of the Kyōto Bunka Hakubutsukan (1991), p. 49.

5 With the arrival of the Portuguese, Christian communities had formed in Kyushu. Heavy taxes levied by the local lords and the persecutions against the Christians provoked a massive revolt by the peasants and minor warriors. After various clashes with government troops, an army of 37,000 Christians led by Masuda Shirō Tokisada (1621–38), a young 17 years old samurai, took refuge in the castle, while the *bakufu* general Itakura Shigemasa (1588–1638) attempted to storm it. The government troops were successfully repelled and Shigemasa himself was killed. The *bakufu* official Matsudaira Nobutsuna (1596–1662) then gathered all the soldiers he could from Kyushu fiefs and laid siege to the castle with an army of 120,000 men. Following several unsuccessful attacks, Nobutsuna laid siege to the castle. After two months the besieged rebels were eventually forced to surrender for want of food and ammunition. The 20,000 survivors – men, women and children – were executed. In Kyoto, the prostitutes, just like the Shimabara rebels, were shut in behind the *yūkaku* enclosure against their will by the *bakufu* representative (Shigemasa was the brother of the Kyoto governor Itakura), and none of them would get out alive.

6 Among many documents that illustrate this point are the *Kyōchō saiken taisei* (Exhaustive compilation of the Capital's details), dated 1831 and published by Takehara Kōbee (179 x 144 cm, coloured, private collection) and the *Zōho saiban Kyō ōezu* (Great illustrated map of the Capital in a new edition, revised and enlarged), dated 1741 and printed by Hayashi Yoshinaga. (This map is in two parts: *Kitayama yori Minami-Sanjō made* (From Kitayama to the south of Sanjō) (120 x 86 cm) and *Kita-Sanjō yori Minami-Fushimi made* (From the north of Sanjō to the south of Fushimi) (117.5 x 87 cm). Both maps are in the library of the department of geography, University of Kyoto.

7 The present day site of the Minamiza theater dates from this time. In the eighteenth century, there were thirty-four such buildings including eleven kabuki theatres and thirteen for *jōruri*.

8 A similar policy would be implemented by the Meiji government after the restoration (Waley 1995).

9 Brothel districts were referred to as *yūkaku*, meaning literally 'pleasure enclosure.' *Keikoku keisei* 'to ruin the states and ravage the fortified place. The powers of a woman's charms' (Couvreur 1890: 54). In Japan, the term was soon attributed to courtesans. As early as 1193, there was an administrative post whose title was 'Administrator to the courtesans' (*keisei bettō*).

10 Based on Kyoto's *ken* of approximately 1.952 metres' length, which give a *shaku* 0.325 metres long.

11 *Kyotofuka yūkaku yuisho* (History of the pleasure districts in Kyoto and its suburbs), a text published in 1872 by Kyoto Prefecture, recounting the history of the licensed districts (quoted in KSMC, p. 942).

12 *Kyōto oyakusho muki taigai oboe-gaki*, quoted in KSCM p. 943.

13 The author is grateful to Nakagawa Kiyo, chairman of the Sumiya Preservation Society (*Sumiya hozon-kai*), for his advice concerning the chapters related to the Sumiya house. Visits to the Sumiya are normally restricted to the first floor; visits to the whole house are by prior arrangement only: Sumiya hozon-kai, 600–8828 Kyoto-shi, Shimogyō-ku, Nishi Shin'yashiki Ageya-chō 32, Tel: 075-351-0024.

14 The original blocks (*chō*) of Heian were about 118 metres square. In the popular districts this square was cut through by an alley, giving two half terrains each about 54 metres deep. Since the land was accessible from either end, the building lots occupied about half of the depth. The fact that ground rent was levied

according to the size of the street facade led to the system of narrow lots being maintained.
15 As well as these oldest parts of the building, the huts and pavilions in the garden have also been classified.
16 In recent years, another pine tree has been planted; interestingly, though, the original trunk had been carefully preserved.
17 The Tokuwaga went so far as to regulate certain architectural elements in terms of social classes (Coaldrake 1983).
18 The sliding partitions and the uprights of the *shōji* are much more recent, probably dating from the beginning of the nineteenth century.
19 *Sukiya* means a tea pavilion and connotes the idea of seeking elegance inherited from the expression of *suki* in classical poetry (Fiévé 1989: 144–66).

References

Pre-1868 Sources

Hito mesengen (1757). In *Kinsei bungei gyōsho*, vol. 10.
Kiryo manroku (1802), by Kyokutei Bakin. In *Nihon zuihitsu taisei*, 1st series, vol. 1.
Kiyū shōran (1816), by Kitamura Nobuyo. In *Nihon zuihitsu taisei*, 2nd series, *Bekkan*, 2 Vol.
Kyō warabe (1658), by Nakagawa Kiun (Jūji). In *Zōho Kyōto sōsho*, vol. 1.
Mita miyako monogatari (1781), by Kimuro Myō'un. In *Nihon zuihitsu taisei*, 3rd series, vol. 4.
Ukiyo monogatari (1660), by Asai Ryō. In *Tokugawa bungei ruijū*, vol. 2.
Yūjōki (eleventh century), by Ōe no Masafusa. In *Gunsho ruijū*, vol. 6, book 135.

Post-1868 Sources

Amino Y. (1994) 'Le Moyen Age japonais et quelques questions qu'il pose aux historiens aujourd'hui.' *Cipango* 3: 125–58.
Coaldrake, W. H. (1996) *Architecture and Authority in Japan*. London: Routledge.
—— (1983) *Gateways of power: Edo architecture and Tokugawa authority 1603–1651*. Ph. D. dissertation. Harvard University.
Couvreur S. (1890) *Dictionnaire classique de la langue chinoise*. New edition (1966), Taipei: Kuangchi Press.
Fiévé, N. (1997) 'Le quartier de Shimabara. Planification urbaine et espaces discriminatoires dans le Japon des Tokugawa.' In J. Pigeot et H.O. Rotermund (eds), *Le vase de béryl. Études sur la Chine et le Japon en hommage à Bernard Frank*. Arles: Éditions Piquier, pp. 373–84.
—— (1996) *L'architecture et la ville du Japon ancien. Espace architectural de la ville de Kyōto et des résidences shōgunales aux XIVe et XVe siècles*. Bibliothèque de l'Institut des Hautes Études Japonaises, Collège de France/Université de Paris 7. Paris: Maisonneuve et Larose.
—— (1995) 'Nascita della città moderna in Giappone: il popolo di Kyoto e la formazione dello spazio urbano.' (Birth of the modern city in Japan: The people of Kyoto and the formation of urban space) *Storia urbana* 70 (*Città dell'Estremo Oriente: Kyoto, Tokyo, Shanghai, Seoul*), pp. 3–28.
—— (1989) *Structure de l'espace des pavillons de thé. Développement des arts et de la pensée à la fin du moyen-âge*. Mémoire de maîtrise de langue et civilisation japonaises. Paris: Université de Paris 7.

Fujioka M. (1956) *Kyōto gosho* (Kyoto imperial palace). Tokyo: Shōkokusha.
Gunji M. (1993) 'Kuruwa no koto' (Concerning the prostitution districts). *Kokubungaku* 38 (9): 6–9.
Hayashiya T. (ed.) (1979) *Kyōto no rekishi* (History of Kyoto), vol. 4: *Momoyama no kaika* (The flourishing of the Momoyama Period), vol. 5: *Kinsei no tenkai* (Development of the early modern period). Kyoto: Kyōtoshi Shuppankai.
Hayashiya T., Murai Y., and Moritani K. (1979) *Kyōtoshi no chimei* (Kyōto's place-names). In *Nihon rekishi chimei taikei*, vol. 27. Tokyo: Heibonsha.
Hérail, F. (1986) *Histoire du Japon. Des origines à 1868*. Paris: Presses Orientalistes de France.
Hyūga S. (1983) *Kinsei Kyōto machiya no keisei to tenkai no katei ni kansuru shiteki kenkyū* (Historical studies on the formation and development process of the Kyoto early-modern *machiya*). Ph. D. dissertation. Kyoto: Kyoto University of Arts and Technology.
Kawashima M. (1994) '*Asobi no kūkan*' (Space for entertainment). In Ashikaga K. (ed.), *Kyōto rekishi atorasu* (Historical atlas of Kyoto). Tokyo: Chūō Kōronsha, pp. 92–3.
Kokubungaku 38–9 (1993). Special issue on *Kuruwa: Edo no sei kūkan* (Prostitution districts: sacred spaces of Edo).
Kyōto Bunka Hakubutsukan (The Museum of Kyoto) (ed.) (1991) *Kyō no kabuki ten: Shijō-gawara shibai kara Minamiza made* (Exhibition on kabuki in Kyoto: From Shijō-gawara to the Minamiza). Kyoto: The Museum of Kyoto.
Kyōto-fu (Kyoto Prefecture) (ed.) (1872) *Kyōtofuka yūkaku yuisho* (History of the pleasure districts in Kyoto and its suburbs). Kyoto: Kyoto Prefecture.
Maës, H. (1964, reprint 1979) *Histoire galante de Shidōken*. Paris: L'Asiathèque.
Naitō A. (1983) *Sumiya no kenkyū* (Study of the Sumiya house). Tokyo: Chūō Kōronsha.
Nishiyama M. (1981) '*Kuruwa no seiritsu*' (The establishment of the prostitution districts). *Kokubungaku* (October): 15–22.
Segawa Seigle, C. (1993) *Yoshiwara: The Glittering World of the Japanese Courtesan*. Honolulu: University of Hawaii Press.
Sekino M. (1980) *Nihon no minka* (Rural houses of Japan), vol. 5: *Kinki*. Tokyo: Gakushū Kenkyūsha.
Swinton, E. de S., *et al* (1996) *The Women of the Pleasure Quarter: Japanese Paintings and Prints of the Floating World*. New York: Hudson Hills Press.
Takada M. (1993) '*Kuruwa no seishin shi: Kugai to akujo*' (Intellectual history of the prostitution district: world of suffering and cursed place). *Kokubungaku* (August): 42–57.
Takahashi Y., Yoshida N., Miyamoto M., and Itō T. (1993) *Nihon toshishi* (History of the cities of Japan). Tokyo: Tōkyō Daigaku Shuppankai.
Tanaka Y. (1992) *Kyōto yūkaku kenmonroku* (Notes of things seen and heard concerning Kyōto's pleasure enclosure). Kyoto: Kyō o Kataru Kai.
Waley, P. (1995) 'Les lieux de passage et les espaces publics dans la ville japonaise.' In P. Bellevaire and A. Gossot (eds) *Japon pluriel*. Arles: Picquier, pp. 319–26.
Waley, P., and E. Tinios (1999) *On the Margins of the City: Scenes of Recreation from the Periphery of the Japanese Capital, 1760–1860*. Leeds: University of Leeds Press.

CHAPTER 3

Urbanisation and the Nature of the Tokugawa Hegemony

Beatrice M. Bodart-Bailey

Introduction

Considering the size of Japan, the number of inhabitants seems scarcely credible or possible ... There are also a large number of cities, the most important of which are tremendously large and very densely built up ... The city and shogunal residence of Edo is of such a size that one may rightfully call her the largest in the world.

(Kaempfer 1712: 482)

These were some of the impressions the German physician Engelbert Kaempfer (1651–1716) returned with from Japan after his visit in 1690 to 1692. Kaempfer's eighteenth-century editor, Christian Wilhelm Dohm, was sceptical. 'This and other descriptions of the size and population of Japanese cities appear almost exaggerated,' he commented (Kaempfer 1777–1779: 2, 398).

No wonder European visitors were surprised. They might have been even more surprised if they had known the population figures available to us today. At the time of Kaempfer's visit the population of Japan was some twenty-six million, while that of England and Wales was not quite six million (Grigg 1980: 165). The population of France, with a much larger area of arable land, was just over nineteen million (Grigg 1980: 203). At the time the well-established trading port of Hamburg had some 70,000 inhabitants (Chandler and Fox 1974: 147), Marseilles some 88,000 (Chandler & Fox, 1974: 115), and Copenhagen 65,000 (Bairoch 1988: 14), while Kyoto had nearly half a million.[1] Edo is likely to have reached the million mark by the time of Kaempfer's visit, and there can be little doubt that at the end of the seventeenth century it was one of the largest cities in the world.

The settlement which Ieyasu (1542–1616) made the seat of his government in 1603 grew rapidly. Around 1609 Rodrigo de Vivero y Velasco (1564–1636) recorded that the city had 150,000 inhabitants (Cooper 1965: 284). But only a decade later Richard Cocks (d. 1624) maintained that Edo was a 'Cittie in Japan as bigg as London' (Cooper 1965: 409). By the close of the century, Edo was nearly twice the size of London, which had some 575,000 inhabitants at the time (Bairoch 1988: 28, 33).

Urbanisation in seventeenth-century Japan is believed to have been more rapid than anywhere else in the world, and this has been referred to as 'one of the most extraordinary periods of urbanisation in world history' (McClain 1982: 1). One of the basic reasons for the concentration of population in certain parts of Japan is the scarcity of flat, arable land. However, in seventeenth-century Japan a number of factors combined to produce not only extremely rapid urbanisation, but also urbanisation differing in significant aspects from that taking place in Europe at the same time.

The last decades of the sixteenth century brought to an end several centuries of warfare. The battles of Sekigahara and Osaka finally set an end to all inter-*daimyō* fighting and marked the beginning of the *pax* Tokugawa. The result was a population explosion of previously unheard-of proportions. Between 1600 and 1700 Japan's population more than doubled (*Kokushi daijiten* 1979: 7, 811). Exact population figures are not available for the sixteenth century, and it is altogether possible that the population might even have tripled in one hundred years, if calculated from the last decades of the sixteenth century (Hayami 1992). This chapter attempts to describe where this overflow population settled and why it settled where it did.

One of the best sources for understanding this process of urbanisation in early modern Japan is the voluminous record left by Engelbert Kaempfer.[2] Residing for two years as physician to the Dutch trading settlement on the man-made island of Deshima in the harbour of Nagasaki, Kaempfer travelled twice from Nagasaki to Edo noting in detail what he saw. As a foreigner he recorded what no Japanese considered worth ink and paper at the time, and his record is now a valuable source of information for Japanese and non-Japanese historians alike.

Engelbert Kaempfer had studied living conditions while working and travelling for a decade in the Near East and Southeast Asia before finally reaching Japan. But it was here in Japan, with its many urban centres, where a comparison with Europe seemed most fruitful. He noted that the structures of everyday life provided many fundamental similarities, and hence he was able to go into great detail explaining the differences without losing his readers.

Kaempfer's report of Japan is in the main a factual account of what he saw and heard. It was written with the intention of publication for a large, non-specialist audience, and, moreover, his was not the age of structural analysis. In this chapter, however, I intend to focus on those factors responsible for shaping Japanese early-modern urbanisation into the form Kaempfer came to observe it. In this process I will, like he, make comparisons with Europe. This is not because I think Europe is the standard against which all developments must be measured, but because it provides a model of a society at a roughly comparable stage of urban development, and thus shows the alternative routes urbanisation could have taken in Japan. In other words, a comparison can sharpen the inquiry into what forces were responsible for creating the patterns urbanisation did take in Japan.

My contention is that Japan's population explosion took place concurrently with important socio-political developments, and that the ensuing urbanisation reflected these paradigmatic changes. These were firstly the institutional division between samurai and commoners and, secondly, the political nature of Tokugawa rule. The two issues overlap in as much as the Tokugawa shogunate, the *bakufu*, inherited and continued strictly to enforce the division between samurai and commoners. As a result the political nature of *bakufu* rule not only determined patterns of settlement but was also partially determined by the socio-political issues this created. Yet while the division of society into classes left its imprint upon urban patterns even before the advent of the Tokugawa hegemony, the newly-built seat of Edo was totally designed to answer the needs of the administration. It is here, therefore, that the fundamental characteristics of the Tokugawa hegemony are most clearly visible.

The Institutional Division between Warriors and Commoners

The paradigmatic shift from a society divided horizontally into opposing regional centres, characteristic of the so-called Age of Warring States (1467–1573), to one uniformly divided vertically into classes, a shift that took place after the 'unification' of Japan at the end of the sixteenth century, had a significant impact on patterns of new urban settlement.

The institutional division into the four classes of warrior, farmer, artisan, and merchant was not new to late sixteenth-century Japan. It dated back to the early Chinese Confucian classics such as the *Spring and Autumn Annals* (Asao 1992: 15), appeared in the eighth-century Yōrō and Taihō codes (Sansom 1966: 29), and was regarded as the norm in the fourteenth-century political writings of Kitabatake Chikafusa (1293–1354) (Asao 1992: 15). However, during the Age of Warring States, famous for the process of *gekokujō* (the low overcoming the high), class divisions became more fluid as strategic skills and military supplies, rather than status or birth, decided the fortune of individuals.

The division between warriors and commoners was given new legal force by Toyotomi Hideyoshi (1536–98) who in his endeavor to unite the country

Urbanisation and the Nature of the Tokugawa Hegemony

used it to quell rioting farmers and create a tax base to finance his campaigns (Asano 1992: 30). An edict of 1588 forced farmers to relinquish all weapons, in what is known as Hideyoshi's sword hunt (*katana gari*).[3] Three years later, this edict was supplemented by one which divided the populace into the three classes of samurai, townspeople and farmers (Asao 1992: 44; Berry 1982: 106). The process was consolidated by land surveys which registered and bound to the soil all those who cultivated it, regardless of whether they were owners, tenants, or helpers (Berry 1982: 118).

Security Measures

(a) Limiting road access to the seat of government

It is shortly after this class division was newly enforced that a new urban pattern in Japanese castle-towns emerged. The scholar Ashikaga Kenryō argued that while in the Age of Warring States the main street of the castle-town ran straight towards the main entrance of the castle, it now bypassed the castle at some distance (see the chapter by Takahashi). Ashikaga saw Fushimi, with its castle built by Hideyoshi, as the first important example of this new layout.[4]

Thanks to the *bakufu*'s production of detailed *nobe ezu* ('extended,' or proportional, maps), this layout can be confirmed also for other castle-towns lining the highways during the Tokugawa period. It might be argued that this was the logical pattern, to avoid obstructing the traffic. But even in a town like Minakuchi (Ōmi province), where the highway forks into three streets running parallel to each other as it enters the town, the castle – which in the early Tokugawa period was administered by the *bakufu*'s representative but in 1690 was conferred to the junior councillor Katō Akihide (1652–1712) (Kuroita 1976: 6, 88) – lies away from the traffic at one side (fig. 18).

The lack of a main traffic artery leading up to the castle gates is also apparent in the plan for a castle town like Kanazawa. Although here the Hokuriku highway had to make a sharp turn to avoid the high ground of the castle, and a direct road to the entrance of the castle would have provided no additional obstruction, the main traffic arteries with their essential change in direction were kept well away from the castle walls.[5]

Historians have seen the change in urban layout as reflecting the shift from local power centres to unified government (Nagahara 1987: 158). But if this were so, how is one to explain that even in Edo, the central traffic artery, Chūō-dōri, the first or final section of the Tōkaidō, does not lead to the castle entrance but runs parallel to it at a considerable distance. As will be discussed in more detail later, even the entrance to Edo Castle – the seat of the shogun – had no direct avenue of approach. Prior to Edo's becoming the all-important seat of the hegemony at the start of the seventeenth

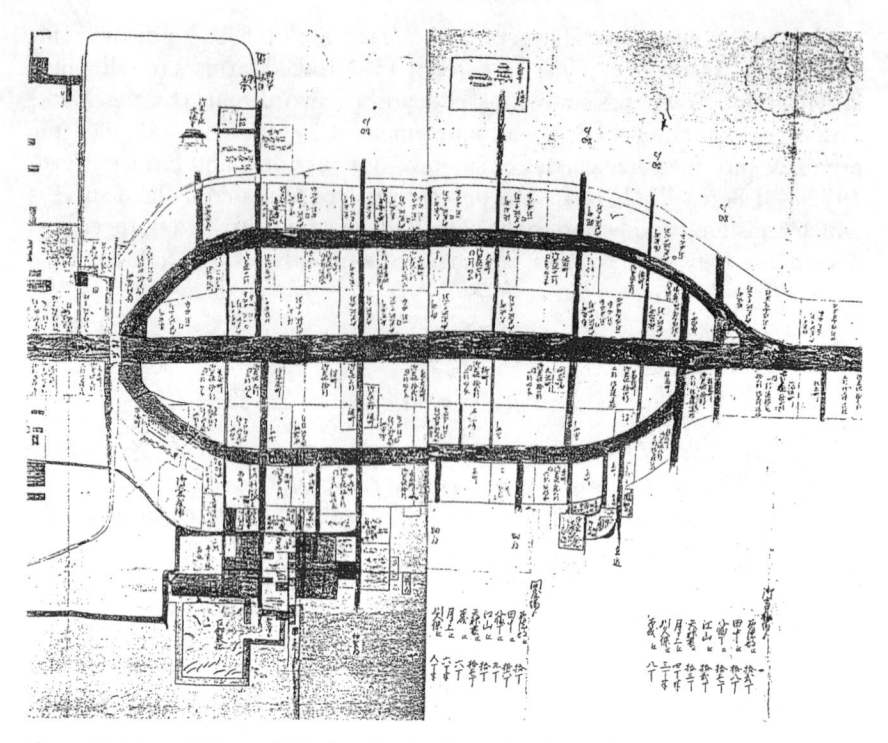

Figure 18 Map of Minaguchi, believed to be from after the Kyōhō era (1716–36). Note the castle in the lower left corner and temples at some distance from the town in the upper part of the map. From Kodama (1977–85) vol. 20, illustration 24–3.

century, however, the main traffic artery leading up to the north of the country, the Ōshū Kaidō, led straight to the castle's main gate.[6]

Hideyoshi's policy of disarming the commoners was a measure to ensure the stability of his administration. It ensured that no rival warlord could easily mobilise a part of the country to fight his government. But the process of strictly enforcing the boundaries of a privileged class entailed at the same time the danger of turning the whole of the less privileged class, the commoners, into the government's enemy. Rapid urbanisation was resulting in an unprecedented concentration of commoners, who by virtue of the uniform policy of a united government, were in turn united by common grievances. I would like to suggest that the urban layout which provided no direct, straight access route to the entrance of the castle, the seat of the administration, was a precautionary defensive measure against possible attack on the part of the commoners.

(b) Creating a human buffer zone

A security measure of a similar nature was the creation of a human buffer zone between the administration and the commoners by restricting samurai settlement to strategic areas surrounding the seat of the administration.

During the Age of Warring States, both townspeople and samurai lived within the enclosure of the castle walls, reflecting the importance of merchants providing the lord with food supplies and weapons. This was originally also the case at Edo, and even when Ieyasu began the reconstruction of the castle, samurai and commoners at first continued to live in the same quarters outside the castle walls (Mizue 1977: 116).

By the beginning of the Bunroku era (1592–96), orders appear in various parts of the country enforcing separate quarters for warriors and merchants.[7] In line with this trend the drainage of Hibiya bay at Edo, which allowed for the greater part of the townspeople to be settled in their own quarters on the flat, lowlying area of reclaimed land, was begun shortly afterwards, in 1593 and 1594 (Haga 1980: 31). But the complete division between the classes in terms of urban settlement was a strategic ideal not easily enforced in a city the size of Edo, as is evident from an order of the 5th Month of 1625 (Kuroita 1976: 2, 344B) threatening that samurai land leased to merchants would be confiscated. The *bakufu*, however, considered the issue important enough to persist, even though seventy years later orders were still necessary in which merchant dwellings on samurai land in Edo were threatened with destruction (Haga 1980: 33).

Nevertheless, this was a method by which not only the housing but also the movement of commoners could be largely controlled through settlement in highly regulated administrative units corresponding to the *machi* or *chō*.

(c) Population control through the *machi*

The concept of the block, *machi* or *chō*, dates back to the Chinese Confucian classics and Japan's earliest capitals. The size of the block varied from city to city, but in the early Heian capital (Kyoto) it consisted of a square city block measuring 40 *jō* on each side (approximately 118 meters). For commoners this was divided into what was termed 'four rows of eight gates' (*shigyō hachimon*), making thirty-two lots (see the Introduction). However, since twelve of these lots had no street frontage, they were generally used as a common area for wells, gardens, and other facilities (Kyōto-shi 1994: 81). Illustrations confirm this pattern also for early urban settlement other than Kyoto.[8] Originally a *machi* was simply one of several units of urban planning and by no means the norm.

In the pre-1600 period of the construction of Edo, the layout of the castle with its moats took priority, and scholars believe that samurai and towns people settled without distinction along the traffic arteries (Mizue 1977: 116). However, by the time Engelbert Kaempfer visited in Japan, the *machi* had developed there and elsewhere into an official, self-contained urban unit, executing and financing its own administration, as well as enforcing land tax collection and strict control over its inhabitants on behalf of the government.

It is interesting to note that artistic illustrations of Edo, such as the well-known *Edozu byōbu* (Illustrated screens of Edo) in the National Museum of Japanese History, show the classical Chinese grid pattern of a square divided by two horizontal and two vertical lines into nine plots, with the central plot being reserved for common amenities.[9] While scholars admit that there is insufficient evidence to determine the rules of *machiwari* (division of streets), they nevertheless believe that a *machi* was less an area than a stretch of road lined by houses on either side, generally measuring sixty, forty, or twenty *ken* (Ogi 1987: 341).[10] This theory is supported by the fact that land tax was levied according to house frontage; the depth of the plot was of no importance, as long as it did not exceeded fifteen *ken*. If it did, the tax was doubled (Kaempfer 1999: 164). Kaempfer noted that in Nagasaki each street consisted generally of ten to fifteen *gonin gumi*, groups of five households owning land. However, each *gonin gumi* might have as many as fifteen households not owning land as tenants under its control (Kaempfer 1999: 158).

Those owning land were responsible for electing the *otona*, or *machi* headman, who was appointed after approval from the *bakufu*'s magistrate had been obtained. His duties consisted in comprehensively controlling the lives of the residents of his *machi*. Kaempfer, who was describing Nagasaki but had been told that the same administrative system existed elsewhere, detailed these as follows:

> He takes care of fires and guards and is responsible for the execution of orders from above. He keeps books and registers of all births, deaths, marriages, departures, removals, and arrivals, in addition to recording people's names, date of birth, religion, and livelihood. He investigates and settles everyday incidents and disagreements, punishes petty crime with chains or imprisonment, has delinquents apprehended by his servants in his own district, and has them imprisoned until the authorities deal with them. He hands over to them all criminal cases, informs them of other important incidents, and is responsible for all occurrences in his street. (Kaempfer 1999: 158)

The *otona* was assisted in his duties by three deputies, the *ōgumi oya* or *ōgumi gashira*, literally, the fathers or heads of the great corporations. Below these were *kogumi oya* or *kogumi gashira*, the fathers or heads of the little corporations. The latter were the elected heads of the *gonin gumi*. The individual members of the *gonin gumi* were in turn responsible for the conduct of the landless individuals that were housed on their plots.

The records kept were sufficiently complex to require the services of a full-time professional scribe. All requests, contracts and oaths were documented in writing, as were the orders, 'testimonials, discharges, and passes' produced by the *otona*. So that the higher authorities could constantly be kept informed of the affairs of the *machi* and orders within the *machi* could be promptly transmitted, the *machi* employed its own messenger. In addition it had its own treasurer (Kaempfer 1999: 159).

The most important task, however, was that of keeping order, for all suffered for crime committed in the *machi*. Kaempfer noted:

> The administrators of the street must atone for the crime of their heads of households, the latter for that of the members of their household, lodgers, and guests; a lord must atone for his servants, a son for his father, a corporation for its members, and neighbors for each other.

Punishment was severe, ranging from torture and execution to confinement within one's house, and was 'incurred so easily without a person's fault or knowledge that almost nobody can live assured that he will be spared' (Kaempfer 1999: 160). If, for instance, a quarrel occurred in the street, it was the duty of the citizens to separate the fighting parties, regardless of whether those fighting were domiciled in the *machi* or not. If one party was killed, the other automatically incurred the death sentence, even if acting in self-defence. The inhabitants of the nearest houses, in turn, would be confined to their dwellings for several months, and the remaining citizens of the street, as well as the *kumi gashira* of the culprit's *machi*, would also receive punishment. This would be more severe if offenders were known for their inclination to brawl, and no preventative steps had been taken (Kaempfer 1999: 162).

With such laws it is not surprising that security was given the utmost attention by all. *Machi* were closed off at each end with heavy gates during the night, and also during the day at such times when there was potential for trouble. At these times nobody was permitted to pass except those carrying a *torifuda*, a branded wooden docket issued by an *otona*. The gates were attended by two guards employed by the *machi*, who would accompany any such visitors through the *machi*. At night the guards constantly made the rounds to watch for intruders and fires. But these two guards were not deemed sufficient, especially when festivals and religious celebrations resulted in large numbers of people on the move. At those times contingents of three citizens staffed an additional guard post in the middle of the *machi*, with even the *otona* and his deputies taking turns when they feared an incident might occur.

European cities were subject to a number of restrictions, preventing movement of people and goods (Chartier 1994: 135), but none would have been quite as exacting as those resulting from the system of mutual responsibility of Tokugawa Japan. The strict rules of the *machi* meant that moving domicile was not easily accomplished. Citizens wanting to sell their plot of land were required to have the potential buyer approved by all land holders of the *machi*. The background and past conduct of would-be buyers was thoroughly investigated, and if even one person of the *machi* voiced doubts about their character, the approval would be withheld. Needless to say, this procedure greatly discouraged the sale of plots, for in-coming citizens too were only acting wisely if they assured themselves first that they would not be liable for punishment on account of their new neighbours. A similar procedure was required even when people not holding land wished to rent lodgings in another *machi*.

The *machi* assumed total responsibility for the lives of their inhabitants. Absence from the *machi* had to be applied for, approved, and documented through the hierarchy of the *machi*, until the *otona* finally set his seal to the necessary travel documents (Kaempfer 1999: 161). Since travel was permitted only for essential purposes, the majority of journeys were termed 'pilgrimage,' which was considered an essential part of life.

Thus urbanisation in early modern Japan was shaped by the strict enforcement of class distinctions, and population growth was concomitantly channelled into the *machi*, which provided both spatial and administrative control. Consequently new, additional housing did not cluster arbitrarily around the periphery of an established centre but was built on both sides of a straight road, closed off by gates at each end. Thanks to this system, a fast-growing city like Nagasaki, located on hilly and irregular ground, developed a neat grid plan, with even Deshima, the man-made island in the harbour of Nagasaki on which the Dutch were forced to live in seclusion, was designed to conform to this pattern. Being more or less self-contained, these units could be added like building blocks and consequently were well suited to the growth of settlements along the arteries of the highways.

Settlements along the highways

Japan's geographic features, especially the elongated shape of the main island, made it essential for any government wishing to control large parts of the country to control and maintain the highways. Thus government orders for the establishment of post and relay stations at regular intervals along highways appear as early as the middle of the seventh century, shortly after the Taika reforms. That these stations developed into a chain of relatively populous centres is evidenced by the fact that by 838 the province of Aki had eleven such post stations with 120 porters each, while in 855 the post station of Sakamoto in the province of Mino is recorded as having had 215 such porters (Kodama 1960: 2). To be able to provide such manpower, settlements surrounding these stations must have had populations of considerable size. The importance and size of these post stations, however, changed in accordance with the political situation, a decline in central power resulting in a general decline of the countrywide highway system, with sections receiving sporadic attention when the local political situation so demanded (Watanabe 1991: 2).

With the reestablishment of central authority under Oda Nobunaga (1534–82) and Toyotomi Hideyoshi, the countrywide highway and post station system underwent renewal. When Tokugawa Ieyasu subsequently established his hegemony with Edo as his administrative capital, gaining control of and reorganising the Tōkaidō highway, linking Edo with Kyoto and Osaka became a government priority. Only a few months after his victory at Sekigahara, he appointed official rest stations along the Tōkaidō and commanded them to keep a supply of horses, to be available free of charge for those carrying his sealed letter (Maruyama 1992: 183, 191; Watanabe 1991: 161).

Especially after Ieyasu had taken the precaution of creating a dual power base, locating the official administration under his son Hidetada at Edo, while he himself retired to Sunpu, he travelled frequently between the two locations, personally inspecting the condition of the road (Maruyama 1992: 198). Moreover, the first three shoguns all travelled to Kyoto on a number of occasions: Ieyasu four times, Hidetada (1578–1632) six times, and Iemitsu (1604–51) three times (Maruyama 1992: 220). The largest of these processions, that accompanying Iemitsu to Kyoto in 1634, is said to have consisted of over three hundred thousand people and, needless to say, required a considerable number of personnel to service the road and the lodgings. *Daimyō*, too, were frequently travelling the highways even in the early years of the *bakufu*, for the most important of them were assigned villas in Edo long before the formalisation of the *sankin kōtai* system. When the latter was formally established in 1635, making travel to Edo on a regular basis compulsory for *daimyō* and high-ranking officials, the volume of traffic increased accordingly. Edo's rapidly expanding material needs, as well as the improved road conditions, led to an increase in travel by the common man, both for business and pleasure. The latter was usually termed pilgrimage, virtually the only form of leisure travel permitted.

Engelbert Kaempfer noted sequentially: 'An incredible number of people daily use the highways of Japan's provinces. Indeed, at certain times of the year they are as crowded as the streets of a populous European city' (Kaempfer 1999: 271). The highways were not just as crowded as 'a populous European city.' Large parts of them were also built up as densely as a city street. He observed that '... very often, a large number of villages continues in one row without a break. On leaving one village, one enters the next, and in this fashion rows of houses built next to each other continue for many miles with merely a change in name' (Kaempfer 1712: 482). What Kaempfer refers to are settlements elongated by the addition of new *machi* units, which were well suited for commercial expansion along the highways.

The highways brought even the smallest village in contact with a large number of potential buyers and led to commercialisation and urbanisation in otherwise remote and poor areas. For instance, Menoke (also Umenoki), a small village outside Kusatsu, became famous for its bitter powders, supposedly curing a large number of illnesses. Kusatsu itself conducted a thriving trade in walking sticks and whips, produced from the roots of a local bamboo. Further up the road, Minaguchi, was famous for its delicately woven hats, coats, and baskets made of split reeds (Kaempfer 1999: 327, 376). If no local handicraft was available, the settlement could always attempt to reach distinction by producing some palatable food. Even though Kaempfer described them as 'a glue-like substance' (Kaempfer 1999: 405), the nearby village of Maeno was famous for its *amakashi* (heavenly cakes). Thus even in this mountainous and otherwise unproductive area, southeast of Lake Biwa between Kusatsu and Kameyama, villages were lining the highway, 'one, so to speak, holding hands with the next' (Kaempfer 1999: 329).

The largest profit, however, was no doubt made by the countless inns that provided the traveller with a great variety of accommodation and entertainment which, even in the seventeenth century, was sold as a 'package.' These 'packages,' many of which included transport, were known as *hatago* (Maruyama 1992: 200). Then as now, travel was a chance to escape the watchful eye of family and friends, and thus 'entertainment' was often included in the price of accommodation. All inns had a number of so-called *meshimori onna*, women 'who attended on the travellers at table and also at night,' as *Kenkyusha's New Japanese-English Dictionary* carefully puts it (p. 1084; also, Vaporis 1994: 81). Some cities were particularly notorious in this respect. Of Akasaka, a city between Okabe and Hamamatsu, Kaempfer wrote:

> Akasaka consists mainly of a long, built-up street, which has many inns, some of which are very fine. The city has a great supply of dressed-up strumpets, especially in the inns, who have to serve the visitors, and this is why it is also called the storehouse of whores. (Kaempfer 1999: 334)

With the increasing importance of travel and transport, the shape of older established cities began to change. Additional population settled in *machi* units strung along the main traffic arteries at the beginning and end of cities. The effect was that settlements located in close vicinity to these population centres began to merge into one large urban sprawl. Leaving Osaka for Kyoto, Kaempfer noted that: 'The road and the surrounding countryside is covered with villages, and not many more are needed to turn the whole road up to Miyako into one urban street' (Kaempfer 1999: 317).

While the official entertainment quarters of the cities were strictly supervised and moved from time to time to more distant and inconvenient locations as Fiévé notes in his chapter on Shimabara, the inns along the highways provided similar services within easy reach. Thus much of the urban sprawl that began to link the major population centres served as unofficial entertainment quarters. Of Hirakata, a town of nearly five hundred houses between Osaka and Kyoto, Kaempfer wrote: 'There are many inns, tea and *sake* houses, and stalls where one can buy all sorts of warm food for a small sum of money, and each inn has a made-up, young prostitute' (Kaempfer 1999: 317). Walking this stretch of the Tōkaidō, one still finds today some of the long rows of gaudily decorated inns, where travellers were entertained from early on in the Tokugawa period until the time when prostitution was outlawed shortly after the Second World War.

The merging of settlements into one gigantic urban landscape was made easy by the fact that even large and strategically important cities like Osaka, Kyoto and Edo had 'neither ramparts nor walls' surrounding them (Kaempfer 1999: 318). Fushimi, Kaempfer observed, was more or less a suburb of Kyoto; Shinagawa, a suburb of Edo. There was no big city gate marking the entrance to Edo. Only the increased number of people, and the more regular pattern of streets, led the foreigners to the conclusion that they had entered the shogun's capital.

The institutional division between warriors and commoners resulted in segregated areas of settlement, with the former creating a buffer zone around the seat of the administration. The latter were housed in strictly administered *machi* units along roads that generally bypassed the castle at a distance and did not lead up to the seat of administration. As linear units, comprising houses on both sides of a stretch of street, the *machi* were well suited as a means of extending the commercial operations of settlements along the highways, resulting in the 'borderless' yet orderly sprawl of settlements Kaempfer observed.

The Tokugawa decision to locate their administrative capital in the Kantō, and the demand that *daimyō* and other high-ranking samurai frequently call upon the *bakufu* and keep their families in Edo, created a large demand for services along the highways, especially the Tōkaidō. The commercial opportunities that resulted led to population concentration of commoners along these roads. Thus the nature of the Tokugawa *bakufu* with its administrative capital away from the commercial hub of the country and strict control over the movement and settlement patterns of both samurai and commoners shaped urbanisation throughout the country.

In Edo, where the blueprint was created according to the government's perceived needs, the imprint of the political nature of the Tokugawa shogunate is even clearer and stronger. Yet the nature of Tokugawa government as expressed in the urban design of its capital is curiously at odds with that which is attributed to it by most scholars.

The Political Function of the Tokugawa *Bakufu* and the Layout of Edo

The straight, orderly streets of the city of Edo greatly impressed European visitors because they reflected the ideals of political absolutism of seventeenth-century Europe. Both in Japan and in Europe it was well understood that straight, orderly streets facilitated autocratic government (Roeck 1999: 20). However, there was the important difference that in Europe straight avenues were generally built in the vicinity and leading up to the seat of authority, while in Edo they were located only in areas at a distance from the seat of the shogun, running parallel and not towards it.

The authoritarian rulers of Europe like the Bourbon kings of France not only used straight avenues physically to control the population but also psychologically to imprint their domination on the populace. The squares of Louis XIV (1638–1715), Ballon notes, 'surrounded by houses of the nobility, deified the king; they magnificently inscribed the cult of the monarch in the form of the city' (Ballon 1991: 145). At the beginning of the seventeenth century, as the complex moat system of Edo Castle was put in place, curved streets in Paris with their maze of small houses were being razed to make room for the Place Dauphine on a plot of some three acres on the Western tip of the central island of the Cité, transforming an area at the back of the palace gardens into a focal point for the large number of aristocrats and commoners who daily crossed the busy Pont Neuf. The square was created to pay homage to the dauphin, the future Louis XIII (1601–43), whose birth assured the continuation of the Bourbon dynasty (Ballon 1991: 125). Its pointed triangular shape cleverly accentuated the lay of the land to lead the eye from one of the main arteries of the city into the direction of the seat of authority. A royal equestrian statue emphasised the symbolism. The visual experience of the passer-by, of both commoners and aristocrats, had become an important dimension of urban design (Ballon 1991: 137).

By the time the fifth Tokugawa shogun was in power and Engelbert Kaempfer visited Japan, city design in Paris had advanced to create the Place des Victoires (1689) and the Place Louis XIV (Place Vendôme, 1699), grandiose squares symbolising the power and glory of the monarch.

Although the shogunate showed similar awareness of the power of spatial and visual symbolism in the design of its palaces, with their awe-inspiring wall paintings and multi-level rooms, it did not use urban design for this purpose when creating its seat of authority. The nearest approach to expressing the authority of the shogun in urban planning was creating a spectacular landmark by building the forty-five-meter tall keep of Edo castle on a stone platform that towered some further twenty meters above the remaining castle buildings (Naitō 1982: 39). One may well argue, however, that this design was based as much on strategic considerations as on any intention to impress the populace. Moreover, when the keep was destroyed in the Meireki fire of 1657, it was not replaced.

Most historians maintain that the castle's keep was not rebuilt after the Meireki fire because the *bakufu* no longer feared a military challenge.[11] Tokugawa authority is generally considered totally secure by this time, leading some historians to conclude that 'the Tokugawa shoguns wielded greater power than did the Bourbon kings' (McClain and Ugawa 1994: 460). Yet this military confidence ascribed to the *bakufu* of the post-Meireki period is neither reflected in any change of policy – such as abolishing the regular compulsory visit and with it the residence of the wives and children of *daimyō* and important officials at Edo – nor any change in the layout of the approaches to Edo Castle.

Not only did the Meireki fire destroy the shogunal castle with its five-storey keep and secondary castles of Ni-no-maru and San-no-maru but also five hundred *machi* and many buildings in *daimyō* compounds, as well as nine thousand rice granaries, sixty bridges, and three hundred temples and shrines (Bodart-Bailey 1998: 46), and resulted in important changes in urban design. But at no point was the maze-like access to the shogun's castle altered to reflect greater security on the part of the *bakufu*, a factor that historians appear to take for granted. Indeed, the opposite was the case. While in Paris squares were built to place the nobility, so to speak, at the feet of the ruler, in Edo the residences of the most important families, the shogun's brothers and the *gosanke* (the three related houses) were moved away from the castle (Ogi 1987: 343). The purpose was to gain a firebreak around the shogun's residence. Yet while in France this firebreak might well have been turned into a stately avenue to direct the gaze of the commoners towards the seat of the ruler, in Edo it became a secluded palace garden.

In the outer precinct of the castle, the *daimyō yashiki*, the large residences of the *daimyō*, were permitted to remain where they were. But at no time were they placed or constructed in such a way as to create a visual effect enhancing the ruler's authority at the cost of easy access to the castle. The road system of this area was so complex that even the experienced cartographer Kaempfer complained: 'It has so many intersections, different moats, and ramparts that I was neither able to work out its ground plan nor properly inform myself by consulting Japanese printed illustrations' (Kaempfer 1999: 353). The main approach to the castle, via Tokiwabashi and Ōtemon, the main castle gate, was winding along multi-cornered streets, in the shadow of tall walls, built to hide rather than express the grandeur of those living behind them (fig. 19). Only the splendour of the gate served as a measure of the occupant's prominence (see the chapter by Coaldrake). Yet while the gate's stateliness indicated the owner's lofty status, its enormous size also effectively concealed the buildings of the residence. Moreover, this area being located behind the large walls lining the outer moat, the common crowd had neither physical nor visual access and hence no occasion to be impressed by these costly gates.

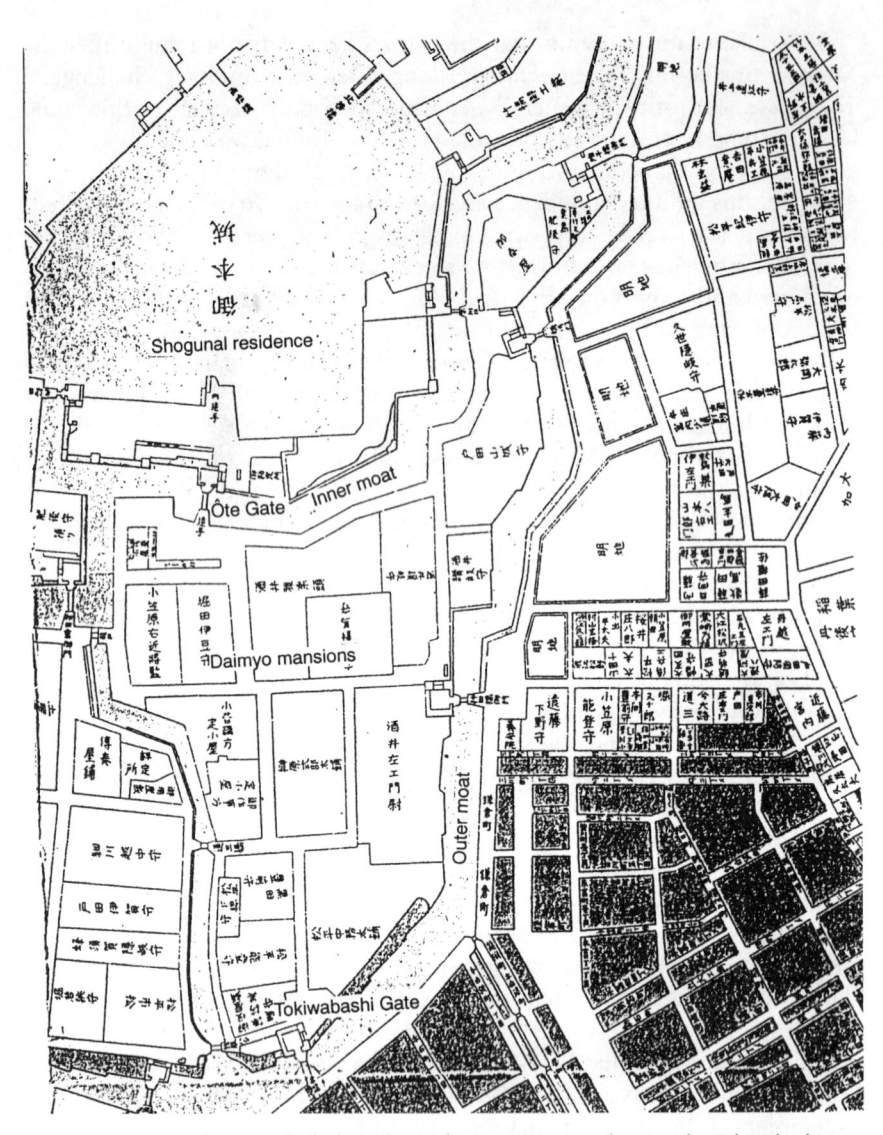

Figure 19 Section of a map of Edo from the Kyōhō era (1716–36) showing the Tokiwabashi gate at the outer moat in the lower part and the Ōtemon gate at the inner moat in the upper part of the map. Note the *masukata* shape of the gates and the fact that the roads do not lead to the gates in a straight line. From Tōkyō shiyakusho (ed.), *Tōkyōshi shikō*, reprint 1994, 1: 121.

Long avenues with imposing vistas were not unknown in Japan. They were present in the layout of the old imperial capitals, Buddhist monasteries, and especially Shinto shrines. The long approach from the sea to Sumiyoshi Taisha at Sakai, as it existed in the Tokugawa period, furnishes an example.

A long avenue of stone lanterns marked by *torii* (ceremonial gates) and bridges – the last of which was (and still is) extremely difficult to cross with its semi-circular arch – led the visitor's gaze to the shrine.

That the shogunate was not oblivious of the need to remind the populace of its authority is indicated by the role assigned to Nihonbashi, the so-called Bridge of Japan. All distances throughout the realm were measured in relation to this bridge at the centre of Edo. Thus even in the remotest part of the country, road signs indicated the precise distance between the ruler and his subjects. But here again, no attempt was made to express political authority in spatial design. The bridge spanned an irregular arm of the complex moat system, which ended up like a twisted appendix, leading vaguely in the direction of the castle. After the Meireki fire, temples and domestic dwellings were relocated away from the crowded centre of the city, roads were redesigned and widened. The necessity for open spaces as firebreaks was clearly perceived, yet no steps were taken to incorporate the famous bridge in an impressive design, with magnificent vistas towards the seat of authority to impress the throngs of people who passed over it daily.

In Paris the construction of the Place Dauphine was financed by merchants, providing residences for the most successful of them closer to the palace. In Edo the commoners, making up over fifty per cent of the city's population, were crowded on some sixteen per cent of the available land. Rather than encourage merchants to invest in stately buildings and squares paying homage to the glory of the ruler, the government punished them and stripped them of their riches if they dared to display their wealth. While urban design in seventeenth-century Paris was meant to enable the monarch to display his wealth and authority and gather the most deserving of his subjects around him, in Edo it attempted to conceal and seclude those in power.

Henry Smith suggests rightly that 'the idea of the city must be approached within a framework of the changing structure of political and economic power' (Smith 1979: 53). The political power of the rulers of Edo and Paris has been approximated, yet the 'idea of the city' varies greatly. In view of this difference, the political function and authority of the Tokugawa *bakufu* must be reexamined.

The Political Function of the Tokugawa *Bakufu* and Edo

Function and Architecture

In his fine study William H. Coaldrake (1996) has shown the link between architecture and authority in early modern Japan. Indeed, architecture as a display of the power to harness the labour and material goods of others has been evident from the dawn of history, expressing itself most succinctly in mortuary monuments, be they the pyramids of Egypt, the enormous stone slabs that make up the mortuary chambers of prehistoric Avebury in Wiltshire, or the large key-shaped tumuli after which the Japanese Kofun period (250–593) is named. These mausoleums, as also the temples at Nikkō, built to commemorate the first and third Tokugawa shoguns, served important ideological and spiritual purposes. But they had, in the strict sense of the word, no practical function. Yet it is the very functionalism of pre-modern Japanese architecture which struck Western visitors to Japan like Bruno Taut, a functionalism that was neglected in Europe. There, not only in the construction of monuments for the dead but also of those for the living, the display of authority was no longer just a by-product of the structure's function but increasingly a means to an end. It was this burden of symbolic and evocative non-functional form which the architects and designers of the Bauhaus attempted to liberate themselves from. The Bauhaus considered itself unique and avant-garde, but Taut saw otherwise when he found that these ideals had already been translated into architectural form in the seventeenth-century Katsura detached villa outside Kyoto (Naitō 1977: 7).

When studying Japanese early modern architecture of a non-religious nature, this functionalism cannot be neglected. Thus while the famous 'goose-flight' patterned layout of the Tokugawa's Nijō Castle in Kyoto no doubt 'heightened the importance of each separate building and provided opportunity for effective use of a sequence of partial revelations for intensifying the dramatic effect of progressing through the building' (Coaldrake 1996: 155), it also had important practical functions. For it not only provided a maximum amount of daylight for every chamber, but also meant that fires – be they accidental or arson – were easier to contain. The gravel which covered the ground of the gardens surrounding each section permitted no visitor to arrive by stealth, and the long corridors with their famous squeaking 'nightingale' floor boards, made necessary by this layout, served the same purpose.

I would like to suggest that the functional component was also a major factor in the urban planning of Edo, not only at the inception of the city but throughout the Tokugawa period.

Edo's Function and the Authority of the Bakufu

Edo's function was, of course, to be a base for rule over Japan. Both the actual record of events and Tokugawa documents tell us that the hegemony exercised political control over the Japanese islands for more than two hundred and fifty years. On the basis of historical sources, historians have concluded that the authority exercised by the *bakufu* was comprehensive, and that military challenge to the regime ended with the siege of Shimabara in 1637–38 (McClain and Ugawa 1994: 460). However, while no scholar would assess the political strength of a modern authoritarian regime on the basis of sources furnished by the government and its supporters, this is what has happened in the case of the Tokugawa. The overwhelming bulk of primary sources available today were written either by those in the employ of the *bakufu* or by men within its ideological orbit. When one adds to this the fact that the historical record was kept primarily for didactic purposes, it becomes obvious why caution is necessary. As Arai Hakuseki (1657–1725) stated, 'Write in history only what is worthy of the record.' If Hakuseki was of the opinion that 'the shame' of the sixth shogun Ienobu dancing Noh should not be recorded in history (Knox 1902: 146; Wildman Nakai 1981: 182), one cannot help but wonder what other incidents of 'shame' were omitted from the record.

Thus, for instance, when the Dutch on Deshima were told in 1680 that a fierce civil war was likely to occur over the question of who was to succeed the dying fourth shogun Ietsuna (1641–80) (Coolhaas 1971: IV, 366), there is no indication of an impending crisis in the otherwise detailed record in the *Tokugawa jikki*, the records of the Tokugawa *bakufu*. The chronicle notes the rumour that the Grand Councillor (*tairō*) Sakai Tadakiyo (1624–81) intended to install an imperial prince as successor instead of Tsunayoshi (1646–1709), the lawful heir as the younger brother of the childless shogun (Kuroita 1976: 5, 354B). But it does not elaborate on the dissent this caused beyond noting without explanation that two days prior to the shogun's death additional guards had been assigned to the Ōte and Sakurada gates of Edo castle, through which the *daimyō* passed (Kuroita 1976: 5, 337B).

When Engelbert Kaempfer visited Japan some ten years later, his Japanese informers told him that the *daimyō* were not content with their subordinate role but 'were thirsting for political authority' (1712: 495). One of the few remaining sources documenting *daimyō* unwillingness to accept *bakufu* commands is a letter by Ikeda Mitsumasa (1609–82) addressed to Sakai Tadakiyo. In it he explicitly cautioned that in the past unjust oppression inevitably led to revolt. He pointed to a number of recent popular uprisings and suggested point blank that even the *daimyō* themselves might rebel (Bodart-Bailey 1993: 310). This letter is contained in Mitsumasa's personal diary of events. However, at the height of the conflict between *daimyō* and *bakufu*, the diary suddenly breaks off. Did it perhaps contain matter that the guardians of the record, historians like Hakuseki, considered 'shameful,' and therefore best to eliminate?

Scholars have argued that Tokugawa legitimacy, and hence its authority, rested on the mandate to govern received from the emperor and on the Confucian concept of *kōgi*, the government's concern with the public good (McClain and Merriman 1994: 10). However, even some nine decades after the event, Ieyasu was portrayed as a usurper to a visitor like Kaempfer (Kaempfer, 1777–79: 1, 247). The Confucian concept of the Mandate of Heaven did not provide justification for the control the *bakufu* exercised very publicly over the emperor and his court at Kyoto (Bodart-Bailey 1998b: 195). Thus a Confucian *daimyō* like Tokugawa Yoshinao (1600–50), lord of Owari and member of the *gosanke*, held the view that the *daimyō*, including the *gosanke*, were not the shogun's retainers but those of the emperor. The shogun was no more than the 'head of the troops' (*hatagashira*). And even though Yoshinao was Ieyasu's son, he instructed his descendants that if the *bakufu* were to take military action against the emperor, as the Kamakura *bakufu* had done in the Jōkyū (1221) and Genkō (1331) wars, they were not to fight against the imperial house. Two hundred years later the fourteenth domain lord, Yoshikatsu (d. 1883), acted on these instructions (Bodart-Bailey 1998b: 195).

Another Confucian *daimyō* and member of the *gosanke*, Tokugawa Mitsukuni (1628–1700), held similar views and is said to have performed regular ceremonial obeisance in the direction of the imperial palace. As is well known, when the choice between shogun and emperor had to be made in the nineteenth century by his descendants, they opted for the emperor, even though a member of their family was occupying the post of shogun (Bodart-Bailey 1998b: 196).

With such sentiments being present among the *gosanke*, the very *daimyō* upon whom the shogunate was supposed to rely for the greatest support, it is not the fall of the shogunate but the length of its hegemony that should surprise us. In other words, it is doubtful whether the *bakufu* and its contemporaries took the stability which historians ascribe to it in hindsight for granted.

With the *a priori* conviction that the *bakufu* was confident in its authority, scholars have interpreted even small changes in the layout of Edo castle as reflecting a change from military to ceremonial rule (for instance Senda 1993: 258, 260). A comparison with Europe draws attention to the *bakufu*'s function and permits a more nuanced judgement.

Edo's Position

Edo has been compared with Paris, London and even St. Petersburg (McClain 1982: 3; Smith 1979). However, it differs in one important aspect from all these cities: Edo was not built at a natural crossroad of traffic but situated in a political, economic, and geographical backwater. Even St. Petersburg, which has been described as having risen dramatically from 'a swampy bog' (McClain 1982: 7), was in fact built where at the close of the seventeenth century the Swedish town of Nyenschanze was developing rapidly due to its strategic commercial location. Already in 1683, years before Peter the Great chose it as the site for his new capital, Engelbert Kaempfer recorded that walls were being constructed for a new city with houses of stone to replace the old town with its wooden buildings (Kaempfer ms 2923, f. 116 v.).

In tracing the historical development of the area later occupied by Edo, the scholar Tamura Akira likens the site to a hole in a doughnut, a place which was least developed compared to neighbouring areas such as Kenukuni (comprising modern Gunma and Tochigi prefectures), Suruga, the Bōsō peninsula, Hitachi, and so on. When Minamoto no Yoritomo (1147–99) established the Kamakura *bakufu* he chose the much more accessible site of Kamakura. In 1457 Ōta Dōkan (1432–86) began the construction of Edo castle, but Tamura points out that this was merely the furthest outpost of the Uesugi domain. The Hōjō family, which ruled over the Kantō area during the Age of Warring States, in turn chose the more conveniently located Odawara for their headquarters (Tamura 1992: 13).

The reason for the unpopularity of the site of Edo was that at the time both the Tone river and the Ara river flowed into Tokyo bay, and their wide deltas, that of the former extending to some sixteen kilometres, formed a formidable natural barrier. The river tributaries permitted navigation only with small boats, and in between the ground was swampy or prone to flooding (Tamura 1992: 14).

In his book *Ieyasu wa naze Edo o eranda ka?* (Why did Ieyasu choose Edo?) Okano Tomohiko at first glance seems to argue exactly the opposite, namely that Asakusa and Shinagawa were already important harbour towns during the Middle Ages, and that the location had some commercial importance. Okano shows that Shinagawa in particular, on the basis of the available sources, had established trading connections with Ise and Kumano (Okano 1999: 72, 140). But when faced with the question of why the site of Edo had not previously attracted attention as a political centre while Kamakura and Odawara had, he explains that the Tone river constituted a formidable barrier, dividing the Kantō area into a northern and southern part, areas culturally different and politically opposed (Okano 1999: 146). Thus due to the Tone river, the site of Edo was an undesirable frontier area, an explanation not incompatible with Tamura's 'hole in the doughnut.'

The fact is that turning the site of Edo into a population center required considerable civil engineering works, including altering the course of rivers, draining parts of the bay and flattening some of the surrounding heights. Unlike other large cities, the site of Edo was not a natural population center, for it offered few advantages for settlement. Yet the very difficulties that had detracted from the site as area for settlement, gave it exceptional strategic value, something which the Tokugawa used to full advantage.

With the difficulty of the site, initial progress on rebuilding Edo castle after it came into Ieyasu's possession in 1590 was slow, especially since Ieyasu himself was called upon by Hideyoshi to assist with the building of Fushimi castle and had to delegate the work to others. Edo of the Bunroku era (1592–96), the scholar Mizue contends, was still simply one of several Tokugawa strongholds (Mizue 1997: 116).

With Hideyoshi's death in 1598, and especially after the decisive Tokugawa victory at the battle of Sekigahara two years later, in which he eliminated the forces that threatened his supremacy, Ieyasu could have chosen a more convenient site. A location like Nagoya or Sunpu, present-day Shizuoka, where he established his retirement seat, would have provided a more accessible and convenient location for the administrative capital of the country. Yet Ieyasu chose to keep his administration at Edo, and rather than making this awkwardly situated location more accessible, he and his successors erected additional barriers to its approach.

The Approach to Edo

If the Tone river had constituted a formidable barrier to the north of Edo in pre-Tokugawa times, the *bakufu* did nothing to ease access to its seat of authority on establishing itself there. If anything, it did the contrary. Soon after the final victory over the Toyotomi forces, in 1616, the *bakufu* erected some fifteen water barriers (*mizuzeki*) with their checkpoints for boats (*jōfunaba*) along the Tone river, maximizing its effectiveness as an impediment to the flow of traffic.[12] The access to Edo along other waterways was similarly brought under the control of the government.

Edo was located on a sheltered bay, and after the swamps had been drained, a large, safe harbour was created. Consequently the bulk of the voluminous amount of supplies required by the population of Edo was transported by the sea route. No *daimyō*, however, was ever permitted to approach the shogun's capital in the comfort of his own fleet. This he could only use as far as Osaka (Edo Tōkyō Hakubutsukan 1997: 69). After this point he had to submit to the strenuous journey by land, enduring the dangers of being carried across rapidly flowing rivers and the odium of being heaved up and down steep mountain passes in his narrow palanquin, as well as the ignominy of passing government inspection points.

Ieyasu began to control the sea approach to Edo even before he had established his authority over the rest of the country. By 1604 he had appointed an officer (*funate*) and a squadron of thirty-nine men to secure the harbour. Five years later, in 1609, he issued an order for the confiscation of *daimyō* ships of a tonnage of five-hundred *koku* and above, and forbid the construction of such vessels. Together with the laws governing the alternate attendance of *daimyō* at Edo, this restriction became part of the 1635 *buke shohatto*, the regulations outlining proper conduct for high-ranking members of the military class (Kōta 1955: 80). Some scholars argue, however, that this law did not apply to freight ships. To ensure that only freighters travelled the route to Edo and did not carry forbidden goods, all ships had to submit to inspection at Shimoda (Watanabe K. 1991: 59; Watanabe N. 1992: 264). To ensure, in turn, that no ship would head out to sea and enter Edo harbour without passing the inspection point at Shimoda, the construction of vessels was limited to a design where the stern was open to the waves when the rudder was lowered. Thus vessels had no choice but to hug the coast and were unable to travel at night when the approach of a storm could not easily be detected (Kaempfer 1999: 254).

The land approach to Edo was controlled with equal severity. The various measures, especially the famous barriers at Arai and Hakone have been discussed in detail by Constantine Vaporis (1994) and need no further elaboration here. With the approach to Edo guarded in this fashion, the city needed no protective walls. The *bakufu*'s defences were much more sophisticated, not just outside, but also inside the city.

Inside Edo

Louis XIV is said to have made Versailles his residence and the seat of government in 1682 because he distrusted the citizens of Paris, himself having had to escape through a window when the palace was besieged by a mob of commoners. To control the mob, European autocrats like Louis XIV built wide avenues where they could display their military and control the commoners, if necessary by force, the logic being that a gun cannot shoot around a corner.

In the *bakufu*'s design of Edo, straight thoroughfares were used in a similar fashion, as a means of control over both population and fire. The administrative division of the *machi* as a linear unit comprising houses on both sides of a street resulted in long, straight streets and a neat grid plan for most parts of the city. Visiting foreigners – Kaempfer, like the earlier visitor Rodrigo de Vivero y Velasco – were greatly impressed by the uniformity and straightness, as well as cleanliness of the streets (Cooper 1965: 284; Kaempfer 1999: 349).

However, the regular pattern of streets stopped at the outer moat of the castle. The roads that led in the direction of the bridges and well-staffed guardhouses that controlled access to the area within the moat were secondary roads, often running at right angles to larger roads. Moreover, these roads did not lead straight to the point of entry but to a place adjacent to it, thus requiring a sharp turn to enter. In Edo there were no great portals at the end of long avenues through which a large army could pass swiftly and easily. Instead the castle was guarded by its famous *masugata mon*. Named after the *masu*, a square measuring box, these entrances consisted of two gates on adjoining sides of a walled square, forming a box-like enclosure. Thus those entering had to turn a sharp corner to exit and moreover could be locked into the enclosure until the desirability of their passage was established. In addition, the inner gate was surmounted by a fortified guardhouse, which could function as machicolation, a construction known as a *watari yagura mon*. Finally a large guardhouse was usually positioned facing the inner exit of the gate (Chiyoda Kuritsu Yonbanchō Rekishi Minzoku Shiryōkan 1990: 4) (fig. 19).

Foreign visitors like Kaempfer were duly impressed by the castle's fortifications. In Kaempfer's eyes the whole area encircled by the outer moat was one large fortress 'with ramparts and moats, gates, bridges and guard towers in which further fortresses with more and superior ramparts, moats, gates, bridges and guard towers were situated.' He noted that the walls of the inner moat 'are built up high with incredibly large square boulders. ... At the back the walls are filled in with soil and on top fortified with long buildings and square multi-storied guard towers. ... The wall itself has guard posts of stone jutting out in accordance with the art of fortification' (Kaempfer 1999: 353). Traversing the outer precinct, where the residences of the most important *daimyō* were located, Kaempfer's party had to pass a great number of fortified gates, moats and bridges. The inner precinct, the area past the Ōtemon gate, had similar fortifications, but was, in addition, separated from the outer precinct by a long stone bridge and 'bastions sealed off twice.' Finally the party 'climbed about twenty paces up a winding road, which was sealed off on both sides with incredibly high walls.' Only then did the party reach the Hyakuninban, the 'guard of one hundred men,' where the visitors were detained for over an hour until the invitation to proceed further was delivered. Passing two further gates and climbing up steps, the party finally reached the forecourt of the shogunal residence (fig. 20). This was 'only a few paces wide,' surrounded by a wall and guarded by a watch tower. Even though the castle was rebuilt after the Meireki fire, the main, ceremonial entrance to the ruler's residence remained a small, difficult-to-reach courtyard, with firing ports in the walls surrounding it. A few steps led up to the entrance door with its Chinese-style gable (*karahafu*), just large enough to provide some protection from the weather to those rare visitors whose lofty status permitted being carried to the very door of the *honmaru*. The arrangement of the entrance with its own extended roof was known as *kurumayose* and, if we can believe Kaempfer's sketch, was no larger and no different in design from similar structures of the houses of nobility and temples.

Sketching parts of the castle and its inner fortifications was strictly forbidden, but Kaempfer did so secretly, providing us with the only extant drawing of the entrance to the main building, the *honmaru*, as it was reconstructed in the Manji era (1658–60) after the Meireki fire (Kaempfer 1999: 358). This structure, in turn, burned down in 1844, before the advent of photography, making Kaempfer's sketch all the more valuable.

A comparison of this modest and strategically hidden entrance to the main building of the shogun's residence at Edo with the splendid portals of European palaces with their commanding views along straight avenues, makes the difference in design and layout and, ultimately, purpose of the

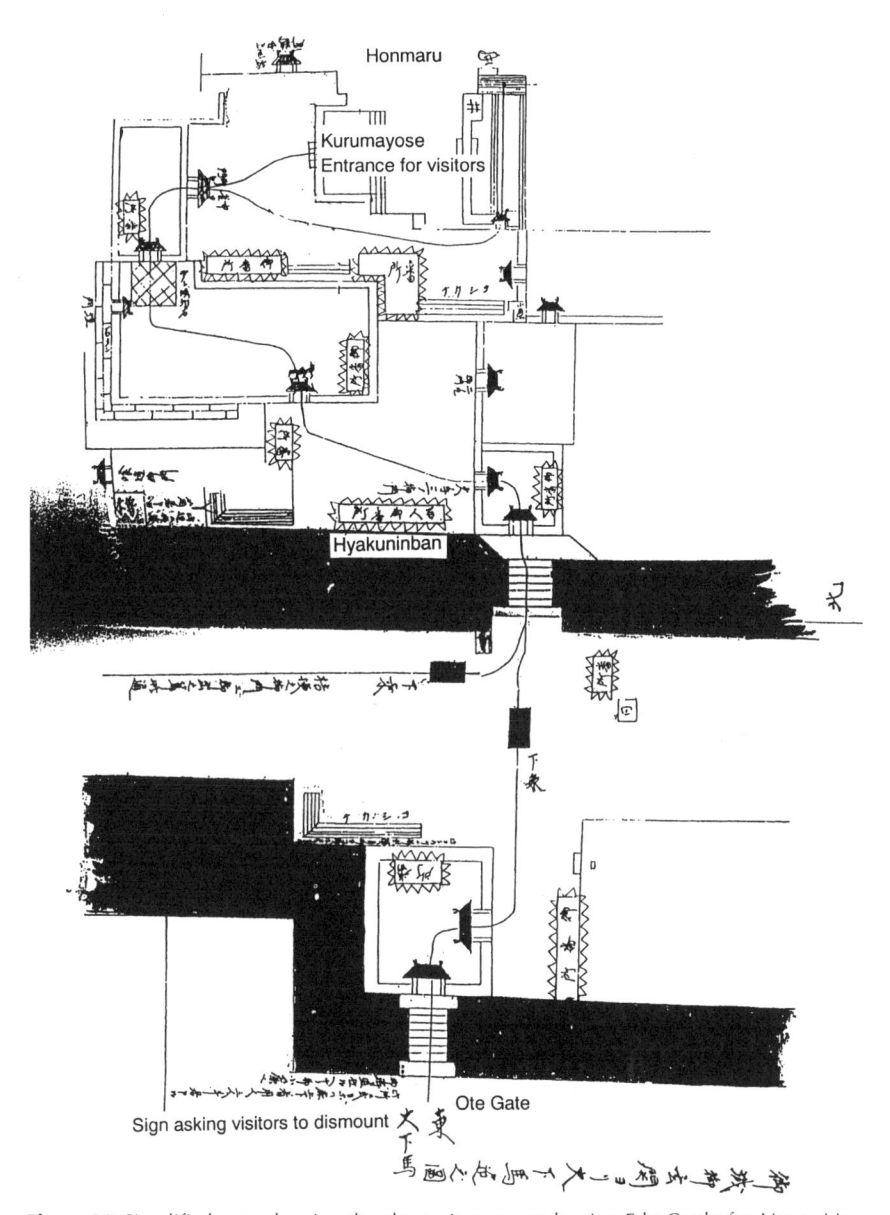

Urbanisation and the Nature of the Tokugawa Hegemony

Figure 20 Simplified map showing the shogun's route on leaving Edo Castle for Ueno. Map adapted by B. M. Bodart-Bailey from Fukai, 1997, pp. 20–1. Original in the National Diet Library, Tokyo. Note the *masukata* shape of the gate. The various guard stations have been surrounded with zigzag lines for identification.

ruler's residence abundantly clear. Moreover, while the design of Edo castle was guarded with utmost secrecy, the plans of Louis XIV's Versailles were liberally circulated and copied by the aristocracy of Europe. If 'the idea of the city,' and by extension the ruler's residence, reflects the structure of political power, then the difference in the structure of authority between the Sun King and his contemporary in Japan, the fifth Tokugawa shogun Tsunayoshi (1646–1709), are amply documented.

The power of the French crown did not last. Louis XVI might well have cursed the urban design of his ancestors as he was led through magnificent avenues and squares to the guillotine in full view of thousands of his subjects. The storming of the Bastille and the events that followed would have been a very different matter in Edo, where the layout did not permit crowds access to military installations and the ruler lived behind solid fortifications. The demise of the shogunate in 1868 followed a very different pattern. Aware of the mounting opposition and an early defeat at Fushimi, the fifteenth shogun handed over his authority voluntarily. With Edo's military fortifications, the final attack on the shogun's castle would have been a long and costly one, and he was enlightened enough to avoid it.

Conclusion

The nature of Tokugawa authority is a complex subject debated by scholars from the time its authority fell and inquiry into and discussion of its structures was finally permitted. The details of the picture undergo change as new primary material becomes available and scholars' political convictions and techniques of interpretation alter. Yet due to the totalitarian nature of the Tokugawa regime and the philosophical concepts of what History ought to be, sources furnishing us with a view not sanctioned by those in authority will always be rare. The demographic record is one of the few sources that could not be manipulated in a similar fashion and one that consequently deserves our attention.

This record tells us that the Tokugawa *bakufu* throughout its existence apprehensively maintained a defensive and well-guarded position towards its subjects. Patterns of settlement throughout the country speak of the strict control it considered necessary over both samurai and commoners. Over samurai as they plied their appointed route at the appointed time to the shogun's seat where the families of the most important among them lived as hostages, over commoners settled in strictly controlled *machi* units, segregated from the samurai and away from the seat of authority, at locations determined by and serving the government's needs. Not interfering with customs of religious worship, this pattern developed without opposition.

The pattern is most obvious in Edo. The *machi* units of the commoners were not only separated from the shogunal castle by a buffer zone of samurai settlements, but a further barrier consisting of moats, walls, and battlements existed. Beyond the castle's outer moat, the roads were straight, facilitating crowd control. They did not, however, provide easy access to the ruler's seat; the main traffic arteries ran parallel to the castle at a distance and not towards the bridges with their guard houses serving as narrow points of entry to the castle. While samurai settlements around the castle served as protection from the commoners, the approaches to the castle within the inner moat indicate that the *bakufu*, nevertheless, did not trust the samurai for its safety. Narrow winding roads and multi-cornered entrance gates hindered rather than assisted the operation of military units. Even though the destruction caused by fires provided the chance for change, the castle's layout remained one designed not for the ruler's military units parading in a display of strength or sweeping aggressively into a crowd but for defensive military fighting and siege.

The Tokugawa *bakufu* lasted for over two hundred and fifty years, but the urban patterns it created belie the claim that it was secure in its hegemony.

Notes

1 For Europe's rapid population increase in the eighteenth century see Zeeden (1981: 102–3).
2 Kaempfer's manuscript *Heutiges Japan*, British Library MS Sloane 3060; English translation C.G. Scheuchzer (1727) *The History of Japan*. London; re-translation B.M. Bodart-Bailey (1999) *Kaempfer's Japan: Tokugawa Culture Observed*. Hawaii University Press.
3 For details see Berry (1982), pp. 102–4.
4 Cited in Nagahara K., *et al* (eds) (1987) pp. 157–8.
5 See map 5: Domain Planning and the Use of Urban Space, 1538–1630 in McClain (1982: 36).
6 See map in Tamai (1988: 40).
7 For instance an order issued by Gamo Ujisato for Wakamatsu. Mizue R. (1977: 116). McClain noted the same development for Kanazawa and points out its importance as a security measure (1982: 28, 35).
8 See, for instance, map no. 10 of the settlement around Zenkōji in Nagano in *Kokushi daijiten* (1979) vol. 13, between pp. 76–7.
9 For an illustration see Coaldrake (1969), p. 131; *Kokushi daijiten*, 1979, XIII, ill. 16, between pages 75 and 76.
10 1 *ken* is approximatively about 1.99 yards or 1.82 meters.
11 This is the standard explanation given by Japanese scholars and also appears in Coaldrake (1996) p. 136.
12 Inoue (1999: 35). For an illustration and detailed discussion of the water barrier at Kanamachi Matsudo see pp. 39–50.

References

Asao N. (1992) '*Kinsei no mibun to sono henyō.*'(Status and change of status in the early modern period) In Asao N. (ed.). *Nihon no kinsei: mibun to kakushiki*

(Japan in the Early Modern Period: Status and Social Standing). Tokyo: Chūō Kōronsha, pp. 7–40.

Bairoch, P. (1988) *La Population des Villes Européennes*. Geneva: Droz.

Ballon, H. (1991). *The Paris of Henry IV*. New York: Cambridge (Mass): MIT Press.

Berry, M. E. (1982) *Hideyoshi*. Cambridge (Mass), London: Harvard University Press.

Bodart-Bailey, (1998a) 'The Economic Plight of the Fifth Tokugawa Shogun.' *Kobe University Economic Review* 44: 37–54.

—— (1998b) 'The Confucian Scholar in Early Tokugawa Japan.' In C. Le Blanc and A. Rocher (eds) *Etat, Société Civile et Sphère Publique en Asie de l'Est*. Montréal: University of Montréal, pp. 191–208.

—— (1993) 'The Persecution of Confucianism in Early Tokugawa Japan.' *Monumenta Nipponica* 48 (3): 293–314.

Braudel, F. (1985) *The Structures of Everyday Life*. London: Fontana.

Cassirer, E. (1974) *The Myth of the State*. New Haven: Yale University Press.

Chandler, T. and G. Fox (1974) *3000 Years of Urban Growth*. New York: Academic Press.

Chartier, R. (1994) 'Power, Space, and Investments in Paris.' In J. McClain, J. Merriman, and Ugawa K. eds. *Edo and Paris: Urban Life and the State in the Early Modern Era*. Ithaca: Cornell University Press, pp. 132–52.

Chiyoda Kuritsu Yonbanchō Rekishi Minzoku Shiryōkan (1990) *Shiryōkan tayori* (Archive newsletter) no. 1. Tokyo.

Coaldrake, W. H. (1996) *Architecture and Authority in Japan*. London and New York: Routledge.

Coolhaas, W. Ph. (ed.) (1971) *Generale Missiven van Gouverneurs-Generaal en raden aan heren XVII der Verenigde Oostindische Compagnie* (General correspondence from the governor generals and advisors to the Council of Seventeen of the Dutch East India Company). S-Gravenhage: Nijhoff

Cooper, M. (1965) *They Came to Japan*. Berkeley: University of California Press.

Edo Tōkyō Hakubutsukan (Edo Tokyo Museum) (ed.) (1997) *Sankin kōtai* (The system of alternate attendance). Tokyo: Edo Tōkyō Hakubutsukan.

Fiévé, N. (1992a) 'Urban Evolution of the City of Heiankyo; A Study of the Iconographic Sources, Part 1.' *Japan Forum* 4 (1): 91–107.

—— (1992b) 'Urban Evolution of the City of Heiankyo; A Study of the Iconographic Sources, Part 2.' *Japan Forum* 4 (2): 285–304.

Fitzgerald, C.P. (1976) *China: A Short Cultural History*. London: Barrie and Jenkins.

Fukai M. (1997) *Edo jō o yomu* (Reading Edo castle). Tokyo: Hara Shobō.

Grigg, D. (1980) *Population Growth and Agrarian Change*. Cambridge: Cambridge University Press.

Haga N. (1980). *Ōedo no seiritsu* (The formation of greater Edo). Tokyo: Yoshikawa Kōbunkan.

Hayami A. (1992) Personal communication with Professor Hayami, International Research Center for Japanese Studies, Kyoto.

Herbert, J. (1967) *Shinto: The Fountainhead of Japan*. London: George Allen and Unwin.

Inoue J. (1999) '*Rikujō kōtsū to sekisho*' (Overland traffic and checkpoints). In Katō T. (ed.) *Ōedo rekishi no fūkei* (The scenery of the history of Greater Edo). Tokyo: Yamagawa Shuppansha.

Kaempfer E. (1777–79) *Geschichte und Beschreibung von Japan* (History and description of Japan). 2 vols edited by Christian Wilhelm von Dohm. Lemgo: Meyer; reprint (1964). Stuttgart: Brockhaus.

—— (1712) *Amoenitatum exoticarum politico-physico-medicarum fasciculi V* (Exotic titbits of political, physiological and medical nature in 5 volumes). Lemgo: Meyer.

——, Sloane ms 2923, manuscript in the British Library, Sloane Collection. London: British Library.

—— (1999) *Kaempfer's Japan: Tokugawa Culture Observed* (ed. and trans. B.M. Bodart-Bailey). Honolulu: Hawaii University Press.

Knox, G. (trans.) (1902) 'Autobiography of Arai Hakuseki.' *Transactions of the Asiatic Society of Japan* 30 (2).

Kodama K. (1960) *Shukueki* (Post-stations). Tokyo: Shibundō.

—— (1955) *Shiryō ni yoru Nihon no ayumi: kinsei* (The course of Japan on the basis of historical material: the early modern period). Tokyo: Yoshikawa Kōbunkan.

—— (ed.) (1977–85) *Tōkaidō bunken nobe ezu* (Proportional map of the Tōkaidō). 24 vols. Tokyo: Tōkyō Bijutsu.

Kokushi Daijiten Henshū Iinkai (ed.) (1979) *Kokushi daijiten* (Large dictionary of national history) Tokyo: Yoshikawa Kōbunkan.

Kuroita K. (ed.) (1976) *Tokugawa jikki* (True record of the Tokugawa). Coll. *Shintei zōho kokushi taikei*. Tokyo: Yoshikawa Kōbunkan.

Kyōto-shi (ed.) (1994) *Yomigaeru Heiankyō* (Bringing back to life the Heian capital). Kyoto: Kyōto-shi.

Maruyama Y. (1992) *Jōhō to kōtsū* (Information and traffic). Coll. *Nihon no kinsei* (Japan in the Early Modern Period), vol. 6. Tokyo: Chūō Kōronsha.

Masuda K. (ed.) (1996) *Kenkyusha's New Japanese-English Dictionary.* Tokyo: Kenkyūsha.

McClain, J. (1982) *Kanazawa, A Seventeenth Century Castle Town.* New Haven: Yale University Press.

McClain, J., J. Merriman, and Ugawa K. (eds) (1994) *Edo and Paris: Urban Life and the State in the Early Modern Era.* Ithaca: Cornell University Press.

McClain, J., and Ugawa K. (1994) 'Edo and Paris: cities and power.' In J. McClain, J. Merriman, and Ugawa K. (eds) *Edo and Paris: Urban Life and the State in the Early Modern Era.* Ithaca: Cornell University Press.

McClain, J., and Ugawa K.(1994) 'Visions of the City.' In J. McClain, J. Merriman, and Ugawa K. (eds) *Edo and Paris: Urban Life and the State in the Early Modern Era.* Ithaca: Cornell University Press.

Mizue R. (1977) *Edo shichū keiseishi no kenkyū* (Research on the history of the formation of the streets of Edo). Tokyo: Kōbundō.

Naitō A. (1982) *Edo no machi I (*Edo town). Tokyo: Sōshisha.

—— (1977) *Katsura: A Princely Retreat* (trans. Charles S. Terry). Tokyo: Kōdansha International.

Nakagawa T. (1990) *Ageya bunka no sumiya* (The culture of entertainment by women and the Sumiya house). Kyoto: Kakuya Bungeisha.

Nagahara K. et al (eds) (1987) *Nihon gijutsu no shakai shi:kōtsū unyu* (The social history of Japanese technology: traffic and transport). Tokyo: Nihon Hyōronsha.

Ogi S. *et al.* (eds) (1987) *Edo Tōkyō jiten* (Edo Tokyo Dictionary). Tokyo: Sanseidō.

Okano T. (1999) *Ieyasu wa naze Edo o eranda ka?* (Why did Ieyasu choose Edo?). Tokyo: Kyōiku Shuppan.

Reynolds, S. (1977) *An Introduction to the History of English Medieval Towns.* Oxford: Clarendon Press.

Roeck, B. (1999) '*Stadtkunstwerke*' (Urban works of art). In Behringer W. and Roeck B. (eds) *Das Bild der Stadt in der Neuzeit 1400–1800* (The image of the city in the modern period 1400–1800). Munich:C.H. Beck, pp. 15–25.

Sansom, G. (1966) *A History of Japan to 1334*. London: Cresset Press.
Senda Y. (1993) '*Shūtaisei to shite no Edo jō.*' (Edo castle as a compilation) *Bulletin of the National Museum of Japanese History* 50: 239–60.
Smith, H. D. II (1979) 'Tokyo and London: Comparative Conceptions of the City.' In A. M. Craig (ed.) *Japan, a Comparative View*. Princeton: Princeton University Press, pp. 49–99
Tamai T. (1988) *Edo, ushinawareta toshi kūkan o yomu* (Edo: Reading the lost space of the city). Tokyo: Heibonsha.
Tamura A. (1992) *Edo Tōkyō machi-zukuri monogatari* (The story of the building of the city of Edo Tokyo). Tokyo: Jiji Tsūshinsha.
Tanigawa A. (1991) '*Edo no bochi no hakkutsu*' (Excavating the graveyards of Edo). In Edo Iseki Kenkyūkai (ed.) *Yomigaeru Edo* (Remembering Edo). Tokyo: Edo Iseki Kenkyūkai, pp. 79–111.
Vaporis, C. N. (1994) *Breaking Barriers: Travel and the State in Early Modern Japan*. Cambridge (Mass): Harvard University Press.
Watanabe N. (1992) '*Fune ni yoru kōtsū no hatten.*' (The development of traffic with reference to ships). In Tsuji T. and Asao N. (eds) *Nihon kinseishi* (The history of early modern Japan), vol. 6: *Jōhō to kōtsū* (Information and Traffic). Tokyo: Chūō Kōronsha.
—— (1991) *Kinsei kōtsū seido no kenkyū* (Study of the traffic system of the pre-modern period). Tokyo: Yoshikawa Kōbunkan.
Watsuji T. (1961) *Fūdo* (Climate and culture) (trans. G. Bownas). Tokyo: Yūshodō.
Weber, M. (1976) *Wirtschaft und Gesellschaft* (Economy and society). Tuebingen: J.C.B. Mohr.
Wildman Nakai, K. (1981) '*Apologia pro Vita Sua*: Arai Hakuseki's Autobiography.' *Monumenta Nipponica*, 36 (2): 173–86.
Zeeden E. W. (1983) '*Das Erscheinungsbild der frühneuzeitlichen Stadt, vornehmlich nach Reiseberichten und Autobiographien des 16. und 17. Jahrhunderts*' (Images of early modern cities, from tavel records and autobiographies of the sixteenth and seventeenth centuries). In Specker H. J. (ed.) *Stadt und Kultur* (Cities and culture). Sigmaringen: Thorbecke.
—— (1981) *Europa im Zeitalter des Absolutismus und der Aufklärung, Studienbuch der Geschichte* (Europe in the century of absolutism and enlightenment). vol. 6. Stuttgart: Klett-Cotta.

CHAPTER 4

Metaphors of the Metropolis

Architectural and Artistic Representations of the Identity of Edo

William H. Coaldrake

The city of Edo became a state of mind as well as the physical focus of the Tokugawa state. The architecture of the elite and the art of the *ukiyo-e* prints exploring themes of the *shitamachi*, or 'downtown' Edo, form both parallel and contrasting metaphors of the identity of that great city. The power this city exerted over the artistic imagination of the populace, rather than the political controls exercised by the *sankin kōtai* system, are its enduring cultural and psychological legacy.

Metaphors serve an elaborate and sometimes perplexing part of social science theory. They belong to the family of tropes, which includes the kindred spirits of metonymy and irony, and revel narcissistically in Saussure's distinction between signifier and signified (Sapir 1977: 3–4). This figurative language helps us understand the architectural and artistic representations of Edo from the seventeenth to the middle of the nineteenth centuries. It will be argued that the development of Edo from 1590, and the arrival of Ieyasu on the Kantō Plain, until the collapse in the 1860s of the *sankin kōtai* system of compulsory 'alternate attendance' by the *daimyō* in the city, stimulated two distinct but inter-related views of its own identity, one born out of high culture ambition, the other spawned by the popular culture. It will be shown that specific metaphors of the metropolis evolved within these two spheres as a direct result of changing political and artistic preoccupations: the creators of early Edo relied on architecture to establish one metaphor of the city, based on an elite vision and sustained metonymically by the representation of order in the architectural attributes of the castle, the palace and the gateway. By the middle of the Tokugawa period, it will be argued, the use of architecture as a metaphor had become more muted. *Daimyō* gatehouses of this era represent a more pragmatic accommodation with reality, while the memory of the earlier, more grandiose city was revived in historicist screen painting depicting the ideal shogunal city, as if to compensate for the loss of authority in actual architecture.

The final stage in this process is the mutation of the elite architectural metaphor with its appropriation by *ukiyo-e* artists in the later eighteenth century and first half of the nineteenth centuries. The locus of both signified and signifier shifts to the *shitamachi*, with the architecture of the shogunal and *daimyō* establishment irreverently re-interpreted in print designs using irony and parody instead of awe and respect to create a new visual iconography of identity expressing the rebellious and rambunctious attitudes of the *Edokko* (children of Edo) and redefining the metaphorical meaning of Edo.

The Early City as an Elite Metaphor

How did the city of Edo serve as a metaphor of elite culture? Architectural form is universally recognised as an effective metaphor, offering a tangible means of constructing an artificial reality (Arnheim 1977; Metcalf 1989; Harbison 1991; Millon and Nochlin 1978; Markus 1993). Edo underwent its primary development in the late sixteenth and seventeenth century as the planned headquarters for the Tokugawa family. From the very beginnings of Tokugawa occupation in 1590 it was conceived as both a metaphor and as a mechanism for Tokugawa authority (Coaldrake 1981). Naitō Akira's ground-breaking work in the 1970s established, on the basis of new documentary discoveries, that there was a close correlation between the Tokugawa socio-political order and the morphology of the city of Edo (Naitō 1972). This was to be seen demonstrated in the zoning of the population according to status within its distinctive spiral moat system, and in a geomantic correlation between the orientation of the city and the perceived order of the universe (Naitō 1972: 16–19). There has been debate about the reliability of Naitō's sources and his emphasis on the 'city from above', but his work has established beyond doubt that the Tokugawa illusion of Edo was as important as the reality of its built environment. The city was consciously created as a tool for buttressing government authority. The physical character of the city was determined by the great state construction projects, begun in the 1590s under the founding shogun Ieyasu and reaching a crescendo in the 1630s under the third shogun Iemitsu (1604–51): the shogunal castle and its surrounding palaces and walls, the Tokugawa family mausolea at Shiba, temples such as Kan'eiji, and the gateways and audience halls which the *bakufu* (shogunate) required the *daimyō* to build for the ritual of *onari*, or shogunal visitation. The city plan was organized on a spiral pattern geomantically orientated to align with the cosmos, thereby establishing a direct equation between Tokugawa rule and the order of the cosmos. Monumental construction projects were imposed on the *daimyō* by the Tokugawa as a mechanism to reduce their resources, in particular the manifold burdens of supplying building materials, excavating moats and constructing walls for Edo castle. Further substance for the Tokugawa metaphor of authority was supplied by the erection of a ring of thirty-six forbidding barbican gatehouses to guard the approaches to the inner city. Not content with fortifications alone to bulwark their establishment, the Tokugawa extended the metaphor of legitimate rule by building sumptuous palaces within the castle walls for the conduct of shogunal government and by requiring the *daimyō* to create palatial residences around the castle, there to receive the shogun and his entourage with all the pomp and panoply of the court. By this stratagem the *daimyō* were housed securely within the physical framework of the new Tokugawa order, put in their place literally and, most significantly for our study, metaphorically.

Official architecture also created an insistent high culture metaphor of ideal government, providing both psychological reinforcement and ritual settings for the enactment of shogunal government. The Tokugawa systematically sought to substitute illusion for reality by the architectural expedient of associating their own palaces and mausolea with Chinese traditions of beneficent rule. This they did by decorating their palaces and mausolea with sculptures depicting legendary Chinese rulers and sages engaged in virtuous acts.

Unfortunately little remains today of the early city of Edo, but three gateways which typify the artistic production of the 1630s surviving at other locations allow us to explore this idea further. These are the Karamon of the Nishi Honganji, Kyoto, and the Yōmeimon and Karamon of the Tōshōgū at Nikkō.

The Nishi Honganji Karamon in Kyoto is dominated stylistically by the sweeping *karahafu* or cusped gables characteristic of the *daimyō* palace gateways at Edo. Like the Edo gateways, decoration covers the entire structure and sculptural reliefs fill every space between. *Kirin*, or mythological creatures with the bodies of giraffes who foretell the coming of sages in Chinese mythology, prance amongst fleeting clouds between the principal tie-beams while *kara-jishi*, or mythological Chinese lions, frolic in a bed of flowering peonies, evoking images of power and wealth. Of particular symbolic importance are the four large sculpted panels set in the side transoms of the gateway. On the east side at the front the sage-ruler Huang Shigong rides a white mule (fig. 21, side elevation), while opposite him on the west transom is his attendant Jiang Liang, one of the Daoist Immortals, who is shown rescuing his lord's boot from a dragon in the sea. At the rear of the gateway the sage Xu Yu, deeply offended by an offer of high office, washes his ears in a waterfall. Opposite him Chao Fu, another sage, turns back from crossing the river sullied by the contents of Xu's ears, pulling his ox with him. These didactic scenes are depicted in brilliantly polychromed sculpture in the round with the type of heroic realism now associated with totalitarian rule. In the Tokugawa context they visually proclaim the association of the Tokugawa with the sagely rule of Confucian allegory.

Power and the Spatial Imprints of Authority

Figure 21 Nishi Honganji Karamon. Front and side elevations. (Source: Bunkachō, *Kokuhō jūyō bunkazai [kenzōbutsu] jissoku zushū.*)

The Yōmeimon and Karamon of the Tōshōgū at Nikkō are even more wilfully ornamental, a visual feast of mythological creatures and Chinese paragons, the pristine, lime-white surfaces of the structures standing out in dramatic contrast to the bracket arms lacquered black with inlaid gold vine patterns. Large *kara-jishi*, carved in the round, thrust aggressively forward from the head of each pillar of the first floor while others prowl the main lintel. Twenty-two separate figural compositions depicting Confucian themes are inserted between the bracket sets above. They include such subjects as the *kinki shoga*, the 'Four Accomplishments' of painting, calligraphy, music and of go, together with a host of Confucian sages and Daoist Immortals. On the Karamon a sculpture of the Duke of Zhou, that paragon of virtuous Confucian rule, is set directly over the front bay of the gateway, an unambiguous message of sagely rule at the entrance to the most sacred precinct in Tokugawa shogunal architecture (fig. 22).

These three gateways may be physically distant from Edo, which helps account for their survival today, but they are closely identified chronologically, artistically and politically with the city of Edo and the world of architectural metaphor. The Karamon of Nishi Honganji was similar in architectural style and political purpose to the ceremonial gateways built by the *daimyō* at the entrances to their Edo palaces to receive the shogun during an official visitation. It was moved and substantially rebuilt at its present location at Nishi Honganji in 1632, in anticipation of an official visit to the temple by Tokugawa Iemitsu, a visit that ultimately never transpired. The Nikkō gateways, for their part, were not only similar in style to contemporary shogunal architecture made in Edo, but were also built under the direction of the same master carpenters and sculptors who were responsible for the greatest Tokugawa palaces and mausolea in Edo itself. There is even a document preserved in Tokugawa records from the period which establishes that the Yōmeimon was prefabricated in an Edo workshop and then transported in parts overland to Nikkō, where it was assembled in its present location (*Nikkō shaji bunkazai hozon-kai* 1974: 9–10).

The shogunal and *daimyō* buildings were deliberately engineered as part of a strategy to construct an illusion of authority using the power of the architectural metaphor to convince the viewer of the legitimacy of Tokugawa rule. In this way Edo reminds us of the rhetorical question posed by Robert Harbison in his challenging study of the meaning of architectural form: '... is it the truth or simply the falsehood of a society which one learns from its monuments?' (Harbison 1991: 37).

The Middle Tokugawa Period and the Artistic Metaphor of the Ideal City

In 1657 the Meireki fire destroyed some eighty percent of Edo. Subsequently the administration of the city became more pragmatic, concerned with the hazard of fire and the realities of managing one of the

Figure 22 Karamon, Tōshōgū, Nikkō. Detail of sculpture (Duke of Zhou).

world's most populous cities, rather than with creating a spectacular urban demonstration of shogunal authority. In political terms, such metaphors were no longer essential. By the 1650s the Tokugawa shogunal dynasty was firmly entrenched and the political imperative for grand architectural metaphors to adorn the city had passed. The rebuilding of the central keep or *tenshu* of Edo Castle itself was postponed after the Meireki Fire, the surest indication of the changing priorities of the new era.

The *tenshu* of Edo Castle may have been physically destroyed in 1657, but it makes a special encore appearance in the definitive work of establishment screen painting of the middle Tokugawa period, the *Edozu byōbu* (Illustrated screens of Edo), now held in the National Museum of Japanese History (fig. 23). Here it rises again above a recreation of the Edo of Iemitsu's shogunate, fabled in its architectural treasures and hallowed in memory.

What was the reason for the pictorial rediscovery of the Edo *tenshu* and its surrounding shogunal city well after its destruction in 1657, and what does this reveal about the artistic and architectural metaphors of mid-Tokugawa period Edo? To answer these questions it is first necessary to understand the reasons for dating the *Edozu byōbu* to the early eighteenth rather than the early seventeenth century.

The *Edozu byōbu* were first identified as a depiction of the city of Edo in the 1970s together with the *Edo meishozu byōbu* (Illustrated screens of famous places in Edo), now in the Idemitsu Museum of Art, Tokyo (fig. 24).

Figure 23 *Edozu byōbu*. Detail of the right two panels of the left screen showing Edo Castle and vicinity. (Courtesy of National Museum of Japanese History.)

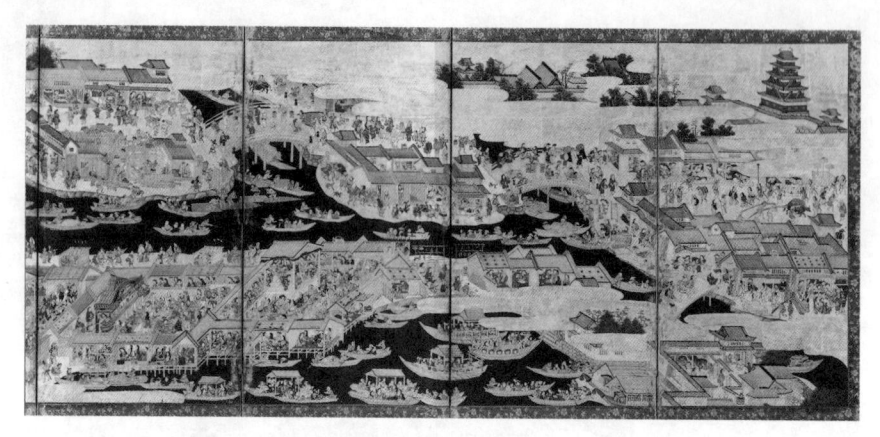

Figure 24 *Edo meishozu byōbu.* Detail of the right four panels of the right-hand screen. (Courtesy of Idemitsu Museum of Art.)

As a result of an understandable enthusiasm for the richness of detail, particularly of Edo castle and its destroyed *tenshu*, both works were tentatively dated to the early era of the Tokugawa city (Naitō and Suwa 1972). More considered analysis of the condition and architectural content of each work now suggests that the *Edozu byōbu* should be dated to the early eighteenth century, or about a century later than the Idemitsu screens. As this different dating significantly changes the metaphor of Edo represented by the *Edozu byōbu* it is important to establish the reasons clearly here.

The Idemitsu screens are appreciably older in condition than the *Edozu byōbu* and the architectural content presents an internally consistent view of Edo in the years 1626 to 1632. For example, they show the Tōshōgū completed at Ueno in 1626 (Naitō and Suwa 1972: 4–5) but omit the Taitokuin Mausoleum built for the second Tokugawa shogun Hidetada (1578–1632) at Zōjōji in 1632 (Coaldrake 1996: 164–80). Further, the scenes of the *shitamachi* show *yūjo kabuki*, banned by the shogunate in 1629, another indication of a date prior to 1630 (Naitō and Suwa 1972: 6). There is always a possibility of depicting activities such as *yūjo kabuki* after their demise, but the coherent and consistent presentation of buildings, together with the condition of the work, point consistently to the years from 1626 to 1629 as the date of the Idemitsu screens.

The *Edozu byōbu,* by contrast, includes two glaring architectural errors which would not have been acceptable in a painting contemporary with the reign of Iemitsu as shogun (1623–51). First, the palace of Tokugawa Tadanaga (1606–33), the younger brother of the third shogun Iemitsu, is shown in a prominent position to the immediate east of the castle (see fig. 23, top right). (Naitō and Suwa 1972, '*Edozu byōbu no sekai,*' section 2).

Tadanaga was disgraced, forced to commit suicide, and his palace dismantled, in 1633. Yet in this painting it still stands in pride of place near the castle of his brother. It is inconceivable for this pariah palace to have been included in a product of the Edo painting establishment during or even shortly after the reign of Tokugawa Iemitsu as shogun. Second, and even more telling, the *tenshu* built for Iemitsu in 1638 is shown with serious mistakes in the arrangement of cusped and triangular gables (*karahafu*, *chidorihafu*) on the visible south and east sides of the building when compared with the architectural drawings made by the Kōra, the family in charge of building works for the construction of the *tenshu* in 1638 (Coaldrake 1996: 132–35). These gables were a key element in the architectural design of the building. Moreover, the large cusped gable on the fourth level of the east side, which completes the hierarchy of gables in the overall design, is completely overlooked. A painting fundamentally flawed in its depiction of the most important building in the city, if not the state, would not have been acceptable for a shogunal or *daimyō* patron while the *tenshu* still stood or memories of the building were still fresh, ruling out the possibility that the screens were painted for Iemitsu or as a tribute to Iemitsu completed shortly after his death.

Judging from the physical condition of the screens, fresher and newer than securely dated early Tokugawa-period works such as the Idemitsu screens, as well as the factual errors, it may be concluded that they date to well after the destruction of the *tenshu* in 1657.

The stylistic similarities between the Idemitsu screens and the *Edozu byōbu* contributed to the initial confusion in dating them both to the early seventeenth century. The similarities – including an elevated viewpoint, tilted picture plane, spatial abbreviation achieved with strategically placed bands of gold leaf clouds, and composition based on the divergent orthogonal mode of representation – arise from the common influence of pervasive traditions in Japanese high culture rather than a similar dating. There were a number of influences on this style of painting. These consisted of 'paintings of manners and customs' (*fūzokuga*), which had their origins in court painting of the Heian period and which flourished in the Momoyama period; the *yamato-e* tradition of depiction of famous beauty sites (*meisho-e*), also dating from the Heian period; the scenes of Kyoto or *Rakuchū rakugai zu*, which celebrated the renaissance of the imperial capital after the devastation of the wars and urban strife of the second half of the fifteenth and first part of the sixteenth centuries (Kyōto National Museum 1966; Tsuji 1991); and the idiosyncratic perspectival system of the Tosa and Kanō painting traditions which may be traced ultimately to Tang dynasty court painting.

Despite these formal similarities, there is an entirely different emphasis in the subject matter of the two works. The Idemitsu screens display a lively interest in the activities and architecture of the people of the city, with the elite architecture positioned at the periphery of the composition to the extent that it was of only marginal psychological concern. Only one *onari* gateway is shown. The influence of the *fūzokuga* tradition is as important as that of the *rakuchū rakugai zu*. By contrast, the *Edozu byōbu* are distant visually and detached psychologically from the people in the city they portray, closer in spirit to the magisterial panorama of Kyoto presented in Kanō Eitoku's (1543–90) definitive Momoyama period *Rakuchū rakugai zu* (held by Yonezawa City) (Okami and Satake 1983). It emphasises the architectural achievements and lifestyle of the elite, from their palaces with the gilded and sculpted *onari* gateways to their boar hunting in the countryside around Edo. This is unmistakable evidence of an overtly rhetorical purpose in reinforcing an establishment metaphor of the meaning of Edo. This rhetorical city of Edo is far removed in time and space from the reality of Edo of the first half of the seventeenth century, which it appears to represent. The *Edozu byōbu* is as much a work of fantasy as fact, a polemical pastiche re-creating a city which never existed at a single moment in the Tokugawa period. Even the cartouches used to 'identify' each of the major buildings in this fantasy 'Edo' are an exercise in documentary deception calculated to give the work a certain verisimilitude to enhance its credibility as a 'document.'

When was this enigmatic work actually painted? An important clue is furnished by comparison with the *Tōkaidō bunken ezu* (Scaled map of the Tōkaidō; Ōta Memorial Art Museum) (Ogi *et al.*, 1987: 5) by the noted early *ukiyo-e* artist Hishikawa Moronobu (d. 1694). This set of printed illustrated maps showing the great coastal highway later to be immortalised by Hiroshige (1797–1858), was published in 1690 (see Chapter 6). It features a view of Edo castle shown immediately above the label for 'Edo.' The *tenshu* is clearly visible, with surrounding walls and towers floating above the city. More than a generation after the destruction of the *tenshu* in the 1657 fire, its memory still lingers as a symbol of Edo in the popular imagination. Significantly for our discussion of the dating of the *Edozu byōbu*, Moronobu, for all his talents as an artist, is guilty of similar errors in depicting the *tenshu*. Moronobu's *tenshu* is shown with four levels, not the five that once existed in reality. This is not only inaccurate but also highly improbable for any Japanese building because of the association of the number four with the word for 'death.' Moronobu, like the artist responsible for the *Edozu byōbu*, also made basic mistakes in the depiction of those troublesome gables, to the extent that only a single triangular gable is shown on his version of the building.

The past was in the air by the turn of the eighteenth century, but it was historicism not history which triumphed. Historical circumstances suggest that the *Edozu byōbu* probably date to the era of influence on shogunal politics of Arai Hakuseki (1657–1725), advisor to the sixth shogun Ienobu (ruled, 1709–13) and seventh shogun Ietsugu (ruled 1713–16). Under

Hakuseki's insistent historicism there was a strong revival of official interest in the Iemitsu *tenshu*. The Tokugawa official chief master builders, members of the same Kōra family that had rebuilt the *tenshu* in 1638, were commissioned by the shogunate, probably in 1712, to make a complete set of technical drawings for a new *tenshu* (Hirai and Itō 1992: 260). These drawings, comprising plans and elevations made meticulously to scale and completed with colour washes, show interest existed in the shogunate in re-establishing the castle *tenshu* as the focal point of the city (Hirai and Itō 1992: figs 10: 1–3, *Ontenshu ezu*, Naikaku bunkō). We know from his dispute with the same shogunal master builders as part of his reforms of shogunal protocol that Hakuseki himself took an informed interest in architectural styles (Nakai 1988: 191–2, 226–7; Coaldrake 1996: 193–7). It seems likely that he was also involved in the plans to rebuild the *tenshu* and perhaps in the commissioning of the *Edozu byōbu* themselves.

The grandiose scheme to rebuild the *tenshu* was soon to be abandoned in the climate of financial stringencies of the Kyōhō era (1716–35) but the *Edozu byōbu* survives, together with the Kōra *tenshu* drawings, as unmistakable evidence of an official desire in the early eighteenth century to revive the memory of the architectural achievements of Iemitsu's Edo as a metaphor of good government and an ideal city. It represents an officially sponsored, consciously contrived recollection of an early age of architectural grandeur. It was an attempt, at an historical juncture when the architectural achievements of the ruling class were disappearing in the face of economic and political change, to re-affirm the validity of the older metaphor of Edo as city of the shogunal establishment using the pictorial tool of a monumental screen painting.

Daimyō Gatehouse Architecture of the Middle Tokugawa Period and the Muted Metaphor of 'Keeping up Appearances'

The creation of an heroic metaphor of early Edo in a work of establishment art of the middle Tokugawa period was in striking contrast to a new accommodation with reality in contemporary establishment architecture. While art sought to revive the memory of the opulence of early Edo, architecture created a more muted metaphor of the establishment by 'keeping up appearances.'

This new metaphor was created using *daimyō* gatehouses as the tool. In the face of the decline in the prestige and economic power of the *daimyō* class with the growth of a money economy, and the perennial and prohibitive cost of rebuilding palaces after fire, copious architectural edicts were issued as part of the periodic waves of reformist zeal which swept the shogunal administration. The objective was to regain political control of the built environment. The priority was to extend the earlier policy of reserving gateway architecture as the exclusive prerogative of the warrior class by specifically regulating the style of *daimyō* gateways. Gateways by their very role as entrances and exits were the most publicly visible buildings in the *daimyō* palace complexes. The strategy of regulating their style according to their owners' status had the virtue of preserving the visible fabric of the Tokugawa status order by standardising the style of *daimyō* architecture according to official rank expressed in *koku*. This offered the *daimyō* a cost-effective means to maintain their claim to a distinct architecture of authority while allowing the shogunate to regulate the *daimyō* hierarchy using a readily legible architectural language.

The result was a radical change in the style of the gateways built at the main entrances to the *daimyō* palaces in Edo, from the exuberant *karamon* of early Edo, to more modest entrances set into the walls of the rowhouses that surrounded the *daimyō* complexes. These gatehouses or *nagayamon* lacked the expressive power of the earlier palace gateways but they assumed new importance as the generic symbol of *daimyō* status. At the same time subtle variations in architectural details spelled out in a specific visual language the precise rank of the *daimyō* for whom they were built.

Detailed regulation of *daimyō* gatehouses began after another major fire in Edo in 1772 which necessitated extensive rebuilding of *daimyō* palaces. After the fire a regulation was issued by the shogunate requiring even the highest ranking *daimyō* to build *nagaya* rather than the more elaborate freestanding style of gateway.[1] As a result the modest rowhouses which flanked the streets around the *daimyō* palace compounds were modified for their new role as principal entry and symbol of rank in the Tokugawa order by the simple expedient of adding guard houses, or *bansho*, beside the main doors (Coaldrake 1988: 397–410). These *bansho* were used to house the guards who supervised traffic through the gateways, but as the focus of attention as well as traffic they became a convenient and cost-effective vehicle for expressing rank within the *daimyō* class.

We can 'read' this new iconography of status and rank using a contemporary guide, the *Aobyōshi* (Blue cover book), a woodblock-printed compendium of rules of protocol and etiquette published in 1840–41 (fig. 25). *Aobyōshi* was a handbook prepared for the convenience of members of the warrior class. One complete section is devoted to *daimyō* gatehouses, itself an indication of their political importance. This section includes a chart of officially approved gatehouse styles, accompanied by written explanations, in much the same way that military forces today publish charts showing badges of rank. Eight diagrams illustrate the various styles, showing the number, style and placement of *bansho*, their roof gables, foundation stones and windows, as well as the number of side doors to be set into the main entrance behind. The accompanying text reprints the most detailed government regulation of gatehouse style issued thirty-one years earlier in 1809.[2] The text sets out in detail the characteristics of gatehouses to be used by *daimyō* of different rank.

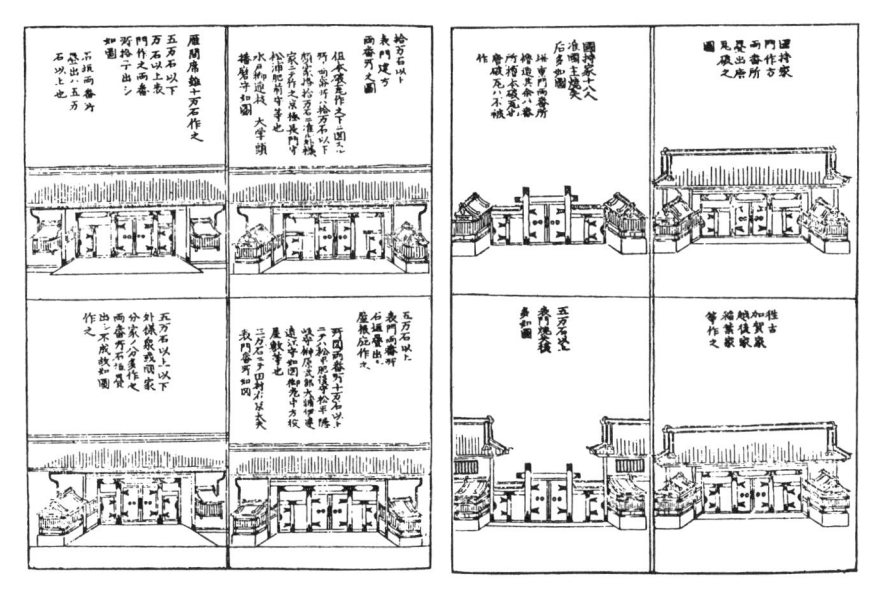

Figure 25 *Aobyōshi*. Detail of *daimyō* gatehouse styles and regulations.

Two of these diagrams serve to demonstrate the official correspondence between architectural form and *daimyō* rank. The diagram at the top right (fig. 25) shows the architecture for a *daimyō* with the high rank of over 100,000 *koku*. He was permitted to use two *bansho*, one on each side of the main entrance, and to cover these with *karahafu*, the cusped gable that had been used for the freestanding ceremonial gateways of the early Edo period.[3]

The diagram second from the left in the lower rank shows the gatehouse for a *daimyō* with a rank of 50,000 to 100,000 *koku* serving as *rōjū* or senior councillor. He was permitted to build a *nagayamon* with two *bansho* but was not allowed to use the all important *karahafu* for his roofs. Instead the *bansho* were to be covered with strictly utilitarian sloping roofs.

Two *daimyō* gatehouses of the types described above miraculously survive to the present day. These confirm the application to actual gatehouses of the shogunal regulations. The first is the Ikedamon, which now stands in the outer wall of the Tokyo National Museum complex at Ueno (fig. 26). It was originally built as the principal entrance to the mansion of the *daimyō* of Tottori to the immediate southwest of Edo Castle.[4] The Ikeda were the *daimyō* of an entire province and had the high rank of 325,000 *koku*. In accordance with the top right diagram it is equipped with two *bansho* each roofed with a *karahafu*.

The second surviving gateway is now located some seventy-five kilometres east of its original site in Edo, rusticating in bucolic isolation at the Yamawaki Gakuen summer camping ground near the coast of the

Power and the Spatial Imprints of Authority

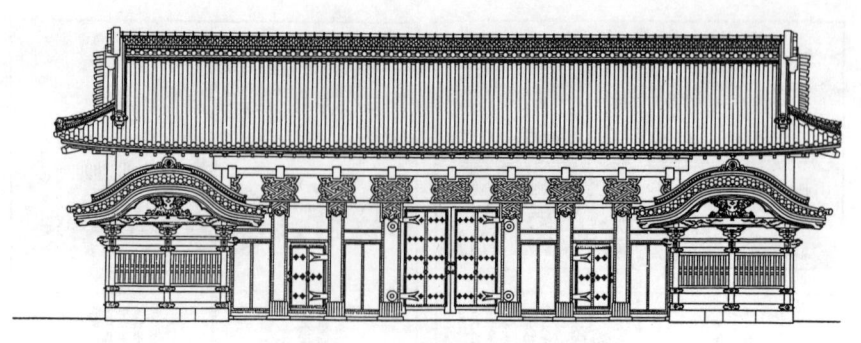

Figure 26 Ikedamon. Precincts of Tokyo National Museum. (Source: Bunkachō, *Kokuhō jūyō bunkazail [kenzōbutsu] jissoku zushū*.)

scenic Bōsō peninsula at Kujūkuri (fig. 27).[5] Records reveal that it was first built as the front entrance to the palace to the immediate south of Edo Castle reserved as the official residence of one of the senior councillors. It may accordingly be named the Gatehouse of the Senior Councillor, or Rōjūmon. The *rōjū* responsible for the construction of this gatehouse had a rank of between 50,000 and 100,000 *koku* and the extant building conforms precisely with the stipulated style for the main gatehouse to the official residence of a *rōjū* of this rank shown in the bottom row of the *Aobyōshi* diagram (Ishii 1982 vol. 3: 137; Coaldrake 1988).

Figure 27 Rōjūmon. Chiba Prefecture.

The Ikeda and Rōjū gatehouses demonstrate the detailed and controlled language of status and rank in the later Tokugawa hierarchy. They were used to convince the viewer of the continuing power of the establishment while masking increasingly serious economic problems. This policy was justified politically with Neo-Confucian rhetoric, particularly with frequent written exhortations in sumptuary edicts to do things 'according to one's status' (*bungen ni ōjite*) (Shively 1964–65). Once again the elite architecture of the city served as a consciously constructed metaphor.

'Stealing the Show' in later Edo: *ukiyo-e* and the Popular Appropriation of the Architectural High Culture

Whatever the pretensions to a convincing presence made by the *daimyō* gatehouses, by the later eighteenth century the architectural theatre of the high culture had become a sideshow in Edo to artistic developments in the popular culture. Conscious high culture metaphors lost their credibility as political reality was redefined as a result of the spontaneous artistic exuberance associated with the patronage of the ebullient *chōnin* sector and the world of gratification of the pleasure quarters. Edo changed inexorably, with a new symbiosis formed between the popular culture and the character of the city. The resulting mass urban culture was literate and visually sophisticated, experimental and wilfully irreverent to the elite culture. Of its own creative volition it refused to be confined by the official city and its carefully constructed political metaphors of order and ownership. It drew from the high culture energetically and indiscriminately: the decoration of the seemingly mundane, such as Hokusai's (1760–1849) printed comb design for the elaborate coiffure of the high ranking courtesan using the motif of the eight-spoked wheel symbolising the paths to Buddhist salvation as a parody on the paths to pleasure (Nishiyama 1997: 16); *ukiyo-zōshi* like Saikaku (1642–93)'s novels of the life and loves of the Shin Yoshiwara written in an irreverent creative dialogue with *The Tale of Genji* (Hibbett 1975: 94–95); and *ukiyo-e* prints of the theatre and amusement districts, and of people at work and play, set against the backdrop of scenes of the city, including its *daimyō* palaces and shogunal castle.

The *Edokko* emerges from the art and literature as the anti-hero larger than life. This denizen of the downtown at work and play became the stuff of legend, to be immortalised in *ukiyo-e* print and popular novel alike, speaking a distinct dialect (Gerstle 1989: 63–84) and regarding the world of the elite with proprietorial bemusement. This character was to be enshrined by the 1780s in the *sharebon* or 'fashionable' books of popular literature. To be a true *Edokko* meant 'to have your first bath in the water of the city aqueduct, and to grow up in sight of the *shachi* (the sculpted roof tile finials) of Edo Castle,' according to the great exponent of *sharebon*, Santō

Kyōden (1761–1816) (Ogi *et al.* 1987: 41–52; Nishiyama 1997: 42). Linking the local water supply with the roof tile sculptures of the castle was neither accidental nor isolated; it goes to the heart of the metaphor for Edo emerging in the later eighteenth and early nineteenth century. Through literary and pictorial devices, the humble origins and daily preoccupations of the *Edokko* were transformed by association with the eviscerated architectural symbols of the elite to express a sense of belonging to the city and an ownership of its built environment, including elite architecture. The city of the *Edokko,* built on low and reclaimed land beside the bay, overcrowded and subject to disease, damp but prey to fire, may have been far removed from the castle and elevated land of the *daimyō* districts. But the life of its narrow streets and alleys, the rowhouses which were at once workplace and residence, the temple fairs, the brothels and the tea-houses, intensified the sense of place and belonging, and moved outwards creatively to encompass and psychologically appropriate the world of the elite. The linking of aqueduct and castle in Kyōden's description of the *Edokko* may have been an enormous conceit but this type of wilful appropriation of elite architecture was to pervade the culture of the populace and transform the city of the elite into part of the visual iconography of identity in *ukiyo-e*.

In this cultural milieu, therefore, *ukiyo-e* became a vehicle for creating a new metaphor for the city of Edo, replacing the official metaphor of benign and omnipotent rule with a metaphor of the urban good life in a city devoted to the pursuit of pleasure. The Edo architectural establishment, sculpted roof tiles and all, was appropriated by *ukiyo-e* as the pictorial setting for the activities and exploits of the floating world rather than the stage upon which the architectural vanities of the Tokugawa order could strut.

The *ukiyo-e* appropriation of Edo as the city of the *chōnin* and *Edokko* is perfectly demonstrated by Hiroshige's view of 'The City Flourishing, Tanabata Festival,' part of his *Meisho Edo hyakkei* (One hundred famous views of Edo) (fig. 28). The city is depicted from the viewpoint of the *shitamachi,* the approach anticipated in the Idemitsu screen. The heavily plastered storehouses and closely set establishments of the merchants and artisans dominate the composition under the legitimating decorations of Tanabata and the sanctifying presence of Fuji. The elite built environment is still visible but seen in the distance, remote from the *shitamachi*. Edo Castle is barely visible in the distance, very much to the side in position and importance. There is no question as to whose city is flourishing in this summertime celebration of reunited celestial lovers, with the castle inseparable but subsidiary to the celebrations of the townspeople.

More mischievously, Hiroshige uses the device of *mitate* or parody to change the meaning of the *daimyō* gatehouses at the very time that the shogunate was issuing copious regulations to reinforce their symbolic importance. In *Toranomon no soto* (Outside Toranomon), part of the series *Edo shōkei* (Scenic Sites of Edo), ca. 1832–34, Toranomon and its

Figure 28 Hiroshige, *'Shichū han'ei Tanabata matsuri'* (The city flourishing, Tanabata festival), *Meisho Edo hyakkei* (One hundred famous views of Edo). (Courtesy of Brooklyn Museum).

protecting moat have become the backdrop for a pleasant promenade by two ladies carrying potted plants back from a shopping expedition.

A similar approach is used for Hiroshige's scene of Hibiya in *Tōto meisho* (Famous places of the Eastern Capital). The same ladies are still promenading, this time without their plants, beside another of the great gatehouses of later Edo. In both scenes the gatehouses are equipped with the symbols of *daimyō* status as set out in the *Aobyōshi*, with which these scenes are nearly contemporary. Yet the ladies' heads are studiously turned away, oblivious to the posturing portals, far more interested in the gossip of the day. This attitude stands in striking contrast to the popular reaction to the official architecture of early Edo, when the gateways built for shogunal visitation became instant *meisho* in their own right, referred to in popular literature such as *Edo no suzume* as *higurashi no gomon*, gateways where one could 'pass the entire day from morning to night' gazing captivated by the marvellous decoration.

At the end of his life, in 1857, Hiroshige had become even less respectful of *daimyō* and shogunal architecture. In 'Hibiya and Soto-Sakurada from Yamashita-chō' (*Meisho Edo hyakkei*) (fig. 29), the imposing facade of another *nagayamon*, that of the Nabeshima, *daimyō* of Saga, together with the inner moat and walls of the castle, are shown in considerable detail (Smith 1986: Plates and Commentaries, 3). Once again the architecture of the elite has been appropriated and its meaning changed. In this New Year scene kites fly disrespectfully over the *daimyō* gatehouse and the walls of the castle. One kite is even entangled in a pine tree on top of the castle battlements, making a mockery of these fortifications which had once been so essential in the consolidation of Tokugawa power. By a trick of spatial juxtaposition, the shuttlecock appears to sail majestically over the *daimyō* and shogunal architecture, flagrantly disrespectful to the authority these buildings try to proclaim. To add insult to injury, the paddle (*hagoita*) is impudently superimposed over the lower half of the castle wall, the smiling face which decorates it becoming graffiti on a shogunal monument, making sure we all appreciate the joke.

The Changing Metaphors of the City

This study of Edo has identified several distinct but inter-related ways in which metaphors were used to define the identity of the city. In the first half of the seventeenth century, elite architecture was instrumental in the creation of an elite metaphor of shogunal authority. Edo was planned and built as an ideal Neo-Confucian city, exemplifying government by virtuous rulers, with the construction of official architecture seen as an enactment of virtuous rule and then as a setting for the rituals of government and control.

After the devastating fires of the second half of the seventeenth century the original architectural metaphor faded from memory. A more muted

Figure 29 Hiroshige, *'Yamashita-chō Hibiya Soto-Sakurada'* (Hibiya and Soto-Sakurada from Yamashita-chō), *Meisho Edo hyakkei* (One hundred famous views of Edo). (Courtesy of Brooklyn Museum).

metaphor was consciously created using gateways and government regulation. If uninhibited splendour was no longer economically feasible, at least consistency in the correlation between status and standardised gatehouse styles could achieve a politically desirable correlation between architectural style and political order. This second architectural metaphor of Edo was tempered by reality but still rendered service to the state. At the same time, as we have seen, the *Edozu byōbu* was painted to recreate the appearance of an ideal shogunal city, as if to compensate for the loss of power in the actual buildings and lend legitimacy to the later shogunate.

The later Tokugawa 'popular' view of the city, seen both pictorially and psychologically from the direction of the *shitamachi*, shared formal pictorial conventions with the high culture but diverged radically in the metaphor of the metropolis it created. This metaphor was created using the pervasive and ultimately more persuasive vehicle of the *ukiyo-e* print. The Edo represented by *ukiyo-e* was heavy with architectural irony, intrinsically critical of the elite but equally wilful in its appropriation of architecture to define popular identity with a new metaphor of the metropolis.

Notes

1 The edict stated: 'Concerning rebuilding in the areas recently destroyed by fire: this should be done in accordance with social status and should not be gaudy throughout... Concerning the front gateways of *daimyō* mansions: a *nagaya* should be built, even in the case of *kunimochi daimyō*' (1772.3.27) (*Zaisei keizai gakkai* (ed.) 1922–23, vol. 4: 748).
2 This analysis is based on the first edition of *Aobyōshi* held in the Archives of the Department of Architecture, the University of Tokyo. I am grateful to Inagaki Eizō, Professor Emeritus of the University of Tokyo, for locating this document for me. Another version of the document is published in *Zōtei kojitsu sōsho henshū iinkai* (ed.) (1928, vol. II: 22–4). The gateway section of the published version is translated in full in Coaldrake 1988: 275–6.
3 The 1809 edict actually banned such extravagance but the *Aobyōshi* diagrams indicate that the upper ranking *daimyō* were ignoring this provision and still using *karahafu*, at least on their *bansho*.
4 The gatehouse was moved to the Tōgū Gosho at Shiba Takanawa in 1891, and to its present site in 1952.
5 It was moved to this site and fully restored in 1973–74. Documents establish that it has been moved three times since 1867, once during the Meiji period when it was drastically reduced in size. See further: *Bunkazai kenzōbutsu hozon gijutsu kyōkai*, 1976.

References

Arnheim, R. (1977) *The Dynamics of Architectural Form*. Berkeley, Los Angeles and London: University of California Press.
Bunkazai Kenzōbutsu Hozon Gijutsu Kyōkai (ed.) (1976) *Jūyō bunkazai buke yashiki mon shūriki* (Restoration record for the gatehouse to a daimyo residence). Chiba: Yamawaki Gakuen.

Coaldrake, W. H. (1996) *Architecture and Authority in Japan*. London: Routledge. Nissan Institute Japanese Studies Series.
—— (1988) 'The Gatehouse of the Shogun's Senior Councillor – Building Design and Status Symbolism in Japanese Architecture of the Late Edo Period.' *The Journal of the Society of Architectural Historians* 47 (December): 397–410.
—— (1981) 'Edo Architecture and Tokugawa Law.' *Monumenta Nipponica* 36 (3): 275–76.
Harbison, R. (1991) *The Built, the Unbuilt and the Unbuildable: In Pursuit of Architectural Meaning*. Cambridge, Mass: MIT Press.
Hirai K. and Itō R. (1992) *Edo jō I: jōkaku*. (Edo Castle I: fortifications) Tokyo: Shibundō.
Hiroshige (1986) *One Hundred Famous Views of Edo*, with preface, introduction and commentaries by Henry D. Smith II. New York: George Braziller, Inc.
Idemitsu Bijutsukan (ed.) (1986) *Kaikan nijūshūnen kin'en meihinten* (Exhibition of famous art to celebrate the tentieth anniversary of the Idemitsu Art Museum). Tokyo: Idemitsu Bijutsukan.
Ishii R. (ed.) (1982) *Bunka bukan* (Warrior heraldry of the Bunka era [1804–18]), vol. 3. Tokyo: Kashiwa Shobō.
Kokuritsu Rekishi Minzoku Hakubutsukan (ed.) (1989) *Kozu ni miru Nihon no kenchiku* (Japanese architecture as seen in old drawings and plans). Tokyo: Shibundō.
Kyōto Kokuritsu Hakubutsukan (ed.) (1966) *Rakuchū rakugai zu* (Illustrations of Kyoto and surroundings) Tokyo: Kadokawa Shoten.
Markus, T. A., (1993) *Buildings and Power: Freedom and Control in the Origin of Modern Building Types*. London: Routledge.
Metcalf, T. (1989) *An Imperial Vision: Indian Architecture and Britain's Raj*. Berkeley, Ca: University of California Press.
Million, H. A., and L. Nochlin (eds) (1978) *Art and Architecture in the Service of Politics*. Cambridge, Mass: MIT Press.
Naitō A. (1972) *Edo no toshi no kenchiku* (The Architecture of the city of Edo). Complementary volume to Naitō A. and Suwa H. (eds) *Edozu byōbu* (Illustrated screens of Edo). Tokyo: Mainichi Shinbunsha.
Naitō A. and Suwa H. (eds) (1972) *Edozu byōbu*. Tokyo: Mainichi Shinbunsha.
Nikkō Shaji Bunkazai Hozon-kai (ed.) (1974) *Kokuhō Tōshōgū Yōmeimon, dōsayū sode-kabe shūri kōji hōkokusho* (Restoration report for the Yōmeimon and flanking walls of the national treasure Tōshōgū). Kyoto: Benridō.
Sapir J. D. (1977) 'The Anatomy of Metaphor.' In J. D. Sapir and C. Crocker (eds) *The Social Use of Metaphor: Essays on the Anthropology of Rhetoric*. Philadelphia, Penn: University of Pennsylvania Press, pp. 3–4.
Shively, D. H. (1964–65) 'Sumptuary Regulations and Status in Early Tokugawa Japan.' *Harvard Journal of Asiatic Studies* 25: 123–65.
Swinton, E. de S. et al (1996) *The Women of the Pleasure Quarter: Japanese Paintings and Prints of the Floating World*. New York: Hudson Hills Press, in assocation with Worcester Art Museum.
Tsuji N. (1991) *Eitoku to shōheiga: Momoyama no eiga kōgei* (Eitoku and wall painting: the glorious decorative arts of Momoyama). Tokyo: Kōdansha.
Wildman Nakai, K. (1988) *Shogunal Politics: Arai Hakuseki and the Premises of Tokugawa Rule*. Cambrdige, Mass: Harvard University Press.
Zaisei Keizai Gakkai (ed.) (1922–23) *Nihon zaisei keizai shiryō* (Historical documents for Japanese finances and economics). Tokyo: Zaisei Keizai Gakkai, 10 volumes, vol. 4.
Zōtei Kojitsu Sōsho Henshū Iinkai (ed.) (1928) *Zōtei kojitsu sōsho, vol. II: Edo sōsho* (The library of old customs and manners) (Revised). Tokyo: Yoshikawa Kōbunkan.

PART TWO

Memory and the Changing Passage of Space

CHAPTER 5

Kyoto's Famous Places

Collective Memory and 'Monuments' in the Tokugawa Period*

Nicolas Fiévé

> *It takes a long time before old aristocratic families, ancient urban patricians, abandon the streets that had been their for as long as they could remember, despite the increasing solitude surrounding them and the development of new opulent areas elsewhere. (…) But nor are the poor easily displaced without resistance, offensive returns, and even when they give in, they leave behind them a part of themselves (….). It is odd to watch it all reappear, even after an interval in which nothing seemed to remain of the past; in districts totally transformed where they no longer seemed to have a place, emerge gradually the pleasure quarters, the small theatres, shops and dealers and obscure places of exchange, etc.*
>
> (Halbwachs 1950: 139)

Introduction: Narratives of the Famous Places of the Capital

The urban *milieu* can be thought of in terms of a relationship, an integrated role, the appropriation of city space being as much symbolic as material. Beyond processes of physical appropriation, there is an interiorization of space in the collective memory and imagination. An urban reality exists in systems of representation and use, in networks of codes as powerful as those of communication, circulation, and distribution. The everyday place has a representational and imaginary structure.

In this chapter my approach to the city will be based on the following premise: place receives its imprint from the group, and, conversely, the

---

* This chapter is a revised and enlarged version of an article published in French (Fiévé 1995). By courtesy of the *Société Française des Etudes Japonaises*.

Memory and the Changing Passage of Space

group is shaped by place. The relationship between place and group is so strong and necessary that the very existence of the group often depends on its being rooted in a place. This can easily be observed in the attachment shown by cultural minorities to an urban territory (exemplified in the Chinese or Italian quarters of American cities), but it applies to any human group. Attachment expresses the consciousness of belonging to a place as a guarantee of the group's existence. That is why the story of cities is made up of resistance, communities refusing to give up the district or the street where their parents and grandparents lived. When socio-economic conditions change, a community will attempt to regroup, clinging to a district or street no longer suited to it, trying once again to find or create a place of its own (Halbwachs 1950: 139).

Cities have always been constituted by these processes and few urban spaces are left untouched by some collective memory that links them to a social class, cultural community, or professional activity. Very often, the toponym is an easily identifiable repository of collective memory. Avenues in Kyoto such as Ichijō, Nijō, and Sanjō are reminders of the old imperial government and the city of the palaces of court families. The meaning of these names – First Avenue, Second Avenue, Third Avenue – recalls their disposition in relation to the imperial palace in the old Heian capital. Some names recall ancient professions: Ōgi-chō (the fan district) is a district around the Shijō–Kawaramachi crossroads at the central hub of commercial activity and named after the fan makers who first settled there in the thirteenth century; Komeya-chō (the rice house district) in Nakagyō-ku, where rice traders lived; and Zaimoku-chō (the timber district) in Shimogyō-ku, were traders and stockists of wood and timber for construction lived, situated near the quays on the Takase river, just near Kiyamachi, the 'district of houses for wood' (see fig. 7).

At the dawn of the Tokugawa period and starting with Kyoto, the Japanese city became the object of study and knowledge, resulting in new pictorial and mapping forms for the representation of urban space. The first map of Kyoto true to scale was produced around 1637. From that time on, the *Heian-jō machinami zu* (Maps of the streetscape of the capital's quarters) were printed and frequently reissued and upgraded. The same concern with mapping soon followed in Edo and other emergent urban centres in early modern Japan. Already in the first half of the sixteenth century, a new choice of techniques and images led to a particularly innovative representation of urban space: the *Rakuchū rakugai zu byōbu* (Screens of the capital and its surroundings), very fashionable during the seventeenth century in the upper echelons of society (Fiévé 1996: 31–61).

This thirst for knowledge, representation, and definition of urban space expresses itself during the same period in a new literary genre, the 'accounts of famous places' (*meisho ki*) and, a bit later, the 'illustrated [accounts] of famous places' (*meisho zue*), a cross between local gazetteers, tourist guides, and practical *vade mecum* in which famous places (*meisho*) of Kyoto and its surroundings were listed and the particularities of individual localities commented upon. A large number of such works were published. Around thirty were issued during the seventeenth and eighteenth centuries on the imperial capital and Yamashiro province, within which Kyoto stood; of these some twenty appeared between 1658 and 1708. The most famous are *Kyō warabe* (The child of the capital; 1658), *Rakuyō meisho shū* (Anthology of famous places of the capital; 1658), *Kyō suzume* (The sparrow of the capital; 1665), *Fusō keika shi* (Annals of the capital of Japan; 1665), *Keishi junran shū* (Anthology of visits to the capital; 1679), *Yōshūfu shi* (Chronicle of Yamashiro; 1684), *Kyō habutae* (The silks of the capital; 1685) and *Yamashiro meishō shi* (Annals of Yamashiro's picturesque sites; 1705).

These narratives are not limited to a list of famous places in a city or a region. They are composite works bringing together a variety of information about the history and geography of the city and province, as well as institutions, tourist attractions, and the everyday life of the area. Thus, they highlight the particular character of a milieu through a simultaneous approach to the spatial and the temporal. They are therefore particularly useful in studying what Augustin Berque has termed '*médiance*,' that is, the qualities identified and the representations made by the group.[1] Let us not forget that there is no milieu as such, only that which is represented, acted upon, and lived.

In many respects, the accounts of the famous places of the capital are reminiscent of Chinese local gazetteers (*fangzhi* or *difangzhi*, in Chinese; *monographies locales*, in French), an ancient literary genre dating back to the Sui and Tang dynasties and very popular under the Ming and Qing (Will 1990; San Juan 1990–91). Some Japanese texts are directly inspired by the Chinese *fangzhi*, the connection being unambiguously revealed by the inclusion in the title of the word *shi* (*zhi*), translated here as annals, chronicles, history, or local monograph. Among these we find several works written in classical Chinese, such as *Fusō keika shi*, *Yōshūfu shi*, *Yamashiro meishō shi*, and *Yamashiro meiseki junkō shi* (Annals of peregrinations through Yamashiro's historical landmarks). Although borrowings are often blatant, Kyoto's accounts of famous places are more eclectic and less thorough than their Chinese counterparts.

The format adopted in all these texts is that of a list of names and words (places or objects), a methodical inventory classified with different headings. Entries are most often toponyms, but sometimes refer to objects, local products, and famous characters. Each entry is followed by a commentary. Some headings are obviously borrowed from the *fangzhi* – for example, 'successive changes in institutions' (*kenshi enkaku*), 'local products' (*miyage*), and 'historic landmarks' (*koseki*). On closer examination, however, one can see that those borrowings are purely formal and that the contents are quite distinct from the Chinese texts. Examples of headings in the first volume of the *Fusō keika shi* (216 pages) are: the capital (*keishi*); Shinto shrines (*jinja*); mountains and hills (*sangaku*); plains and moors, forests and woods, ways and crossroads (*gen'ya, shinrin, kaiku*); rivers and swamps (*sentaku*); and fences and bridges (*kanryō*). Among headings in the second volume, we find: imperial residences (*kyūshitsu*); villages and hamlets (*kyōyū*); Buddhist monasteries (*jiin*); mausoleums and imperial graves (*byōryō*); and graves (*funbo*). In the third volume we find historic landmarks (*koseki*) and vegetation (*sōmoku*) – essentially pines and cherry trees.

The authors review everything that has to do with the physical existence of places (buildings, mountains, rivers, etc.) and areas (districts, towns, quarters, etc.), information that can usually be found in the Chinese *fangzhi* under headings such as 'successive changes' (*yange*), 'mountains and rivers' (*sanchuan*), 'territories' (*yudi*), 'local products' (*wuchan*), 'historic landmarks' (*guji*), and 'miscellaneous' (*zaji*). However, the Chinese headings concerning 'land and taxes' (*tianfu*), 'officials' (*zhiguan*), 'literary works' (*yiwen*), 'personalities' (*renwu*), 'biographies' (*liezhuan*) and 'examinations' (*xuanju*) do not appear in the Japanese texts. But differences in style between the Chinese and Japanese texts are due to a lack of orders emanating from the Japanese state as to the contents of *meisho ki*. Authors were therefore free to choose their style in depicting the capital, while in China *fangzhi* were the product of the Chinese imperial state's determination to provide an exhaustive record of the entire country (San Juan 1990–91: 4).[2] Similar differences exist even with the local gazetteers written by individual writers such as *Wujun zhi* (Annals of Suzhou), written by the poet and traveller Fan Chengda (1126–93) (Will 1990: 2).

The freedom of style that the 'accounts of the famous places' acquired especially in the eighteenth century allows for great heterogeneity and undoubtedly explains the wealth of material they contain. A text such as *Meisho miyakodori* (Famous Places of the Sea Gull; 1690), written in classical Japanese in the style of earlier topographies, lists, identifies and comments upon a number of important toponyms from Yamashiro province.[3] Moreover, a poem (*waka*) is related to each of the names quoted, and the entire work is classified under thirty-seven headings: mountains (*yama*); rivers (*kawa*); plains (*no*); ponds (*ike*); hills (*oka*); wells (*i*); waterfalls (*taki*); roads (*michi*); bridges (*hashi*); forests (*mori*); springs (*mizu*); rocks (*ishi*); mountain peaks (*mine*); meadows (*shiba*); islands (*shima*); famous trees (*meiki*); valleys (*tani*); hillsides (*saka*); high mountains (*take*); hamlets (*sato*); plains (*hara*); foothills (*o*); woods (*hayashi*); mountain passes (*tōge*); cultivated fields (*ta*); fringes, borders (*fuchi*); sanctuaries, temples, sacred enclosures, and gardens (*miya, yashiro, in, sono*); miscellany (*zatsu*); dikes (*tsutsumi*); paths crossing a mountain (*etsu*); ancient forts (*kojō*); mounds, hillocks (*tsuka*); paths between fields (*nawate*); gardens (*sono*). Texts such as *Kyō warabe* or even *Kyō suzume* have a literary background; they are based on an evocative – but not necessarily exact – depiction of historical background and interesting popular anecdotes and beliefs. As Jurgis Elisonas put it, 'At its best, as in the case of the *Kyō warabe*, the topographical *kanazōshi* comes close to achieving the kind of completeness that one might expect of a modern-day *Guide Michelin*: while being overtly instructional, it manages to entertain; the facts it chattily presents to the reader are intermingled with a lot of pleasant fiction; often wrong in the historical description of the places one 'must see,' it is nonetheless a welcome companion to the foot-weary as also to those who merely visit famous sites in spirit' (Elisonas 1994: 260–61).

Famous Places Listed in the *Shūgaishō*

The starting point for our investigation is the text *Shūgaishō* (The compendium of fragments, in *Shintei zōho kojitsu sōsho* 22: 220–227), a kind of encyclopaedia attributed to Tōin Kinkata (1291–1360) and completed by his descendant Tōin Sanehiro (b. 1409), in which eighty famous places (*meisho*) in the capital are listed with one or two line commentaries. The work was written three hundred years before the *meisho ki* of the Tokugawa period, almost one century before the great urban fires of the Ōnin War, in which about three-quarters of the city was destroyed.[4] After searching the *meisho ki* and *meisho zue* of the Tokugawa period for each of the toponyms quoted in the *Shūgaishō*, we find that out of thirty works consulted, five of them reproduced the original list complete. These five consist of four texts written in classical Chinese and *Kyō habutae oridome* (Epilogue on the capital's silks; 1685) written in classical Japanese. The toponyms in question are classified under the heading 'historic landmarks.' The other *meisho ki* consulted make a cursory reference to the famous places listed in the *Shūgaishō*. In order to investigate this further, we will place the contents of the *Shūgaishō* alongside those of the first 'accounts of the famous places' of the Tokugawa period, *Kyō warabe*, published in Kyoto in 1658. *Kyō warabe* introduces eighty-seven famous places in Kyoto.

Famous Places of 'Historical' Value

Memories of famous buildings

Kinkata, himself a court noble, seems to focus mainly on the famous dwellings of high dignitaries of the Heian period. The dwellings, which are always referred to by name, were mostly destroyed when the *Shūgaishō* was compiled. Although the occasional palace was still in existence when the book was written, the texts indicate that their value always sprang from a glorious past rather than from their present qualities. One example – still famous nowadays – is the Kawara-no-in, the palace built in the ninth century by Minamoto no Tōru (822–95), in which Tōru had reproduced, on a reduced scale, the landscape of the bay of Shiogama, itself classified at that time as one of the three most famous landscapes in the country. Tōru had the garden pond filled with sea water brought from the bay of Naniwa and enjoyed having salt extracted from it. Amongst others were the palace of Ōnakatomi no Sukechika (954–1038), the Rokujō-no-in at Rokujō, in the garden of which the famous landscape of Ama-no-hashidate had been reproduced, and the Kan'in, the famous palace of Fujiwara no Fuyutsugu (775–826), with its garden for which the painter Kose no Kanaoka (active, end of ninth century) had designed a stone assemblage symbolising water.

This first category of famous places constitutes the majority of the *meisho* quoted in this work. The main characteristic is that their value as reminders lies in the historical significance of the place. This significance does not depend on a desire to create an object of commemoration in the first place but on the subjective choice of later generations, those of Kinkata or his descendant Sanehiro. This subjective choice was made by a courtier, a member of the fallen aristocracy resisting the ascendance of the ruling military class through the power of its imagination, putting down roots in the places that used to reflect its strength.

A further characteristic of this category of famous place lies in the physical absence of any original building or monument. According to the maps and texts of the time, they have often been replaced by a new dwelling or have even become districts inhabited by commoners. One can assume that very few ruins remained in place as nowhere are they a separate heading, and they do not appear to have any particular significance.

Memories of ancient beliefs

A second category of famous places consists of places of ill repute (*akusho*), such as Yamano'i-tei and Oni-dono palaces or the well known as Naiki-no-i. The so-called Oni-dono (Palace of the Devil) was a cursed house (*kyōtaku*). Situated near the crossroads of the Sanjō and Higashi-no-tōin avenues, it had been the mansion of the court noble Fujiwara no Arisuke (d. 1131). But the origin of the superstition dates back to when the capital was founded, to the occasion when a man was changed into a ghost after being struck by lightning on the spot where he stood.

The value of this second category as reminders also lies in the historic value of the place, but, as opposed to the memories of famous buildings, the reference is to an event rather than an object (such as a palace), an event the origin of which lies in the transmission of popular beliefs extending beyond the boundaries of aristocratic culture.

Focal Points of Prosperity in the Contemporary City as Famous Places

Commoners' districts make up a third category of famous places in this section of *Shūgaishō*. Sakura-chō, the 'cherry blossom district,' is described in the following terms: 'It is said that near the Tsuchimikado–Made-no-kōji crossroads is the cherry-blossom district with a south-facing garden overflowing with flowers. It has been so called since olden times. The house of the poet Ki no Tsurayuki (868?–945?) was once here.' Mikura-chō, situated west of Sanjō–Karasuma crossroads is also indicated; it is described as one of the most lively centres of the capital, probably owing its name to the cotton traders' guild, linked to the Gion sanctuary. This district in the lower city (*shimogyō*) was important as a result both of the prosperity and of the influence of its inhabitants, who were in charge of seating arrangements for the shogun so that he could contemplate the Gion festival parade in 1571. These famous places, although existing within the contemporary city, have a value as collective memory through their association with long-established activities related to a flourishing economy and trade and 'golden ages' of prosperity. Besides, in these two examples, the toponymy issues directly from the very aspects that qualify them as famous places, and although the history of Sakura-chō may have its origins in the dwelling of a courtier, the value of both places lies in their prosperity within the contemporary city.[5]

Famous Places quoted in *Kyō warabe*

Kyō warabe (The child of the capital) was written by the poet and physician Nakagawa Kiun (1636?–1705) and published in Kyoto in 1658. It was the first example of an 'account of famous places' and became a model for a lot of guides of the famous places of early modern Japan. The commentaries included in *Kyō warabe* are more substantial texts (from ten lines to three pages) than those found in *Shūgaishō* and they provide quite detailed descriptions of related places and both historical and popular anecdotes.

Focal Points of Prosperity in the Contemporary City as Famous Places

As with *Shūgaishō*, a first category of famous place consists of renowned popular sites and districts, the two main ones quoted being Shijō-gawara and Keisei-chō, the pleasure district of early modern Kyoto. Shijō-gawara was famous for its theatres, especially *kabuki*, as was Keisei-chō, known as Shimabara, for its prostitution (see my chapter on Shimabara and figs. 30, 31 and 32). The descriptions of these 'famous places' inaugurate a new form of presentation made of both historical background about theatres, *kabuki*, and prostitution as practical information about the sites, a style which will be copied later in other 'accounts of famous places' (Elisonas 1994: 258).

Figure 30 Nishimura Chūwa, Sakuma Sōen, and Oku Bunmei '*Sumiya, yukigeshiki*' (Snow landscape at the Sumiya house). From Akizato Ritō's *Miyako rinsen meishō zue* (Illustrated collection of the picturesque gardens of the capital), vol. 5 (1799).

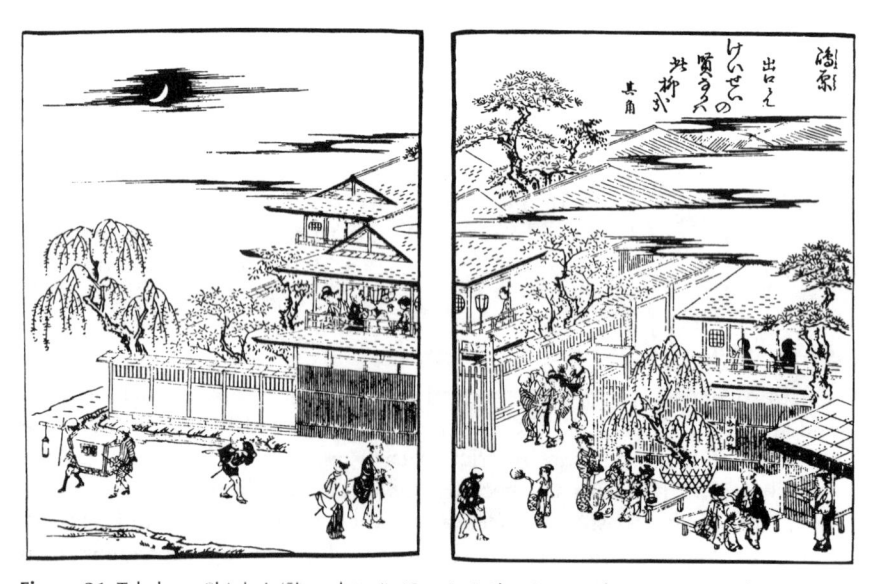

Figure 31 Takehara Shinkei (Shunchōsai) '*Sumiya*' (the Sumiya house). From Akizato Ritō's *Miyako meisho zue* (Illustrated collection of famous places of the capital), 1780.

Figure 32 '*Shimabara.*' From Nakagawa Kiun's *Kyō warabe* (The child of the capital), 1658, vol. 2.

Figure 33 '*Shijō-gawara.*' From Nakagawa Kiun's *Kyō warabe* (The child of the capital), 1658, vol. 1.

With the descriptions of Shijō-gawara (fig. 33) and Keisei-chō, we are dealing not with any original 'intended' value nor with any 'historical' value of a famous place, but with prosperity within the contemporary city. Leisure, performing arts, commerce, and craft activities define the level of significance of the sites. These are the districts with a cultural life involving all levels of society, districts that show the important place in urban life of the commoner class and entertainers coming from discriminated classes (Zōho Kyōto Sōsho [abbreviated to ZKS] vol. 1, *Kyō warabe*: 7–10; 32–3).

Famous Places with a 'Historical' Value

The second category of 'famous place' referred to in *Kyō warabe* concerns places made famous by the presence of a famous figure in popular history. Prominent among these are Buddhist saints such as the founders of the Amidist movement, which was very popular amongst the commoner classes of Kyoto. One example of this type of *meisho* is the Hyakumanben monastery, where Hōnen (1133–1212), founder of the Amidist strain of the Pure Land school, stayed (ZKS vol. 1, *Kyō warabe*: 13–14).[6] Another is the Mieidō, where the immensely popular preacher Ippen (1239–89) resided for a while.[7] Further examples are the Ryōsen and Sōrinji temples, where Kokua (1314–1405), one of Ippen's later followers, lived (ZKS vol. 1, *Kyō warabe*: 16–17). As for the Rokuhara site, celebrated for its connection to the Taira family, the author only mentions the Rokuhara-mitsuji temple and Kūya (903–72), hardly mentioning the name of Taira, with whom the place has close historical connections (ZKS vol. 1, *Kyō warabe*: 21–2).[8] These are, therefore, places with value as 'historical' reminders, but a value that does not originate in the creator's will, emerging instead from the subjective choice of later generations. The characters thus remembered belong to the popular imagination (see fig. 7).

Famous Places with an 'Intended' Value

Some *meisho* were invested with a value that was intended from the start of their existence rather than being dependent on events and values imposed at later stages in their history. Prominent among these are Shinto shrines and Buddhist temples, religious institutions whose fame reached all layers of society. Such are the famous pilgrimage sites of Kitano Tenmangū and Gionsha, also known as Yasaka Jinja (ZKS vol. 1, *Kyō warabe*: 37–42; 11–13) (see fig. 7).

Kitano Tenmangū was founded in the tenth century to appease the soul of Sugawara no Michizane (845–903), courtier and man of state who died in exile in Kyushu. Later, Michizane came to be associated with the celestial divinity Tenjin and venerated by peasants as a deity protecting crops against the elements. He also came to be revered by all as the protector of literature.

During the Middle Ages, he became the patron saint of yeast for *sake* brewers and is still venerated in the weaving world of the Nishijin district of Kyoto (Ōtoneri guild).

Famous since the Heian period in every layer of society, the Gion sanctuary was founded at the end of the ninth century. During the tenth century, the Buddhist and Shinto cults were brought together in the same temple. In 970, the first 'meeting to appease the souls' (*Gion goryō-e*) took place, organized following epidemics and disasters that had struck the whole country. This rite is the origin of the Gion festival, which by the seventeenth century had become one of the pivotal events of the calendar for the city's artisans and traders, the *chōnin*. In 1533, the festival had been banned by the authorities, but subsequent riots allowed the *chōnin* to prevail and organize the festival the following year, thus confirming their power. This sanctuary always gathered numerous devotees, testimony to the bonds created by some places of worship with all sections of society. Enshrined here were some of the founding deities of Japanese mythology, in this case, Susanoo no Mikoto and Kushinada Hime.[9] There was also a privileged relationship with the imperial family. Gion Shrine was, since the eleventh century, one of the sanctuaries to which the court presented offerings. Similarly, Kitano Tenmangū's cult ceremony had been receiving offerings from the court since the tenth century and had been often visited by members of the imperial family.

The value of the Kitano shrine lies in its institutionalisation of the memory of Michizane and the various ceremonies conducted there to appease his soul. Gion enshrines a variety of the founding deities of Japanese mythology. In both these cases, the physical building is important, but less for its age than because it allows for the everlasting execution of ceremonial rites.

Two sub-categories of place with an 'intended' value appear in *Kyō warabe*. The first are urban statues or images – among examples of these are Haraobi no Jizō and Meyami no Jizō – and other places of worship such as Shimogoryō (fig. 7). Of the Haraobi no Jizō, *Kyō warabe* tells us that this clay statue of the bodhisattva Jizō was located in the Seitaiji temple. Haraobi no Jizō was worshipped by pregnant women (ZKS vol. 1, *Kyō warabe*: 5), hence its name – a *haraobi* being the sash tied around the belly from the fifth month of pregnancy. The temple was situated in the Haraobi-chō district, since renamed Higashigawa-chō (in present-day Nakagyō-ku). Haraobi no Jizō is mentioned in the *Chūsaku keishi chizu* (Map of the ancient capital), drawn by Mori Kōan (dates unknown) in 1750, which depicts the city after its destruction in the Ōnin era (1467–69). Of Meyami no Jizō, *Kyō warabe* tells us that it was situated in the Keikōji, a temple no longer remaining. Meyami no Jizō is now the main deity of Chūgenji, a temple of the Pure Land school (Gion-machi Minami-gawa, Higashiyama-ku). The name *meyami* is derived from *ameyami*, 'stopping the rain.'

Meyami no Jizō has its origins in the disastrous floods that devastated the city in 1228. During the 8th Month, the prayers of the people to stop the rains were answered, and the floods receded. And as for Shimogoryō, among the deities quoted in the text, the eight deities worshipped here were the tutelary patron saints (*ubusunagami*) of the imperial palace. These are the spirits of Kibi no Makibi (693–775), Sawara Shinnō (later known as Sudō Tennō; (750–785), Fujiwara no Hirotsugu (d. 740), Iyo Shinnō (d. 807), his mother Fujiwara Yoshiko (dates unknown), Tachibana no Hayanari (d. 842), Fun'ya no Miyatamaro (dates unknown), and, again, Sugawara no Michizane. All where court nobles from the Nara period (710–784) and from the begining of the Heian period. The spirits of these tutelary patron saints were moved to their present site (Shimogoryō-chō, Nakagyō-ku) in 1589 on the orders of Toyotomi Hideyoshi (1536–98) during the great works carried out to restructure the city (ZKS vol. 1, *Kyō warabe*: 10–11).

The other sub-category are the graves and tumuli erected in memory of a person, a famous deity, or a particular event. *Kyō warabe* lists a number of these. *Izumi Shikibu no kofun* is assumed to refer to the grave of the Heian period woman poet Izumi Shikibu (active end of the tenth, begining of the eleventh centuries) (ZKS vol. 1, *Kyō warabe*: 4–5) which is today located in the cemetery of the Seishin'in (Shingon school), south of Seiganji (today in Nakasuji-chō, Nakagyō-ku).[10] *Shōgun tsuka*, 'mound of the shogun,' is another entry in this category (ZKS vol. 1, *Kyō warabe*: 15–16) (see fig. 7). So as to secure the establishment of the Heian capital on its site, the city's founder, Emperor Kanmu (737–806), had the effigy of a protecting deity buried there. The anecdote is told in the thirteenth-century classic *Heike monogatari* (Tale of the Heike):

> 'Since ancient times and throughout the ages, sovereigns have indeed established numerous capitals in many different provinces and sites, but no place lends itself better to it than this one!' exclaimed Kanmu Tennō after deliberating with ministers, dignitaries, and all sorts of experts. So as to secure his choice of settlement forever, he ordered an eight-foot clay figure with human shape, had it dressed in a black iron armour, armed with a bow and arrows made of the same metal, and had it buried facing west at the top of the eastern mountains. Whatever may happen in time, should the capital have to be transferred to another province, let this be its protecting god! (*Heike monogatari*, Book Five, Transfer of the Capital).

By the time *Kyō warabe* was written, the story seems to be have been well known, and many *meisho ki* mention it. The mound is located in what is now Awatayama Minami-chō (Higashiyama-ku, Awata-guchi). During the Heian period, this site used to be a cemetery and has since been the focus of much veneration. When the surroundings were excavated in 1905, sarcophagi and diverse funerary objects were unearthed. Another entry in this category is *Toba no koi-zuka* (ZKS vol. 1, *Kyō warabe*: 60–2). This is, most likely, the 'grave of the one who died of love' (*koi-zuka*), located within the walls of Koizuka-dera (at Shimotoba-mura, today in Fushimi-ku), where Kesa Gozen is thought to be buried. According to this story from the late twelfth century, Endō Moritō (1139–1203) fell in love with Kesa Gozen (dates unknown), the wife of Minamoto no Wataru (dates unknown), a third class military civil servant with the imperial guard. He mistakenly killed his beloved when he meant to murder her husband, and the long life of suffering he led thereafter has been a theme extensively exploited by the theatre. Later, Moritō became a monk, first taking the name of Jōa and then that of Mongaku, by which name he is best known today.

In the sub-category of graves and tumuli, the material element may be a monumental building (like the grave of Izumi Shikibu) or a simple grass covered mound (as with the *Shōgun tsuka*). As we have seen, in these examples, collective memory is generally linked to the world of court nobles. Yoshida hill would fit this category, celebrated not because the poet and author Yoshida Kenkō (1283?–1350?) lived there, but mainly because it was forbidden territory containing many imperial graves (SZKS 1: 50).[11]

Conclusion: Famous Place as Collective Creation

In his authoritative essay *Der moderne Denkmalkultus* (The modern cult of monuments) written in 1903, Alois Riegl defined three categories of monuments. There are 'intended monuments,' buildings destined by the will of their creator to commemorate a precise moment or a complex event from the past. Secondly, there are the 'historical monuments' that refer back to a particular moment, the choice of which actually comes from the subjective preferences of later generations. Lastly, the 'ancient monuments' is a category useful as a description of any human creation, independent of its original meaning or intention, the only criterion being that the monuments should bear witness to the weathering effect of time.

In the light of these classifications, we have shown that examples of the first two categories, 'intended monuments' and 'historical monuments,' were largely represented in the early modern city, with the difference – and it is a big difference – that the monumentality of the place does not accrue from the buildings themselves. This characteristic of famous places in Japan is of interest for two reasons. First of all, on a theoretical level, it clearly brings out certain aspects of the attachment of a group to a place, emphasising how the collective memory of urban society at the beginning of the early modern period inscribes itself in space and time, providing the group with an image of itself intimately linked with its past. There is also a multi-faceted historical interest. The famous places in *Shūgaishō* reveal how important the aristocracy and its cultural traditions were for the collective memory, despite their being as much as four centuries old at the time the work was written and eight centuries old when it was reprinted. As for *Kyō warabe*, it shows in every aspect an already deeply rooted plebeian culture. On the other hand, it is surprising to see how few traces are left by the warrior class in the famous places of urban memory. The Nijō castle of the Tokugawa is quoted but with a succinct description (ZKS vol. 1, *Kyō warabe*: 36–7) (fig. 34). Conversely, we have noted the position assigned to places whose existence or history is related to tutelary deities of the imperial

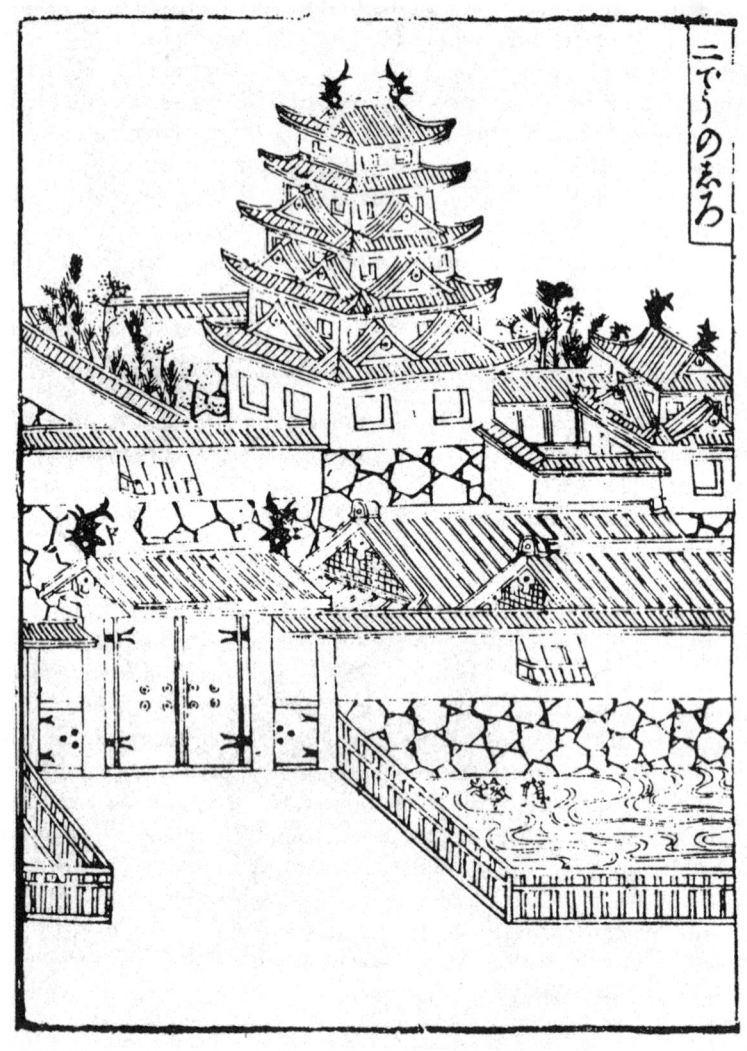

Figure 34 '*Nijō no shiro*' (Nijō Castle). From Nakagawa Kiun's *Kyō warabe* (The child of the capital), 1658, vol. 2.

family or to reminders of aristocratic culture (for example ZKS vol. 1, *Kyō warabe*, Dairi: 1–2; Shinsen'en: 36).

Another point of interest is related to the complete absence of value of 'ancient monuments,' as defined by Riegl, in the monuments (buildings, works of art) of the Japanese capital. This value, highly esteemed in the West since the Italian renaissance and the cult of antique ruins, is not apparent in Japan. Most of the examples quoted here show how authenticity, and even the actual existence of an ancient building, mattered little. The material monument with its parade of evocations increasing with the passage of time is only minimally apparent in these early guides to famous places (see also Fiévé 1999: 340–3).

We tend to accept nowadays that the monuments (in the sense of monumental buildings) in our cities are far from being representative of the spatial marking of a collective memory. Monuments are in general tools for the recognition of political authority. Indeed, like traditions they are the manifestation of an expressive will attempting to inscribe themselves on the passage of time but effective only because they belong to the present. Finally, the function of a monument is not to incarnate duration but rather to set up parallels between different temporalities; they often serve as the articulation between the instantaneous nature of authority and authority's desire for recognition in the passage of time. Vernacular architecture is not actually made up of monuments.

The value of a famous place does not strictly speaking depend on the material building and the symbolic relation of place to building. Above all, it emerges from a collective creation, the first condition of its very existence. Its origins lie in certain forms of grandeur, of heroism, of images etched into popular beliefs and even in the mechanisms of habit, ways of being and acting, practices transmitted from generation to generation. But place is not simply a collective space, and the role of attendance (very strong in the early modern period) must be emphasized, the slow consecration of a place through the mere passage of people. Once consecrated, the famous place becomes a witness to consciousness and the tool through which people find their roots (actual or mythical) and recognize themselves in the other. To borrow, in conclusion, an idea from the French historian Alphonse Dupront, the famous places 'originate from a double reality: a living collective memory and a therapy of belonging' (Dupront 1990: 65).

Notes

1 This term was coined by Augustin Berque when translating into French the idea of *fūdosei* (Berque 1996: 86–94).
2 The determination of the state to provide local gazetteers is still a widespread practice in contemporary China (Vermeer 1992: 438–67).

3 *Miyako-dori* is an ancient literary term for a sea gull and is written with the characters for 'capital' and the 'bird.' The title is reminiscent of the more famous *Kyō suzume* (The sparrow of the capital) published some years before, in 1665, by Asai Ryōi (1612–?).
4 *Shūgaishō* was itself re-issued several times during the Tokugawa period with the addition of several maps in the Keichō (1596–1614) and Kan'ei (1624–43) eras. Among these is a reconstitution of the map of the old capital where the famous place are quoted (Fiévé 1996: 35).
5 It is interesting to note that places of worship – Buddhist temples and Shinto shrines – only appear in sections one and nine of the third volume of *Shūgaishō*. There five monasteries are mentioned, but for historical reasons and for their associations with the court aristocracy.
6 This refers to the Chionji (Tanakanishi Hinokuchi-chō, Sakyō-ku), a monastery including four temples: Chionji, Shōjōke'in, Konkaikōmyōji, and Chion'in. The place used to be known as Kawaraya and a statue of Shakamuni was venerated there. Hōnen settled here for a while, then Genchi, one of his disciples, turned it into a space for religious practice. The place was then named Kōtoku'in Chionji (according to the *Yōshūfu shi*). During the year 1331, Amida's invocations are said to have been chanted about a hundred times to ward off an epidemic, whence the popular name of Hyakumanben.
7 The temple was situated in the present Mieidō-chō (Shimogyō-ku); it then covered parts of the land where the Kawara-no-in used to be.
8 This is the Rokuhara-mitsuji temple, originally founded by Kūya (its name was then Saikōji). The temple was located on a plot of land where the Taira later built a palace in the years 1160 to 1180, when at the peak of their power. The temple still houses a very famous wooden statue of Kūya, a Buddhist monk from the middle of the Heian period who preached the invocation to Amida through the streets of Kyoto.
9 *Kyō warabe* quotes Inada Hime, Izanagi no Mikoto and Izanami no Mikoto.
10 At the origin of the Jōshin'in was probably the Komidō, a retreat for Izimi Shikibu built by Fujiwara no Michinaga (966–1027). Formerly situated at Higashi Kyōgoku–Imadegawa, the temple was later transferred in the compounds of the Seiganji. It is indicated at that place in the 'Map of the Ancient Capital' drawn by Kōan.
11 The ancient name for the area is Kagura-oka. These forbidden lands, forbidden because of the imperial graves, were originally under the control of the minister for religious affairs (*Jingikan*).

References

Pre-1868 Sources

Most of the local gazetteers and accounts of famous places in the former capital are included in *Zōho Kyōto sōsho* (abbreviated to ZKS; Collection of Books on Kyoto). I have used in this study the edition published in Kyoto by Kyōto Sōsho Kankōkai from 1933 to 1938 (some of them are reprinted in a more accessible edition: Takemura T. (ed.) *Nihon meisho fūsoku zue*, vol. 7 (1979): *Kyōto no maki 1*; vol. 8 (1981); *Kyōto no maki 2*. Tokyo: Kadogawa Shoten.

Dairi hina (Summary of Knowledge of the Imperial Palace) (or *Dairi hina miyako no hana, Yamashiro meisho jisha monogatari, Yamashiro meisho dairi hina, Yamashiro meisho dairi hina jisha monogatari*), 1717 (Kyōhō 2), 6 vols ZKS vol. 2.

Kyoto's Famous Places

Dekisai kyō miyage (Things brought back from the capital by the monk Dekisai) (*Kyō miyage, Yamashiro meishoki*), 1677 (Enpō 5), 7 vols, ZKS vol. 4.

Fusō keika shi (Annals of the capital of Japan), foreword dated 1665 (Kanbun 5). 3 vols, by Matsuno Genkei. ZKS vol. 2.

Horikawa no mizu (The stream of Horikawa), 1692, 3 vols, by Rogetsuan Jisen. ZKS vol. 9.

Keijō shōran (Beaming glance on the capital) (or *Kyōto meguri*), foreword dated 1706 (Hōei 3). 2 vols, by Kaibara Ekiken (Tokushin). ZKS vol. 5.

Keishi junran shū (Collection of visits to the capital), 1679 (Enpō 6), by Jōgu (Rokkadō Sekichō). 15 vols, ZKS vol. 4.

Kinki rekiran ki (Records of walks in the Kinki) (date unknown), by Kurokawa Dōyū (Gen'itsu). ZKS vol. 3.

Kyō habutae (The capital's silks), 1685, by Suiundō, 6 vols, ZKS vol. 6.

Kyō habutae oridome (Epilogue on the capital's silks), 1689, by Suiundō, 6 vols, ZKS vol. 6.

Kyōmachi kagami (Mirror of the districts of the capital), 1674 (Enpō 6), by Hakurotei Shujin. 2 vols, in vol. 2, ZKS vol. 10.

Kyō no mizu (The stream of the capital), 1790 (Kansei 2). 2 vols and maps, by Akizato Ritō (no reprint).

Kyō suzume (The sparrow of the capital), 1665 (Kanbun 5). 7 vols by Asai Ryōi. ZKS 1.

Kyō suzume atooi (The sparrow of the capital, sequel), 1678 (Enpō 6). 3 vols (no reprint).

Kyōto bō mokushi (Inventory of the Kyoto districts), by Usui Kosaburō. ZKS, vol. 13 to 16 and vol.18.

Kyō uchi mairi (Going round the capital), 1708 (Hōei 8), by Shusetsusai. ZKS, vol. 9.

Kyō warabe (or *Kyō waranbe*) (The child of the capital), 1658 (Meireki 4). 6 vols by Nakagawa Kiun (Jūji). ZKS vol. 1. Takemura T. (ed.) (1979). *Nihon meisho fūsoku zue*, vol. 7: *Kyōto no maki 1*. Tokyo: Kadogawa Shoten.

Kyō warabe atooi (The child of the capital, sequel), 1667 (Kanbun 7), by Nakagawa Kiun (Jūji). ZKS vol. 1. Takemura T. (ed.) (1979). *Nihon meisho fūsoku zue*, vol. 7: *Kyōto no maki 1*. Tokyo: Kadogawa Shoten.

Meisho miyakodori (Famous places of the 'sea-gull'), 1690 (Genroku 3).

Miyako kagetsu meisho (Famous places for entertainment in the capital), 1793. 1 vol., by Akizato Ritō (Koseki). ZKS vol. 2.

Miyako meisho guruma (Going through the famous places of the capital), 1714, by Tōritei Shujin (Ikeda Masayoshi). ZKS vol. 9.

Miyako meisho zue (Illustrated collection of famous places of the capital), 1780, by Akizato Ritō (Koseki), illustrations by Takehara Shinkei (Shunchōsai). 6 vols, in vol. 6. ZKS vol. 11. Takemura T. (ed.) (1981). *Nihon meisho fūsoku zue*, vol. 8: *Kyōto no maki 2*. Tokyo: Kadogawa Shoten.

Miyako meisho zue atooi (Illustrated collection of famous places of the capital, Sequel). 1786, by Akizato Ritō (Koseki). 4 vols, ZKS vol. 12.

Miyako rinsen meishō zue (Illustrated collection of picturesque gardens of the capital), 1799 (Kansei 11), by Akizato Ritō (Koseki). In *Nihon zue zenshū*, 2nd series, vol. 3.

Rakuyō jūnisha reigen ki (Miraculous stories from the twelve shrines of the capital), 1827, 1 vol. by Ōki Anshu (Matsuura Kōshū). ZKS vol. 5.

Rakuyō meisho shū (Collection of famous places of the capital) (or *Miyako monogatari*), 1658. 12 vols, by Yamamoto Taijun. ZKS vol. 1; *Kadogawa bunko*; *Nihon zukai zenshū* (2nd series) vol. 1.

Shūgaishō (Compendium of fragments), *Shintei zōho kojitsu sōsho*, vol. 22. Yoshikawa Kōbunkan (1952), middle part, section 20, pp. 220–27.
Tsuginefu, 1684. 8 vols, by Kitamura Kigin. ZKS vol. 5 (Tsuginefu is a *makura-kotoba* for Yamashiro).
Yamashiro meiseki junkō shi (Annals of peregrinations through Yamashiro's historical landmarks), 1754, 12 vols, ZKS vol. 10.
Yamashiro meiseki shi (Annals of Yamashiro historical remains). 1705. By Hakkei. 12 vols ZKS 19 et 20.
Yamashiro meisho jisha monogatari (see Dairi hina).
Yamashiro meishō shi (Annals of Yamashiro's picturesque sites), 1705, by Ōshima Takeyoshi, 21 vols + maps. ZKS vol. 7 and 8.
Yōshūfu shi (Chronicle of Yamashiro), foreword dated 1684. 10 vols, by Kurokawa Dōyū (Gen'itsu). ZKS vol. 3.

Post-1868 Sources

Berque, A. (1996) *Être humain sur la terre: principes d'éthique de l'écoumène*. Paris: Gallimard.
Burgier, A., and J. Revel (1993) *Les formes de la culture*. In Histoire de la France, vol. 4. Paris: Éditions du Seuil.
Choay, F. (1992) *L'allégorie du patrimoine*. Paris: Éditions du Seuil.
Cruellier, M. (1991) *La mémoire des français: recherches d'histoire culturelle*. Paris: Veyrier éditeur.
Dupront, A. (1990) 'Au commencement, un mot: lieu.' In M. Crépu and R. Figuier (eds) *Hauts lieux: une quête de racines, de sacré, de symboles*. Paris: Éditions Autrement, pp. 58–66.
Elisonas, J. (1994) 'Notorious places: a brief excursion into the narrative topography of early Edo.' In J. McClain, J. Merriman, and Ugawa K. (eds) *Edo and Paris: Urban Life and the State in the Early Modern Era*. Ithaca: Cornell University Press, pp. 253–91.
Fiévé N. (1999) 'Architecture et patrimoine au Japon: les mots du monument historique'. In R. Debray (ed.) *L'abus monumental: actes des entretiens du patrimoine*. Paris: Fayard, Éditions du Patrimoine, pp. 323–43.
—— (1996) *L'architecture et la ville du Japon ancien: espace architectural de la ville de Kyōto et des résidences shōgunales aux XIVe et XVe siècles*. In Bibliothèque de l'Institut des Hautes Études Japonaises, Collège de France/Université de Paris VII. Paris: Maisonneuve et Larose.
—— (1995) 'Le récit sur les hauts lieux de la capitale: essai sur le rôle du meisho dans la constitution d'une ville-mémoire.' In P. Bellevaire and A. Gossot (eds) *Japon pluriel*. Paris: Éditions Piquier, pp. 305–18.
—— (1992a) 'Urban evolution of the city of Heiankyo: a study of the iconographic sources, part 1.' *Japan Forum* 4 (1): 91–107.
—— (1992b) 'Urban evolution of the city of Heiankyo: a study of the iconographic sources, part 2.' *Japan Forum* 4 (2): 285–304.
Halbwachs, M. (1968) *La mémoire collective*. Paris: Presses Universitaires de France.
—— (1971). *La topographie légendaire des évangiles en Terre Sainte*. Paris: Presses Universitaires de France.
Lapierre, N. (ed.) (1989) *Communication, n. 49. La mémoire et l'oubli*. Paris: Éditions du Seuil.
Namer, G. (1987) *Mémoire et société*. Paris: Méridiens-Klinksieck.
Needham, J. (1959) *Science and Civilisation in China, vol. 3: Mathematics and Sciences of the Heavens and the Earth*: Cambridge: Cambridge University Press.

Nora, P. (1986) *Les lieux de mémoire.* 7 vol. Paris: Gallimard.
—— (ed.) (1994) *Le débat,* n. 78. *Mémoires comparées.* Paris: Gallimard.
Pigeot, J. (1982) *Michiyuki-bun, poétique de l'itinéraire dans la littérature du Japon ancien.* Bibliothèque de l'Institut des Hautes Études Japonaises, Collège de France. Paris: Maisonneuve et Larose.
Riegl, A. (1903) *Der moderne Denkmalkultus.* French translation by D. Wieczorek (1984), *Le culte moderne des monuments.* Paris: Éditions du Seuil.
San Juan (Sanjuan), T. (1990–91) *Les monographies locales de la préfecture de Canton (1864–1949): dépouillement de documents historiques en vue d'une étude de géographie régionale et culturelle.* D.E.A Dissertation in Social Sciences. Paris: E.H.E.S.S.
Vermeer, E. (1992) 'New county histories: a research note on their compilation and value.' *Modern China,* 18 (4): 438–67.
Will, P.-E. (1990) 'Local Gazetteers.' Lectures on methodological approaches for historical research on modern China, 19–27 June. Oslo. 26 pages.

CHAPTER 6

Representing Mobility in Tokugawa and Meiji Japan

Jilly Traganou

If within the condition of modernity the map was regarded as a fixed point of reference, a reflection of the expansive nature of universal space, in the contemporary dissolution of such unities the objectivity of the map, as well as of the described space, has been frequently questioned. The unidimensional surface of maps has been seen instead as a 'deep-text,' a text that demands interpretation and recontextualization. On the level of appearance, maps use precise systems of signification in order to describe selected aspects and relations within a given space. However, the information to be found on the surface of a map is rarely limited to the codified data indicated in the legend but rather expresses prior assumptions and ideologies. A careful analysis of cartographic signification can reveal a surplus of non-cartographic systems of representation which are employed in the making of a map. These are susceptible to diverse interpretations, depending upon the contexts of time, place, language, and the viewer's identity.

The cartographer J.B. Harley, basing himself on Michel Foucault (1926–84), has claimed the necessity of exploring the cartographic *discourse* through a broader *iconological* perspective that positions maps within the 'value-laden images' contributing to the social construction of the world. Such a perspective can address the relation between maps and power, or more broadly, the overall ideological discourses that envelop map production (Harley 1988: 277). In this chapter, I apply these ideas to a discussion of representations of the Tōkaidō and other routes during the passage from the Tokugawa period (1603–1867) to the Meiji era (1868–1912), or in other words during the Tōkaidō's transformation from highway to railway (for a description of the structure of urban areas along the Tōkaidō during the Tokugawa period, see the chapter by Bodart-Bailey).[1] A comparison between highway and railway maps produced during these two periods will reflect not only physical transformations along the route and changes in cartographic representation but will also offer insights regarding the changing ideological function of space during these two periods.

The History of Mobility

The development of infrastructure is usually narrated as a history of technological progress. In the case of the Tōkaidō, historians and geographers have examined the transformation of the route from being principally a highway to a railway (1889) and recently (1964) to a super-express bullet train line. Parallel to this, a number of historians have indicated the instrumentality of the infrastructure within the national goals of each period, considering at the same time the practices and the fantasies of the travelers, based on literary and visual accounts of the two eras (Vaporis 1994; Erickson 1996).

Mobility, and consequently its cartographic representation, has not only taken different forms throughout Japanese history, but has also been handled by changing institutional bodies, for each of which it has been a means for expressing diverse national ideals. The high degree of mobility during the Tokugawa period, which reached the level of a 'travel boom,' can be considered as a sign of departure from the feudal condition towards the creation of a modern society. Although the system of highways and post stations had initially been reinforced as a means of facilitating the territorial control of the Tokugawa authorities and the centrality of Edo, it soon overcame its administrative character and became an arena of play and release for the commoner population.

In the Meiji era, the highway system was replaced by the railways, an infrastructure that facilitated the civic and military scope of Meiji rule. It is important to note that the Tōkaidō was eventually selected as the first trunk line in the country, the construction of which was completed in 1889, after the agreement of the military had been obtained.[2] It is true, however, that the railway did not replace the highway from one day to the next, but rather that the two systems coexisted for an extensive period of time, each of them being associated with distinctive social classes and life-styles. In short, the highway was the realm of backwardness or in some cases even of the indecent (due to the concentration of outcaste groups such as prostitutes, entertainers, and so on), while the railway was the canal of 'Civilization and Enlightenment' (*bunmei kaika*). During this period, the Tōkaidō became the route of middle-class tourism and new Western-style leisure activities. At the same time, the Tōkaidō became a focus of industrialization, as well as other more pervasive types of mobility. Migration from rural to urban areas, a major characteristic of modernity worldwide, was encouraged as a new model of individual and public well-being.

The Rhetoric of Mobility

Since its establishment, the railway has been presented as symbolic of the repression and anguish of rationalized modern life. In Europe, Flaubert described the boredom of the railway traveler in comparison to the previous excitement of journeys on foot. In the Meiji era, when the railway was introduced to Japan, a number of prominent Japanese saw the train as a major expression of the negative side of modernity. Natsume Sōseki (1867–1916), who believed there was nothing more typical of twentieth-century civilization in its contempt for individuality than the train, wrote in 1906:

> Whenever I see the violent way in which a train runs along, indiscriminately regarding all human beings as so much freight, I look at the individuals cooped up in the carriages, and at the iron monster itself . . . and I think, 'Look out, look out, or you'll find yourselves in trouble.' The railway train which blunders ahead blindly into pitch darkness is one example of the very obvious dangers which abound in modern civilisation. (Natsume Sōseki 1865: 181)

The geographer David Harvey argues that the sensuous qualities of space representation within the 'enduring' time of pre-modern ages were eliminated by the objectivity and rationalization of modernity (Harvey 1989: 240). Within the same framework, according to Schivelbusch, the railway network deprived the traveler of a holistic perception, reducing the position of the individual to that of passive observer. The aversion towards the railway is followed by an apotheosis of the 'sensual' character of preindustrial modes of perception and representation. Traveling by railway is considered to have 'annihilated' the traditional space-time continuum which characterized an old transport technology 'organically embedded in nature' (Schivelbusch 1979: 45). The traveler-walker (voyager) had once perceived space in its duration (*durée*, or time understood not as an objective mathematical unity but as subjective perception) as a living entity. De Certeau (1925–86) praises 'walking practices' as 'pedestrian speech acts,' contrary to the railway, which is considered 'a speculative experience of the world,' 'a module of imprisonment that makes possible the production of an order' (De Certeau 1984: 97–111). Therefore a set of antithetical polarities is being assumed: walker versus railway traveler, tradition versus modernity, natural versus artificial, continuous versus fragmented, sensual versus rational, individualistic versus massive, intensity versus abstraction, be there versus be nowhere. In what follows, I will suggest that most of the negative characteristics that have been commonly attributed to the mechanized mode of railway travel may be seen to originate, at least in Japan, in the structure and representation of traveling of the pre-railway era.

As historians have indicated, the borders between the Tokugawa period and the Meiji era are not clear-cut, and a fusion of ideas and forms may be easily detected (Jansen and Rozman 1986; Jinnai 1995). Therefore, besides seeking analogies or contrasts between forms, one should also observe the changing ideological framework within which seemingly unchanged forms are being inserted, and consequently detect the 'mobility' of their meaning. In order to proceed to such a comparison, we will consider two interrelated issues: first, the changing relations between producing bodies (map-makers, art market, organizers of infrastructure, commercial agencies) and observers (users, consumers, potential or physical travelers) from one era to the other; and secondly, the connections between representation and the wider epistemological and socio-political framework within which it operates. Although the railway traveler perceives the time and space of a journey in a manner undoubtedly different from the walker, we should also be aware of the fact that the history of representation does not necessarily correspond to the history of vision and might have little to do with the actual field of perception or 'physical reality.'[3] Rather it is related to symbolic sources and procedures that mediate between regulations upon space and practices within space, the notion of space being apprehended as a material, a mental and a social field (Lefebvre 1991: 11–12).

The present inquiry will proceed through the following steps. It begins by distinguishing between the spatial perception of popular and official maps of the Tokugawa period, trying to detect the different meanings that space and traveling acquired reflecting the interests of different social classes. By examining a wide range of travel artifacts of the Tokugawa period, I will deconstruct established preconceptions according to which the walker enjoys a sensuous, holistic spatial appreciation in contrast to the railway traveler who perceives space in fragments. Similar characteristics can be detected in most examples of visual and literary representation of traveling in the popular arts of the Tokugawa period, and therefore they should not be regarded as results of technological modes of mobility. In discussing rail travel in the Meiji era, I will suggest that there are two major types of cartographic representation: railway charts, which are based on spatial abstraction, and geographical railway maps, which are based on geographical precision. We will see that both systems of representation (railway charts and railway maps) participate within the modern economic restructuring of 'abstract space,' within which geographical precision plays much more than a symbolic role. This can be related to Japan's position on the international political scene rather than solely to the technical demands of representing the operation of the railway system. I will conclude by suggesting that the analogies of forms which can be detected between Tokugawa and Meiji road maps do not entail analogies in ideology. If Tokugawa-period popular production is related to the narrative qualities of a cultural landscape that I will argue is fragmented and discontinuous, in the Meiji era cartography is based on a totalizing system of measurable observations idealized by the modern state.

Road Maps in the Tokugawa Period

The maps of the Tokugawa period displayed a high degree of accuracy. They were initially made by means of traditional surveying methods learned from China, supplemented by so-called *nanban* (Spanish and Portuguese) techniques, and the help of instruments that had been introduced from Europe before Japan's period of seclusion. Around the middle of the eighteenth century, *rangaku*, the study of Western sciences through Dutch scholarship, developed and was often tapped into by the government. Maps of the Tokugawa period are divided into five categories according to the scale of the region represented: national maps of the whole country (*teizenzu* or *Nihon sōzu*), domain maps (*kuni ezu*), regional maps (*chihōzu*), city maps (*toshizu*), and road maps (*dōchūzu*). The maps of the whole country were based on separate domain maps, ordered by the Tokugawa from each province. During the Tokugawa period they were revised four times. Revisions were necessary to meet changes in geographical or man-made features and social and political changes.[4] Domain maps showed the geographical demarcation of provinces and districts. They indicated villages, which were represented by small oval shapes (*muragata*), together with the indication of total village production (*muradaka*); topographical features such as rivers, seas, lakes, swamps; and man-made works, such as castles, shrines, temples, inns, and roads. Those maps did not include depictions of ordinary buildings and houses, a type of data that appeared in road and city maps. They provided however the base for much of the information that was necessary in order to produce all other maps.[5] Road maps followed the *heikō chokusen shiki* (parallel method), a method which lined up all highways down the length of Japan as parallel straight lines with connections routes (Wattenberg 1988: 58).

In the Tokugawa period, road maps of the country's five main highways, the *gokaidō*, were an important instrument for administration and military security and a practical tool for official traveling. Road maps can, therefore, be broadly divided into two categories, the official and the popular. Among official travel-related artifacts we should consider maps and other material patronized by the emperor, the shogun, or *daimyō* (provincial lords). The travels of the *daimyō*, under the *sankin kōtai* policy, required precise road maps with information on roadside facilities such as the location of inns, resting places, and sharp turns in the road, similar to the ones described by Bodart-Bailey in her chapter in this book. Like other artifacts produced for officials in the political conditions of the Tokugawa period, such maps were drawn, stored, and positioned in an extremely careful manner reflecting the authority and power of the owner and viewer.

During the Tokugawa period, the Tōkaidō, being the busiest road in the country, appeared in the public consciousness as a ground of escape, play, and release from the repression of everyday life. The Tōkaidō became the subject of numerous popular maps, guidebooks, humorous narratives, and *ukiyo-e* prints. These were not only meant to facilitate traveling but also included pictorial or fictional forms that used traveling as their subject matter. It is worth bearing in mind in this context the transformation of the *ukiyo-e* and the culture of traveling from an autonomous, potentially subversive, popular expression in the Genroku era (1688–1704) into what can be characterized as a mass culture by the end of the Tokugawa period.[6] Road maps of the Tōkaidō were produced in various formats including screens, fans, plates, games, mirrors, cases, or kimono. In addition to practical information, maps of the Tōkaidō included famous places (*meisho*) that lay along the road and had been celebrated since the classical era in literary and visual arts, such as Tago-no-ura, Miho-no-matsubara, Yatsuhashi, Nakayama, Utsunoyama/Tsuta-no-hosomichi.[7] Given the limits of this chapter, we will focus on selected map examples. However, we should bear in mind that this material belongs to a much broader matrix of travel-related artifacts that started as schematic diagrams (*dōchūki*), which as the popularity of travel developed, were integrated more and more with genres of both pictures and fiction.

The origin of all travel artifacts was the *dōchūki*, a linear, diagrammatic book format that followed the itinerary of the road. The first two *dōchūki* were published in 1655 and 1659.[8] *Dōchūki* mentioned the names of towns, villages, and post-stations and the distances between them, rates for horses, prices of inns, and the names of post-station administrators (*ton'ya*), who were appointed by the Tokugawa. More detailed *dōchūki* listed important landmarks, names of *daimyō*, tips for travelers, as well as legends and historical information about each locality (Bresler 1975: 135). A development of the *dōchūki* was the *dōchūzu*, which was elaborated in a pictorial manner and often contained additional pictures or charts (*zu*), indicating visual or practical information (for example, high and low tides and rates charged at inns). *Dōchūki* were produced in a variety of shapes: oblong booklets opening horizontally; accordion-like, folding maps; single folded sheets; and fan-shaped maps. The style in which they were drawn could be schematic (usually based on frames that corresponded to the sequence of post-stations) or it could be a continuous sketch of scenery. The orientation of the *dōchūki* was not fixed and reflected various symbolic systems of the Tokugawa period, or simply practical necessities. There were numerous systems of orientation used at the time.[9] The most relevant to the case of the Tōkaidō (a road running east-west) is the orientation system that refers to the cosmology of the east-west axis. According to Buddhist beliefs, the west is the direction of heaven (the Pure Land), and therefore important places were positioned on the left-hand side. In Tōkaidō itineraries, Kyoto is positioned on the left, not only because of its location west of Edo, but also because it was revered as an important place. Later *dōchūki* abandoned the 'linear method' and became precise geographical maps of Japan, but in general most *dōchūki* positioned the itinerary in diverse layouts that neglected the system of geographical coordinates. *Dōchūki* usually included one or two highways, but sometimes included the whole highway system of the country indicating the points of intersection.

Tōkaidō bunken ezu

The *Tōkaidō bunken ezu* (Proportional map of the Tōkaidō) was a woodblock-printed *dōchūzu* map with high pictorial elaboration that included elements of a guidebook. According to Cortazzi, it derived from an official map of 1651 made by Hōjō Ujinaga (1609–70) (Cortazzi 1983: 33).[10] The map's first edition in 1690 was drawn at a scale of 1:12,000 and was published by Hangiya Shichirōbee (dates unknown) in Edo (Matsumoto 1977: 5). The map was divided into five folded volumes and its total length was about thirty-seven metres. The pictorial illustrations were made by the *ukiyo-e* artist Hishikawa Moronobu (d. 1694). Although the first publication was entitled *Tōkaidō kōmoku bunken no zu* (Proportional map of the Tōkaidō in detail) (fig. 35), the numerous reprints of the map that followed carried the name *Tōkaidō bunken ezu*. The first version of the map clearly follows the division of the 53 stations. The post-stations are identified through a label carrying their name, the name of the *ton'ya* and travel charges,[11] and a schematic representation of row-houses in the area of the post-stations but not in the cities. Other place-names, tea-houses (*chaya*), temples and shrines are merely marked without further elaboration. Not all shrines and temples along the route are noted, only the most famous or those known to the map-makers. The map also includes geographical elements (such as mountains and rivers), as well as trees planted by the *bakufu* (the shogunal administration), which are distinguished by kind: pine trees (*matsu*; *Pinus densiflora* Sieb. and Zucc.), Japanese cypress (*hinoki*; *Chamaecyparis obtusa* Endl.), and hackberry trees (*enoki*; *Celtis sinensis* Pers.). The distances between the stations, length of bridges, and positions of mile-markers (*ichirizuka*) are accurate, as well as the directions.[12] Square blocks with the four points of the compass were drawn for each major area of the map.[13]

The map combines precise geographical description with vigorous details of life. The illustrations added by Moronobu transform the map into a vivid pictorial demonstration of the culture of traveling in the Tokugawa period. Such illustrations focus on the celebrated 'floating' aspects of the culture of the road, elements which are ephemeral and changeable. The map depicts various types of travelers along the road, including *daimyō* processions and commoners traveling back and forth, as well as incidents for which the Tōkaidō was well known in popular culture. The map also depicts meteorological conditions such as the Ōi river in flood, snow on Mount Fuji, and rain in Hara. A major difference between this map and our

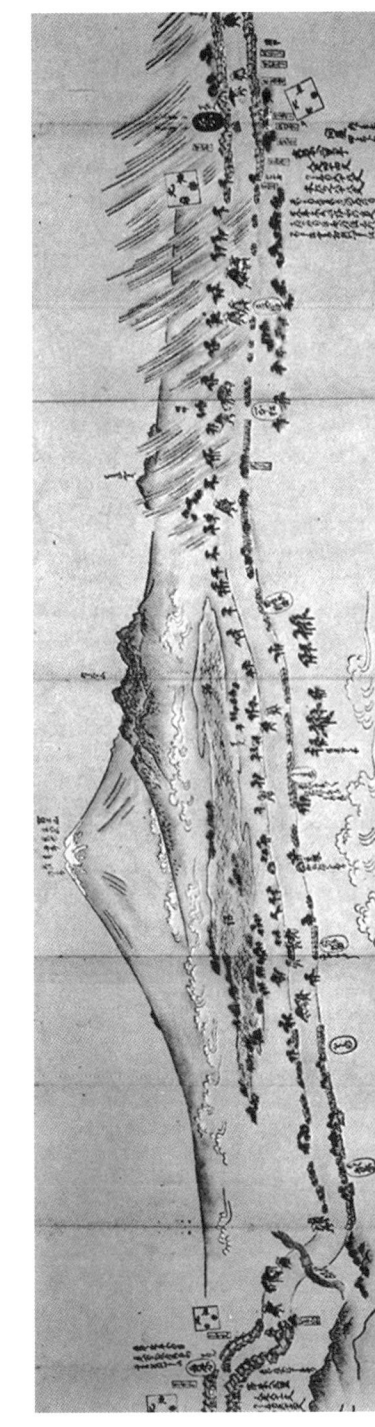

Figure 35 Ichikochi Dōin and Hishikawa Moronobu, 'Tōkaidō kōmoku bunken no zu' (Proportional map of the Tōkaidō in detail), Hara, 1690, detail of woodblock print, hand color, folded book, 5 volumes, cover page 26.7 x 14.9 cm (Courtesy of Tokyo National Museum).

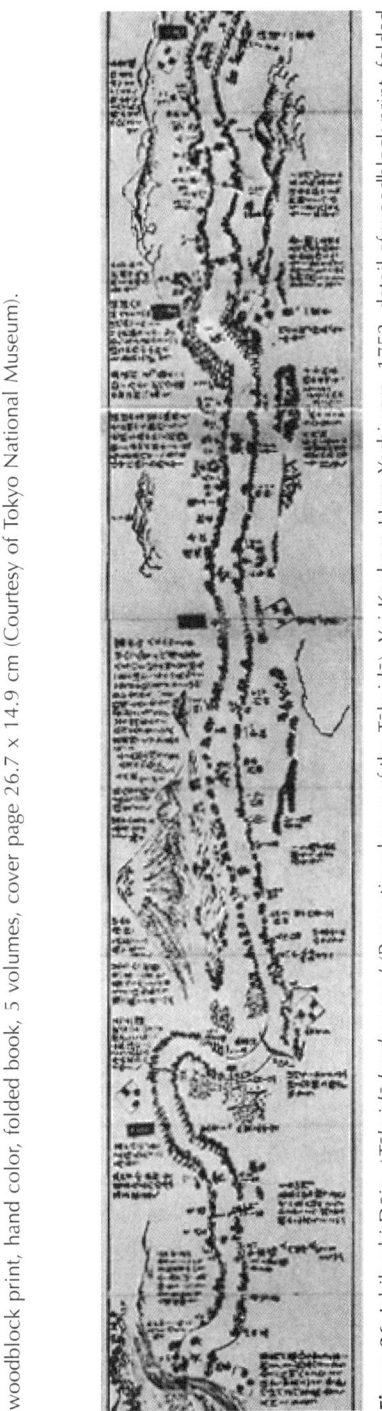

Figure 36 Ichikochi Dōin, 'Tōkaidō bunken ezu' (Proportional map of the Tōkaidō), Yui-Kanbara-Hara-Yoshiwara, 1752, detail of woodblock print, folded book, 1 volume, cover page, 15.7 x 9.3 cm (Courtesy of Tokyo National Museum).

contemporary geographical standards is the depiction of certain elements more than once. As Nitschke has remarked, Mount Fuji appears more than ten times on the map in spots from which it is visible (Nitschke 1993: 55). To this we should add the repeated appearance of Mount Ōyama, famous in the popular mythology of Edo. This view represents an understanding of space that is different from the Cartesian one, according to which each element is represented in a single location upon the map. The representation of *Tōkaidō bunken ezu* incorporates aspects of topological space according to which the spatial qualities remain unaltered even if geometrical attributes change.

If we make a more detailed inquiry into the spots where Mount Fuji has been depicted, we realize that the selection of these places has not necessarily been based on the actual experience of the artist, but most of these views appear in previous representations well known to the public. These spots should rather be interpreted through the poetic legacy of the famous places rather than as records of traveling. The significance of the *meisho* becomes more obvious in the later version of *Tōkaidō bunken ezu* published in 1752 (fig. 36). Besides scale and other differences that were meant to please the traveler, this version assumed a more decorative manner.[14] While the first version is determined by the space division of the post-station system and simply contains toponymies, the second version is enriched with a plethora of non-practical information that introduces the cultural landscape of the Tōkaidō. It incorporates comments, *haiku*, and short stories that relate to the famous places of the route rather than just the stations.

As a result of representations of famous places that lie in proximity to the road, the travelers are reminded of places that they know from poems, paintings, and history. By celebrating such localities, the spatial journey becomes a journey into national time. Such places punctuate the landscape of Japan, not being familiar through actual viewing but through poetic memory and preexisting knowledge. As Katō Kunio has remarked, there is a double projection taking place through such conventions: at the same moment, 'we are going to the landscape, while the landscape is coming to us. This double projection makes us dwell,' bridging the perceptual with the cognitive, individual experience with collective knowledge (Katō 1997). The prevalence of the *meisho* in the popular culture of the Tokugawa period can be understood as a result of the movement of National Learning (*kokugaku*), in which the nation was comprehended through its historical continuity since the ancient era. According to Konishi, the idea of the *meisho* originates from the ancient age of Japanese literature (604 to 905), when the Emperor and his courtiers traveled to important places in order to perform the ritual of *kunimi*, beholding the country (Konishi 1984: 238). During the Middle Ages (1185–1573), the privileged traveler changed from the aristocrat to the Buddhist ascetic, who searched for aesthetic satisfaction, and finally in the Tokugawa period to the commoner, who searched for escape from feudal repression and used the pilgrimage as a pretext for traveling. The appropriation of *meisho* within the hedonistic culture of *ukiyo-e* commercialized them and related them with new places of fame. The brothels of places like Akasaka, described by Bodart-Bailey in her chapter, and Mishima were now described as *meisho* and entered the pages of guidebooks such as the *Tōkaidō meisho zue* (Illustrations of the Famous Places of the Tōkaidō; 1797) by Akisato Ritō. On the other hand, previously respected localities were now mocked and parodied, especially in works of late Tokugawa popular literature such as Jippensha Ikku's *Tōkaidōchū hizakurige* (By shank's mare along the Tōkaidō; 1802–21).

Besides such perceptions of landscape as text, as a narrative of Japanese cultural continuity, history, and mythology, there is a further tendency that we can observe in some of the landscape representations of the Tokugawa period. This is the perception of space as a visually grasped reality, a realm of observation, that is different from what is simply known or contemplated. This is related to the comprehension of the land as a terrain of productivity, development, and progress, and has to be seen in connection with the broader political and epistemological framework of the end of the Tokugawa period. The political conditions of the Tokugawa period necessitated the detailed recording not only of history but also of space, including the national borders and the interior structure of the country.[15] Next we will view a map of the Tōkaidō made by the shogunal authorities in the early nineteenth century, visualizing survey data that derive from the actual field rather than from received readings and conventions.

Tōkaidō bunken nobe ezu

Both versions of the *Tōkaidō bunken ezu* differ greatly from the official maps drawn for administrative purposes. The *Tōkaidō bunken nobe ezu* (Proportional linear map of the Tōkaidō) (fig. 37) is such an official map. It was a part of the *Gokaidō sono hoka bunken mitori nobe ezu* (Proportional linear maps of the Gokaidō), which included the whole *gokaidō* system in separate volumes.[16] It was produced by the *bakufu* office for roads (*bakufu dōchū bugyōsho*) in 1806 and was drawn to the scale of 1:1800. The decision to produce this *gokaidō* map was taken in 1800. The information was collected through a primary survey of the condition of the roads, and at the same time a separate book about each post-station was prepared. The Nakasendō, which ran through the mountains of central Japan, was the first road to be surveyed, while the research for the Tōkaidō started in 1802. The surveys proceeded in parallel. In 1843, the research was repeated in order to compare the changes between these periods, registering the population and number of houses at each post-station.[17] The *bakufu* ordered that no shrine, temple, river, or bridge should be excluded and that not even farmers' houses should be overlooked, covering an area that went beyond the strict

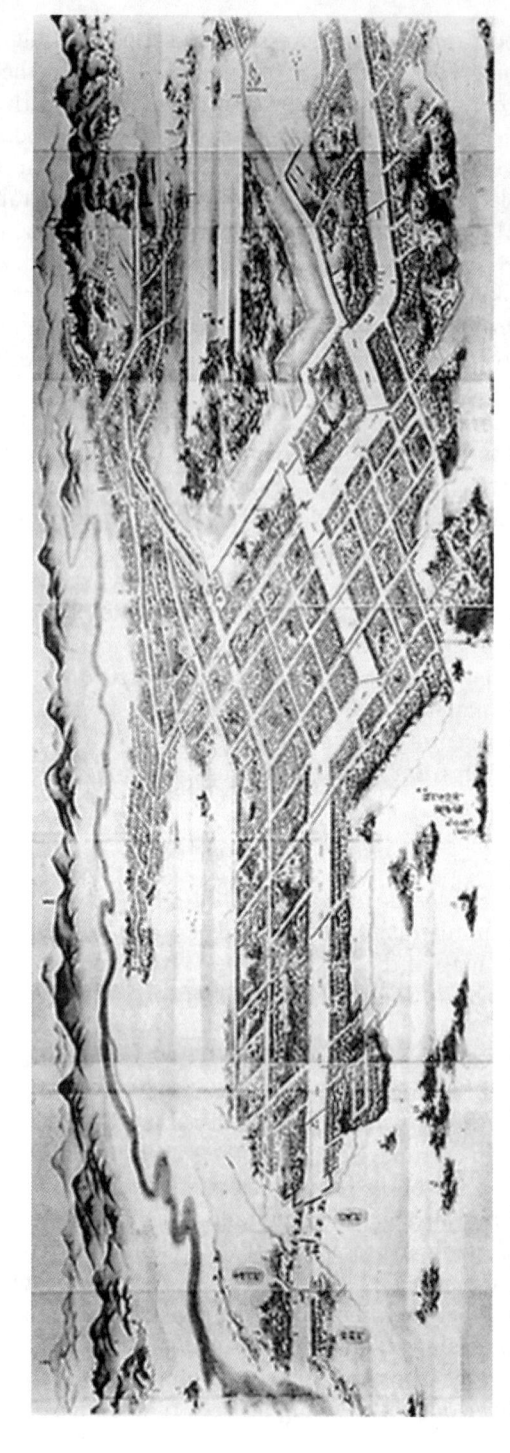

Figure 37 Bakufu Dōchū Bugyōsho (Magistrate of the Bakufu), 'Tōkaidō bunken nobe ezu' (Proportional linear map of the Tōkaidō), Fuchū, 1806, hand color on paper, detail, 60.1 × 2546 cm (Courtesy of Tokyo National Museum).

limits of the road. It is obvious that the intentions of this project much exceeded the function of the usual road maps, which were meant to facilitate the journey of the *daimyō*. There were three original copies of these maps, one kept in Edo Castle and the other two by the *bakufu* officer for roads. The restricted usage of these maps makes for a sharp contrast with the numerous reproductions of the popular maps discussed above.

Tōkaidō bunken nobe ezu is a precise topographical map, a land survey drawn in a consistent codified manner, including both iconography and texts. The manner of drawing is basically on a plane, but the map includes many iconographic symbols drawn in elevation or schematic axonometric views with exaggerated proportions. The depiction of the Tōkaidō itself is just such an exaggeration, since it is drawn much wider than it actually is, making it look disproportionately large in comparison to bridges or rivers. Special attention is given to the right-angle turns in the road in the approaches to post-stations and castle-towns, a technique used for defense and screening purposes and discussed in her chapter by Bodart-Bailey. Iconographic symbols denote architectural typologies (shrines, temples, castles, houses), topographical features (trees, fields), and elements in the road infrastructure such as bridges or mile-markers. Three types of bridge are shown: stone, wood, and earth. The names of the post-stations and the distances between them, the location of hotels for the *daimyō* (*honjin*) and their followers (*waki honjin*), and the location of the offices of the *ton'ya* (*ton'ya ba*) are marked precisely.

Political maps use size and symbolism as a means of imposing their authority, while at the same time important information is concealed for reasons of military security. In *Tōkaidō bunken nobe ezu*, shogunal properties – for example, Fuchū Castle (in present-day Shizuoka Prefecture) – appear larger than they do in other maps, while details within the castle are covered under the conventional cloud technique. The viewers of this map were shoguns and administrators, thus the emphasis is not on the practical aspects of traveling but on a high degree of accuracy regarding particular spatial information: visibility, exact demarcation of the road and turns, positioning of landmarks, and the structure of bridges. All the above information was particularly critical not only for administration but also in the case of war. The whole series of *gokaidō* maps, as well as most of the official scroll-maps, were made with hand-painted additions in colour, which was done in a proper manner according to the high status of the viewers. Their elaboration is very detailed and refined and is obviously a product of team work that included a large number of artists.

Narrative Itineraries – Territorial Maps

The Japanese terrain is usually depicted as a coherent landscape of rivers and hills, united by the passage of highways. However, the method employed in each of these maps in order to achieve this coherence is significantly different. In *Tōkaidō bunken ezu* the road is floating on the surface of the map and functions as a narrative device. It lacks the grounded character that the second map has due to its being drawn in a combination of a plan and axonometric view. The road is drawn in the foreground, being a territory of its own, with its distinct character and life. In *Tōkaidō bunken nobe ezu*, the territory is a spatial continuum that is not limited to the strict borders of the road. Such national unification had been a matter for dispute and conflict in the past. During the Momoyama period (1575–1603), before the centralization implemented by the *bakufu*, the roads were intentionally abandoned as a means of securing the borders between different domains, and high tolls were imposed at the barriers.

One of the novelties of the Tokugawa regime was road unification and maintenance. The *daimyō* processions to and from Edo down the highways that crossed different provinces were a symbolic reminder of the pragmatic policy of the centralization of power in Edo. In a similar manner, road maps, besides their function as traveling tools, can be viewed as campaigns to reinforce the image of unification between different provinces whose borders are not drawn in any of these maps. Despite their diversity, therefore, both maps are making a claim for unification. This unification in *Tōkaidō bunken ezu* is realized through the creation of the image of a woven-into-myth landscape that binds the major geo-cultural symbols in a coherent narrative reinforcing the collective consciousness of Japanese history. *Tōkaidō bunken nobe ezu*, on the other hand, has a strictly territorial objective and is the product of a survey. The differences between the two maps are, therefore, mainly a consequence of the different objectives of the institutions that produced them.

These differences can be expressed through Michel de Certeau's distinction between maps and itineraries. According to de Certeau, a map is a 'plane projection' that reflects 'totalizing views from above,' while an itinerary is a 'discursive series of operations' and expresses the movement of bodies in the realm below (de Certeau 1984: 119). *Tōkaidō bunken nobe ezu* is a map produced through observation of the structures from above, namely the scientific and governmental authorities of the time. It also presents and preserves the established order and law, the grid of administration, and infrastructural regulations. *Tōkaidō bunken ezu*, however, although also drawn as a panoramic view derived from the cartographic data of a governmental map, subverts any objective of surveillance and incorporates elements that negate any governmental intent. This map functions as the mental itinerary of a collective traveler rather than as a record of an 'immobilized totality' seen from above. In it, the Tōkaidō is not a political territory but a 'field of practices' realized by the travelers. Mythical, historical, and bodily time coexist upon the same surface. Therefore, while the domain of *Tōkaidō bunken nobe ezu* is strategic, based on accuracy and observation, the domain of *Tōkaidō bunken ezu* is that of bodily perception and collective memory. Despite its illustrative character, *Tōkaidō bunken ezu* should not be considered a pictorial work. Its illustrations have a schematic character, and its format remains diagrammatic despite its elaboration. Although it includes pictorial elements, it does not cease being a *dōchūki*, a topological diagram that assumes a variety of linear forms. On the other hand, *Tōkaidō bunken nobe ezu*'s iconographical qualities are products of measurability, an aspect that is closer to our contemporary cartographic definition.

Panorama

If both the above road maps had to be approached in a sequential order, as texts rather than as images, the following picture-maps were meant to be approached in a reverse order: primarily visually, focusing on their macroscale, and only secondarily as texts, focusing on their micro-scale. This approach was inspired by the increasing interest of artists in a combination of views: first, a realistic representation based on the capacities of the human eye, which from a distant viewpoint can afford a macroscopic perspective; and secondly, the illusionist possibilities created by the use of magnifying lenses, such as telescopes, that expanded the eye's capabilities to penetrate into the microcosm of life within its separate parts. Such combinations succeeded in a remarkable transformation of the traditional Japanese preoccupation with detail, which can be seen in the screens of the capital (Kyoto) and its surroundings (*rakuchū rakugai zu byōbu*) produced during earlier periods.

In the nineteenth century, most probably based on Kuwagata Keisai's (1764–1824) panoramic view of the whole of Japan, *Nihon meisho no e* (A picture of the famous places of Japan; fig. 40), described by Henry Smith as a 'leap of vision' (Smith 1988: 17), *ukiyo-e* artists produced panoramic topographic images of the whole Tōkaidō. Examples of such panoramic views of the Tōkaidō are Hokusai's (1760–1849) *Tōkaidō meisho ichiran* (Famous places of the Tōkaidō at a glance) drawn in 1818 (fig. 38) and Kuwagata Shōi's (d. 1855) *Tōkaidō saiken ō ezu* (Large picture map with detailed views of the Tōkaidō; fig. 39).[18] None of those panoramic pictures is limited to the post-stations alone. On the contrary, they all mark numerous famous places along the road. Although the panoramic views of the Tōkaidō seem to be using perspective, they actually pay too little attention to the laws of perspective, and even perform major geographical distortions. It is obvious that the use of perspective in them is decorative rather than technical. The panoramic views drawn by Kuwagata Shōi and Hokusai show a particular similarity with Kuwagata Keisai's view in that they represent the topography of Japan in the conventional terms of mountains and an array of tiny settlements, almost 'as a work of landscape art' (Smith 1988: 17). In contrast to the apparent clarity of the horizontal

Memory and the Changing Passage of Space

Figure 38 Hokusai, '*Tōkaidō meisho ichiran*' (Famous places of the Tōkaidō at a glance), woodblock print, Kadomaruya Jinsuke (publisher), 1818, 43 x 58 cm (courtesy of Leiden University, Oriental Collections, ex-Philipp. Franz von Siebold Collection, Ser. 373).

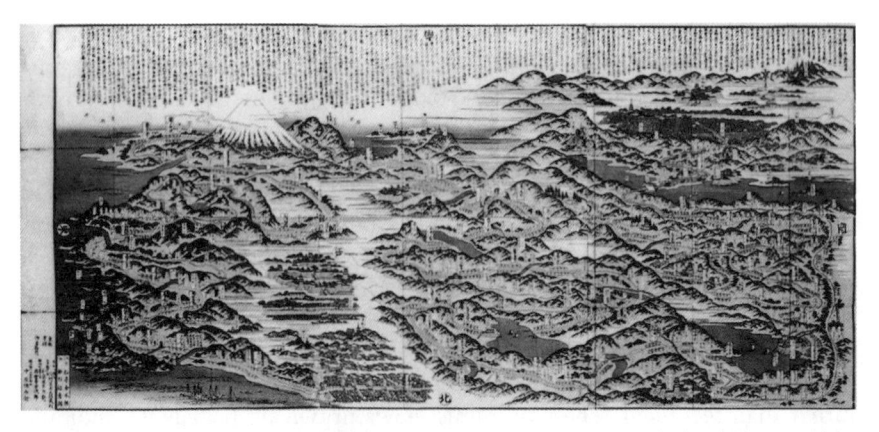

Figure 39 Kuwagata Shōi, '*Tōkaidō saiken ōezu*', (Large picture map with detailed views of the Tōkaidō), Shōtei Kinsui, mid nineteenth century, 69.8 x 141.5 cm, woodblock color print (courtesy of the Kobe City Museum).

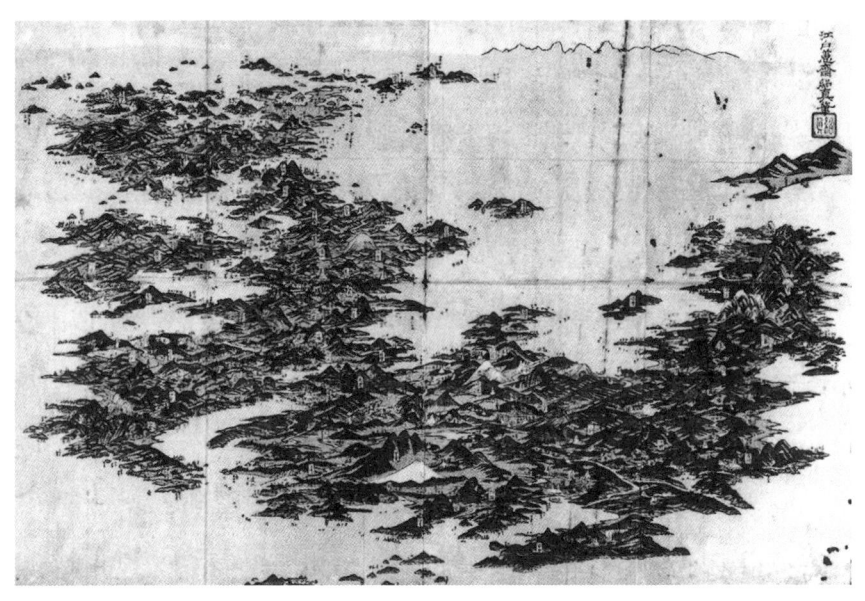

Figure 40 Kuwagata Keisai, '*Nihon meisho no e*' (A picture of the famous places of Japan), early nineteenth century, 39.8 x 57.4 cm, woodblock color print (courtesy of the Kobe City Museum).

scroll maps, they convey the sense of a labyrinthine journey. Although the panoramas of the Tōkaidō are geographically incorrect (distorting topographical features and ignoring geographical coordinates), one cannot overlook the fact that as itineraries they are topologically precise: both the sequence of place-names and the intersection of the road with major points such as bridges and lakes correspond to reality. The artists could without doubt have used the perspective technique (which was already known to them) or simply make a copy of just a part of Kuwagata Keisai's panorama, should they have wanted to be technically precise. The symbolic content of these panoramas is stronger than any attempt to be realistic.

The panoramas of the Tōkaidō, produced after Hokusai's first print series of the route (1812), are a reconciliation of map and picture, text and vision. By creating a hypothetical vista of the whole route at a glance (although unachievable in reality), they superimpose the landscape of the road upon the land(-scape) of the nation. Although issues of national territoriality were not necessarily a direct concern of the artists, a broader climate of increasing national consciousness must have influenced them (see footnote 15). At the same time in those panoramas, the itinerary becomes a microcosm that symbolizes the whole of Japan, while the imaginary journey resembles the labyrinthine layouts of the *sugoroku* games, for which movement in space does not depend of temporal linearity.[19] In spite of their geographical imprecision, and unlike many maps and series of the Tōkaidō in the Tokugawa period, these panoramas include only one depiction of Mount Fuji, which with its eminent, central position connotes symbolically the whole nation. It is possibly through the uniqueness of Mount Fuji that the path towards the uniqueness of Japan as a whole is illuminated.

Aspects of Travel Representation in the Popular Production of the Tokugawa Period

Common characteristics of the representations we have been looking at are the incorporation of a temporal element, the use of multiple orientations, and the fragmentation and distortion of the route based on principles of topological spatial perception rather than geometry. These examples indicate that topographical truthfulness and geographical precision are not essential attributes of the road map function. Moreover, the techniques of fragmentation and distortion of the route do not prevent the conveyance of information necessary for the process of traveling. Such characteristics demonstrate a space perception that is related to topological space. Within such spatial perception, 'one's position relative to the larger, outside world is indiscernible' (Inoue 1985: 145). Despite their differences in shape, all *dōchūki* are, therefore, equivalent to each other, transferring a space perception which in its simplest form can be described as a long unfolding line. This line may be bent, squared, or fragmented without change, while it may also incorporate diverse contents.

Such characteristics can be demonstrated in a number of literal and visual works on the Tōkaidō. Writers of Tokugawa period travel literature such as Jippensha Ikkū in his picaresque novel *Tōkaidōchū hizakurige* scarcely offered any direct descriptions of the landscape, limiting their references to a simple mention of the toponymy and the famous place and products (*meibutsu*) of the route while paying much more attention to descriptions of extravagant episodes, often bearing little relation to their setting. Hiroshige (1797–1858) and other late *ukiyo-e* artists used the pretext of the post-stations' toponymies to introduce diverse subjects varying from precise topographical descriptions to the mention of famous places that did not exist any longer during the Tokugawa period, and even subjects only loosely related to the topography, such as beautiful women (*bijin*) and kabuki actors (*yakusha*).[20] Through such devices as representation of the road in various seasons (as we find in *Tōkaidō bunken ezu* and in Hiroshige's print series) and the absence of plot in comic popular culture of the Tokugawa period, traveling is captured and portrayed in terms of the pursuit of the illusory, the otherworldly, and the legendary rather than through a 'holistic' appreciation of a 'real' landscape perceived directly by the sensory organs of the traveler. Despite the significance that the body acquired in Tokugawa period popular art, spatial representation is not based on the subjective, visual perception of the artist-traveler. Even when landscape is depicted in pictorial form (for example, in the landscapes with figures), it is still often viewed from selected codified spots, most of which are famous places rather than views that derive from observation or direct experience.

Besides the mythological subtext of space, we can detect an emerging consciousness of spatial characteristics that derive from a visually grasped landscape, the perception of the national land as a terrain of productivity and the growth of geographical knowledge that became widespread by the end of the Tokugawa period, a source of material for landscape artists.[21] Those diverse layers of spatial perception can be found to a different degree incorporated in most of the representations of the Tōkaidō in the late Tokugawa period, deriving either from the official or the popular arts. Such characteristics should be attributed not only to an increase in traveling and the direct experience of the artists but also to a growing consciousness of 'nation' within the international environment of the nineteenth century. On the other hand, while traveling within a popular cultural milieu became synonymous with an act of escape or even political resistance, by the end of the period the commercialization of travel and the role of religious co-fraternities in providing an infrastructure for travelers paved the way for the regulation of traveling under new, normative procedures.[22] During the subsequent Meiji era, not only was the realm of mythology within travel subordinated within an objectified, geographical reality, but also a new division was imposed with regard to the agents of representation. With this, representation, as well as space itself, became a tool of ideology.

Railway Maps in the Meiji Era

In the Meiji era, the railways facilitated not only the economic and military restructuring of Japan but also the promotion of new, westernized tourist models. New modes of traveling were promoted by both state-sponsored applications (infrastructure) and private initiatives (the building of hotels, advertizing, organizing tourist offices such as The Welcome Society of Japan).[23] With this, traveling was appropriated by official ideology and lost any subversive potential that it had retained as a part of the popular culture of the Tokugawa period.[24] The Meiji state's endorsement of modernity produced not only a division of disciplines and institutions that dealt with distinct aspects of the state's operation, but each of them used diverse systems of representation and scientific or artistic languages. The development of distinct disciplines such as geography, cartography, ethnography, and the arts, each of which had its own methodology and scope, facilitated the division of travel-related production into categories non-existent in the Tokugawa period, when a fusion of forms was predominant. Each of the established categories was addressed to different audiences and facilitated different functions: maps, guide-books, multi-colored woodblock prints (*nishiki-e*), applied arts, Western-style painting (*yōga*), Japanese-style

Memory and the Changing Passage of Space

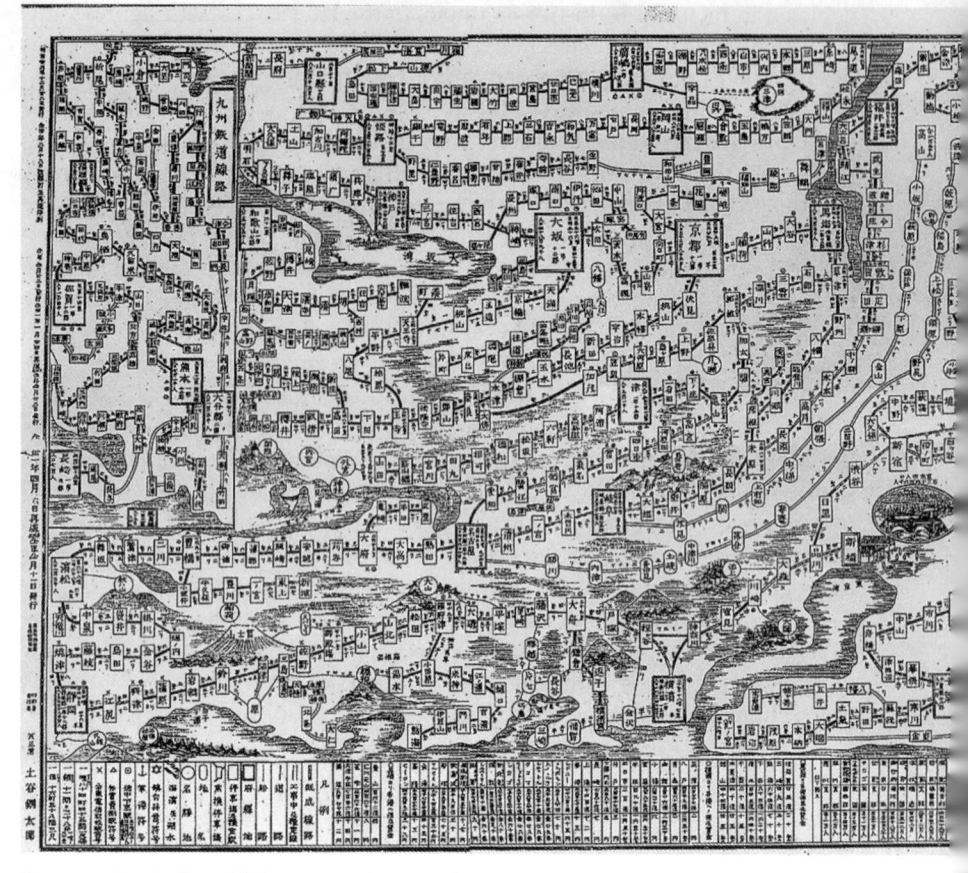

Figure 41 Tenshodō (Publisher), '*Tetsudō senro chinsen ritei hyō*' (Railway distances and fares chart), 189? 35 x 76.3 cm (courtesy of the Tenri University Sankōkan Museum).

painting (*nihonga*), caricatures, and so on. As a result, the realm of 'popular culture' was greatly altered. What was previously described as popular culture gradually entered the sphere of mass culture, being controlled by the new railway or tourist authorities, advertizing scientific and engineering achievements, and being used for commercial ends. Art became the preserve of artistic and cultural circles, galleries, and fine arts schools, while mass culture became a means for consumption and the propagation of a national ideology, mediating between the realms of authorities-producers on the one hand and populace-consumers on the other.

Mapping under the new Meiji government (although largely based on major cartographic developments of the Tokugawa period and in particular the cartographic achievements of Inō Tadataka [1745–1818]) was realized by three independent agencies: the Geographical Bureau of the Home

190

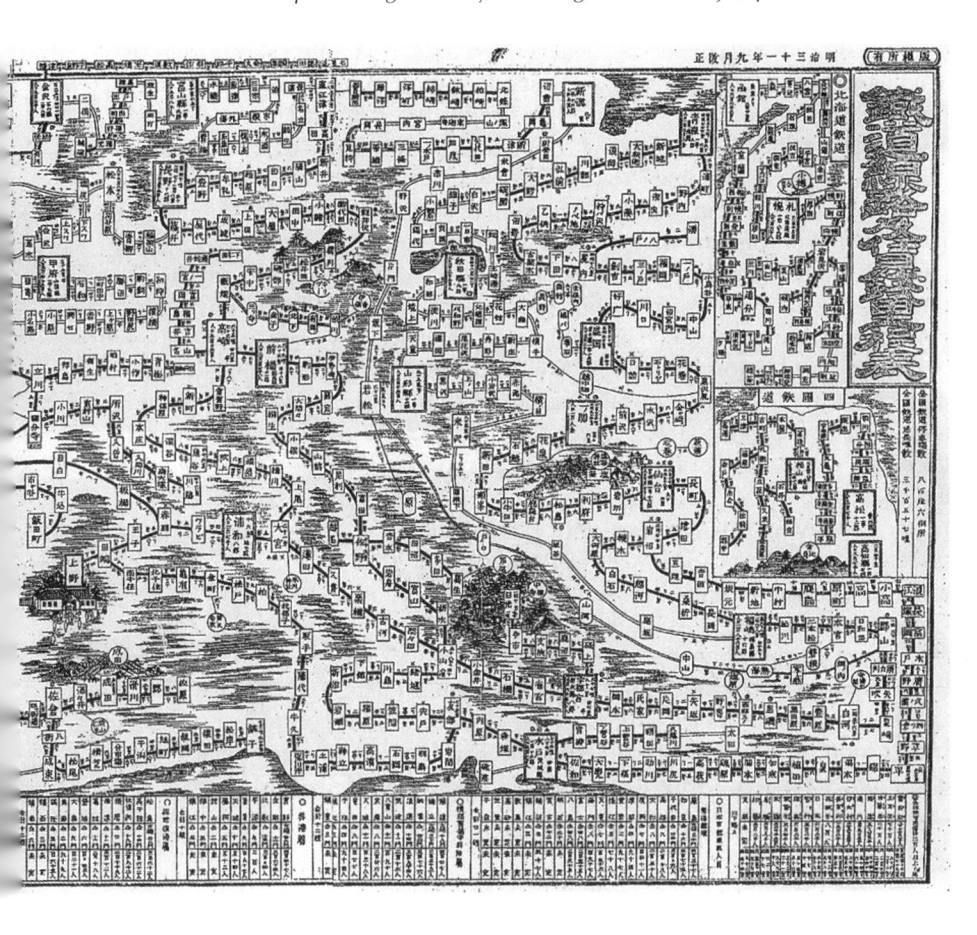

Ministry, established in 1874 and responsible for making cadastral maps at a scale of 1:600 in 1877 showing land use and tenure (*chikenzu*); the Land Survey Department of the Army, which started work in 1869; and the Hydrographic Department of the Navy, established in 1855.[25] If in the Tokugawa period, travel maps functioned as both practical traveling tools and symbolic representations that were part of the broader *ukiyo-e* culture, in the Meiji era, travel maps were mainly produced by state institutions (the railway company and subsidiary tourist offices) and thus reflected official national ideals. In what follows, we will review two railway map typologies that were developed due to the particular technological and political context of the Meiji era. I will call the first railway charts, in order to highlight their attention to measurement, and the second geographical railway maps, in order to emphasize their relation to precise geographical descriptions.

This should not make us believe however that influences from the Tokugawa period's cartographic and iconographic system were abandoned. On the contrary, not only in the Meiji era but even much later in the early Shōwa era in the 1930s, popular road maps were still based on Tokugawa models. At the same time, Tokugawa-style cartography was repositioned within the new system, so that it signified what was considered uniquely Japanese in contrast to what was seen as foreign, connoting thereby ethical national elements rather than progress and science. Therefore, despite the undoubted changes brought about by the new state, we should not neglect persisting continuities. Such examples can be viewed in small-scale railway maps produced before the completion of the Tōkaidō railway line, in maps that combined railway and highway routes, and in a plethora of graphic arts material, produced for advertizing and other commercial purposes (tickets, posters, signs). It is also important to note that the Tōkaidō – now a railway line as well as a road – continued to appear as the exclusive theme of Meiji railway maps, at least until about 1890, often indicating points of intersection between those parts of the railway that had been completed and the highways, still the preserve of those traveling on foot and of horse-carried vehicles. This is understandable, not only as a vestige of the Tokugawa cartographic practice of depicting single routes but also because the Tōkaidō was the first railroad constructed in Japan. Indeed, most of the railway maps that depict only the Tōkaidō, which was completed in 1889, were produced before the completion of other lines. However soon after the development of a railway network, the Tōkaidō appears less often as the exclusive theme of railway cartography.

a. Railway Charts

The railway charts indicate the itineraries of railway lines and their points of intersection in a diagrammatic manner that disregards the geographical characteristics of the Japanese territory, such as its overall shape, topography, coordinates, and the actual distances between locations. These charts are composed as labyrinthine arrangements of an elastic railroad network whose deformed shape is difficult to explain. An example of such an odd arrangement can be seen in the railway chart showing times and fares 'Tetsudō senro chinsen ritei hyō' (Railway distances and fares chart), produced in 1898 (fig. 41 above). This chart distorts the railway routes as well as the (hypothetical) map of Japan, which is presumed to form a background to the railway network. This distortion can be clearly understood if we focus our attention on the relative positioning of places such as Kyoto and Tokyo. Their positioning in this chart corresponds to no familiar system of representation. Nor can it be explained by reason of practicality either – as was the case for many *dōchūki* of the Tokugawa period, which for reasons of simplification assumed a linear development. The formal aspects of such

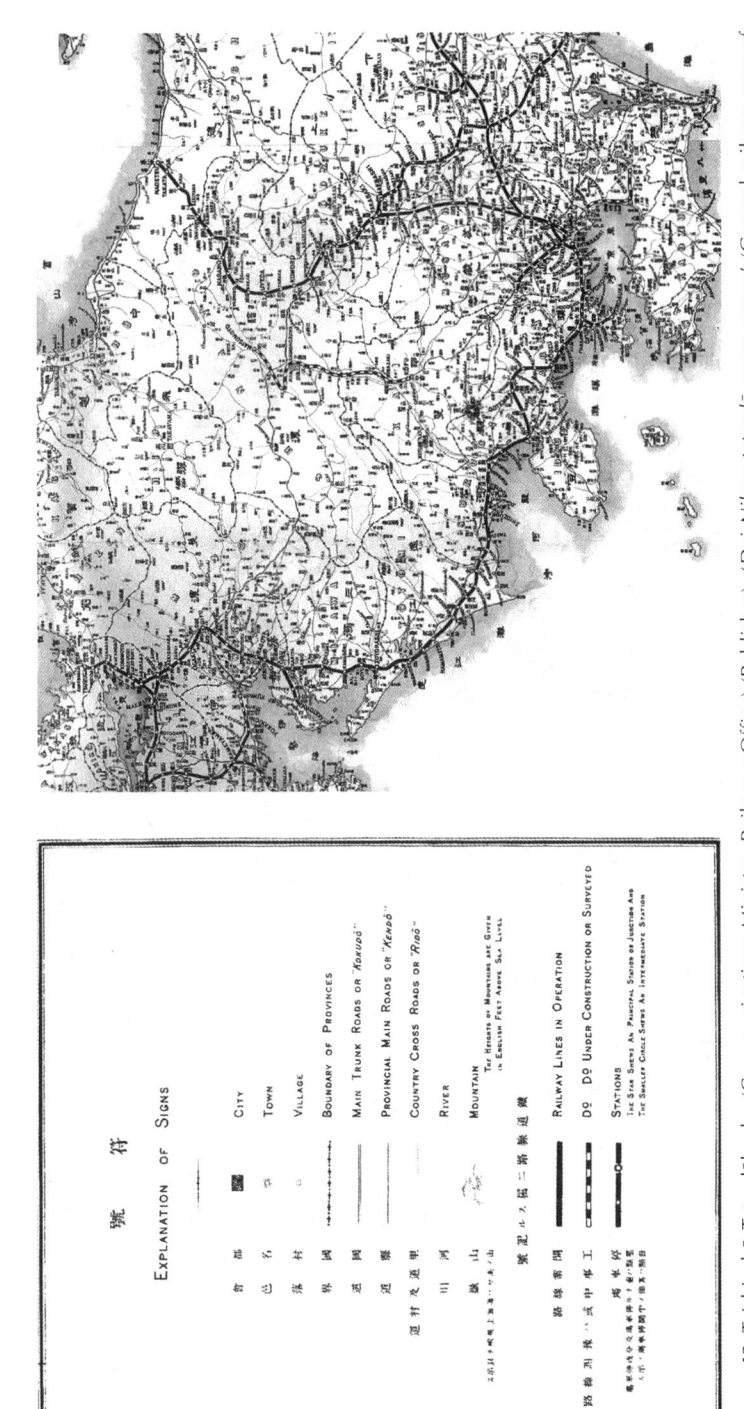

Figure 42 Teishinshō Tetsudōkyoku (Communications Ministry, Railways Office) (Publisher), '*Dai Nihon tetsudō senro zenzu*' (General railway map of Japan), 1902, New Edition (first published 1891), 248 × 88 cm (courtesy of the British Library).

distortions may be reminiscent of arrangements we have noticed in Tokugawa panoramas or *sugoroku* games; they are due however to significantly different symbolic frameworks, as we will see in the sections below.

In the railway charts, the expansion of the land is indicated by the white surface of the paper, while the outline of the Japanese archipelago is not always suggested. Upon the blankness of the paper (which operates as an imperceptible if instantly understood, map of Japan), the railway network functions as the sole figure. However, due to its dense distribution, such a figurative impression is simultaneously negated, and the railway network appears more as a 'second (artificial) ground,' rather than as a figure upon the ground (= land/paper). Thus, it is no surprise that so few topographical and man-made landmarks are to be found on such charts. Rather, the primary function of the charts is to indicate price and time measurements. That is why they are usually followed by a second page where all distances, prices, and measures are codified and illustrated in tables. In contrast to travel in the Tokugawa period, fares are now determined by distance and class division, which corresponds to the social class distinction of the Meiji era.[26] Therefore, the two parts (network and price list) are usually complementary, and the visual quality of the first is converted into the measurable data of the second.

b. Geographical Railway Maps

In contrast to the railway charts, the geographical railway maps represent either the whole of the network or part of it as it is positioned upon the geographical map of Japan. This is done with geometrical precision and attention to the geographical coordinates. These maps are distinguished by their intention to take into consideration the cartographic developments of the time and new knowledge concerning the exact outline of the Japanese archipelago. Some of these maps adopt a decorative character due to their function as travel guides, while others, such as the '*Dai Nihon tetsudō senro zenzu*' (General railway map of Japan; fig. 42 above) adopt a system of signification that is reminiscent of the technical methods used by scientific or military maps.

Railway maps are based on a triple-scale figurative composition: the macro scale, constituted by Japan as a whole or part of it, appearing as a clear shape upon the surface of the paper, and surrounded by sea; the meta scale of the railway network upon the map of Japan; and the micro scale of stations and topographical or urban landmarks. The difference between this type of representation and the charts discussed above is that the railway network in the charts coincides with the ground – indeed could be said to be the only ground – creating its own topological enclosure and ignoring everything else that might exist outside the network. On the contrary, in geographical railway maps, the railway network is represented in accordance with the national territory, which seems still to hold the major significance and is usually represented by naturalistic, iconic elements. As we will see below, besides their geographical precision, these maps show an attention to a system of place classification that is based on the new national hierarchy introduced by the Meiji government, an aspect that cannot be found in the rather homogeneous railway charts. This fact shows that such maps function as media that can imprint in the collective consciousness of Meiji citizens ideas of national hierarchy and differentiation that are important for the operation of the new system.

Representational Character

The symbols and signs used in Meiji era maps adopt many of the graphic elements current in the Tokugawa period such as tags of various shapes and colors (oval, round, rectangular) indicating localities or railway stations according to their size and importance. There is however a difference in the distinctions marked on the maps of each era, as well as in the clarity of their distinction system. In the road maps of the Tokugawa period, we notice the marking of qualitative differences, such as castle-towns (local power), post-stations (centralized authority), barriers, pilgrim sites, routes of various types (major, minor, pilgrimage), as well as selected topographical features (mountains, lakes, and rivers). All these elements are marked as either icons or texts, but are rarely codified in a legend, at least not before the end of the Tokugawa period. Although most of the railway charts of the Meiji era show a relative homogeneity in the signification of different stations, the railway maps of the same era are based on more systematic differences, reflecting the new hierarchical divisions of Meiji geography. Some of the geographical railway maps in particular (such as the one in figure 42) include not only stations and railway lines but also the new administrative classifications of city (*shi*), town (*chō*), and village (*son*) and main trunk road (*kokudō*), provincial main road (*kendō*), and country road (*ridō*). All these distinctions are classified on a legend. On the other hand, topographical elements such as rivers, lakes, and mountains are usually drawn in an iconographical manner – either in elevation or in plane – and are usually not included in the legend.

The representational manner of both railway charts and maps is basically diagrammatic, abandoning the picturesque intentions of earlier *dōchūki*, which showed a continuous topography. This is not to say that iconic elements are not being employed but rather that such elements are superimposed in a clipped, discontinuous manner and are positioned selectively and out-of-scale at the points of major interest. The purpose of railway maps and charts is not to register the full topography of the land, but rather to mark the major landmarks and possible destinations in direct or indirect relation with a network facilitating movement. We can identify three types of iconic element that these maps include, each of which adopts a distinct representational system: urban landmarks, which are usually presented in the form of Western-style vignettes; natural features, such as mountains, lakes, and rivers, drawn pictorially in plan or elevation and usually adopting Tokugawa-period stylistic conventions; and man-made elements, such as bridges, tunnels, and stations, which are considered as achievements of engineering related to railway technology.

On the other hand, we should not fail to notice that besides the major reconstruction of the spatial (geographical) and temporal (historical) structure of Japan during the Meiji era, ideas and preconceptions of the Tokugawa period are still present even within the renovated framework of modernization. We should not be surprised therefore to find toponymies characteristic of Tokugawa-period geography even in official documents of the Meiji era, despite their having been abolished by the new government. Among examples of this are the names of the domains, which often appear in Meiji maps even though they were replaced by newly named prefectures. Moreover, the urban landmarks that are being represented in Meiji maps are often landmarks characteristic of the Tokugawa period or places important within the earlier highway network. These places are a part of the collective memory and therefore difficult to neglect or discard. An example is Nihonbashi, the bridge in Tokyo that had served as the starting point of the five major highways, the *gokaidō*, which remain a feature of many of the railway maps of the Meiji era. However, the starting point of the Tōkaidō railway line in Tokyo was Shinbashi station, which had its own distinctive toponymy. However, it has less significance as a landmark in Tokyo in comparison with the much older bridge, Nihonbashi.

If we attempt to evaluate Tokugawa and Meiji road-maps in terms of their legibility, we must first recognize that none of the maps discussed above fails to transfer adequately the required information. Therefore we cannot talk about improvement of the legibility of these maps from one period to the other. The actual differentiation between the representational systems of Tokugawa and Meiji Japan is not a matter of formal characteristics, but it should rather be sought in the manner that broader socio-political contexts are reflected in the symbolic function of these maps. There are two major characteristics that we will discuss below as the main distinctions between the cartographic material of the two eras. One relates to the issue of abstract space – a result of Japan's adopting the new international standards of modern capitalism – and the other to the use of geography, as a symbolism of a reconfigured national idea.

From Absolute Space to Abstract Space

A major aspect of the railway maps is their emphasis on totalized views and the dependence of each part on the whole. This is a characteristic that can be observed in late Tokugawa period road maps as well. Although most road maps of the Tokugawa period lack a sense of the overall shape of Japan and its geographical coordinates, a change is observable from the early nineteenth century, with an emphasis on the shape of the country as a whole and sometimes even the inclusion of Hokkaido, which does not appear in earlier maps (see note 15). A new emphasis on coastal sites can be observed in such maps, betraying an increasing consciousness of borders and even signs of future imperialism – in the same manner that Renaissance maps during the age of exploration included many more coastal sites and ports than places within the mainland. The transformations from Tokugawa to Meiji maps relate in not insignificant ways to the sort of cartographic ideas that shaped the thinking of Ptolemy, who is often regarded as the founder of Western cartography. Ptolemy distinguished between 'geographic' and 'chorographic' maps, the first showing the whole world, using diagrammatic features, and the second representing smaller areas, using pictorial elements. According to this division, the role of chorography is to deal separately with a part of the whole, whereas that of geography is to survey the whole in its just proportions. Upon this basic distinction, P.D.A. Harvey has based his review of topographical maps that 'set out to convey the shape and pattern of landscape, showing a tiny portion of the earth's surfaces as it lies within one's own direct experience' (Harvey 1985: 9). Tokugawa-period *dōchūki* were meant to facilitate the sequential experience of the parts without subordinating them to the whole. This accords with the position of the highway journey in the popular mythology of the Tokugawa period as a journey whose purpose, if it can be said to have one, is escape and release rather than arrival at a particular destination.[27]

Based on this, if we attempt to compare Tokugawa-period labyrinthine layouts such as *sugoroku* games and panoramas with the geographically distorted railway charts, we realize that despite their similarities in spurning what we would take today to be geographical accuracy, Meiji-era charts express a fundamentally different condition: not the enclosure of play and escape any more, but rather the transformation of space into time through the means of 'measurability,' that is to say of money. As David Harvey and before him Henri Lefebvre have argued, one of the major aspects of capitalism is the transformation of space into time through the mediation of money (Harvey 1985). While the Tokugawa network of movement represented by the roads functioned as a marginal, differentiated ground of escape that was separated from the realm of the ordinary, the railway network appropriated traveling space through the economic logic of modern capitalism. With this, traveling was removed from its marginalized realm and the destination of the journey became the ultimate goal. As we saw, the railway charts ignored geographical coordinates, acknowledging only their own operational logic, a fact that was not different in nature from the evaluation of space conducted by the state. The purpose of the railway charts was to indicate the fare according to two laws: social class and distance. Within the overall homogenized system, space and time were transformed in their relations one with the other through the mediation of money. The railway chart is symbolic of the abstract character inherent in capitalism. The labyrinth of endless traveling has been transformed into a regulated mechanism. For this, space is measured as distance, distance is measured as time, time is measured as money. Therefore, traveling cannot be aimless any more but becomes instead a means to an end.

Hierarchical classifications, totalizing views, and the dependence of space on time and money signifies the emergence of homogenized space, or, in the words of Lefebvre, the passage from absolute to abstract space. Absolute space is symbolic space, made up of natural fragments chosen for their intrinsic qualities, being populated by political, military, and religious forces that mediate between what lies out there and what exists here. On the other hand, abstract space is the institutionalization of a homogenous, isotropic space, established by capitalism, one that expands as a *tabula rasa* throughout a measurable terrain (Lefebvre 1991: 48–53). Such spatial homogenization can be found in the blunt expansion of the railway network that we observed in the railway charts. It goes without saying that the principles that such charts expressed are incorporated in geographical railway maps. These principles thus become naturalized, placed upon a geographical map (decorated, though it may be, with topographical motifs), reinforcing a monetary definition of space and the national hierarchies recognized by the railway network.

It is indeed hierarchy and difference rather than uniformity that complements the expansion of homogeneous space. Abstract space needs and capitalizes upon differences and thus uses qualities of absolute space as means of establishing hierarchies and representations. Therefore, as Lefebvre has shown, it is an intention inherent in capitalism, rather than a contradiction, that homogenized abstract space can accept fragmentation in isolated segments. Homogenization and pulverization, unity and fragmentation are the major characteristics of modern capitalist space. This is expressed through the divisions of zoning and the specialization of space, which is realized 'under the umbrella of a bureaucratically decreed unity' (Lefebvre 1991: 317). Such applications can be found within the borders of the city but also in the compass of divisions within the national territory, where the dichotomies between sites of consumption and production are established, based on differences between agricultural, industrial, tourist, and other modes. If at the national level the metropolis was a locale of consumption, selected spots in the country became its objects of consumption. That is to say, not only were products, raw material, and labour transported from the countryside to the city, but selected spots of the countryside became objects of (tourist) consumption. The homogenization of abstract space was thus followed by hierarchy and fragmentation. Not only were distance and money valued in the overland transport network of the Meiji era, but each particular locality was assessed through its role within a hierarchy of national functions. With this a further spatial pulverization occurred. The development of the tourist industry, trading upon historical or mythological notions that reinforce the national identity, is indicative of the incorporation of absolute values (Fuji, *meisho*, tradition) within undifferentiated abstractions (space-time-money). The abstract labyrinthine layouts and the clipped images of the railway charts of the Meiji era clearly illustrated this procedure.

Symbolic Geography

From our experience we all know that geographical precision does not necessarily facilitate the transferral of information regarding the operation of a mechanical network such as a railway or subway system (see for example the diagrammatic subway maps drawn with straight lines that do not correspond to the actual topography of the cities). A question that emerges then is what the aim was in building a degree of geographical veracity into the railway map if not the operation of the railway, which was the primary objective of these maps. This said, however, it must be borne in mind that in most of the geographical maps, the shape and outline of Japan's territory is highly schematized.

The geographical railway maps are one more example of spatial representation being appropriated as a source of ideology. In the Tokugawa period, popular road maps expressed the mythological, narrative aspects of the Japanese cultural landscape, while official maps reflected the military and administrative needs for detailed spatial survey. In the Meiji era, both specialized and popular railway maps are produced by authorized bodies (railway and tourist agencies) rather than by individual artists or the demands of a buying public. With this a double procedure was taking place. At one level, destination sites were selectively established upon the national land, according to a new national hierarchy (Tokyo, the centre of the country; Kyoto and Nara, the historical cities; Ise, the holiest religious site; Hakone, the first western-style resort; and later, Yokkaichi and Yawata, major industrial spots). Those new functions were realized through engineering works, tourist establishments, historical preservation – in other words, through materialized nation-markers that contrasted with immaterial, imaginary notions celebrated in the Tokugawa-period *meisho*. At a second level, representation, advertizing, and promotion of new models were the means through which the above hierarchies became public knowledge.

The interest in geography as a science was an innovation of the time. Geographical learning was highly valued, and many thinkers saw geography as a means of benefitting the nation and expanding the horizons of knowledge towards the West. This view was perfectly in accordance with the evaluation of the sciences made by one of the Meiji apostles of Western thinking, Fukuzawa Yukichi (1835–1901), who ranked them in their order of importance as follows: geography, physics, chemistry, and arithmetic in the first rank, followed by history, economics, and ethics (Miwa *et al.* 1970: 11). The railway maps certainly did not function in a vacuum but were embedded in a broader framework that fostered geographical knowledge as national knowledge. Geographical knowledge imprinted an image not only of national unification but also of national territoriality, supported by a plethora of geographical treatises, textbooks, guidebooks, advertizing materials, and school songs.[28] The imagery of the Meiji era mythologized the new engineering achievements of Japan, and such views now appear on the foreground of the diachronic, symbolic images of Japanese land. Mount Fuji, famous places, legendary spots, mist and clouds were now merged with man-made elements that reconfigured the conception of natural beauty. From a legendary landscape, Japan proceeded to a new idealization of the natural field, which was not simply based on notions of beauty but also on scientific explanations of topographical, geological, and geographical factors that produced 'unique' views and settings.[29] Scientific, analytical tools were used not only as precise means of observation but much more in order to investigate new methods of exploitation of nature leading to national prosperity and progress. Therefore natural beauty is now found not in images of pure nature but rather in nature transformed, nature worked upon, through renovated agricultural or technological means of productivity. Such notions, having developed from the late Tokugawa period, found institutional foundation in the Meiji era and became crucial to the formation of the Japanese national identity (see footnote 21).

Conclusions

When the railway was established, Japanese people saw in it an extension of 'democratic' free public space. Inside the train, 'dignified gentlemen arose to make a political speech and, when the train officials attempted to stop them, refused to yield on the grounds that freedom of speech was their privilege' (Yanagita 1957: 147). Moreover, the train figured for the populace as a new illusory device, a new way to see the world, not different from the optical machines that were imported from the West and were displayed in the renowned carnivals of the Tokugawa period. It was through the civic aspirations of the Meiji state that the railway was incorporated within the new framework of civilization and enlightenment, introducing new disciplinary models of public behaviour.[30] The mechanized wheels became symbolic of ideological changes that affected both individual and masses.

Earlier we noticed that representational forms of spatial surveillance can be found during the pre-railway era as well. This we noted in the example of the Tokugawa road maps, which functioned as instruments of territorial control. Despite the different means of traveling, these early maps are not different from the geographical maps of the Meiji era. What unites them is the reconfiguration of the notion of visuality from the partial experience to the panoptic, totalizing machine. Therefore, what should be considered as the source of such spatial representations is the authoritative vision itself rather than the speed of the wheel and the mechanization of traveling (which, on the other hand, has been an empowering apparatus that facilitated such procedures). The question thus becomes: when did the paradigm of totalized spatial representations as means of surveillance and control become the dominant paradigm and by what means was this established? The crucial point here lies in the modern disqualification of a wider population from expressing their aspirations by means of spatial representation, or indeed, their exclusion from exercising any form of command over space. Spatial representations as well as spatial production are undertaken by particular institutional bodies, based on specialized methodologies that are less and less accessible, more and more ineligible to wider audiences. At the same time, while the majority of the population has a decreasing capacity to express its own spatial experience, the meaning of space becomes codified in an overall, all-encompassing set of values and jurisdictions, and the space of the individual or the group becomes more and more limited. The inhabitant, user of transport, or traveler in space becomes a measurable entity, to be enumerated, manipulated, and finally neutralized from any spatial representation or expression.

From a study of the above material, we can see that the notion of space developed from a textual, narrative entity that had been based on mythologies transmitted in oral and written fashion towards visual configurations that were based on observation and measurability. The causes of these transformations have been Japan's exposure to Western scientific methodologies and, even more important, Japan's growing awareness of the new international setting and its codification. This codification was based on the economic principles of modern capitalism and the modern categories of specialized, scientific disciplines and institutions. In short, we can see that it is through inquiry into the positions adopted by the institutional bodies which authorize cartographic representation that we should undertake an investigation into cartographic change rather than through a strict analysis of stylistic forms and methods. Forms may be repeated, and in the process their meanings subjected to modification. Based on the above, we can try to interpret our contemporary reexamination of Tokugawa and other historical stylistic conventions and uncover the reasons that necessitate such revisions. The new meanings that such forms acquire should then be sought in Japan's postmodern return to a 'pristine' and 'unique' past, which has been greatly removed from the socio-political contexts that produced such forms (Gluck1993: 72; Harootunian 1989: 78). On the other hand, the mixture of high and low culture as well as the lack of borders between existing domains of endeavour that characterized cultural production in the Tokugawa period – both features that were gradually abandoned in the modern era – may also explain the contemporary interest in Edo culture.

Notes

1 The Tōkaidō is the 500-kilometer-long road that connects Edo-Tokyo and Kyoto. Since the Tokugawa period it has been the major highway of Japan, and in the Meiji era it became the first and foremost trunk rail line in the country.
2 After a preliminary survey by Meiji officials, it was concluded that it would be more useful to construct a trunk route along the Nakasendō instead of the Tōkaidō. This would be a way of promoting the development of the mountainous regions through which the Nakasendō passed, but most of all it was a solution that had the approval of the military authorities, who were afraid that a coastal railway would be vulnerable to foreign attack. Soon however this decision had to be revised in favour of the Tōkaidō, since the opening of a railway along this route was less expensive and technically easier.
3 According to cultural studies theorists such as Stuart Hall, representation cannot be simply seen as a reflection of the world but rather as a constitutive action that takes part in the construction of the world (Hall 1997).
4 The first whole map of Japan was made in 1605 (Keichō era), at a scale of 1: 280,000 and is preserved today in the Diet Library. The second was made in 1644 (Shōhō era), at a scale of 1: 432,000, and was based on maps of the provinces drawn to a scale of 1: 21,600. The third was made in 1697 (Genroku era), and since it was considered to be inferior to the previous one, it was corrected in 1719 (Kyōhō era) by the mathematician Tatebe Katahiro (1664–1739), using high mountain peaks as points of reference, and drawn to a scale of 1: 21,600. The fourth was made in 1831 (Tenpō era) in 148 sheets. These were not compiled into a whole map, since Inō Tadataka had provided adequate outlines of the Japanese islands in 1821. Kawamura mentions one more revision produced in 1633. Besides the official projects, another epoch-making map of Japan was that compiled by Nagakubo Sekisui (1717–1801) in 1799 at a scale of 1: 1,300,000, employing meridians and reducing decorative elements but still uninfluenced by his knowledge of contemporary Europe (Muroga 1973: 170; Kawamura 1989: 70).
5 Since the 1570s, domain maps had become standardized. They distinguished between main roads and bye-ways by using varying thickness of red lines. They depicted all mile-markers with two small black dots running bilaterally along the road and inns for the lords with a circle or a rectangle. The domain boundaries were indicated by different colors, a division that does not appear in the road maps, and was abolished in the Genroku era. Unlike the maps produced for public circulation, the official *kuni ezu*, which the Tokugawa ordered from each province, were drawn in color with an intricate finish, suitable for the high status of commissioners (Kawamura 1989: 71).
6 According to Marilyn Ivy 'popular culture' is characterised as a spontaneously arising, communally based culture of the 'masses,' while 'mass culture,' as theorised by Adorno, is an administered, commodified culture, pre-targeted and produced for large number of consumers. In this general sense, mass culture arose together with industrial capitalism, for it is predicated on those technologies of material and social production that are entwined with large-

Representing Mobility in Tokugawa and Meiji Japan

scale production, dissemination, and consumption. (Ivy 1993: 239). For the diffusion of traveling practices during the Tokugawa period, see Vaporis (1995).

7   For an introduction to *meisho* within the context of Kyoto, see the chapter in this book by Nicolas Fiévé, 'Kyoto's Famous Places.'

8   The first *dōchūki* had 52 pages and included only 3 illustrations. These had little more than very minimal descriptions referring to place-names, distances, names of officers, and listings of the 'suspicious and inauspicious days for setting out,' according to the superstitions of the period. The second *dōchūki* added a lot of new information, texts, and haiku for each station. The style of the text is still abbreviated, but it shows a development from a list of information towards a narrative (Bresler 1975: 136).

9   The administrative maps of the Tokugawa period were usually viewed on the floor by a group of people who were sitting around them. Therefore the orientation of the lettering of the maps is different on each side in order to be easily read. The indications north, south, east, and west were either written in the margins of the maps or represented by the twelve signs of the eastern zodiac. Through another symbolic order, prominent structures and important topographical elements had to be positioned at the top of the picture. According to Nanba, the Japanese inherited both the Chinese belief that the Pole Star was the center of the Universe, and the *Yi Qing* division of *yin*-north-earth and *yang*-south-heaven. Thus we can find both types of maps that either position the north on the top or maps of southern orientation, for which south was the symbol of heaven. There are, in addition, maps with an easterly and westerly orientation (Nanba 1973: 155; Narazaki 1969: 11; Suizu 1984: 10).

10 There are many different opinions regarding the identity of the map maker, who also signed a precise map of Edo, *Edo Kanbun zu (bunken)*, drawn in 1657. Some researchers argue that the map maker was a samurai from the Tōyama domain named Fujii Hanchi who worked as a surveyor under Hōjō, or even that the word Dōin means a kind of a map-measuring method. For various discussions on that topic, see Kurimoto (1960); Matsumoto (1977); Hasegawa (1993).

11 These are the fees for river crossing, carriage fees for transferring different kinds of luggage or people, and use of horse or man-power.

12 This map is considered to be quite precise, since it depicts 103 out of the 120 mile-markers on the road (Kurimoto 1960).

13 A similar technique was used in the European road maps of the nineteenth century. See John Ogilby's *Britannia* map, where, for graphic convenience, the route has been converted into an almost straight line neglecting the turning points. For this, a type of compass is drawn at its curve.

14 This map was produced in a single scrolled volume, drawn to a scale of 1 : 36,000. Various differences exist in the place-names, the figures of the travelers and topographical features, such as Yoshida castle, which is drawn on the right-hand side of the road in the early version and on the left-hand side in the later one. The second version classifies travel fees (which had doubled since Genroku era) in an appendix at the end of the map and not next to each post-station.

15 Such territorial interests can be seen in official expeditions, such as the one undertaken by the artist Tani Bunchō (1763–1840), who accompanied the government's official Matsudaira Sadanobu (1758–1829) on an inspection tour of coastal defenses in order to prepare for a possible attack from the Russians (Takeuchi 1998: 328). During the same period, the astronomer Hayashi Shihei (1738–93) produced his *Sangoku tsūran zusetsu* (Illustrated outline of the three countries; 1785) which according to Tessa Morris-Suzuki was the first attempt to define Japan and distinguish it clearly from the Ryūkyūs and Ainu lands. According

to Hayashi's suggestions, these regions should be colonized by Japan. Such attitudes were further expanded after Japan's 'wholehearted entry into the modern world,' with the incorporation of the Ainu lands into the Meiji state in 1869, as Hokkaidō, and the Ryūkyū in 1879, as Okinawa prefecture (Morris-Suzuki 1998: 23).

16 The Tōkaidō occupies 24 volumes (originally 13 rolls), while the *gokaidō* occupy 91 volumes.
17 Twenty-five officers were involved with the making of this map. Groups of three officers collaborated in surveying each post-station under the guidance of the *ton'ya* (post-station administrator).
18 Kuwagata Shōi was Kuwagata Keisai's son. Although the exact date of Kuwagata Shōi's map is not known, we should assume that it was produced after Kuwagata Keisai's '*Nihon meisho no e*,' which, according to Henry Smith, was made around 1805 (Smith 1988: 257).
19 *Sugoroku*, usually played on New Year's Day, is equivalent to the Western 'snakes and ladders' board game. The board represented a combination of pictures gathered in a single paper in a spiral layout, composing a hypothetical travelogue.
20 Examples of famous places that were still celebrated although they did not exist during the Tokugawa period are Yatsuhashi (the eight-fold bridge) and Hamana bridge. Such places were famous for their 'historical' or poetic value rather than any physical remains from the past.
21 As has been discussed by Toshio Watanabe, throughout the Tokugawa period the tradition of the *meisho* was gradually altered towards a 'modern' perception of nature that avoided places famous for their depiction in poetry and attempted to 'objectify nature' – for example, to record local customs, vegetation, and geology (Watanabe and Kikuchi 1997: 278). Moreover, according to Tessa Morris-Suzuki, 'a speculative view on nature, as a field of resources, had started already in the Tokugawa period. Philosophers and scholars of the time expanded the concept of *kaibutsu* (opening up of nature) far beyond the limits of agriculture to include the making of textiles, dyes, pottery, metals, and paper, the building of ships, the forging of armaments, and the brewing of wines and beers' (Morris-Suzuki 1998: 45).
22 A league or co-fraternity (*kō*) consisted of people from one or more villages with the common goal of religious worship. Each member of the league made a contribution towards traveling costs and representatives used the money for the pilgrimage. *Naniwa-kō*, *Santō-kō*, and *Azuma-kō* were among the best-known leagues. For Kanzaki the leagues help to explain the contemporary group tourism in Japan (Vaporis 1995: 36; Kanzaki 1995: 42).
23 The Welcome Society of Japan was formed by Shibusawa Eiichi (1840–1931) and Masuda Takashi (1848–1938), the head of Mitsui, who believed that Paris flourished because of the city's successful system for attracting foreign tourists and money (Nakagawa 1998: 22).
24 Travelers in the Tokugawa period, used the pretext of pilgrimage in order to escape from the repression of their daily life. Vaporis discusses numerous examples of amoral and anarchic conditions that challenged the official morality and ethics (Vaporis 1995: 32).
25 These maps produced by metal printing show more detail and new information, such as the elevation of the land, creeks, flora (bamboo groves, farmland, tea, and mulberry fields), details of the ex-*daimyō* grounds, telegraph lines, and railway networks (Watanabe 1980: 59).
26 Tokugawa-period travel fees depended upon the difficulty of the route, weather conditions, load, etc. High-ranking samurai did not have to pay any fee, but it was a custom to offer big presents.

27 According to Ihara Saikaku's (1642–1693) descriptions of the pilgrimage to Ise, travelers 'at Ise failed to visit the Inner Shrine or the sacred beach at which homage is paid to the Sun, stopping only at the Outer Shrine for a few minutes and purchasing as their only souvenirs a purification broach and some sea-weed' (Ihara 1956: 33).

28 According to Kamei Hideo the purpose of the school songs was both bodily and moral improvement. The songs aimed to improve the pupils' health, correct their posture and strengthen their lungs, adopting European vocalization, while at the same time, they heightened the pupils' sentiments, using refined words that praised the natural beauty of their motherland. In 1900, the classical scholar Ōwada Takeki (1857–1910) wrote the 'railway songs' (*tetsudō shōka*). These songs, which narrated railway travelogues, were intended to help students strengthen their national consciousness through learning geographical facts and cultivating 'a collective illusion of nature' (Kamei 1994; Fujioka 1982: 84, 134; Harada 1983: 30; Traganou 1997: 24).

29 One of the most influential such treatises is Shiga Shigetaka's *Nihon fūkei ron* (Japanese Landscapes), published in 1894. This book offers a renovated perception of the Tōkaidō, based on scientific explanation of its scenery, as a landscape of vapor. Shiga's perception also contributed to the establishment of a national mythology about the uniqueness of the Japanese land in comparison with other countries.

30 Various prohibitions within the train were issued in order to secure proper behavior. Moreover, the operation of a rail system introduced a time discipline not existing in the Tokugawa period.

References

Akisato R. (1925) *Tōkaidō meisho zue*. (Assorted pictures of the famous places of the Tōkaidō), Coll. *Nihon zue zenshū* (Complete collection of assorted pictures of Japan), vol. 5. Tokyo: Yoshikawa Kobunkan. First published in 1797.

Bresler, L. (1975) 'The Origins of Popular Travel and Travel Literature in Japan.' Unpublished Ph.D. dissertation. Columbia University.

Cortazzi, H. (1983) *Isles of Gold, Antique Maps of Japan*. Tokyo: Weatherhill.

Crary, J. (1990) *The Techniques of the Observer: On Vision and Modernity in the 19th Century*. Cambridge (Mass): MIT Press.

Certeau, M. de (1984) *The Practice of Everyday Life* (trans. Rendall S. F.). Berkeley, Los Angeles, and London: University of California Press.

Erickson, S. (1996) *The Sound of the Whistle: Railroads in Meiji Japan*. Cambridge (Mass): Harvard University Press.

Fujioka K. (1982) *Tōkaidō no keikan to henbō* (Tōkaidō's landscape and transformations). Tokyo: Kokon Shoin.

Fujitani T. (1973) '*Okagemairi*' to '*ee-ja-nai-ka*' ('*Okagemairi*' and '*ee-ja-nai-ka*'). Tokyo: Iwanami Shoten.

Gluck, C. (1993) 'The Past in the Present.' In Gordon A. (ed.) *Postwar Japan as History*. Berkeley: University of California Present, pp. 64–98.

Gottmann, J. (1961) *Megalopolis: The Urbanized Northeastern Seaboard of the Unites States*. New York: The Twentieth Century Fund.

Hall, R. B. (1937) 'Tōkaidō Road and Region.' *The Geographical Review* 27 (3). (pp. 353–377).

Hall, S. (1997) *Representation: Cultural Representations and Signifying Practices*. London: Sage Publications.

Harada K. (1983) *Meiji tetsudō monogatari* (Tales of Meiji railroads). Tokyo: Chikuma Shobō.

Harley, J. B. (1988) 'Maps, Knowledge and Power.' In D. Cosgrove and D. Stephen (eds) *The Iconography of Landscape*. Cambridge: Cambridge University Press, pp. 277–312.

Harootunian, H. D. (1989) 'Visible Discourses/Invisible Ideology.' In H. Harootunian and Miyoshi M. (eds) *Postmodernism and Japan*. Duham: Duke University Press, pp. 63- 92.

Harvey, D. (1989) *The Condition of Postmodernity: An Inquiry into the Origins of Cultural Change*. Oxford: Blackwell.

—— (1985) *Consciousness and the Urban Experience: Studies in the History and Theory of Capitalist Urbanization*. Baltimore: Johns Hopkins University Press.

Hasegawa K. (1993) 'Road Atlases in Early Modern Japan and Britain.' In J. Sargent and R. Wiltshire (eds) *Geographical Studies and Japan*. Folkestone, Kent: Japan Library, pp. 15–24.

Honda R. (1996) '*Tōkaidō bunken nobe ezu sakusei no kiso chōsa*' (Basic research into the making of *Tōkaidō bunken nobe ezu*). In Shizuoka-ken Chiikishi Kenkyūkai (ed.), *Tōkaidō kōtsūshi no kenkyū* (Research on the transportation history of the Tōkaidō) Osaka: Seibundō Shuppan, pp. 269–99.

Ichiko N. and Yokoyama S. (1979) *Tōkaidō meishoki (Record of the Famous Places of the Tōkaidō)*, Coll. Kinsei bungaku shiryo ruiju, *Kohan chishi hen* 7, Tokyo: Benseisha.

Ihara S. (1956) *Five Women who Loved Love (Koshoku gonin onna)*. (trans. T. De Bary). Tokyo: Tuttle. First published in modern edition in 1868.

Inoue M. (1985) *Space in Japanese Architecture*. Tokyo: Weatherhill.

Ivy, M. (1993) 'Formations of Mass Culture.' In A. Gordon (ed.) *Postwar Japan as History*. Berkeley: University of California Press, pp. 239–58.

Jansen, M. B. and G. Rozman (eds) (1986) *Japan in Transition: From Tokugawa to Meiji*. Princeton (NJ): Princeton University Press.

Jinnai, H. (1995) *Tōkyō: A Spatial Anthropology*. Berkeley: University of California Press.

Jippensha I. (1960) *Dōchū Hizakurige* (translated as *Shank's Mare* by T. Satchell). Tokyo: Tuttle. (First published in 1802–1804).

Kamei H. (1994) 'Meiji Literature and the Transformations of Sensibility: A Case of Sensibilities and Nature' (presentation at the Harvard Meiji Studies Conference, Cambridge MA, 8 May 1994).

Kanzaki N. (1995) 'A Comparative Analysis of the Tourist Industry.' *Senri Ethnological Studies* 38: 39–49.

Katō K. (1997) '*La structure spatiale de Kyōto*.' Unpublished lecture given to École des Hautes Études en Sciences Sociales, Paris.

Kawamura H. (1989) '*Kuni-ezu* (Provincial maps) Compiled by the Tokugawa Shogunate in Japan.' *Imago Mundi* 41: 70–5.

Kodama K. (1977) *Tōkaidō bunken nobe ezu* (Proportional linear map of the Tōkaidō). Tokyo: Tōkyō Bijutsu.

Konishi J. (1984) *A History of Japanese Literature, vol. 1: The Archaic and Ancient Ages*. Princeton (NJ): Princeton University Press.

Kurimoto K. (1960) *Tōkaidō bunken ezu 1* (Proportional map of the Tōkaidō). Tokyo: Kohan Edozu Shūei Kankō Kai.

—— (1960) *Tōkaidō bunken ezu 2* (Proportional map of the Tōkaidō). Tokyo: Kohan Edozu Shūei Kankō Kai.

Lefebvre, H. (1991) *The Production of Space* (trans. D. Nicholson-Smith) Oxford: Blackwell.

Matsumoto S. (1977) '*Dōin to Tadataka: chizu no senkaku sha*' (Dōin and Tadataka: Pioneers of Map-making). In Nishimaki K. (ed.) *Kochizu sanpo Edo-Tōkaidō* (Walking Along the Old Maps of Edo and Tōkaidō). Taiyō Collection 1. Tokyo: Heibonsha.

Miwa K. (1970) *Shiga Shigetaka (1863–1927), A Meiji Japanist's View of and Actions in International Relations.* Tokyo: Sophia University, Institute of International Relations, Research Papers.

Morris-Suzuki, T. (1998) *Re-Inventing Japan: Time, Space, Nation.* New York: M.E. Sharpe.

Muroga N. (1973) 'The Development of Cartography in Japan.' In Namba M. (ed.) *Old maps in Japan.* Osaka: Sogensha, pp. 158–76.

Nakagawa K. (1998) 'Prewar Tourism Promotion by Japanese Government Railways.' *Japan Railway and Transport Review* 15: 22–7.

Namba M. (ed.) (1973) *Old maps in Japan.* Osaka: Sogensha.

Narazaki M. (1969) *Masterworks of Ukiyo-e: Hiroshige, The Fifty-three Stations of the Tōkaidō.* Tokyo: Kōdansha International.

Nitschke, G. (1993) *From Shinto to Ando: Studies in Architectural Anthropology in Japan.* London: Academy Editions.

Nosco, P. (1990) *Remembering Paradise: Nativism and Nostalgia in Eighteenth Century Japan.* Cambridge (Mass): Harvard University Press.

Schivelbusch, W. (1979) *The Railway Journey* (trans. A. Hollo). New York: Urizen Books.

Smith, H. D. II (1988) 'World Without Walls: Kuwagata Keisai's Panoramic Vision of Japan.' In G. L. Bernstein and H. Fukui (eds) *Japan and the World: Essays on Japanese History in Honor of Ishida Takeshi.* Basingstoke: Macmillan, pp. 3–19.

Sōseki N. (1965) *The Three-Cornered World,* (trans. A. Turney) (first published in 1906). New York: Putnam.

Suizu I. (1984) 'The Codes of Japanese Landscape: An Attempt at Topological Geography.' *Geographical Review of Japan* 57B (1): 1–21.

Takeuchi K. (1993) 'The Decline and Survival of Academic Geography: Publications in the Early Stages of Academic Geography in Japan (1907–1945).' *Hitotsubashi Journal of Social Studies* 25: 63- 81.

Takeuchi M. (1998) 'Travel and Landscape: Catalogue 185.' In *Edo Art in Japan 1615–1868.* Washington: National Gallery of Art.

—— (1992) *Taiga's True Views: The Language of Landscape Painting in Eighteenth-Century Japan.* Stanford: Stanford University Press.

Traganou, J. (1997) 'The Tōkaidō: Scenes from Edo to Meiji Eras.' *Japan Railway and Transport Review* 13 (September): 17–27.

Tsukahira T. G. (1966) *Feudal Control in Tokugawa Japan: The Sankin Kōtai System.* Cambridge (Mass): Harvard University Press.

Vaporis, C. N. (1995) 'The Early Modern Origins of Japanese Tourism.' *Senri Ethnographical Studies* 38: 25–38.

—— (1994) *Breaking Barriers: Travel and the State in Early Modern Japan.* Cambridge (Mass): Harvard University Press.

Watanabe A. (1980) 'An Outline of the Development of Cartography in Japan.' In The Japanese Organizing Committee of the 10th International Conference of the International Cartographic Association (ed.) *Geography in Japan* Tokyo: Japan Map Center.

Watanabe T. and Kikuchi Y. (1997) 'Introduction.' In Watanabe T. (ed.) *Ruskin in Japan 1890–1940: Nature for Art, Art for Life.* London: 'Ruskin in Japan 1890–1940' Exhibition Committee.

Wattenberg, U. 'Maps and Map Collecting in Japan.' In Y.-Y. Brown (ed.) *Japanese Studies, Papers Presented at a Colloquium at the School of Oriental and African Studies, University of London, 14–16 September 1988.* London: The British Library, pp. 53–65.

Yanagita K. (1957) *Japanese Manners and Customs in the Meiji Era.* (trans. C. Terry) Tokyo: Ōbunsha.

CHAPTER 7

By Ferry to Factory

Crossing Tokyo's Great River into a New World

Paul Waley

Ferries crossing a river represent a link with a past era. They cross time as well as a spatial divide. The ferries that crossed Tokyo's main river, the Sumida, once known simply as the Great River (Ōkawa), represented collectively a cultural landscape that was in the throes of abrupt change. At the same time, each stood in its own way for a different era, having differing associations and resonances, imbued with different topographical references. No artist would think of depicting the Hashiba ferry without some pictorial reference to white sea birds. The Takeya ferry evoked the amorous license of the late Tokugawa period. The ferries at the mouth of the river, the offspring of an industrializing city, came later to symbolize the early years of industrialization, before the construction of bridges and the filling-in of canals. The writers in whose works the ferries figure most prominently are people like Nagai Kafū (1879–1959) and Akutagawa Ryūnosuke (1892–1927), whose sensibilities were nourished by a deep attachment to a cultural landscape undergoing a wrenching process of change.[1] Like the print artist Kobayashi Kiyochika (1847–1915) a few decades previously, they sensed in the ferries a whole jumble of meanings from which they were steadily being forced away.

Ferries were a prominent motif in a rapidly changing vernacular of landscape. In the exceptionally rich topographical language of the city of Edo-Tokyo, the ferries that crossed the Sumida became one of the most evocative symbols of landscape change, as we will see in the pages that follow. They stood both for continued links with the city of Edo, the shoguns' capital, and for the many features of the cultural landscape that were disappearing in a rapidly industrializing city. And yet during the decades of transformation and industrialization that Tokyo experienced between about 1880 and 1920, there were more ferry services carrying as many passengers as ever before. The passage from an early modern urban centre of power and consumption to a modernizing, industrializing imperial capital has been cast in terms of change from a water-based urban culture and economy to a land-based one, and from one fashioned out of wood to one built of steel, from the fluid spontaneous rhythms of flowing water to the solid, angular patterns of functional planning (Hasegawa 1985; Maeda 1982). Within this shifting cultural landscape the ferries of the Sumida river provided a memory of the gentle motions of the water-based city and a reference to its rich topography.

Hashiba Ferry: Floating through History

Although never occupying a central position in the city, the Sumida served as a focus for the artistic and topophilic imagination as no other feature of the city or surrounding area. The earliest settlements were established near its mouth in order to afford a crossing point close to the temple to Kannon at Asakusa, at a point where the marshy land along the bay gave way to firmer alluvial deposits. According to contemporary literary sources as well as later, sixteenth, seventeenth, and eighteenth century topographies, a ferry carried traffic across the Sumida along the main road to the north of the country from about the ninth century onwards (Sumida-ku 1978: 338). At this time, the river was about as far as any place in the literary imagination of the Japanese, for whom the Heian Capital (Kyoto) and its environs represented a finite world in which topographical features were associated with emotions and experiences. So distant was this river that its exact location was sometimes forgotten. In her memoirs written in the eleventh century, the Sarashina Lady tells the story of a journey she made back to the capital: 'After crossing hills and fields, which were a desolate waste of reeds, we finally reached the Sumida river on the border of Musashi and Sagami.... We crossed by boat to the province of Sagami.' The geographical reference is confused, as the Sumida river lay on a different provincial border.[2] In her memoir the Sarashina Lady makes reference to a still older literary appearance, in *Ise monogatari* (Tales of Ise), a series of romantic episodes built around the verse of the legendary ninth-century poet Ariwara no Narihira (825–80). In this story, a group of courtiers from the capital are reminded of their loved ones by the appearance of white sea birds as they are crossing the Sumida river on board a ferry. The story later became a sort of pictorial cliché, to the point where no mention of the river and its banks along this stretch would be complete without a reference.[3]

As the decorous world of the Heian court collapsed, Minamoto no Yoritomo (1147–99), one of the architects of the new order, is said to have had his troops cross the river here in 1180 by constructing a floating bridge of boats.[4] The floating bridge (*ukihashi*) is a recurrent metaphor in the

Memory and the Changing Passage of Space

Japanese literary imagination. In their initial act of creation of the world the two deities, Izanagi and Izanami, 'are standing on the floating bridge of heaven' (*ama no ukihashi*), a metaphysical structure linking heaven and earth.[5] The floating bridge reappears frequently, both as a metaphor in poetry anthologies like the *Manyōshū* and as a real construction allowing passage across rivers for armies on the march and, in later times, processions like those of the shogun or of visiting Korean emissaries. Indeed, the broad, shallow, island-strewn, turbulent, flood-prone nature of the lower stretches of Japan's rivers often meant that a crossing was best effected by a variety of means, including boat, bridge, piggy back, or a combination, and a common combination was of boat and bridge.[6]

The means were perhaps of less significance than the act of crossing a river. The idea of the river and its banks as an area of enhanced spiritual power has been proposed by various writers including Higuchi Tadahiko and Augustin Berque, as has the symbolism of crossing a river by means of bridge or ferry (Higuchi 1981: 30, 154; Berque 1986: 76). The notion of rivers as a border, as a liminal strip, a belt of enhanced spiritual power, is a widespread one, potently symbolized by Charon ferrying the souls of the dead across the Styx to Hades. In Japan, the bodhisattva Jizō (Kshitigharba) was popularly believed to escort the spirits of dead children across the riverbed to safety (Hayami 1975: 152).

In later times, the Hashiba ferry was, according to the official shogunal administrative topography *Gofunai bikō* (Preparatory notes on Edo) of 1829, operated by a certain Gon'emon from the village of Terajima on the far bank, but responsibility for the service, with its two boats and two ferrymen, was subsequently handed over to the village of Hashiba on the near bank, north of Asakusa (fig. 43). Nagai Kafū wrote of the Hashiba ferry's landing place, its rickety legs supporting a platform that jutted out into the river to a point beyond the mudflats. Only a few years later, in 1913, a wooden bridge was built by private interests a short distance north of the ferry, and a toll charged to those who crossed. That signalled the end of the ferry service.

Takeya Ferry: Passage to Pleasure on the Edo Periphery

From the Hashiba ferry, the waters of the Sumida flowed past a mixed scenery. The right bank was urban, lined by the grey-tiled roofs of modest dwellings. The left bank, by contrast, was largely rural, with a scattering of temples, shrines, and suburban retreats of retired poets, generals, and industrialists. Later, in the early 1900s, this was to become an area of rapid industrialisation. A mile or so south of the Hashiba ferry, another ferry threaded its way through sandbanks across the river from a landing stage on the west bank, at the mouth of the Sanyabori inlet (fig. 44). The Takeya ferry was started in 1803 by Takeya Tetsugorō (dates unknown), the owner

By Ferry to Factory

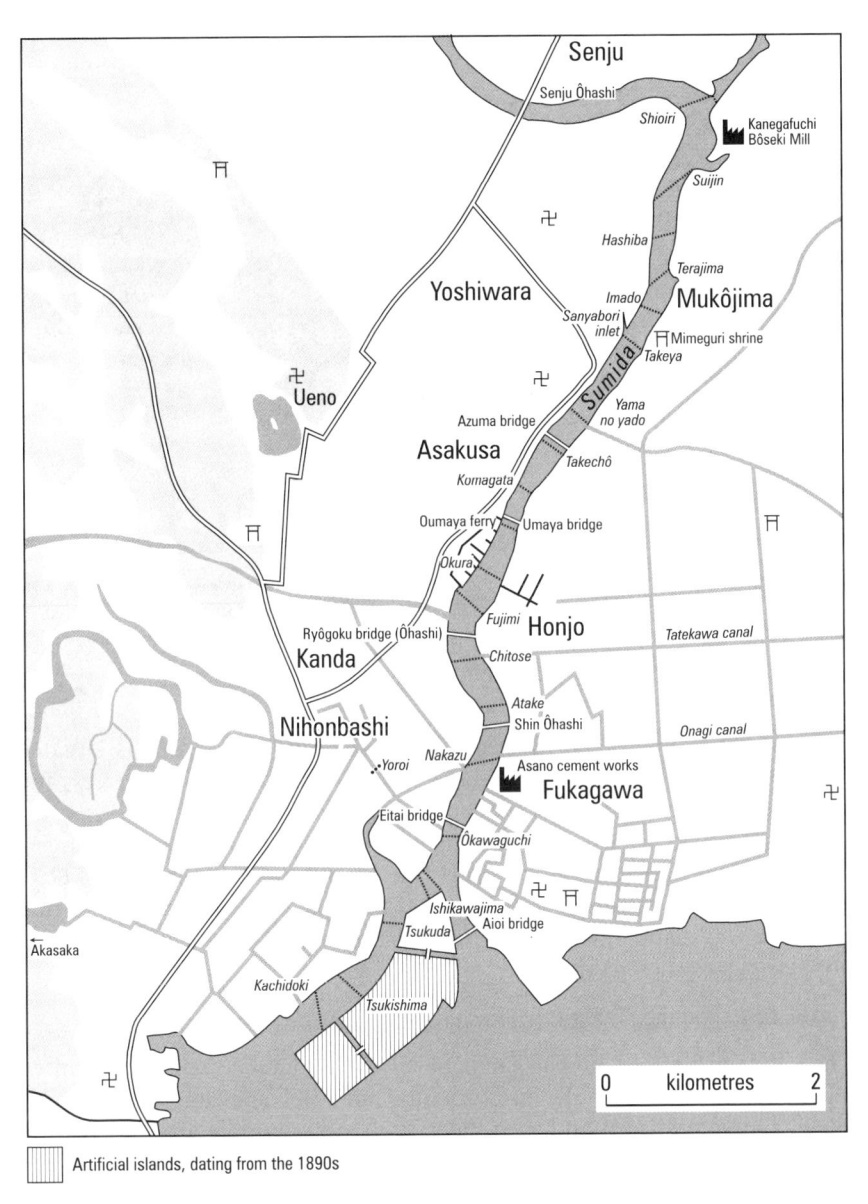

Figure 43 Ferries and bridges across the Sumida from Senju bridge downstream, *ca.* 1860–1910.

Figure 44 The Sumida river and the entrance to Sanyabori canal showing the Takeya ferry landing stage and various types of river craft. Ogawa Isshin, *Scenes in the Eastern Capital of Japan* (1911). By courtesy of the Tokyo Metropolitan Records and Archives Institute.

of a local boathouse. On the east bank, the landing stage was situated adjacent to the Mukōjima embankment, celebrated for its cherry trees, and near the entrance to the well-known Mimeguri Shrine.[7] In the 1830s, a tea stall was set up by the landing stage. Whenever there were passengers waiting on the east bank for the ferry, the proprietor of the stall would call out 'Takeya' at the top of her voice. So familiar did her cry become that reference was made to it in a best-selling story, and it became the subject of popular verses such as this one:

> The face shouting 'Takeya' is blossom pink in the evening sun

The Mimeguri shrine on the far bank of the Sumida river and the raised levée along the river here bore equally powerful associations, with the cherry blossom festival and with the vaguely otherworldly air of recreation on the periphery of the city. The Sanyabori inlet was closely associated with the licensed brothel district, Yoshiwara, and a number of boat-houses were situated at its mouth. Customers bound for its brothels would board small boats called *chokibune* near Ryōgoku bridge in the centre of town for the short journey north, disembarking here at the mouth of the Sanyabori, before completing the short journey on foot.

Ferries were but one of a number of different types of vessel on the rivers of east Japan, each type a slightly different size and bearing a different name. The boats of the Sumida were described by the politician and patron of horse-racing Arima Yoriyasu (1884–1957) in an essay entitled 'Sumidagawa no fune' (The boats of the Sumida river) written in 1916 and first published in *Kyōdo kenkyū* (Local research). Arima had a villa along the river in Hashiba, and no doubt it was from there that he observed the variety of boats. The little water-borne taxi boats known as *chokibune* ('boar's tooth boat,' named, according to one theory, for its resemblance to the tusk of a wild boar) had, Arima wrote, all but disappeared. Equally, the old *yakatabune* were hardly to be seen any longer. These were the pavilioned pleasure boats under whose elegant eaves *geisha* entertained summertime party-goers.[8] Arima described the various types of fishing boat still in use and the boats for the transport of goods, including the *takasebune*, only recently introduced to the Sumida, with their large high bow making them look from the front like a toad, whence their alternative name of *gamabune*, or toad boat. These were used for the transport of potatoes, grains, beans, and firewood from Kawagoe. The most common form of vessel was the *denmasen*, conveying goods between markets and wholesalers. The *chabune*, 'tea boat,' was a smaller equivalent used mainly as a lighter to carry goods from larger boats down the waterways to the quays in town.

Coastal transport was of great importance in the Tokugawa period, as most goods had to be shipped up to Edo from the older cities of the west of the country, principally from Osaka. The coastal vessels on which were transported these provisions (rice and *sake* foremost among them) were anchored in the bay away from the sediment washed out by the river. From there, goods were transferred onto lighters (*hashike*) and carried down the city's network of waterways to the quayside stores of merchants and military lords. As the eighteenth century wore on, production and commerce in the east of the country grew more vigorous, and many of the goods sold in the city's quayside markets were shipped directly by riverine vessels (*takasebune* and *godairiki*) down the waterways of the Kantō plain of east Japan.

As for the ferry boats themselves, Arima commented, 'the shape of these boats is extremely flat so that they can pass freely through shallow water, carry a lot of people on board, and at the same time roll as little as possible.' The ferry boats of early modern Japan are described by the Swedish traveller Charles Peter Thunberg (1743–1828). They have, he wrote, 'flat bottoms made of thin planks, or boards, which, if in the passage the boat runs on a stone or shallow, will yield, and let it slip over.'[9] According to documentation published in 1894, the Takeya ferry boats were 29.6 *shaku* in length (about 9 metres), and had a maximum width of 6 *shaku* (1.82 metres) and a depth of about 1 *shaku* 4 *sun* (about 40 cm). These measurements appear to have changed little over time, although some of the boats carrying traffic along national and prefectural roads were somewhat bigger (Tōkyō-to Kōbunshokan 1991: 50). The Takeya ferry boat would take about 50 passengers seated at stern and bow, on both sides, and on one transversal bench. The boat was propelled by a scull attached to a fulcrum in the stern.

Until 1872, the Takeya ferry would pull out on demand, but from that date on, a regular service was instituted between five in the morning and eight at night (Honjo-ku 1931: 264). In 1905, the crossing cost 8 *rin* per person. The writer Kōda Rohan (1867–1947) commented on the fine scenery in his essay '*Mizu no Tōkyō*' (The Tokyo of water), written in 1908. 'From the middle of the river if you let your gaze wander,' he wrote, 'on a clear day you can see Mount Tsukuba far beyond the surface of the river. . . . It is hardly surprising that this ferry has been depicted by artists and others.' A few years later, in 1913, officials from Asakusa Ward applied to the Minister of Home Affairs for permission to run the ferry as a municipal enterprise on the grounds that the increasing amount of river traffic and especially the steamer boats were causing inconvenience and danger and that the success of the municipal Tsukishima ferry could be replicated. Permission, it seems, was not granted (Tōkyō-to Kōbunshokan 1991: 70). The ferry ceased operating on 10 February 1928, on completion of the new Kototoi bridge.

Takechō Ferry: Growing Regulation of Ferry Services

From the mouth of the Sanyabori inlet, the Sumida flowed south past Asakusa, an important centre of worship, festivity, entertainment and commerce near the northern outskirts of the city. There were several ferries linking Asakusa to the east bank, among them the Takechō ferry. Also known as Hanagata, Narihira or Nakanoe ferry, the Takechō was one of the oldest across the Sumida, continuing to operate despite the construction of Azuma bridge in the 1770s immediately to the north and not ending regular service until 1876. Along with the Oumaya, the Takechō ferry was the only service across the Sumida to have an official designation (*sadame watashibune*), with special duties such as the dispatch of boats during floods.[10] At the landing place for these two ferries, official notices were displayed, as they were at the feet of major bridges.

Regulation of ferry services in the Tokugawa period appears to have been patchy at best.[11] Ferries were generally privately run. They charged a variety of fares, although they were normally free for samurai. The first attempts at standardization, made in the early years of Meiji rule, suggest how haphazard practice had previously been. In 1873, the Ministry of Finance issued guidance to the effect that all ferry services should operate even if they only had one passenger. Four years later, it was announced that all ferry services were to have notice boards with fares displayed, a maximum number of passengers, and a pledge to cross the waterway on request (Tōkyō-to Kōbunshokan 1991: 10). In 1892, it was agreed that the operating hours of the Sumida's ferries should be shortened, but that in exceptional circumstances (for example, during flooding) services would continue after normal working hours with passengers accepted free of charge in an emergency.

Ferry prices appear to have risen only sporadically. However, as prices soared in 1918, ferry operators applied for rises, and permission was granted in 1919. Fares on the Takeya ferry were doubled to 2 *sen* for an adult and 1 *sen* for a child (age 5 to 10), to 2 *sen* for a bicycle, and to 4 *sen* for a rickshaw (this at a time when a bowl of noodles cost 8 *sen*) (Tōkyō-to Kōbunshokan 1991: 30). With the promulgation of the Road Law (*Dōro hō*) at about this time, a new policy came into force, one of bringing ferry services into public hands. Nevertheless, with the construction of bridges and the termination of services in the late 1920s, only the three ferries at the mouth of the river became municipal operations, the greater breadth of the river and the lack of bridges making the service here the more essential.

It would seem that right up until 1910 or so the number of ferry services increased. Five new services were started in 1872, four across the Sumida and the fifth, interestingly enough, across a shrinking pond in Akasaka, in the west-centre of town. In the following year, a further twenty-two applications were made for new ferry services, mainly to replace bridges that were closed for repair. In all, there were 166 applications for permission to operate a ferry service in Tokyo between 1872 and the early Taishō years, around 1914. Many of these were in the 1870s and were applications for temporary services to replace bridges undergoing reconstruction. Several other applications were made for special services for temple markets and image unveilings. Others were for the reinstatement of ferries that had once been in operation.

A number of factors make it difficult to establish the exact number of ferries operating throughout the city of Tokyo in the period from 1870 to 1930. Records are of variable reliability; many of the services were temporary, a few were for private use; landing stages were frequently moved; and ferry names often changed. In 1876, the government of Tokyo prefecture commissioned a survey of ferry numbers. Ferries were divided into three categories, those conveying traffic along national or prefectural roads, 'work' ferries for farmers and local use (*sakujō watashibune*), and normal service ferries (*eigyō watashibune*), which included the ferries crossing the Sumida. The survey came up with the following figures: six ferries on national or prefectural highways, twenty-eight 'work' ferries, and twelve 'normal service' ferries, with a further varying number similar to 'work' ferries (*sakujō watashi ni rui suru mono*) (Tōkyō-to Kōbunshokan 1991: 19). Figures for ferry services in the Tokyo statistical yearbooks for

Memory and the Changing Passage of Space

the first two decades of this century suggest a sustained weight of activity on the waterways (tables 1, 2, and 3).

The situation for the ferries crossing the Sumida, with which we are concerned here, is clearer. There appear to have been about ten at the end of the Tokugawa period, and their number grew steadily over the following forty years or so, to reach a maximum of about twenty, before declining over the succeeding decades (table 4). Although the evidence presented in maps is contradictory, it seems that twelve ferries remained at the time of the 1923 earthquake. After 1923 four new road bridges were built over the river, and by 1930 there were only four ferries left crossing the lower reaches of the river, the Shioiri at the north end near Senju and the Tsukuda, Tsukishima, and Kachidoki ferries at the south end, linking islands and new landfill at the river's mouth to the centre of the city. As with so much else in

Table 1 Municipal ferry boats average crossings and passenger numbers per day

	Crossings			Passengers		
	1906	1916	1926	1906	1916	1926
Tsukishima	371	479	204	14,413	37,748	11,534
Kachidoki*	72	81	116	972	3,093	5,502
Tsukudajima**		95			3,809	

* Figures for the Kachidoki ferry show a sudden increase in 1917, presumably caused by the introduction of steam boats. Tsukishima ferries were already steam.
** Transferred to municipal ownership in 1926.
Source: *Tōkyō-shi tōkei nenpyō* (Tokyo city statistical yearbook) 1907, 1913, 1919, 1928

Table 2 Selected private ferries, showing boat numbers and average crossings and passenger numbers, per day

	No of boats		Crossings		Passengers	
	1911	1918	1911	1918	1911	1918
Hashiba*	3		46		234	
Takeya	3	6	24	82	227	767
Okura	4	4	21	68	125	136
Chitose	3	3	20	20	39	57
Nakasu	5	4	7	91	339	56
Tsukuda	9	8	190	356	950	1,780

* The two tables include various discrepancies and omissions, indicating the improvised and changeable nature of private ferry operations.
Source: *Tōkyō-shi tōkei nenpyō* (Tokyo city statistical yearbook) 1913, 1919

Table 3 Numbers of private ferry boats, annual crossings and passenger numbers, and fares charged – totals for Tokyo in selected years

	Boats	Crossings	Passengers	Fares
1908	54	378,304	2,220,640	¥17,605
1913	41	380,455	1,290,325	¥9,510
1918	37	577,400	1,745,910	¥13,771

Source: *Tōkyō-shi tōkei nenpyō* (Tokyo city statistical yearbook) 1913, 1919

Tokyo, change would have occurred without the earthquake, but as a result of the subsequent construction effort, it was vastly accelerated.

Oumaya Ferry: Ferries and Bridges

South from the Takechō ferry, both banks of the river were fully urbanised from at least the eighteenth century on, lined by quays on one of which a large vegetable market was held. Long stretches of the banks of the Sumida river, as it flowed through the city, were lined by stone banks and open spaces, quayside roadways that allowed for markets to develop or for the temporary placement of goods loaded off boats and destined for nearby stores. The majority of these stores belonged to the shogunal government or to the domainal lords, who were compelled to maintain family and retinue in Edo and to spend periods of attendance there themselves. The domainal stores, some of which occupied a compound in a block of streets, generally had gates opening onto the quayside spaces. The shogun's stores tended to abut directly onto the river. Such was the case immediately south of the Oumaya ferry, where, on the right bank, the shogunal rice stores were located. The Oumaya ferry, one of the two officially designated ferries, was named after the shogunal stables (*oumaya*), situated at some point here (but it is not clear exactly where) in the city's early years (fig. 45). The ferry itself ceased operating in 1874 on completion of Umaya bridge.

While there were numerous bridges across the smaller waterways, Umaya bridge was only the sixth to be built over the lower reaches of the Sumida. The first, Senju Ōhashi (Senju Great Bridge), was completed in 1596 and carried the main highway to the north of the country across the river. The first bridge downstream of Senju and within the city bounds stood about one kilometre south of the Oumaya ferry. It was completed after the Great Meireki Fire of 1657, when the lack of a means of escape across the river had contributed significantly to the casualty toll. Popularly called Ōhashi (Great Bridge), although it was officially known as Ryōgoku bridge, it became an important centre for streetside entertainment and riverine transport. Within the following one hundred years, three more

Table 4 Ferries across the Sumida from Senju Bridge downstream, showing dates for which records indicate services were operating

Ferry name	Start-end dates	A	B	C	D	E
Shioiri	1890–1971			1907	1916	1922
Suijin	?–?		1897	1907	1916	1922
Hashiba (Sumidagawa)	8thc?–1914	1870s/2#	1897	1907*	1916?	
Terajima (Shirahige)	1891–1920s			[1907*]	1916	1922
Imado	1880s–1920s	(occasional service?)				1922
Takeya (Matsuchi)	1830s?–1928?	1870s	1897	1907*	1916	1922
Yama no yado (Makurabashi)	1876–1920s	1870s/3	1897	1907*	1916	1922
Takechō (Hanagata/ Narihira)	early 1600s?–1876			1907		
Komagata	?–1910s?	1870s/4	1897	1907		
Ōumaya	1700s?–1874					
Okura (Yokoami)	1896–1927			1907*	1916	1922
Fujimi	1870s?–1910s	1870s/3	1897	1907*	1916?	
Chitose (Ichinohashi/ Hitotsume)	?–1920s	1870s/3	1897	1907	1916	1922
Atake (Hamachō)	1873–1920s	1870s/4	1897	1907*		
Nakazu	?–1928	1870s/5	1897	1907*	1916	1922
Ōkawaguchi (Ōwatashi)	1600s–1910s?	1870s/4		1907		
Ishikawajima	?–?			1907		
Tsukuda	?–1964	1870s/2		1907	1916	1922
Tsukishima	1896–1940			1907	1916	1922
Kachidoki	1905–1940			1907	1916	1922

\# Denotes the number of boats.
* Asterisked ferries are those listed in *Tōkyō annai*, published in 1907.

Columns

A. 1870s, *Tōkyō-to Kōbunshokan* (1991: 39), based on contemporary records.
B. 1897, *Tōkyō-shi 15 ku kinbō 34 chōson banchi sakai iri* (The 15 ward of Tokyo City and 34 towns and villages with borders between blocks). 1:5000. Tōkyō yūbinkyoku (Tokyo Post Office). Modern edition: no date given. Tokyo: Jinbunsha.
C. 1907, *Tōkyō-shi 15 ku kinbō 34 chōson banchi sakai iri* (as in column B).
D. 1916, *Tōkyō hyakunen shi* (vol. 4, p. 782), based on an unnamed 'Taishō era record.'
E. 1922, *Zaishinshiki Dai Tōkyō chizu banchi iri* (New format map of Greater Tokyo with block numbers). 1:100,000. Tokyo: *Tōkyō nichinichi shinbun.*

All save the Shioiri ferry in the north and the three southernmost services were terminated on the completion of bridges in the 1920s, as a result of the reconstruction programme following the Great Kantō Earthquake of 1 September 1923.

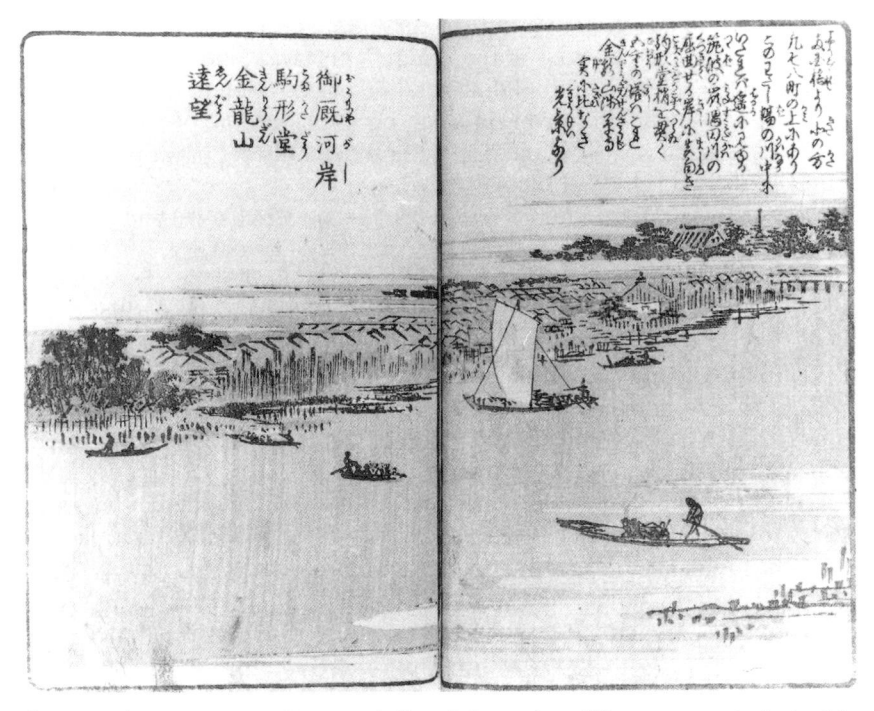

Figure 45 The Oumaya quay, Komagata hall, and distant view of Kinryūzan temple. In the right hand foreground is the Oumaya ferry. Hiroshige. *Ehon Edo miyage* (Illustrated books of Edo souvenirs), vol. 1. 1850.

bridges were built across the Sumida, Shin Ōhashi and Eitai and Azuma bridges. Ryōgoku bridge was an important centre of entertainment and riverine transport, not unlike London Bridge, which until 1750 was the only link to the south bank of the Thames.

In any early modern city, the administration of bridges was a complicated but vital matter.[12] In Edo, the aim of the shogunal government was generally to ensure that the expense for upkeep and repair was shouldered, if possible, through tolls or levies on local districts. In Osaka, known as the 'city of 808 bridges,' the situation was simpler. Of its 150 or so bridges, the shogunate maintained twelve, while most of the rest were the responsibility of the quarters (*chō*, or *machi*) at either end (Wakita 1994: 72). Whichever of Japan's largest cities one looks at, the difference with medieval and early modern Europe is striking. In European cities, bridges, generally of stone not of wood, were built by the city or central authority. As on the Ponte Vecchio in Florence, roadside space on bridges was often let out to shopkeepers in order to recoup some of the cost of construction (Girouard 1985: 57). In Edo, the central point on the bridge was sometimes adorned by a hut for the bridge-keeper, although this was more often located at a foot of the bridge. Otherwise, the wooden bridges of Japan were kept free of buildings and other encumbrances. The land at their feet was supposed to be kept clear, both for freedom of passage in an emergency and as space for the display of official notices (as at the landing stages of the Takechō and Oumaya ferries services).[13]

Despite the apparent importance of bridges, only two were built over the Sumida between the change of regime in 1868 and the earthquake of 1923.[14] These were the Umaya and Shirahige bridges, both of which replaced ferries, making for a total of six bridges in the lower reaches of the river. The first railway bridge over the Sumida was not completed until 1931, followed by a second the following year.

Even where bridges existed, they seldom facilitated the transport of goods by land. The old humped wooden bridges had been one of the principal obstacles to wheeled transport. In Edo, edicts were periodically issued reinforcing restrictions on the use of ox carts, and human portering was routinely considered more practical. It was only in 1872 that passage over the Sumida bridges was permitted for wheeled transport, be it rickshaw or cart, and new flat wooden and then steel bridges were built, so the volume of wheeled transport grew. The limited use of wheeled road transport meant the continued transport of goods by boat to the city's markets, most of which retained, at least until after the 1923 earthquake, their original quayside location. Even the burgeoning rail network, from the 1880s on, was closely integrated with the waterways. Most of the city's main stations were located alongside waterways, allowing for the easy transfer of goods from train to boat but leaving passengers to find their own way across.[15]

One of these stations was Ryōgokubashi, situated about five-hundred metres south of Umaya bridge, terminus for the railway line from points east of the city. There was no bridge at this point, and when a petition was launched for a ferry service here, the main reason cited was the large number of students and workers commuting across the river from the railway station. The petition was successful, and the Okura ferry came into service in 1896.

Fujimi Ferry: Symbol of a Vanishing Order

The number of ferries across the Sumida had started to decline by the early 1910s. Gone were the Oumaya and Takechō ferries, to be followed at about this time by the Hashiba, Komagata, Atake and Ōkawaguchi ferries and shortly after by the Fujimi ferry, which first started operating in the 1870s and traversed the Sumida just south of the Okura ferry.

For Akutagawa Ryūnosuke, the ferries were symbols of a vanishing order, and their suppression was like a stab in the cultural soul. 'If I remember correctly,' wrote Akutagawa in 1914 in a piece entitled 'Ōkawa no mizu' (The waters of the Great River), 'there were five ferries between Azuma Bridge and Shin Ōhashi [when I was a child]. Three of these – Komagata, Fujimi, and Atake – disappeared one by one. Now only two are there as they always have been: the [Chitose] ferry from Ichinohashi to Hamachō and the ferry that crosses from Okura Bridge to Sudachō [Okura ferry]. . . . Only these two ferries, with the same flat-bottomed boats and old boatswains on board ply back and forth every day across the willow-green waters of the river, just as they always used to' (Sumida-ku 1967: 655).

In an uncompromisingly bleak essay, 'Honjo Ryōgoku,' written in 1927 just before his death, Akutagawa describes a return to the area near the river where he was brought up. With everything destroyed in the earthquake and then hastily rebuilt, there is nothing familiar in the landscape. All links with the past have been broken. 'I recalled that the Fujimi ferry had surely been somewhere around here. But nowhere could I see anything resembling the hut at its landing stage. I decided to ask a man of about thirty who was peeling potatoes there at the side of the road whether the landing stage for the ferry still existed. He had, however, not heard of the Fujimi ferry, let alone its landing stage.'[16]

Ferries were one among many elements in the landscape vocabulary of the city. The sandbanks were another. 'Compared with when I was a child,' wrote Akutagawa in the passage quoted above from the essay of 1914, 'the flow of the river has changed and the occasional sandbanks with their profusion of reeds have been buried without a trace.' Yet another were the stakes that lined the river at various points. On the left bank of the river north of Ryōgoku Bridge had stood a disorderly platoon of stakes known as *hyappongui* (hundred stakes). They had been planted there to protect the bank at a point where there was a bend in the river. The stakes were portrayed in prints by two great artists of the city, Hiroshige (1797–1858) and, memorably, by Kobayashi Kiyochika, who seemed to find in them a haphazard quality that symbolized the city of the past and stood in contrast to the order of the new urbanism. Kōda Rohan referred to them in his essay '*Mizu no Tōkyō*.' They were, he wrote, a favoured spot for anglers fishing for carp. The stakes disappeared along with the sandbanks when new banks were constructed for the Sumida in the 1910s.

As the sandbanks sank and the stakes were stripped, so a new vocabulary of landscape emerged, ponds, ditches, and collections of dirty liquid waste to the fore. Pools of stagnant water crop up in various accounts; one, for example is mentioned by the poet Masaoka Shiki (1867–1902) in his description of the area around a train station (Sumida-ku 1978: 736). Ditches were another common feature of the east bank landscape. They are clearly shown in maps of east Tokyo in these years. By 1930 these ponds and ditches had become the principal features of the informal waterscape of the industrialising east of the city, putrid in summer, dry in winter, and discoloured by run-off from local factories. Streams, ditches, ponds, pools, and puddles all provided a breeding ground for mosquitoes, and many of them were drained, covered, or culverted in the 1930s and successive decades.

Chitose Ferry: Losing out to Steam

Here and there, riverside areas were appropriated by purveyors of prostitution or of those establishments (like boat-houses and tea-houses) that provided a range of entertainment services to a male clientèle. As the river flowed south past the storehouses and depots, it reached Yanagibashi, just south of the Okura and Fujimi ferries, where the banks burst into life. On the right bank, the boat-houses from which customers were sculled the short distance upriver to the brothel district of Yoshiwara grew later into one of the city's more exclusive *geisha* districts. In the second part of the nineteenth century and on until after the Second World War, the river here and the streets behind were lined with restaurants where *geisha* poured the rice wine and plucked the strings of their *samisen*.

Immediately downstream lay Ryōgoku bridge. Before the new imperial government brought in a regime of traffic regulation and the purposive use of public space, the open ground at the bridge's feet appears to have been in a state of permanent congestion. Crowds gathered, goods were bought and sold, and a rich variety of entertainment was on offer. The river was 'opened' each year on the 28th day of the 5th Month with a fireworks display, and for the next three months, its waters were busy with boats whose passengers were involved in the summer ritual of keeping cool with fans, music, food and drink. The bridge was thus a focal point for the river as a locale for celebration and festivities (Markus 1985; Smith 1986a, 1986b). In later years, the bridge remained a hub of riverine transport. From a landing stage at its feet, steam boats with paddle wheels set off for points to the east of Tokyo, Matsudo, Nagareyama and all the way to Chōshi on the coast.

The bridge straddled the river halfway between the Fujimi and Chitose ferries, mentioned by Akutagawa in the passage quoted above as being one of the two services still functioning. The east bank landing stage for the Chitose ferry was situated a short distance down the Tatekawa canal, which cut directly eastward through the city, part of the grid of canals that characterized Tokyo east of the Sumida river. These canals were serviced by a number of boats conveying people further along the city's waterways. These were the *hayabune*, express boats, sculled vessels about the same size as the ferry boats. The official *Tōkyō annai* (Tokyo guide), published by the city office in 1907, lists eight *hayabune* routes. Several of these routes followed the Tatekawa canal on its route through the rapidly industrializing east of the city (Tōkyō-shi 1986: 1–214). In a little vignette of a story, written in 1909, Nagai Kafū describes a journey on an express boat from Ryōgoku bridge down the canal to a peony garden. On the way, 'in the middle of the river we brushed prows with the ferry to First Bridge [the Chitose ferry]' (Seidensticker 1965: 221). The next moment, 'our little boat rocked in the wake of a passing steamer, and the flat-bottomed ferry rocked yet more violently. ... The spray, threatening to break over the embankment into the street, was clear from across the river.'

The steamer that Kafū refers to was generally known as *issen jōki*, the 1-*sen* steamer, named after the fare originally charged. By the time Kafū was writing, steamers had become a prominent feature of the city's waterscape. In many a woodblock print, they appear as resplendent inflated symbols of new mechanical power, reminiscent of their rendition in the paintings of European artists like Monet who sought to represent the impact of industrialization on the landscape.[17] They appear too in the writings of Nagai Kafū and Akutagawa Ryūnosuke. In his story '*Reishō*' (Cold smile), published in 1910, Kafū writes of a trip in a *ponpon* steamer (named after the sound of its siren) and describes the passengers, an old lady in from the nearby countryside, a woman with baby from the poor backstreets, and a retired gentleman. 'The river,' he writes, 'seems even broader than it does when sitting on one bank and looking across. The brick buildings of the Sapporo brewery rise red against a blue sky, and the rickshaw pullers wait like small but well-formed toys in the sun at the waterside' (Sumida-ku 1967: 530).

The first Tokyo steamer started operating in 1885, when a certain Furukawa Koshichi (active mid to late Meiji era) was given permission for a service from Hatchōbori, near the centre of town, up the Sumida river to Asakusa in the north (Tōkyō-to Kōbunshokan 1991: 114, 130, 134). By then steamers were already linking the city with its immediate environs, among these being the Tsūun Maru service that operated first five and soon eight sailings a day down the Onagi canal to Gyōtoku. These and other services were a response to government promotion of new forms of transport in the 1880s.

Over the following two decades, Furukawa Koshichi appears to have built up something of a monopoly of 1-*sen* steamer services in Tokyo, having founded the Sumida Maru and Ōkawa companies and then merged them in 1898. Two years later, his monopoly was ended by the Senju Azuma steamer company, whose boats conveyed passengers north from Asakusa to Senju. These two were joined in 1911 by the Kōtō Junkō company, with 13 fuel-powered boats on a loop route from Azuma bridge through east-bank areas and then back along the Tatekawa past the landing stage of the Chitose ferry to Ryōgoku bridge and up the Sumida to Azuma bridge.

The steamers, whose engines had a habit of catching fire and spewing flames out of their funnel, inevitably drew passengers away from other water-borne forms of transport, express boats in particularly but also ferries. It appears, however, that their impact extended onto land. According to newspaper reports published in the period just after the start of steamer operations along the Sumida, demand for rickshaws in districts near the river plummeted. This was at a time when rickshaws had become an increasingly common form of transport, their numbers in Tokyo reaching a peak of almost 50,000 by the turn of the century. Their subsequent decline was accompanied by a growth in the number of bicycles in circulation as well as in the tram network. Tram lines were routed across the Ryōgoku and Umaya bridges from 1906 and the Shin Ōhashi and Eitai bridges by 1920. A combination of trams and steamers, bicycles and rickshaws would surely have dealt a fatal blow to the ferries, even without the construction of more bridges in the 1920s. The steamers continued to provide a service up until the war and beyond but eventually fell to competition from the railways.

Nakazu and Ishikawajima Ferries: Conveying Workers to the Factory Gates

In the short term, it was the industrialisation of the east bank that led to an increase in the number of ferry services and crossings and, so far as it can be gauged, passengers. In this sense, it is perhaps ironic that ferries were adopted by writers like Kafū as symbols of a preindustrial day.

For the nation's first industrialists, situating factories near the seat of government bore a number of advantages, and the choice of a site along the Sumida and the waterways of the east bank was a natural one, given the cheapness of the land and the ease of transport afforded by the water. This was a pattern that had been started by the shogunate, with the foundation in 1853 of the shipbuilding yards at Ishikawajima at the mouth of the Sumida. The nation's first cement works, later to become Asano cement, were sited by the river in Fukagawa. In the case of both these factories, direct links with the west bank of the Sumida were effected by a ferry, the private Ishikawajima ferry and the Nakazu ferry.[18]

It was by no means only near the mouth of the river that factories were being built. Further upstream, the Kanegafuchi Bōseki mill was founded in 1889 on the east bank of the Sumida north of the Hashiba ferry. The following year, a ferry service was started at Shioiri, carrying workers over to the new factory. By this time there were already eight other industrial enterprises located on either side of the three-kilometre-long Mukōjima embankment that ran south from the mill. By 1920, there were sixty-eight. In 1891, a successful application was made to the Tokyo prefectural government for a new ferry service to cross the Sumida between the Hashiba and Imado ferries, to serve as another link between the Mukōjima embankment and the west bank. The request was made on the grounds that the growing number of factories had led to a general increase in activity and movement to and from the centre of town but that this was impeded by the distance of the two existing ferries (Tōkyō-to Kōbunshokan 1991: 77).

Industrialization of the urban periphery led to land subsidence and to a significant intensification of flooding. By the 1880s flooding, or at any rate water seepage, had become virtually an annual event in the east and northeast of the city. Severe flooding occurred along the east bank at least fourteen times between 1870 and 1923. The 1885 floodwaters were violent enough to carry away chunks of the Senju and Azuma bridges. Ryōgoku Bridge and Shin Ōhashi were also damaged (Sumida-ku 1967: 1131). The floods of 1907 and 1914 were particularly serious, but the most catastrophic of all was that of August 1910, when the whole of the east bank remained under water for at least ten days. The estimated cost of the damage was 1.34 million yen in Honjo Ward and 1.80 million yen in Fukagawa. The total cost of the damage wrought by the flooding in the east of Japan in August 1910 was 120 million yen, at a time when the national income stood at 290 million yen.[19]

It was after the 1907 flood that work was stepped up on the construction of concrete banks for the Sumida. The process took many years, but by about 1920 the river had become considerably narrower, and maps of this time no longer show the sandbanks that had so enchanted Akutagawa Ryūnosuke. The new banks did at least provide a solution to one of the more pressing problems presented by the steamers (alluded to by Nagai Kafū in the passage quoted above), the wash from the boats flooding the river banks and eroding the soil. This was an issue that had been taken up with the police and the Tokyo government in 1900 by a neighbourhood association representing residents of the flood-prone land in the fold of the river at Shioiri before it turned south toward Hashiba.

After the 1910 flood, it was decided to build a new outlet for the river, an enormous enterprise that was near enough to completion to avert flooding in August 1923, only a few weeks before the earthquake that devastated the city. The new Arakawa outlet itself, with a width that increased from two to five hundred metres near its mouth, occasioned the start of a number of new ferry services.

For a few decades, then, the process of industrial urbanization – outstripping, one might say, that of urban modernization – actually led to an increase in the number and use of ferry services. Cheap to operate and flexible, the ferry proved an invaluable means of carrying workers across the city's waterways to its growing number of riverside factories. As the process of industrial urbanization spread outward, so new ferry services were started, and ferries that had been used principally by farmers became filled with workers in the factories of the urban periphery. Ferries, then, had their place in the new landscape of the industrializing city.

Tsukuda, Tsukishima, and Kachidoki Ferries: Municipal Ferries and Modern Cities

Two of the three ferries that crossed over from central Tokyo to the islands at the mouth of the Sumida were more recent services – inevitably, since they linked land that had been built out of the bay around the turn of the century. The three ferries – Tsukuda, Tsukishima, and Kachidoki – were the only means of travelling direct from the centre of the city to the islands and landfill at the river's mouth, and they were heavily used by the workers in the many factories that were located there. The other link was across Aioibashi, a bridge completed in 1903, vital for power supplies to the newly reclaimed land but inconvenient in terms of access to the city centre.

The only one of the three that predated the landfill work was the Tsukuda ferry. This was an old service probably dating from the early years of settlement on the island of Tsukuda, at the mouth of the river. The origins of the ferry and its importance to the inhabitants of the island led to a dispute over its operation (Tōkyō-to Kōbunshokan 1991: 58). In the Tokugawa period, it was said to be the joint possession of the Tsukuda landowners (*jinushi no kyōyū butsu*), but as forms of municipal governance changed in the Meiji era, so this practice came to be seen by local residents as fundamentally unjust. Eventually they took their case to law and won; the court ruled that the ferry service belonged to all the residents of Tsukudajima, and so any operating profits should be divided between them.[20]

The ferry started regular service in 1883, under the management of the Ōkura-gumi company. It cost 5 *rin* to use, about half the price of a large bowl of *soba*.[21] Operations were handed over to the Tokyo government in 1925, and two years later the ferryman's overworked scull was relieved through the addition of a steamer to tug the ferry most of the way across. By December 1928, the number of daily crossings had been increased to 166, with 262 carts, 2188 bicycles, and 10,199 passengers making the short journey each day (Table 2). This was the last of the municipal passenger ferries, ceasing operation in 1964 on the completion of a bridge linking the island of Tsukudajima to the heart of the city.

The Kachidoki ferry went into service in 1905 and was named to commemorate the capture of Port Arthur in the Russo-Japanese War. The ferry was initially operated by Kyōbashi Ward but was soon handed over to the Tokyo city government, its scull being supplemented with paddles and a steam-powered engine in 1914. Years later, the writer and historian Kishii Yoshie wrote of his memories of the Kachidoki ferry. 'The ferry I knew had a steamer like a locomotive engine and two old-style boats [*wasen*]. One of these would be sculled out by the boatman once the passengers were on board. At a certain point, the steamer would arrive, throw out a rope, and pull the boat, until – approaching the far bank – the rope would be released and once again the boat would be sculled by the boatman.' Then the steamer would tug the other boat back. Bicycles used to be taken on board, but Kishii never saw carts or horses on the Kachidoki ferry. The service continued until the completion, much delayed, of a bridge by the same name, in 1940 (Kishii 1977: 95).

It was in a restaurant, the Eitai Pavilion, near the landing stage of the Tsukuda ferry, that a group of young writers met in the years between 1908 and 1912. They called themselves *Pan no kai*, the Bread Society, to broadcast their embrace of an exotic Europeanism and their acceptance of the influence of the new cultural landscape that was transforming the city in which they lived. Several of their number, which included the poets Kitahara Hakushū (1885–1942), Kinoshita Mokutarō (1885–1945), and Ishikawa Takuboku (1886–1912), the sculptor and poet Takamura Kōtarō (1883–1956), and the novelist Tanizaki Junichirō (1886–1965), used the city as a point of reference in their literary explorations. Their city, home of the retreating shadows of Edo, was also a bright, dynamic capital, shimmering with new possibilities, with the Sumida river as the principal geographical backdrop for their artistic imaginations (Kubota 1996: 95; Suzuki 1995: 163). For a number of reasons, the landscape at the mouth of the Sumida was resonant with symbols of the West and of modernity. Here on the west bank, the first Western residents of the city had been briefly corralled in the 1860s and many of their institutions remained, while on the east bank stood the new factories of a rising industrial power. It was appropriate therefore that a ferry should appear in one of Kinoshita Mokutarō's better known poems, contrasted with the whistle of the steamer and the lights of the hotel:

> Setting off for Bōsu, or going to Izu?
> A whistle can be heard – to which, that whistle?
> As the ferry ferries over to Tsukudajima,
> The lights of the Metropole shrine bright.[22]

Symbol and Landscape Vocabulary

Ferries formed part of an unusually rich vocabulary of landscape that enabled writers and artists to articulate their fears and feelings about the changing world around them. In the works of people like Nagai Kafū and Akutagawa Ryūnosuke, the elimination of ferries and their replacement by bridges is symbolic of cultural change at a higher level. Even at a time, in the 1910s when there were as many ferries as ever before, both these writers were full of premonitions. 'Disappear [the ferries] surely must as Tokyo is ordered and bridges built,' wrote Kafū in his 1914 topography of the city. 'Already there are only woodblock prints to remind us of the Ōkawaguchi, Oumaya, and Yoroi ferries' (Nagai 1961: 342).

The multiplicity of boats that had once plied the river provided a rich source of terminology with which to express change within the cultural landscape of the city. The roll call of names of the different types of boat is a frequent feature of topographical writing in the modernizing city, often expressed as a litany for a variety and richness that is fast disappearing. This richness of vocabulary is reflected in an equally abundant toponymy. Each ferry had a name, and each name a repository of associations. Some ferries indeed had more than one name. Such an abundant toponymy suggests a deeply topophilic sensibility.

Together, the ferries, lighters, and pleasure boats, sandbanks, stakes, and inlets offered a vocabulary of landscape that was subsumed into a much broader idiom of cultural change – change from a world of water and wood to one of land and steel. This is the overarching language of landscape into which the vocabulary of ferries and boats is set. Kafū's writing reflects the tension inherent in this change. For Kafū, the writer for whom, more than any other, artistic inspiration was bound up with the city, water was the essence of the city's sensuous charm. 'Water remains as it has been since the Edo period the main element for preserving an aesthetic quality in Tokyo. In earlier days, lacking the convenience of land transport, it goes without saying that the naturally flowing Sumida and its many artificial tributaries were the lifeblood of Edo commerce. And together with this, for the people of the city, it provided pleasure for the four seasons and sometimes formed the substance of poems and paintings of some worth. But in today's city of Tokyo, the waterways are simply there for transportation, and they have lost all their former aesthetic value' (Nagai 1961: 331). Water has become functional at best; at worst, it is insanitary and putrid.

In the same passage, Kafū lamented the disappearance of ferries and the construction of bridges. 'Railways,' Kafū wrote, 'take the emotion out of travel for people born in the previous era [*kinsei*]. Bridges deprive you of the gentle emotions of ferries.' The piquancy of change is evoked in a passage from the official *Honjo kushi* (History of Honjo Ward), published in 1931: 'Now as a result of the construction of bridges and the development of land transport systems, small boats are becoming ever rarer, and the ferries of the Great River will soon be nothing but a memory. Of course, this sort of change is surely to be desired. But even if it is little more than the name of a ferry, there is no denying the sadness of a break with these slender links to the traditions of Edo' (Honjo-ku 1931: 264).

Some writers, however, like the poet Kinoshita Mokutarō, were more willing to engage with the potentialities of changing urban cultures. With a copy of a recently purchased treatise by Le Corbusier (1887–1965) in his hand, Mokutarō set off on a June day in 1930 to examine the new steel bridges over the river, publishing his impressions in the *Tōkyō Asahi* newspaper. Although he could not accept Le Corbusier's message of functionalist structuralism, he did find features to admire in the new bridges, one of which, Eitaibashi, he declared to be 'the technical masterpiece of Tokyo's reconstruction' (Unno 1983: 18). Other sources gave voice to a more unambiguously triumphalist mood in tune with what might be called official thinking. Glorying in the new steel structures built across the main waterways in the years following the 1923 earthquake, a publication of the *Asahi* newspaper contained the following trumpet blast: 'With its abundance of rivers, Tokyo is now recognised in particular as a "capital city of bridges".... In its number of bridges, it is surely first in the world' (*Asahi shinbun* 1932).

Although Tokyo's ferries may seem an unusually arcane inlet of topographical inquiry, they tell us much about attitudes towards change in the cultural landscape and in the culture of urban life. In the first place, they indicate the importance placed on the constituent elements of the phenomenal environment. A way of life is here symbolised not in moral codes or religious beliefs but in the spatial patterns described by the objects around us. The ferries are mourned because of their power as symbols of a vanishing world; they are mourned even before they lose their function and disappear from the waters of the river. The ferries remind us too that conceptualisations of the objects that form our material surroundings are fluid, dependent on our memories. 'I certainly can't say that the waters of the Great River were clean when I was young. But it was the dirt of soil, mud, not the chemical dirt of now.'[23] The ferries and boats of the Sumida succeed each other as visual symbols of a cultural landscape. As the boats of Edo fade into memory, so their place is taken by the tugs and the 1-*sen* steamers.

Underpinning it all, however, is an attitude to change that prefers to lament – and equally, as a consequence to celebrate – the passage of time and its effects on the manifest world rather than to attempt an institutionalised act of preservation. 'Wooden ferries and their aged ferrymen are revered treasures and should be preserved as one would old trees and temples,' wrote Kafū in his 1914 topography *Hiyori geta* (Daytime clogs), knowing full well that they would not be preserved any more than old trees and temples were in this city rapacious for change (Nagai 1961: 343).

Notes

1 Much of Nagai Kafū's literary *oeuvre* deals with the theme of passing time and the changing cultural geography of Edo-Tokyo. It resonates with an elegiac feeling for times and places past. All this is well represented in Edward Seidensticker's biography-cum-anthology, *Kafū the Scribbler: The Life and Works Nagai Kafū, 1879–1959* (1965). Kafū's representation of the city is discussed in Pierre Faure's *La Sumida par Nagai Kafū* (1974). A provocative recent commentary is provided by Tomi Suzuki, *Narrating the Self: Fictions of Japanese Modernity* (1995), pp. 135–51. In Japanese the work of Maeda Ai is

Memory and the Changing Passage of Space

illuminating, in particular, *Toshi kūkan no naka no bungaku* (Literature in urban space) (1982).

For an account of the short life of Akutagawa Ryūnosuke, see Graham Healey's introduction to the translation of Akutagawa's *Kappa* (1971).

2 Literary references to the Sumida are discussed by Kubota Jun in his *Sumidagawa no bungaku* (1996). This passage is discussed on page 217. Lady Sarashina's memoirs were translated into English by Ivan Morris under the title *As I crossed a bridge of dreams: Recollections of a woman in eleventh-century Japan* (1975).

3 A translation of the story is given in Waley (1996: 395). A fuller treatment of the topography of the city can be found in P. Waley, *Tokyo: City of Stories* (1991).

4 The story is mentioned in one of the city's early topographies *Edo sunago onko meiseki shi* (Gold-dust memories of famous sites in Edo), published in 1732. The reference here is taken from Imai (1969: 120).

5 The creation story is told in the *Kojiki* (Records of ancient matters). The translation into English by Basil Hall Chamberlain, originally published in 1883, was reprinted in 1973 by the Asiatic Society of Japan.

6 In discussing travel and transport under the Tokugawa shoguns (1603–1868), Japanese historians have been divided over the reasons for the paucity of bridges along the country's main highways, with some arguing that their number was kept to a minimum in order to impede the advance of a hostile military force. In a recent monograph on travel in Tokugawa Japan, the American historian Constantine Vaporis questions the evidence for this argument. 'Geographical and technological issues,' he writes, 'rather than political philosophy, lay at the heart of Tokugawa policy towards rivers and bridges' (Vaporis 1994: 152).

7 For an account of the layers of narrative and visual topography constructed around the Mukōjima embankment, see Waley (1996).

8 This and other quotations concerning the Sumida river appear in *Bokutō gaishi: Sumida* (Sumida: an unofficial history of the east bank of the river), an anthology published by Sumida Ward Office in 1967.

9 Charles Peter Thunberg, *Travels in Europe, Africa, and Asia*, quoted in Vaporis (1994: 49).

10 Details of names and dates of these and other ferries are taken from volume 13 (Tokyo) of *Kadokawa Nihon chimei daijiten* (1978).

11 For a detailed account of ferry services, dates of operation, and fares, see the work compiled and published by Tōkyō-to Kōbunshokan (Tokyo Metropolitan Records and Archives Institute), *Kindai Tōkyō no watashi-bune to issen jōki* (The ferries and 1-*sen* steam boats of modernizing Tokyo) (1991).

12 So expensive were bridges to build that reconstruction after flooding was often tardy. Vaporis relates how the Rokugō bridge on the main Tokaidō highway carrying travellers from Osaka, Kyoto, and the west into Edo was washed away and rebuilt many times in the sixteenth and seventeenth centuries. It was destroyed by flooding in 1688 and replaced by a ferry service. A new bridge was not built until 1868, and that one too was washed away not long after its completion. Eventually a steel bridge was constructed in 1925 (Vaporis 1994: 52).

13 The administration of open spaces, such as at the foot of bridges is discussed by Itō Yoshiichi in his *Edo no machikado* (Edo's streeet corners) (1987: 28).

14 Much of the detailed information on bridges and transport across the Sumida is taken from a chronology published by the Sumida Ward Library called *Sumida no kōtsū ōrai* (The changing traffic of Sumida) (1984).

15 In 1926, a peak year in the volume of goods transported into and out of the city by train, some 45 per cent of these products were transferred onto boats at the city's eight central goods stations (Okajima 1989: 500).

16 The essay forms part of an anthology by various authors 'rediscovering' the rebuilt city and published as *Dai Tōkyō hanjōki* (Accounts of prosperity in Greater Tokyo). The book was republished in 1976 by Kōdansha.
17 'A popular contemporary symbol for industial progress' is how Paul Hayes Tucker describes the steamboats of 1860 France in his book *Monet at Argenteuil* (Tucker 1982: 62).
18 The Nakazu ferry was named after an islet built out of the river in the 1770s, on which were situated tea-houses, bath-houses and restaurants. A few years later, in 1789, the whole island was vacated, an affront to public morality, but the memory remained (Smith 1986a: pl. 57).
19 Details on flooding in Tokyo can be found in volume 4 of the 6 volume *Tōkyō hyakunen shi* (History of 100 years of Tokyo) compiled by the Tokyo Metropolitan Government (1979: 1012).
20 Occasionally (but perhaps inevitably) problems continued to arise as a result of an excess of ferry services. According to the *Tōkyō Asahi* edition of 12 October 1892, the police inspected ferry landing places following a dispute between ferry operators plying the Onagi canal. Respective ferry operators organised themselves into 'black banner' and 'red banner' groups. Other disputes were occasioned by differing interpretations of the need to send out emergency services at times of flooding.
21 All comparisons of prices are taken from *Shūkan Asahi* (ed.) *Nedan shi nenpyō* (An annual catalogue of the history of prices) (1988).
22 The Metropole Hotel had been built in Akashi-chō, on land vacated by the American consulate, when the latter moved to its present site in Akasaka. Akashi was a celebrated area of coastline near where the city of Kobe now stands and from where the district's first inhabitants are said to have been brought. See Kubota, (1996: 60) and Suzuki (1995).
23 These comments come from an essay entitled 'Ōkawa' (The great river), written by Nakajima Mamoru in 1961 and quoted in Sumida-ku 1967, page 930.

References

Akutagawa R. (1971) *Kappa*. With an introduction by G. Healey. Tokyo: Tuttle.
Asahi shinbun (ed.) (1932) *Shin Tōkyō daikan* (A panorama of the new Tokyo). Tokyo; Tōkyō Asahi Shinbun.
Berque, A. (1986) *Le sauvage et l'artifice: Les Japonais devant la nature*. Paris: Gallimard.
Chamberlain, B.H. (1973) *Ko-ji-ki: 'Records of Ancient Matters.'* Tokyo: Asiatic Society of Japan. First published in 1883.
Faure, P. (1974) *La Sumida par Nagai Kafū*. Paris: Gallimard.
Girouard, M. (1985) *Cities and People*. New Haven: Yale University Press.
Hayami T. (1975) *Jizō shinkō* (Belief in Jizō). Tokyo: Hanawa Shobō.
Higuchi T. (1981) *Nihon no keikan* (The Japanese landscape). Tokyo: Shunshūsha.
Honjo-ku (Honjo Ward) (1931) *Honjo kushi* (History of Honjo Ward). Tokyo: Honjo kuyakusho.
Imai K. (1969) *Shōsetsu Edo meisho ki* (A detailed explanation of the accounts of famous places in Edo). Tokyo: Shakai Shisōsha.
Itō Y. (1987) *Edo no machikado* (Edo's streeet corners). Tokyo: Heibonsha.
Kishii Y. (1977) *Taishō no Tsukijikko* (Tsukiji child of the Taishō era). Tokyo: Seiabō.
Kubota J. (1996) *Sumidagawa no bungaku* (The literature of the Sumida river). Tokyo: Iwanami Shoten.

Maeda A. (1982) *Toshi kūkan no naka no bungaku* (Literature in urban space). Tokyo: Chikuma Shobō.

Markus, A. (1985) 'The carneval of Edo: *misemono* spectacles from contemporary accounts.' *Harvard Journal of Asiatic Studies* 45: 499–541.

Morris, I (trans.) (1975) *As I Crossed a Bridge of Dreams: Recollections of a Woman in Eleventh-Century Japan*. London: Penguin.

Okajima K. (1989) '*Kindai Tōkyō ni okeru shinai suiun ni tsuite*' (Concerning urban water transport in modernising Tokyo), *Jinbun chiri* 41 (6).

Seidensticker, E. (1965) *Kafū the Scribbler: The Life and Works of Nagai Kafū, 1879–1959*. Standford: Stanford University Press.

Shūkan Asahi (ed.) (1988). *Nedan shi nenpyō* (An annual catalogue of the history of prices). Tokyo: Asahi Shinbunsha.

Smith, H.D. II (1986a) *Hiroshige: One Hundred Famous Views of Edo*. New York: Braziller.

—— (1986b) 'Sky and water: the deep structures of Tokyo.' In M. Friedman (ed.) *Tokyo: Form and Spirit* New York: Abrams.

Sumida-ku (Sumida Ward) (1978) *Sumida kushi, zenshi* (History of Sumida Ward before its foundation). Tokyo: Sumida Kuyakusho.

—— (1967) *Bokutō gaishi: Sumida* (Sumida: an unofficial history of the east bank of the river). Tokyo: Sumida Kuyakusho.

Sumida-ku toshokan (Sumida Ward Library) (1984) *Sumida no kōtsū ōrai* (The changing traffic of Sumida). Tokyo: Sumida Kuyakusho.

Suzuki T. (1995) *Narrating the Self: Fictions of Japanese Modernity*. Standford: Stanford University Press.

Takeuchi R. (ed.) (1978) *Kadokawa Nihon chimei daijiten* (The Kadokawa complete dictionary of Japanese place names). Tokyo: Kadokawa Shoten.

Tōkyō-shi (1986) *Tōkyō annai* (Tokyo guide). 2 vols. Tokyo: Hihyōsha. First published, 1907, by Tōkyō Shiyakusho.

Tōkyō-to (Tokyo Metropolis) (1979) *Tōkyō hyakunen shi* (History of 100 years of Tokyo) Tokyo: Gyōsei.

Tōkyō-to Kōbunshokan (Tokyo Metropolitan Records and Archives Institute) (1991) *Kindai Tōkyō no watashibune to issen jōki* (The ferries and 1-*sen* steam boats of modern Tokyo). Tokyo: Tōkyō-to Kōbunshokan.

Tucker P.H. (1982) *Monet at Argenteuil*. New Haven: Yale University Press.

Unno, H. (1983) *Modan toshi Tōkyō: Nihon no 1920 nendai* (Tokyo the modern city: the 1920s in Japan. Tokyo: Chūō Kōron.

Vaporis, C. (1994) *Breaking Barriers: Travel and the State in Early Modern Japan*. Cambridge, Mass.: Harvard University Press.

Wakita O. (1994) *Kinsei Osaka no keizai to bunka* (The economy and culture of pre-modern Osaka). Kyoto: Jinbun Shoin.

Waley, P. (1996) 'On the far bank of the river: places of recreation on the periphery of the pre-modern Japanese city.' *Ecumene* 3(4): 384–407.

—— (1991) *Tokyo: City of Stories*. New York: Weatherhill.

CHAPTER 8

From a Shogunal City to a Life City

Tokyo between Two Fin-de-siècles*

Mikako Iwatake

In the wake of the by-now celebrated volume edited by Hobsbawm and Ranger (1983), the contributors to which discussed the extent to which traditions could in fact be considered modern inventions, there have been a number of studies on the issue of invented traditions in the context of modern Japan (Fujitani 1996; Vlastos 1998; Shirane and Suzuki 1999). The ideas originally advanced in the Hobsbawm and Ranger book have since been modulated and developed, to the point where tradition today is regarded as more an act of redefinition in the light of changing circumstances than an outright fabrication. Following on from this more nuanced reading of the significance and meaning of tradition, this chapter discusses the (re)making of identity and the (re)writing of history in Tokyo over the last one hundred years. For this purpose, I will draw upon seven major anniversaries held in Tokyo by the Tokyo Metropolitan Government (TMG) and earlier by the Tokyo City Government between 1889 and 1989. As the following table shows, Tokyo has not celebrated its anniversaries regularly, on the basis of a single historical origin of the city. Rather, the making of identity has been the primary political goal, which then has appropriated historical events of different temporal orders.

---

*The writing of this chapter was made possible by grants given by the Nordic Institute of Asian Studies in 1995 and 1996. I would like to express my gratitude to the Institute. A different version of this chapter was published in *Suomen Antropologi* 1998 23(2): 37–53.

Major anniversaries celebrated by Tokyo Metropolitan (City) Government

Year	Event	Desired City Identity
1889	Edo 300th Anniversary	(Ambiguous)
1898	30th Anniversary of the founding of the capital	Imperial City
1919	50th Anniversary of founding of the capital	Imperial City
1940	2600th Anniversary of the imperial stater	Imperial/World City
1956	Greater Tokyo 500th Anniversary	(Ambiguous)
1968	Tokyo Centennial	Modern City
1989	Edo Tokyo 400th Anniversary	World/Cultural City

This chapter also discusses the emergence of a heroic narrative about the city during the post-World War II years and the political meanings of this narrative. Recently Lisa Yoneyama has discussed how postwar Japan discursively constructed an image of a peace-loving, harmless nation by emphasizing victimization by atomic bombings in Hiroshima and by masking nation's history of military aggression (Yoneyama 1999). Events in Tokyo during the postwar years tend to bear out this interpretation. While the imperialization of historical memory was a critical task until World War II, the de-imperialization of historical memory became an urgent undertaking in the postwar years. In this process, the TMG has produced a narrative for the city which presents it as a victim of a series of catastrophes and a phoenix that comes back as a world city. The various postwar anniversaries have provided an opportunity to represent such a narrative.

In Edo, disjointed and contesting temporal orders – most notably imperial time and shogunal time – have existed side by side. The city's passage from shogunal capital into imperial capital created its own historical consciousness. Each temporal order has been influenced by Judeo-Christian conceptions of time, such as the decade, century, centennial, millennium, anniversary, solar calendar, and the Christian era. In a process aligning itself with the Western powers, Japan adopted the Judeo-Christian temporal system in 1872, after which it was internalized in the assertion of 'indigenous' temporal orders.

Anniversary celebrations might not necessarily be a primary driving force for social change. They often have carried multiple and contradictory meanings and messages. Yet symbolically they have played a vital role in shaping, presenting, and representing a desired identity for a territory, whatever its dimensions. An examination into Tokyo's various anniversaries reveals how the organization of time and political power are closely related, and how the (re)writing of history is a contested terrain, depending on whose historical memory and which temporal order is presented and represented, and for which political end.

The Emperor and the Shogun, Their Time and Their City

Except for the Greater Tokyo 500th Anniversary (*Kaito gohyakunen kinen dai Tōkyō sai*), all anniversaries celebrated either imperial or shogunal time. I would like to give a brief outline of the conflicting relationship between the emperor and the shogun, and their competition over both temporal management and cities.

Around the seventh century, the imperial family of today established itself as the dominant clan. Their power started to decline around the tenth century, and political power shifted to land-holding warrior families, the leading representative of which started to rule in the twelfth century. This did not, however, mean the end of imperial authority. Although deprived of political power, the emperor embodied symbolic and ritualistic authority. In the period of shogunal rule, which continued through to the mid nineteenth century, one of the few arenas where the emperor's power was manifested was the control of time. The setting up of a *nengō* (era name) and the issuing of a calendar were imperial prerogatives.

The *nengō* system is said to have originated in imperial China around the second century AD. It had spread throughout the Chinese cultural world and had started to be used in Japan between the mid seventh and the eighth century. The adoption of *nengō* in written records was a means by which the imperial family represented itself as the ruler of the country domestically as well as internationally in the wider East Asian world order (Tokoro 1996: 3–13).

Before the Meiji era (1868–1912), the emperor adopted and changed *nengō* at critical moments during his reign. *Nengō*, which always consisted of two Chinese characters, were changed upon a new emperor's enthronement as it was seen to symbolically mark the start of the new era. *Nengō* were also changed after an earthquake, flood, famine, epidemic, fire, the appearance of a comet in the sky, or war. After natural as well as man-made catastrophes, a new era name was given and within it the first year started anew. This act was thought to nullify the polluted time and to bring in new time and order (Miyata 1992: 104–108).

In any social organization, time is one of the most fundamental organizing principles. Those who regulate time have power to rule, and for this reason there have been fights over the power to control time.[1] Many attempts were made by the shogun as well as other warriors to obtain the power to regulate time (Miyata 1992: 108–112). For example, in the early part of the Tokugawa period (1603–1867), when the shoguns came to their post the *nengō* was changed even though the shogun's accession to power should not have brought a change of *nengō*.

The adoption of imperially defined time was also resisted. For example, in the twelfth century, regional warriors refused to use a new *nengō* as a sign of challenge to the new emperor, and they dated documents according to the old *nengō*. In the early seventeenth century, peasants in rebellion or those who were converted to Christianity were known to have used what is called a 'private *nengō*' (*shi nengō*) or a 'false *nengō*' (*gi nengō*) to record their deeds. However, the validity of these attempts at creating their own era name remained local, and their *nengō* did not become authoritative, official, or binding (Akasaka 1988: 182–191).

In addition to the setting up of a *nengō*, the issuing of a calendar was also an important task for the imperial house – not that it made the calendar itself as it lacked the sophisticated astrological technology. Instead, it continued importing the Chinese calendar until early modern times. The imperial court issued the calendar and distributed it to various regions. Those who observed the imperial calendar symbolically became imperial people, and the land they lived in, imperial territory.

However, the making of a calendar was also challenged and threatened. In the Middle Ages, Buddhist temples and Shinto shrines in various regions started to create their own calendars and distribute them to the people. Many of these were based upon local agricultural practices. They did not necessarily match with the imperial calendar based on astrological observations but were better suited to the life cycle of the people. For the convenience of those who could not read, calendars only with signs and pictures were made. The fatal blow came in 1684, when the astrology office of the Tokugawa shogunate created the first 'Japanese' calendar independent of the Chinese almanac. After this, the power to create a calendar shifted to the shogunate and the authority of the imperial calendar diminished (Akasaka 1988: 186).

Just as there has been a competition over the management of time, there has been competition over the power of place (especially the city). The Tokugawa were the third shogunal house but the first to establish themselves in Edo. By the mid eighteenth century, the city of Edo had grown into one of the largest urban centers in the world, with a population of over one million. With growing economic prosperity, people in Edo entertained a sense of being in the center. Yet Kyoto officially remained the imperial capital, being a city of incomparably greater historical depth. The emperor's residence remained in Kyoto even though the emperor himself was unknown and obscure in the minds of ordinary people throughout the Tokugawa period.[2]

The Tokugawa regime faced a serious crisis in the 1850s and 1860s as it could not cope with the increasing pressure from the western powers and Russia as well as domestic upheavals. The emperor, long cast into obscurity in the popular memory, was rediscovered by antishogunal leagues of warriors for his potential political use in overthrowing the Tokugawa shogunate and was made the symbolic focus of the movement. The forces that coalesced to crush the shogunate 'restored' the ancient imperial order in 1868.

From a present-day perspective, it is often assumed that Tokyo became the capital in 1868. However, this is not the case. For the first time in history, the emperor, then a 15-year-old boy, moved from Kyoto to Tokyo to take up occupancy of Edo castle in 1868. The court families in Kyoto were vehemently opposed to the move. In fact, a 'dual capital system' continued for a few decades as both cities asserted their status as the capital (Ogi 1988: 16–18). The emperor remained in Tokyo and that fact gave Tokyo an advantage in its competition with Kyoto.

Following the Meiji Restoration in 1868, a new emperor and *nengō* system were created. The emperor served for life and was no longer to be threatened by political power games, and on his death, he was to be succeeded by his oldest son. A *nengō* was to start at the time of the new emperor's enthronement and remain unchanged until his death. The significance of this system is that time is fixed to the emperor's body. Instead of encompassing plural *nengō* within his time, one emperor has one *nengō* and indeed is made to represent one era. Although in present-day Japan both *nengō* and the Gregorian calendar are in use side by side, significant moments of personal life (for example, date of birth, marriage, and death) as well as social events are officially registered according to imperial time only.

Celebration of Shogunal Memory in 1889

The Edo 300th Anniversary (*Edo sanbyakunen sai*) in 1889 celebrated the 'entrance' into Edo of the first Tokugawa shogun Ieyasu (1542–1616) in 1590. Why was the celebration of Tokugawa memory found necessary at a time when the Tokugawa regime no longer existed? And why was it celebrated on this particular occasion?

The Meiji Restoration in 1868 inflicted great social turmoil. After the Restoration, a wave of emigration took place. By 1872, the city's population had dropped to 580,000, which was almost half of what it had been. The recovery was a long and gradual process. It was around 1889 that the population figures climbed back to the highest level in Edo, more than one million (Ogi 1991: 18).

After the Meiji Restoration the residences of the military, which occupied almost seventy per cent of residential land in the city, were abandoned and left to decay. Remaining castle buildings were burnt down by fire in 1873 and were not rebuilt for over eleven years. For all these years, the emperor lived in a temporary residence in one of the decaying mansions of a former *daimyō* lord. It was in 1889 that the construction of the new imperial palace was completed, after five years of work. It was also around this time that the physical rebuilding of a dilapidated city started in earnest (Fujitani 1996: 67–82).

Having been rebuilt in time for the promulgation of the Meiji Constitution in February 1889, the new palace had a symbolic significance in the emerging emperor cult. Only a year later, the Education Rescript (*kyōiku chokugo*) was issued. It was in these two events that the relationship between the emperor as divine ruler and the people as subject was first publicly promulgated. The making of an absolutist imperial system was underway, blending the Prussian monarchical system and Shintoist principles. The emergence of emperor-centered nationalism was around the corner. In terms of demography, the city's symbolic topography, and the shaping of an emperor cult, the late 1880s mark the last stage of a transitional period.[3]

Internationally Japan was struggling to change its position in relation to Asian neighbors as well as the Western powers. The Tokyo City Government and those who were in influential positions had been ambitious in their visions for the city. For example, a commentator wrote that 'Edo had grown into a city with an imperial palace, central government, commercial and artistic centers, the national capital of Japan, and a first-class city in Asia' (*Edo kai shi* 1889: 4). In this wishful portrait of the city, some of the elements which will later constitute a world city are already present, although the term itself was not yet used. Indeed, Tokyo as a first-class city in Asia and further in the world has been the recurring theme over the last century. The aspiration was that Tokyo should be reshaped in the image of great Western cities like London, Paris, Berlin, and New York.

In reality, however, Tokyo started as a 'semi-colonial-type city' (Ishizuka 1991: 23–31).[4] A consensus grew that the only way to get out of a semi-colonial status was to fashion oneself as a colonialist. In the late nineteenth century, Japan emerged as a colonial empire. While striving for the status of a great empire in Asia, it was also important to correct relationships with the Western powers. Attempts were made by the national government to amend 'unequal treaties' imposed by the West in the last years of the shogunal regime.

In this domestic and international situation, motivations behind the 300th anniversary were not necessarily unified. It is possible to locate at least two different kinds of motivations. The first is a rejection of the new order, which was smoldering among former Tokugawa retainers who looked back nostalgically to the memories of shogunal rule. They created an organization called *Edo kai* (Edo Association) and published several journals featuring articles on the virtues of Edo society and culture. The second and more important motivation was that some of the organizers of the anniversary seemed to have been seeking a bridge between the two political orders. They included Maejima Hisoka (1835–1919) and Enomoto Buyō (1836–1908) who were important former Tokugawa retainers and who also successfully found political positions in the Meiji government. These people helped shape the symbolic occasion in a transitional period.

First advocated by people of different motivations, the idea of the 300th anniversary immediately obtained support from the Tokyo City Government. It was considered important at this time to have a public event that would lift regional consciousness and give a chance to put on display to the guests, who included a number of Western diplomats, the city's glorious history.

The nature of the celebration was, however, problematized and even caricaturized by newspaper commentaries. First conceived as the Edo (or Tokugawa) 300th Anniversary, the plan met with criticism because Tokugawa was an abolished regime. A new name, Tokyo 300 Years (*Tōkyō sanbyaku nen*), was proposed but that did not escape criticism on the grounds that Tokyo was only twenty-two years old. As the nature of the anniversary became problematic, many variations started to circulate. The headlines of the newspaper coverage of the day of the anniversary ceremony were varied – Tokyo Festival (*Tōkyō sai*), Edo Festival (*Edo sai*), 300th Anniversary of the Founding of Tokyo City (*Tōkyō kaifu sanbyakunen sai*), and the 300th Festival (*Sanbyakunen sai*) were among the names used.

Despite the ambiguity and confusion in the nature of the anniversary, however, there was no doubt that it celebrated Tokugawa Edo. The Tokugawa family members as well as previous Tokugawa retainers were among the most important guests at the ceremony. The emperor was not invited, but the crown prince was, showing respect for the imperial family. When the ennobled Tokugawa Ietatsu made a congratulatory speech at a buffet-style banquet after the ceremony, he was received by a 'viva Tokugawa' as well as 'viva Tokyo' chorus (TMG 1987: 205).

The anniversary ceremony took place at a building in Ueno on a clear August day.[5] The building was decorated in the style of Edo castle. In addition to several congratulatory speeches, the day's program included various entertainments. Mixed with Western-style gaiety such as balloons were entertainments spiced with the flavor of Edo – performances by firefighters (on whose clothes were marked the Tokugawa family's *aoi* crest) and dances by Kabuki actors and geishas.

If Shinto was to be made to serve the imperial state soon, the 300th anniversary was predominantly Buddhist. Many of the important temples closely associated with the Tokugawa, such as Kan'eiji, Zōjōji, Dentsūin in Tokyo as well as the Tōshōgū in Nikkō held religious services. In addition, at Zōjōji, a service for the 300th Anniversary of the city's founding was held in the morning, attended by over one hundred monks. Many of them had traveled to Tokyo, some by train, from other parts of the country. Monks clad in robes decorated with a small Tokugawa family crest were seen at railway stations.

As I have shown, symbolic codes for the 300th Anniversary were strikingly mixed and confused. The confusion extended to the finances of the occasion. The Imperial Agency endowed 300 yen, the largest sum of all the donations to the '300th Anniversary of the Founding of the Shogunate.' This was much more than Tokugawa Ietatsu's donation of 200 yen (TMG 1987: 735).

Many ordinary people were not even informed of what the event was all about. Those who were aware of the anniversary celebrated the occasion by hanging lanterns at their doors and windows. The lanterns were of mixed nature. Some had the *hinomaru* flag on them, others the Tokugawa family crest but bearing a caption reading 'celebrating the Meiji Constitution,' whose promulgation had occurred earlier the same year (*Jiji shinpō* 29 August 1890).

The 300th Anniversary purported to re-create continuity against the perceived discontinuity caused by the Meiji Restoration in 1868. It served to give a sense of historical depth to a city whose memory had been seriously disrupted. The paradox of the 300th Anniversary is that shogunal time was brought in at the same time as the shaping of an imperial city was underway. The 300th Anniversary, celebrating the Tokugawa, was possible during this transitional period when Tokyo was still under the shadow of the memory of the Tokugawa, and Tokyo's identity as an imperial city had not yet been fully established.[6]

Creating Discontinuity between Edo and Tokyo in 1898 and 1919

Unlike the 300th Anniversary, which created historical continuity, both the 30th and 50th anniversaries of the foundation of Tokyo (*Tento sanjūnen sai*, *Tento gojūnen sai*) as the national capital assumed disruption between Edo and Tokyo. And unlike the former, which celebrated shogunal time, the latter celebrated imperial time – counted on the basis of the emperor's residence in the city of Tokyo (fig. 46).

Both the 30th and the 50th anniversaries were meant to establish Tokyo's status as an imperial city. The commemoration of shogunal time was possible in 1889 but would no longer be so in 1898, when the emperor cult was taking a more distinct shape. Tokyo was increasingly heading in militarist directions. Victories in the Sino-Japanese war (1894–95) and the Russo-Japanese war (1904–05), coupled with the consequences of World War I (1914–18), brought Japan more colonial acquisitions and international recognition. Along with these advances, the 'unequal treaties,' embarrassing reminders of Japan's inferior position vis-à-vis the Western powers, were finally amended in 1899.

In celebration of the occasion, the Association for the 30th Anniversary writes that 'our Tokyo now competes in its grandeur with London and Paris, the great cities of the world' (Tento Sanjyūnen Shukuga Kai 1898: 2). The emperor and empress attended the commemoration ceremony held near the imperial palace, to which Western diplomats were invited. The opening speech in praise of the emperor made by the chairman of the anniversary celebrations was delivered in a strikingly formal, classical Chinese style of expression. Entertainment programs after lunch were, in turn, imbued with strong a flavor of Edo and included processions of samurai and maids-in-waiting, acrobatic displays from firefighters, and the singing of *nagauta* songs.

Figure 46 30th Anniversary of Tokyo. Ueno on the day of the festival. *Fūzoku gahō* (Illustrated journal of customs) 25 April 1898, No. 163, special issue for the 30th Anniversary.

Ordinary people were not invited but decorated their homes and streets and organized various entertainment. The city center was crowded and business was brisk for traders selling drinks, foods, and other items (figs 46 and 47). Judging from what newspaper commentators wrote, however, the anniversary organizers did not welcome these festive expressions by ordinary people, who were described by the organizers as looking shabby and plain. Commentators were not only critical of what they saw as official narrow-mindedness, but they also expressed their skepticism about organizing this kind of anniversary event in itself (*Hōchi shinbun*, 12 April 1898).

During the thirty years in which the emperor had been living in Tokyo, the city had been functioning administratively as the capital city. Physically it was made an 'imperial city' through the construction of monuments, museums, and military facilities that glorified imperial memories. Yet there was a cautious note to the holding of the two anniversaries. On both occasions the word '*tento*' was used instead of '*sento*.' The former term, which today is out of use, means 'to found a capital city in a certain place,' while the latter means 'to relocate a capital city' (Tokyo City Government 1926). By using the former, Tokyo's status as the capital subsequent to Kyoto is implied. In fact, even as late as in 1919, on the occasion of the 50th

Anniversary, one historian strongly argued that the distinction between *tento* and *sento* had to be maintained (Okabe 1919). The establishing of Tokyo as an imperial city and Japan's capital was a long process, one that was only concluded in the first decades of the twentieth century (fig. 47).

One of the major differences between these two anniversaries is that the absolutist imperial system was much more firmly established by the time the latter was held. Advocacy of the ideology that the emperor was the divine ruler of a dynasty which had continued for over two millennia was much more strongly advanced in the 50th Anniversary.

Another difference is that the 50th was a smaller event than the 30th. On the occasion of the 30th Anniversary, two of the influential journals of the day, *Taiyō* and *Fūzoku gahō*, issued special numbers dedicated to the anniversary. In the 50th, no such numbers were published. Both anniversaries were held in conjunction with other celebrations, the 30th Anniversary, that of the introduction of a new administrative status for the city, and the 50th, the coming of age of the crown prince among others.

Celebration of Imperial Time in 1940

At first glance, the 2600th Anniversary (*Kigen nisen roppyakunen saiten*) does not appear to have any connection with the other celebrations because of its extraordinarily long time span. However, it has an ideological link

Figure 47 30th Anniversary of Tokyo. Nihonbashi on the day of the festival. *Fūzoku gahō*, 25 April 1898.

with the preceding 30th and 50th Anniversaries as well as with the Meiji Centennial, organized by the national government in 1968. All these celebrated imperial time, albeit according to different calendars. The 2600th Calendar Year is based on the myth that Japan's first emperor, Jinmu, ascended to the throne in 660 BC.

The 2600th Anniversary was held immediately before Japan's full-fledged entry into World War II at a time when emperor worship had reached its zenith. According to the imperial ideology, the Japanese imperial family was descended from the mythical figure of Jinmu and reigned without a single break for 2600 years. The idea was propagated that such continuity was unprecedented in the world, and it was used to demand complete devotion from the people. Further, it was used to legitimize the colonial rule of the Great Japanese Empire over the Greater East Asian Co-prosperity Sphere.

My major interest here is to point out a striking similarity between the 2600th Anniversary and the Edo Tokyo 400th Anniversary (*Edo Tōkyō yonhyakunen kinen*). The 2600th Anniversary was a national event of commemoration. However, the Tokyo City Government (TCG) busied itself working closely with the national government. In addition to various ceremonies, commemorative events such as sports days in the style of Nazi sport festivities were organized by the TCG.[7] Although the Tokyo Metropolitan Government (TMG) later dismissed the earlier occasion as sheer absurdity (TMG 1972: 1516), there is a striking parallel between the 2600th Anniversary of 1940 and the Edo Tokyo 400th Anniversary of 1989 in terms of their ultimate goal. Both shared the same vision of Tokyo as a world city. A world city as described in both the TCG and TMG literature means a hegemonic city which serves as a sort of node in a network of important cities in a perceived new world order.

As we will see later, there are also differences in the concept of world city as used in the 1940s and 1980s respectively. One of the major differences between the two, in their application to Tokyo, is that in 1940 the world order refers primarily to the Greater East Asian Co-prosperity Sphere, while in 1989 the world order is extended to the global scale. Another difference is that in 1940, a world city meant an imperial city. In 1989, however, the world city is deimperialized and presented as a sort of 'autonomous' city-state. Yet another difference is that in the former Edo is not given any significance, while in the latter it holds a central position.

Celebration of Tokyo's Medieval Foundation in 1956

The Greater Tokyo 500th Anniversary (*Kaito gohyakunen kinen Dai Tōkyō sai*) is the only one in which the object of commemoration is a medieval warlord, Ōta Dōkan (1432–86). The anniversary on the surface celebrated the year when he built his castle at Edo, upon which later the Edo castle of

Memory and the Changing Passage of Space

the Tokugawa shogunate was built. However, the real intention of the anniversary lay elsewhere.

The end of World War II in 1945 brought the emperor cult to an end. Japan was 'democratized,' and the imperial system was reformed under the guidance of the U.S. Occupation Army. The Greater Japanese Empire had collapsed, and the colonies were lost. The imperial past quickly became a dark side of history. Although Tokyo remained the capital, it was no longer an imperial city. In this context, the celebration of imperially defined time and memory was completely irrelevant, and a historical consciousness independent of imperial time had to be created.

Eleven years after the defeat in the war, Tokyo was recovering from the devastation and starting to show signs of economic growth. A symbolically charged occasion was required to give a sense of regeneration to the city. When the Tokugawa memory could not provide an apt anniversary for the occasion, Ōta Dōkan provided a handy object of celebration.[8] Instead of calling the event the 10th anniversary of the postwar period, the 500th Anniversary of Greater Tokyo gives an image of increased historical depth to a city of which large parts had been burnt down.

The 500th Anniversary was politically significant in that it also provided a historical framework in which the immediate past, the history of the fifteen years of war from 1931 to 1945, occupied a minor place. By stretching the history of Tokyo over 500 years, the significance of the immediate past becomes smaller. Of the several speeches made at the opening ceremony of the 500th Anniversary, hardly any referred to the fifteen years of war. The sole reference was made by Tokyo's Governor Yasui Seiichirō(1891–1962), who stated that 'we were at a loss in the city, which was completely burnt down in the wartime fires' (TMG 1957: 2). His speech presented the city in a way which appealed to the emotions and concealed the complex historical realities.

It was in this speech that the idea of Tokyo as a victim to a series of catastrophes was first publicly presented. Having referred to the Meireki Fire of 1657, the Great Kantō Earthquake of 1923, and the fierce American air raids of 1945, the Tokyo governor encouraged people to work together for the future prosperity of the city (TMG 1957: 2). During wartime, the experience of the Great Earthquake was often referred to as a trope for invincibility and recovery not only for Tokyo but for Japan. While his speech can be understood as a continuation of this line of rhetoric, other disasters were newly added in order to enhance a sense of victimhood. If the Meireki Fire of 1657 had been the first significant event worth mentioning in the space of 500 years, it would have left the first 200 years of Tokyo history empty. Yet the 500th Anniversary provided an opportunity to publicly state a new historical portrait of the city in terms of catastrophes. Presenting Tokyo primarily as victim of a series of catastrophes over the three centuries is a way to conceal Tokyo's aggressive role as a military center before and during the war. It is also a way to de-imperialize the historical memory.

Tokyo's past as an imperial city was long forgotten until Aramata Hiroshi's lengthy best-selling novel *Teito monogatari* (Story of an imperial city) came out in the mid 1980s. The fact that Tokyo once was officially called an imperial city appeared as strikingly fresh, especially for the younger generations. While this attests to people's forgetfulness, it also indicates success in the de-imperialization of the city's history.

The TMG gave up the idea of making Tokyo an imperial city, yet the vision that Tokyo would find its place among dominant Western cities was repeated in the Anniversary. In celebrating the 500th Anniversary, the chairperson of the metropolitan assembly of the TMG stated that Tokyo should not just be Japan's capital but a cultural city of the world. As was the case before, Paris and London provided points of reference (*Nikkan tosei shinbun* 15 September 1956).

Unlike its immediate predecessor (the 2600th Anniversary) and successor (the Meiji Centennial), the 500th Anniversary was not a controversial occasion. The focus of commemoration was a lesser figure, a local warlord who was not linked to the imperial period nor to some other politically charged time. Although the 500th Anniversary did contain political rhetoric and historical manipulation, it succeeded in appearing more or less innocent and benign.

Celebration of 'Modern' Japan in 1968

Two centennial celebrations, the Tokyo Centennial (*Tōkyō hyakunen sai*) and the Meiji Centennial (*Meiji hyakunen sai*), were held in October 1968. One was organized by the national government, the other by the TMG. According to the TMG, the Tokyo Centennial was held 'independent of the Meiji Centennial' (TMG 1972: 351) as the centennial of Tokyo as capital of Japan. This independence can be doubted, though, as the relationship between the two was not a simple question. Before examining the Tokyo Centennial, however, I would like to discuss the Meiji Centennial.

The Meiji Centennial, celebrating the 100th anniversary of the Meiji Restoration, triggered a wave of criticism and protest from 'leftist' parties, regional governments, scholars, teachers' unions, and students. A peculiar feature of the Meiji Centennial was its combination of the celebration of both 'modern' and ancient Japan. The Meiji Centennial, on the surface, appeared to concern the celebration of 100 years of 'modern' Japan, but this was only one aspect of it.

A more critical goal of the Meiji Centennial was the celebration of the imperial institution and its imagined continuity from ancient times. This aspect becomes clearer when we look into the focal point of the celebration. When the national government was planning the Centennial, six crucial occasions in the Meiji Restoration were put on the agenda: (1) the day of the coronation of the Meiji Emperor (1852–1912), 13 February 1867; (2) the day the emperor accepted the 'restoration' of political power, 10 November; (3) the day the imperial restoration and the establishment of a new imperial rule was promulgated, 3 January 1868; (4) the day the Five Article Ordinance was issued, 6 April 1868; (5) the day the coronation was held, 26 August 1868; and (6) the day the *nengō* was changed to Meiji (23 October 1868).[9] Of these, the last one was finally chosen as the day to be commemorated (Ienaga *et al.* 1967: 14).

In a speech at the start of the ceremony, the emperor stated that 'we have developed remarkably as a modern nation in the one hundred years *since the nengō was changed to Meiji*' (*Asahi shinbun* 23 October 1968; my emphasis). The emperor seemed to be saying that it was the regeneration of time brought about by the change of *nengō* that had become the driving force of Japan's modernization. He seemed to be thus referring to the power thought to be inherent in the act of the changing of *nengō* since ancient times. In this way, the Meiji Centennial can be understood as a celebration of imperial time.

The celebration of imperial time over one hundred years creates an image of historical continuity which in return covers up historical disruption within that period. The modern imperial system underwent a substantial reformation in the post World War II era. The concept of the Meiji Centennial concealed this grave historical break and celebrated the imperial order as it was created in the early Meiji era, giving thus the impression that the imperial system had continued intact.

Yet with the exception of 'leftist' scholarly and educational circles, the idea of the Meiji Centennial was widely accepted. Ironically, the TMG wrote that a 'history boom' had been created, and soon the Meiji Centennial became a 'national key word' and a 'slogan' (TMG 1972: 343). A huge amount of publications and many television and radio programs featured the Centennial. The popularity of the Centennial and the general acceptance of the historical view it encapsulated was founded, among other things, upon the fact that it had become common for the Japanese people to talk about personal and family history in relation to three *nengō*, the three imperial generations of Meiji (1868–1912), Taishō (1912–26), and Shōwa (1926–89). The time span of one hundred years between Meiji and Shōwa had become a naturalized – although ideologically charged – temporal concept, which penetrated into the sphere of personal life and became a popular reference point for personal and family narratives.

Celebration of 'Modern' Tokyo in 1968

The TMG emphasized that the Tokyo Centennial was 'independent' of the Meiji Centennial and was a celebration of one hundred years of Tokyo as an 'autonomous regional body' and as Japan's capital (although, as I have shown above, that was not necessarily the case) (TMG 1972: 351). However, the meaning and role of the Tokyo Centennial in relation to national celebration is open to question. Here I will first summarize some of the TMG's critical assessments of the Meiji Centennial as they appeared in the *Tōkyō hyakunen shi* (History of one hundred years of Tokyo), which was published to commemorate the Tokyo Centennial, and then discuss the Tokyo Centennial itself.

The TMG was critical of the 'historical manipulations' and the political use of history by the national government. In the 1960s Japan was enjoying a booming economy. The Olympic Games had been held for the first time in Asia in Tokyo in 1964; one dimension given to them was that of celebrating Japan's postwar economic recovery. Following the Olympic Games, the World Exposition was scheduled to be held in Osaka in 1970. The TMG maintained that the Meiji Centennial was designed to link the two nationally significant events and to keep up the nationalistic momentum that these events created (TMG 1972: 342-3).

The TMG argued that a link existed between the Meiji Centennial and the national government's effort to make 11 February a holiday as National Foundation Day (*Kenkoku kinen no hi*). This was a controversial issue because of its clear link to the prewar emperor cult. Despite strong opposition, however, it was announced in December 1966 that this date would henceforth be a national holiday (TMG 1972: 342-3).

Overall, the TMG's criticism remained limited. As to the political use of history by the national government, the TMG itself could hardly escape from this kind of criticism. The second point, concerning the link between the Meiji Centennial and the setting up of a new national holiday, was never addressed in an explicitly critical fashion but was merely mentioned in a descriptive statement of governmental procedure. The TMG dared not address the essential question of the imperial institution itself in the manner done by scholars such as Ienaga Saburō (Ienaga *et al.* 1967). Although the TMG emphasized its status as the head of an 'autonomous' regional state, officials were aware that they were operating within the national government. In their comments, the essential contradiction of the Meiji Centennial remained unaddressed.

Furthermore, despite the TMG's criticism of the Meiji Centennial and its claim that the Tokyo Centennial was an 'independent' celebration, it has been argued that the Tokyo Centennial was in fact a 'miniature version' (Yoneda 1968: 60), a 'brother' (Yoneda 1968: 59) or even a 'handmaiden' (Tōkyō Rekishi Kagaku Kenkyūkai Iinkai 1969: 63) to the Meiji Centennial. There were indeed similarities. Preparations started in the same year, in 1966, when the similarly named Tokyo Centennial and Meiji Centennial Preparation Committees, were set up. Much of the membership overlapped.

The commemorative ceremony for the Tokyo Centennial, held on 1 October also indicated a link to the national state.[10] The invited guests who attended included foreign diplomats, politicians, representatives from regional and local groups, and ordinary citizens. The ceremony began with a performance of the *Kimigayo* (Your Reign), the controversial hymn with a status close to that of national anthem. This was followed by the song of the Tokyo Metropolis. The Crown Prince made a congratulatory speech following that of the governor of Tokyo. This format indicated that the Tokyo Centennial was not merely a celebration of Tokyo as an autonomous regional body but of a city within the national state. When the ceremony marking the Meiji Centennial was held three weeks later, the two centennials appeared to be linked, with the Tokyo Centennial serving as an introduction to the national event.

The Tokyo Centennial was overshadowed by the Meiji Centennial and failed to obtain the same level of publicity and attention. Ordinary people did not bother to separate analytically two centennials held within the same month. In public consciousness the two became entangled and were perceived as the same sort of event. To the extent that this was the case, the Tokyo Centennial ultimately supported the ideology of the Meiji Centennial, despite the TMG's criticism.

The Centennial celebrations revealed a continuation of the same historical self-portrait as presented earlier at the 500th Anniversary as well as the emergence of the idea of Tokyo as phoenix. In the early stages of preparation for the occasion, the TMG published a report, which included the following comment:

> During the last hundred years, our Tokyo met with a number of catastrophes such as the Great Earthquake and the War. However, having endured them, the city *rose like a phoenix* and developed with miraculous scale and speed. (Tōkyō Rekishi Kagaku Kenkyūkai Iinkai 1969: 63; my emphasis)

In the 500th Anniversary celebrations the idea of phoenix was there, but the word was not used. It now succinctly epitomizes the city's self-portrait. As I will discuss later, this line of historical interpretation continued in the subsequent Edo Tokyo 400th Anniversary.

The Tokyo Centennial celebrated the hundred years of 'modern' Tokyo. By defining the beginning of modern Tokyo in 1868, this line of historical interpretation inevitably marginalized Edo (the pre-1868 era) as premodern. In the *Tōkyō hyakunen shi*, we read the following:

> The birth of self-government was simultaneous with the dismantling of the Tokugawa feudal system and Japan's emergence as a modern nation after the Meiji Restoration. The history of one hundred years in Tokyo, in a sense, can be understood as the history of one hundred years of modernity in Japan. (TMG 1972: 576)

What is also implied here is that Japan's modernity was brought about by 'westernization' following the Meiji Restoration. In the Edo Tokyo 400th Anniversary of 1989, such an orientalist historical interpretation is officially corrected.

Recreating Continuity between Edo and Tokyo in 1989

Unlike the previous anniversaries, no commemorative ceremony was held for the Edo Tokyo 400th Anniversary. Instead, various anniversary projects (a series of public lectures on the cultures of Edo and Tokyo, the construction of the Edo Tokyo Museum, etc.) were conducted over a number of years and were presented as a part of the larger Tokyo Renaissance Campaign, which was held between 1989 and 1997. Both the Edo Tokyo 400th Anniversary and the Tokyo Renaissance were image-making campaigns which were intended to transform Tokyo into a world city (Iwatake 1993).

In the 1980s, the concept of world city as a control center in the global economy gained much scholarly attention in urban studies (Friedmann and Wolff 1982; Friedmann 1986). On the level of urban administration, the concept has provided a strategy for urban regeneration. After a serious financial crisis in the 1970s, New York City employed the concept as a revitalization strategy in the early 1980s. Taking models mainly from New York, London, and Paris, Suzuki Shun'ichi (b. 1910), who was governor from 1979 to 1995, strongly advocated the idea of world city as Tokyo's identity. The idea of Tokyo as a world city was first made public in the Second Long Term Plan (*Dainiji chōki keikaku*) of 1986.

As we have seen, world city was not a new concept in the 1980s but was advocated in conjunction with the 2600th Anniversary in 1940 as well as in preceding and succeeding years. On an international level, one of its earlier advocates is said to have been the scientist and urban planner Patrick Geddes (1854–1932), who discussed the concept in 1915 (Hall 1984: 1). However, world city in the 1980s was a concept that differed from earlier usage. In the 1980s, world cities were seen as more than just pre-eminent capital cities but as cities increasingly controlled by transnational corporations working beyond the frame of the nation-state (Hall 1984). An examination of the literature published by the TMG shows that the TMG has a composite vision of world city, one that includes the 'classical' idea of world city (*Tokyojin* 1989: 24–35). Whatever the TMG's understanding of world city, its strategy can be seen as an extension of its ambition to make Tokyo one of the world's dominant cities.[11]

While economic and financial power is a decisive factor in a world city, a world city is not only an economic concept; its role as a cultural, artistic, and ideological center is also seen to be crucial. However, Tokyo's cultural profile had been low compared to rival world cities such as New York,

London, and Paris (Hannerz 1990). Culture is often associated with history, and the idea behind the Edo Tokyo 400th Anniversary has helped to re-create a historical depth needed in a cultural city.

The scholars who were called in to attend the planning of the Edo Tokyo 400th Anniversary helped radically reinterpret Edo. Among the vast potentialities of Edo society and culture, those aspects that were considered to be immediately relevant to the present were selectively underscored. For example, Edo was re-defined as an information society and a consumption society (Ogi 1991). It was argued that Edo, with its material wealth and huge population of over a million, foreshadowed present-day Tokyo in its prosperity.

This line of historical interpretation fits well into an explosive general interest in Tokyo and Edo which started in the early 1980s. The phenomenon known as 'Edo Tokyo Boom' helped to promote a new view of Tokyo as the most exciting city in the world and Edo as Tokyo's precursor (Gluck 1998). The anniversary drew upon, utilized, and further shaped this discourse.

The new historical interpretation has both domestic and international implications. Domestically it served to differentiate the city from Kyoto. Edo culture was represented predominantly as plebeian in the Edo Tokyo 400th Anniversary projects. For example, in Edo Tōkyō Jiyū Daigaku (Edo Tokyo free university), a series of public lectures on the cultures of Edo and Tokyo, Edo culture was discussed in terms of popular literature, popular music, popular theater, popular religion, and popular entertainment. Typically, Edo people were depicted as argumentative, short-tempered, consumption-oriented and unpretentious. Such a representation makes a sharp contrast to the generally-held view of Kyoto culture and people as being aristocratic and pretentious.

In the international context, such an interpretation, which was imbued with a strong 'counter-Orientalist' overtone, redefined the relationship between Edo-Tokyo and the West. It negated the widely held historical view that 'premodern' Edo underwent 'modernization' through Westernization (Reischauer 1981). In fact, some influential scholars have argued that Edo was already modern or even postmodern (Tanaka 1986: 230–245; Karatani 1988).[12] Throughout the Edo Tokyo 400th Anniversary, the argument was made that it was the continuity between Edo and Tokyo – and not Western influence – that prepared the ground for Tokyo's own development into a world city.

Within the recent writings of anthropologists and others, 'postcolonial' histories have taken a central position within academic and related production. In many parts of the world histories are being rewritten in such a way as to make a counter statement to hegemonic modernist narratives (Foster 1991). The way in which Edo has been appropriated in the Edo Tokyo 400th Anniversary can be understood within this context.

The heroic historical narrative that was presented earlier in the 500th Anniversary and in the Tokyo Centennial was reinforced in the Edo Tokyo 400th Anniversary. In spite of a number of catastrophes – repeated fires in the Edo era, 'unequal treaties' imposed by the Western powers, the Great Earthquake of 1923, and the American air raids in 1945 – Tokyo rose like a phoenix and grew into a world city.[13] These historical interpretations – Edo-Tokyo continuity and Tokyo as a victim and a phoenix – are now officially sanctioned by the TMG and put on display most visibly in the Edo Tokyo Museum, the first historical museum of the city, opened in 1993 as part of the Edo Tokyo 400th Anniversary.

The Edo Tokyo 400th Anniversary celebrated shogunal time. In re-creating an identity for the city, the TMG chose regional time based on the Tokugawa legacy, which was independent of imperial time. Shogunal time was seen to be more suitable for current political purposes than imperial time or the time of a lesser warlord. By emphasizing Tokyo's status as a world city directly linked to other core cities of the world, the TMG wished to take what might be thought of as a city-state attitude vis-à-vis the national government. The celebration of national imperial time became irrelevant in this connection. However, this does not mean that imperial time had lost its legitimacy. As I have shown above, imperial time continues officially to bind and regulate social and personal lives in Japan.

Tokyo as a Life City

Aoshima Yukio (b. 1932), who served as governor of Tokyo from 1995 to 1999, harshly criticized the former Suzuki administration for being a product of the speculative 'bubble economy' of the 1980s. Aoshima maintained that the idea of world city placed priority on economic achievement over people's real interests such as welfare and environmental concerns. He put forward the idea of a *seikatsu toshi* (life city or quality life city) to replace Tokyo's identity as a world city (TMG 1997).[14]

Aoshima's policy did, however, represent a partial continuation of the strategies of the Suzuki administration. The idea of a quality life city had already been advocated by Suzuki in 1993 as an integral part of world city (TMG 1993). The idea was also in line with the new national policy made public by the national government in the Quality Life Country (*seikatsu taikoku*) Plan of 1992 (Keizai Kikakuchō 1992). Although the TMG tries to be 'autonomous' where it can, its policy is set within the larger national domain. The Aoshima administration can be seen as a revision and continuation of already existing policies.

A parallel shift of emphasis can also be observed in scholarly discourse. Recent urban studies have taken a critical attitude to the concept of world city or global city for its focus on economy and have redirected attention to such issues as class, gender, and ethnicity, which are seen to be of concern to more people (King 1996). [15]

Concluding Remarks

The present chapter has discussed anniversaries as political action and rhetorical means by which performers attempt to accomplish practical and symbolic goals. In Tokyo the (re)making of identity and the (re)writing of history have been conscious and interventive strategies. There has not been a single agreed point of origin for the city. At important moments in the city's existence, historical pasts of different temporal origins have been appropriated for desired political ends.

Of the anniversaries discussed here, the Edo Tokyo 400th Anniversary seems to have been one of the most successful in mobilizing and attracting general interest. This is partly because it drew upon an already existing explosive interest in Edo and Tokyo and succeeded in not appearing to be a mere imposition from above.

The term Edo Tokyo 400 Years articulates the relationship between Edo and Tokyo in a way in which the previous anniversaries did not. The Edo 300 Years was a name which caused bewilderment. The concept of Greater Tokyo 500 Years included Edo in its timespan but told its audience little about Edo and its relationship to Tokyo. The 30th and 50th Anniversaries and the Tokyo Centennial did not include Edo at all in Tokyo's history. The Edo Tokyo 400 Years, on the other hand, situated Edo at the very foundation of Tokyo and underlined historical continuity (instead of disruption) between the two.

This in return marginalized the impact of Japan's 'Westernization' – it did not interrupt the historical continuity between Edo and Tokyo. The root of Tokyo's present-day prosperity – it was saying – is situated not in the borrowings from the West but in indigenous Edo experiences. The success of the Edo Tokyo 400th Anniversary can also be attributed to the fact that the concept captured the postmodern and counter-Orientalist mood in Tokyo quite well. If Edo was the past which was marginalized in a process of Westernization, a postmodernist turn rediscovers it and embraces it.

While the Edo Tokyo 400th Anniversary tried to minimize Western influence in the history of Tokyo, the strong identification with a handful of prominent Western cities has prevailed in the imagining of an identity for Tokyo. All the anniversaries of different temporal orders share one thing in common, that Tokyo should find its place among these cities. Such a longstanding and one way aspiration seems to have been finally realized in the 1980s, when international scholarly circles started to discuss Tokyo as a 'world city' (Friedmann and Wolff 1982) or a 'global city' (Sassen 1991).

When one looks at Tokyo in the Asian context, it is easy to notice that neighboring cities in Asia have never been a frame of reference in the making of Tokyo's identity. As famously enunciated in the slogan coined by the Meiji era educational Fukuzawa Yukichi (1835–1901), '*datsua nyūō*' (out of Asia, into Europe), Asia was not an object of Japanese aspiration.

The heroic self-portrait of the city as victim to a series of catastrophes assumes a most significant meaning when Tokyo is situated in an Asian context. Before and during World War II, Tokyo was an imperial city and a colonial center which dominated many parts of Asia. One of the most significant turning points in the history of Tokyo is the postwar era, when the relationship between Asian countries had to be renegotiated. Tokyo's heroic self-portrait emerged during the postwar years as a way to redefine Tokyo's position as a victim and not an aggressor, de-imperializing, in the process, historical memory.

The making and remaking of Tokyo's identity then has a domestic dimension. Domestically, it has been critically important to redefine the city's relation to Kyoto. Starting second to Kyoto, Tokyo needed to establish itself first as an imperial city. After World War II, Tokyo was no longer an imperial city and a new identity was needed. The idea of world city separates Tokyo from Kyoto, as the latter is not Tokyo's rival in the hierarchy of world cities.

The strong identification with a handful of Western cities, distancing from Asia, and the making of an identity distinct from Kyoto have been some of the most critical elements in the cultural politics of the city of Tokyo. It is within these international and domestic complexes, which are mutually interconnected, that the (re)making of identity and (re)writing of history is undertaken.

Notes

1 The fight over temporal control is not specific to Japan. Zerubavel discusses the relationship between the calendrical system and political power, and points out how in the French and Bolshevik revolutions, the setting up of a new calendar was seen to be an integral part of social reformation (Zerubavel 1981: 82–95).
2 Today historians agree that ordinary people knew very little about the existence of the emperor during the Tokugawa period. Even in the early Meiji period, the emperor was not linked to national consciousness nor were his political and representational roles articulated yet (Fujitani 1996: 7–9).
3 A sense of the transition is also manifested in the way in which the city was named. In the period approximately between 1868 and 1889, the same Chinese characters which today are pronounced 'Tōkyō' were read 'Tōkei.' The city was no longer Edo but not quite Tokyo yet (Ogi 1988).
4 According to Ishizuka, the presence of French and British troops, the guarantee of immunity for Westerners, and unequal trade conditions are some of the indicators of the city's 'semi-colonial' status (Ishizuka 1991: 23–31).
5 Ueno was symbolically Tokugawa territory as Kan'eiji temple, one of the most important temples for the Tokugawa, was located there. The remaking of Ueno into imperial territory was undertaken later through the construction, for example, of the Imperial Museum (Fujitani 1993: 96–97; 1994: 80–81).

6 In recent years, Fujitani Takashi has argued that the imperialization of historical memory between the late nineteenth and twentieth centuries has been central in the crafting of national unity in Japan (Fujitani 1993; 1994; 1996). One of his points is that contrary to an often-held view that the imperial institution is an age-old tradition, it is a new invention in Japan's modern experience. He is critical of the idea that history and culture for the Japanese have always centered on the imperial institution. However, in an ironical way, his study gives an impression that in the (re)writing of modern national history, if not earlier history, the emperor was indeed a central figure. He writes that his work is an attempt at 'deconstructing official memories' (Fujitani 1993: 105). He seems to equate official memories with imperial memories, giving thus supreme power to the imperial memories that he tries to deconstruct. The 300th Anniversary indicates that there was also a pull toward a different kind of historical memory.
7 It had originally been hoped that the first Olympic games in Japan would be held in 1940 in conjunction with the 2600th Anniversary. However, the plan was not realized until 1964.
8 However, this is not to say that the TMG has not paid a tribute to Ōta in other ways. Ōta was sometimes presented as a 'founding father' of the city. There was a statue of him in front of the former TMG building.
9 Dates are translated from the original lunar calendar into the solar calendar.
10 1 October is the Day of the Citizen of Tokyo (*Tōkyō shimin no hi*), commemorating the fact that the citizens obtained the right to elect a governor on 1 October 1945. Before then, the national government had appointed a governor.
11 As has been pointed out by Anthony King, the concept of world city has a strong association with that of former colonial centers (King 1990, 1991).
12 For a critique of rosy illusions about Edo, see Koyano 1999 and Sakurai 2000.
13 Such a presentation successfully influenced the way in which scholars look at Tokyo (Ishizuka 1991: 2; Cybriwsky 1991: 7, 78–93).
14 Aoshima did not launch another anniversary event because the Tokyo Renaissance Campaign, which succeeded the Edo Tokyo 400th Anniversary, officially continued through the spring of 1997. Nor did Aoshima's governorhood change the way in which the history of Edo and Tokyo was represented in the Edo Tokyo Museum.
15 In 1999, Ishihara Shintarō (b. 1932) was elected Tokyo's governor. Enjoying great popularity, he has made an number of public comments in which he has indicated, among other things, disdain for Korean and Chinese residents in Tokyo and for handicapped people. His vision of Tokyo appears to share common features with the imperial city of the Japanese colonial empire in the 1930s and 40s.

References

Akasaka N. (1988) *Ō to tennō* (King and Emperor). Tokyo: Chikuma Shobō.
Cybriwsky, R. (1991) *Tokyo: The Changing Profile of an Urban Giant.* London: Bell.
Edo kai shi (Journal of Edo Association)(1889). 'Hachigatsu nijyūroku-nichi o shukuse (Celebrate August 26.) 1(1): 4–6.
Foster, F. (1991) 'Making National Cultures in the Global Ecumene.' *Annual Reviews of Anthropology* 20: 235–260.
Friedmann, J. (1986) 'The World City Hypothesis.' *Development and Change* 17(1): 69–83.

Friedmann, J., and G. Wolff. (1982) 'World City Formation: An Agenda for Research and Action.' *International Journal of Urban and Regional Research* 6 (3): 309–344.
Fujitani, T. (1996). *Splendid Monarchy: Power and Pageantry in Modern Japan.* Berkeley, Ca: University of California Press.
—— (1994) *Tennō no pegento: kindai Nihon no rekishi minzokushi* (Emperor's pageant: historical ethnography of modern Japan) (Trans. L. Yoneyama). Tokyo: Nihon Hōsō Shuppan Kyōkai.
—— (1993) 'Inventing, Forgetting, Remembering: Toward a Historical Ethnography of the Nation-State.' In H. Befu (ed.) *Cultural Nationalism in East Asia: Representation and Identity.* Berkeley, Ca: University of California Press.
Gluck, C. (1998) 'The Invention of Edo.' In S. Vlastos (ed.) *Mirror of Modernity: Invented Traditions of Modern Japan.* Berkeley, Ca: University of California
Hall, P. (1984). *The World Cities.* London: Weidenfeld and Nicolson.
Hannerz, U. (1990) 'The Cultural Role of World Cities.' Paper presented at Symposium on The Age of the City: Human Life in the 21st Century, Osaka.
Hobsbawm E. and Ranger T. (eds) (1983) *The Invention of Tradition.* Cambridge: Cambridge University Press.
Ienaga S. et al. (eds) (1967) *Kindai Nihon no sōten* (Controversial issues of modern Japan). Tokyo: Mainichi Shinbunsha.
Ishizuka H. (1991) *Nihon kindai toshi ron: Tokyo, 1868–1923* (On the Modern Japanese City: Tokyo, 1868–1923). Tokyo: Univerity of Tokyo Press.
Iwatake, M. (1993) 'The Tokyo Renaissance: Constructing a Postmodern Identity in Contemporary Japan'. Unpublished Ph.D. dissertation, University of Pennsylvania.
Karatani K. (1988) 'One Spirit, Two Nineteenth Centuries'. *The South Atlantic Quarterly.* 87(3): 615–628.
Keizai Kikakuchō (Economic Planning Agency) (ed.) (1992). *Seikatsu taikoku gokanen keikaku – chikyū shakai tono kyōzon o mezashite.* (A 5-year plan for quality life country: toward a co-existence with global society) Tokyo: Economic Planning Agency.
King A. (ed.) (1996) *Re-presenting the City: Ethnicity, Capital and Culture in the 21st-Century Metropolis.* London: MacMillan.
King A. (1991) *Urbanism, Colonialism, and the World-Economy: Cultural and Spatial Foundations of the World Urban System.* London and New York: Routledge.
—— (1990) *Global Cities: Post-Imperialism and the Internationalisation of London.* London and New York: Routledge.
Koyano A. (1999) *Edo gensō hihan* (Critique of illusionary Edo). Tokyo:Shinyōsha.
Miyata N. (1992) *Hiyorimi* ('Weather vane') Tokyo: Heibonsha.
Ogi S. (1988) *Tōkei jidai* (Tōkei Period). Tokyo: Nihon Hōsō Shūppan Kyōkai.
—— (1991). *Edo Tōkyōgaku kotohajime* (Introduction to the study of Edo Tokyo). Tokyo: Chikuma Shobō.
Okabe S. (1919) '*Tōkyō tento wa sento niarazu.*' (*Tento* in Tokyo is not *sento*) *Rekishi chiri.* May: 502–6.
Reischauer, E. (1981) *Japan: The Story of a Nation.* Tokyo: Charles Tuttle.
Sakurai S.(2000) *Edo no noizu: kangoku toshi no hikari to yami* (Noise in Edo: light and darkness of prison city). Tokyo: Nihon Hōsō Shuppan Kyōkai.
Sassen, S. (1991) *The Global City: New York, London, Tokyo.* Princeton, NJ: Princeton University Press.
Shirane H. and Suzuki T. (1999) *Sōzō sareta koten: kanon, kokumin kokka, Nihon bungaku* (Invented tradition: canon, nation-state, Japanese literature). Tokyo: Shinyōsha.

Tanaka Y. (1986) *Edo no sōzōryoku* (Imagination of Edo). Tokyo: Chikuma Shobō.
Tento Sanjyūnen Shukuga Kai (Association for the 30th Anniversary) (ed.) (1889) *Tento sanjū nen shukuga kaishi* (Record of the 30th anniversary celebration). Tokyo: Nichibunsha.
Tokoro I. (1996) *Nengō no rekishi: gengō seido no shiteki kenkyu* (History of era names: a historical study of the *gengō* system). Tokyo: Yūzankaku Shuppan.
Tokyo City Government (1926) *Zassho* (Miscellaneous Records). 3 (3).
Tōkyōjin (1989). '*Suzuki Shun'ichi: Tōkyō Runesansu ga sekai toshi o hiraku*' (Suzuki Shun'ichi: The Tokyo Renaissance opens up a world city) 24: 24–35.
TMG (Tokyo Metropolitan Government) (ed.) (1997) *Seikatsu toshi Tōkyō kōsō* (A plan for a life city Tokyo). Tokyo: Tokyo Metropolitan Government.
—— (1993) *Tōkyōto chiiki jōhōka suishin keikaku no kōsei: hito ni yasashii, jōhō toshi Tōkyō NETS* (A plan for advancement of informational Tokyo region: human-friendly information city Tokyo NETS). Tokyo: Tokyo Metropolitan Government.
—— (1987) *Tōkyō-shi shikō: shigaihen* (Historiographies of the city of Tokyo: Towns). Vol. 78. Tokyo: Tokyo Metropolitan Government.
—— (1972) *Tōkyō hyakunen shi* (History of one hundred years of Tokyo). Vol. 6. Tokyo: Tokyo Metropolitan Government.
—— (1957) *Dai Tōkyōsai kinen arubamu* (Greater Tokyo celebration album). Tokyo: Tokyo Metropolitan Government.
Tokyo Rekishi Kagaku Kenkyūkai Iinkai (ed.) (1969) '"*Tōkyō hyakunen kinensai*" *ni hantai shi, kakushin tosei o sodateyō*' (Toward a radical metropolitan policy, in protest against the Tokyo Centennial) *Rekishi hyōron* 222: 57–64.
Vlastos, S. (ed.) (1998) *Mirror of Modernity: Invented Traditions of Modern Japan*. Berkeley. Ca: University of California.
Yoneda S. (1968) '"*Tōkyō hyakunensai*" to "*Tōkyō hyakunenshi*" *o meguru mondaiten*' (Problems concerning the Tokyo Centennial) *Rekishi hyōron* 216: 59–65.
Yoneyama. L.(1999) *Hiroshima Traces: Time, Space and the Dialectics of Memory*. Berkeley, Ca: University of California.
Zerubavel, E. (1981) *Hidden Rhythms, Schedules and Calendars in Social Life*. Berkeley, Ca: University of California Press.

CHAPTER 9

Time Perception, or the Ineluctable Aging of Material in Architecture

Murielle Hladik

The flow of the river is ceaseless and its water is never the same. The bubbles that float in the pools, now vanishing, now forming, are not of long duration: so in the world are man and his dwellings. It might be imagined that the houses, great and small, which vie roof against proud roof in the capital remain unchanged from one generation to the next, but when we examine whether this is true, how few are the houses that were there of old. Some were burnt last year and only since rebuilt; great houses have crumbled into hovels and those who dwell in them have fallen no less. The city is the same, the people are as numerous as ever, but of those I used to know, a bare one or two in twenty remain. They die in the morning, they are born in the evening, like foam on the water.

Kamo no Chōmei, *Hōjōki* (trans. Keene 1955: 197)

In this chapter I would like to investigate the relationship between time perception and concepts surrounding the preservation of buildings.[1] In the West, buildings are generally thought of in terms of aging and the ensuing problems of conservation, relying on a linear concept of time, the origins of which lie in Christian eschatology. In Japan, however, the idea of cyclical time underlies the conscious awareness of the perishability of matter and the potential renewal of form. This idea of cyclical time is related both to the seasonal and agrarian cycles venerated in Shintōism and to the Buddhist concept of cyclical time and rebirth. In Buddhist texts, time is not perceived as a linear process but as cyclical. The 'four aspects of duration' are 'apparition' (*sho*), 'duration' (*jū*), 'deterioration' (*i*) and 'disappearance' (*metsu*) (Girard 1990: 406). In the human life cycle, we have the image of birth, living, aging and death. I would like to outline an analogy with the life span of a building: 'apparition' is the moment of construction, 'duration' is when the building is inhabited (*sumu*, living), 'deterioration' is linked with the weathering process, or aging, and 'disappearance' is the ruin or the death of architecture. Once the construction is finished, the building will irremediably enter into a process of degradation. One can project one's own finite life-span in objects, buildings, or the environment. According to David Lowenthal, 'Most attitudes toward aging suppose a similitude between human beings and things of natural and human make. The human body has habitually served as an image for everything around us.... Organic analogies often go beyond metaphor. Cosmos, church, and state were long believed to be creatures animated with life' (Lowenthal 1985: 127). Furthermore, Lowenthal analyses two types of reactions to aging: one is a total rejection, a 'distaste for age,' the other is an appreciation for the 'look of age' through the contemplation of the traces of time. The first attitude articulates a desire for newness and a distaste for decay: thus the image of death will be avoided. The second attitude first emerges in the West with the discoveries of Roman ruins during the fourteenth and fifteenth centuries. It was in the eighteenth century that the 'beauty of patina' was first perceived as bringing into the present all memories of a glorious past (Lowenthal 1985).

Human beings would like to fight against this process of deterioration, against the 'virtual death' of a building. As organic matter, the human body is doomed to an ineluctable end, while buildings, as human artifacts, can be restored. It is possible to do a partial renovation, to replace a roof or some other parts of a building. It is also possible to do a total reconstruction of entire buildings.[2] But will the building remain the 'same' entity after this total reconstruction? Architecture is conceived as a match between a 'design concept' and the physicality of the building. Therein lies the ambiguity of architecture. It is both an artistic work and a craft objet, concept and matter. If the architecture can be reproduced, then can its products be considered 'unique' works of art?[3] Does its original material existence certify the authenticity of the monument? An architectural project first conceived on paper (with plans, sections, and drawings) can be later reproduced. But, as it is also conceived with material, once it is constructed the building is related to time (and history), and it is difficult to rebuild it without the disappearance of this historical background.

While in the West, 'reconstruction' is related to the alteration of the original, that is, to a copy in a pejorative sense, in Japan, 'reconstruction' (*fukugen*), repetition (*fuku*) of the original (*gen*), is almost synonymous with 'conservation' (*hozon*). From a philosophical point of view even the notion of original (*gen*) is problematic. What is thus, in Japan, the meaning of an identical reproduction? How is it possible to refer to an 'original state'? As pointed out by Augustin Berque, in the West, 'to rebuild entirely anew and on an identical model would be an act of falsification violating the authenticity of the monument and is equivalent to a 'demonumentalisation' by the abolition of memory' (Berque 1994). In a recent survey on *Architectural and Urban Conservation in Japan*, Niels Gutschow analyses this 'quest for the original state' (Enders and Gutschow 1999: 28–71). This was also the main topic of the Nara Conference of Authenticity, where the contributors tried to come up with a definition of a new concept of 'authenticity' that could make the connection between the UNESCO World Heritage (and ICOMOS) definitions of conservation and the specificity of Japanese culture and its history of preservation (Larsen: 1995). In Europe in 1903, Riegl introduced the concept of 'age value' (*Alterswert*) in his work, *Der moderne Denkmalkultus* (The modern cult of monuments), which ushered in a modern attitude towards the contemplation of the past. According to him, the age value attributed to a monument is not simply limited to its historical value (its style, its position in art history), but also includes a perception of the presence of time. The flow of time exudes from the monument and transports modern individuals to former periods. Authenticity is transferred into the actual physicality of a monument. The contemplation of a monument transformed by the passage of time brings individuals face to face with a natural law, an inevitable return to nature. For Riegl, restoration should always be based on an equilibrium between three factors: 'historical value,' 'contemporary value' (often linked to function), and 'age value,' in other words, authenticity of form, authenticity of function, and authenticity of matter. The preservation of the original materials is contradictory with the conservation of the original form, since by allowing the process of natural degradation to take place, the building itself is progressively destroyed. Conversely, 'historical value' emphasizes the authenticity of form and does not take into account the authenticity of matter. Any restoration must, therefore, compromise between the different kinds of value.[4]

Through the example of Theseus' ship, David Lowenthal analyses the ambiguities of the notion of 'original matter.' According to Plutarch's *Lives*, Theseus' ship was preserved for more than a thousand years, and during this period of time, they took away the old planks as they decayed, putting in new and stronger timber in their place.[5] Does this ship remain the same 'entity,' after all these renovations? Assuming that the identity of an object lies in the continuity of form, and not in its ephemeral and fragmentary matter, will the authenticity of the ship be certified? In the words of Lowenthal, 'Being a part of Theseus' old ship was only a phase in the lifetime career of the old planks' (Lowenthal 1989: 69). Thus, the importance and the original value of this ship as historical treasure resides more in its identity as a ship (its form) than in the fact that it is a framework of planks (its material aspect). Discussions among philosophers about the identity of matter began with this example. The perennial question as to whether form or substance is more important, or whether the whole is more important than the parts, has led us to question of the status of the frame.[6]

Partial or complete renovation implies that it is culturally acceptable for an object to retain its 'identity' through the continuity of space and/or time, and this beyond the occasional changes and modifications of the original matter.

In the context of Japan, the contrast between the conservation of form and the conservation of matter is much starker.

In the case of the Ise Shrine (fig. 48), the original materials are entirely replaced, while in most other wooden buildings, Buddhist temples as well as

Figure 48 Ise Shrine. When the Ise Shrine, Japan's main Shinto sanctuary was entirely rebuilt in 1993, the visitor could observe a phenomenon which only occurs every twenty years. Two buildings standing face to face have exactly the same shape. Their difference is not a formal one but a temporal one. Comparing the freshly cut hinoki wood with the wood exposed over twenty years to weathering processes, observation shifts from form-difference to time-difference. © 1993, M. Nordström.

Time Perception, or the Ineluctable Aging of Material in Architecture

Shinto shrines, only some of the original parts are periodically renovated. This illustrates the two opposed attitudes towards the conservation of buildings in Japan reflecting distinct categories: on the one hand the periodical renewal of forms to be found in Shinto ritual alongside the importance of purification and, on the other hand, in the case of Buddhist temples and other Shinto buildings, the partial renewal of materials as the need arises. Already, in the latter category, some original parts of the overall building will be maintained and acquire value as traces of history or 'age value' (Riegl 1903). This is why I would suggest (following Sclatsas 1981) creating a third category, one which would encourage the contemplation of the traces of time.

In his commentaries on 'Identity, Origin and Spatiotemporal Continuity,' Theodore Scaltsas analyses the interrelation between object and time and discusses 'the significance of the history of an object and its recoverability (from destructive damage) for the preservation of the identity of the object' (Scaltsas 1981: 395). One of his first examples – concerning an ancient vase (destroyed), reconstructed from its fragments, and preserved in a museum – leads us to the question: how far (and to what extent) is this reconstructed vase the 'same' as it was in its first stage (before the destruction)? How far is its identity and origin preserved in spite of the temporary interruption of its 'wholeness'?[7] In response, Theodore Scaltsas proposed the following analytical scheme:

> Two objects can be found to be different phases of one and the same object if:
>
> (a) The form of that object remains spatio-temporally continuous throughout the two phases and the interval (if any) between them. Or,
> (b) The parts of that same object remain spatio-temporally continuous throughout the same period. Or,
> (c) The matter of that object remains spatio-temporally continuous throughout that period. (Scaltsas 1981: 400)

The first category (spatio-temporal continuity of form) can just as easily be applied to the case of Theseus' ship as to the identical reconstruction of Shinto shrines, both based on continuity of form. In the case of shrines, the building's identity is authenticated by Shinto rituals of renewal.

The second category (spatio-temporal continuity of parts) can be observed – in the Japanese context – in the partial renovation and replacement of materials in major religious or historical buildings. This process of dismantling and reconstruction is linked to the physicality and vulnerability of wood. The third category (spatio-temporal continuity of matter) applies to building materials exposed to the passage of time. This ineluctable aging of materials can be appreciated in terms of perception and aesthetics (see below).

1 Spatio-temporal Continuity of Form: Periodical Renewal and the Ise Shrine

The Ise Shrine is reconstructed every twenty years, and, through this process, its original form dating to the seventh century has been preserved. Based on apparently simple and sophisticated jointing, the archaic style of architecture is retained despite the destruction of the original materials.[8] Form (*katachi*) thus seems to be eternal while matter is highly perishable. Before the traces of degradation appear on the building and before it is destroyed, an identical reproduction of itself is built on the adjacent plot. Here, the reconstruction ritual (*shikinen zōtai*), another kind of form (*keishiki*), is what provides the building with an identity. The apparently eternal nature of the Ise Shrine is thus made of successive cycles in which matter, *hinoki* wood, is transformed and displaced, while form is continuous in time. If the identity of matter is not important, emphasis must be placed on the continuity of the form over time.[9] The periodical reconstruction of the Ise Shrine in identical form epitomizes the Japanese concept of time. With the regular renewal of matter, the identity of the building refers far more to an original form than to original substance, to mythological origins and eternal time rather than to particular moments of history (fig. 1).

The paradox of Ise Shrine – the contradiction between the eternal form of the building and its ephemeral character – is well expressed in the title of a recent monograph by Svend M. Hvass, *Ise: Japan's Ise Shrines, Ancient yet New* (Hvass 1999). In these words, 'ancient yet new,' resides the fascination exercised by this building, thirteen centuries old but constructed from material never more than twenty years old. This in turn leads us to wonder how the continuity of time is perceived in spite of the destruction of material. Every twenty years, with the rebuilding of Ise Shrine, a new construction arises which is paradoxically always the 'same' as the one it replaced. In thirteen hundred years, sixty-one 'occurrences' of the same edifice materialized. Hvass includes in his book a comparative chronology, expressing graphically in a linear representation the cyclical time of Ise. But while this schematic representation allows us to 'turn the pages of history,' it demonstrates the subjective nature of a linear concept of time.

The first stage in the reconstruction consists in choosing the trees, Japanese cypress, *hinoki* (*Chamaecyparis obtusa*), that will serve the purpose. Deep religious meaning is associated with this primary stage of the process, expressed in the ceremony of *yamaguchisai*, 'the expiatory prayers offered to the *kami* of the mountain where the sacred trees to be used in the construction are felled' (Coaldrake 1900: 5). It is also very important for the master carpenter to choose the tree on the site and note the position and orientation which will be the 'characteristic' (*kuse*) of this specific trunk. This will in turn determine the way the wood is used on the building site. Before any of the construction work can begin, all the different elements of the building are first of all prepared according to traditional techniques by a team of specialist carpenters who work on site. The preparations for the reconstruction of the new sanctuary can last up to nine years during which thirty-two major ceremonies and rituals take place (Kobayashi 1981; Coaldrake 1990). In the course of the reconstruction ritual, and during one of the last ceremonies, the relics are moved from the old to the new shrine thus providing the latter with a sacred value. The building is, therefore, nothing but a temporary envelope containing the sacred relics.

The reconstruction is motivated by a desire for purification. The building, both in its temporary and eternal nature, is preserved undefiled by time. As Kobayashi has explained, in ancient forms of Shintoism no permanently consecrated spaces were specifically dedicated to the gods; instead, a sacred space was occasionally defined by enclosing a plot of land with rope. During religious celebrations, a piece of wood was temporarily erected to provide a support for the deities (*kami*) who were not represented in human form but identified through natural elements. In time, these temporary supports became increasingly fixed and elaborate until eventually they became actual buildings. As the deities were not supposed to reside in a building prone to deterioration, impurities, and defilement (*kegare*), it was periodically rebuilt. It is very likely that most of the old sanctuaries were reconstructed every twenty to thirty years, but nowadays this only applies to those buildings that are part of the Ise sanctuary.[10] An explanation for the twenty year period put forward by Kobayashi is that this corresponds to the span of a generation, in other words, the necessary time required for craftsmen to transmit their skills to their successors (Kobayashi 1981: 186).

To understand the necessity for the reconstruction ritual, I will refer to Tamakoshi Oshio, who, in his article entitled '*Basho to keishiki*' (Place and form), analyses two types of building rebuilt for temporary periods (Tamakoshi 1979). One called the *Nihinaheya*, was reconstructed for the celebration of renewal every new year. The second, the *Dainahegū*, was constructed only for the celebration of the enthronement of each new emperor. Tamakoshi shows that the *Nihinaheya* type of building represents both the concept of eternity (*kyūeisei*) and the concept of ephemerality (*kasetsusei*). These notions are in radical opposition, but the specificity of this type of building is that it joins together the two contradictory notions. Ephemerality can be understood through the structural aspect of the building: the structure was probably made with rough timber tied with plant fibre ligaments and roofs thatched with straw. The posts were put directly in the ground without foundations. All these materials can deteriorate rapidly.[11] Furthermore, the ephemeral aspect is also directly linked to the fact that these buildings were to be destroyed after the ceremony. Tamakoshi notes that during the Heian period, the *Dainahegū*, a temporary rustic building, was constructed inside the imperial palace for the ceremony of enthronement of a new emperor, in front of more sophisticated buildings covered with tiles in the Chinese style of this period, thus highlighting the contrast between these two types of buildings. Since the ceremony of enthronement was very important, we can assume that the ephemeral quality was intentional, expressed through the rustic image of a hut (*iho*). Through this ceremony, the emperor transcended the ephemeral qualities of his human body (*utsutsumi*) and took on the eternal life of the Gods to become Son of Heaven (*tenson*). This transformation echoes the relationship between the ephemeral and the eternal character of the building where the ceremony takes place (Tamakoshi 1979). The conflicting and complementary aspects of ephemerality and eternity are also exemplified in the buildings of the Ise Shrine, the imperial sanctuary which has been rebuilt every twenty years for more than a thousand years. Negating the perishable quality of the architecture through repeated reconstruction, the Ise Shrine represents metaphorically the eternal nature of the imperial line.[12]

2 Spatio-temporal Continuity of Parts: The Periodical Dismantling and Maintenance of Wooden Buildings

In the *Hōjōki*, Kamo no Chōmei (1155–1216) describes his own dwelling. Of small proportions, it was built without foundations. All structural elements, posts and beams, could, if necessary, be dismantled for moving.

> I laid a foundation and roughly thatched the roof. I fastened hinges to the joints of the beams, the easier to move elsewhere should anything displease me. What difficulty would there be in changing my dwelling? A bare two carts would suffice to carry off the whole house, and except for the carter's fee there would be no expenses at all. (Kamo no Chōmei, *Hōjōki*, trans. Keene 1955: 206)

The building is perceived as perishable and its constituent parts are consequently fitted with a view to being later dismantled. This applies not only to smaller provisional buildings such as Kamo no Chōmei's dwelling, but equally to larger structures such as temples and palaces that were designed to last. The flexibility of the joints is also calculated to improve resistance to earthquakes.

Most temples in Japan are regularly dismantled and renovated; *tatenaosu* implies both reconstruction and maintenance. Complete restoration of a whole building (*zen-kaitai*) is required every 300 to 400 years, while partial renovation (*han-kaitai*) is carried out every 150 to 200 years by entirely dismantling and restoring the roof and the walls but keeping the structural frames (Larsen 1994: 68–73). Finally, according to necessity, occasional restorations are carried out on the more vulnerable parts of the building, mainly those exposed to the wind and the weather.[13] These days, it is deontologically recommended to conserve as much of the original

Time Perception, or the Ineluctable Aging of Material in Architecture

Figure 49 Walls of Ryōanji. The walls of the Ryōanji temple show a superimposition of several strata, each altered in a different way. A segment of the roofing material, hinoki wood, has been restored recently. © 1995, M. Hladik.

materials as possible (Figs 49, 50, and 51). Dismantling is literally the deconstruction of a building and will, therefore, be the basis not simply for its conservation but also for an analysis and understanding of its history. As with the dissection of a body, sections and structure appear through the dismantling of a building. The historian Asano Kiyoshi (1905–91) worked on the restoration of the Hōryūji from 1930 onwards and defined the scientific criteria for the conservation and systematic dismantling of wooden buildings (Larsen 1994: 106). As a building is dismantled (*kaitai*), every different stratum of past restorations appears and can be analysed; changes carried out at different periods become visible such as when some members are re-used and dispersed.[14]

Larsen analyses the case of the Kondō in the Hōryūji in Nara. In 1949, a fire destroyed nearly the whole ground floor of the building. Restoration began in 1950 under the leadership of the master-carpenter Nishioka Tsunekazu (1908–95). Before reconstruction began, the burnt remains were consolidated with resin and moved to a separate site for conservation (Larsen 1994: 28). The restored building is now a National Treasure (*kokuhō*), while the burnt structure from the first floor (the ruin) is also preserved as Important Cultural Property (*jūyō bunkazai*). The Kondō is thus divided into two separate entities: one, the ruin, continues to preserve

Figure 50 Detail of a rafter. Manshū'in, Kyōto. The detail shows a very precise intervention on an old rafter. The new part fits into the existing wood like an inlay would fit into a tooth. © 1995, M. Hladik.

the original materials, while the new building is entirely renovated. On the floors above where the burnt remains used to stand, some original elements date from the seventh century, but most of the building has been dismantled and restored. There have been two major restorations carried out since it was first built, one in the twelfth century and the other in the early seventeenth century. There could still be as much as fifteen to twenty per cent of the original materials in place (Larsen 1994: 27–9).

Successive acts of dismantling were not simply based on restoration but were also adapted to the evolution of the use of the building. In the past,

Time Perception, or the Ineluctable Aging of Material in Architecture

Figure 51 Basement of pillar. Tōkōji temple in Hagi (built in 1698), Yamaguchi Prefecture. On the lower part of this column, which has detoriated due to weathering, restoration has been undertaken. Only the damaged part has been replaced by fresh wood. © 1995, M. Hladik.

master carpenters did not hesitate to alter the structure and add or change proportions and volumes. In the beginning of the Meiji era, with the introduction of modernization, Japan established a new relationship with its own history. Buildings which had religious functions or represented the former feudal system were initially abandoned or even destroyed (Nishimura 1995). This rejection of the past, illustrated by an iconoclastic surge, was only gradually replaced by its preservation, exemplifying the alternation between on the one hand decline and neglect and, on the other, legislation which only partially compensated for the disappearance of systems of production. The first legislation for the protection of the national heritage was implemented in 1897 and only covered religious buildings: Buddhist temples and shrines (*Koshaji hozon hō*). The way the legislation is formulated implies a return to an 'original form' such as must have existed before any restoration took place. This is a striking contrast with the traditional practices which had prevailed until then and which allowed for the evolution of a building's design through time. The legislation can be partly explained by the influence of Western concepts of heritage based on the perceived disjunction between past and present. It formed a part of the nineteenth century debates on what constituted restoration, debates between those who advocated the restitution of an original model and those in favour of preserving and presenting historical strata through the materials themselves.

These issues are discussed by Niels Gutschow (1999). He suggests that before the time of the law of 1897 the form of a building was modified as its function evolved – either partially transformed during the dismantling process or reconstructed, on the same site, as a totally different building. From this time on, however, conservation becomes part of the work of architects and is seen to entail an obliteration of previous strata of history in order to return to a pre-supposed 'original state.'[15] Gutschow refers us to the example of Shin Yakushiji in Nara, 'restored' in 1898, and he argues that this desire to return to an 'original state' is linked to the construction of a national identity. The construction of a national identity is correlated with the emergence of the notion of historical monument In their introduction to the same book, Enders and Gutschow write that, 'The "idea" of a building is in any case more important than the material. It can be removed and replaced to restore the original state.' Thus, 'the notion that a ruin or a deformed temple is beautiful would be absurd' (1999: 7).

The 1897 legislation is part of a long Japanese tradition in which preservation plays an important role. Traditionally, the dismantling and reconstruction of complex structures is primarily based on the preservation of necessary skills and techniques. Coaldrake, introducing *The Way of the Carpenter*, shows how apprenticeship engages both body and mind as two notions that are not radically opposed. This influence of Buddhism is partly reinforced by the etymology of the term 'tools' in Japanese, *dōgu*, which refers originally to the implements used in the transmission of Buddhist ritual knowledge (Coaldrake 1990: 4). The transmission of knowledge is based on the repetition of gestures in the relationship between masters (*iemoto*) and apprentices, thus preserving skills across generations.[16] With the impact of modernization and changes in methods of construction, there has been a progressive demise of traditional skills, once again only partially counteracted by legislation for the protection of intangible heritage, which the Japanese were the first to implement. Put in place after World War II and focusing on skill-based knowledge, it complements the legislation concerning material heritage and nominates outstanding masters as 'holders of intangible cultural properties' (*jūyō mukei bunkazai*), referred to in everyday parlance as 'living national treasures' (*ningen kokuhō*). This colloquial expression emphasizes the importance of the body in the transmission of knowledge. The concept of intangible heritage is what Ogino Masahiro has referred to as 'the logic of actualization' – in Japan, conservation is not a fixed notion linked to a linear concept of time, but is something that is constantly brought to the fore in the practice of skills which repeatedly 'actualize' intangible knowledge in the present and evolve with time (Ogino 1995). Time is thus permanent flux and process.

3 Spatio-temporal Continuity of Matter: 'Age Value' and the Aesthetics of the Perishable

In Japan, the positive attitude towards aging finds its origins in classical literature and medieval aesthetics, a 'tradition' that was reinvented during the Tokugawa period and even more so during the Meiji era.[17] Thus, one of the characteristics of Japanese aesthetics suggests that beauty does not disappear with time but actually increases in refinement. The perishable characteristic of daily life provides an awareness of the process of aging and an understanding of impermanence in this world. The traces of the passage of time, signs of wear and tear at the hands of human contact, confer a superior form of beauty transcending daily life through aesthetic contemplation. Beauty increases with age, and the ephemeral and perishable reflect process, flux, and flow, all adding to the perception of the passage of time.

This aesthetic of degradation was also valued in the 'way of tea' (*chadō*). Organic materials such as straw and puddle clay used for the construction of tea pavilions, bring to mind the fact that all buildings will vanish one day. The irregular surface of the walls, where pieces of straw and wattle are mixed with clay and left exposed, confer to these small buildings the appearance of a rustic hut in the mountains or a hermit's pavilion. On occasion, iron fillings are placed in the mud wall (*tsuchikabe*), and, as they rust, these small bits of iron express artificially the process of aging.[18] This ephemeral aspect of the building is related with an ideal of ascetic life. To attain enlightenment, novices were supposed to reject the material nature of this world. In this sense, the way of tea is also conceived as a process to attain detachment. Taian, the tea pavilion supposed to have been built by Rikyū (1522–91), was probably conceived as a temporary building. But it is nowadays preserved as 'national heritage' (*kokuhō kenzōbutsu*).[19] This small building was recently restored and the original material of the mud wall has been preserved. The clay was remodeled, and the wall then reconstructed with the same material. Similarly, during the restoration of the Shōiken tea-room in the Katsura Villa, some parts of the existing wall were delicately removed and put back after the dismantling and restoration of the entire structure. This shows that conservators and architects are more and more concerned with the preservation of original material (Larsen 1994: 95).[20]

During the Muromachi period, within the aesthetics of tea pavilion – thatched roof, rough mud walls and undressed timber – were used in order to create a new typology of buildings related to an unpretentious beauty, referring to the style of a farm house (*minka*) rather than to the architecture of the mansions of noble families. But under a rustic appearance, the construction of tea pavilions was quite sophisticated. During the Tokugawa period, fresh timber inside tea-rooms was even painted in order to artificially age it. As noted by Larsen, 'as early as the seventeenth century, interior members of tea-rooms were treated in order to give them an old, rustic appearance' (Larsen 1994: 57). But it is difficult to consider this 'fake-patina' as a normal process; on the contrary it appears mainly as a deformation of the philosophy of tea. Furthermore, the tea ceremony took on a different significance with increasing formalization.[21]

The beauty of patina must definitely include an awareness of impurity and sullied image. In the tea ceremony, some objects refer to an old history (author, provenance, history), while others must be fresh and pure.[22] The memorial charge of history is conferred on one object, whereas other objects and materials will be frequently renewed or replaced in order to give an image of purity. Inside the building, some components must be replaced regularly, such as *tatami* mats (with their fresh herbal smells), *shōji* or, more specific to the tea pavilion, *koshigami* (the paper which covers the mud wall up to a height of some eighty centimetres to protect seated persons leaning against it). As Lafcadio Hearn (1850–1904) wrote in 1896:

> Generally speaking, we construct for endurance, the Japanese for impermanence. Few things for common use are made in Japan with a view to durability. The straw sandals worn out and replaced at each stage of a journey; the robe consisting of few simple widths loosely stitched together for wearing, and unstitched again for washing; the fresh chopsticks served to each new guest at a hotel; the light shōji frames serving at once for windows and walls, and re-papered twice a year; the matting renewed every autumn, all these are but random examples of countless small things in daily life that illustrate the national contentment with impermanence. (Quoted by Keene 1995: 38)

Today it has become more and more expensive (but no less important) to renew components of buildings in this way. Although the aesthetics of freshness and perishability (contrasting with oldness) have been interrupted by modernity and overturned, it is still possible to appreciate in contemporary examples how a refined sense of beauty can be produced by the contrast between an aesthetic of patinaed old age and an expression of freshness.[23] This dual structure appears in classical literature as ancient as the eleventh century *Makura no sōshi* (The pillow book). Sei Shōnagon (965?–1021) noted in her diary that there are on the one hand 'things that seem pure' and on the other hand 'things that are reminders of a sentiment of past.'[24]

The refinement and detachment of tea ceremony utensils was first related to a natural and unintentional beauty. An object used in daily life, such as a rice bowl from Korea, may be used in the tea ceremony; through this displacement or transfer, the value of a common object will be extended to the purest aesthetic creation.[25] This specific object had been used for another purpose and had been touched by many hands, conferring on it the authenticity of patina and the traces of history. Irregularity can be found in objects with an imperfection, an irregular shape, or missing parts. Described as an 'aesthetic of imperfection,'[26] this actually forms the basis of the celebration of a process of natural degradation. The tea bowl known by the name of Ido Kizaemon (Korea, Yi dynasty, sixteenth century) described by Yanagi is not only an example but also a model of beauty.[27] 'The foot-ring of an Ido-bowl is exceptionally beautiful, but to set out to copy its spontaneous irregularities is fatal; the beauty vanishes' (Yanagi 1989: 194–5).

Yanagi Sōetsu strongly protested against the misunderstanding perpetrated by those tea masters who tried to copy the irregularity found in the unintentional and transform and deform it, thus creating a 'fake' irregularity. Through the example of a tea bowl that has been restored with gold, Donald Keene shows that this piece, first broken and then restored, acquired more aesthetic value with the 'appreciation of perishability' and 'signs of wear and tear.' 'A pottery bowl that has been cracked and mended, not invisibly but with gold, as if to call attention to the cracks, is human, suggesting the long chain of people who have held it in their hands – more human than a bowl that looks as if it might have been made very recently' (Keene 1988: 38–9) (fig. 49).

The signs of the passage of time must be natural and not intentional. Indeed, there is an essential difference between an object consumed by time and another that has been voluntarily broken.[28] When perfection of form is only slightly interrupted, this 'imperfection' is where the beauty lies.[29] From imperfect or unfinished objects, it is possible to imagine what the whole would have been like and thus transcend the idea of beauty. Through imperfection on the one hand and the unfinished quality on the other, beauty refers to the past (what the object was) or to the future (what it will be). Whereas the idea of present time (the 'instant') is impossible to catch; projection through past and future by means of imperfection provides an allegorical image of the flow of time, consuming and passing away.[30]

Epilogue

Different attitudes towards conservation of architectural forms in Japan can be identified. Besides the fact that wooden architecture represents today a very small number of building structures, the question arises inevitably from the discussion above as to how to preserve this heritage otherwise doomed to vanish. I have not set out to answer this question. Possible answers (or the failure to find any) are discussed by Yamasaki Masafumi and Kinoshita Ryōichi in their chapters in this volume. Here, in the above pages, I have attempted to elucidate the nature of the conceptual issues involved by setting out a three fold analytical scheme that seeks to place buildings and objects and an appreciation of their value within a spatio-temporal flow.

First, in the case of the Ise Shrine, the 'identity' of the building lies not in its materiality but in its form. It is firstly the shape or appearance of the building, form, secondly the gesture of the carpenters, repeating the same skills from generation to generation, and finally the formalization of the ritual that authenticate the 'identity' of the building. The absence of a precise original time of foundation – what Derrida would call 'blindness' (Derrida 1990) – makes possible the practice of renewal and the conception of an eternal time. As in the example of Theseus' ship, where the old planks were replaced but the identity of the ship remained the same, the identity of the whole is far more important than the identity of the part.

Secondly, apart from the very specific case of the Ise Shrine, other buildings such as temples and shrines are periodically dismantled and renovated. Some parts will be renewed while others will stay in their original state. But besides the fact that in former times it was possible to modify the design through this periodic renovation, since the normalization of legislation on the conservation of heritage, the priority has been placed on the 'quest for an original form' (Enders and Gutschow 1999). The conservation of gesture is valorized but not the 'actualization' of the shape (fig. 50).[31]

Third, looking at the beauty of 'age value,' it appears that this aesthetic value of 'weatherworn material' is counterbalanced by the 'freshness' or 'newness' of elements or members that have been replaced. The beauty of 'oldness,' the trace of history lies only in some parts of the building. Rustic and ephemeral structures are supposed to vanish and it is therefore the perishability of things and impermanence which is valued. There is always a balance between 'old age' and the traces of time in contrast with 'newness' and a sense of purity.

Through its degradation, matter projects an image of decomposition and decay, just as every 'moment' of time is supposed to vanish and pass away. In a philosophy of 'becoming' and 'flux' (*nagare*), how is it possible to understand the nature of time in its movement? By its very nature, it is impossible to capture what is submitted to fluctuation (fig. 51).

Notes

1 This chapter is based partly on research under the direction of Professor Katō Kunio, Kyoto University (1996–97) with the support of Japan Ministry of Education. I am very much grateful to Sara Pimpaneau (British Museum) for her help with the English translation.
2 To pursue the analogy, it is also possible to 'replace' parts of the human body today with polyester limbs or through heart transplants, etc. Artificial skin grafting has also made it possible to avoid the 'look of age' and to appear much younger. But of course, in the case of human beings, it is still impossible to create an entire body.
3 G. Genette distinguishes two different modes of art: one is 'autographic' and supposes unity and authenticity, the other one is 'allographic' where the copy has the same value as the original. Architecture, considered in a classic way, fits into this first category (Genette 1994).
4 The authenticity value of a work of art is determined not only on the basis of matter, form and original function, but also on the role of the 'author' in the process of production. Although matter is useful as a means of authenticating the origin of an object, it is its generic properties (author, production, provenance, history) which make it possible to separate the authentic item and its reproduction.
5 Theseus, after killing the Minotaur, came back to Athens with this ship. Therefore as a symbol of Athenian independence, it became the centre of a ritual ceremony. In order to commemorate this event, the ship was reconstructed continuously and regularly for more than thousand years (so the story is told in Plutarch's *Lives*).
6 The question surrounding this 'collection of planks' (Lowenthal 1989) will help towards an understanding of the relation between a part and the totality. In Buddhist philosophy, the whole is much more important than the parts. Winston L. King, in his foreword to Nishitani's *Religion and Nothingness*, gives a good example of this: 'Fa Tsang illustrated it by his hall of mirrors in which all mirrors (individual beings) reflect (or 'contain') the central image of Buddha as well as every other mirror in the hall (the universe). Thus the whole can be said to be in the part as truly as the part is in the whole. These and many similar figures clearly suggest a living body rather than an intricate machine.' (Nishitani 1982: xii).
7 'Since the broken pieces of the vase that was restored in the museum were the connecting link between the ancient and its restoration in the museum we can speak of them as being the medium for the preservation of the identity of the vase' (Scaltsas 1981: 295). Thus, fragments ('broken pieces') are conceived as a connection between the ancient and the renewed object. Another medium, one that permitted the reconstruction of the object, is the space – the space of the museum in this case, but in another case it might be the Earth where 'broken pieces' are found. The reconstruction of the object is, in any case, an attmept to negate the irreversibility of time. The possibility of fighting against the flow of time is, however, limited, for as Scaltsas writes, 'Not every product of the destruction of the vase can serve as a medium. For example, if the vase was pulverised or shattered no restoration procedure would record the initial vase' (Scaltas 1981: 296). However, to reconstruct or to copy does not allow one to make the original object.
8 The art of joinery is both simple and sophisticated, 'rustic' and 'sacred.' The Ise Shrine, based on the model of a granary, refers to the agrarian cycle (festivals and

rice harvest). The massive structure and sharp-edged joints provide us now with a very old and archaic image, while at the time the shrine was built, they would have appeared as very sophisticated buildings executed with much knowledge and art. According to Coaldrake 'the importance of smooth, pristine surfaces for ritual purity' was made possible only with the emergence of new tools such as the planing knife and a new type of chisel (Coaldrake 1990: 98–102).

9 Although, in a sense, it is always the 'same material' which is used (*hinoki* wood) throughout the periodic reconstructions, it is nevertheless not the same tree, thus not exactly the same 'matter.' Just as in Heraclites' comments about the flow of the river, where the water flowing 'is never the same' (even though it is always 'water' and always the same 'river').

10 This team of carpenters works on the restoration of all the sanctuaries under the dependency of Ise. Some pieces can sometimes be reused in smaller sanctuaries, in which case a thin skin of eroded surface will be scraped off with a planing knife. The art of the carpenters requires them to have very considerable skills. Nowadays, the durability of matter and process of degradation are the subject of experiments on the building site under the direction of Prof. Iida who is in charge of the reconstruction of Ise Shrine. (I am very much indebted to Prof. Iida for allowing me to visit the carpenters' work site in 1995). These experiments include the application of resin to the straw material used for the roofing as it seems difficult to maintain this material over the twenty year period. The wooden posts of the foundations, directly driven into the earth, are the part most vulnerable to erosion, so there has been a suggestion to cover underground sections of the posts with a copper surface. Besides the desire for a 'pure' and 'clean' aspect, these experiments appear nonetheless to be contradictory to the renewal ritual.

11 Tamakoshi refers to *Manyōshū* poems 1637 and 1638, where it is said that 'from an ancient past,' (*yorozuro*, a poetic expression referring to a distant past) sunken rooms (*muro*) were built with black wood (*kuro guittsu kuri no ie*) and covered with straw (*obana sakabuki*) (*Manyōshū*, *Nihon no koten*, 1984: 288–89).

12 This could explain why the Japanese refuse to allow the Ise Shrine to be recognized by UNESCO as a World Heritage Site.

13 'As a matter of fact, damage occurs in limited areas, such as the bottom of post, joints connecting timbers, etc., and most other parts survive without any damage for long periods of time' (Itō 1995: 43).

14 To continue the analogy between architecture and body, one could make a comparison between *kaitai*, dismantling, and *kaibō*, dissection.

15 This practice is in a sense not so far away from what happened in Europe too, where nineteenth century strata have sometimes been erased in the process of restoration of stones buildings. The intention is to return to an original state that is supposed once to have been existed (even if in Europe the 'official discourse' of preservation is radically different from Japan).

16 The term '*iemoto*' appears only in the eighteenth century, when the rule of the master and the hierarchy inside the school or craft tradition had become much more rigid.

17 In this sense, as Iwatake Mikako argues in her chapter in this volume, 'looking back' and 'tradition' are always a reinterpretation. Further research is required into changes in the field of aesthetics at the turn of the century. A rich example of this process of inventing tradition can be found in the works of Motoori Norinaga (1730–1801) in his reinterpretation of the meaning of ancient words in Japanese (*Kojiden*) or his explanations of the *Tale of Genji*.

18 The verb *sabiru* means 'rusting' or 'aging' while *sabi*, expresses both 'serenity', within the Aesthetics of Tea defined during Muromachi period and, especially nowadays, 'rust.'
19 Sen no Rikyū (1522–1591) elaborated his concept of reduction and simplicity (*wabi*). The term *wabi* can be translated as spirit of poverty, but there are also many other meanings and implications related to Zen philosophy. 'Wabi means lacking things, having things run entirely contrast to our desires, being frustrated in our wishes,' wrote Jyakuan Sotaku in the *Zencharoku* (1828), quoted by Kōshirō (Kōshirō 1995: 246). The historical evolution of the definition of *wabi* and *sabi* aesthetics has been well described by many scholars.
20 Previously, renewing wattle and daub panels was favored, because those panels play a important role in case of earthquakes by absorbing the shocks and vibrations. In this sense the preservation of the original material is also in conflict with the preservation of the whole building.
21 With the disappearance of strict rules, many playful elements (*asobi*) began to appear in buildings during the Tokugawa period (round windows, curves, etc.). Different species of wood were used. The pillar of the *tokonoma* alcove was extended and often made of silver birch or cherry, wood that is both tender and perishable.
22 According to Sylvie Guichard-Anguis, tea utensils (objects) were more often preserved than buildings. This dual attitude is reflected in the etymology of the French words *meuble* (movable heritage) and *immeuble* (real estate). Historical value lies in objects and their pedigree (objects related to the tea ceremony: their makers and a list of owners), whereas buildings were frequently reconstructed. Thus, 'the protection of objects allowed the conservation of a series of wrappers, of which buildings would be the last layer. Maintenance and reconstruction of many buildings, such as tea-rooms, monasteries, castle keeps, storehouses, etc., only play the role of containers for the precious objects: tea ceremony utensils, religious statues, etc.' (Guichard-Anguis 1996: 187).
23 As for example, the beauty of a flower beyond age: in Zeami's theories about Noh plays, the first grade of Beauty can be found in the freshness and youth of the 'flower' (*hana*), but the ultimate stage will only be found after much experimentation and in the ability of an old actor to reinterpret and retranscribe the image of this first 'flower.' Zeami then uses the term *sabi* to describe the emotional impact of this first occurrence. The flower reappearing on an old branch – similarly in Tanizaki's work *The Diary of a Mad Old Man* (*Fūten rōjin nikki*, 1961) in which the freshness of a young woman is only remarkable in its contrast with a decrepit old man.
24 Sei Shōnagon, refers to the 'Things That Give a Clean Feeling' (like 'an earthen cup... a new wooden chest') in opposition to the 'Things that Give an Unclean Feeling' (*The Pillow Book*, trans. Morris, 1967, p. 168). But she also notes, 'Things which are no longer used but which recall the past,' such as 'a flower mat, old, worn and frayed at the edges.... In the garden of a pretty house, a fire has burnt the trees. The pond had kept some of its primitive appearance, but was soon taken over by duckweed and aquatic plants.' (Morris 1967: 186).
25 This phenomenon, consisting in detaching the object from its environment, can be compared with the 'distanciation' of an object when it is designated a 'work of art' and inserted in a collection (or museum). But in this case, the object is still 'in use' in the tea ceremony, and seen at a distance only by *connoisseurs*.
26 Yanagi Sōetsu (1889–1961) in *The Unknown Craftsman*, wrote about 'the beauty of irregularity' (Yanagi 1972: 119–26) and Okakura Kakuzō (1862–1913) in *The Book of Tea* (1906), 'the art of imperfection' (1989). With

lacquerware, the patina of time can also be read in the accumulated strata of lacquer (Tanizaki 1977). It is probably not a coincidence to find a reinterpretation of classical literature and aesthetics appearing in at the beginning of the twentieth century with authors such as Yanagi, Okakura or Tanizaki. At this turning-point between a Western influence (modernity and its historical background) and an Eastern one (in classical literature), they were able to locate themselves at the critical distance required for the contemplation of the past and redefinition of the East.

27 Not simply an example, but an exemplar in which the unique, the singular, takes on a generic value.

28 'There are important aesthetic differences between a vase whose handle broke off by accident, and an identical vase whose handle was intentionally broken off. Chips and cracks on a tea bowl have different aesthetic connotations depending upon whether they are due to a natural aging process or a part of the calculated design' (Saitō 1997: 378).

29 When the image of a circle is not totally finished, it is always possible to imagine what the entire figure (i.e., perfection) might be. The same feeling emerges from the irregularity of the curves of a tea bowl. As noted by Saitō, the aesthetics of imperfection presupposed a strong definition of the notion of perfection (i.e., classicism) itself.

30 A comparison between Saint Augustine's (354–430) and Dōgen's (1200–53) conceptions of time is suggestive. According to Tamba, they had diametrically opposed concepts on a spiritual level: for Dōgen, individuals experience the relativity of time, while for Augustine there is only the eternity of God. Their common point is in their understanding of the 'instant' (*shikin* for Dōgen and *praesentia* for Augustine) as the only possible moment to 'grasp' time: that is, past, future, and present (Tamba 1997: 96).

31 To go beyond the opposition between 'form' and 'substance,' it is important to keep in mind the non-dualistic Buddhist concept. Yuasa Yasuo analyses non only the dualistic opposition between soul and body characteristic of Christianity but also emphasizes the unity of body and mind in 'practice' as in Buddhism (Yuasa 1987).

References

Berque, A. (1994) 'Des Thermes à Nanterre. Figures de l'être parisien.' *Le Débat* 81: 85–93.

—— (1993) *Du geste à la cité. Formes urbaines et lien social au Japon*. Paris: Gallimard.

Bock, F. G. (1974) 'The Rites of Renewal at Ise.' *Monumenta Nipponica*, vol. 34 (1): 55–68.

Choay, F. (1995) 'Sept propositions sur le concept d'authenticité et son usage dans les pratiques du patrimoine historique.' In Larsen, K. E. (ed.) *Nara Conference on Authenticity*, pp. 101–20.

—— (1987) 'Mémoire de la ville et monumentalité.' In Berque, A. (ed.) *La qualité de la ville. Urbanité française. Urbanité nippone*. Tokyo: Maison franco-japonaise, pp. 121–9.

—— (1982) *L'allégorie du patrimoine*. Paris: Seuil.

Coaldrake, W. H. (1990) *The Way of the Carpenter*. New York and Tokyo: Weatherhill.

Derrida, J. (1990) *Mémoires d'aveugle. L'autoportrait et autres ruines*. Paris: Musée du Louvre, Réunion des Musées Nationaux.

Enders, S., and N. Gutschow (eds) (1999) *Hozon: Architectural and Urban Conservation in Japan*. Köln: Axel Menges.

Fiévé, N. (1996) *L'architecture et la ville du Japon ancien. Espace architectural de la ville de Kyōto et des résidences shōgunales aux XIVe et XVe siècles*. Coll. Bibliothèque de l'Institut des Hautes Études Japonaises, Collège de France/ Université de Paris VII. Paris: Maisonneuve et Larose.

—— (1995) 'Le récit sur les Hauts-Lieux de la capitale. Essai sur le rôle des Meisho dans la constitution de la ville-mémoire.' In *Japon Pluriel*. Arles: Philippe Piquier, pp. 305–17.

Gallian, C. (1987) 'Système de protection du patrimoine dans la ville japonaise.' In Berque A. (ed.) *La qualité de la ville. Urbanité française. Urbanité nippone*. Tokyo: Maison franco-japonaise, pp. 139–46.

Genette, G. (1994) *L'Oeuvre de l'art. Immanence et transcendance*. Paris: Seuil.

Girard, F. (1996) 'La vie et la mort au Japon.' In *La vie et la mort. Actes du XXIVe Congrès de l'Association des Sociétés de Philosophie de Langue Française*, Poitier: Société Poitevine de Philosophie, pp. 189–93.

—— (1990) *Un moine de la secte Kegon à l'époque Kamakura, Myōe (1173–1232) et le Journal de ses rêves*. Paris: Publications de l'école française d'Extrême-Orient (vol. CLX).

Guichard-Anguis, S. (1996) 'Les objets du thé. Un patrimoine national au Japon.' In Shimizu Ch. (ed.) *Les Arts de la Cérémonie du thé*. Paris: Faton, pp. 158–187.

Gutschow, N. (1999) 'Quest for the Original State: Reconstruction and Restoration to an Earlier State in Japanese Conservation.' In Enders and Gutschow (eds) *Hozon: Architectural and Urban Conservation in Japan*. Köln: Axel Menges, pp. 28–73.

Hvass, M. S. (1999) *Ise: Japan's Ise Shrines, Ancient yet New*. Holte: Aristo.

Itō N. (1995) 'Authenticity Inherent in Cultural Heritage in Asia and Japan.' In K. E. Larsen (ed.) *Nara Conference on Authenticity*. Trondheim, Norway: Tapir Publishers. Published by ICOMOS International Wood Commitee, pp. 35–46.

—— (1981) 'Wood as Material for Japanese Buildings.' In *Nessun Futuro senza Passato* (No future without the past), Acts of the Sixth General Assembly of the International Concil on Monuments and Sites. Rome: ICOMOS, pp. 391–97.

Jokilehto, J. (1995) 'Authenticity: A General Framework for the Concept.' In K. E. Larsen (ed.) *Nara Conference for Authenticity*. Trondheim, Norway: Tapir Publishers. Published by ICOMOS International Wood Commitee, pp. 17–34.

Keene, D. (1955) *Anthology of Japanese Literature: From the Earliest Era to theMid-Nineteenth Century*. New York: Grove Press.

—— (1995) 'Japanese Aesthetics.' In N. G. Hume N (ed.) *Japanese Aesthetics: A Reader*. New York: State University of New York Press, pp. 27–41.

Kobayashi, B. (1981) 'The case of the Ise Grand Shinto Temple in Japan.' In *Nessun Futuro senza Passato*, (No future without the past), Acts of the Sixth General Assembly of the International Concil on Monuments and Sites. Rome: ICOMOS, pp. 185–91.

Koshima N., Kinoshita M., and Satake A. (eds) (1984) *Manyōshū*. Coll. *Kanyaku nihon no koten* (vol. 3). Tokyo: Shōgakkan.

Kōshirō H. (1995) 'The *Wabi* Aesthetics through the Ages.' N. G. Hume (ed.) *Japanese Aesthetics: A Reader*. New York: State University of New York Press, pp. 245–78.

Larsen, K. E. (1994) *Architectural Preservation in Japan*. Trondheim: ICOMOS International Wood Commitee and Tapir Publishers.

Larsen, K. E. (ed.) (1995) *Nara Conference on Authenticity*. Trondheim: Tapir Publishers and UNESCO World Heritage, Agency for Cultural Affairs (Japan), ICCROM, ICOMOS.
Leatherbarrow, D., and M. Mostavi (1993) *On Weathering: The Life of Building in Time*. Cambridge, Mass: MIT Press.
Lowenthal, D. (1995) 'Changing Criteria of Authenticity.' In K. E. Larsen (ed.) *Nara Conference on Authenticity*. Trondheim: Tapir Publishers and UNESCO World Heritage, Agency for Cultural Affairs (Japan), ICCROM, ICOMOS, pp. 121–36.
—— (1989) 'Material Preservation and its Alternatives.' *Perspecta* 25: 67–77.
—— (1985) *The Past is a Foreign Country*. Cambridge: Cambridge University Press.
Nishimura Y. (1995) 'Evolution du concept d'authenticité dans l'histoire de la conservation au Japon.' In K. E. Larsen (ed.) *Nara Conference on Authenticity*. Trondheim: Tapir Publishers and UNESCO World Heritage, Agency for Cultural Affairs (Japan), ICCROM, ICOMOS, pp. 185–93.
Nishitani K. (1982). *Religion and Nothingness* (transl. by Jan Van Bragt). Berkeley, Ca: University of California Press.
Nitschke, G. (1993) *From Shinto to Ando*. 'Daijosai and Shikinen sengu: First Fruits Twice Tasted.' New York: A.D. Academy Group, pp. 8–33.
Ogino M. (1995) '*La logique d'actualisation. Le patrimoine et le Japon*.' *Ethnologie française* ('*Le vertige des traces. Patrimoines en questions*') 25 (1): 57–63.
Owen, S. (1986) *Remembrance: The Experience of the Past in Classical Chinese Literature*. Cambridge, Mass: Havard University Press.
Petzet, M. (1995) 'In the full richness of their authenticity: The Test of Authenticity and the New Cult of Monuments.' In K. E. Larsen (ed.) *Nara Conference on Authenticity*. Trondheim: Tapir Publishers and UNESCO World Heritage, Agency for Cultural Affairs (Japan), ICCROM, ICOMOS, pp. 85–99.
Plutarch (1961) *Vies* (French trans. R Flacière). Paris: éditions des Belles lettres.
—— (1967) *Vie parallèles des hommes illustres* (French trans. J. Amyot). Paris: Gallimard.
Pons, P. (1988) *D'Edo à Tōkyō, Mémoires et modernités*. Paris: Gallimard.
Riegl, A. (1903) *Der moderne Denkmalkulturs*. French translation by D. Wieczorek (1984) *Le culte moderne des monuments*. Paris, Éditions du Seuil.
Ryckmans, P. (1986). 'The Chinese Attitude Towards the Past'. The Forty-Seventh George Ernest Morisson Lecture in Ethnology. Camberra: The Australian National University.
Saitō Y. (1997) 'The Japanese Aesthetics of Imperfection and Insufficiency.' *The Journal of Aesthetics and Art Criticism* 55 (4): 376–385.
Scaltsas, T. (1981) 'Identity, Origin and Spatio-temporal Continuity.' *Philosophy* 56: 395–402.
Sei Shōnagon (1966) *Makura no sōshi, Notes de chevet* (recueil du IXe siècle). (French trans. Beaujard A.). Paris: Gallimard/UNESCO.
Tamakoshi O. (1979) '*Basho to keishiki*' (Place and form). *Risō* 558: 80–92.
Tamba A. (1997) '*La conception du temps-existence ou yūgi chez Dōgen*.' *Daruma* 2: 89–105.
Tanizaki J. (1977) *L'éloge de l'ombre*. (French trans. R Sieffert). Paris: Presses Orientalistes de France.
—— (1967) *Le Journal d'un vieux fou*. (French trans. Renondeau G.). Paris: Gallimard. (*Fūten rōjin nikki*, Tokyo: Chūō Kōronsha, 1961).
Yanagi S. (1972) *The Unknown Craftsman: Japanese Insight into Beauty* (adapted by B. Leach). Tokyo: Kodansha International.

Yoshida Kenkō (1968). *Tsurezure gusa. Les heures oisives.* (1283–1350). (French trans. C. Grobois and Yoshida T.). Paris: Gallimard.

Yuasa Y. (1987) *Toward an Eastern Mind-Body Theory.* New York: State University of New York.

PART THREE

Place Between Future and Past

CHAPTER 10

The Past in Tokyo's Future

Kōda Rohan's Thoughts on Urban Reform and the New Citizen in Ikkoku no shuto *(One nation's capital*[1]*)*

Evelyn Schulz

Introduction

From their beginning cities have functioned as centers of technical and cultural achievement and of social differentiation, as places of diversity, change, and fluidity. Due to the process of modernization – the unparalleled expansion of cities, increased industrialization and growth of urban population that started both in Europe and in Japan during the nineteenth century – urban reality became more and more fragmented and complex. At the turn of the twentieth century the modern age was characterized by scientific progress on the one hand and by cultural pessimism on the other. Rising nationalism, fear of war, the alienating effects of industrialization and urban growth on daily life, the deepening gap between rich and poor – all these factors contributed to the perception of modern, and mainly urban, life as a condition of alienation, discontinuity, and acceleration. People recognized a deep break with the past and felt that they were living in a time of transition and crisis. Furthermore, in the age of imperialism, the capital cities became not only important sites for the representation of national identity, but also melting pots in which the individual was forced to find a new self-identity in accordance with the ideology of building a nation. In the latter half of the nineteenth century, in urban discourse as well as social and political thought, the question of the citizen and his or her relationship to the urban community and the nation gained importance.[2]

Both in the West and in Japan the description of urban phenomena was (and still is) an important tool for the social and political criticism of modernity and of modernization in general. With the Meiji Restoration Edo was renamed Tokyo and became Japan's capital. Here the processes of modernization and nation-building were very intense and the intellectuals' perception of Japan's modernization was mainly shaped by their experience of Tokyo. Countless works of art, literature and political and social criticism focused (and do so still today) on Tokyo, the political, economic and cultural center of modern Japan, as the evocative symbol for the expression of contemporary conditions and ideas of future improvements. The discourse of Japan's modernity and future is often linked to the discourse of Tokyo's modernity and future.

Compared to Western countries, Japan's modernization was slow at first, but then caught up. This process is reflected in countless fictional and non-fictional texts about urban features. From the 1880s on, urban phenomena were described in a way not unlike that found in Western contemporary writings about the city. Tokyo was mainly represented as a space of social diversity and rapid changes. The urban newcomer who had left his rural home behind, hoping for a splendid future, and followed the goal of *risshin shusse* (rise in the world) was a common figure (Kinmouth 1981).[3] In Japan as in the West the individual's loneliness in the crowd was a common topic, reminiscent of Georg Simmel's analysis of the mental condition of the city dweller.[4]

Attempts have recently been made in the West to rethink the Enlightenment and to question universal concepts. Now one prefers to speak of 'global modernities' than of one path to modernity (Featherstone, Lash and Robertson 1995). Urban discourse emphasizes that neither is there a definition of the city which is independent of its cultural background, nor can a clear-cut method for analyzing the city as an abstract, universal concept be developed.[5] In modern Japan reflection on urban matters is even more complicated than in the West because the discourse is polarized between the East and the West on the one hand, and between tradition and modernity on the other. In general, one has to question how definitions rooted in a North American or Western European context can be useful tools for analyzing the city in other cultures. For example, as Max Weber pointed out in *Economy and Society* (*Wirtschaft und Gesellschaft*; 1921–22), in East Asia the city in European terms does not exist (Weber 1976: 733–38). This seems to be an extreme statement, but at least it suggests that Western ideas of the city have to be carefully applied to the urban situation in Japan. They can be helpful tools, but one has to keep their limits in mind. Rather than using a Western definition of the city out of context to find out how urban features are conceptualized in Japan, it could well be more appropriate to analyze the way urban pictures are depicted in Japanese texts.

In this light, I would like to investigate Kōda Rohan's (1867–1947) depiction of Tokyo and his thoughts on urban reform and the creation of a new urban community as revealed in *Ikkoku no shuto* (One nation's capital), written and published at the turn of the twentieth century. Rohan was not only a celebrated writer of fiction but also an intellectual who was concerned about the problems of his time. In this treatise of nearly 180 pages

Rohan analyzes Tokyo's role as Japan's national capital. Focusing on the city's growth due to migration and industrialization as well as the importance of the identification of the individual with the urban community, this text is not only unique in Rohan's work but also in the whole corpus of Meiji literature on urban features.[6]

This text reflects the difficulty of conceiving the city as an abstract idea. It convincingly shows the problems connected with the use of pre-Meiji vocabulary and its underlying precepts for the explanation of modern urban phenomena. Rohan uses abstract terms such as *toshi* or *tokai*, both meaning 'city,' but when it comes to concrete depictions of Tokyo he mainly uses contextualized images of diversity, change, and fluidity rooted in Japanese and Chinese tradition. He develops an idea of Tokyo's future on the basis of concepts from the past.

Tokyo's Growth and Reorganization During the Latter Half of the Nineteenth Century

Unlike Europe, Japan was already economically and culturally determined by urban phenomena from the mid eighteenth century on. At that time the city of Edo was inhabited by more than one million people – some researchers even estimate a population of more than 1.4 million – and was therefore the largest city in the world. At the beginning of the nineteenth century no city in Europe had such a large population. The largest Western city at that time was London (850,000 residents), followed by Paris (550,000), and Vienna and Moscow (both 250,000).

In 1862, however, the abolition of the *sankin kōtai* (alternate attendance)[7] destroyed the foundation of Edo's prosperity. Due to the political and social turmoil in the years around the Meiji Restoration in 1868, more than half of Tokyo's population left the city and returned to their hometowns. Only 500,000 people remained. One can imagine that Tokyo, which from a Western point of view had never looked much like a great capital, was in a poor state at the very moment when the emperor moved there and the city became the nation's capital.

The transition to a new political and economic system began rather slowly, but then proceeded very quickly. In the 1870s and 1880s the economic situation improved and more and more people moved back or migrated to the city. Due, both to more births than deaths and accelerated industrialization, Japan experienced extreme urban growth from the 1880s on. Tokyo was most affected by changes brought up by the modernization policy of the Meiji government because all important political, economic and cultural functions had to be moved from the Kansai area to the Kantō area (Yazaki 1968: 418–21). In 1890 more than one million people lived in Tokyo, and at the turn of the century it already had a population of 1.4 million, which means that it had returned to its demographic size of the

18th century when the city was at its cultural prime. The population of Tokyo doubled from 1895 to 1923, reaching almost four million by the eve of the 1923 earthquake. Such explosive growth severely strained the already inadequate infrastructure of the city and disrupted familiar patterns of urban space.

In the age of imperialism cities were regarded as symbols of the progress of mankind and as the embodiment of modern civilization. Capital cities were physical representations of the power and wealth of the nation-states then competing with each other. Much as today, they were objects of the discourse of nation-building and modernity on the one hand, and its criticism on the other. Japan, like Victorian England and Germany, followed the ideology of progress and nationalism. Images of historical and hence cultural continuity in architecture and historiography served the construction of a unified Japanese national identity. Tokyo's reorganization was a national goal, and the city was to become a symbol of Japan's participation in the competition amongst the 'enlightened,' 'civilized' nations of the West. The designing of Tokyo as the capital city had important nationalistic implications (Fujitani 1996). It was regarded as the *teito* (imperial capital), an old Nara period term which became popular again around the time of the Meiji Constitution promulgated in 1889. This term suggests a Tokyo viewed less as a city than as a symbol of the nation.[8]

During the latter half of the nineteenth century most of Europe's major cities such as Barcelona, Berlin, Vienna, and Brussels, were modernized. Also modernized were non-European capital cities such as Mexico City and Hanoi. Paris, the so-called 'capital of the nineteenth century', which was newly constructed during the 1860s, became a kind of archetype of city planning.[9] It was grand, permanent, and monumental. It was the model for the new Tokyo, too.[10] Tokyo's infrastructure was insufficient and urgently had to be improved. From the 1880s on, the city's population suffered from the lack of a sewage system, from overpopulation and diseases, and from the ongoing danger of fire.[11] Several plans for modernizing the city were discussed.[12] Japanese planners even used the expression 'Parisation of Tokyo' (*Tōkyō no Parika*) (Fujimori 1990: 444), and tried to adapt essential elements of the French model, such as the construction of broad boulevards and a sewage system. The government attempted to design the city center following the model of German neoclassical and historical architecture, with the aim of representing the nation's identity and the government's authority. Under the guidance of foreign architects, most of the new institutions, such as banks, schools, theatres, libraries, and ministries, were built in Western style in order to document Japan's successful process of building the nation.[13] Monuments such as triumphal arches and memorials were erected in Tokyo's central districts after Japan's victories in two wars (in 1895 against China and in 1905 against Russia) to represent the power of the emerging nation-state. Furthermore, they constituted not only a new network of visual orientation in the cityscape but also places where modern Japan's collective identity was being officially located. As Fujitani Takashi pointed out Tokyo was reconstructed into a 'ceremonial center' of the nation and became an important tool for 'disciplining the memory' of the past as well as creating visions for the future (Fujitani 1996: xi). However, a plan for the entire city never existed as in Paris and Berlin. There were only plans for the modernization of representative areas such as Hibiya, the new center of administration and government, and the Ginza, the 'shop window' of modern Japan. Apart from financial problems, Tokyo's particular topography and social segregation prevented a complete adaptation to Western models.

On the one hand, Tokyo was a showcase to display the latest fashions and inventions from the West, and on the other a testing-ground for institutional innovations (Smith 1978: 53). Not only the city's outer shape but also its internal structure was reformed. The local government system of 1888 as applied to Tokyo was revealing in two respects. First, Tokyo (along with Osaka and Kyoto) was granted less autonomy than ordinary cities through a special law, which was soon abolished in the face of local protests in 1898. Since then Tokyo's mayor has been elected by the municipal council and not by the central government as before (Mikuriya 1996: 23). Second, local municipal administration extended only as far down as the new 'borough' (*ku*), leaving the neighborhood level (*chō*) unattended, which had been so closely regulated in Edo. The city was thus identified with the state at the top end but left to its own devices at the bottom (Smith 1978: 53).

Rohan's *One Nation's Capital*

When analyzing Rohan's thoughts on Tokyo, it is important to keep two biographical facts in mind. First, Rohan belongs to the generation of Meiji intellectuals who were among the last to become adults under the traditional education system, and the first to confront the full impact of modern ideas. Second, he was born into an Edo family of craftsmen and combined both eagerness for progressive change and strong hostility towards the migrant samurais, who often had no love for Tokyo but used it for the advancement of their own ambitions (Smith 1978: 56).

Rohan argues against two positions: pro-Edo sentiment and government technocracy. On the one hand he condemns the antiurban attitude of contemporary writers who tended to criticize the city as the source of all evil and praised the village as 'paradise on earth' (Kōda 1993: 11). At the end of the 1880s and into the 1890s there was a revival of Edo culture and literature (Kornicki 1981; Lane 1968). In a series of magazines nostalgic reminiscences and reprinted sources on Edo history appeared in an antiquated and rather sentimental mode (Smith 1978: 56). Rohan criticized the conservative sentimentalists who longed for old Edo and concentrated on the evocation of the past instead of creating a vision of Tokyo's future. He postulates that the intellectuals' most important task should be the development of a method for the city's improvement (Kōda 1993: 12).

Rohan's treatise is also a harsh criticism of the government's technocratic policy for Tokyo's reorganization. From the Meiji Restoration until around 1900 the dominant concept of Tokyo was that of a passive object to be viewed from the outside. Most of the people who were involved in the modernization had a mechanistic view of the city. The emphasis was on the construction of a representative imperial capital through monumental architecture, broad avenues, and public spaces. Tokyo's modernization was a challenge to be met with modern technology. The question of the citizen's function within the process of social reorganization which accompanied the rebuilding of the city did not appear in the government's considerations. One reason for this was that Tokyo's ruling elite mostly came from the western part of Japan and therefore had no personal link with the history and culture of the city. Due to the Freedom and People's Rights Movement (*Jiyū minken undō*)[14] and the promulgation of the constitution in 1889, political and social focus shifted from the technical aspects of modernization to the role of the individual in the constitution of society and the nation-state.[15]

One Nation's Capital can be regarded as Rohan's contribution to the discussion of the new citizen and citizenship in general, which at that time was not only widely discussed in Japan but also in China and in the West.[16] Rohan focuses on Tokyo's social modernization; therefore, there are neither descriptions of architecture or streets in his work, nor does he mention the role of the emperor in the designing of the city. He requires a new spirit, a teleology, for Tokyo's and Japan's future in order to compensate for the losses modernization has brought to the mental life of Tokyo's citizens and their attitude towards the city. These losses are the reason for the disorganized condition of the city. Rohan's ideas concentrate on individuals and their responsibility for Tokyo's present condition and future. In particular, he emphasizes the question of how each citizen can be brought to participate in the creation of an urban community based on the citizens' emotions for the city. Rohan's thoughts on the urban community show surprising similarities with those of contemporary social thinkers in the East and West, such as Kang Youwei (1858–1927), Liang Qichao (1873–1929), Ferdinand Tönnies (1855–1936), Ebenezer Howard (1850–1928) and even Edward Bellamy (1850–98).[17] It appears that Rohan was familiar with the urban discourse in the West, and he probably studied some Western treatises on urban problems and larger social questions.

Rohan's reflections on Tokyo are set in the context of those Western ideas that were transmitted to Japan during the Meiji period, and of the Japanese and Chinese thought forming the epistemological background to the reception of these Western ideas. His image of Tokyo's contemporary condition as chaos originates in Daoism. His evaluation of the city's condition is based on Confucian moral thought, and his conceptualization of time and his view of the future share important elements with the Western idea of history as progress. However, when a Japanese thinker of this period uses Western or Chinese ideas, it should never be taken for granted that they have the same meaning as in their original context. Modern Japanese ideas are usually a complex mix of indigenous Japanese ideas and interpreted Western ideas. This amalgamation stemming from different cultures and historical periods reflects the general circumstances of Meiji intellectual discourse. The intellectuals perceived their period as being a time of transition and they had to conceptually cope with tremendous change and diversity in epistemological, social and cultural terms.

Despite the convincing modernity of Rohan's ideas of progress and his orientation towards the future, his style of argumentation, the argument's structure and his moralizing diction remain reminiscent of classical Chinese rhetoric, such as in *Daxue* (Jap.: *Daigaku*; The great learning). His mode of thought is basically shaped by the principles of Confucian ethics. Rohan not only often points out the positive consequences of his advice, but also warns of the negative consequences if his advice is not followed (Kōda 1993: 48).

How does Rohan approach the problem of rebuilding Tokyo as Japan's capital city? He divides the urban space into two spheres: the 'material' or 'visible' (*yūkei*) and the 'immaterial' or 'invisible' (*mukei*). He states that, compared to Edo, astonishing progress has been achieved in a lot of 'things' (*jibutsu*), and that customs and public morals have changed tremendously. He points out that there is 'progress' (*shinpo*) in the material sphere but 'decline' (*daraku*) in the immaterial sphere (Kōda 1993: 15–16).

Rohan's View of History: Past, Present, and Future

Although *One Nation's Capital* is not divided into chapters, the content can nonetheless be divided into three parts:

1. In the first part (pp. 7–68) of the text Rohan asks what terms are suitable for describing Tokyo's condition. What constitutes a city in general? What ought to be the basis for the citizen's relationship to the city? Here Rohan's thoughts focus on the future and reflect the Western ideas of the individual, the community, and the nation. The terms he uses to express these ideas are either neologisms coined during the Meiji era, such as *shakai* (society), or categories of premodern Japanese thought, such as *jikaku* (self-awareness or self-awakening), originally a Buddhist term which during the Meiji era became the accepted word for the Western idea of the individual.

2. In the middle part (pp. 68–139) of the text Rohan describes new elements of the city's infrastructure, such as the organisation of waste removal and a sewage system. He thinks both are necessary for Tokyo to function as Japan's capital city, representative of standards of hygiene (pp. 88–94). His consideration of communal institutions such as public parks and kindergartens show his concern for the needs of the inhabitants.
3. The last part (pp. 139–185) of *One Nation's Capital* importantly differs from the other sections. Here Rohan outlines the history of Edo's pleasure districts and its prosperous popular culture, and claims that these caused Edo's decline. He points out the negative influence on the inhabitants' morals caused by the pleasure districts of Edo that spread all over the city. For Rohan, Tokyo's golden age was the beginning of the seventeenth century, when Edo was founded under Tokugawa Ieyasu and the urban community was well organized (p. 139). In his eyes, the history of Edo becomes a history of moral decline. This judgement forms the basis of Rohan's criticism. He warns that Tokyo might decline like Edo did, and he offers proposals about how such a decline could be averted, and how Tokyo's history could become a history of success and prosperity. Here no obvious connections with modern Western thought in terms of borrowed words and neologisms can be found. Rohan's ideas and language seem to belong to the past. He is talking about a future which is determined by an immoral past.

Rohan's view of history is based on the construction of a polarity between Edo and Tokyo. He perceives Edo and Tokyo as two different cities and emphasizes the discontinuities caused by the Meiji reforms. In the Japanese paradigm for criticizing modernity, it is a common feature to use the split in Tokyo's history as an instrument for criticizing the changes brought by the Meiji reforms against the background of the past. Edo thus serves as a mirror of Tokyo's modernity. In contrast to Rohan, authors like Tanizaki Jun'ichirō (1886–1965) and Nagai Kafū (1879–1959), who also based their criticism on this polarity, depict Edo's pleasure districts as harmonious, homogenous urban spaces. In their works this part of Edo serves as a counterworld to modern Tokyo, which they describe as a place of fragmentation, disruption and uncontrolled dynamics. Rohan, on the other hand, used the Edo Tokyo polarity for a different criticsm of modern Tokyo. Here the history of Edo is a history of moral decline and Edo serves as the negative model for Tokyo's future.

It is astonishing that Rohan's argument in this part of the text is so one-dimensional and his view of history so deterministic and inflexible. Rohan's outline of history primarily seems to work in the service of ethics. The events of the past are only interesting to him in so far as they provide practical examples of the moral principles enshrined in the Chinese classics.

Rohan seems not to have the slightest interest in the various factors that determined politics towards the end of the Tokugawa period (1600–1867), such as the tremendous social problems or the pressure from outside. According to Rohan, Edo declined simpply because of its pleasure districts. He regards Edo's popular culture, which considerably contributed to the city's fame, as harmful to the citizens' morals. This negative judgement of premodern popular culture is a modern view which combines elements of Confucianist and Protestant moral philosophy.

Images of Tokyo in *One Nation's Capital*

For Rohan Tokyo is in a general state of 'chaos' (*konton*) and looks like an 'unfinished product' (*miseihin*) (Kōda 1993: 14). This is due to the fact that even the idea of what the capital city should be is 'chaotic and without shape' (*konton mushō*) (p. 51). In Rohan's thinking chaos is the means for describing Tokyo's contemporary condition and serves as the image of crisis. Here crisis is to be understood as a situation in which nothing has yet been decided and everything is open to change. In Daoist thought 'chaos' (*hundun* in Chinese; *konton* in Japanese) is a central concept and it means a condition 'that has its own internal principles of organization, change, order, and life' (Girardot 1983: 59). It has similarities with the current discourse on chaos theory in the natural sciences and in city planning (Zibell 1995). The idea of 'chaos' allows Rohan to depict the city as being in a state of permanent change and flux. Actually, one of Tokyo's most urgent problems at that time was not only its population growth but also the fact that the city's borders had not yet been defined (Kōda 1993: 69–71). *Konton* is etymologically related to the notion of water (Girardot 1983: 95). Rohan's remark that Tokyo is 'flooded' (*hanran*) by people who have migrated from all over the country (Kōda 1993: 72), and that it is getting filled with 'people who are in flux' (*ryūdō no sei aru mono*) (p. 79), is reflected in the image of *konton*. Furthermore, *konton* implies a cycle of creation and destruction which is linked to the idea of a perfect society (Girardot 1983: 69). Thus, Rohan's exhortations for Tokyo's future have utopian traits.

Rohan makes an allusion to a very famous passage in the *Zhuangzi* which most of his contemporary readers were probably familiar:

> Is not the reason for this that Tokyo is in a chaotic (*konton*) condition, but has not yet got the seven holes (*shichikyō*)? (Kōda 1993: 14)

'Seven holes' is a reference to the story of 'Emperor Hundun of the Center' in the Zhuangzi. It means the seven openings of the senses: two ears, two eyes, two nostrils, and the mouth. The story of Emperor Hundun throws light on the theme of 'returning to the beginning' and thus clarifies one of Rohan's intentions when he describes Tokyo as 'chaos':

The Emperor of the South was called Shu. The Emperor of the North was called Hu. And the Emperor of the Center was called Hundun. Shu and Hu at times mutually came together and met in Hundun's territory. Hundun treated them very generously. Shu and Hu, then, discussed how they could reciprocate Hundun's virtue saying: 'Men all have seven openings in order to see, hear, eat, and breathe. He alone doesn't have any. Let's try boring him some.' Each day they bored one hole, and on the seventh day Hundun died. (Girardot 1983: 81)

Various interpretations of this passage exist but one of the most convincing with regard to Rohan's citation is that of the sinologist Marcel Granet. Granet stresses the significance and prestige of becoming completely human or civilized by having the seven openings of the senses that give one a face (pp. 83–84).

During the Meiji era *konton* (chaos) and the metaphor of *shichikyō* (seven holes) not only had a Daoist connotation, but were also important terms in the discourse of civilization which was deeply influenced by the Western theory of progress, positivism and Social Darwinism. There *konton* had a completely different meaning than in Daoism. It meant primitive chaos and pointed to the lowest stage of barbarism.[18] For example, Katō Hiroyuki (1836–1916) in his treatise *Bunmei kaika* (On civilization, 1874) also stated that the senses or *shichikyō* are an asset of civilization. Katō writes that,

> Even if the head is not a tenth of the whole body it must be viewed as the most important part, as ears, eyes, nose, and mouth, all important things, are arranged there. The idea that the human soul is located in the head is an interesting idea. In former times it was said to be found in the breast.... There is nothing as important [in the human body] as the head. (Quoted in Iyama 1996: 10)

Applied to Tokyo's condition as depicted in *One Nation's Capital* the Daoist meaning of the word *konton*, as well as its meaning in the Meiji discourse on civilization, describe a similar situation: not yet 'civilized.' Through this double-bound quotation Rohan criticizes the government's policy of 'civilization.' Although in Rohan's view Tokyo, the 'capital city' (jap.: *shuto*; literally: 'head-capital') is 'not yet civilized,' which means that the government's policy of modernization has not yet shown satisfying results, he regards Tokyo's condition of chaos positively. The city provides material which could yet be formed. But how should it be formed?

In contrast to the image of chaos to describe Tokyo's condition, Rohan uses the image of an organism as the matrix for discussing the central functions that the capital city must fulfil. He focuses mainly on the function of the city as a social organism. He perceives the city as a living entity with all of its parts interconnected and dependent on each other as in an organism.

A variety of texts dealing with urban topics exists from the Meiji era, but as far as I know none of them presents the city as a community in the same social or political terms as Rohan. His image of the city as an organism seems to be a novelty. Conceiving the city by means of analogy with the proportions of the human body has a long tradition in European thought.[19] But it seems that especially during the nineteenth and twentieth centuries the image of the city as organism gained new meaning. Due to important nineteenth century inventions in the natural sciences as well as the central position of biologism, organicism, and Darwinism, the organism became a common metaphor for the conceptualization of the city and society. Imagining the city as an organism opens a whole set of categories for describing various kinds of urban phenomena. On account of the tremendous growth in population, the cities' size in this era lost every link to anthropometrical proportions. A city conceived of as an organism no longer meant that it should be designed on the basis of human proportions, but rather that it could be seen as a living being with characteristics such as movement, fluidity, and diversity, which allowed one to cope conceptually with its growing size and changing structure.

In the nineteenth century discourse of urban reform in the West as well as in Japan, hygienic and medical aspects of city life were essential topics. Thus, the metaphor of illness often appears in descriptions of the living conditions in cities and in criticism of Japan's modernization in general. It was common to talk about the 'disease of civilization' (*bunmeibyō*) (Gluck 1985: 161 and 177; Loftus 1985: 191). The city was not only a source of disease for its population, but was also ill itself and longing for a cure. The image of the city as an organism fits the view of history as decline which was common in the nineteenth century.[20] Because of this image's biological character, its basic condition is first growth and then decline. Furthermore, it was a useful tool for discussing the city in social and political terms both in the West and in Japan. It implies a correlation between city, urban society, and nation.[21] Consequently, Rohan's criticism encompasses not only Tokyo but the whole nation. How does Rohan use the image of the organism? In *One Nation's Capital* he writes,

> One nation's capital (*shuto*) is like the head of a human being. It is equipped with all kinds of high-grade facilities and is the place from which all activities arise and to which they return. Therefore, because the capital city's influence on the whole country is exceedingly strong, the good or bad situation of the capital city becomes instantly the good or bad situation of the whole country. This is the same as the fact that the good or bad situation of the head becomes instantly the good or bad situation of the whole body. (Kōda 1993: 9)

Shuto literally means 'head-capital' and was introduced as the word for the capital city in the Meiji era. Furthermore, the usage of *shuto* reflects an important shift that had taken place in the nineteenth century in Western thought. Instead of the heart, the brain was now regarded as the most important part of the body and it became a central metaphor in social and political thought. This metaphor is directly connected with the Meiji expression for the capital (*shuto*) (Iyama 1996: 9–12) and is also linked to the idea of *kokutai* (national polity), the myth of continuity which described Japan's distinctive national identity (Gluck 1985). *Kokutai* connotes the spiritual component of nationhood, based upon the emperor's genealogical descent from the gods. The use of *shuto* as well as of *kokutai* was a uniquely nineteenth century product.

Rohan correlates the capital, the nation, and the citizen through the image of the organism and positions Tokyo in the center of the network that constitutes the nation. The capital serves not only as a model for the whole country but also leads it in everything. If the capital is in bad shape, the rest of the country is, too. On the basis of this equation Rohan constructs a network of correlations amongst all parts of society. According to Rohan, every event that takes place in Tokyo influences the whole country. The capital city transmits to the periphery not only material novelties but also changes in the mental world:

> Also it is obvious that the capital city has a great influence on the language and public morals of the people of the nation, on their ideas and customs, and on the system. (Kōda 1993: 9)

Thus no hierarchy exists between the capital city and the periphery. Their 'relationship is mutual' (*sōgō no kankei*) (p. 10), which means that it is organized horizontally, not vertically, as is typical of Confucian thought. Because of this close mutual relationship, a 'rich' (*furyoku*) country has 'virtue' (*tokuryoku*) and 'knowledge' (*chiryoku*), and therefore will never have a 'bad' capital city:

> Therefore, one can also say that the capital city is an instrument for inspecting the state of health of the nation (*kokumin*). That is to say that the capital city represents the nation. (p. 10)

Rohan describes Tokyo's condition mainly on the basis of aesthetic categories that are deeply rooted in Confucian thought. The city is not a machine that can be reformed merely through modern technology. It is an organism that has to become 'good' from the inside. The binary terms 'good' (*zen/zenbi*) and 'bad' (*aku*) are Rohan's means of judging Tokyo's state in aesthetic, moral and hygienic terms (pp. 12–13). In his opinion the city is 'bad' at present and requires the 'good' for its future. In Confucian thought the 'good' (*zen*) means shape, system, order, and harmony.

It is interesting to note that in the propaganda of the hygienic movement in Europe during the nineteenth century 'good' meant hygienic as well as moral cleanliness (Berndt 1987: 143) and social engineers strove to replace morals with hygiene (Sennett 1994: 256). This equation of ethical with ontological principles is typical for Confucian thinking and was also common in nineteenth century Western social thought, which was influenced by Protestantism and Puritanism. These streams of thought share common characteristics and contributed important elements to the Meiji discourse on urban reform.

For Rohan cleanliness is similar to order. He talks about 'the way of hygiene' (*eisei no michi*) and thus integrates hygienic matters into the Confucian social order. Aside from the abstract connotation of 'clean' as morally good, Rohan makes concrete suggestions of how the hygienic situation in Tokyo could be improved, as for example through the construction of a sewage system and the organisation of waste removal (Kōda 1993: 88–94). Even if in Rohan's opinion the situation of Tokyo has improved in hygienic and aesthetic terms, there is still a lot to do in order to achieve real progress (pp. 93–94).

An important aspect of the image of the city as an organism is the implication that it is a subject which is able to act. According to Rohan Tokyo urgently needs reform because there is a lack of 'purposeful movement' (*mokuteki aru undō*). Only this will create a 'capital city that is alive' (*seimei aru shuto*) and make it prosper from day to day (p. 48). Edo serves as the negative model:

> When Edo was moving with purpose, it was prospering. But when it slowed down in the activity that desired the good (*zenbi o yoku suru no undō eisaku*), it soon declined (*tsui ni horobiru*). (p. 48)

The idea of 'purposeful movement' belongs to the nineteenth century idea of history as progress. Rohan perceives the city not as static but as permanently moving. This image of movement is quite unusual for Meiji texts about Tokyo.[22]

Community and the Citizen

Rohan mainly conceptualizes Tokyo with the metaphors of chaos and the organism. Both share the quality that their condition is never fixed and that they are always in flux. These metaphors are thus appropriate means of perceiving the city, which was the space where the changes brought about by modernization took place very intensively. Rohan applies these images to his description of Tokyo's community. On account of migration into the city and the evolution of new social structures after the abolishment of the feudal system, Tokyo's citizens consist of a combination of people who had lived there before and people who had come from all over the country. In Rohan's view, the lack of a shared identity caused the formlessness of the city.

He compares Tokyo's situation to that of Edo, where everyday thousands of people moved in and out. Due to the *sankin kōtai* system Edo's population was very diverse like that of Tokyo.[23] But according to Rohan all of these people became 'natives of Edo' (*Edokko*) after having settled there for a while. He suggests that the same will happen with Tokyo's population; it will soon become the 'people of Tokyo' (*Tōkyō no tami*). He expects that in Tokyo, as in Edo, all these different people will fuse together in a 'huge melting pot' (*ichidai rutsubo*) to form the 'capital city's people' (*shuto no tami*) (p. 45).

The image of Tokyo as an organism implies not only that the city is an active subject but also an object of love. In Rohan's view there are two reasons for the 'decline of the city' (*tofu no daraku*): the citizens' passive attitude towards the city and their egoism, which prevents them from caring for anything but personal matters (p. 62). He regards it as the duty of the 'Empire's people' (*teikoku no tami*) to contribute to the city's good and to reform the bad. Tokyo's prosperity and its moral and aesthetic condition depend not only upon the buildings, but also on the people's emotions for the city (p. 13). In order to improve, Tokyo needs its citizens' 'love' (*ai*) (pp. 12–14). Ai is a central term in Confucian thought. Rohan demands a close-knit relationship between Tokyo and its citizens. He makes the city a beloved object through anthropomorphization and thus reduces the emotional distance between the city and the citizens. The 'love' for Tokyo is a tool for organizing commitments among strangers. The city becomes the space where diverse identities melt into a new 'Tokyo identity.'

Rohan regards the diversity of Tokyo's population in a very positive light. The city is a place where individuals have countless opportunities to make contact with each other. Therefore, Tokyo's people will have 'many things in common as well as many different things' and the amalgamation of their thoughts will create a new consciousness for the city (pp. 48–49). He stresses that it is important for Tokyo's prosperity that its citizens think in different ways.[24] In Rohan's opinion it is the citizen who creates the city:

> There is no need to discuss the fact that the question of whether the city is beautiful or not, or whether it is good or not, also depends on the awakening (*jikaku*) of the individual (*kojin*) towards the city (*tofu*). Therefore each self is a particle of the capital city, and the acts, words, and thoughts of each self influence and greatly stimulate the outer shape and the inner content of the city. To develop consciousness of the things that make the city ugly or beautiful, is it not true that someone has to live there and have enough spare time to sing of the city in an emotional and poetic way not profit oriented? Following the light of self-awareness the self should discover a number of dark points that are mistakes of past times and then develop the feeling that these must be corrected and reformed as fast as possible and, following this, it could busy itself with the realization.... The people of the city (*tomin*) are its owners. The city is a huge tassel composed of many fine threads. Whether the city shines or not depends on whether each single person in the city possesses light or not. Whether the city is clean or not depends on whether every single person loves cleanliness or not. The selves and the city are like one body. (pp. 37–39)

The Western idea of the autonomous individual had an enormous impact on the Meiji discourse of civilization and of modernization. Rohan's call for 'self-awakened,' 'self-aware,' independent and moral citizens fits into the mainstream of Meiji intellectual thought. Particular to his considerations is the fact that he extends the idea of the individual to the urban citizen who is equipped with a sense of responsibility towards the community where he lives; he is, furthermore, a citizen of the nation. From Rohan's point of view the people of Tokyo are in a state of diversity and flux and therefore the consciousness of building a community has not yet evolved. The city struggles with a lack of 'love' (*ai*) and its citizens have no identity as citizens of Tokyo. Tokyo's future depends on the development of the ideal citizen who would also serve as a model for the whole nation. Thus, Rohan's idea of citizenship is an expression of urban community on the one hand, while it defines the relationship between the state and the individual on the other.

The question of what individuals should be and how they should relate to the state was one of the most prominent topics in Meiji intellectual discourse. It can be found in nearly every text on society, culture, and philosophy. Especially after the introduction of the writings of Jean-Jacques Rousseau (1712–1778), John Stuart Mill (1806–1873) and Social Darwinist thought, the idea of the individual and the new citizen, or the search for an 'Ethics for the New Society' (Havens, 1970: 141), became a central topic. These discussions appear in the works of thinkers such as Fukuzawa Yukichi and Nakamura Masanao (1832–1891), Meiji Japan's leading interpreters of English liberalism, and Katō Hiroyuki, who was deeply involved in the study of Social Darwinism. All were prominent members of the *Meirokusha* (Meiji 6 Society), founded in 1874.[25] Their shared assumption was that radical reform of the morals and spirit of the Japanese people was the first essential task for Japan's modernization. They were in search of a new 'spirit of civilization.' 'Civilization' was not regarded as a matter of material base, but of the way people thought. In 1872 Fukuzawa wrote in *Gakumon no susume* (An encouragement of learning),

> Schools, industries, armies and navies are the mere external forms of civilisation. They are not difficult to produce. All that is needed is the money to pay for them. Yet there remains something immaterial, something that cannot be seen or heard, bought or sold, lent or borrowed. It pervades the whole nation and its influence is so strong that without it none of the schools or the other external forms would be of the slightest use. This supremely important thing we must call the spirit of civilisation.[26]

In 1898 Fukuzawa reflected on the relationship between 'independence and self-respect' (*dokuritsu jison*) and 'the independence of a nation' (Huang 1972: 91). He believed that to acquire national dignity the Japanese must adopt a new set of morals patterned on that of England. This statement reflects the influence of Samuel Smiles' *Self-help* (1859), a small but important book translated by Nakamura Masanao and published in 1871, which successfully propagated Victorian morality (p. 91). Katō Hiroyuki postulated that modern national power stemmed from the energies of Western individuals and societies and that a representative government must be built upon certain definite qualities of the people (p. 90). The source of the immense power of modern nation-states lay for him in the unification of state and society. Representative institutions were dependent on the existence of a politically conscious and active body of citizens. The secret of Western power and progress lay in the distinctive character of Western people as individuals.

The shift from the concentration on the technical aspects of modernization to the individual and its role as a constitutive element of the nation-state forms the background of Rohan's thoughts on the citizen. He stresses the idea of self-cultivation. Individuals should possess the desire for self-improvement as well as moral and intellectual strength to realize it. This is reminiscent of the *Daxue*, which explicitly addresses the renewal of the people, meaning essentially their moral rectification (Zarrow 1997: 17). In the twelfth century this concept was integrated into neo-Confucian thought, which postulates the self-disciplined and morally autonomous individual. These ideas laid the foundations of the Tokugawa discourse of the individual and his relationship to society.[27] Rohan's three 'powers' that constitute the country – the 'power of wealth' (*furyoku*), the 'power of virtue' (*tokuryoku*), and the 'power of knowledge' (*chiryoku*) (Kōda, 1993: 10) – can also be regarded as the main characteristics of the new citizens. They must cultivate a capacity for acting as members of the community by developing a national consciousness and a regard for public welfare. Rohan summarizes the predominant characteristics of the new citizen with the term *jikaku* (self-)awareness or (self-)awakening. The metaphor of awakening is central to his thoughts on modernization, nationhood and individuality.[28] For Rohan *jikaku* means 'real knowledge, real morality, and real emotion' (*shinchi, shintoku, shinjō*) (Kōda 1993: 31). *Jikaku* is related to the entire social world – science, morality, and art – and acts as the magic formula for Tokyo's social reorganization. According to Rohan, *jikaku* creates 'ideals' (*risō*) and 'faith' (*shinkō*) (p. 47). Both combine to form a 'purposeful movement,' or telos, that 'facing the light [will] advance' (*kōmei ni mukatte o susumuru*) (pp. 47–48). The aim of such movement is a 'capital city that is alive' (*inochi aru shuto*) and changing day by day (p. 48).

The Meaning of *One Nation's Capital* in the Context of Present-Day Urban Discourse

From the time of the foundation of the Japanese nation-state in 1868 to the present, the discourse about Tokyo and its function as the capital city implies criticism of Japan's process of modernization. It is also directly linked to the discourse of Japan's national identity. Tokyo serves not only as a space for the invention of a collective Japanese past but also of a collective future. Rohan wrote his treatise at a time when Japan's modernization has reached a peak. At this point, industrialization and urbanization created serious social problems and the quest for national identity already showed signs of incipient nationalism. Due to the diversity of intellectual trends at the turn of the century, Rohan's text is an amalgamation of contemporary Western and (Sino-)Japanese ideas about the 'hard city,' its architecture and infrastructure (i.e. the city that can be located in maps and statistics) as well as of the 'soft city,' the city of illusion and aspiration.[29] Rohan criticizes the government's mechanical view of the city and its policy of treating Tokyo as an object. It is essential to Rohan's criticism that he was born into an old Edo family and despised the newcomers from western Japan because of their 'provincialism.' He advocated social rebuilding of the city instead of the show-case reforms of the government. His idea of the individual and his emphasis on self-cultivation probably is a reaction against the 'selfish person' created by industrialization. *One Nation's Capital* can be read as Rohan's attempt to overcome the alienation caused by Japan's modernization in the creation of a new urban community.

Rohan's broad perception of the complexity of Tokyo's modernization narrows again at the end of his treatise. The autonomous individual disappears from his thoughts. His view of history seems to follow the pattern of a 'history of decline,' which is not only characteristic for nineteenth century European thought but is also rooted in Chinese tradition. His enthusiastic view of the future and his will for overcoming the chaotic condition of the present, seen as the result of the process of decline in the recent past, is reminiscent of Kang Youwei's view of history as expressed in *Datongshu*. In this text Kang elaborates the notion of a historical process in three stages. The present is a state of crisis and chaos, which serves as the basis for the creation of a splendid future, itself linked to a past which was well ordered and was destroyed in a process of decline.[30] In this respect *One Nation's Capital* is not a universal treatise on the modern city. In line with Confucian thought, Rohan refers to the real and concrete aspects of Tokyo, the city where he lives.

As the publication of the paperback edition in 1993 indicates, Rohan's treatise has not lost its pertinence.[31] The image of the city as chaos, organism, and community are Rohan's tools for conceptualizing the city and its problems. It is interesting to note that recently Western city planning has adopted elements of chaos theory in order to break through the all too rigid norms of modern architecture and city planning. The postmodern use of chaos theory resembles Rohan's idea of chaos to a certain extent. The search for a 'hidden order' in the aestheticized chaos of Tokyo is a common feature in Western and Japanese writing on Tokyo.[32] Furthermore, in the past few years the concept of citizenship has come under renewed historical and theoretical scrutiny. In spite of the vagueness of the word, or perhaps precisely because citizenship can mean so many things, it seems to be an appropriate tool for analyzing varying contemporary issues from the status of minorities, the underclass, and women to civic and ethnic identity, regional and global cooperation, and the future of democracy (Zarrow 1997: 6).

From the Meiji Restoration on, Tokyo has been the space in which the Japanese nation is formed and represented. Rohan's appeal to build a 'Tokyo of the world' (sekai no Tōkyō; Kōda 1993: 67) shows that he had not only the realm of Japan in mind, but also the rest of the world. During the twentieth century Tokyo experienced tremendous growth and has become a 'world city' (Sassen 1991), one faced with the expectation of creating a home for migrants and melting their diverse identities into one national identity. The problem of *Tōkyō no tami* ('people of Tokyo'), i.e. the problem of creating a 'Tokyo identity' as it was articulated by Rohan still exists today. In the 1980s and 1990s discourse of postmodernism as well as activities of city planning and architecture, attempts have been made to construct a unified Tokyo identity. The search for a concrete as well as a spiritual home surfaced in the discourse of Japan's re-Asianization and the so-called 'Edo boom' as well as in the politics of national memory and native place-making (Robertson 1997). In dozens of publications, and through newly built landmarks such as the Edo Tokyo Museum (Edo Tōkyō Hakubutsukan, opened to the public in 1993) and the Tokyo Metropolitan Government Offices (Tōkyō Tochōsha, completed in 1991), attempts were made to construct a cultural continuity between modern Tokyo and the Edo period. In the same years, the Tokyo Metropolitan Government launched its long-term project *My Town Tōkyō* and *machi-zukuri* ('making neighborhood') became a common catchphrase.[33]

But as the city is in a permanent state of flux and change and therefore is too complex to freeze into a fixed identity as was historically intended by the role of Western architecture and city planning, the discourse about Tokyo has produced a diversity of often opposing identities. This very dynamic, continuously changing process is not unique to Japan. Rather, it is occurring in nearly every nation and is characteristic for an age which is motivated in general by two sets of forces: the push for globalization and universalistic criteria on the one hand, and a fundamentalist interest in preserving ethnic and racial purity on the other (Mouer and Sugimoto 1995: 237). Most of Asia's cities are more than ever in a state of flux and diversity. They are 'cities on the move'[34] and challenge common ways of thinking the city.[35]

In Western as well as non-Western countries discourses about the relationship between national identity, citizenship, politics, architecture and city planning gain importance in the age of globalization.[36] As Peter G.

Zarrow notes, the transnational movements of people, ideas, goods, and images now heightened by the globalization of capital is highly disruptive to the sense of community that lies behind citizenship (Zarrow 1997: 7). Not only nations but also cities are 'imagined communities.'[37] The modern notion of citizenship consists of membership in a nation-state with its attendant legal, social, and moral rights and obligations, and of participation in public life. Furthermore, it includes sharing in the destiny of the political community (p. 8). In this respect, Rohan's ideas on the urban community gain universal meaning. *One Nation's Capital* can also be regarded as a manifestation of Confucian thinking in the modern age. Rohan probably wanted to show that categories such as 'love' (*ai* or *aijō*), 'virtue' (*toku*) and 'knowledge' (*chi*), which stem from Chinese thought, are not only still valid both for the description of modern urban phenomena and for the conception of modern citizenship, but that they gain importance in the face of the alienation experienced in modern urban society. Viewed from the present, Rohan's treatise convincingly shows that cities are not only made up of buildings, streets, and other infrastructures but also of the people who live there. In this sense, modern urban society requires not just more new technologies in order overcome its problems but first and foremost a new idea of community.

Notes

1 The title is translated as suggested by Smith (1978: 56), who incidentally gives the year 1898 as the date of publication. However, according to the introduction in the Japanese edition used here (Kōda 1993: 227) the text was written in the summer of 1899. It was published in the magazine *Shin shōsetsu* (New novel) from November 1900 to March 1901. See also Kōda Rohan's *Zenshū* (Collected works), vol. 27, pp. 3–168 (Kōda 1979).

2 Michel Foucault points out that 'from the eighteenth century on, every discussion of politics as the art of the government of men necessarily includes a chapter or a series of chapters on urbanism, on collective facilities, on hygiene, and on private architecture.... [At the beginning of the seventeenth century] the city was no longer perceived as a place of privilege, as an exception in a territory of fields, forests, and roads. The cities were no longer islands beyond the common law. Instead, the cities, with the problems that they raised, and the particular forms that they took, served as the models for the governmental rationality that was to apply to the whole of the territory.... The model of the city became the matrix for the regulations that apply to a whole state.' (Foucault 1984: 240–1)

3 See for example the story of Kikuchi Shintarō, the hero of Tokutomi Roka's *Omoide no ki* (Footprints in the snow, 1901) (Tokutomi 1970) and Natsume Sōseki's (1867–1916) *Sanshirō* (1908) (Natsume 1977). It is interesting to note that most of those authors who depicted the newcomer's insecure position played a central role in the naturalistic movement after 1900 and came from the periphery or the countryside. See for example Kunikida Doppo's (1871–1908) short story *Kyūshi* (Death in anguish, 1907) (Kunikida 1984) and Ikuta Kizan's (1876–1945) *Tokai* (The city, 1908) (Ikuta 1957).

Place Between Future and Past

4 In his famous speech 'The Metropolis and Mental Life' at the Congress of City Planning in Dresden in 1904, Georg Simmel (1858–1918) focused on the urban individual and his or her state of mind. In contrast to the rural world the density and diversity of the city constantly put the individual in touch with possibilities unknown outside the city. The assumption in Simmel's analysis is that the city dweller is mobile and resourceful. Gliding over the urban landscape, picking and choosing the associations that create a particular, individualised social world, the city dweller belongs to many different groups and thus has to produce multiple personal identities. (Simmel, 1957).

5 Mayer, (1971) gives 14 different definitions of the city.

6 As far as I know, no extensive study of *One Nation's Capital* has yet been published. Maeda (1983) deals with this text in one short chapter (pp. 164–74). Mikuriya (1996: 18–23), Ōoka (1983: 3–27); Haga (1992: 137–84) and Koseki (1986) outline their ideas of this text. It is surprising that Rohan's treatise is not even mentioned in Yoshihara Naoki's *Toshi no shisō* (Ideas of the city, 1993) although he discusses Mori Ōgai's and Katayama Sen's ideas on urban reforms, both contemporaries of Rohan (see Takahashi 1993 and Sekino 1993).

7 This is a rule of the Tokugawa shogunate (1603–1867), whereby *daimyō*, or territorial lords, were required to reside in alternate years at Edo in attendance on the shōgun. This system was devised to maintain control over the more than 260 *daimyō*. They were obliged to attend the shogunal court in Edo at fixed intervals, dividing their time equally between the capital and their domains. To perform this obligation, the *daimyō* had to maintain residential estates (*yashiki*) in Edo, where their wives and children were permanently detained by the shogunate. The journeys and the upkeep of a *daimyō*'s Edo estates consumed about 70 to 80 percent of his income.

8 Smith (1978) outlines the idea of Tokyo as Japan's capital.

9 See *Paris s'exporte: modèle d'architecture ou architectures modèles* (1995).

10 Tokyo was the only Japanese city that was redesigned on Western models in the Meiji period. It was not until the 1910s that plans were made to redesign other cities (Jujimori 1990: 413).

11 As in the West, also journalistic writings in Japan documented poverty and slums in the cities. Yokoyama Gennosuke's (1871–1915) *Nihon no kasō shakai* (Japan's lower classes, 1899) and Matsubara Iwagorō's (1866–1935) *Saiankoku no Tōkyō* (Darkest Tokyo, 1893) investigations of the living conditions among the poor show convincing similarities with contemporary Western reports of the dark sides of city life, such as *How the Other Half Lives* (1890) by Jacob Riis, a police reporter from New York, and Henry Mayhew's *London Labour and London Poor* (1864).

12 Most of the discussions centred on the question of which major functions Tokyo should fulfil, e.g. trade city, harbour city, or imperial city. All of them together were subsumed as *Shiku kaisei* (Reorganization of the City Boroughs) (Fujimori 1990: 3–205 and 425–53). Fukuzawa Yukichi (1835–1901) was involved in this discussion as well as Mori Ōgai (1862–1922). Both published several articles on the relationship between city planning and health policy. See for example Fukuzawa (1959a, 1959b and 1959c) and Mori (1974). Johnston (1995) discusses tuberculosis as an urban disease and its impact on health policy in Japan.

13 It is worth mentioning that Japan adapted not only the latest style in architecture but also rather 'old-fashioned' styles. For example, as late as 1910 the Akasaka Palace was built in a style reminiscent of Versailles. At that time, nobody in Europe would have built a municipal building in a style of the sixteenth or

seventeenth century. See Stewart (1987: 13–62), Fujimori (1993) and Coaldrake (1996: 208–50) for a general outline of Western style architecture in Meiji Japan.

14 There is no precise definition of this movement, as it included a diversity of loosely organised groups claiming the promotion of citizenship rights. In Japanese historical scholarship, popular movements in the period between 1874 and the 1880s are usually lumped together as *Jiyū minken undō*.

15 Koseki (1996) notes that some treatises on society and the individual written after 1900 focused on the improvement of the living conditions and the life-style of the urban individual (pp. 9–10). An important example for this discussion is Sakai Toshihiko's (1871–1933) collection of essays *Katei no shinfūmi* (A new way of home and family life, 1902). It probably was influenced by the contemporary life reform movement in Europe. Furthermore, after the turn of the century socialism gained importance in the discussion on urban reform. See for example Katayama Sen's *Shisei to shakaishugi* (City government and socialism, 1899) and *Tōkyō shi to shakai shugi* (The city of Tokyo and socialism, 1902). For an outline of Katayama's treatises see Sekino (1993).

16 Tilly (1996) is a compilation of articles on 'Citizenship, Identity and Social History' from a comparative perspective. Ikegami Eiko's contribution on 'Citizenship and National Identity in Early Meiji Japan, 1868–1900' in particular provides important background information (Ikegami 1996). Fogel and Zarrow (1997) is a compilation of articles which approach from different angles the concept and idea of citizenship in China in the years from 1890 to 1920.

17 Kang Youwei evolved utopian ideas about society in *Datongshu* (Book of the great community), posthumously published in 1935; as early as 1902 in *Gongmin zizhi pian* (Citizen self-government) he provides a definition of citizenship (Zarrow 1997: 20). He and Liang Qichao were forced to flee Japan after the collapse of the Hundred Days of Reform in 1898. There they continued their work on the Chinese reform movement. Liang Qichao published his serial essay *Xinminshuo* (Treatise on the new people) between 1902 and 1904 in *Xinminbao* (New citizen journal). The German social thinker Ferdinand Tönnies in 1887 published *Gemeinschaft und Gesellschaft* (Community and society) and Ebenezer Howard brought out his famous *To-morrow: A Peaceful Path to Real Reform* in 1898. Edward Bellamy published *Looking Backward, 2000–1887* in 1888 and it was translated into more than 20 languages. The Japanese translation, published in 1903, also came to the attention of a younger generation of Chinese students who stayed in Japan (Fitzgerald 1996: 59).

18 See Blacker (1964: 34). Carmen Blacker points out that Fukuzawa Yukichi divided the lower stages of barbarism into four 'kinds,' the lowest called *konton*. According to Fukuzawa the aborigines of Australia and New Guinea belong to this group.

19 For example, the fifteenth-century architect Filarete was the first to introduce anthropometrical proportions into the construction of cities and to depict the city as a human body. This image became the reference point of Renaissance architecture (Kruft 1992: 58). Francesco di Giorgio Martini, an early Renaissance theorist of architecture, relates the analogy between city and house, as postulated by Leon Battista Alberti (1404–72), to the proportions of man who himself contains the cosmic order (p. 63). This correlation between earth, man, and cosmos is also characteristic for traditional Chinese thought. In the Middle Ages the European city was supposed to be a faithful copy of the human beings' internal structure and thoughts (Taut 1995: 93). Due to scientific progress in biology and physiology during the eighteenth century, the city

Place Between Future and Past

(Sennett 1994: 255–70), such as Paris, came to be described in biological terms (Lees 1984: 70). This tradition of perceiving the city as an organism continues into the twentieth century.

20 See for example Edward Gibson's *The History of the Decline and Fall of the Roman Empire* (1776–88) and its impact on later historiographic writing.

21 In his famous treatise *Gesellschaft und Gemeinschaft* Ferdinand Tönnies described the city, urban life and society in biological terms and defined the city as a 'social organism' (Tönnies 1995: 126). Johann Kaspar Bluntschli (1808–81), a specialist in public law whose writings were known in Japan, developed the idea in *Allgemeines Staatsrecht* (General constitutional law, 1852) that the order of the state is comparable to that of the human organism. The German architect Gottfried Semper (1803–79) referred to premodern city planning in a critique of classical city planning and used the expression 'state organism' (*Staatsorganismus*) (Schumann 1995: 96).

22 For comparison, see the documents about the discussion of *Shiku kaisei* in Fujimori (1990: 3–205). Here Tokyo is only seen from the point of view which functions the city should fulfil. See also note 14.

23 See note 9.

24 This is reminiscent of Richard Sennett's dictum that the city has a 'culture of difference' (Sennett 1991).

25 This was an intellectual society founded on February 1, 1874 (Meiji 6) for the purpose of 'promoting civilization and enlightenment.' Through its journal, the *Meiroku zasshi* (Meiji 6 Journal) and public lectures, the society played a leading role in introducing and popularizing Western ideas during the early Meiji era. Its 33 members included some of Japan's most eminent educators, bureaucrats, and thinkers.

26 Quoted from Blacker (1964: 31). For the original see Fukuzawa (1959a: 58).

27 For further information on this topic, see Maruyama (1974).

28 The use of this metaphor is not particular to Rohan. Rather, it is a common term in the discourse of individualism in the Meiji period. See for example *Kichōsha no nikki* (Diary of one who returned to Japan, 1909), a diary-like essay criticizing Japan's modernization by Nagai Kafū (1879–1959). Here *jikaku* refers to the 'awakened' individual, regarded as an asset for the creation of a modern Japanese culture (Nagai 1992: 158). For an analysis of Kafū's criticism, see Schulz (1997).

29 The expressions of 'soft city' and 'hard city' were originally used by Raban, (1988: 10).

30 It is interesting to note that the view of history in the romantic movement shares similarities with Rohan's and Kang's concept of history. The present is conceived as chaos and disunity; the future then represents the regaining of harmony and unity similar to that in the past before decline began (Stäblein 1989: 43).

31 This volume, besides *Ikkoku no shuto*, also contains the essay *Mizu no Tōkyō* (The Tokyo of water), written in February 1902 (Kōda 1993: 1189–212).

32 See, for example, Ashihara Yoshinobu's *Kakureta chitsujo*, translated as 'The Hidden Order' (Ashihara, 1989); the special edition on Tokyo of *Casabella* (1994), an Italian magazine on architecture (especially the article 'A dis-oriented modernity' by Vittorio Gregotti); and *Arch+*, No. 123, (1994), a German magazine on architecture, on 'megalopolis Tokyo.'

33 See the following publications by the Tokyo Metropolitan Government: *Long-term plan for the Tokyo Metropolis: 'My town Tōkyō' – Heading into the 21st century*, TMG Municipal Library No. 18 (1984), *The 2nd Long-term plan for the Tokyo Metropolis: 'My town Tōkyō' – A new evolution toward the 21st century*,

TMG Municipal Library No. 22 (1987), *The 3rd long-term plan for the Tokyo Metropolis (outline): 'My town Tōkyō' – For the dawn of the 21st century*, TMG Municipal Library No. 25 (1991).
34 This was the title of an exhibition shown at the Musée d'art contemporain de Bourdeaux, France (1997) and at the Wiener Secession in Vienna, Austria (1997/98). See the catalogue by Hou and Obrist (1997). The title of the exhibition is reminiscent of a book with the same title written by the historian Arnold Toynbee as early as 1970 (Toynbee, 1970).
35 In October 1996 in Tokyo the symposium *'Ajia ga toshi o koeru* [Asia: Overcoming the City] – Asia: Redefining the City' tried to take up these questions. The keynote speaker was the Dutch architect Rem Koolhaas; participants came from Thailand, Singapore, Malaysia, Hongkong, etc. For the Japanese translation of the papers, see *Ajia ga toshi o koeru* (1997). There exists an English edition, too.
36 See Vale (1992) and Abel (1997) Both give examples of architecture and city planning in non-Western countries such as Sri Lanka, Kuwait, Bangladesh, etc. as a tool for designing power and identity.
37 This term was coined by Anderson (1983).

References

Abel C. (1997) *Architecture and Identity: Towards a Global Eco-culture*. Oxford: Architectural Press.
Ajia ga toshi o koeru (1997). Tokyo: TN Probe (TN Probe vol. 5).
Anderson B. (1983) *Imagined Communities: Reflections on the Origins and Spread of Nationalism*. London: Verso.
Arch+, September 1994, vol. 123 (special topic: 'Megalopolis Tokyo').
Ashihara Y. (1989) *The Hidden Order: Tōkyō through the Twentieth Century*. Tokyo: Kōdansha International.
Berndt H. (1987) 'Hygienebewegung des 19. Jahrhunderts als vergessenes Thema von Stadt- und Architektursoziologie' (The hygiene movement of the 19th century as a forgotten topic of urban sociology and the sociology of architecture). *Die alte Stadt: Zeitschrift für Stadtgeschichte, Stadtsoziologie und Denkmalpflege* (The old city: Journal for urban history, urban sociology and preservation of monuments), 14: 140–63.
Blacker C. (1964) *The Japanese Enlightenment: A Study of the Writings of Fukuzawa Yukichi*. Cambridge: Cambridge University Press.
Casabella, January/February 1994.
Coaldrake W. H. (1996) *Architecture and Authority in Japan*. London: Routledge (The Nissan Institute/Routledge Japanese Studies Series).
Featherstone M., Lash S. and Robertson R. (eds) (1995) *Global Modernities*. London: SAGE Publications.
Fitzgerald J. (1997) *Awakening China: Politics, Culture and Class in the Nationalist Revolution*. Stanford: Stanford University Press.
Fogel J. A. and Zarrow P.G. (eds) (1997). *Imagining the People: Chinese Intellectuals and the Concept of Citizenship, 1890–1920*. New York: M.E. Sharpe.
Foucault M. (1984) 'Space, knowlege, and power.' In Rabinow P. (ed.) *The Foucault Reader*. Harmondsworth: Penguin Books.
Fujimori T. (1990) *Toshi kenchiku* (City – architecture). Tokyo: Iwanami shoten (Nihon kindai shisō taikei; 19).
Fujitani T. (1996) *Splendid Monarchy. Power and Pageantry in Modern Japan*. Berkeley: Univesity of California Press.

Fukuzawa Y. (1959a) *Gakumon no susume* (An encouragement of learning). *Fukuzawa Yukichi zenshū*, vol. 3. Tokyo: Iwanami shoten.

—— (1959b). *Shufu kaizō to kōkyo go-zōei to* (Reorganizing the capital city and constructing the imperial palace). *Fukuzawa Yukichi zenshū*, vol. 9. Tokyo: Iwanami shoten.

—— (1959c). *Tōkyō ni chikukan subeshi* (There must be a harbour in Tokyo). *Fukuzawa Yukichi zenshū*, vol. 9. Tokyo: Iwanami shoten.

Girardot N. J. (1983) *Myth and Meaning in Early Taoism: The Theme of Chaos (hun-tun)*. Berkeley: University of California Press.

Gluck C. (1985). *Japan's Modern Myth: Ideology in the Late Meiji Period*. Princeton: Princeton University Press.

Haga N. (1992) *Dai Tōkyō no shisō* (The idea of Greater Tōkyō). Tokyo: Yūzankaku.

Havens T. R. H. (1970) *Nishi Amane and Modern Japanese Thought*. Princeton: Princeton University Press.

Hou H. and Obrist H. U. (1997) *Cities on the Move*. Ostfildern-Ruit: Hatje.

Huang Ph. (1972) 'Liang Ch'i-ch'ao: The idea of the new citizen and the influence of Meiji Japan.' In Buxbaum D. C. and Mote F. W. (eds) *Transition and Permanence: Chinese History and Culture. A Festschrift in Honor of Dr. Hsiao Kung-ch'üan*. Hong Kong: Cathay Press.

Ikegami E. (1996) 'Citizenship and national identity in early Meiji Japan, 1868–1889: A comparative assessment.' In Tilly C. (ed.) *Citizenship, Identity and Social History*. Cambridge: Cambridge University Press.

Ikuta K. (1957) 'Tokai' (The city). *Meiji shōsetsushū*. Tokyo: Chikuma shobō (Gendai Nihon bungaku taikei; 84).

Iyama H. (1996) '*Nōbyō no shinwa: 'Nōka' shakai no raireki*' (The myth of the illness of the brain: The history of the 'brain' society). *Nihon bungaku*, 45 (11): 10–18.

Johnston W. (1995) *The Modern Epidemic: A History of Tuberculosis in Japan*. Cambridge, Mass.: Harvard University Press.

Kinmonth E. H. (1981) *The Self-made Man in Meiji Japanese Thought: from Samurai to Salary Man*. Berkeley: University of California Press.

Kōda R. (1993) *Ikkoku no shuto* (One nation's capital). Tokyo: Iwanami shoten.

—— (1979). *Ikkoku no shuto* (One nation's capital). *Rohan zenshū*, vol. 27. Tokyo: Iwanami shoten.

Kornicki P. (1981) 'The survival of Tokugawa fiction in the Meiji period.' *Harvard Journal of Asiatic Studies*, 41 (2): 461–82.

Koseki K. (1986) '*Kōda Rohan Ikkoku no shuto kō*' (Reflections on Kōda Rohan's *One nation's capital*). *Nihon shigaku shūroku*, 3 (9): 7–12.

Kruft H.-W. (1991) *Geschichte der Architekturtheorie: Von der Antike bis zur Gegenwart* (History of the theory of architecture: From antiquity to the present). München: Beck.

Kunikida D. (1984) *Kyūshi* (Death in anguish). Tokyo: Chikuma shobō (Chikuma shobō gendai bungaku taikei; 6).

Lane R. (1968) 'Saikaku and the modern Japanese novel.' In Skrzypczak E. (ed.) *Japan's Modern Century: A Special Issue of Monumenta Nipponica*. Tokyo: Sophia University.

Lees A. (1984) 'The metropolis and the intellectual.' In Sutcliffe A. (ed.) *Metropolis 1890–1940*. London: Mansell.

Loftus R. (1985) 'The inversion of progress: Taoka Reiun's *Hibunmeiron*.' *Monumenta Nipponica* 40: 191–208.

Maeda A. (1983) *Kindai Nihon no bungaku kūkan: Rekishi kotoba jōkyō* (The literary space of modern Japan: History language condition) Tokyo: Shin'yōsha.

Maruyama M. (1974) *Studies in the Intellectual History of Tokugawa Japan.* Tokyo and Princeton: Tokyo University Press/Princeton University Press.

Mayer H. M. (1971) 'Definitions of "city".' In Bourne L. S. (ed.) *The Internal Structure of the City.* Oxford: Oxford University Press.

Mikuriya T. (1996) *Tōkyō: Shuto wa kokka o koeru ka* (Tōkyō: Is the capital overcoming the state?). Tokyo: Yomiuri shinbunsha.

Mori Ō. (1974) *Shiku kaisei wa hatashite eiseijō no mondai hi zaru ka* (Is the Reorganization of the City Boroughs finally not a problem of hygiene?). *Ōgai zenshū,* vol. 28, Tokyo: Iwanami shoten.

Mouer R. and Sugimoto Y. (1995) '*Nihonjinron* at the end of the twentieth century: A multicultural perspective.' In Arnason J. P. and Sugimoto Y. (eds) *Japanese Encounters with Postmodernity.* London: Kegan Paul International.

Nagai K. (1992) *Kichōsha no nikki* (Diary of one who returned to Japan). *Kafū zenshū,* vol. 6. Tokyo: Iwanami shoten.

Natsume S. (1977). *Sanshirō: A novel.* Trans. Jay Rubin. Seattle: University of Washington Press.

Ōoka M. (1983) 'Kōda Rohan no Tōkyōron' (Kōda Rohan's treatise on Tokyo). In Ōoka M. (ed.) *Hyōgen ni okeru kindai: Bungaku geijutsu ronshū.* Tokyo: Iwanami shoten.

Paris s'exporte: modèle d'architecture ou architectures modèles (1995). Paris: Ed. du Pavillon de l'Arsenal.

Raban J. (1988) *Soft City.* London: Collins Harvill.

Robertson J. (1997) 'Empire of nostalgia: Rethinking "internationalization" in Japan today.' *Theory, Culture & Society,* 14 (4): 97–122.

Sassen S. (1991) *The Global City: New York, London, Tokyo.* Princeton, New Jersey: Princeton University Press.

Schulz E. (1997) '*Tagebuch eines Heimgekehrten*' (1909) *von Nagai Kafu: Der Entwurf ästhetischer Gegenwelten als Kritik an der Modernisierung Japans* ('Diary of one who returned to Japan (*Kichōsha no nikki*)' (1909) by Nagai Kafū: The conception of aesthetic counterworlds as a means of criticising Japan's modernization). Münster: Lit (Ostasien – Pazifik. Trierer Studien zu Politik, Wirtschaft, Gesellschaft, Kultur).

Schumann U. M. (1995) '*Die Freiheit zu bauen. Bürgerarchitektur des 19. und 20. Jahrhunderts*' (The freedom to build: Bourgeois architecture of the 19th and 20th century). In Salden H. (ed.) *Die Städelschule Frankfurt am Main von 1817 bis 1995.* Ausstellungskatalog Städelsches Kunstinstitut Frankfurt/M.

Sekino M. (1993) '*Katayama Sen no toshi shakaishugi*' (Katayama Sen's urban socialism). In Yoshihara N. (ed.) *Toshi no shisō: Kūkanron no sai-kōsei ni mukete.* Tokyo: Aoki shoten.

Sennett R. (1991) *Civitas: Die Großstadt und die Kultur des Unterschieds* (Civitas: The metropolis and the culture of difference). Frankfurt/M.: Fischer.

—— (1994) *Flesh and Stone: The Body and the City in Western Civilization.* New York: Norton.

Simmel G. (1957) '*Die Großstädte und das Geistesleben*' (The metropolis and mental life). In Landmann M. and Susman M. (eds) *Brücke und Tür: Essays des Philosophen zur Geschichte, Religion, Kunst und Gesellschaft* (Bridge and door: Essays of the philosopher on history, religion, art and society). Stuttgart: Köhler.

Smith H. D. (1978) 'Tokyo as an idea: An exploration of Japanese urban thought until 1945.' *Journal of Japanese Studies,* 4 (2): 45–80.

Stäblein R. (1989) '*Zwischen Auflösung und Erlösung des Ich: Zur Wiederkehr einer romantisch-modernen Bewußtseinskrise bei Clemens Brentano und Hugo von Hofmannsthal. Mit einem methodischen Vorspann nach Walter Benjamin*'

(Between dissolution and salvation of the I: On the return of the romantic-modern crisis of consciousness on Clemens Brentano and Hugo von Hofmannsthal). In Klinger C. and Stäblein R. (eds) *Identitätskrise und Surrogatidentitäten: Zur Wiederkehr einer romantischen Konstellation* (Crisis of identity and surrogate identities: On the return of a romantic constellation). Frankfurt/M.: Campus.

Stewart D. B. (1987) *The Making of a Modern Japanese Architecture: 1868 to the Present*. Tokyo: Kōdansha International.

Takahashi H. (1993) '*Mori Ōgai to toshi eisei shisō*' (Mori Ōgai and thoughts of urban hygiene). In Yoshihara N. (ed.) *Toshi no shisō: Kūkanron no sai-kōsei ni mukete*. Tokyo: Aoki shoten.

Taut B. (1995) 'Die Stadtkrone' (The city crown). In Lampugnani V. M. *Texte zur Geschichte des Städtebaus* (Texts on the history of city planning). Band IV: 20. *Jahrhundert. Tradition und Avantgarde* (The century of tradition and avant-garde). Zürich: Eidgenössische Technische Hochschule.

Tilly C. (ed.) (1996) *Citizenship, Identity and Social History*. Cambridge: Cambridge University Press.

Tokutomi R. (1970) *Footprints in the Snow*. Kenneth Strong. Rutland, Vermont: Tuttle.

Tönnies F. (1995) '*Gemeinschaft und Gesellschaft*' (Community and society). In Lampugnani V. M. *Texte zur Geschichte des Städtebaus* (Texts on the history of city planning). Band IV: 20. *Jahrhundert. Tradition und Avantgarde* (The century of tradition and avant-garde). Zürich: Eidgenössische Technische Hochschule.

Toynbee A. (1970) *Cities on the Move*. London: Oxford University Press.

Vale L. J. (1992) *Architecture, Power, and National Identity*. New Haven: Yale University Press.

Weber M. (1976) *Wirtschaft und Gesellschaft. Grundriß der verstehenden Soziologie* (Economy and society: An outline of interpretive sociology). Tübingen: J.C.B. Mohr (Paul Siebeck).

Yazaki T. (1968) *Social Change and the City in Japan: From Earliest Times through the Industrial Revolution*. Tokyo: Japan Publications.

Yoshihara N. (ed.) (1993) *Toshi no shisō: Kūkanron no sai-kōsei ni mukete* (Ideas of the city: Toward the restructuring of the discourse on space). Tokyo: Aoki shoten.

Zarrow P. G. (1997) 'Introduction: Citizenship in China and the West.' In Fogel J. A. and Zarrow P. G. (eds) *Imagining the People: Chinese Intellectuals and the Concept of Citizenship, 1890–1920*. New York: M.E. Sharpe.

Zibell B. (1995) *Chaos als Ordnungsprinzip im Städtebau. Ansätze zu einem neuen Planungsverständnis* (Chaos as a principle of order in city planning: Approaches to a new understanding of planning). Zürich: vdf Hochschulverlag (ORL-Bericht 99/1995).

CHAPTER 11

Visionary Plans and Planners

Japanese Traditions and Western Influences

Carola Hein

Since Meiji times, Western comprehensive planning ideas have been introduced to Japan and have stimulated some large scale visions. Planning the capital city, Tokyo, for example, gave Japanese architects and planners chances to discuss new urban concepts and develop planning ideas. Further occasions were provided by the Japanese occupation of Manchuria and other neighboring countries, particularly in the 1930s, but also by the reconstruction period after World War II. Similar chances for visionary planning generated numerous ideas and discussions in the West, the number of planning visions in Japan is however small and their influence on urban reality is limited. What is more, these visions do not seem to have functioned as long term guidelines and have not induced particular historic and scientific interest.

What are the reasons for this relative absence of architectural and planning visions in Japan? What is the history, status, and theoretical debate on planning visions in Japan? Which major examples exist and how do they reflect Japanese traditions and Western influences? These are the guiding questions of the present chapter. Following some general reflection on the term 'vision' and an overview of planning visions in Japanese urban history, three examples of visionary planning in Japan will be analysed, including two which are largely unknown in the West. The examples chosen concentrate on the reconstruction period after World War II, a period in which architects and planners in other war-damaged countries produced numerous visions and worked towards the implementation of new ideas.[1]

Visionary planning often concentrates on the capital as the national showcase. In this context, the competitions and plans for the rebuilding of Tokyo, inspired by one of the central figures in Japanese planning, Ishikawa Hideaki (1893–1955), are given as an example. Visionary plans for regional cities are more rare; they nevertheless exist. As the first city destroyed by atomic bombing, Hiroshima is a particular case, for which the reconstruction proposals by the internationally known architect Tange Kenzō (b. 1913) are discussed. Finally, the attempts to generate an overall debate on visions will be analyzed in the more theoretical reflections by Nishiyama Uzō (1911–94), professor at Kyoto University and in many respects the 'godfather' of Japanese planning and housing (Hein 1998a).

Planning Visions

A comparative analysis of Western and Japanese planning and their relationship requires a definition of the term 'vision,' which can be seen as an essential part of Western planning. In fact, urban planning particularly in Europe has often aimed at long term, large scale comprehensive ideal plans. Religious and secular leaders as well as citizens have generally tried to express their power and status in the design of buildings and urban space. The built environment thus reflects a city's history and gives identity to its citizens. This particular relationship between the people and the urban environment is projected into the future through visions in writing or as ideal projects. In Europe, large scale comprehensive visions are often seen as a necessary basis for discussion and a guideline for urban development, not only in regard to esthetics but also in a socio-economic and political sense. They give a background to planning discussions and may sometimes be realized only in part or even centuries later.

In Japan, however, urban planning is less a means for the creation of identity and the long-term orientation of society than a pragmatic instrument for the organization of the city-space. The word 'vision' in its positive Western usage does not have an exact translation in Japanese. '*Maboroshi*,' or any word combination including the Chinese character read as *gen* or *maboroshi* in Japanese, indicates something not really existing and is thus closer in meaning to 'phantom' than it is to vision. The Western meaning inherent in the word 'vision' might be best expressed in Japanese by '*nozomashii miraizō*,' that is, a 'desirable image of the future,' although this formula still does not include the desire for realization usually connected to the idea of vision as a long term goal. Instead of this long and complicated but still insufficient explication, Japanese tend to use the transcription of the English word with Japanese syllables, resulting in the *katakana* word '*bijon*,' which is not only shorter but also has a much appreciated international sound to it.

Like the word 'vision', comprehensive and large-scale urban projects that might be called 'visionary plans,' when prepared by Japanese planners, were traditionally a reflection of Western concepts and were often used to show that Japan had attained the same level of cultural, political and economic development as the leading Western countries. These plans, however, only exceptionally led to realization. Comprehensive planning visions that responded to Japanese reality of the urban scene in Japan were rare and only served as guides to city development in exceptional cases.

One possible explanation for the different approaches to city design in Europe and Japan may be that, due to the existence of a strong social hierarchy in Japan, urban representation is less important. The social structure remains in place even when the individuals change, whereas urban signs related to a particular figure have to be replaced. The reconstruction of cities due to earthquakes might be mentioned as another reason, but Western cities were also destroyed numerous times following natural disasters or wars. They, however, were mostly replanned and sometimes reconstructed with a long term vision and on a coherent overall plan. The contrast of approaches becomes even clearer from the comparative experience of Europe and Japan during World War II and during the occupation and reconstruction periods. In areas where the existing general constraints could be ignored or where a destroyed city seemed to invite a new design, planners in the West often produced large-scale projects and partial applications while Japan developed few comprehensive and visionary projects and only piecemeal answers.

Designed urban space, which is typical for many European cities, with boulevards, squares, and monumental architecture, came to Japan only in the Meiji era (1868–1912) alongside the profession of architect. This late introduction may be another reason for the lack of representative urban space. In Japan, architects lack the support that a long historic tradition can give, and they do not enjoy the support of society's leading groups as they do in the West. Urban planning, understood primarily as providing infrastructure and not as a three dimensional art of city design, is dominated by engineers and technical personnel. This may be seen as a result of the Japanese aim to emulate the advanced Western countries, a goal proclaimed since the opening of the country to the West.

The dominance of technical planning and the lack of a Western-style urban vision, which continue to characterize Japanese planning today, was noticeable as early as 1924 when the urban planner Fritz Schumacher (1869–1947) from Hamburg wrote an article on plans to rebuild Tokyo after the Kantō Earthquake in 1923. He criticized the lack of a comprehensive plan for a rail network, which would have been the basis for an overall traffic system. He also remarked on the absence of a systematic plan for parks and other green areas as well as of a coherent concept for future growth and the connection of Tokyo and Yokohama. Schumacher regretted the absence of spatial design particularly in such important spaces as the approach to Tokyo station and pointed to the absence of architectural and urban places to give specific character to parts of the cityscape. This reference to the overall form of the city touches another difference between Western and Japanese urban planning. While

Western cities confer identity to their inhabitants through the city's form and silhouette, Japanese concentrate on natural elements, shrines, or temples in their neighborhood to identify themselves with. As to the need for planning vision, which was self-evident for Schumacher (1924), he insisted that although financial and administrative problems accompany large scale and design projects, an idea has to be born in spirit so that it can become reality one day.

Short History of Urban Planning Visions and Reality in Japan

'Grand Design' without Vision

Foreign realizations in neighboring colonial states, projects completed by foreigners in Japan, the experiences of Japanese planners in the West, and the observations of the Iwakura mission that toured Europe and north America in 1871 to 1873 are just some channels through which Western planning ideas were introduced to Japan. The Japanese were particularly fascinated by the transformation of the French capital from a medieval city with small and dirty streets into a metropolis with tree-lined boulevards. However, while they looked at the 'grand design' – the street network, the parks with trees, fountains, and sculptures, and the connection between architecture and urban planning – they tended neither to see it in terms of French history nor to reflect on the appropriateness of these forms for Japan (Ishida 1992a). However, experience rapidly taught them that these approaches did not correspond to the Japanese tradition and culture.

The initial disapproval that greeted the new Ginza boulevard and brick houses was a first lesson (Ishida 1988a, 1988b; Fujimori 1990). A more immediate failure was the attempt to monumentalize Tokyo through the creation of a government district in Hibiya, designed by the German architects Wilhelm Böckmann (1832–1902) and Hermann Ende (1829–1907). This project was dropped in favor of the First Plan for the Urban Improvement of Tokyo (1889) therewith ending the first phase of 'grand design' in Japan (Ishida 1992a, 1992b; Hein and Ishida 1998). The First Plan for the Urban Improvement of Tokyo addressed the overall transformation of the city, like Haussmann had done in Paris. A building law, which might have initiated a process of regulation of the three dimensional appearance of the city, was postponed, however, and the first step towards the separation of urban planning and building regulations which became emblematic of Japanese urbanism was taken.

Steps towards a Japanese Planning Idiom

While the first projects by Western planners introduced the notion of 'grand design' to Japan, Japanese planners were trying to establish a planning idiom that was capable of implementing such a concept. On several occasions, urban techniques which had been designed for the West were imported. However, they did not necessarily fit Japanese reality and necessities.

A good illustration of a failed introduction of planning techniques which would have combined the laying out of new streets with the control of building design is 'zone expropriation', particularly in a form which concerns the expropriation of areas alongside newly built streets, known as 'chōka shūyō' in Japanese. Such a procedure had been used during the transformation of Paris under Haussmann. The Japanese version was adopted as an urban planning tool for the Tokyo Urban Improvement Ordinance (*Shiku kaisei jōrei*) of 1888, which was the basis for the above-mentioned First Plan for Urban Improvement of Tokyo of the following year. However, although the upper chamber, the *genrōin*, included these methods in the law, they were never applied during the thirty years of implementation of the plan.[2]

An example of a far reaching combination of Japanese traditions and Western concepts, on the other hand, is land readjustment, a technique of creating infrastructures and replotting land which includes the reduction of individual building sites and which has become the central instrument of Japan urban planning (Hein and Ishida 1998).

Planning Technique Replaces 'Vision'

Japan's first planning law was enacted in 1919, although it was promulgated slowly and partially through the major cities. The first test case for the new planning law and a chance for large scale rebuilding came in 1923, when the Great Kantō Earthquake of 1923 destroyed large parts of Tokyo and Yokohama. Gotō Shinpei (1857–1929), an important actor in Japanese urban planning who was mayor of Tokyo at the time, returned to his former post as minister for home affairs. For his first reconstruction plan he took up the ideas expressed in the New Tokyo Plan, elaborated by Fukuda Shigeyoshi (1887–1971) in 1918, ideas that can be considered to represent the first Japanese planning vision, encompassing as they did a whole city and its surrounding region. In fact, Fukuda proposed a comprehensive plan for the extension of Tokyo towards the west, which was to be realized over a period of fifty years. City growth was to be primarily orchestrated through infrastructure construction, although a basic land-use plan existed. The size of the city was to be limited to ten kilometers, equivalent to a one hour commuting time. Fukuda's major suggestion, however, was the creation of several satellite cities on a ring road surrounding the city along the route of the present Ring Road 7. Decentralization had been promoted in many countries since the diffusion of Ebenezer Howard's (1850–1928) garden city concept, and this had led to the creation of satellite towns as mainly self-contained entities separated by green belts from major cities. Fukuda's proposal aimed at the decentralization of commercial functions to the rim of the city, thus opening it up for further extension. This project may be seen, in fact, as a predecessor of the decentralization of central city functions on the Yamanote loop, which has come into existence during the last decades, concentrating, however, on tertiary functions. It is interesting to note that it was Fukuda who had informed Schumacher about the official projects for the rebuilding of Tokyo after the Kantō Earthquake.

Gotō's comprehensive reconstruction plan even included areas that were not touched by the earthquake. However, such ideas were swept away by the necessity for rapid rebuilding. In order quickly to set up a basic infrastructure despite limited financial means, the government resorted to land readjustment and enacted the Ad Hoc Town Planning Law (*Toshi keikaku hō*) of 1923, which provided supplementary measures in order to apply the land readjustment system to built-up areas, and created a planning agency. Of three thousand hectares designated for land readjustment about two-thirds were affected between 1923 and 1930, constituting the first large scale planning intervention and one that became a precedent often discussed later. The only general concepts that guided city planning at that point concerned the amelioration of infrastructure for greater economic efficiency and a greater resistance to disasters, especially fires.

From the 1920s on, the techniques of urban engineering became ever more appropriate for Japanese cities. However, steps towards an overall concept for the Japanese city were not taken. The failure of 'grand design' and the absence of vision on the one hand and the establishment and the pragmatic application of planning techniques on the other became an obstacle to exchange with Western planners. Foreigners no longer got a chance to practice in Japan, and Western criticisms, when not invited, were generally rejected. Nevertheless, some Japanese planners continued to observe Western discussions, concentrating particularly on large scale regional and national planning and to turn for advice to Western masters. Fukuda, for example, discussed the rebuilding plan for Tokyo after the Kantō earthquake in 1923 with Schumacher; and Ishikawa Hideaki, at that time an engineer in the Ministry of Home Affairs assigned to the town planning of Nagoya, consulted Raymond Unwin (1863–1940) during his trip to Europe in 1923 to seek advice on a master plan for Nagoya (Shōji 1993: 25–30).

From the 1920s to the 1940s, Nagoya was the center and the motor of urban planning, with a focus on land readjustment. Two master plans were prepared, which concentrated mainly on infrastructure, assuming an increase in population to 1.3 million. They proposed a new separation of functions, establishing trade and office activity in the center, proposing the harbor area for industrial use, and concentrating housing in peripheral areas. This new urban structure was to have been bound together by a system of streets and canals connecting several new parks. It was a comprehensive concept, which reflected international planning discussions about infrastructure networks and parks as well as zoning. It was realized in large part, and did not remain a two dimensional plan.

The first plan was set up by the Commission for Urban Planning in Aichi Prefecture, an organization for prefectural planning under the Ministry of Home Affairs. The members of this commission included such important figures of urban planning as the above-mentioned Ishikawa and Kaneiwa Den'ichi (1899–1970), a civil engineer and planner who also became prominent in the communist party. Until he left for Tokyo in 1933, Ishikawa made important contributions to the urban planning of Nagoya through his theoretical and practical works. Thanks to his influence, Nagoya has become one of the few Japanese cities with a strong sense of urban planning, shared by the administration as well as the general public. Urban planners educated under Ishikawa's leadership worked in later years all over the country and spread the spirit of Nagoya urban planning, a phenomenon which requires analysis in another study.

In fact, Ishikawa was also strongly engaged in the field of theory. He was at the center of the Group for Town Creation, established in 1926 within the Commission for Urban Planning. This group published the magazine *Toshi sōsaku* (Town creation), which had a wide distribution and strong influence. In a centralized country like Japan it is unusual for a local magazine to become a trendsetter and for initiatives to be taken by a city other than the capital. Although the main figures of this magazine were also engineers of the Ministry of Home Affairs, the journal can be considered an open publication, with a range of topics and a variety of opinions. In that, it contrasted with the official publication on urban planning, *Toshi kōron* (Public opinion on cities) which was published by the *Toshi kenkyū kai* (Study group for cities), a body affiliated to the Ministry of Home Affairs, from 1914 to 1945. The main aim of *Toshi kōron* was to spread information on urban planning from the national level to the cities and regions.

The Nagoya magazine, lacking the support of a central institution, ceased publication in 1930. However, five years later, a new magazine entitled *Kukaku seiri* (Land readjustment) came to life under the leadership of Kaneiwa. While *Toshi sōsaku* contained land readjustment proposals as well as articles on urban form and European examples, *Kukaku seiri* concentrated, as its name suggests, on land readjustment. This magazine coined the oft-quoted phrase: '*Kukaku seiri wa toshi keikaku no haha, tochi kaihatsu no kagi*' (Land readjustment is the mother of urban planning and the key to land development), which reflects Japanese planning with particular acuity. What could have been a regional initiative and a basis for discussion on urban planning concepts thus ended up as a powerful promoter of land readjustment. The tool of land readjustment was becoming well defined, but a general political, social, and cultural concept of the city and city life that could inform such a tool was absent.

As to other comprehensive proposals prepared during this period, the Tokyo Green Space Plan (*Tōkyō ryokuchi keikaku*) has to be mentioned. In fact, the creation of a system of parks and green areas in the densely built-up Japanese cities had been discussed since the beginning of the century. Initially established in the prewar era to ameliorate the quality of urban life, this concept was taken up for military purposes at the end of the 1930s. Following the laws of air defense of 1937 (revised in 1941), only projects of military importance could be realized. Important to the war effort was railway construction as well as the decentralization of industry and relocation of workers. City planning was reduced to the creation of new military settlements outside the cities. Low building density together with the green belts was supposed to create free corridors. Land readjustment was used to create spaces for building munitions plants. In this sense, the Tokyo Green Space Plan, which had been discussed since 1932, was not implemented until 1939. It proposed the creation of a green zone at about fifteen to twenty kilometers around Tokyo, reflecting greenbelt planning of the previous generation and simultaneous European discussions on regional planning.

Freedom of Planning in the Colonies

Planning in Japan had to take into account the existing urban structure and had to focus mainly on corrections or extensions to the urban structure. In the 1930s, it became even more restricted than before, as it was tuned to the needs of defense. Simultaneously, however, the colonies afforded Japanese architects the chance to plan on a supposedly empty terrain, and this relative freedom gave a boost to large scale plans (Hein 1998b: 352–57). In fact, in contrast to the attitude towards the first colonies, Taiwan and Korea, where the Japanese concentrated on administration including planning techniques such as land readjustment, the occupation of Manchuria and parts of China in the 1930s was seen as a chance for architects and planners to discuss urban concepts, develop planning ideas, and sometimes even apply them. The proposals prepared for the colonies give a good account of the state of visionary planning in Japan.

Work in the colonies was seen by the architects as a way to escape the political and professional constraints of the Japanese mainland. There they could experiment in regard to urban design as well as building and planning law. Simultaneously with the construction of the Siberian railway and its extension to Dairen, several cities under the control of the Japanese colonial forces were built or extended. The city of Changchun, like others in this region, had been created by the imperial Russian government as a linear railway town consisting of rectangular blocks cut with diagonals spreading out from a semicircular plaza in front of the station and crossing other diagonals at traffic intersections. This first plan, on which work was begun in 1912, became the basis of urban and regional plans for Shinkyō, the name given to Changchun during the Japanese occupation, a name which means 'new capital' and translates the function of the city as capital of Manchuria in the 1930s. The different projects for Shinkyō reflect the main topics of the Western planning discussion (Koshizawa 1990: 1991). Japanese planners proposed green belts, also included huge round plazas and axes derived from the monumental proposals of French colonial planners, and designed housing districts influenced by Le Corbusier.

Most of these plans, however, appear like academic exercises, the planning of Datong (Daidō in Japanese) in Manchuria, being a typical example. In 1938, Utida Yosikazu (1885–1972), professor at Tokyo University, who was engaged in the planning of several towns in the Japanese colonies, was invited to prepare a plan for this city (Kawai 1976). His son Utida Yosifumi accompanied him, along with Sekino Masaru (b. 1909) and Takayama Eika (1910–99). After earning his diploma, Takayama spent a half year collecting, copying, and organizing examples of planning from foreign magazines. When he went to Datong, he was thus familiar with the latest foreign concepts. The final drawing however was established under the leadership of Utida Yosifumi (1913–46) after their return to Japan in 1938.

The proposal for Datong is remarkable in several regards (fig. 52). Despite its academic character, the project includes regional planning, zoning, separation of types of traffic, the design of neighborhood units, and even the conservation of the old city. Takayama prepared a financial plan, which was aimed at preventing speculation. He proposed the complete purchase of the area to be planned and its sale at a later time in order to finance further development – a proceeding which was largely applied in the colonies but strongly resisted on the mainland. The most interesting element is the intricate design of the neighborhood unit, which is, however, not a Japanese product. In fact, it is a nearly identical copy of an American garden-city neighborhood realized in Detroit in 1931 (Takayama 1936).

In contrast to European projects in occupied territories, which were generally aimed at manifesting the occupants' culture, the Japanese proposals mixed Western concepts and local traditions. Utida Yosikazu insisted, for example, on the planning of local style courthouses and even Tange Kenzō in his competition entry for a cultural center in Bangkok adapted his design to Thai forms. While the export of land readjustment to Korea and Taiwan may be considered a transfer of Japanese planning, these proposals, although a product of the Japanese occupation, are a reflection of Western cities and colonial attitudes not of a particular vision of a Japanese or Asian city, whose appearance and historical basis are distinct.

Place Between Future and Past

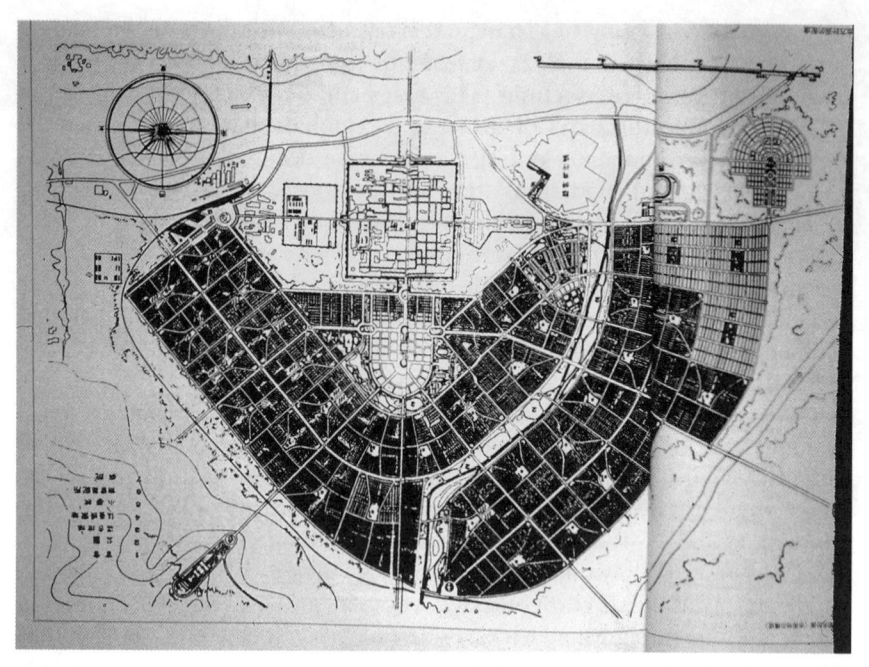

Figure 52 Utida Yosikazu, Utida Yosifumi, Takayama Eika, *et al.*, 'Urban Plan for Datong,' 1939. From: Utida Yosikazu Sensei biju shikaku kinen sakuhin shū kankōkai (The Editors Group for 'Selected Works of Professor Utida Yosikazu in Architecture and Planning) (1969) *Utida Yosikazu Sensei sakuhinshū*, (Collection of the Works of Professor Utida Yosikazu. Tokyo: Kajima Kenkyūjo Shuppankai, 1969, pp. 170–71.

The Reconstruction Period

Dominance of Pragmatic Rebuilding

Considering the planning projects prepared before 1945 for the mainland and the colonies, it could have been expected that the destruction of Japanese cities during World War II would induce planners to prepare large scale plans for reconstruction or elaborate visions of future city life. Ishikawa Hideaki said as much when he proclaimed that 'Hiroshima has a resource that cannot be easily obtained even in hundreds of years and which must be utilized for the future. It is this vast, open land' (Ishimaru: 63). In contrast to their European counterparts, the great majority of architects and planners, however, did not share this feeling.

The reconstruction in Japan was under the direction of a national central planning office for reconstruction, which had been created on 5 November 1945. Only a few cities, including Tokyo and Toyama, elaborated their proposals before national guidelines were established. In Japan, however, no earlier concepts existed that might have become a basis. A first program for reconstruction had been prepared by members of the National Land Development Department of the Ministry of Home Affairs (Naimushō Kokudokyoku), and on 30 December 1945 the Fundamental Policy for Reconstruction Planning (*Sensaichi fukkō keikaku kihon hōshin*) was promulgated, defining several aims for reconstruction. These included reducing urban density, which had reached extreme levels before the war, the development of small and middle sized cities, and urban designs that were both esthetic and functional.

Cities destroyed by the war were to establish reconstruction plans that aimed among other things at creating streets and parks by means of land readjustment. Even if realizing the whole plan took years, the Japanese considered land readjustment to be urgent, and its importance increased during the postwar period of rebuilding. Officials proposed that 65,000 hectares be rebuilt, compared to the more than the 50,000 hectares in 115 cities that had been officially marked for reconstruction, a figure which included areas that had not been touched by bombing. However, in the end, the War Damage Rehabilitation Plan (*sensai fukkō toshi keikaku*) reached only 102 cities and 28.000 hectares.[3] The Special City Planning Act (Tokubetsu toshi keikaku hō), established in September 1946, allowed land readjustment procedures to be applied in those inner cities areas which had not been destroyed. Reconstruction therefore laid a long term basis for the planning of most Japanese cities although it did not give rise to fundamental discussions about city planning.

Even Osaka and Nagoya, cities with an important history of urban planning, did not develop particular visions for reconstruction after World War II. Some roughly sketched ideas for regional decentralization were produced; the construction of boulevards and the future harbor were discussed for Osaka in newspapers, but they never contained elements which could not be found in the projects for other Japanese cities (Hasegawa 1995). Some small scale projects exist, however, which show the variety of ideas included in discussions about reconstruction. While the project of a four storey shopping street with arcades proposed by Takizawa Mayumi (1896–1983) recalls traditionalist European examples and found large support, there were also projects which followed a modernist tradition like Nishiyama Uzō's project for Tennōji Ward or the fifteen storey skyscraper proposal by Ishihara Masao for Minami Ward, both of them in Osaka (Hasegawa 1995).

As to the reconstruction plan for Nagoya, it was a reduced variant of plans from the 1920s. It did, however, introduce a new feature: the 100 meter wide boulevard with a 66 meter wide, planted median strip, two 10 meter wide roadways on both sides, and tree-lined sidewalks (Nagoya 1991) (fig. 53). In fact, 24 boulevards of 100 meters length each had been planned after the war in Japan. Four were realized, two of them in Nagoya.

Place Between Future and Past

名古屋市戦災復興計画図（1946年決定）
Reconstruction Plan of Nagoya 1946   After the War Damage

Figure 53 'Reconstruction Plan of Nagoya,' 1946. From: Committee on Historical Studies in Civil Engineering, Japan Society of Civil Engineers (1991) *Reconstruction Plan of Nagoya 1946 After the War Damage* (*Nagoya shi sensai fukkō keikaku zu*). Commentary by Koshizawa Akira. Nagoya: Nagoya City Public Works Bureau.

Most of these boulevards were planned in areas where inhabitants had been evicted and buildings demolished to create firebreaks. Large empty areas were therefore available for road-building. Most of the time, only streets under 50 meters wide and small parks were realized as the financial and symbolic support for larger realizations was missing.

The creation of the Nagoya boulevards was the result of several particularities. Officials in charge thought that a large scale operation was necessary for future commercial activities. What is more, the city's cemeteries were thoroughly reorganized and were concentrated in one large specially created park-like public space in the city. The urban land needed for this new cemetery was in the hands of only a few owners, and this facilitated the reorganization. The experiences of the 1920s had prepared both the authorities and the public in Nagoya, insofar as urban planning in general and land readjustment in particular were well accepted in the city. Of the initially projected 4400 hectares, 3450 were finally rebuilt.

The Nagoya proposal is unique in its scale. However, in spite of opposition movements, public discussion – for example through competitions – was missing as well as the integration into a larger political, socio-economic, and cultural urban vision. During the prewar period a comprehensive project had been sketched out in the form of a park system for the whole city, and the new boulevards could have been connected with the canals, the castle park, and other parks into a large pedestrian network, but no one seems to have thought of that. The reconstruction of Nagoya is thus less visionary and forward-looking than the 1920s project on which it is based.

The official account of rebuilding is documented in an administrative publication entitled *Sensai fukkō shi* (History of disaster rebuilding). This impressive publication of ten volumes fails, however, to relate the history of planning ideas and omits discussion of thirteen model cities entrusted to independent architects (Kensetsushō 1959). Young planners, including Tange Kenzō and Takayama Eika from Tokyo University as well as Take Motō (b. 1910) from Waseda University and others, were called to prepare model projects for cities such as Hiroshima, Maebashi, Wakkanai, Nagaoka, and Nagasaki. Several of these planners also took part in the competitions for Shinjuku and Ginza in Tokyo and prepared model plans for educational districts around the major universities. More than the reconstruction of Osaka and Nagoya these proposals have a visionary character and could have contributed to a discussion on the basis of Japanese city form and function. Further research is necessary, however, to give an overall appreciation of these projects.

There were various reasons why architects and young practitioners became involved in the reconstruction effort. It is due, at least partly, to the disorganization of planning procedures immediately after the war. Those traditionally responsible – engineers and technical personnel – could not cope with the work load, even though additional professionals returned from Manchuria. University departments had been closed or were riven with internal fighting about responsibility for wartime events.

Some of the leading figures of Japanese urban planning promoted planning visions in the postwar period and in rare examples could even realize them, as the following three case studies will show. First of all, we will see how Ishikawa Hideaki, the director of urban planning in Tokyo, tried through his own work and through the promotion of competitions to introduce design qualities into the rebuilding and establish the capital city as a model for the rest of the country. Due to his own personality and the importance of Tokyo, competitions were held; realization, however, was extremely limited. The only other city in Japan which received similar attention and which is even better known on an international scale is Hiroshima, mainly as a result of Tange Kenzō's project for the Peace Park and the Peace Boulevard. That his plan was realized can be attributed to the way in which it was oriented towards garnering international support and appreciation; it is a very rare example of a realized visionary intervention into the city. Finally, attempts to promote visionary planning through individual proposals and to define basic criteria for Japanese urban planning based on the traditional urban structure are seen as characteristics of the work of Nishiyama Uzō.

Ishikawa Hideaki's Vision for Tokyo

During his years in Nagoya, Ishikawa contributed to the development of land readjustment as the major urban planning device in Japan. In his work in Tokyo from 1933 to 1951, however, he insisted on the need to combine land readjustment with design aspects and an overall concept of the city. Although he was himself an engineer trained at Tokyo University, he thought that land readjustment alone was not sufficient for the creation of a well-balanced city plan and, thus, tried to enforce the cultural and humanist as well as esthetic aspects of rebuilding. Ishikawa wanted to set examples, whether they could be realized or not. As he did not have any political influence to bring to bear on the general rebuilding process, he tried at least to give urban design a larger place in the rebuilding of the Tokyo metropolitan region.[4] Just before the announcement in March 1946 of the outline plan for the rebuilding of the capital, Ishikawa opened competitions for some major areas in Tokyo, which were followed by consultations on the educational districts.

The Tokyo Rebuilding Plan

The film *Tokyo in 20 Years' Time (20 nen go no Tokyo)*, which explains the basic concepts of the overall plan for the rebuilding of Tokyo in 1946, shows that Ishikawa's initiatives for Tokyo were based on an overall vision for the capital. This plan recommended that Tokyo be developed as an industrial city. Political and economic functions were to be decentralized to cities inside a 40 kilometer radius area from the city center, while culture was to be concentrated in cities at a radius of one hundred kilometers. These functions were to promote the development of existing cities into centers of 100,000 to 200,000 inhabitants. With this system, Ishikawa aimed at creating specialized cities which then would work together in a network. As to Tokyo, he suggested a reduction of the number of inhabitants from 6.5 million before the war to 3.5 million as a maximum (fig. 54)!

The city was to be reconstructed following a strict zoning concept, with industrial functions close to the harbor and the Sumida river, clearly separated from housing and other functions. Major amusement and commercial functions were to be placed in Ginza as the international center, in Shinjuku as the amusement area for white-collar workers, and in Asakusa as the old downtown. Other major centers were to spring up along the Yamanote loop line, at Ikebukuro, Shibuya, Gotanda, and Ōmori. Many of these centers in the decentralized form suggested by Ishikawa – and before him by Fukuda on a ring further out – have come into being. The big commercial centers named by Ishikawa would provide mainly specialized goods, whereas some shopping areas for daily use were to be placed close to the stations in the middle of neighborhood units. Housing was to be created between the other functions, using building forms which would allow sun and air to enter.

The whole city form was still largely based on the Tokugawa period street pattern. The rebuilding plan proposed to bind it together included an overall network, including eight ring roads and numerous radial roads leading towards satellite towns. In the center of the city Ishikawa suggested several 100 meter wide streets and a loop line with extensions crossing Shinjuku and Ueno responding to functions as diverse as esthetics, traffic capacity and disaster prevention. Thus, a monumental avenue was provided through west Shinjuku, which is nowadays one of the city's most important business districts. These major thoroughfares then continued as 80 meter wide streets as a part of the city's overall network. In fact, the strangest feature of this plan was the 100 meter wide street in the east of Tokyo, running north-south through Kōtō Ward. Although it connected two radial avenues, its northern end had no connection with the network. Its main purpose, in fact, was to act as a firebreak.

Ishikawa not only thought about the necessities of the car but wanted at the same time to promote the pleasures of life in the city; thus he proposed 10 meter wide pedestrian walkways and an extended green network designed to provide further firebreaks. A network of parks was to be created with 34 public squares of 30,636 hectares providing the city with

Place Between Future and Past

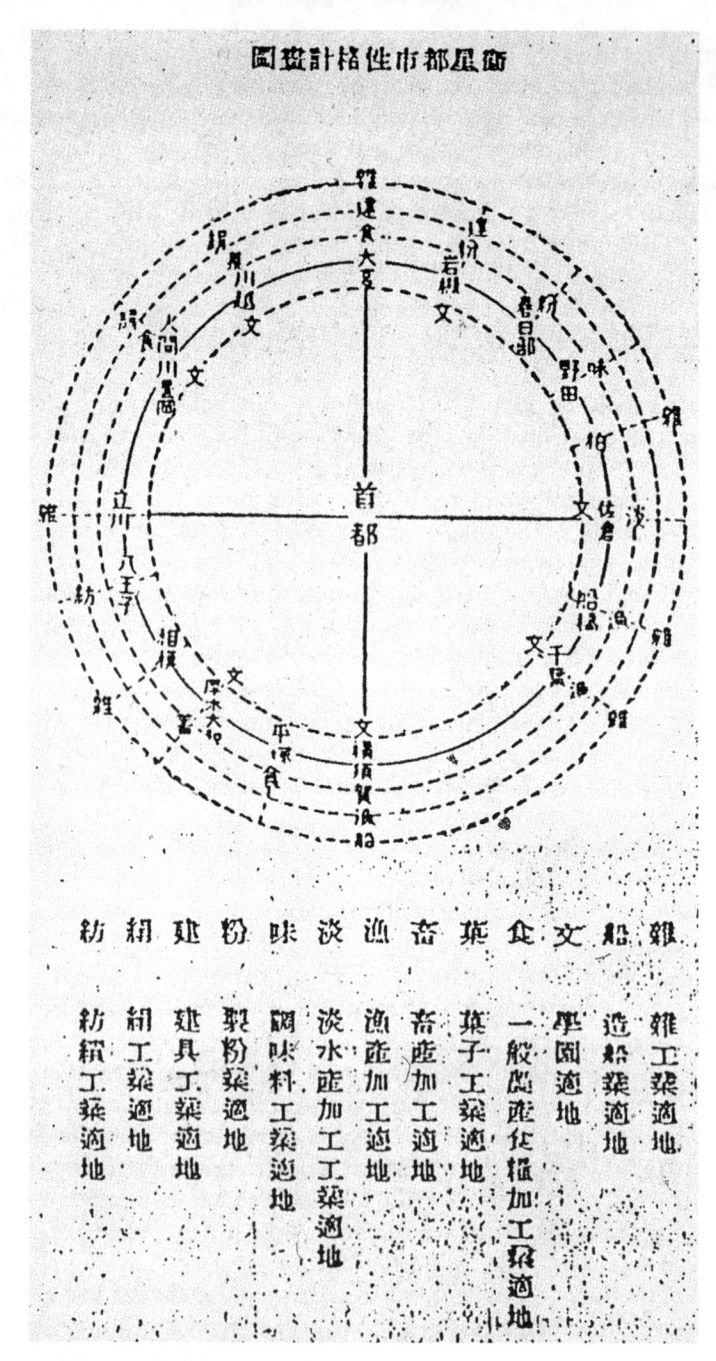

Figure 54 Ishikawa Hideaki, 'Satellite Cities Concept,' 1946. From: The City Planning Institute of Japan (1988) *Centenary of Modern City Planning and Its Perspective*. Tokyo: Shōkokusha, p. 39.

more than 10 percent of its green space. Numerous large private parks were to be opened for public use, including Shinjuku Gyoen, Shirogane, and the Outer Garden of the Imperial Palace, while military sites were to be transformed into parks. This was for Ishikawa an important step towards the transformation of Tokyo into a cultural city. In July 1948, the Tokyo Metropolitan Government finally designated a plan for 18,010 hectares of green zones in the periphery of the ward area. Ishikawa's plan proposed land readjustment on 20,130 hectares, out of which 15,840 hectares had been burned down. Following the publication of his plan, 6,100 hectares were suggested for land readjustment, which were reduced to 3,000 hectares in November 1947. In the end, only 1,380 hectares were implemented. As Ishikawa had indicated himself, land ownership was to be the major problem for the rebuilding.[5]

Competitions and Consultations for the New Tokyo

Tokyo, then, had a reconstruction plan which was based on urban planning theory, explained through visual images of the future city, and publicized through a film. What is more, Ishikawa tried to give life to the overall plan by initiating urban planning competitions and consultations. The areas chosen by Ishikawa were in fact zones to which he had attributed particular functions in his overall plan, like Ginza, Shinjuku, Asakusa, Shibuya, Shinagawa, and Fukagawa. Only two competition entries are still known today. Both were prepared by the above-mentioned Utida Yosifumi, a member of the Datong planning group; they received first prize. For Shinjuku, which was to become Tokyo's high-rise business district, Utida suggested several steps for the reconstruction of the western and the eastern sides of the station. In a first phase, the eastern side was to be redeveloped with large scale, high rise buildings. For the western side Utida suggested a grand axis with a Le Corbusier type building as an 'eye-stop.' With uncanny prescience, he proposed that this building should be the Tokyo Metropolitan Government headquarters. Its decentralization had been suggested by Ishikawa earlier on. Further skyscrapers resembling Le Corbusier's Antwerp proposal – probably for residential use – would have surrounded it and would also have taken the place of low-rise residential areas. If this master plan had been accepted, it would have provided a large scale context to the development of a business district in west Shinjuku, a transformation that soon occurred as a result of piecemeal planning decisions taken on a day to day basis (fig. 55).

Furthermore, educational districts were singled out for special attention in the overall master plan by Ishikawa. Waseda, Hongō, Mita, Kanda Surugadai, and Ōokayama were to become culture and education zones with libraries, museums, research institutions, and housing for the professors. Each university was asked to prepare an urban plan for its

Place Between Future and Past

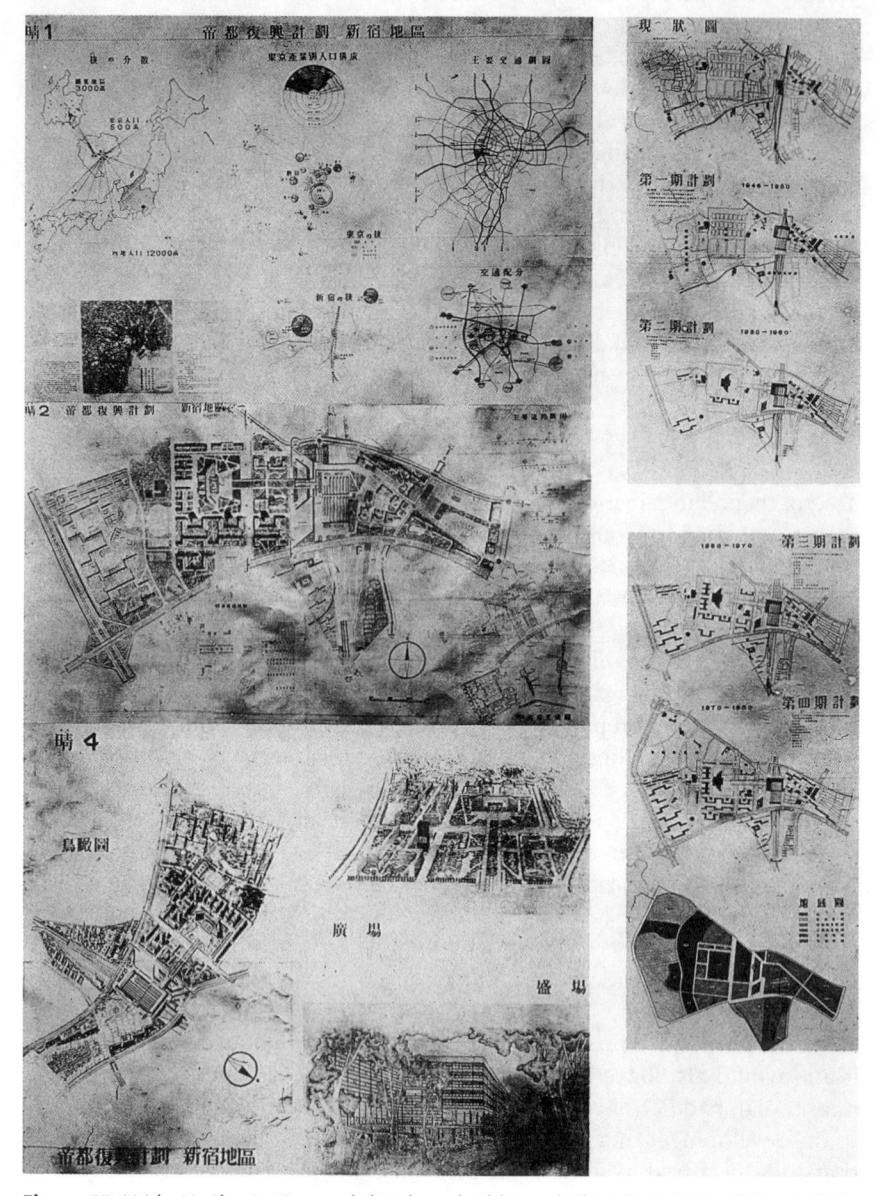

Figure 55 Utida Yosifumi, 'Proposal for the rebuilding of Shinjuku,' (*Teito fukkō keikaku Shinjuku-chiku*) 1946. From: Utida Yosikazu Sensei Biju Shukaku kinen sakuhin shū kankōkai (The Editors Group for 'Selected Works of Professor Utida Yoshikazu in Architecture and Planning) (1969) *Utida Yosikazu Sensei Sakuhinshū*, (Collection of the Works of Professor Utida Yosikazu). Tokyo: Kajima Kenkyūjo shuppankai, 1969, p. 185.

campus and surroundings, and this job was generally taken up by the architectural faculties. All proposals were given a basic urban form. However, only the drawings of four projects remain. Generally speaking, they translated Ishikawa's attempt for a new city into a 'grand design,' as Takayama, one of the authors of the Hongō plan mentions.[6] All were based on the idea of creating large axes and vistas as well as eye-stop and high rise buildings. Major plazas and important sports facilities give structure to the overall plans.

The design for a limited area around the Hongō campus of Tokyo University was made by Takayama Eika, Tange Kenzō, Ikebe Kiyoshi (1920–79), Asada Takashi (1921–90), and Ōtani Sachio (b. 1924) (fig. 56). As to the delimitation of the area, Ishikawa stated that they should cover one and a half kilometers outside the campus area and that Tokyo University should be connected with the area of Ueno Park and the Koishikawa Botanical Garden. The reasons for the delimitation of the area are unknown; they do not reflect administrative boundaries and seem to be based mainly on the desire to integrate neighboring universities and nearby green areas. The boulevard-like main streets of the project followed more or less the infrastructure designs Ishikawa had imagined for Tokyo. As to the architectural indications contained in the plan, the high rise buildings and the spiraling square of the never-ending museum, a form proposed by Le Corbusier and called the Mundaneum, can be understood as badges which show the authors' admiration for modernist ideas and especially the projects of Le Corbusier, but do not reflect a real architectural proposal. These projects, while important in local postwar planning discussions, remained unrealized and are unknown to international planning history. They lacked the symbolic value and design ideas of the plans for Hiroshima, to which we now turn.

Hiroshima – Monumental Planning

An Exceptional Case

The best known example of Japanese reconstruction is the rebuilding of Hiroshima following the proposals of Tange Kenzō and his group for the Peace Park (1946–52). It is discussed here as a unique example of urban design, as an object for international appreciation, and as a sign of modernization and westernization. As such, it recalls plans from the Meiji era, like that for the Ginza, or western-style plans for a government center in Hibiya. The architects conceived the Hiroshima project for an international audience, and it became one of the rare examples of Japanese urbanism known abroad. Presented to the CIAM meeting in 1951, it earned praise as an important example of postwar planning, although international commentators did not understand that the project was unique. However,

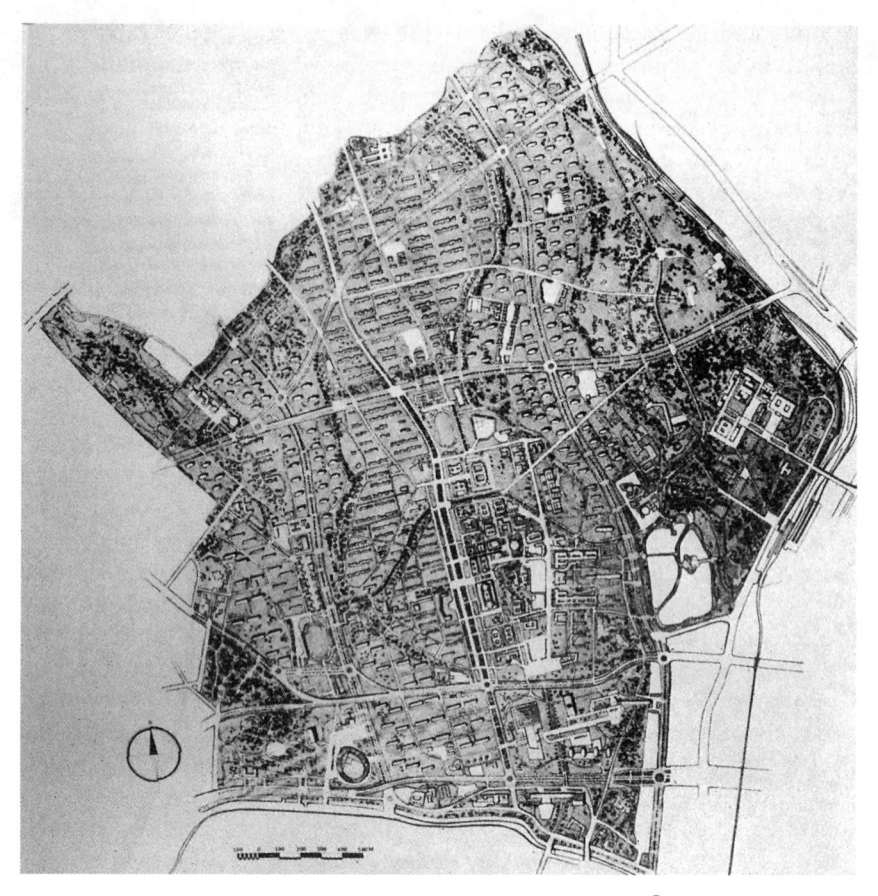

Figure 56 Takayama Eika, Tange Kenzō, Ikebe Kiyoshi, Asada Takashi, Ōtani Sachio, 'Proposal for the Hongō educational district,' 1946. From: Kawakami Hidemitsu, Ishida Yorifusa (1960) *Henbō suru toshi: toshi wo mukaeta sengo Nihon no toshi keikaku* (Changing cities: postwar urban planning in Japan as directed towards cities). Tokyo: Tokyo Bijutsu Shuppansha, pp. 33–88.

the Hiroshima project is also an illustration of Japanese planning as a technical device based on practical necessity – the creation of firebreaks – a matter ignored by western observers.

What is more, the Hiroshima project could only be conceived as a result of strong outside support. The idea that the planning of Hiroshima was a highly symbolic project was reinforced by foreign planners and journalists, and its realization depended on American permission for a special treatment of the city and thus an increase in funding (Ishimaru: 27). However, the Japanese themselves also found it important to reflect on the future of the city, as the surprising number of proposals for the city shows.

Visionary Plans and Planners

Many people wondered whether the terrain of a city demolished by an atomic bomb could be reinhabited within a few years, and several publications proposed conserving the ruins as monuments. Kora Tomiko (1896–1993), the deputy mayor of Kure, suggested that a new Hiroshima be created elsewhere and that the old city be preserved only as fragments; this idea recalls the proposals of Max Taut (1884–1967) for Berlin. Kuwabara Ichio, former president of Asahi Industries, promoted the preservation of the destroyed area as a monument and symbol of world peace, surrounded by cultural and religious institutions.[7] Tōge Sankichi (1917–53) proposed a plan for a green, decentralized city. In regard to its urban form, however, it was based on the monumental design concepts of the nineteenth century, whereas the buildings showed a wide variety of forms and styles (fig. 57). Such general approaches did not induce further debate and were quickly rejected.

Figure 57 Tōge Sankichi, 'Hiroshima in 1965'. From: Hiroshima Toshi Seikatsu Kenkyū Kai (1985) *Reconstruction of Hiroshima: Pictorial History of Forty Years since Atomic Bombing (Toshi no fukkō, Hiroshima hibaku 40 nen shi)*, p. 44.

Pragmatic Rebuilding of the Entire City

The discussions of the planning commission concentrated on questions such as the population density in the new Hiroshima. Most of the planners thought that without military industry, Hiroshima could not survive economically. They therefore expected a population of about 100,000 to live there, in contrast to the prewar population of 420,000 (or 500,000 including military personnel). Tange, one of the specialists invited to give an opinion, prepared a land use plan for from 300,000 to 350,000 inhabitants. Only Watanabe Shigeru, who was also invited by the reconstruction commission, thought already in 1946 that 700,000 inhabitants would be possible, and that only if skyscrapers were erected. In the end, no effective measures were taken for limiting the city's population, and Watanabe was proved the most prescient.

The debate on the future size and form of Hiroshima led to the land use plan prepared by the Tange group and published in the *Chūgoku* newspaper in 1947. Infrastructure planning and zoning were the main topics of this project. It partly referred to existing plans, but the zoning into seven functional units was new. The main elements of this plan were integrated into the administrative plan of 1949. The zones were, however, reduced to three. The general difficulty of developing a comprehensive urban concept can be partly explained by the youth of the Japanese planning movement. The urban planning law of 1919 was only applied in 1922 in Hiroshima and the first *toshikeikaku dōri* (urban planning streets) were designed in 1928 and realized after the 1930s. Thus, before the construction of the 100 meter wide boulevard, urban planning did not have a long tradition in Hiroshima. The streets proposed in the 1930s were only partly realized, because during the war projects of military importance came first.

Even the famous Peace Boulevard is less a reference to Western monumental axes than the result of the customary Japanese clearance done to create a firebreak and thus the result of military planning. After the bombing of German cities and especially Hamburg, the creation of further firebreaks was ordered. The city authorities of Hiroshima put this order into effect in 1944. In Hiroshima the demolition of buildings was carried out mainly according to the street plan of 1928. The straight 100 meter boulevard was not part of these plans but was created as a firebreak where initially a street 15 meters wide had been proposed. Though conceived as a firebreak and green strip, when the boulevard was constructed, its symbolic character became integral to the project. This explains the failure to construct a second, identical 100 meter wide boulevard that was planned south of the city center after the war. Even the network of parks and green areas, which is impressive by Japanese standards, was not so much the result of a concept for the amelioration of urban quality but based on the necessity to create free space for use in an emergency (fig. 58).

Visionary Plans and Planners

Figure 58 Tange Kenzō, et al., 'Hiroshima City Reconstruction Plan and Land Use Plan,' 1947. From: Hiroshima Toshi Seikatsu Kenkyū Kai (1985) *Reconstruction of Hiroshima: Pictorial History of Forty Years since Atomic Bombing* (*Toshi no fukkō, Hiroshima hibaku 40 nen shi*).

The symbolic character of reconstruction, which was anchored in the Hiroshima Peace City Construction Act from 1949, was a basis for urban planning visions. However, the vision has only survived in parts. Many buildings which were not destroyed by the atomic bomb were torn down later, and generally speaking, the city does not show the beauty, harmony, and high quality of life to which those in charge had aspired. The peace park, museum, and boulevard exist but have been absorbed into an ordinary Japanese city without an overall design, outstanding architectural landmarks, or some overall urban response to its particular history (Hiroshima 1996).

The Peace Park as Part of International Planning History

The functional elements of city planning went largely unnoticed on an international level. The design for the peace park, however, found worldwide interest. Its design was the result of an architectural competition which was set up after the financing had been decided. As Ōtani Sachio explains, Tange did not want to insist on the land use plan for fear of loosing the chance to participate in the competition for the peace park.[8] A total of 145 designs were introduced in August 1949. Tange's proposal was exceptional. Reflecting Le Corbusier's architectural language, it presents three buildings on pilotis connected by bridges. In its axis a huge arc frames the view towards the so-called A-bomb dome, that is the cupola of the Hiroshima Industry Promotion Hall, a brick and steel building standing close to the center of the explosion, the ruins of which, including the steel frame of the dome, survived the bombing and have been maintained as a symbol of the war (fig. 59).

The peace park is unique in the history of Japanese reconstruction and it stands as a reminder that city planning can include identifiable landmarks and local particularities. It came into existence in the short period of time when the ordinary framework of Japanese urban planning was dissolved,

Figure 59 Tange Kenzō, et al. (Tange Kenzō, Asada Takashi, Ōtani Sachio and associates in the Planning Research Group, Architectural Department, Tokyo University), 'Model of the competition project for the peace park,' (1st prize) 1949. From: Hiroshima Toshi Seikatsu Kenkyū Kai (1985) *Reconstruction of Hiroshima: Pictorial History of Forty Years since Atomic Bombing* (*Toshi no fukkō, Hiroshima hibaku 40 nen shi*), p. 92.

leaving room for new solutions. Tange himself states that, '[the] peace park is not that heart of an ideal city to which we have been mentally so attached. It represents an unusual and fortunate opportunity in Japan. For it has been possible to gain the co-operation of various administrative and governing interests and get them to agree to act together as a single body so that the realization of this project may be possible' (Riani 1969: 8–10). This window of opportunity closed when the administration rebuilt itself. It is nevertheless surprising that architects did not take additional advantage of the situation, however briefly it endured. Apart from esthetic debates, the reconstruction could have been used to anchor social concepts in urban planning, to reinforce the construction of housing and promote public facilities. That would have been an even better expression of the peace city. Although land readjustment existed as a strong instrument for planning, the necessary individual initiatives and the theoretic planning background were missing.

Nishiyama Uzō – Urban Visions Based on Japanese Traditions

While the Hiroshima plans strove for an urban form, the visions elaborated by Nishiyama referred mainly to the traditional structure of Japanese cities, the organization in small neighborhoods, and as such, they are probably the closest to a Japanese planning vision. Nishiyama was also one of the rare planners to reflect on the term vision. In his text *Bijon kara kōsō keikaku e* (From vision to conceptual plan), he pointed out that the Japanese word bijon has often been used as a catch phrase and needs to be analysed with care (Nishiyama 1990). A beautiful presentation called a vision, aimed at making people dream, he wrote, is often based on lies or inaccuracies and may be used to hide the real intentions of its authors or the negative impacts of a project. In particular, futuristic visions lack concrete indications for their realization and a basic set of human values to orient them. As example, Nishiyama mentioned the 'vision' of motorization that brought cars to Japan, where a separation of traffic functions and an appropriate street network did not exist and where the traditional roads were used as a place for community activities, a room to play and to meet, treated like an extension of the home. The negative effects of car traffic, noise, and air pollution, the need for parking spaces and similar problems had not been discussed beforehand. In spite of the negative usage made of the word *bijon*, Nishiyama strongly recommended the existence of a vision which lays out basic principles and gives an overall aim to individual initiatives.

While Tange was internationally acknowledged, Nishiyama is largely unknown in the west. However, he has influenced generations of Japanese planners through his numerous books and articles, his visionary and realistic projects, as well as his teaching activities at Kyoto University, all of which reflect his broad humanist-communist ideas. His writings remain an important basis for schoolbooks and scientific studies on urban planning. Nishiyama had not the international presence of theoreticians such as Patrick Geddes (1854–1932), Lewis Mumford (1895–1990), or Werner Hegemann (1881–1936), and he wrote neither a fundamental planning theory nor an international history of urban planning. He did not influence the development of planning through exhibitions. All the same, he has in Japan a comparable status, being seen as an influential critic and initiator of urban planning projects.

Nishiyama is a planner who was educated as an architect between 1930 and 1933. During his studies he became interested in the social dimension of architecture and felt a resistance to its character as an elitist art for a small number of persons. Thus, he participated in the magazine *Dezam*, which tried to connect architectural topics with social studies. Nishiyama's strong engagement with housing in later years probably also derived from this period (Nishiyama 1975, 1976, 1980). Nishiyama is one of the rare Japanese planners whose proposals are based on a comprehensive and long term concept of society and one of the few to have transformed his ideas into visions.

Visualization as a Means of Communicating and Discussing Ideas

His interest in the visualization of his ideas, however, made him vulnerable to criticism, and not all his ideas were either politically sensitive or feasible. Thus, in 1942 he entered the competition for a monument for the Greater East Asian Co-prosperity Sphere (the Japanese imperialist area of control), without concerning himself about the policies behind it. Four sites had been proposed and in contrast to Tange, whose project for a location close to Mount Fuji is better known, Nishiyama situated his proposal in Asuka, in Nara Prefecture. The creation of a completely new city is a rare opportunity in Japan, and just as with his visionary planning in Manchuria, Nishiyama's approach to this topic differed from that of the other competitors. Instead of creating an isolated monument, he connected the new city closely with the existing village. In regard to the contents, he chose a kind of permanent Olympic village, sketching out a meeting and festival capital offering cultural and sports facilities for all the different people who had come under Japanese authority. The design combines monumental and modern elements, proposing a compact infrastructure connected by green routes, reminiscent more of the projects in Fascist Italy than of those in Germany (Nishiyama 1942, 1943; Fujimori 1986) (fig. 60). It is interesting to note that neither Nishiyama nor Tange has been strongly criticised by later writers for participating in these politically motivated competitions.

In 1946, reacting to the real and the planned increase in inhabitants as well as the hardship and the need for food after World War II and based on the idea of self-reliance in food production, Nishiyama argued that further

Visionary Plans and Planners

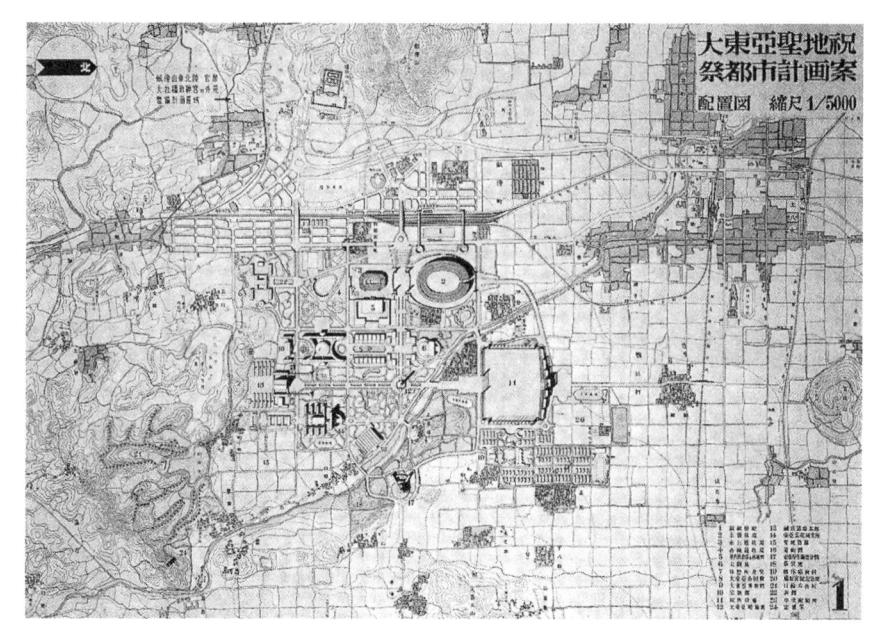

Figure 60 Nishiyama Uzō, 'Monument for the Greater Asian Hemisphere' (*Dai tōa seichi shukusai toshi keikaku an*), 1942. From: Fujimori T. (1986) *Japon des Avant Gardes 1910–1970*. Paris: Editions du Centre Pompidou, p. 208.

land was needed for cultivation. In Japan, however, where three-quarters of the territory is accounted for by steep mountainsides, this is a request difficult to fulfill. Therefore he proposed the creation of cities on mountain slopes, to keep the plains free for agriculture and thereby guarantee the nourishment of the population (Nishiyama 1978). Some twenty new cities for 50,000 inhabitants could be created each year in his opinion. After demonstrating that inclined skyscrapers allow for better insulation of neighboring houses, he proposed to erect high rise buildings on south-facing slopes (fig. 61). This project contained many questionable elements, some of which were already anticipated by Nishiyama, who opposed the notion of landscape preservation with that of feeding the people and opted for the latter alternative. For all their problematic elements, these proposals are an important example of individual ideas made public and left for discussion and thus as a starting point for the creation of an overall concept for Japanese cities.

The Neighborhood as the Basic Japanese Life Sphere

All of Nishiyama's written texts were based on his readings. He read widely, for example, in Russian and German. He never traveled abroad in prewar

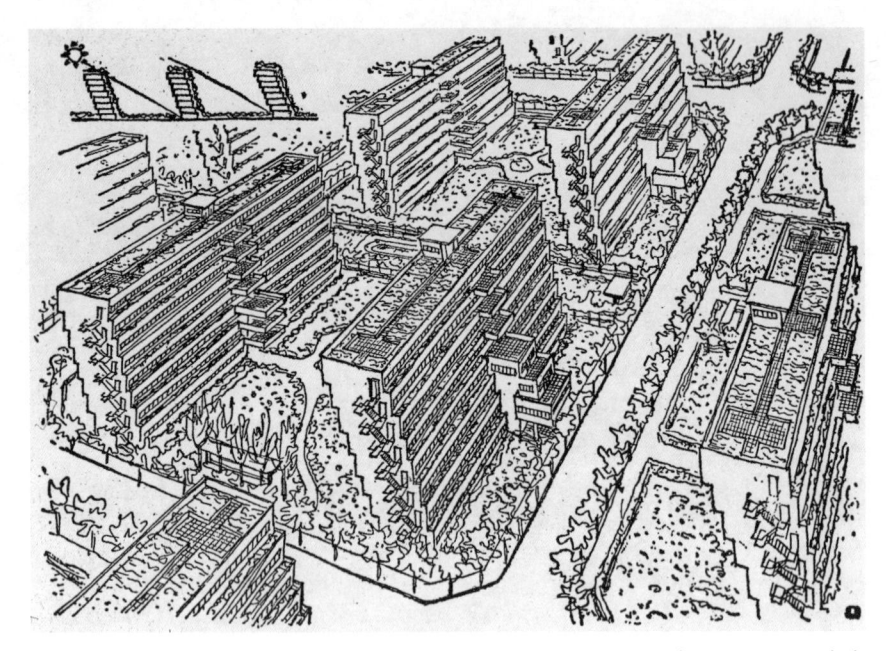

Figure 61 Nishiyama Uzō, 'Cities on mountain slopes,' 1946. From: Nishiyama (1968) *Chiiki kūkan ron* (Reflections on urban, regional and national space). Tokyo: Keisō Shobō, p. 284.

days, however, and thus did not have an opportunity to meet the authors of the texts and discuss his ideas with them. He did not even participate in international planning groups. Although books circulated between Japan and the West, the network of planners integrated Europeans, North Americans, and South Americans but did not include Japanese. Even the contacts which had been created as results of emigration or student exchange were limited. The similar cultural background and the cooperation of western planners since the 1920s allowed the emigration of prominent German architects to the USA and their later intervention in the reconstruction of Germany. Japanese rebuilding, however, did not find specific foreign support except at Hiroshima.

Neighborhood planning was one idea dear to Nishiyama. In fact, in 1942 Nishiyama was analysing the problem of the big city as locale for a concentrated workforce, trying to find a new organizational form for the Japanese city. In this connection, he analysed the major urban planning discussions in the west. The material he presented was chosen without regard to the political context that engendered it, whether capitalist America, socialist Russia or fascist National-Socialist Germany. He compiled his findings and interpretations in an article entitled *Seikatsu kichi no kōsō* (The structure of life-units) (Nishiyama 1968). In that text, first of all he rejected urban concepts featuring skyscrapers and higher density of population in the cities, as had been advocated by Le Corbusier or Ludwig Hilberseimer (1885–1967), calling the first, a simple reorganization of the city without seeking solutions to the density problems and the second a transposition of the capitalist American cities. Beaux-Arts projects like the plan for Canberra were also rejected as purely esthetic concepts. Although not mentioned in this particular article, he also rejected the monumental urban design proposals by Albert Speer and others.

The garden city and the neighborhood concept, however, appealed to Nishiyama. Both ideas had been developed in the west as answers to the problems of the big city and were studied, just like housing problems, more or less simultaneously in Japan. The works of Clarence Perry (1872–1944) and Thomas Adams (1871–1940) promoting the neighborhood theory were especially well known (Perry 1929; Adams 1934). The creation of largely independent urban units is close to the traditional form of the Japanese city. It is thus not surprising that the neighborhood concept found considerable interest in Japan. In fact, Japanese cities are organized as a patchwork, based on the historic urban unit of the *machi* (the neighborhood block).

As a basis for Japanese urban planning Nishiyama conceived of the garden city in a form similar to that initially developed by Ebenezer Howard. He appreciated the formal design, which was well known in Japan, but concentrated on the economic and social background (Watanabe 1980). The main problem identified by Howard – the question of how to develop a complete new town with local employment and to prepare enough housing space for a growing number of urban inhabitants – was similar in Japan. The solutions Howard proposed, such as public ownership, autonomy, and distances which can be covered by foot, were taken up by Nishiyama. However, he did not consider these sufficient. He looked also to the linear city as it was developed by N.A. Miliutin in the Soviet Union.

Nishiyama was searching for a concept that could be applied both to new and also to existing cities, and in this regard he very much appreciated Gottfried Feder's (1883–1941) proposal outlined in his book *Die neue Stadt* (The new city), published in 1939. German planners concentrated at that time on topics like housing and air defense, which were of interest also for Japan. In fact, Feder proposed urban units for 20,000 inhabitants divided into nine autonomous units and surrounded by agricultural areas. The institutions necessary for daily life were listed in detail, ready to be used as an introduction to city building. Feder wanted this technical project to be connected with the art of city planning, as shown in the subtitle of his book, *Essay on the Creation of a New Art of City Planning, Based on the Social Structure of Its Inhabitants* (*Versuch der Begründung einer neuen Stadtplanungskunst aus der sozialen Struktur der Bevölkerung*). However, the esthetic part of this project and the reference to medieval forms were not appropriate to Japan, and Nishiyama therefore ignored them.

It may be thought that the political relationship between Germany and Japan at that time might be at the basis of this interest for the Feder concept. The rejection of the Nazi monumental design, however, suggests that it was more the technical approach to planning which intrigued the Japanese or the possibility of adopting ideas of an Anglo-American background through this German book. Nishiyama's reference to Feder's book seems to have had a lasting influence on the Japanese interpretation and analysis of Western history of town planning. In fact, ever since the 1950s most Japanese urban planning textbooks have given Feder's 'new city' a prominent place in a lineage that included Howard and Perry.[9] In the 1940s, when Nishiyama wrote his article, such a genealogy might have been comprehensible, as the project was new and needed to be explained in detail. In regard to the history of town planning, however, it seems somewhat misplaced. This is a typical example of the misunderstandings and shortcomings which regularly occur in the transmission of planning concepts from the west to Japan.

It is often said that the book had a strong impact on Japanese urban planning and particularly on the creation of new towns. Details on how the book's recommendations were translated into planning reality are, however, never given, and it is clear that there was a certain ignorance of its contents. Feder himself insisted that the data given for an ideal new city can be used also for the creation of neighborhoods inside existing cities, for renewal as much as for rebuilding. This ignorance becomes particularly evident in an article written by Ishikawa in 1943.[10] Criticizing the ideas of Feder for not being applicable to existing cities, he develops his own concept of dividing existing cities into smaller units separated by green areas and agriculture, a concept which strongly resembles in fact the German planning debate on the *Stadtlandschaft* or 'urban landscape,' as developed in the drawing by Hans Bernhard Reichow (1899–1974) for Posen, which itself is connected to Anglo-American neighborhood concepts. Due to the war, however, these origins could not be identified by name. It is surprising, however, that the central figures in this debate, people like Reichow or Konstanty Gutschow (1902–78), find no mention, although their projects strongly resemble Japanese concepts (Durth and Gutschow 1988).

As to Nishiyama, he developed several projects concerning the organization of the city in decentralized, self-governed neighborhoods, which he called life spheres. Just like his western counterparts he opposed unnecessary traffic and suggested the creation of small urban units. However, he did not criticize the big city itself. On the contrary, and this is typical of Japanese planners, he tried to find a way to maintain the multifunctional big cities and make them more liveable. In spite of his generally positive attitude towards big cities, he stressed the need for equilibrated growth and the existence of an appropriate number of

Visionary Plans and Planners

workplaces, welfare facilities, and the like, in order to prevent sprawl. In regard to their organization and size, he suggested that about ten school catchment areas should form one working unit, which would account, for example, for the workers needed by one industry. For cities of a million inhabitants that means about ten major working units.

In a sketch from 1946 Nishiyama showed how such a city could be organized. In fact, his plan is very similar to that for his mountainside city. Industrial establishments are sited alongside the river and cut off from the city by a green strip. The residential districts are divided up by a grid of major roads which connect them to the industrial areas. The central boulevard is lined with trees and leads up to a zone with 'welfare' facilities such as hospitals. Underground parking lots and shopping and cultural facilities are concentrated around the main intersections. The housing areas themselves are designed some with high and others with low rise housing, generally organized around a school and connected by green routes. In order to realize such neighborhoods inside existing cities, however, large-scale demolition would be necessary to create free space. This was accepted by Nishiyama without hesitation. Altogether this project can be seen as based on the tradition of the Japanese city as well as on foreign concepts (fig. 62). Nishiyama's analysis of the neighborhood in the sense of *machi* certainly had a major influence on the importance given to this element of the Japanese city in the last decades.

National Decentralization

In regard to the city as a whole, Nishiyama outlined an organization close to Western concepts. Reserving the city center for commercial and public administrative functions, he proposed a network of small monofunctional urban units, industrial, cultural, and harbor facilities, located along major lines of transportation, principally railway lines, and separated from other urban areas by green strips. Exclusively residential districts were further spaced out, and became themselves centers for the surrounding villages. In contrast to Ishikawa, Nishiyama calculated distances between the different units in temporal and not spatial terms. In fact, distances of between one hundred and five hundred kilometers can be traveled by high speed trains and planes, which connect the big cities, whereas highways and railway lines connect the smaller ones and cover distances of between thirty and fifty kilometers. Ordinary streets and trains lead to the villages, taking about an hour to travel twenty kilometers. Even the villages, however, should be at a maximum traveling time of three hours from the capital. This idea reflects a particularly Japanese notion of day trips from the capital to any place in the country and is virtually a reality today.

As to regional planning, the ideas of the German geographer Walter Christaller (1893–1969) were first introduced in Japan in the 1930s and

Place Between Future and Past

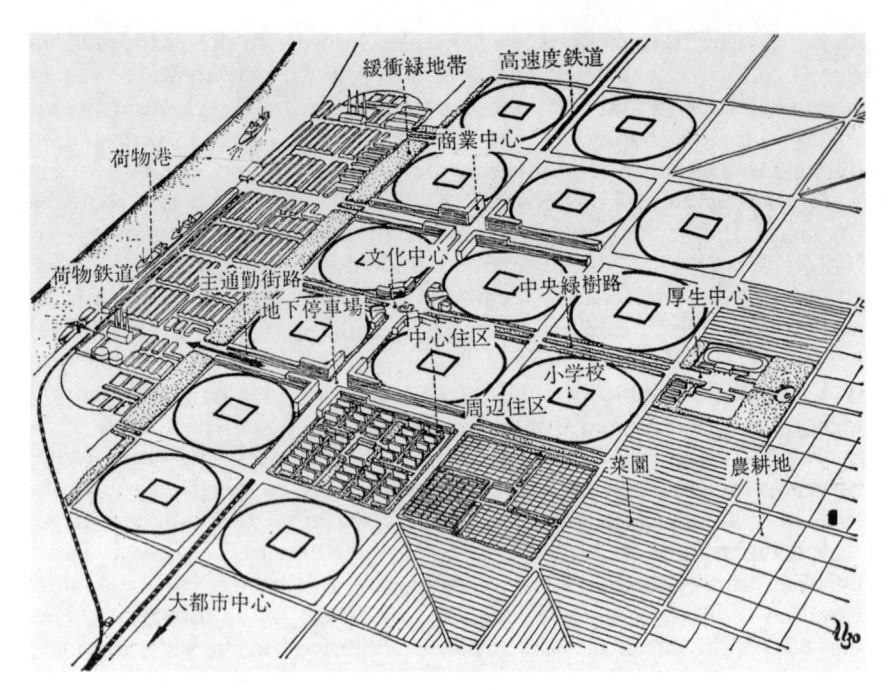

Figure 62 Nishiyama Uzō, Neighborhood unit, 1946. From: Nishiyama (1968) *Chiiki kūkan ron* (Reflections on urban, regional and national space). Tokyo: Keisō Shobō, p. 229.

were met with great interest. However, again in contrast to Ishikawa who was concerned with the same topic, Nishiyama explained that due to the very limited area of land which could be urbanised, such concepts of small cities dispersed over the whole nation could not be realized as no space would remain in between. Promoting development along preestablished lines, Nishiyama proposed cities of between one and two hundred thousand inhabitants. Each of these cities would be the center of one of twelve central regions structuring the national space and connected to form a network. Some of these cities already existed; others had to be created. Given Japan's narrow, elongated form, Nishiyama proposed in place of Christaller's scheme a spindle-like system. The overall aim was to create a culturally and industrially balanced system (fig. 63). As a proposal for decentralization, Nishiyama's concept is still valid today.

In later years, Nishiyama became interested in environmental questions and was a prominent member of citizens' movements, fighting for example against a new high rise building for Kyoto station. The amelioration of the conditions of urban life and a better distribution of social wealth was a major concern for him. In contrast to the usual method of proceeding of Japanese urban planners, he asked for a general concept that was not only

Visionary Plans and Planners

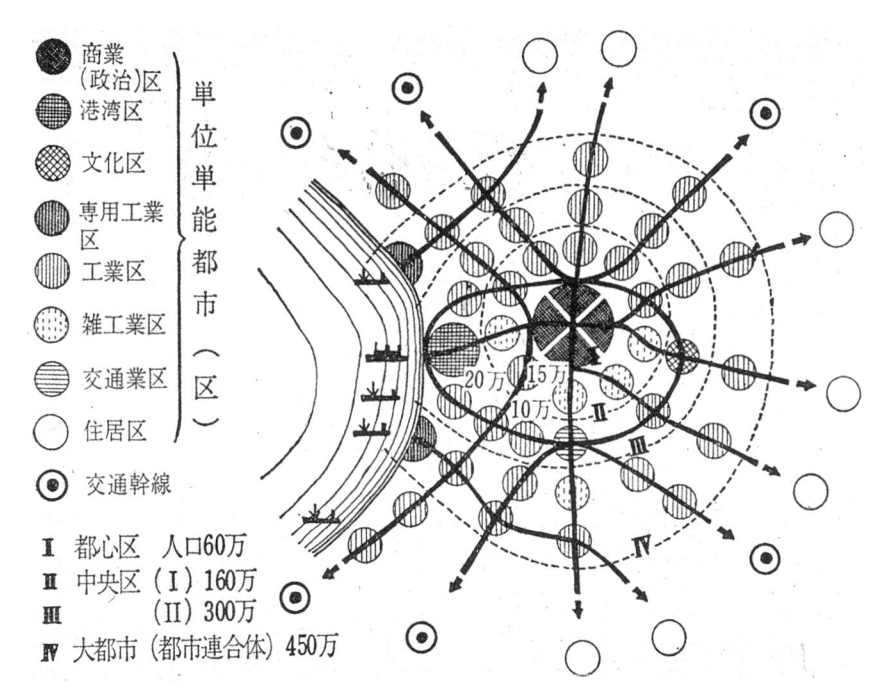

Figure 63 Nishiyama Uzō, Zoning of a metropolis, 1946. Nishiyama (1968) *Chiiki kūkan ron* (Reflections on urban, regional and national space). Tokyo: Keisō Shobō, p. 232.

oriented towards economic development but also integrated concerns for quality of life as well as urban functions before plans were drawn up for new roads. Planning visions were for Nishiyama an important means for urban design, and he was one of the rare planners to request them (Nishiyama 1990). An analysis of Nishiyama's writings and work shows that independent of western theories, Japanese visions and individual activities existed in the fields of housing and planning, and these were transmitted to a large group of students and may hopefully contribute to a renewal of urban and regional planning in the future.

A Vision for Japanese Cities?

The few visionary proposals developed for the reconstruction of Japanese cities were only very partially realized. Nevertheless they are still characteristic of the approaches to the Japanese city in recent years. While Ishikawa's ideas for a reduction of the population could not be fulfilled, his notion of creating specialized centers inside the city has materialized in the officially designated metropolitan sub-centers on the Yamanote loop line such as Shinjuku and Shibuya, each with its distinct characteristics. A recent addition to these sub-centres, completed in 1994, is the business, department, and amusement center in Ebisu called the Yebisu Garden Place. With its French-style chateau, German-style red brick building, and steel and glass covered central space, which resembles a large European train station and binds the whole together, the Yebisu Garden Place, with its air of a foreign island in the Japanese landscape, reminds us of the 'grand design' competition entries that were elaborated on the initiative of Ishikawa

As to the Hiroshima project of Tange, its core element, the Peace Park was built, and its design is outstanding, but it had no influence either on the surrounding city or on planning in Japan in general. It may be seen as representative of the tradition of architectural objects which are erected without connection to their built environment and often even in confrontation with it. This tradition found its apotheosis in the bubble years of the 1980s, when new buildings came to be seen as elements in a so-called chaotic city, forming the expression of Japanese urbanism as it is best known abroad.

Nishiyama's intervention in favor of the neighborhood, *machi*, was not a direct reaction to wartime destruction; it transcended this period and had a strong influence on *machi-zukuri*, the movement for neighborhood or community planning, which includes social as much as physical aspects.

In fact, one might say that many characteristics of planning from the Meiji era have survived today. With a few special exceptions, urban planning and building design are still dissociated. Concerns with infrastructure and disaster prevention prevention remain dominant. Urban planning is still subject to short term interventions, and projects which would have needed long term commitment like the Tokyo waterfront are reduced to pragmatic interventions. *Machi-zukuri*, as local participation in decision-making and small scale urban amelioration programs are called, is a first step towards a more humanized planning. It does not, however, replace a comprehensive vision based not only on economic concepts but on a set of comprehensive social and political ideas for a balanced society. Such a vision does not have to be interpreted in a Western sense as a monumental and esthetic concept but can have a distinctive but still-to-be-defined Japanese character. That means also reviving local characteristics, which have been largely lost following the engineering-led reconstruction after World War II. In fact, Japan still has to analyse, create, and coordinate an overall policy, a vision for its cities.

Notes

1 For an analysis of reconstruction in the West see also Cohen and Frank (1986–89); Diefendorf (1990); Diefendorf (1993); Durth and Gutschow (1988); von Beyme (1987); and von Beyme, Durth, Gutschow, Nerdinger, and Topfstedt (1992).

2 Suzuki Eiki and Ishida Yorifusa (1987) *'Tōkyō shiku kaisei tochi tatemono shobun kisoku no seiritsu ni tsuite'* (On the creation of the regulation regarding selling and buying of building sites and buildings in the Tokyo law on urban renewal) *Kenchiku gakkai keikaku keiron bunshū* 376. Quoted in Hein and Ishida (1998).
3 All data on the damages during World War II excludes Okinawa.
4 Ishida Y. (1988). *Sensō kara sengo no fukkō e* (From War to Reconstruction). Interview with Takayama Eika (in Ishida 1988a: 229–35).
5 *Tokyo in 20 years*, Film 1946.
6 Interview by Professor Ishida Yorifusa with Eika Takayama (quoted in Ishida: 1992).
7 See Ishimaru (no date); material here is also taken from interviews by the author with Ishimaru Norioki and members of the urban planning administration in Hiroshima as well as with Professor Ōtani Sachio.
8 Author's interview with Prof. Ōtani Sachio on 27 September 1996 in Tokyo.
9 See for example Toshi Keikaku Kyōiku Kenkyū Kai (1987, 1995, 1996); Akiyama (1980, 1985, 1993); Higasa (1977, 1985, 1986, 1992, 1993, 1996); Katsura, Adachi, and Zaino (1975, 1988); Takei (1958); Ishikawa (1943 and 1951); Itō (1942 and 1943).
10 Ishikawa gets mixed up with the first and last name and speaks of 'Professor Gottfried.' In regard to the theory, he also spoke of the day/week/month center (Ishikawa 1943).

References

Adams, T. (1934) *The Design of Residential Areas*. Cambridge, Mass: Harvard University Press.
Akiyama M. (1980, 1985, 1993) *Toshi keikaku* (Urban planning). Tokyo: Rikō Tosho.
Beyme, K. von (1987) *Der Wiederaufbau* (The reconstruction). Munich: Piper.
Beyme, K. von, W. Durth, N. Gutschow, W. Nerdinger, and T. Topfstedt (1992) *Neue Städte aus Ruinen* (New towns from ruins). Munich: Prestel.
Cohen, J.-L., and H. Frank, (eds) (1986–89) *Deutsch-französische Beziehungen 1940–1950 und ihre Auswirkungen auf Architektur und Stadtgestalt, Forschungsprojekt* (German-French relations 1940–1950 and their impact on architecture and city form, research project).
'*Dai Tōa kensetsu kinen eizō keikaku*' (Competition results in the Greater East-Asian Co-prosperity Sphere). *Kenchiku zasshi* December 1942.
Diefendorf, J. (1993) *In the Wake of War*. New York: Oxford University Press. (1990) *Rebuilding Europe's Bombed Cities*. London: Macmillan.
Durth, W., and N. Gutschow (1988) *Träume in Trümmern* (Dreams in ruins). Brunswick: Vieweg.
Feder, G. (1939) *Die neue Stadt* (The new city). Berlin: Verlag von Julius Springer.
Fujimori T. (1990) *Meiji no Tōkyō keikaku* (Tokyo planning in the Meiji era). Tokyo: Iwanami Shoten.
—— (1986) *Architecture et Design de 1910 à 1945: Le Japon des Avant-Gardes 1910–1970*. Paris: Centre Pompidou.
Hasegawa J. (1995) '*Nihon ni okeru sensai fukkō toshi keikaku no sakutei: Ōsaka no jirei o chūshin ni*' (City reconstruction in Japan and the decisions on planning: with particular reference to the case of Osaka). Tokyo: Center for Business and Industrial Research, Hosei University (31 March).
Hein, C. (1998a) 'Uzō Nishiyama: the 'Godfather' of Japanese Housing and Planning.' Paper presented at the conference of the Society of Architectural

Historians in Los Angeles, April. Revised version published as: C. Hein (2000) *Nishiyama Uzō to Nihon ni okeru seiyō riron no denba* (Nishiyama Uzō and the spread of Western concepts in Japan). Tokyo: Inax Shuppan.

—— (1988b) 'Japan and the Transformation of Planning Ideas – Some Examples of Colonial Plans.' In R. Freestone, ed. 'The Twentieth Century Urban Planning Experience.' Proceedings of the 8th International Planning Society Conference and 4th Australian Planning and Urban History Conference, Sydney, 1998, pp. 352–57.

Hein, C., and Ishida Y. (1998) *Japanische Stadtplanung und ihre deutschen Wurzeln*. (Japanese urban planning and its German roots) *Die alte Stadt*. Stuttgart: Verlag W. Kohlhammer.

—— (1997) '*Machi* and *toshi*: cities' divisions in Japan.' Paper presented at the City Words conference, organized by the CNRS and UNESCO, in Paris, December.

Higasa T. (1977, 1985, 1986, 1992, 1993, 1996). *Toshi keikaku* (Urban planning), 3rd vol. Tokyo: Kyōritsu Shuppan.

Hiroshima City (1996) *Architectural Witnesses to the Atomic Bombing: A Record for the Future*. Hiroshima: Hiroshima Peace Memorial Museum.

Hiroshima Toshi Seikatsu Kenkyū Kai (1985) *Toshi no fukkō: Hiroshima hibaku 40 nen shi* (Reconstruction of Hiroshima: pictorial history of forty years since atomic bombing). Hiroshima: Hiroshima City.

Ishida Y. (1992a) '*Nihon toshi keikakushi ni okeru gurando dezain*, (Grand design in Japanese planning history.' *Toshi keikaku/City Planning Review* 175.

—— (1992b) *Mikan no Tōkyō keikaku* (Unfinished plans for Tokyo). Tokyo: Chikuma Shobō.

—— (1988a) *Tōkyō seichō to keikaku 1868–1988* (Tokyo growth and planning). Tokyo: Toritsu Daigaku Toshi Kenkyūjo.

—— (1988b) *Tokyo Urban Growth and Planning 1868–1988*. Tokyo: Tokyo Metropolitan University, Center for Urban Studies.

—— (1987a) '*Tōkyō shiku kaisei no shisō*' (The idea of the urban improvement of Tokyo). In *Nihon kindai toshi keikaku no hyakunen* (100 years of modern planning in Japan). Tokyo: Jichitai Kenkyūsha.

—— (1987b) *Nihon kindai toshi keikaku no hyakunen* (100 years of modern planning in Japan). Tokyo: Jichitai Kenkyūsha.

Ishikawa H. (1951) *(Shintei) Toshi keikaku oyobi kokudo keikaku* (Urban planning and national planning). Tokyo: Sangyō Tosho.

—— (1943) *100 nengo no toshi* (Cities in 100 years). In Ishikawa H. (ed.) *Toshi no seitai*. Tokyo: Shunjūsha.

Ishimaru N. *Post-War Reconstruction Planning in Hiroshima*, manuscript without date.

Itō G. (1942, 1943) *Nachisu doitsu no toshi keikaku* (Urban planning in Nazi Germany), *Kenchiku zasshi* November 1942 and January 1943.

Kasugai M. (1986) *Stadtentwicklungsprozesse in den Agglomerationsräumen Ōsaka und Frankfurt* (Urban development processes in the conglomerations of Ōsaka and Frankfurt). Beiträge der Fachgruppe Stadt, TH Darmstadt: Fachbereich Architektur.

Katsura H., Adachi K., and Zaino H. (1975, reprint 1988) *Toshi keikaku* (Urban planning). Tokyo: Morikita Shuppan.

Kawai Z., ed. (1976) '*Kindai Nihon toshi keikaku shi: hito to shisou – jōkyō*' (History of urban planning in modern Japan: people and ideas – conditions) *Toshi jūtaku*, TJ 7604 No. 102 Tokyo: Kajima Shuppankai.

Kawakami H. and Ishida Y. (1960) *Henbō suru toshi: toshi o mukaeta sengo Nihon no toshi keikaku* (Changing cities: Postwar urban planning in Japan as directed towards cities). Tokyo: Tokyo Bijutsu Shuppansha.

Kensetsushō (1959) *Sensai fukkōshi* (The history of war reconstruction). Tokyo: Toshi Keikaku Kyōkai.

Koshizawa A. (1991) *Manshū koku no shuto keikaku* (Capital city planning in Manchuria). Tōkyō: Nihon Keizai Hyōronsha.

—— (1990) *Harupin no toshi keikaku* (Urban planning of Harbin). Tokyo: Sōwasha.

Larsson G. (1993) *Land Readjustment*. Aldershot: Avebury.

Minerbi, L., P. Nakamura, K. Nitz, and J. Yanai (1986) *Land Readjustment: The Japanese System*. Boston, Mass: Oelgeschlager, Gunn + Hain.

Nagamine H. (1986) *Urban Development Policies and Programmes*. Nagoya: United Nations Centre for Regional Development.

Nagoya City Public Works Bureau (1991) *Nagoya shi sensai fukkō keikaku zu/ Reconstruction Plan of Nagoya 1946 After the War Damage*. Nagoya Municipal Government.

Nishiyama U. (1990) '*Bijon kara kōsō keikaku e*' (From vision to structural planning). In Nishiyama (ed.) *Machizukuri no kōsō* (The structure of community building). Tokyo: Toshi Bunkasha.

—— (1978) '*Sangaku toshi*' (Cities on mountain slopes). In Nishiyama (ed.) *Chiiki kūkan ron* (Reflections on urban, regional and national space). Tokyo: Keisō Shobō. (Original in *Atarashiki kokudo kensetsu, dai 3 hen, sankaku toshi-ron, Shinkenchiku*, June 1946).

—— (1975, 19 76, 1980) *Nihon no sumai* (Housing in Japan), 3 vols. Tokyo: Keisō Shobō.

—— (1968) '*Seikatsu kichi no kōsō*' (The structure of life-spheres). In Nishiyama (ed.) *Chiiki kūkan ron* (Reflections on urban, regional and national space). Tokyo: Keisō Shobō. (Original in *Kenchikugaku kenkyū* 110 and 111, 1942.)

—— (1943) '*Dai tōa seichi shukusai toshi keikaku an oboegaki*' (Plan for a holy and festival place for the Greater East Asian Co-prosperity Sphere). *Shinkenchiku* (January).

—— (1942) '*Dai tōa kensetsu kinen eizō keikaku*' (Design for the greater East Asian coprosperity sphere memorial place) *Kenchiku zasshi* (December).

Olmo, C., ed (1993) 'The Reconstruction in Europe after World War II.' *Rassegna* 54 (2).

Osaka City (1991) *Ōsaka no machizukuri, kinō, kyō, asu* (Community creation in Osaka, yesterday, today, tomorrow). Osaka: Ōsaka Shiyakusho.

—— (1958). *Ōsaka shi sensai fukkō shi* (The history of the reconstruction after the war in Osaka). Osaka: Ōsaka Shiyakusho.

Perry C. A. (1929) 'The Neighborhood Unit.' In *Regional Survey of New York and Its Environs*, vol. VII. New York: Committee on Regional Survey of New York and Its Environs.

Peace City Hiroshima, without place or date. Introduction: Mayor of Hiroshima

Riani, P. (1969) *Kenzō Tange*. London: Hamlyn.

Schumacher F. (1924) 'Der Plan zum Wiederaufbau von Tokyo,' *Deutsche Bauzeitung* 96, 29 (November): 33–37.

Shōji S. (1993) 'The Life of Hideaki Ishikawa.' *Toshi keikaku/City Planning Review* 182.

Stewart D. (1987) *The Making of a Modern Japanese Architecture: 1868 to the Present*. Tokyo: Kodansha International.

Takayama E. (1936) *Gaikoku ni okeru jūtaku shikichi wari ruireisyū* (A Collection of Plans for Housing Districts Abroad). Tokyo: Dōjunkai.

Takei K. (1958/1960) *Toshi keikaku* (Urban planning). Tokyo: Kyōritsu Shuppan.

Toshi Keikaku Gakkai (City Planning Institute of Japan) (1993) 'The Centennial Issue of the Birth of Dr. Hideaki Ishikawa.' *Toshi keikaku/City Planning Review* 182.
—— (1988) *Centenary of Modern City Planning and Its Perspective.* Tokyo: Shōkokusha.
Toshikeikaku Kyōiku Kenkyū Kai (1987/1995/1996), *Toshi keikaku kyōkasho*, vol. 2 (Urban planning textbook). Tokyo: Shōkokusha.
Utida Yosikazu Sensei Biju Shukaku Kinen Sakuhin Shū Kankō Kai (The Editors Group for 'Selected Works of Professor Utida Yosikazu in Architecture and Planning') (1969) *Utida Yosikazu Sensei sakuhin shū* (Collection of the works of Professor Utida Yosikazu) Tokyo: Kajima Kenkyūjo Shuppankai.
Watanabe S. (1980) 'Garden City Japanese Style: The Case of Den-en Toshi Company Ltd., 1918–28.' In G.E. Cherry, (ed.) *Shaping an Urban World: Planning in the 20th Century.* London: Mansell.

CHAPTER 12

Kyoto and the Preservation of Urban Landscapes

Yamasaki Masafumi, with Paul Waley

Introduction

Among the larger cities of Japan, Kyoto and Kanazawa are the only two that were not heavily damaged by air raids during World War II. Nevertheless, many of their historic buildings have been lost in the decades since. The municipal government and people of Kyoto have been working for the preservation and conservation of what remains. This effort, however, has been insufficient. If it has been insufficient, it is not for want of a regulatory framework. The contemporary conservation system for historic landscapes in and around Kyoto is made up of several layers, and the central ordinance regulating Kyoto's landscape was significantly altered in 1996. In this chapter, I will introduce the recent changes first, before examining two highly controversial developments that occurred shortly before the changes came into effect, and then finally travel forward again in time to consider some of the problems issuing from an anti-conservation ethos reflected in an underlying and implicit hostility to traditional wooden structures.

The origins of regulation to protect and preserve important historic buildings go back to the Meiji era, in the late nineteenth century. The prefectural government of Kyoto first started to control changes to its historic scenery in 1930, through the designation of Landscape Zones (*fūchi chiku*) covering about one quarter of the municipal area of Kyoto and surrounding areas to the west, north, and south. Landscape Zones had been included as one of several types of zones in the first City Planning Law, enacted in 1919. The purpose of these zones was to preserve both woodland and historic natural scenery. Kyoto's Landscape Zones included temples and the terrain around them at the base of the hills surrounding

Kyoto, hills that are visible from the central parts of the city. In these areas, the government retained considerable power to control or sometimes forbid development. After World War II, however, the implementation of city planning measures for Kyoto moved from the prefectural to the municipal government while national government retained control of the legislative framework.

The Preservation Systems for the Traditional Cityscape

From the mid 1960s, with development proceeding apace, the protection and conservation of historic districts and landscapes came to be regarded as an issue in many cities in Japan. In 1966, as a result of popular pressure, a new national law was enacted, known for short as the Old Capital Conservation Law (*Koto hozon hō*), covering Kyoto, Nara and other sites in the Yamato basin, and Kamakura. Under this national law, Kyoto designated sixty square kilometres of Conservation Zones for Historic Landscapes (*rekishiteki fūdo hozon chiku*), of which a growing proportion was singled out as being of special status, meaning that approval was needed for alterations to buildings rather than only a notification. In extreme cases, when a landowner wanted to develop his land in an unsuitable way, the municipality could buy the land to protect it (fig. 64).

It was at a local level that most activity occurred, both at the level of local government and that of professional city planners and architectural historians. This activity reached its peak around 1970. The cities of Kurashiki and Kanazawa were the first to pass ordinances for the protection of historic townscapes in the late 1960s. Then a few years later, in 1972, the municipal government of Kyoto passed its own ordinance, but here it was intended to make it more comprehensive and have it include a control system for big new buildings besides the preservation of historic townscapes. The Urban Landscape Ordinance (*Shigaichi keikan jōrei*) brought into being three new zones: an aesthetic zone (*bikan chiku*) in which the design of buildings was controlled, a zone for the preservation and visual restoration of the townscape (*tokubetsu hozen shūkei chiku*), and a zone for the regulation of large structures other than buildings (*kyodai kōsakubutsu kisei chiku*). The last type of zone was created after the bitter experience of the 131 meter high Kyoto Tower, the construction of which had gone ahead because it was not regarded as a building and so not controlled by the Architectural Standards Code.

In 1975, the national government enacted a system for the preservation of historic townscapes through a revision of the Law for the Protection of Cultural Properties (*Bunkazai hogo hō*). This involved the creation of what are known officially in English as Important Conservation Districts for Groups of Historic Buildings (*jūyō dentōteki kenzōbutsugun hozon chiku*).

Kyoto and the Preservation of Urban Landscapes

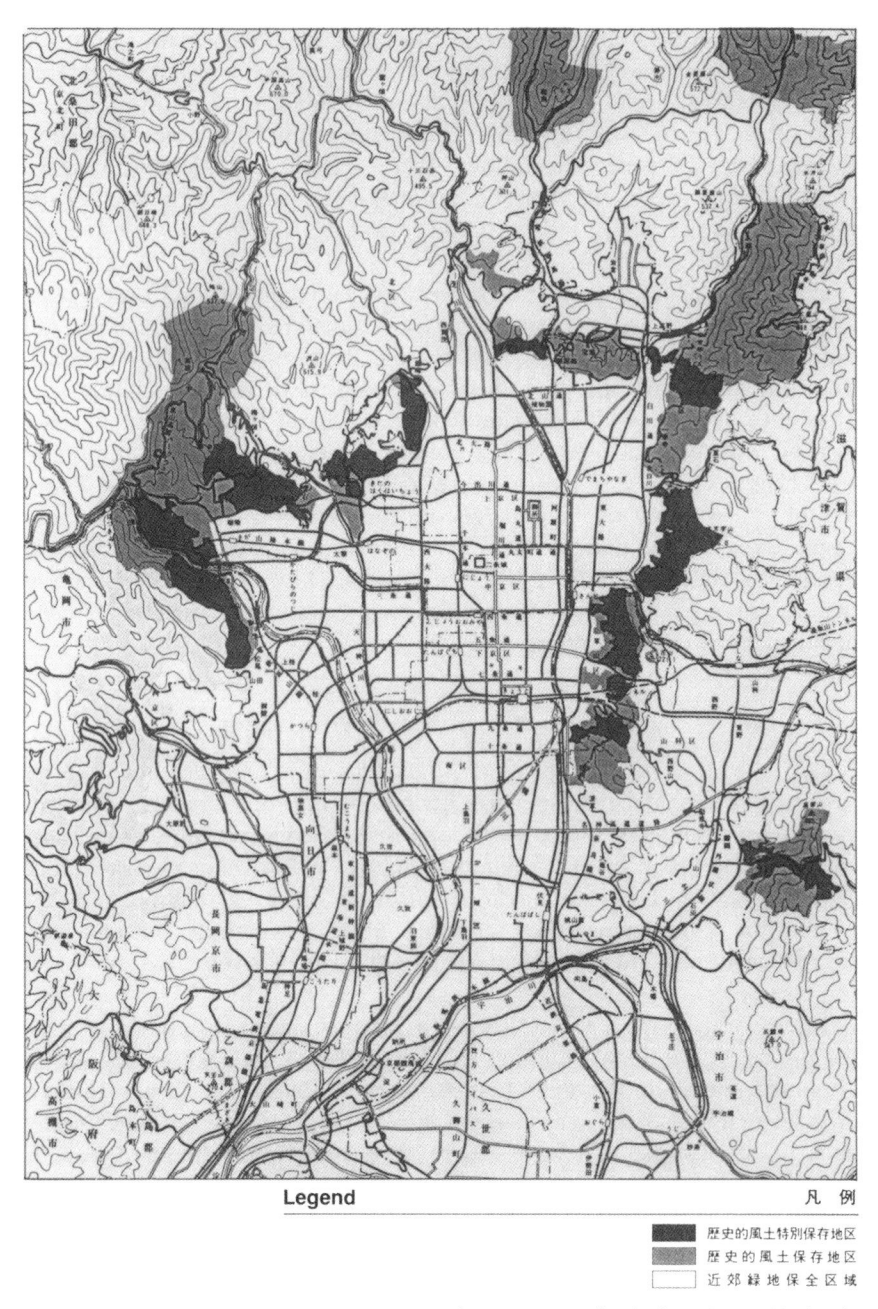

Figure 64 Map showing Conservation Zones and Preservation of Suburban Green Districts in and around Kyoto.

Originally, officials at the Agency of Cultural Affairs (Bunkachō) had been keen to respect the regional characteristics and conditions enabling historic towns to be preserved. Each regional government had been left to preserve (or not) its own urban landscapes as it chose, through its own ordinances. In Kyoto's case, this was the Urban Landscape Ordinance, which applied to the three types of zones listed above. As a result of the 1975 revision to the Cultural Properties Law, however, national standards were drafted for the Important Conservation Districts, and regional governments were strongly expected to respect them.

Four districts in Kyoto have now been designated Important Conservation Districts, and these are accordingly administered through municipal ordinance under the national Law for the Protection of Cultural Assets. The four are Sanneizaka and Gion Shinbashi (designated in 1976), Saga Toriimoto (1979), and Kamigamo Shakemachi (1988). The Sanneizaka district was extended in 1995, giving a total area for the four of 14.9 hectares. The first two of these had been designated Special Zones for the Preservation and Visual Restoration of the Townscape (*tokubetsu hozen shūkei chiku*) under the 1972 municipal ordinance. Now all four are designated under the national law. They remain, however, under the care of the urban landscape section of the department of city planning and not the department of cultural affairs.

The Kyoto Style of Facade Preservation

Back in the late 1960s and early 1970s, the question had been how historic townscapes should be preserved. Officials of the municipal government, aware that architects tended to be opposed to conservation at this time, consulted the urban history laboratory led by Professor Nishikawa Kōji at Kyoto University. I was among those consulted. The method of preservation of historic townscapes then adopted after discussions between the consulting group and the municipal government of Kyoto was unique in some respects.

In drawing up the 1972 ordinance it was decided that only the style of the facade of traditional buildings such as *machiya* (town-houses) should be preserved, giving up the idea of conserving buildings themselves with their original materials. The reason for this was that wooden buildings easily become rotten and tend to have structural problems in one hundred years or so unless they are well made buildings with comparatively big timber frames such as temples or the town-houses of wealthy merchants. At the same time, it was a basic tenet that a town should appear active and lively and that its buildings should not be preserved merely in order to maintain a museum atmosphere. It was made possible in the 1972 ordinance to demolish old buildings if they were to be replaced by facades with historic designs made of traditional materials. This approach to preservation was clearly different from that adopted for individually designated cultural properties, and, as we have seen, within Important Conservation Districts, it was to some extent superseded by the new approach stemming from the Cultural Properties Law.

Sanneizaka district near Kiyomizu temple was selected as the first place to be designated under the 1972 ordinance. A number of typical models were abstracted and classified according to the type of second floor facade they had – for example, low second floors with heavily mullioned windows (*mushiko*) or tall second floor facades with wooden lattice works (*kōshi*). Then each type was classified into the open shop type and house type with openings covered with *kōshi*. New facade designs with glass windows were prepared for each type, to be adopted by restaurants or coffee shops built to cater for the increase of tourists anticipated after the start of preservation work. With three basic types of facade – full open facade, half open facade with glass windows, and the closed facade with *kōshi* – it was expected that it would be possible for people to construct buildings for any use in the preservation district.

The adjustment of the townscape was planned to be achieved over a considerable period of time in an organic process dictated by the needs of property owners to repair or rebuild. The municipal government prepared a grant to give to the owners of buildings in the preservation districts, due to the fact that wooden facades cost more to maintain than contemporary buildings. This method of preservation is still in force, with one significant exception. To comply with the 1975 legislation, old buildings in preservation districts are designated as traditional buildings. The original facade and structure must be maintained in line with instructions from the Cultural Affairs Agency, and repairs must be carried out at a time that accords with government plans (fig. 65).

The 1996 Ordinance for the Regulation of the Urban Landscape

The Kyoto Urban Landscape Ordinance of 1972 was greatly amended in 1996. Its name was changed to the Ordinance for the Regulation of the Urban Landscape (*Shigaichi keikan seibi jōrei*). The new ordinance has brought into being the followed revised zones.

(A) Zoning for Control of the Urban Landscape

The control of the cityscape is basically operated through zoning systems and designated districts. This basic zoning can be divided into three categories, of which this is the first. Districts covered by these zoning systems can be considered important, either as a result of their history and cultural significance or of their geographical centrality. These areas are designated by the city government in accord with the 1996 ordinance.

Place Between Future and Past

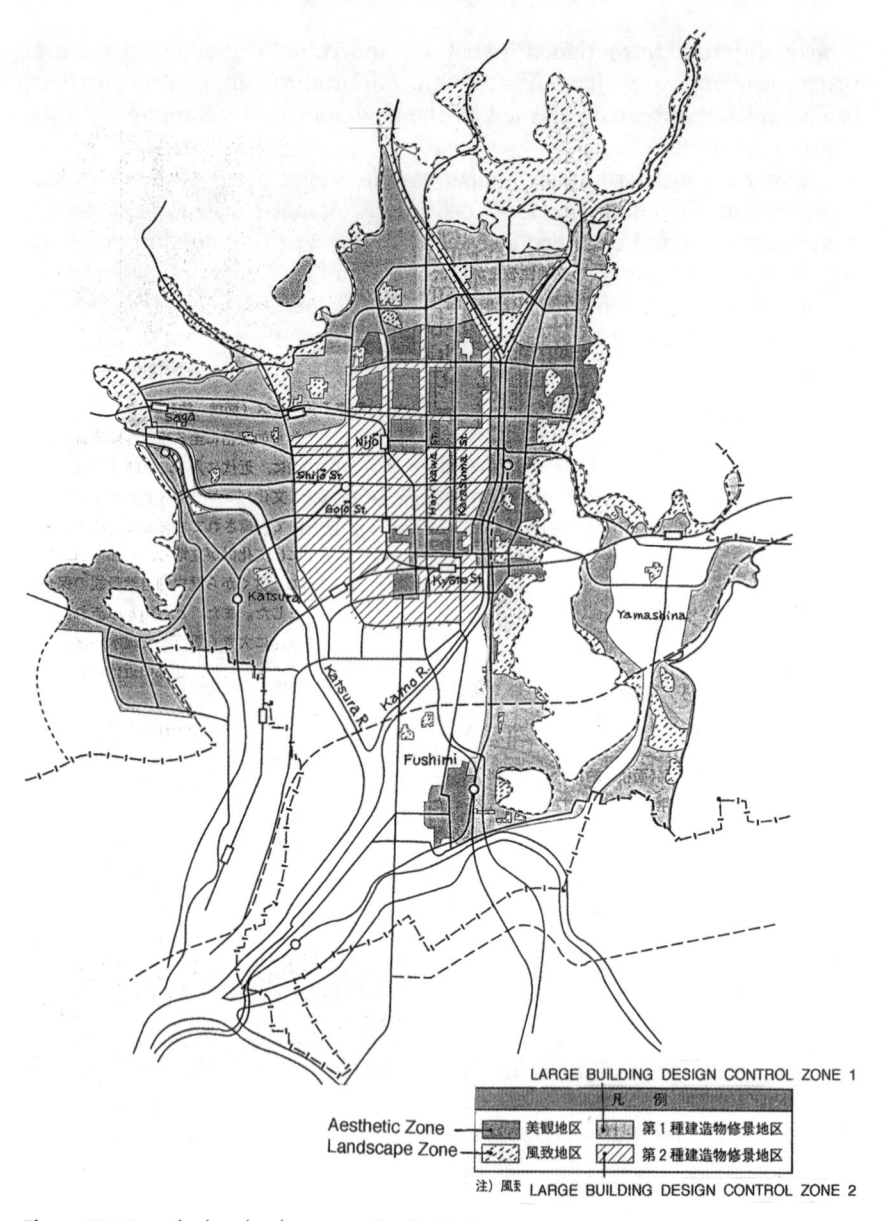

Figure 65 Map of urban landscape zoning in Kyoto.

(A–1) Aesthetic Zone (*bikan chiku*): These areas, extending over 1,804 hectares, correspond to those defined by the 1972 ordinance, and they are designated under national legislation, but the details of operation as stipulated by this ordinance are conducted according to local decisions.

352

Within these areas controls are placed on the design of buildings so as to conserve urban landscapes. Aesthetic zones are made up of five categories, two of which were in the 1972 ordinance. They include some of the most important landmarks and the terrain around them, the historic area in and around Nishijin famous for the production of fabrics for kimono, the area between the Kamo river and Higashiyama, and Fushimi, which was originally a castle town located south of Kyoto. The design standards for buildings are given in the ordinance, and there are common standards for all the categories and standards for each category (fig. 66).

(A–2) Buildings and Townscape Adjustment Zone (*kenzōbutsu shūkei chiku*): This designation covers 6,873 hectares in which the construction of buildings over twelve meters high involves notifying the mayor. In parts of these areas (Category 1), buildings over twelve meters tall need approval from the city government, while in other parts (Category 2) this applies to buildings over twenty meters tall. These designations susbsume the aesthetic zones and are wider in the amount of land they cover. The areas close to the surrounding hills are designated as Category 1. Most southern areas of the city are outside the designated areas. The city government plans to promote higher density development in the south of the city with a laxer regulatory regime (figs. 67 and 68).

(B) Additional Zones for Control of the Urban Landscape

The following zones consist of much smaller districts where either local residents or the government wish to enforce conservation rules or acquire a measure of control over the cityscape in the neighbourhood. Even if these places are small and relatively insignificant, they can be legally protected by the following designations, which are authorized by the city government. While grants are not available for buildings in aesthetic zones, funds can be accessed for work on buildings in the following areas.

(B–1) Roadside Landscape Formation Zone (*endō keikan keisei chiku*): This designation is intended to aid in the creation of better contemporary streetscapes along main roads in the central area of Kyoto. A section of Oike avenue between Kiyama and Horikawa has been proposed for this category.

(B–2) Historic Landscape Preservation and Adjustment Zone (*rekishiteki keikan hozen shūkei chiku*): The name is different but this designation is almost the same as the former Special Zones for the Preservation and Visual Restoration of the Townscape (*tokubetsu hozen shūkei chiku*). This designation was created to promote the preservation of historical townscapes usually composed of those town-houses that are not suitable for preservation under the strict regulatory framework of the Conservation Districts for Groups of Historic Buildings. A more flexible method for conservation is applied in this zoning system. For example, construction of a three storey building in a traditional style would be allowed in this designation. Details

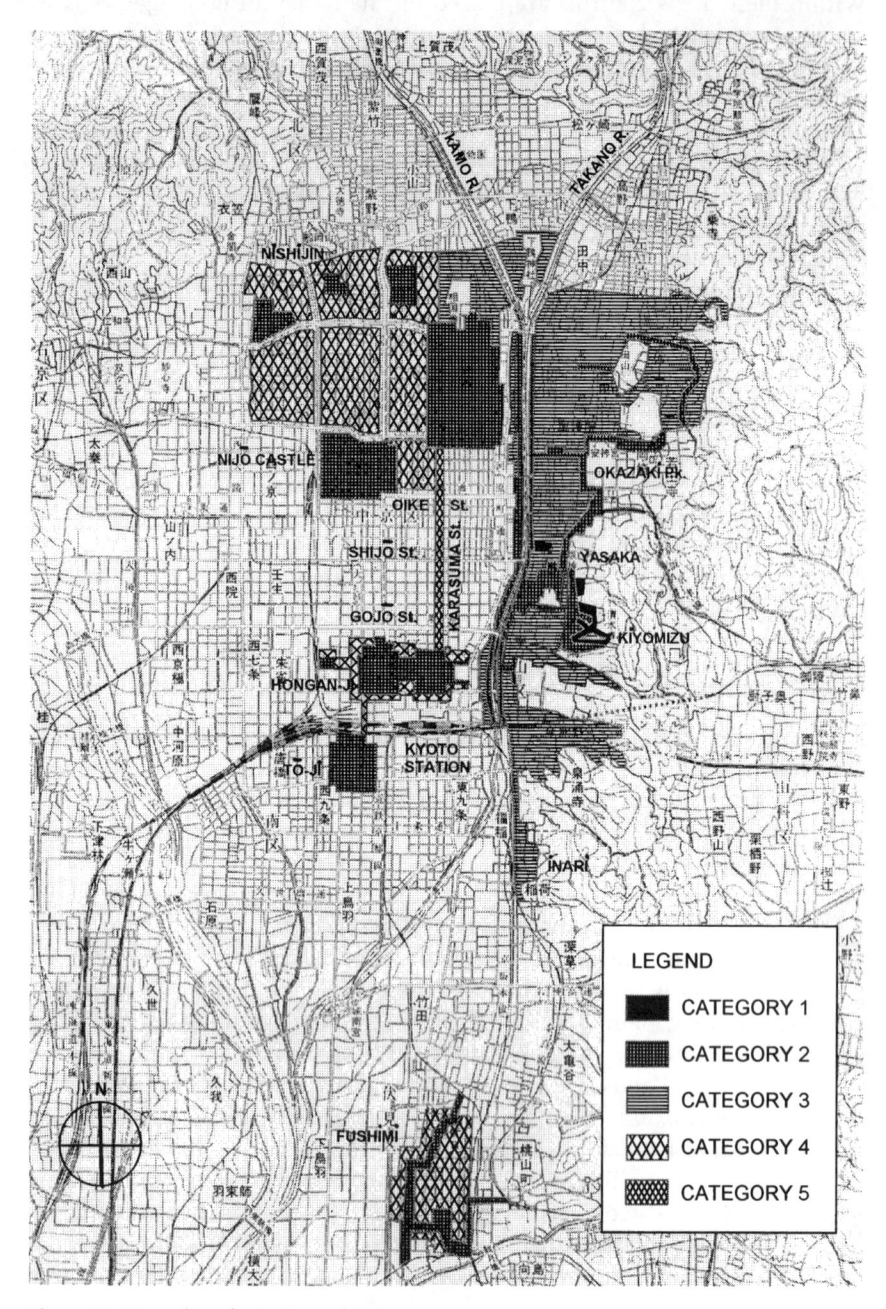

Figure 66 Map of Aesthetic Zones in Kyoto.

Kyoto and the Preservation of Urban Landscapes

美観地区の種別景観整備イメージ

ADJUSTMENT MODELS FOR AESTHETIC ZONES

第1種地域　京風町屋の町並み景観の保全・整備
1　Conservation and adjustment of Kyoto style street-scape

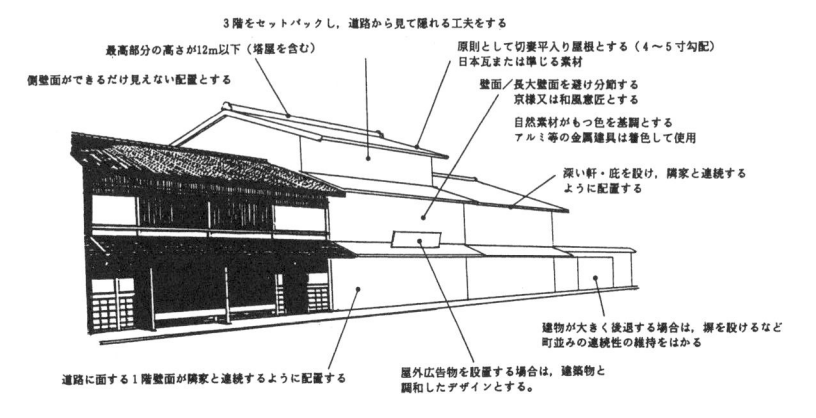

第2種地域　歴史的建造物と調和する和風町並み景観の整備
2　Creation of harmony with historic buildings

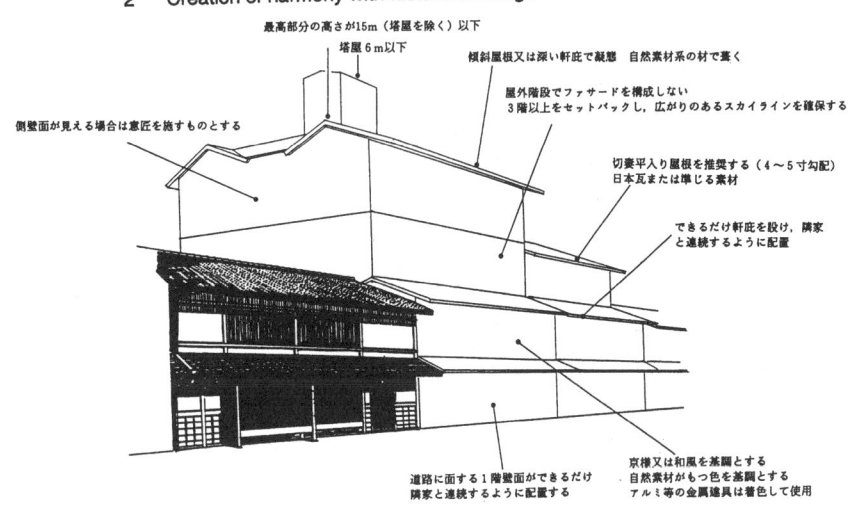

Figure 67 Adjustment models for Aesthetic Zones 1 and 2.

Place Between Future and Past

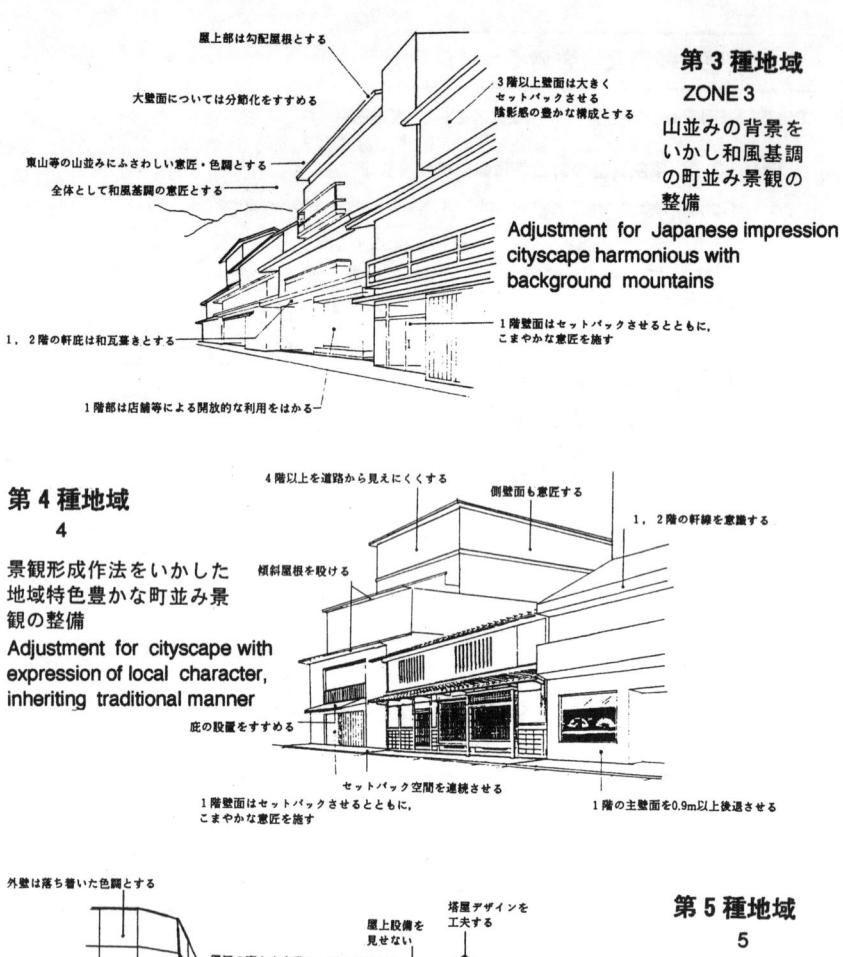

第 3 種地域
ZONE 3

山並みの背景を
いかし和風基調
の町並み景観の
整備

Adjustment for Japanese impression cityscape harmonious with background mountains

第 4 種地域
4

景観形成作法をいかした
地域特色豊かな町並み景
観の整備

Adjustment for cityscape with expression of local character, inheriting traditional manner

第 5 種地域
5

中高層建築物の群と
しての構成美の整備

Adjustment for harmony and beauty of composition of high-rise buildings

Figure 68 Adjustment models for Aesthetic Zones 3, 4, and 5.

356

for design control are made independently for each district. The residents can get grants at the time of repair or construction of their houses.

(B–3) Historic Atmosphere Regulation Zone (*kaiwai keikan seibi chiku*): Districts with specific features or distinctive characteristics such as those in front of temples or clusters of shops selling traditional articles are to be protected to maintain the traditional feel of the district. In this case the municipal government designates some important buildings or scenically unusual places, and grants are made available. Three zones were selected: Sanjō-dōri (6 hectares), Kamigamo (22 hectares), and Fushimi (25 hectares).

(B–4) Buildings with Historic Designs (*rekishiteki ishō kenzōbutsu*): Where a house is considered historical but not worthy enough to be designated as a cultural asset, or where the owner does not want to have the property designated as a cultural asset, it is now possible for the city government to give support through the provision of grants and advice. Flexible ways to make the buildings last longer are applied. This system is applied only to individual buildings, but the city government can use it is as a way of preserving the urban landscape. The traditional atmosphere in the central area of the city largely depends on the existence of town-houses (*machiya*), even if they are no longer to be seen in a row.

(C) Support for Urban Landscape Agreements

This is a new system designed to support any community that intends to conserve or otherwise look after its neighbourhood. The city government sends a specialist to help the community draw up the agreement (*kyōtei*). Thus, these agreements, known as *shigaichi keikan kyōtei*, are generally authorized by the city government.

Conservation of the Hills Surrounding the City

The surrounding hills of Kyoto are called Sanzan, or three mountains: Higashiyama to the east, Kitayama to the north, and Nishiyama to the west. There are no hills to the south of the Kyoto basin. These mountainous areas are protected by several superimposed systems. The municipal government's Urban Landscape Ordinance of 1972 was accompanied by a second ordinance that controlled developments in the Landscape Zones (*fūchi chiku*). The original, national law had left regulatory methods to local government. In Landscape Zones the proportion of land covered by buildings is strictly restricted in order to protect the landscape, this being the main purpose of the law. At the same time it has been used to control building designs to preserve the historic atmosphere around temples. The degree of control exercised was quite strict for some years. Afterwards it grew less so, as the national government issued new national standards that were weaker compared to those in place in Kyoto.

In 1995 the city government introduced a new Kyoto Natural Landscape Preservation Ordinance (*Kyōto-shi shizen fūkei hozen jōrei*). This ordinance widens the old Landscape Areas, reinforces the regulation of these areas, and makes it possible for the government to buy land if necessary. Many of these areas, especially those composed of important landmarks and the natural environment located at the foot of the hills that surround the city, had been designated as Special Conservation Zones for Historic Landscapes (*rekishiteki fūdo tokubetsu hozon chiku*) under the 1966 Old Capitals Conservation Law.

This is not the only system operating to protect the landscape of the hills surrounding Kyoto. Under the 1968 Town Planning Act (*Toshi keikaku hō*), this is an Urbanization Control Area (*shigaika chōsei kuiki*), with the result that development activities are severely circumscribed (but not altogether prohibited). Some western parts of the hills are protected under a law for the Preservation of Suburban Green Districts (*kinkō ryokuchi hozen kuiki*) (fig. 64). The city government found, however, that it was still difficult properly to protect the surrounding hills even with all of these laws. As a result, it declared most them Areas for the Preservation of Natural Beauty. With this designation the city government can compel landowners to plant trees and impose a severer penalty on illegal developers than under other laws.

All these complicated systems suggest that much of the legislation to protect green areas is actually weak. It also shows that the people of Kyoto have been very concerned about the protection of the surrounding hills. In comparison, measures to protect central historical areas of town have lagged behind. This may indeed be one of the characteristic features of Japanese culture in the modern age, showing that the Japanese respect natural areas while believing in the modernization and 'westernization' of urban districts – even in Kyoto.

Kyoto Hotel and Planned Development Design System

Much thought went into the preparation of the 1996 ordinance, and the whole system for the conservation of the traditional cityscape is much more comprehensive than it once was (I participated in the preparation of the draft). Two particularly controversial developments showed how urgent was the need for a more thorough system. We will now briefly examine these issues before moving onto a concluding discussion of the problems that remain to be solved before a truly effective conservation policy can be adopted. The two controversies concern the reconstruction of the Kyoto Hotel and the Kyoto Station Building. Today these two buildings cast their gigantic silhouettes over the historic townscape of the city. While the basic problem might be shared, these two controversies exposed contradictory processes and systems for the control of the townscape. There was a lively discussion among citizens about these huge buildings, all of which had an important impact on the drafting of the 1996 ordinance, but the causes of these controversies have yet to be properly analysed.

The new Kyoto Hotel was able to rise sixty meters above the surface of the city without infringing any legislation. It could do this because it adhered to the Planned Development Design System (*sōgō sekkei seido*). This is a system of planning gains that allows for the relaxation of city planning regulations so long as certain conditions are met, including the construction of an open public space in the form of a garden. The extra floors are the obvious bonus for developers. Open public space would be its biggest merit in the eyes of government officials. It is a national system applied all over Japan. In the case of the Kyoto Hotel plans, the Kyoto city office decided to relax the height limitations together with the regulations covering the floor to plot size ratio, making it possible to build a building fifty per cent higher than the height regulations would normally allow despite the design difficulties in creating a public garden beside a building of this size. Nevertheless, the site stood on the very spot where an entrance staircase to a station on the new underground line as well as a new underground shopping mall and car park had been planned.

Kyoto Hotel was a case in which the deregulatory approach to planning had serious repercussions for the townscape. The hotel is near the Kamo river and the Higashiyama hills, some of which are only about fifty meters high. The ensuing protests from Kyoto residents and others concerned about the preservation of the city's historical landscape was predictable. And equally predictable was the eventual outcome, the failure of the protests to halt or radically modify the construction of the hotel. The idea of the planned development system itself seems unsuitable for historic towns. One problem is the centralization of the government system in Japan. But it is also true that it is not only central government officials and others in Tokyo but also many of the city planning specialists in regional governments who believe in making cities with open spaces and skyscrapers like those the early modernist architects dreamed of.

Kyoto Station Building and the 1200th Anniversary of the Historic Capital

It seems natural that an authority feels like constructing a monument at the time of an important anniversary, even if it is difficult to pinpoint the precise necessity (see the chapter in this book by Iwatake). The year 1994 was the 1200th anniversary of the establishment of the capital of Heian-kyō, the first name for Kyoto, and so was a prime candidate for a monument. While many ceremonies and events were planned for the anniversary, the municipality was not wealthy enough to build a monument by itself. The national government had no plans to help Kyoto financially for this anniversary. It has consistently taken the line that Kyoto is to be treated as merely one of Japan's regional cities. Only the West Japan Railway Company was ready to undertake a monumental project to be completed in the year of the anniversary.

An international competition was held for the design of the project. The competition rules called for the design of a very big building. The actual railway station was to occupy only five percent of it. A department store would occupy most of the rest, and an auditorium was to be added. Citizens movements emerged to oppose the project. Argument revolved almost exclusively around plans to waive restrictions on the height of the building. I heard many professional planners and architects say that those campaigning against the building were doing so on trivial grounds because the height of the building was merely one of many characteristics to be debated, including its shape, color, and other factors. I personally think that the height of the building has a special meaning when it is twice as tall as other buildings in the city. Such a monument is destined to become a symbol for the whole city. The prominent height of a building has a special hold over people. The existing limit on the height of buildings in the area of Kyoto Station was only thirty-one meters. The Planned Development Design System would allow for a height of forty-five meters, but it was impossible to accommodate the desired floor area within these limits. The City Planning Bureau promised that the city planning regulations would be changed to suit the winner's design for the building. However, no research was conducted to determine the impact of a giant building at this location.

A number of famous international architects submitted their designs. The jury selected Hara Hiroshi's entry, which was in the loud controversial movement. Hara's building, a little lower than 60 meters high, was the lowest among the proposed designs but was as long as 470 meters. It was, and remains, an extremely big building within the context of Kyoto. The City Planning Bureau designated the site a Special Zoning Urban Block Area (*tokutei gaiku*) to enable it to be built legally. This makes it possible to introduce new land use regulations for this one block, and even building controls are treated in an exceptional way.

The municipality of Kyoto had made it a policy in the 1960s to control development in the central and northern parts of the city to preserve the historic townscape and to promote development in southern areas. The border was formed by the Tōkaidō railway line on which Kyoto Station Building is located. This had been a policy accepted by local citizens. The new Kyoto Station Building, however, runs contrary to this policy. Like a great wall, this building stands on the north side of the railway facing the northern part of the city. It shows its long rear wall to the southern part of town, looking to all the world like the southern boundary of the city. This is the sense it will give to Kyoto's inhabitants in the future. I have heard young people say that Kyoto Tower is the representative symbol of their native city, which sees them off when they leave Kyoto and welcomes them when they return. This role will be transferred to the gigantic Kyoto Station Building from now on. It will deeply influence the imaginations of future generations of inhabitants of the city. The new building might well give people the impression that it is the realization of the ideal of the future city dreamed of in the mid twentieth century – an optimistic belief in large scale structures, functionalism, and an aesthetic of appreciation of the astonishingly new. In this sense the Kyoto Station Building will have a much bigger influence on the future of the city than Kyoto Hotel.

It is to be regretted that the national government did not help Kyoto with this opportunity to create a monumental development in the southern part of the city. It could have been a key project to spur development in the south leaving the north historical. The national government, apparently, is not interested in conservation of the historical environment of Kyoto.

The Kyoto Station Building project has had an unexpected impact on the city. As the enlarged store was almost twice as big as other existing department stores in Kyoto, the two major rivals have expanded their floor space. The total floor area of these department stores is now twice what it was before. We now see small stores disappearing from the streets as a result. This development pattern is contrary to that of some European countries, where the conservation of attractive historical streets is respected. There is as yet no consensus for the future image of the city of Kyoto. It is difficult but necessary to have a real creative imagination to dream a future image of a Japanese city. In the concluding section to this chapter, we will try to find out a few of the reasons why this should be so.

The Property Owner's Right to Say No

The belief is widespread in Japan that a person can do anything they want with their property, build anything they wish on their land. In a sense this is true. Except for in the stricter category of residential zones, which are generally concentrated on the outskirts of a city, it is normally possible to build a building as tall as four or five storeys high, even when most of the surrounding structures are wooden houses two storeys high. Perhaps we are to find an explanation for this state of affairs in the desire to modernize Japan as quick as possible at the beginning of the modern era. Anyone who had the wealth and the opportunity to build a tall modern or western style building was expected to do so even if it was in a very traditional district with two storey buildings.

The strongly held belief in the rights of the property owner help to explain why the agreement of the owner of a building is needed before it can be designated a cultural asset. If the owner is disinclined to preserve his or her dwelling as a historic house, no one can force the issue. The Agency of Cultural Affairs obliges local governments to obtain the agreement of all the landowners of a district before designating it a Conservation District, making such a designation difficult in many places. In Kyoto, residents have tended to be sympathetic, but this has not been the case in towns such as Sakamoto district in Ōtsu city, Shiga prefecture, not far east of Kyoto. There, the designation of a Preservation District had to wait nineteen years after the initial investigation because a few persons out of about two hundred residents were opposed. The municipal government ended up by designating half of the district after giving up on the other half when they could not get the agreement of all of the residents.

Of course, it is not necessarily the case that a landowner can build whatever he or she wants. Urban land and the buildings built on it are subject to the usual planning regulations, affecting such matters as plot size to floor ratio, land coverage ratio, and the function of the building. The preferences of landowners are not always respected. When land use zones are considered for redesignation, the plans are shown to the public for a certain period before changes are executed. The government has strong powers when it comes to moving people away to build a road or some other public facility, although in fact it seldom uses them. As far as the aesthetic of scenery is concerned, however, the right of the landowner is very well protected. The landowner's use of the space over his land is largely unrestricted as long as he or she does not neglect a small number of regulations clearly written in the statute books. Usually the regulations are prepared by the government, often after a consultation exercise led by a committee composed of people of experience and academic standing (*gakushiki keikensha*).

The national government in Tokyo dislikes obstructing the right of private property owners. This is an outstanding difference between the Japanese and the Europeans, whose designation of historic monuments and conservation districts is in most cases effected without regard to the opinion of residents. In the United States, a number of cities have ordinances on the preservation of historic districts, again without the necessity of obtaining the prior agreement of local residents. The Japanese government has seen old buildings as antithetical to a smooth and quick process of modernization. It has designated only a small number of buildings as cultural assets or historical monuments compared with European countries and the United States. These few are to be preserved entirely as exceptions while all other buildings are to be modernized.

The picture in Europe could not be more different. In France, for example, the *Architectes des Bâtiments de France* have great power in controlling and conserving historical sites. All alterations to building designs and plans for new buildings need their permission within a radius of five hundred meters of a designated monument and in all conservation districts. The rules governing acceptable design are not written down. In Britain, planning policy is shown in the form of a plan rather than as regulations. This means that land owners do not know what they can build on their land until their application for development has been considered and the local government officers have decided what is acceptable for the site. The officers have strong powers of discretion over private plots of land. Similar powers are also held by government officials in other European countries, but this situation would be regarded as unacceptable within a Japanese context, where most property owners will not abide by any decision that affects their building differently from that next door. They demand 'even treatment.' This sense of the rights of property owners causes serious difficulties for conservation in Japan.

The Problem of Protecting Views and Surroundings

These problems of policy and attitude find expression in serious inadequacies involving the rules that govern the protection of the surroundings of the city itself and of its historic buildings on the one hand and the conservation of the buildings themselves on the other. As we have already seen, the importance of preserving the hills around Kyoto has been widely recognized. But this awareness has not been reflected in recent policy decisions, as the case of the Kyoto Hotel made amply clear. The city government has failed to protect the views out toward important landmarks such as Yasaka pagoda or the slope of Mount Daimonji, on which bonfires are lit in an annual festival. The view of the much loved Higashiyama hills from the bank of the Kamo river will also soon be lost. In 1972, research was conducted on how to protect this view. It was found that buildings along the Kamo river should be less than two storeys high, but it was considered impossible to persuade people to accept this height restriction. At that time, the government gave up on protecting the view. It is still possible to protect the view of Mount Daimonji or some other parts of the hills from certain viewpoints such as from famous bridges. Important unprotected views exist not only in Kyoto but in other parts of the country too. Indeed, the protection of views is an urgent issue throughout Japan.

A similar problem affects the protection of the immediate surroundings of historic buildings. Such cultural assets almost always exist alone without any buffer zone. On the same site as a temple where an important cultural asset is located, we sometimes find brash modern buildings. Frequently we see inharmoniously designed and unattractive buildings next door to a designated building or a historic garden. Moreover, without some form of protection, no one can tell when a large apartment house will appear in the background of a quiet temple garden.

The old Landscape Zones (*fūchi chiku*) originally introduced in 1930 cover some of the sites of temples and shrines and a small surrounding area. The more extensive Aesthetic Zones (*bikan chiku*) cover many of the historic buildings in the centre of town and their immediate surroundings. Among these buildings are the old Imperial Palace, Nijō Castle, Higashi

Honganji and Nishi Honganji temples, and Tōji temple. Fortunately quite a few cultural assets are located in Landscape Zones, and in other cases in residential areas where the construction of large buildings is forbidden under normal land use zoning regulations. There are however many other historic buildings and gardens whose immediate surroundings are unprotected. It would appear desirable that buffer zones be set around these cultural assets, but it is often argued, especially by government officials, that local residents would not agree to regulations that benefited others and not themselves. If this were the case, then some consciousness-raising exercise would be in order.

The Problem with Wooden Buildings and Narrow Streets

The fundamental tendency of city planning in Kyoto is towards modernization of the historic central areas through the construction of big buildings in precisely those areas where many traditional town-houses still stand. Indeed, I would argue that one of the fundamental targets of city planning in Kyoto seems to be to erase the traditional *machiya* houses from the central historical area. The most central part of the city is an area known informally as Ta-no-ji district after the grid pattern of the Chinese character (*ji*) for a field (*ta*), bordered by Kawaramachi avenue in the east, Horikawa avenue in the west, Oike avenue in the north, and Gojō avenue in the south, with Karasuma and Shijō avenues dissecting it. The Ta-no-ji district is entirely a commercial district. The permitted plot size to floor ratio is 700 per cent along the main streets and 400 per cent on backstreets, where many traditional *machiya* houses are located, including the most beautiful ones (the plot size to floor ratio is also affected by the width of the road on which the building stands). Taller buildings make more commercial sense.

There are a whole range of obstacles to the successful conservation of wooden town-houses in Kyoto, some of which obstacles, such as the inheritance tax, are examined by Kinoshita Ryōichi in his chapter. There are, however, a number of additional difficulties relating to planning regimes that I would like to discuss here. In the first place come the various fire regulations. It is forbidden to construct new buildings in traditional *machiya* style in historic urban areas of Kyoto. This is for protection against fire. Almost all the historic urban areas of Kyoto fall within Fire Protection Category 2. In these areas the construction of wooden buildings is permitted, but it is forbidden to make wooden frame doors or windows within three meters of the border of the site or the center of the road. Wooden lattice work on the facades is, as we have seen, one of the representative designs of the *machiya*, but it is forbidden in almost all the areas of urbanized Kyoto. It is only allowed in the suburban areas. If you see a new *machiya* house with beautiful *kōshi*, it is illegally constructed.

Efforts to protect cities against fire are of course right. We have the chemical process to make inflammable wood, but it is ignored by the law. The law has turned its back on wood as a material. The Historic Buildings Preservation Districts give the impression of forbidding many activities, but it is more a case of their 'allowing' the construction of fully wooden buildings only in designated districts. Not only this, wooden buildings are limited by means of scale too. The Building Standards Law (*Kenchiku kijun hō*) forbids the construction of wooden buildings over thirteen meters high except according to structural standards that do not conform to traditional Japanese temple and town-house architecture. This law is applied all over Japan. When one intends to build a tea-house in the traditional style, one has to make a false application to the government, saying the structure will be used for storage only. This is because the height of the ceiling of the traditional tea-house is too low and infringes the Building Standards Law.

Hand in hand with the problem of preserving wooden buildings goes that of safeguarding the intimate atmosphere of narrow roads. The Building Standards Law stipulates that a building should be set two meters back from the center of the road where the road is narrower than four meters (article 42). This means that narrow streets with a characteristic atmosphere, such as those of Ponto-chō, are under pressure. Ponto-chō along the Kamo river is one of the most attractive places in Kyoto, with traditional *machiya* houses and refined *kōshi* windows. Not only in Ponto-chō but also occasionally in other parts of town we come upon the intimate, agreeable space of narrow roads. This unexpected pleasure will no longer exist in the future.

Would it be really impossible to make a safe city with narrow roads in certain limited districts? Is it beyond the capacity of government to come up with a few simple solutions such as small fire cars, emergency water supplies, or an emergency access road? Most of these issues should be solved by the national government, but at the same time the citizens of Kyoto should become more aware of these issues and make their opinions known.

These various problems exist for at least two basic reasons. In the first place, the functionalists' ideas of city planning are still alive and well, a holdover from the time of Japan's postwar rehabilitation and the reconstruction of those cities destroyed by air raids (amongst whose number Kyoto is not to be found). Planners and developers inhabit and reproduce a world inimical to conservation. How can we continue the tradition of wooden building in the face of hostile national laws drafted so as to force us to abandon our tradition of wooden architecture? This should be one of the basic issues of contemporary Japanese culture. In the second place, the national laws for city planning and building standards are common to all Japanese cities including both postwar modern cities and historic towns such as Kyoto and Kanazawa. The process of conservation, whether of rural, suburban, or urban landscapes as well as of individual buildings, historical or modern, is beset with obstacles because the basic premise of social activity still rests on development-oriented systems. In the economic climate of contemporary Japan, we can hope that both the government and the people will eventually shift from a development-oriented approach to a more thoughtful system of conservation, control, and renewal of our environment.

References

Fukushima N. (1990) 'A study of landscape zones in Kyoto.' In *Toshi kenkyū, Kyōto* 2: 84–96.

Kyoto City Government, Department of Cityscape (ed.) (1996) *The Cityscape of Kyōto: Conservation, Revitalization and Creation.* Kyoto: Kyoto City Government.

—— (1993). *The Research Report of the Review of the Scenic Control Systems of Kyōto.* Kyoto: Kyoto City Government.

Kyoto Prefectural Goverment, Department of City Planning (ed.) (1990) *The Guide Book for the Control of Scenic Zoning.* Reprinted in 1990 by The Section of the Scenic Control. Kyoto: Kyoto City Government.

Yamasaki M. (1994) 'The Movement of Preservation for the Historic Townscape from the View Point of Imaichō.' In Watanabe S. (ed.) *The Townscape of Imai.* Kyoto: Dohosha Shuppan, pp. 141–8.

Yamasaki M. (ed.) (1994) 'Kyoto, its Cityscape Traditions and Heritage.' *Process Architecture* 116.

CHAPTER 13

Preservation and Revitalization of *machiya* in Kyoto

Kinoshita Ryōichi

Kyoto is on the verge of extinction as a historic city. Although wars, great fires, and natural disasters frequently devastated the ancient capital of Kyoto, it was always able to rebuild and reestablish itself as the great cultural center of Japan. The destruction during the last half of this century, however, is not a result of war or disaster but of unchecked development, and Kyoto's ability to maintain its status as a great historic city is in question. Just over fifty years ago, during World War II, Japan's urban areas were targeted for bombing. The U.S. military decided not to bomb Kyoto because it recognised the importance of Kyoto's cultural and architectural heritage. Kyoto was spared the destruction of war but suffered greatly from the indiscriminate destruction that came later as a result of the postwar economic boom. The insensitive and haphazard development of the last thirty years has devastated the harmonious quality that was found on the streets and in the communities of the ancient capital.

The History of *machiya*

Kyoto is well known as a beautiful city of temples and gardens within unique natural surroundings of mountains and rivers. Among its most notable natural features are the *machiya*, or traditional town houses. These low rise wooden buildings, with tiled roofs and congruous exterior features, blend together to give the street a cohesive harmonious quality that once awed visitors and was the pride of its inhabitants. When we look at the history of Kyoto's *machiya*, we find that the origins of the classic architectural form we now call *machiya* can be seen in small structures that blended various aspects of urban life – both residence and business – and that lined the roads of the capital in the late Heian period (794–1185).

These include the huts of the common people, small shops (*misedana*), festival viewing stages (*sajiki*), and so forth. By looking at various paintings from the late twelfth century, such as *Nenjūgyōji emaki* (Picture scrolls of annual festivals), we can tell that a typical structure was about four to six meters wide and eight meters deep, that it had gabled roofs made of wooden boards, was built contiguously in the form of a row-house, and was already divided into two sections: one earth-floored (*doma*) and the other having a wooden floor (*itajiki*). We can also see in these paintings that the strict, grid-like urban planning system used in Japan since the eighth century (*jōbōsei*) had begun to change as the functions of the city itself changed. In the spaces along the roads we find stalls and other small structures being built, and even cases in which the earthen walls surrounding aristocratic residences (*shinden*) were taken apart to fit in festival viewing platforms.

During the Kamakura period (1185–1333), the urban culture of merchants and craftsmen begins to gain prominence, and wealthy townsfolk are granted the right to own land. The old system of large city blocks with a grid-patterned infill of narrow alleyways (*shigyō hachimon sei*) breaks down in favor of the development of narrow row-houses lining the streets. In the *Kasuga gongen kenki emaki* (Picture scroll of miracles of the Kasuga Gongen), a work from that period, we see large scale residences containing main residences as well as storehouses standing next to rows of small commoners' huts which line the streets. By the mid sixteenth century, when the *Rakuchū rakugai zu byōbu* (Screens of the capital and its surroundings) folding screens were painted, things had progressed further. In these paintings we find large shops along the street that have wooden lattices on the windows and cloth banners (*noren*) hanging in front of the entrances. The rear of the properties show various other uses such as wells, places for airing the washing, and other communal spaces, as well as other outer buildings such as thick-walled storehouses (*kura*) and secondary residences (*hanare*). We also find walled gardens and long alleyways that lead from the street to the rear, all of which reveals the complexity of the development of the *machiya* by this era.

Machiya Form

The spatial relationships within the *machiya* – indoor/outdoor, light/dark, active/solemn – create complex and poetic spaces. The variety of spaces include the main entry, entrance garden, shop, formal entry, entry room, small interior garden, private entry, passageway, kitchen, sitting room, main room or guest room, main garden, and storehouse. This clear progression of space, public to private, from shop to storehouse, reflects the practical needs of the traditional inhabitant and also embodies a spiritual hierarchy. Active daily spaces such as the shop, kitchen, and passageway are the closest to and most accessible from the street. Traditionally, these areas were paved, like the streets once were, with compacted earth. Although found 'inside' the house, they are used like outdoor areas. Occupants wear their regular outdoor shoes when in these parts of the house. More private areas, however, are always a step up from the ground and are covered in *tatami* mats or wooden floors.

Deep in the *machiya* are the most private, protected, and sacred spaces. These include the main room, main garden, and storehouse. The main room contains the most spiritually significant spaces, the *tokonoma* or display alcove and the *butsudan* or family altar. Traditionally, the main room, also called the guest room, was the living area of the master of the household and was used to entertain only the most important guests. The room is situated next to the main garden, providing light and a formal scenic composition for the pleasure of the viewer. Just beyond the main garden is the storehouse where family treasures are kept. The shop served as intermediary space linking the public and private zones of street and house, respectively. It was the place where neighbors would stop in to talk and do their daily shopping. The *kōshi mado* or wooden lattice window on the front facade enabled the inhabitant to observe street activity while obscuring the public view into the house. It maintained privacy, but could also be removed during business hours to give a clear view into the shop to attract customers. The *kōshi mado* and other architectural features of the *machiya* fostered commerce and encouraged daily personal interaction, both integral parts of the complex equation that makes a healthy urban community (fig. 69).

Social Aspects of *machiya*

Machiya usually refer to buildings which were constructed by wealthy merchants and craftsmen, collectively known as *machishū*, as their own residences. They also include those that were built by the *machishū* as rental units for people who worked in their businesses, as well as government workers, servants, and skilled craftsmen. The latter type of *machiya* falls into two groups: those that faced out onto a street, called *omote jakuya*, and those built along an alleyway, called *ura jakuya* and *ura nagaya*. *Machishū* who owned homes and property are referred to by the term *mochiie sō*, literally meaning house owning class and therefore 'landed class.' Only by being part of the *mochiie sō* could one obtain the right to make decisions as official members of a local street-block community (*chō*) or a group of such communities (*machigumi*).

It was customary to use the term *machiya* in reference to the architecture of property owners, and that custom continued even after the official dissolution of the four-tiered class system – samurai, farmer, craftsman, and merchant – at the end of the Tokugawa period (1603–1867), and we can see

Place Between Future and Past

Figure 69 Recently built, traditional *machiya*-style shop, Kyoto.

a separation between owned properties and rental units even today. Whether or not a person was a property owner would decide if they could become a decision-making member of a community. The size of their property, or more specifically the width of the frontage, would determine the taxes they paid. If Japanese society up through the Tokugawa period is compared with that of the Meiji era (1868–1912), or even post World War II, it is clear there have been many major changes and yet when the basic form of Kyoto's *machiya* as it exists today is considered, the social and cultural influence of the wealthy property owners is undeniable.

For better or worse, the development of *machiya* is in many ways synonymous with the development of the *mochiie sō* and the feudal class system that fostered them. Furthermore, the structures we currently term *machiya* are often the grand residences associated with the *mochiie sō*. However, we will consider here not only those structures but all of the traditional wooden structures, whether they be the residences of the *mochiie sō*, residences of the aristocracy and samurai, temple and shrines, or the more humble rental residences which were originally lived in by the worker/servant class. When considering issues of Kyoto's townscape and its historical environments, traditional wooden architecture must be understood in its totality.

Kyoto was the imperial capital of Japan for over a thousand years, and as the center of Japanese culture, it was the stage for the development of various arts and crafts. As a result, the various craftsmen who worked to build the city, and the guilds (*shokkata seido*) that they established, became highly organized. During the Tokugawa period, for instance, carpenters in Kyoto were organized into two categories: carpenters who were responsible for the building of temples and shrines, called *dōmiya daiku*, and carpenters responsible for the construction of *machiya*, who were known as *Kyōto machiya daiku*. There were twenty groups, called *kumi*, in each of the two categories, and each *kumi* was responsible for a specific area of Kyoto. In this way the *kumi* had the sense of being local, community-based organizations, but at the same time, there was a city-wide consciousness as well by which they were seen to be builders and conservators of the city as a whole. Historical records held by carpenters who participate annually in festivals such as the Gion Festival and who are now often owners of or employed by modern construction companies contain evidence of a continuous succession from the guilds of the early modern era to the present day. Despite these remaining links, for the most part the dramatic social changes that have taken place in Japan in the modern era, especially since World War II, have almost completely destroyed the traditional system of craftsmen. The knowledge and skills maintained by the remaining elderly craftsmen is on the verge of being lost forever. The fact that traditional skills still exist even to some extent in Kyoto is a point of pride for the city because in most other cities and regions in Japan, those same skills have completely disappeared.

Machishū culture developed from an intimate relationship between the privileged classes – the courtiers, samurai, temple and shrine priests – and the more influential townspeople (merchants and artisans) through the necessities of mercantile life. This intra-social contact produced the varied aesthetics of the *machishū* and cultivated the creativity of the artistic cultures of many ages. Absorbing cultures from outlying provinces, the *machishū* digested and revised them in Kyoto, then sent back to the provinces. These layers of culture gathered in Kyoto form the cultural base of the *machishū* and *machiya*, and *machiya* districts as a whole served as the stage for this development. From medieval times through to the modern period, the seed, growth, fruition, and rebirth of various aspects of Japanese culture such as literature, painting, theater, crafts, and music can be seen to have happened as part of Kyoto's urban life. Kyoto's *machishū* culture was a result of both the popularization of the culture of the imperial court, characterised by a graceful elegance called *miyabi*, as well as the gradual refinement and sublimation of the raw, energetic culture of the townspeople and lower social echelons. Kyoto's *machiya* are of course only one form of the many commoners' residences (*minka*) that can be found throughout Japan, but they are more refined than those that will be found in other, outlying provinces and in as much are representative of Kyoto's aesthetic in general. The *machiya* contain aspects drawn from many other forms of architecture – the *shinden-zukuri* style of the Heian court families and the *shoin zukuri* style of temples and samurai residences – and yet they also established their own unique aesthetic forms of beauty of strength resulting from their spiritual simplicity (see the chapter on Shimabara by Fiévé).

Despite being confined by the severe limitations of the urban plan – specifically building sites that were narrow in frontage and long in depth – the *machiya* were functionally organized to allow for the necessary rooms, passageways, and gardens both large and small. This is entirely different from the 'functionalism' proposed by the modern architecture movement in that both the structure and the spaces of the *machiya* were developed, as it were, organically. The internal plan of one *machiya*, the way that one building relates openly to the street, the manner in which a group of *machiya* relate as a block community, the further relation of many blocks within the city, and finally the relation of the city to the surrounding landscape – all of these stages express the organic quality of a '*machiya* city.' The materials used in the *machiya* were various: Japanese cypress (*hinoki*: *Chamaecyparis obtusa*) and Japanese hemlock (*tsuga*: *Tsuga sieboldii*) for the posts; pine (*matsu*: *Pinus densiflora*) for the beams and other cross-pieces; Japanese cedar (*sugi*: *Cryptomeria japonica*) for light braces within the walls and for roof understructure; bamboo and clay for the walls; and reduction-fired clay tiles for the roof.

As long as these structures were properly maintained they could last for several hundred years. Because of a large fire that spread through central Kyoto in 1864 (known as *don-don yaki*), most of the *machiya* that still exist in Kyoto are only a few decades over one hundred years old. As long as these are protected from rot and insect damage, they could easily last another hundred years. After the large earthquake that devastated Kobe and the Awaji island area in 1995, the earthquake viability of wooden architecture became a topic of interest on a national level. For the first time since World War II, the earthquake resistance of wooden structures has become the object of serious research in both university and government centers. The results of this research are sure to testify to the earthquake viability of traditional wooden architecture. *Machiya* are built entirely from natural materials and so from the point of view of economic use of our natural resources, *machiya* have again become a topic of national interest. The revitalization of *machiya*, based on plans that respect the basic structure while developing aspects of their modern usefulness, are receiving attention.

Regulatory Structure for the Landscape

Part of the beauty and power of the *machiya* lies in the relationship between the dwelling and the larger urban context. Recognizing the unique quality of Kyoto's harmonious landscape now that virtually all other cities had been destroyed, the municipal government quickly realized that such a beautiful city had tremendous economic value in terms of tourism. In 1950, the city government introduced an ordinance that declared Kyoto an International Cultural and Sightseeing City and promoted tourism and activities to beautify the city. Ironically, the same postwar city government established policies and regulations that have brought about the destruction of historic Kyoto and the *machiya*. After the war, central Kyoto between Oike Avenue in the north and Gojō Avenue in the south, one of the most historic parts of the city, was designated a commercial zone. Falling outside the Aesthetic Zone (*bikan chiku*), discussed by Yamasaki in his chapter, buildings are allowed to be as high as thirty meters, and the overall floor area of a building can be as much as six hundred per cent of the overall site area along the main streets. The introduction of these and other zoning measures caused land values in the downtown area to skyrocket. This, as a result, prompted land owners to tear down low rise *machiya* to replace them with large buildings which are obtrusive within the traditional townscape and disfigure views of the city's scenic surroundings. At the same time, strict building regulations have hindered revitalization efforts. Any new construction or renovation of wooden buildings in the downtown area is prohibited, even if the building is clad in fire proof material.

In 1995 Kyoto City revised its planning for land use and landscape control and introduced the Kyoto System for the Regulation of the Urban Landscape (*Kyōto shigaichi keikan seibi seido*), dividing the city into three zones labelled conservation (*hozen*), renaissance (*saisei*), and creation (*sōzō*) zones. Roughly speaking, the preservation zone includes the northern part of the city and runs along the mountains that ring the city on the east, north, and west sides; the renaissance zone occupies the center of the city north of Kyoto station; and the creation zone lies south of the station. In order to protect the existing natural environment and historical structures in the preservation zone from random destructive development, the new ordinance increased the existing areas of the Special Conservation Zones for Historic Landscapes (*rekishiteki fūdo tokubetsu hozon chiku*), revised the Landscape Zone system (*fūchi chiku seido*) originally established in 1930, and established the Natural Landscape Preservation Ordinance (*shizen fūkei hozon jōrei*).

The 1995 system involved a restructuring of the Urban Landscape Ordinance (*shigaichi keikan jōrei*), which, when established in 1972, was the first of its kind in Japan. The new ordinance – issued in 1996 – provides for five categories of Aesthetic Zone (*bikan chiku*), a Buildings and Townscape Adjustment Zone (*kenzōbutsu shūkei chiku*), a Roadside Landscape Formation Zone (*endō keikan keisei chiku*), a Historic Landscape Preservation and Adjustment Zone (*rekishiteki keikan hozen shūkei chiku*), and a Historic Atmosphere Regulation Zone (*kaiwai keikan seibi chiku*) (all of these are described in more detail in the chapter by Yamasaki). The various, cumbersome names for all these areas give an insight into the nature of conservation in Kyoto. With regard to the preservation of historical natural landscapes and structures, as well as the four strict conservation zones (*dentōteki kenzōbutsugun hozon chiku*) that lie outside the central urban areas, it can be said that this ordinance represents an improvement. In addition, with regard to urban areas, Kamigyō Ward was designated in its entirety as an Category 4 Aesthetic Zone, which the City Planning Bureau department states as being a 'zone where buildings of unique shapes and designs which have grown out of Kyoto's traditional urban lifestyles constitute attractive landscapes' (Kyōto Toshi Keikakukyoku Toshi Keikanbu 1997). Within this category, buildings over twenty meters in height cannot be built and buildings over twelve meters in height must adhere to certain aesthetic design regulations. All of these are desirable changes in the regulatory system. However, the scope of application of these new regulations does not include other urban areas, such as Nakagyō Ward, in the center of the city, and Shimogyō Ward, to the south, in which high concentrations of traditional *machiya* still exist. In these areas the regulatory system is as deficient as before. At the same time, these areas are designated Building Adjustment Zones (*kenzōbutsu shūkei chiku*). Buildings within these areas are not simply to be preserved in their existing condition; their condition should be improved by 'adjusting' the townscape by gradual changes as buildings are rebuilt or repaired. Unfortunately the regulations governing these revisions are extremely vague, requiring nothing more than that developers planning buildings over twenty meters in height in the central urban areas must file an official notice with the mayor's office and that they do their best to refrain from using garish colors or decorations that would not fit in with the surrounding townscape. Even in the parts of the city with the longest history, and despite the fact that they may have a special status as a Landscape Zone or Aesthetic Zone, the unfortunate reality is that apartment buildings and office towers which destroy the townscape are being put up in increasing numbers.

With regard to the central districts of Nakagyō, Shimogyō, and Higashiyama wards, where *machiya* are still to be found in great numbers, there is simply no effective system for protecting individual traditional *machiya* or traditional *machiya* townscapes. It is essential that a new system of regulations be established that are not based on the old vision of a city of fire-proof buildings but rather on the ideal that wooden architecture is a great gift to our present society. Only in this way will we be able to establish a sound policy on the urban landscape. This new policy should include a revision of the regulations regarding fire districts in Kyoto while at the same time augmenting fire-fighting measures throughout the city. The policies should also include a rethink of the land use planning system and a downsizing of square footage, volume, and heights of buildings with relation to their property sizes. Finally, the new regulations should create a blanket protection for traditional townscape areas by instituting a protection zone that could be entitled something like 'Kyoto *Machiya* Conservation and Revitalization District.'

Inheritance Tax (*sōzokuzei*)

Another major factor to which the decline of *machiya* can be attributed is the inheritance tax. Those who inherit property must pay exorbitant taxes and are often forced to develop their property, sell it, or relinquish it to the government. Part of a recent survey performed by five university research groups on traditional buildings and with assistance from volunteer citizens in central Kyoto focused on the opinions of residents.[1] When asked if they felt they could go on living in *machiya* in the future, the major reason listed for not being able to continue was the national inheritance tax. Compared to the recent past, the cost of land and the quantity of real estate transactions have lessened. However, from the standpoint of residents of *machiya*, the enormous inheritance taxes levied in relation to the size of their properties is an inescapable problem (figs. 70 and 71).

I will give as an example the case of a friend who lives in central Kyoto, whose father-in-law passed away in 1992. The property is located a few hundred meters northwest of the intersection of Shijō and Karasuma avenues, near Kyoto's central business district. The residence faces out onto

Figure 70 Destruction of a traditional *machiya*.

Figure 71 Disappearance of traditional urban landscape of the Kyoto *machiya*.

a northwest street, and, as it is traditional, the property is deep and narrow. The local area is known for its concentration of businesses related to the kimono wholesale trade. In the case of my friend as well, the building facing the street (*omoteya*) and was rented out some time ago to a company in the kimono fabric wholesale business. The family lives in the other buildings that are on the rear of the site (*omoya*).

When the head of the family passed away, he left five heirs: his widowed wife, two children, and two grandchildren. This is important because the inheritance tax is calculated based on the numbers of heirs. The property was 848 square meters, of which 148 square meters were rented out to the fabric company in the front, and 700 square meters were used as the family residence. At the time, the cost of land for the front portion of the site used as a business was 1,801,800 yen per square meter, which was charged against the inheritance at 72 per cent of total value, making that portion of the land worth 192,648,456 yen. The rear portion of the property was valued at 1,155,772 yen per square meter, making the value of that portion of the property, after a special deduction of 60 per cent on 200 square meters, 670,255,298 yen. In addition, the estate included the value of the buildings – 4.2 million yen – and monies in the bank – 10 million yen – making the total unadjusted value of the estate 877,103,754 yen.

From this there was taken a standard deduction of 48 million yen, which means, in other words, that people whose estates are valued at less than 48 million yen are essentially excluded from the inheritance tax. There was also a deduction for each heir at 9.5 million yen per person, bringing the adjusted value of the estate to 781,603,754 yen. Based on this estate value, and some other special adjustments given to the widow, the tax levied on the heirs was as follows: 173,429,400 yen for the widow, 39,556,400 yen each for the two children, and 15,246,550 yen each for the two grandchildren, for a total tax of 283,035,300 yen. At an exchange rate of approximately 120 yen per US dollar this translates as a total estate value of approximately 6,513,365 dollars, on which an inheritance tax of 2,358,628 dollars was levied.

In the above case, the amount of tax weighed against the total adjusted value of the estate amounts to about 35 per cent of the value of the estate, but the tax ranges from 10 per cent (for estates valued under 7 million yen) to 70 per cent (for estates valued over 1 billion yen). The government extends the period over which this tax can be paid, but the enormous size of the tax usually means that for a person living on a salary, or ordinary business profits, the tax burden is unbearable. The result is that in a majority of cases the land (and of course the *machiya* on it) are sold off to pay for the tax.

The tax is calculated primarily on the price of the land the *machiya* sits on, and the land price, in turn, is heavily affected by the height and size of buildings allowed for in that district by the city planning regulations. In an area zoned for ten storey buildings, the owner of a two storey *machiya* becomes the object of severe pressure to remove their residence. One approach to conserving *machiya* would be, in areas where *machiya* remain in large concentrations, to link the upper limit of square meter land valuation to, or base it on, the potential financial profits possible in a two storey structure.

A citywide survey of architecture in Kyoto shows that in the decade between 1978 and 1988 alone, over fifty thousand prewar wooden residences were destroyed. In the central districts of Kamigyō, Nakagyō, Shimogyō, and Higashiyama wards, which comprise the old city of Kyoto, over 6,400 such structures were destroyed (Nishikawa, Funo, and Yokoo 1988: 29). It can be clearly seen that the 'bubble economy' years were very hard indeed on Kyoto *machiya*. Despite this, in these same four districts of central Kyoto, there are over 32,000 prewar wooden residences still standing. The areas lining the main roads have been developed with tall buildings in recent years, but according to research being undertaken now, the number of *machiya* left in areas just adjacent to those is much higher than expected. Especially along the alleyways (*roji*) that lead back from the street and are inaccessible to automobile traffic there can still be found many styles of *ura jakuya*. Within a few years, at the completion of the aforementioned study, we will come to understand just how many *machiya* in the central areas of Kyoto have been destroyed and how many still remain.

Momochitarukan: An Example of a Revitalization Project

There are a handful of architects, of whom I am one, who see the *machiya* as a building type that can be renewed and reused to help revitalize the socio-economic fabric of the city. One such project I was involved in is called Momochitarukan (fig. 75). It is a mixed-use project of old and new structures which I designed so that it would blend into the traditional context in central Kyoto. With the client, I developed this complex comprising an arts and crafts factory, showroom, residence, restaurant, and a stage for Noh theater. On the street side of the site we relocated and rebuilt a wooden *machiya* that had been previously discarded. Here at its new location, the front shop is a popular bar and restaurant. Behind the front shop is a garden that connects with the main building, a five storey house for complex functions. The large structure is set back and only the front shop is visible from the street. The roof of the structure is scaled down and sloped like the roof of a *machiya*, and all the roofs are tiled. These simple design techniques minimize obstruction to the skyline and help the building blend in with its surroundings. The complex of buildings, garden, and passageway are finished in natural materials and colors using traditional methods.

In relation to this modern *machiya* renewal project, I would like to point out some problems as regards Japan's basic architectural planning laws and regulations. Both the client and the architect on this project, in an attempt to create a design which would be in keeping with the traditional streetscape of the area, wished to build a two storey wooden structure facing the street. However, according to the Architectural Standards Law (*Kenchiku kijun hō*), a national regulation that sets basic requirements for architectural work and is applied uniformly throughout Japan, any structure which is three stories or more and will contain public functions is required to be built of fireproof materials and must allow fire-fighters direct access from the street to the inside of the building. Furthermore, the site is in one of the central wards of Kyoto which is designated as a Fire Protection Zone (*bōka chiku*), where the construction of wooden structures in the traditional manner is prohibited as all structural members of the building must be covered by a layer of fireproof material. There is also a basic stipulation in the Architectural Standards Law that declares that on any one site only one structure may be built. If this project had been designed according to commonly accepted methods, the result would have been a four-storey modern building fronting the street. Because of our strong desire to include *machiya* revitalization as part of the overall plan, a different route was taken, which involved strict review by various government agencies but resulted in the following plan. The site is typical of that part of Kyoto, narrow and deep. The structures built on it were broken into three units (already a divergence from the 'one site/one structure' regulation) to allow for spatial and visual complexity as seen from the street as well as from within the site itself. The building that faces directly onto the street was designed as a two storey wooden structure to be used as a shop, the middle building is a five storey, mixed-use steel structure, and in the rear is a four storey steel storehouse. Between these three architectural units there are open spaces that contain gardens and terraces. Some of the regulatory hurdles we had to overcome in order to receive building permits involved the construction of a steel bridge over the roof of the forward wooden structure to the third floor of the middle steel structure to be used as an access route for fire-fighters. The wooden structure along the street had to be entirely surrounded by fireproof walls, as well as to have fireproof doors or shutters at all access points. In addition, we had to install emergency sprinklers and a large water cistern to hold emergency fire-fighting water. The existing architectural regulations put adverse pressure on this project, which was trying to achieve what could be considered an ideal form for Kyoto town planning. For its part, the city government should really designate these central districts of Kyoto, where many traditional structures still exist, as *machiya* preservation and revitalization zones, creating conditions that would encourage the preservation and restoration of old *machiya*, and the construction of new ones as well. It is time to rethink and restructure the singular, conformist national architectural legal structure that was set up after World War II. (figs 72, 73 and 74).

Some other architects are also involved in the revitalization of *machiya*. Unfortunately, most architects who design buildings in Kyoto give in to the demands of the builders and developers. Hence, almost all new projects are built to maximum height, full site coverage, and maximum floor area. Successful methods used in historic cities in other parts of the world include designing buildings with suitable shapes, volumes, and set backs; using natural finish materials; and giving back part of the site to the community by including non-commercial public space. In Kyoto, however, there are no regulations or incentives to promote the use of such techniques; consequently, they are rarely incorporated into new projects (fig. 75).

Place Between Future and Past

HATA RESIDENCE
594 Taishiyama-cho
Aburakoji-dori Bukkoji Sagaru
Shimogyo-ku, Kyoto 600

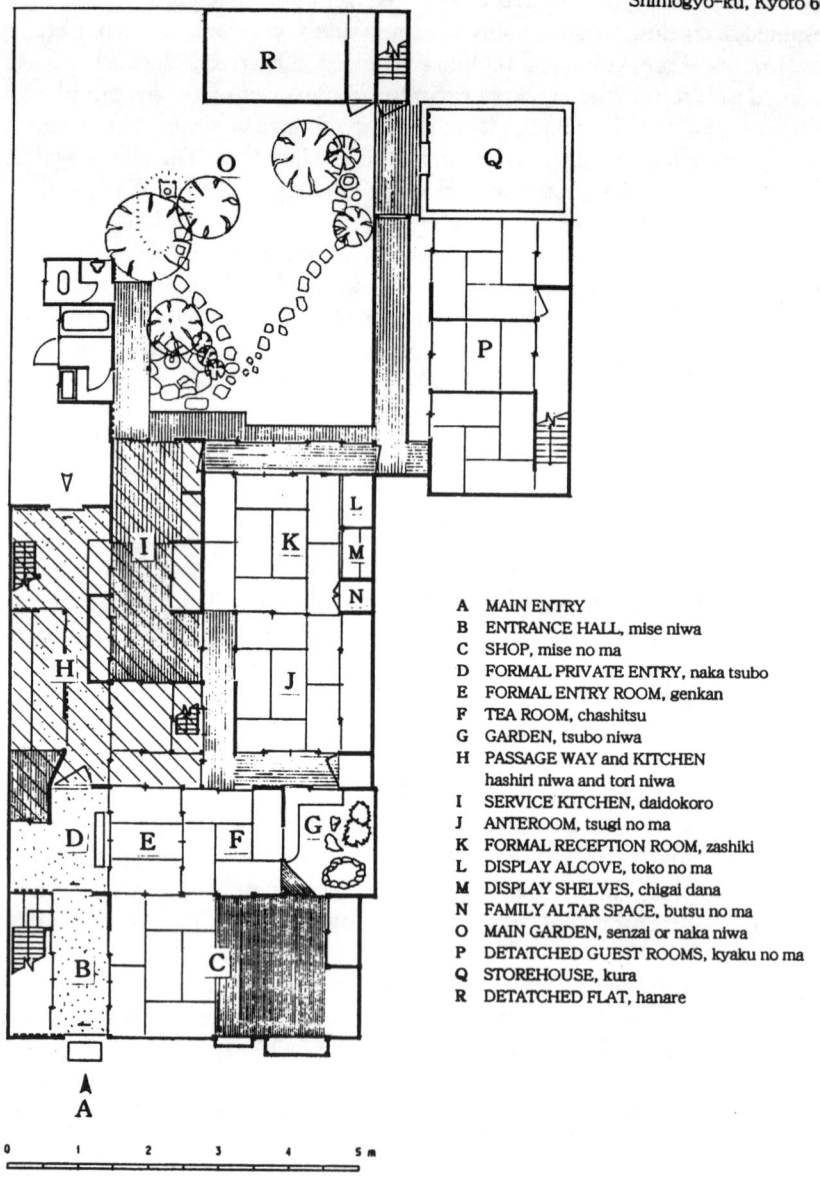

A MAIN ENTRY
B ENTRANCE HALL, mise niwa
C SHOP, mise no ma
D FORMAL PRIVATE ENTRY, naka tsubo
E FORMAL ENTRY ROOM, genkan
F TEA ROOM, chashitsu
G GARDEN, tsubo niwa
H PASSAGE WAY and KITCHEN
    hashiri niwa and tori niwa
I SERVICE KITCHEN, daidokoro
J ANTEROOM, tsugi no ma
K FORMAL RECEPTION ROOM, zashiki
L DISPLAY ALCOVE, toko no ma
M DISPLAY SHELVES, chigai dana
N FAMILY ALTAR SPACE, butsu no ma
O MAIN GARDEN, senzai or naka niwa
P DETACHED GUEST ROOMS, kyaku no ma
Q STOREHOUSE, kura
R DETACHED FLAT, hanare

Figure 72 Layout of the Hata residence (first floor) (Shimogyō-ku, Kyoto).

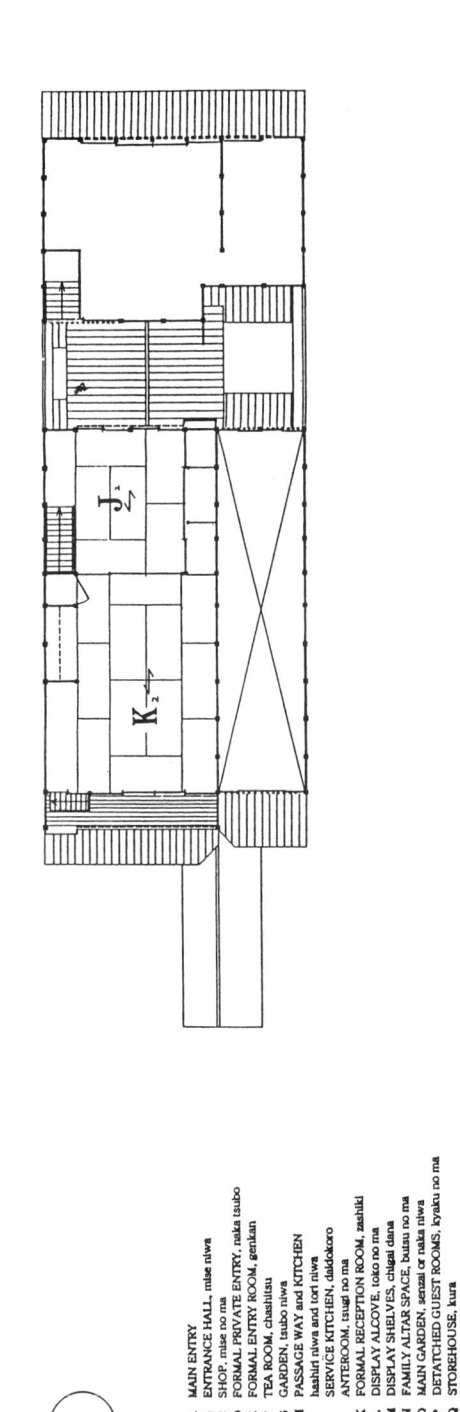

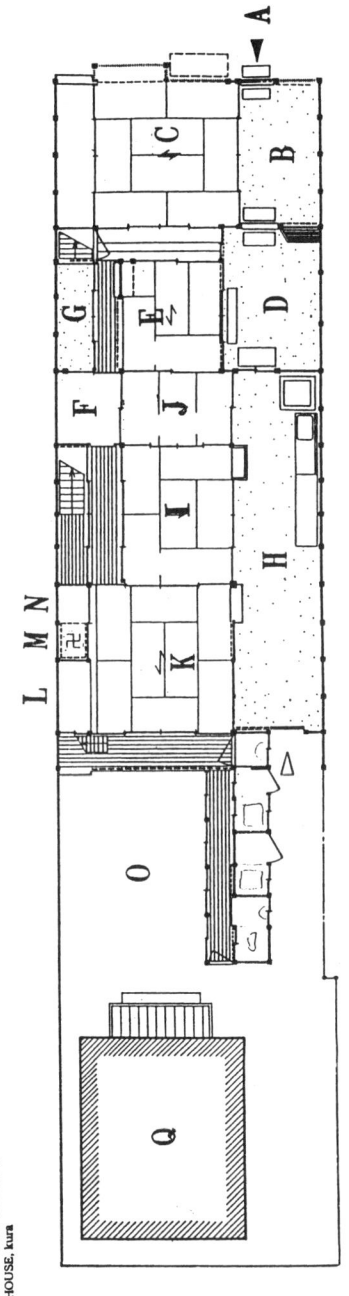

A MAIN ENTRY
B ENTRANCE HALL, mise niwa
C SHOP, mise no ma
D FORMAL PRIVATE ENTRY, naka tsubo
E FORMAL ENTRY ROOM, genkan
F TEA ROOM, chashitsu
G GARDEN, tsubo niwa
H PASSAGE WAY and KITCHEN
    hashiri niwa and tori niwa
I SERVICE KITCHEN, daidokoro
J ANTEROOM, tsugi no ma
K FORMAL RECEPTION ROOM, zashiki
L DISPLAY ALCOVE, toko no ma
M DISPLAY SHELVES, chigai dana
N FAMILY ALTAR SPACE, butsu no ma
O MAIN GARDEN, senzai or naka niwa
P DETATCHED GUEST ROOMS, kyaku no ma
Q STOREHOUSE, kura

Figure 73 Layout of a traditional Kyoto *machiya* (ground floor and first floor). Design Atelier Ryo, Kyoto.

Place Between Future and Past

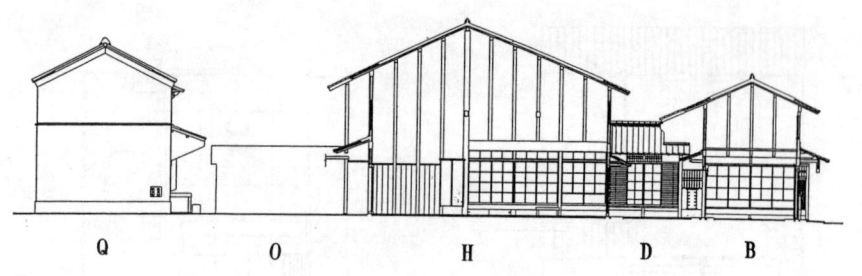

Figure 74 Section of a traditional Kyoto *machiya*. Drawing: Atelier Ryo, Kyoto.

Figure 75 Model for modernization of a traditional *machiya*. Momochitarukan, Kyoto. Design Atelier Ryo.

Citizen's Movements

Among the organizations working to preserve and revitalize Kyoto is the Kyoto Townhouse Revitalization Society, which was started in 1992 and consists of 120 professionals and Kyoto residents, mostly Japanese. The group meets regularly to research and do field documentation of remaining *machiya*. We promote the renewal of *machiya* and have been involved with several projects where *machiya* have been renovated into shops, galleries, or restaurants.

Kyoto Mitate (fomerly, International Society to Save Kyoto), formed in 1994, is a group of 290 foreigners and Japanese living all around the world.

The group's mission is to maintain Kyoto's remaining historic environment by showing that it is still a vital part of modern life. There are four annual meetings and many smaller meetings in between. The larger seasonal gatherings are held somewhere in Kyoto with historical connections to show one aspect of Kyoto's traditional culture in a new light, specifically, how that culture can be part of our lives today. For instance, at Myōrenji members explored the potential uses of *furoshiki*, the carrying-cloths that are infinitely more beautiful and ecologically friendly than plastic bags. On another occasion, in a 'modern' *machiya* (a traditional structure with a sculpture by Noguchi Isamu in the inner courtyard) members enjoyed newly reinvented *namafu* cuisine.

Another group, recently established, is the Kyoto International Committee of Art and Cultural Exchange (KICACE). The group's goal is to organize regular cultural and international events in Kyoto *machiya*. We feel that by creating pockets of cultural activities – concerts, contemporary art exhibitions, and lectures – more people will have meaningful experiences in these traditional buildings. Through these experiences people will develop a better understanding of the *machiya* and realize the value of maintaining and reusing them. These are the kinds of experiences that build strong communities, and we hope they will help reestablish a healthy urban environment in Kyoto.

Of late, in some areas of Kyoto like the textile district of Nishijin, a movement has begun to rent out to artists old *machiya* that are no longer being lived in. This process is being increasingly supported by local communities. Likewise, in central Kyoto, many old *machiya* that were once closed up are now being renewed as cafés, restaurants, and galleries attracting the attention of a whole new set of young people, and now, much more than before, one can also find real estate brokers who have information about available townhouses. Thanks to these recent developments, the communities in districts with a concentration of old town-houses, once on the verge of dying out, are now experiencing a revival. There has also been a palpable change in the attitude of the Kyoto city government toward the preservation and revitalization of old wooden town-houses.

No one is suggesting that Kyoto be transported back to its prewar state. Modernization is both important and undeniable. However, the *machiya*, symbols of Kyoto's urban vitality, are disappearing by the thousands, and there is little support to reintegrate the remaining *machiya* into the needs of modern Kyoto. What we hope to achieve is balance and desire to preserve the essence of Kyoto not just for the people of the city but for the whole world. We need to foster a relationship where modern and traditional can coexist in a positive way to create a beautiful city, and we need to enlist the support of the younger generation because soon it will be their city, and, like us now, they will be the ones responsible for maintaining and passing on traditions, customs, and a healthy and active community.

Note

1 The survey was made under the direction of the Kyoto-shi Keikan Machizukuri Sentâ (Kyoto city landscape community planning center).

References

Kyōto Toshi Keikakukyoku Toshi Keikanbu (Kyoto City Planning Bureau) (1997). *Kyōto no keikan: hozen, saisei, sōzō* (The landscape of Kyoto: Conservation, renaissance, and creation). Kyoto: Kyoto City Government.

Nishikawa K., Funo S., and Yokoo Y. (eds) (1988) '*Machiya saisei ni kakawaru bōka shuhō ni kansuru chōsa kenkyū hōkokusho*' (Research on fire prevention methods with regard to revitalization of wooden town-houses). Machiya Bōka Shuhō Kenkyūkai, Nihon Kenchiku Sōgō Shikensho (Research Association into Fire Prevention Methods for Wooden Town-Houses, Japan Architecture General Laboratory).

CHAPTER 14

Conclusion

Power, Memory, and Place

Paul Waley

This book began with a discussion about one building, but it was not any building. The castle built first by Yoshiteru and then by Yoshiaki and Oda Nobunaga on the main road linking the two parts of Kyoto can be considered a harbinger of the early modern period, the first hesitant essay in central control. Not long after its two-fold demise came the short-lived triumph of Nobunaga's castle of Azuchi, on the banks of Lake Biwa, followed by the more sustained attempt by Hideyoshi Toyotomi, not only to build a castle in Kyoto but also to convert the city into a new and different form of urban settlement. Even this was to prove inconclusive. However much Kyoto had recovered from the ravages of earlier periods, it had lost its position as centre of political power. The affirmation of Tokugawa control, which came with the victory at Sekigahara in 1600, led inevitably to the final ascendancy of Edo and to an eastward move in the axis of power.

Transcience, movement, flux – these are all clichés of the Japanese urban scene. But these abstractions have concrete meanings too. Buildings were frequently dismantled and moved elsewhere. Some even changed their function in the process. Regular destruction of buildings through fire led inevitably to an appreciation of memories as evoked by the name of a place or a story. The great Japanese cities like Kyoto and Edo-Tokyo have stories where other cities have monuments. This is a narrative urbanism, and an urbanism of narrative. Japanese cities are fast reinvented and redefined. At one level, this is reflected in a shaping and moulding of collective memories. At another, it simply means that buildings are frequently torn down and replaced by something more profitable. Land is a powerful tool of capital accumulation. Preservation of buildings and landscapes is a task fraught with difficulties. Visions of a better urban order soon become torn and tattered, blasted by the dirty air from millions of air conditioners.

These are some of the themes dealt with either explicitly or implicitly by the contributors to this book. They are the underpinnings for an understanding of the dynamics of Japanese urbanism in the early modern and modern periods. In the pages that remain, these themes will be brought together in an attempt to place Japan's two great capitals in a broader context.

Power and the Spatial Imprints of Authority

Political and military regimes have always sought to represent their authority in spatial terms. Thus, cities reflect the locus of power and the patterns it projects over larger territories. There is, you might say, nothing so significant about this. The Romans projected power through city-building projects and then reinforced it with a process of urban planning. The picture is repeated whether one looks to the cities of North America or to the urban centres of Soviet power. The modernist planning idiom is predicated on the spatial manipulation of populations in order to respond to political ideas and social needs. There are, however, certain reasons why the Japanese case stands out. It is exceptional, first, in the thoroughness with which the social and the spatial were conflated by those who held power, and it is unusual because of the limited nature of monumental representations of political authority.

This writing of a social order onto the map of the city inevitably entailed a certain amount of clustering, with people of similar occupation or social status brought together to share the same territory. In medieval Japanese castle towns, local power-holders surrounded their own fortified compound with the residences of retainers. Temples have tended to be situated in close mutual proximity, the main foundation surrounded by branch temples. Merchants tended to live and work in close proximity to each other from early times. Wakita Haruko writes about the clustering of merchant warehouses in Watanabe port, the settlement that was later to become Osaka (Wakita H. 1999: 30). In Kyoto in the years of strife in the fifteenth and sixteenth centuries, merchants and artisans crowded together for self-defence.

The centralizing pressures exerted by Oda Nobunaga and Toyotomi Hideyoshi changed the nature of Japanese urban development. With the advent of the early modern castle towns, the conflation of the spatial and the social was taken to new levels, never to be attained again in Japan. This was made possible in large part because so many of these settlements were new urban centres, a *tabula rasa*, onto which a new model of urban development could be inscribed. The prime examples of course were Osaka and Edo, both of them carved out of the marshes at about the same time, in the 1590s. Even Kyoto, as Fiévé and Takahashi have indicated, was the subject of a sustained attempt to stamp political power onto the urban landscape.

Castle towns were unusual for a number of other but related reasons. Perhaps the most extraordinary point is simply that so many new urban settlements were built in such a short time – more than two hundred from 1580 to the 1620s (McClain and Wakita 1999: 14). In the light of this, it is hardly surprising that these new settlements were characterised, as suggested in the Introduction, by a uniformity in the application of a model. The castles themselves around which the settlements were built differed one from the other, although the difference was still one of degree. The topographical setting inevitably varied, even if the castle was normally set on an eminence. But the overall layout, with its careful layering of the compounds of vassals and the quarters inhabited by merchants and artisans, was replicated throughout the country. Patterns occasionally differed, but the model was the same.

At the heart of the scheme of these castle towns lay the imperative of self-defence. As Bodart-Bailey reminds us, access to the castle was rendered as tortuous as possible through the simple expedient of a complicated approach that made its way in zigzag fashion and then at right angles through barbican-style gateways. The urban jigsaw puzzle referred to in the Introduction was a feature not only of those parts of Edo (the capital of castle towns, so to speak) occupied by the shogun's retainers and the compounds of the feudal lords but also of the much more restricted stretches of city land on which the commoners' quarters were located. Here it was not possible, nor was it necessary, to be quite so insistent on exercising control through control of space. Nevertheless, the gates that impeded night-time passage down the main streets and barred access to and from the backstreets were but one of several physical manifestations of the projection of political power onto the urban landscape and its translation into social control. This was backed up by a network of paternalistic supervision that was constantly revised and renegotiated.

Fiévé in his chapter on Shimabara, the licensed brothel district of Kyoto, draws our attention to further means of buttressing this system of control over urban space. Those activities that were less open to regulation and close scrutiny or that carried a high potential for destabilization were moved to the urban periphery. In Kyoto as in Edo, the district within which prostitution was legalized was carefully located on the outskirts of the city. In the case of Edo, urban sprawl resulted in the further move of the licensed district of Yoshiwara to a new location outside the fast-growing city (Tinios and Waley 1999). Temples too were potential sites of transgressional activity, and their grounds represented urban space over which control was harder to exercise (Markus 1985). They represented, therefore, less of a risk if they were located on the urban periphery. The Tokugawa approach to control over space was well illustrated in Edo, but it extended throughout the country and into the sea lanes. Bodart-Bailey points out that the provincial lords were banned from travelling by sea; Traganou draws our attention to some of the controls that were placed on travelling overland.

To represent the castle town in terms of an inscription on urban space of political power might suggest that these settlements suffered from excessive rigidity, with segregated spaces creating a population cowering impotently before their lord. While it is true that even at the end of the long Tokugawa rule, foreign visitors to Edo commented on the austere and forbidding atmosphere of those central parts of town where the more powerful *daimyō* had their compounds, all the evidence suggests that, taken as a whole, Edo was a vibrant and dynamic city. Furthermore, as Coaldrake argues through his reference to metaphors of power, it was a city in which the merchants and artisans came increasingly to the fore, and while it would be an exaggeration to claim that they imposed their values on urban life, they were nevertheless instrumental in forging, along with those elements of the military population who were permanently stationed there, an unusual hybrid urban culture. In the end, one of the principal causes of the fatal fatigue of Edo and the edifice of Tokugawa rule was the fundamental anomaly represented by a military caste who depended on the services provided by a merchant elite.

Memory and the Changing Passage of Space

What makes Edo so unusual is the fact that, with the exception of the occasional gatehouse, we have no physical reminder of what the city looked like, and therefore far less idea of what it felt or smelt like. Even Kyoto with its many pre-modern temple buildings provides only slight clues since it too bears only a distant relation to the historical capital city of the emperor. Tokyo and Kyoto, as well as other large Japanese cities, fascinate and perplex the Western observer in equal measure because they require recourse to a different form of historical imagination.

Meanings for the urban landscape must be sought not in the visual memories represented by material objects such as buildings and monuments but in a narrative of change and continuity. The collective memory of which Fiévé writes is recorded not engraved, narrated not enshrined. Or perhaps one should say that the collective memory *was* recorded and narrated. A voluminous topophilic and topographic literature evolved in the eighteenth century, as did a rich new tradition of visual representations of the urban landscape. These developments were spurred by advances in printing techniques and by the growth of a market among both commoners and samurai. Topographies, guides, and gazetteers were published in growing numbers in the nineteenth century, the format and styles moving east to Edo from Kyoto (Mizue 1973; Elisonas 1994). There were calendric guides to the seasonal rituals of nature and comprehensive illustrated topographies that covered the famous sites of the city. Alongside these, polychrome prints came increasingly to reflect the growing topophilic interest, and landscape became an accepted subject for sets of woodblock prints. The works of Hiroshige are of course the archetypes in this genre (Smith 1986).

This topographic literature was built on a much older literary tradition of poetic reference to place, that of the *meisho*, or famous place, discussed by both Fiévé and Traganou. A different reading of the two characters that make up *meisho* gives us *na-dokoro*, or named place, and the concept has its origins in an epithetical coupling in Heian court poetry of place with emotion (Pigeot 1982). A reference to a particular emotion would be tied so closely to a specific place that mention of the place alone would be sufficient to convey the emotion. Over the passage of the centuries, *meisho* came to refer to celebrated sites that the tourist or simply the urban resident would want to visit. Traganou explains how *dōchūzu* maps of the Tōkaidō portrayed in one long image all of the many famous places along the highway, presenting thus a narrative of a journey within a schematized topographical representation.

In a world without the substantive material reminders of the past, collective meanings are derived too from place-names. I have tried to suggest in my chapter on the disappearance of Tokyo's ferries how a rich topophilic imagination was formed around the evocative impact of the names of ferry services. Affection for place was evinced through an act of elegiac commemoration. The role-call of names symbolized not only features of the landscape but a whole way of life that was seen to be disappearing. In a landscape of material impermanence, continuities and discontinuities were wrapped up in place-names.

The various topographical traditions continued into the modern era, and I have drawn on a number of them in my chapter. Their contemporary avatars are the voluminous and increasingly scholarly local histories that are compiled and published by local government offices throughout the country. But, as Iwatake has argued in this book, when commemoration involves celebration of the intangible, of events and occasions, it is all too easily manipulated (although it needs to be recognized that manipulation is anyway the hand-maiden of memory). The various celebrations held to mark major moments in the story of Edo-Tokyo read like a history of contemporary political trends. Historic monuments have been used often enough to glorify modern political regimes (one need think no further than Mussolini and ancient Rome), but where there are none, the task of redefining celebrations of the collective memory are all the easier.

Japan, then, as both Fiévé and Hladik have pointed out, lacks the historic monuments that some other countries possess. Instead, it possesses a culture in which people write individual and collective narratives of their lives without a regular reference to the material structure of buildings. Hladik distinguishes between continuity of form, continuity of parts, and continuity of matter. She sees a dichotomy between an appreciation of the value of age in an object and a need for freshness and newness. This dichotomy is resolved through a recognition that it is in its very perishability that an object gains its age value, and as a result, it is the 'impermanence which is valued.'

Place, between Future and Past

This poses problems in modern urbanism, dominated, as it is, by a Western-inspired aesthetic that cherishes the old and at the same time assigns to old objects and structures a monetary value that reflects and valorizes their age. Any regime of preservation and conservation is going to face difficulties in a country that values impermanence. Some of the consequences of this impasse have been examined in these pages by Yamasaki and Kinoshita, both of whom belong to a substantial corpus of professional planners, architects, and academics who are appreciative of Japan's heritage and who are well versed in the conceptual underpinnings of the Western approach (or approaches) to these issues. They can also see some advantages in compromise with the dominant Japanese ideology, with its emphasis on development fuelled by construction. They are acutely aware of the various difficulties that a tradition of building in wood poses in terms first of preservation and then of conservation. They are realistic as to the chances of success.

Yamasaki writes about 'the basic premise of social activity still [resting] on development oriented systems.' These systems have their nerve centre in Tokyo, the national capital. Tokyo indeed dominates patterns of thought and practice throughout Japan. We have already noted the growing conformity of design in the early modern castle town. This process has been accentuated in the modern era (not only, of course, in Japan) by the unitary nature and centrality of the state, whose organs are located in the national capital. It has also been driven forward, as Yamasaki has pointed out, by the centralizing forces of state-regulated construction. In these pages, Yamasaki has stressed the continued grip exercized over planners, engineers, and architects by an unimaginative brand of functionalism, and certainly a walk through any Japanese city provides copious evidence to support this argument. This rather arid variant of modernism affords countless opportunities for cost-cutting replication. It also negates the local and the regional in favour of the central and national. The shadow of the modern capital has fallen particularly heavily on the historical capital as the one large city with the most that was heterodox and distinctive.

It is not only *the* capital that casts its shadow over the country, but also capital that does so. City planning is generally effected in tandem with corporate interests. Large businesses are able to inject massive amounts of capital into urban investments, as we saw in the rapid reconstruction of Kobe after the 1995 earthquake. The slow dismantling of the notion of collective memory, stemming in part from the greater penetration and indeed the suffusion of capital in the urban fabric, has prompted (or so I would argue) a collapse in the collective ethos that is essential if urban planning is to work in a contemporary context. Instead, it has been replaced, as Yamasaki argues, by a stubborn adherence to the rights of individual property holders. As the centre of capital accumulation, the national capital is indeed all-powerful in today's Japan.

References

Elisonas, J. (1994) 'Notorious places: a brief excursion into the narrative topography of early Edo.' In J. McClain, J. Merriman, and Ugawa K., (eds) *Edo and Paris: urban life and the state in the early modern era*. Ithaca, NY: Cornell University Press.

Markus, A. (1985) 'The Carnival of Edo: *Misemono* Spectacles from Contemporary Accounts.' *Harvard Journal of Asiatic Studies* 45. Pp. 499–541.

McClain, J., and Wakita O. (eds) (1999) *Osaka: The Merchants' Capital of Early Modern Japan*. Ithaca: Cornell University Press.

Mizue R. (1973) '*Shoki Edo no annai ki*' (Guides to early Edo). In Nishiyama M. (ed.) *Edo chōnin no kenkyū* (Research into Edo commoners) vol. 3. Tokyo: Yoshikawa Kōbunkan.

Pigeot, J. (1982) *Michiyuki-bun: Poétique de l'itinéraire dans la littérature du Japon ancien*. Paris: Editions G.-P. Maisonneuve et Larose.

Smith, H.D. II. (1986) *Hiroshige: One Hundred Famous Views of Edo*. New York: Braziller.

Tinios, E., and P. Waley (1999) *On the Margins of the City: Scenes of Recreation from the periphery of the Japanese Capital, 1760–1860*. Leeds: University of Leeds Press.

Wakita H. (1999). 'Ports, markets, and medieval urbanism in the Osaka region.' In J. McClain and Wakita O., (eds) *Osaka: The Merchants' Capital of Early Modern Japan*. Ithaca: Cornell University Press.

Glossary

ageya 揚屋
Ageya-chō 揚屋町
ai 愛
Aichi 愛知
aijō 愛情
Ajia ga toshi o koeru アジアが都市を超える
Akasaka 赤坂
Aki 安芸
Akisato Ritō 秋里離島 (active end of the 18th c., beginning of the 19th c.)
aku 悪
akusho 悪所
Akutagawa Ryūnosuke 芥川龍之介 (1892–1927)
Ama no ukihashi 天の浮橋
Amakashi 天菓子
Amakusa Shirō, see Masuda Tokisada
Amakusa 天草
Ama-no-hashidate 天橋立
ameyami 雨止
Andō Hiroshige 安藤廣重 (1797–1858)
aobyōshi 青表氏
Aogai no ma 青貝間
Aoshima Yukio 青島幸男 (b. 1932)
Arai Hakuseki 新井白石 (1657–1725)
Arima Yoriyasu 有馬頼寧 (1884–1957)
Ariwara no Narihira 在原業平 (825–880)
aruki miko あるき御子 (歩神子, 歩巫)
Asada Takashi 浅田孝 (1921–1990)
Asai Ryōi 浅井了意 (b. 1612)
Asakusa 浅草
Asano cemento (cement) 浅野セメント

Asano Kiyoshi 浅野清 (1905–1991)
Ashihara Yoshinobu 芦原義信 (b. 1918)
Ashikaga Yoshiaki 足利義昭 (1537–1597)
Ashikaga Yoshiharu 足利義晴 (1511–1550)
Ashikaga Yoshiteru 足利義輝 (1536–1565)
asobi 遊び
asobime 遊び女
Asuka 飛鳥
Atake ferry, or Atake no watashi 安宅の渡し
Azuchi castle or Azuchijō 安土城
Azuchi 安土
Azuma bridge 吾妻橋
Baishun bōshi hō 売春防止法
bakenjō 馬見場
bakufu kanryō sei 幕府官僚制
bakufu 幕府
bansho 番所
basho to keishiki 場所と形式
bijin 美人
bijon ビジョン
bikan chiku 美観地区
Bikuni 比丘尼
Biwa lake, or Biwako 琵琶湖
bō 坊
Böckmann, Wilhelm (1832–1902)
bōka chiku 防火地区
Bōsō peninsula, or Bōsō hantō 房総半島
Bōsu 房州
Bueijin-chō 武衛陣町

Glossary

Buei-tei 武衛邸
bugyō 奉行
buke shohatto 武家諸法度
buke yashiki 武家屋敷
Bunkachō 文化庁
Bunkazai hogo hō 文化財保護法
bunkazai 文化財
bunmei kaika 文明開化
bunmeibyō 文明病
bushi 武士
butsu tsugi no ma 仏次の間
butsudan 仏壇
byōryō 廟陵
chabune 茶舟
chadō 茶道
Chang'an 長安
Changchun (Jap. Chōshun) 長春
chanoyu zashiki 茶の湯座敷
Chao Fu 巣父
chashitsu 茶室
chaya 茶屋
chi 智
Chiba 千葉
chidorihafu 千鳥破風
chihōzu 地方図
chiken 地券
Chionji 知恩寺
Chiryoku 智力
Chitose ferry, or Chitose no watashi 千歳の渡し
chō (or *machi*) 町
chōgumi (or machigumi) 町組
chōka shūyō 超過収用
chokibune 猪牙船
chōnin 町人
Chōshi 銚子
Chōshū 長州
Chōshun (see Changchun)
Chūdōji 中堂寺
Chūdōji-chō 中堂寺町
Chūgenji 仲源寺
Chūō-dōri 中央通り
Chūsaku keishi chizu 中昔京師地図
chūsei 中世
Dai Nihon tetsudō senro zenzu 大日本鉄道線路全図
Daidō, see Datong
daidōgei 大道芸
daigaku 大学
Daigokuden 大極殿
Daijōsai 大嘗祭
Daimon 大門

Daimon-chō 大門町
daimyō 大名
Dainahegū 大嘗宮
dainiji chōki keikaku 第二次長期計画
Dairen (Chinese, Dalian) 大連
daraku 堕落
Datong 大同
datsua nyūō 脱亜入欧
dekasegichi 出稼地
Demizu 出水通
denmasen 伝馬船
Dentōteki kenzōbutsugun hozon chiku 伝統的建造物群保存地区
Deshima 出島
difangzhi 地方志
Dōchūki 道中記
Dōchūzu 道中図
Dōgen 道元 (1200–1253)
dōgu 道具
dokuritsu jison 独立自尊
doma 土間
Dōmiya daiku 堂宮大工
Donsu no ma 緞子の間
dosan 土産
du (Jap.: *to*) 都
Ebisu 恵比寿
Echigoya 越後屋
Edo castle, or Edojō 江戸城
Edo kai 江戸会
Edo Tōkyō Jiyū Daigaku 江戸東京自由大学
Edo 江戸
Edokko 江戸っ子
eigyō watashibune 営業渡し船
eisei 衛生
Eitai bridge, or Eitaibashi 永代橋
endō keikan keisei chiku 沿道景観形成地区
Endō Moritō 遠藤盛遠 (1139–1203)
Enomoto Buyō 榎本武楊 (1836–1908)
enoki 榎
eta 穢多
Etsu 越
Fan Chengda 范成大 (1126–93)
fangzhi 方志
fūchi chiku seido 風致地区制度
fūchi chiku 風致地区
fuchi 縁
Fuji river, or Fuji gawa 富士川
Fujieda 藤枝
Fujii Hanchi 藤井半知
Fujimi ferry, or Fujimi no watashi 富士見の渡し
Fujisan 富士山

Fujiwara no Arisuke 藤原有佐 (d. 1131)
Fujiwara no Fuyutsugu 藤原冬嗣 (775–826)
Fujiwara no Hirotsugu 藤原広嗣 (d. 740)
Fujiwara no Michinaga 藤原道長 (966–1027)
Fujiwara or Fujiwarakyō 藤原京
Fujiwara Yoshiko 藤原吉子 (dates uncertain)
Fukagawa 深川
Fukuda Shigeyoshi 福田重義 (1887–1971)
fukugen 復元
Fukuzawa Yukichi 福沢諭吉 (1835–1901)
Fun'ya no Miyatamaro 文室宮田麻呂 (dates unknown)
Funaoka 船岡
funate 船手
funbo 憤墓
furoshiki 風呂敷
Furukawa Koshichi 古川孝七 (active mid of late Meiji era)
furyoku 冨力
Fushimi 伏見
Fusō keika shi 扶桑京華志
fusuma 襖
fūzokuga 風俗画
gakumon no susume 学問のすゝめ
gamabune がま船
Ganku 岸駒 (1756–1838)
garyō 臥龍
geisha 芸者
gekokujō 下剋上, 下克上
gen'ya 原野
Genchi 源智 (1183–1238)
genkan 玄関
Genrōin 元老院
gi nengō 偽年号
Ginza 銀座
Gion goryō-e 祇園御霊会
Gion Matsuri 祇園祭
Gion Shinchi 祇園新地
Gion 祇園
Gion-machi 祇園町
Gionsha 祇園社
Godairiki 祇園社
Gofunai bikō 御府内備考
Gojō av. (-ōji, -dōri) 五条 (大路, 通)
Gojō bridge, or Gojō ōhashi 五条大橋
Gonchūbō 言注房
gonin gumi 五人組み
Gorgio Martini, Francesco, di (d. 1502)
gosanke 御三家

gosho 御所
Gotanda 五反田
goten 御殿
Gotō Shinpei 後藤新平 (1857–1929)
goyōtashi 御用達
guji (Jap. koseki) 古蹟
Gyōtoku 行徳
hagoita 羽子板
haiku 俳句
Hakone 箱根
Hamachō 浜町
Hamamatsu 浜松
han kaitai 半解体
hana 花
hanare zashiki 離れ座敷
hanare 離れ
Hangiya Shichirōbee 版木屋七郎兵衛 (dates unknown)
hanran 氾濫
Hara Hiroshi 原弘 (1936–)
Hara Sanzaaemon 原三郎左衛門 (dates unknown)
Hara 原
Haraobi no Jizō 原帯地蔵
Haraobi-chō 原帯町
hashi 橋
hashi 端し
Hashiba ferry, or Hashiba no watashi 橋場の渡し
hashike 艀
hatago 旅篭
hatamoto 旗本
Hatchōbori 八丁堀
hayabune 早舟
Hayashi Mata'ichirō 林又一郎 (dates unknown)
Hayashi Shihei 林子平 (1738–1793)
Hayashi Yoshinaga 林吉永 (end of 17th c., beg. 18th c.)
Hayashi 林
Heian capital, or Heiankyō 平安(京)
Heianjō machinamizu 平安城町並図
Heijō capital, or Heijōkyō 平城京
Heike monogatari 平家物語
Hibiya 日比谷
Higashigawa-chō 東側町
Higashi-no-Tōin 東洞院
Himeji 姫路
hinin 非人
hinoki 檜
Hirakata 枚方
Hiroshige, see Andō Hiroshige

394

Hiroshima heiwa kinen toshi kensetsu hō 広島平和記念都市建設法
Hiroshima 広島
Hishikawa Moronobu 菱川師宣 (d. 1694)
Hiyori geta 日和下駄
Hō 保
Hōjō Ujinaga 北条氏長 (1609–1670)
Hokuriku 北陸
Hokusai 北斎 (1760–1849)
Hōnen 法然 (1133–1212)
Honganji 本願寺
Hongō 本所
honjin 本陣
Honjo 本所
Honkakuji 本覚寺
Honkokuji 本国寺
honmaru 本丸
Hori-no-uchi-chō 堀之内町
Hōryūji 法隆寺
hozen 保全
hozon 保存
Huang Shigong 黄石公
Hyakumanben 百万遍
Hyappongui 百本杭
i 井
i 異
Ichijō av. (-ōji, -dōri) 一条 (大路, 通)
ichirizuka 一里塚
Ido Kizaemon chawan (Korea. Yi dynasty, XVIth. century) 井戸喜左衛茶碗
iemoto 家元
Iga 伊賀
Ihara Saikaku 井原西鶴 (1642–1693)
Iho 廬
Ike 池
Ikebe Kiyoshi 池辺陽 (1920–1979)
Ikebukuro 池袋
Ikeda Mitsumasa 池田光正 (1609–82)
Ikkoku no shuto 一国の首都
Ikuta Kizan 生田葵山 (1876–1945)
Imado 今戸
in 院
Inō Tadataka 伊能忠敬 (1745–1818)
Ippen 一遍 (1239–1289)
Ise Jingū or Ise shrine 伊勢神宮
ishi 石
Ishihara Masao (dates unknown)
Ishikawa Hideaki 石川栄耀 (1893–1955)
Ishikawa Takuboku 石川啄木 (1886–1912)
Ishikawajima 石川島
issen jōki 一銭蒸気

itajiki 板敷
Itakura Katsushige 板倉勝重 (1545–1624)
Itakura Shigemasa 板倉重昌 (1588–1638)
Itakura Shigemune 板倉重宗 (1585–1656)
Iwakura mission, or Iwakura shisetsudan 岩倉使節団
Iyo Shinnō 伊予親王 (d. 807)
Izu 伊豆
Izumi Shikibu no kofun 和泉式部の古墳
Izumi Shikibu 泉式部 (end of the 10th c., begining of the 11th c.)
Izumi 和泉
jibutsu 事物
jiin 寺院
jikaku 自覚
Jinaichō 寺内町
jing (Jap, *kyō*) 京
jinja 神社
Jinmu Tennō (Empreor) 神武天皇
jinushi no kyōyū butsu 地主の共有物
Jippensha Ikkū 十返舎一九 (1765–1831)
jishi menkyo 地子免許
jishisen 地子揃銭
jiyū minken undō 自由民権運動
Jizō Bosatsu 地蔵菩薩
jō 条
jōbōsei 条坊制
jōkamachi 城下町
jōruri 浄瑠璃
jū 住
Jurakutei, or Jurakudai 聚楽亭(第)
jūyō bunkazai 重要文化財
jūyō dentōteki kenzōbutsugun hozon chiku 重要伝統的建造物群保存地区
jūyō mukei bunkazai 重要無形文化財
Jyakuan Sōtaku 寂庵宗沢
Kabuki 歌舞伎
Kachidoki ferry, or Kachidoki no watashi 勝鬨の渡し
Kachōkin 下賜金
Kadeno-kōji 勘解由小路
Kadono 葛野
Kagura oka 神楽岡
kaibō 解剖
kaifu 開府
Kaikō Takeshi 開高健 (1930–1989)
kaiku 街衢
kaitai 解体
kaiwai keikan seibi chiku 界隈景観整備地区
kakegoya 掛け小屋
kakoi no ma 囲いの間
kakoi, or *kakoi jorō* 囲い女郎, 囲恋女郎

395

Glossary

Kakureta chitsujo 隠れた秩序
Kamakura 鎌倉
Kameyama 亀山
kami 神
Kamigyō no kamae 上京構え
Kamigyō 上京
kamikura 神座
Kamo no Chōmei 鴨長明 (1155–1216)
Kamo river or Kamo gawa 加茂川
kamuro 禿
Kan'in 閑院
Kanagawa 神奈川
kanaya 金屋
Kanazawa 金沢
kanazōshi 仮名草子
Kanda 神田
Kanegafuchi Bōseki 鐘ケ淵紡績
Kan'eiji 寛永寺
Kaneiwa Den'ichi 兼岩伝一 (1899–1970)
Kang Youwei 康有為 (1858–1927)
Kanmu Tennō (Emperor) 桓武天皇 (737–806)
Kanō Eitoku 狩野永徳 (1543–1590)
kanryō 関梁
Kansai 関西
Kantō daishinsai 関東大震災
Kantō 関東
karahafu 唐破風
karamon 唐門
karashishi 唐獅子
Karasuma av. (-ōji, -dōri) 烏丸 (大路, 通)
kasetsusei 仮設性
Kasuga Gongen Reigenki emaki 春日権現霊験記絵巻
Kasuga no tsubone 春日局
Kasuga-kōji 春日小路
katachi 形
katana gari 刀狩り
Katayama Sen 片山潜 (1859–1933)
katei no shinfūmi 家庭の新風味
Katō Akihide 加藤明英 (1652–1712)
Katō Hiroyuki 加藤弘之 (1836–1916)
Katsura Rikyū (detached imperial villa) 桂離宮
Katsura river, or Katsura gawa 桂川
Katsushika Hokusai (see Hokusai)
kawa 川
Kawachi 河内
Kawaramachi 河原町
Kawaramono 河原者
Kawara-no-in 河原院
Kawaraya 河原屋

Kazusa 上総
Kazusaya 上総屋
kegare 穢
kei 京
Keijūin 慶壽院
Keikaku kyoku dōro kachō 計画局道路課長
Keikaku kyoku 計画局
keikoku keisei 傾国傾城
keisei bettō 傾城別当
keisei 傾城
keisei-chō, or *keisei-machi* 傾城町
keiseiya 傾城屋
keishi junran shū 京師巡覧集
keishi 京師
keishiki 形式
ken 間
kenchiku kijun hō 建築基準法
kendō 県道
kenshi enkaku 建置沿革
Kenzōbutsu shūkei chiku 建造物修景地区
Kesa Gozen 袈裟御前 (dates unknown)
Ki no Tsurayuki 紀貫之 (868?–945?)
Kibi no Makibi 吉備真備 (693–775)
Kichōsha no nikki 帰朝者の日記
kimon 鬼門
Kinai 畿内
kinenbutsu 記念物
kinki shoga 琴棋書画
kinkō ryokuchi hozen kuiki 近郊緑地保全区域
Kinoshita Mokutarō 木下杢太郎 (1885–1945)
kinsei jōkaku 近世城郭
kirin 麒麟
Kitabatake Chikafusa 北畠親房 (1293–1354)
Kitahara Hakushū 北原白秋 (1885–1942)
Kitano Kami Shinchi 北野上新地
Kitano Tenmangū 北野天満宮
Kitanosha 北野社
Kiyamachi 木屋町
Kiyomizu dera 清水寺
Kobayashi Kiyochika 小林清親 (1847–1915)
Kōchi 高知
Kōda Rohan 幸田露伴 (1867–1947)
Kogen'in 光源院
Kōhakubai zu byōbu 紅白梅図屏風
Koizuka dera 恋塚寺
Kojima Yahei 小島弥平
kojō 古城

koki kyūbutsu hozon fukoku 古器旧物保存布告
koku 石
Kokua 国阿 (1314–1405)
kokudo keikaku kihon hōshin 国土計画基本方針
kokudō 国道
kokugaku 国学
Kokuhō hozon hō 国宝保存法
kokuhō kenzōbutsu 国宝建造物
kokuhō 国宝
kokumin 国民
kokutai 国体
Kōma Jinja 高麗神社
Komagata ferry, or Komagata no watashi 駒形の渡し
Komeya-chō 米屋町
kondō 金堂
Konoe (ōji/dōri) 近衛 (大路／通)
konton 混沌
Kora Tomiko 高良富子 (1896–1933)
Kose no Kanaoka 巨勢金岡 (end of the ninth century)
koseki (Chin. *guji*) 古蹟
Koseki Kenshi 小石健司
koshaji hozon hō 古社寺保存法
kōshi 格子
koshigami 腰紙
kōshimado 格子窓
Koto hozon hō 古都保存法
Kototoi bridge, or Kototoibashi 言問橋
kozashiki 小座敷
ku 区
kuge 公家
kugigakushi 釘隠し
Kujō av. (-ōji, -dōri) 九条 (大路, 通)
Kujō no yūri 九条の遊里
kukaku seiri 区画整理
kumi gashira 組頭
kumi 組
Kunikida Doppo 国木田独歩 (1871–1908)
kunimi 国見
kura 蔵, 倉
Kurama guchi 鞍馬口
Kure 呉
Kuritayama Minami-chō 栗田山南町
kurumayose 車寄せ
kuruwa 廓
Kusatsu 草津
kuse 癖
Kushi[i]nada Hime 櫛稲田姫, 櫛名田比売
Kuwabara Ichio 桑原市男 (1904–1988)

Kuwagata Keisai 鍬形恵斎 (1764–1824)
Kuwagata Shōi 鍬形紹意 (d. 1855)
Kūya 空也 (903–972)
Kyō habutae oridome 京羽二重織留
Kyō habutae 京羽二重
Kyō suzume 京雀
Kyō warabe 京童
kyō 京
Kyōbashi Ward, or Kyōbashi-ku 京橋区
Kyōgen 狂言
kyōiku chokugo 教育勅語
Kyokumokutei 曲木亭
Kyokutei Bakin 曲亭馬琴 (1767–1848)
Kyō machiya daiku 京町家大工
Kyō machiya saisei kenkyūkai 京町家再生研究会
kyōtaku 凶宅
Kyōto 京都
Kyoto (see Kyōto)
Kyōto shigaichi keikan seibi seido 京都市街地景観整備制度
Kyōto shoshidai 京都所司代
Kyōto wo mamoru kai 京都を守る会
Kyōto-shi shigaichi keikan jōrei 京都市市街地景観条例
Kyōto-shi shigaichi keikan seibi jorei 京都市市街地景観整備条例
Kyōto-shi shizen fūkei hozen jōrei 京都市自然風景保全条例
kyōyū 卿邑
Kyū Nijōjō 旧二条城
kyūeisei 久遠性
kyūshi 窮死
kyūshitsu 宮室
Kyūshū 九州
Liang Qichao 梁啓超 (1873–1929)
Liezhuan 列傳
maboroshi 幻
machi-zukuri まちづくり
machi 町, 街
machigumi 町組
machi-kōji 町小路
machishū 町衆
machiwari 町割
machiya 町屋, 町家
Made-no-kōji 万里小路
Maebashi 前橋
Maeda Gen'i 前田玄以 (1539–1602)
Maejima Hisoka 前島密 (1835–1919)
Maeno 前野
Mariko 丸子
Maru 丸

Maruyama Ōkyo 圓山応挙 (1733–1795)
Masaoka Shiki 政岡子規 (1867–1902)
Masuda (Shirō) Tokisada 増田 (四郎) 時貞, or Amakusa Shirō 天草 四郎 (1621–38)
Masugatamon 枡形 (升形, 斗形)門
matsu 松
Matsubara Nijūsankaidō 松原二十三階堂 (1866–1935)
Matsudaira Nobutsuna 松平信綱 (1596–1662)
Matsudaira Sadanobu 松平定信 (1758–1829)
Matsudo 松戸
Matsumoto 松本
Matsunaga Hisahide 松永久秀 (1510–1577)
matsuri 祭
meibutsu 名物
Meiji hyakunen kinen 明治百年記念
Meiji Tennō (Empror) 明治天皇 (1852–1912)
Meiji 明治
meiki 名木
Meireki 明暦
meiroku zasshi 明六雑誌
Meirokusha 明六社
meisho ki 名所記
meisho zue 名所図会
meisho miyakodori 名所都鳥
meishō 名勝
meisho 名所
meisho-e 名所絵 (会)
Menoke 梅木
meshimori onna 飯盛り女
metsu 滅
Meyami no Jizō 目疾地蔵
michi 道
michisuji 道筋
Mie 三重
Mieidō 御影堂
Miho-no-matsubara 三保の松原
Mikawa 参河 (三川)
Mikura-chō 御倉町
Mikuriya Takashi 御厨貴
Mimeguri Jinja, or Mimeguri shrine 三囲神社
Minaguchi 水口
Minami-ku 南区
Minamiza 南座
Minamoto no Tōru 源融 (822–895)
Minamoto no Wataru 源渡 (dates unknown)

Minamoto no Yoritomo 源頼朝 (1147–1199)
Minamoto no Yoshitsune 源義経 (1159–1189)
Minatomachi 港町
Minatosaki-machi 港先町
mine 峰
minka 民家
Mino 美濃
Minobu 身延
Mise 店
Misedana 見世棚
Miseihin 未製品
Misemono 見世物
Mishima 三島
Mita 三田
Mitamura Engyo 三田村鳶魚 (1870–1952)
mitate 見立て
Mitsui 三井
miya 宮
miyabi 雅
miyage 土産
Miyako rinsen meisho zue 都林泉名所図会
miyako 都
Miyoshi Nagayoshi 三好長慶 (1522–1564)
Miyoshi Yoshitsugu 三好義継 (d.1573)
Mizu no Tōkyō 水の東京
mizu 水
Mizuzeki 水関
mochiie sō 持家層
Momochitarukan 百千足館
Mongaku, 文学 see Endō Moritō
Mori Kōan 森幸安 (dates unknown)
Mori Ōgai 森鴎外 (1862–1922)
Mori 森
Mount Fuji, see Fujisan
mukei 無形
Mukōjima 向島
mune 棟
muradaka 村高
muragata 村形
muro 室
Muromachi av. (-kōji, -dōri) 室町通 (小路, 通)
Muromachi bakufu 室町幕府
Muromachi dono 室町殿
Musashi 武蔵
mushō 無象
Myōkakuji 妙覚寺
Myōrenji 妙蓮寺

Nagai Kafū 永井荷風 (1879–1959)
Nagakubo Sekisui 長久保赤水 (1717–1801)
Nagaoka 長岡
nagare 流れ
Nagareyama 流山
Nagasaki 長崎
Nagauta 長唄, 長歌
Nagayamon 長屋門
Nageshi 長押
Nagoya 名古屋
Naiki-no-i 内記井
Naimushō kokudo kyoku 内務省国土局
Nakagawa Kiun 中川喜雲 (1636?–1705)
Nakagyō-ku 中京区
Nakamikado-kōji 中御門小路
Nakamura Masanao 中村正直 (1832–1891)
Nakamuraya 中村屋
Naka-no-chō 中町
Nakasendō 中線道
Nakayama no michi 中山の道
Nakayama 中山
Nakazu ferry, or Nakazu no watashi 中洲の渡し
Namafu 生麩
Nanban 南蛮
Nando 納戸
Naniwa 難波
Nanzenji 南禅寺
Nara 奈良
Natsume Sōscki 夏目漱石 (1867–1916)
nawate 畷
nengō 年号
nenjūgyōji emaki 年中行事絵巻
nihinaheya 新嘗屋
Nihon fūkei ron 日本風景論
Nihon no kasō shakai 日本之下層社会
Nihonbashi 日本橋
nihonga 日本画
Nijō av. (-ōji, dōri) 二条 (大路, 通)
Nijō Castle or Nijō-jō 二条城
Nijō gosho 二条御所
Nijō Shinchi 二条新地
Nijōdai 二条第
Nijō-Horikawa 二条堀川
Nijō-yanagi-machi 二条柳町
Nijō-yanagi-no-banba 二条柳馬場
Nijū nengo no Tōkyō ２０年後の東京
nikai zashiki 二階座敷
Nikkō 日光
ningen kokuhō 人間国宝

Ni-no-maru 二丸
Nishi Honganji 西本願寺
Nishi Shin'yashiki 西新屋敷
Nishijin 西陣
Nishikawa Kōji 西川幸治 (b.1930)
nishiki-e 錦絵
Nishi-no-Tōin 西洞院
Nishioka Tsunekazu 西岡常一 (1908–1995)
Nishiyama Uzō 西山卯三 (1911–1994)
Nissaka 日坂
niwa 庭
no 野
Nobe ezu 延絵図
Noren 暖簾
Nozomashii mirai zō 望ましい未来像
O 尾
Ōbori 大堀
Oda Nobunaga 織田信長 (1534–1582)
Odawara 小田原
odoi お土居
Ōe no Masafusa 大江将匡房 (1041–1111)
Ōgi-chō 扇町
Ōgumi oya 大組 親
Ōgumigashira 大組頭
Ōhashi 大橋
Ōi river or Ōi gawa 大井川
Ōiso 大磯
Oka 岡
Okabe 岡部
Okakura Kakuzō (Tenshin) 岡倉覚三 (天心) (1862–1913)
Ōkawa 大川
Ōkawaguchi ferry, or Ōkawaguchi no watashi 大川口の渡し
Okazaki 岡崎
okiya 置屋
oku gosho 奥御所
oku mune 奥棟
oku no zashiki 奥座敷
okujochū 奥女中
Ōkura ferry 大倉の渡し
Ōmi 近江
Ōmiya (in Kyoto) 大宮
Ōmiya (in Tokyo) 近江屋
Omoide no ki 思出の記
Ōmori 大森
omote jakuya 表借家
omote mune 表棟
omoteya 表屋
omoya 主屋
Onagi canal 小名木川

Ōnakatomi no Sukechika 大中臣輔親 (954–1038)
Onari 御成
Oni dono 鬼殿
Ōnin War, or Ōnin no ran 応仁の乱
Onmyōdō 陰陽道
Ōoka Makoto 大岡信
Ōokayama 大岡山
Osaka (see Ōsaka)
Ōsaka 大阪
Ōsakaya 大阪屋
Osue 御末
Ōta Dōkan (1432–1486) 太田道灌
Ōtani Sachio 大谷幸夫 (b.1924)
Ōtemon 大手門
Otona 乙名
Oumaya ferry, or Oumaya no watashi 御厩の渡し
Oumaya 御厩
Ōwada Takeki 大和田建樹 (1857–1910)
Owari 尾張
Pan no kai パンの会
Ponto-chō 先斗町
Rakuchū ezu 洛中絵図
Rakuchū rakugai zu byōbu 洛中洛外図屏風
Rakuchū rakugai zu 洛中洛外図
rakuchū 洛中
rakugai 洛外
Rakuyō meisho shū 絡陽名所集
Rangaku 蘭学
Rashōmon 羅城門
Reizei av. 冷泉 (小路)
Rekishiteki fūdo hozon chiku 歴史的風土保存地区
Rekishiteki fūdo tokubetsu hozon chiku 歴史的風土特別保存地区
Rekishiteki ishō kenzōbutsu 歴史的意匠建造物
Rekishiteki keikan hozen shūkei chiku 歴史的景観保全修景地区
renwu 人文
ridō 里道
risō 理想
risshin shusse 立身出世
Roji 路地
Rōjumon 老中門
Roku-chō 六町
Rokugō 六郷
Rokuhara 六原
Rokuhara-mitsuji 六波羅蜜寺
Rokujō-misuji 六条三筋
Rokujō-misuji-machi 六条三筋町
Rokujō-no-in 六条院
Rokujō-yanagi-machi 六条柳町
Rokuon'in 鹿苑院
rōnin 浪人
Ryōgawa-machi 両側町
Ryōgoku bridge 両国橋
Ryōgokubashi station 両国橋駅
Ryōsen 霊山
ryūdō 流動
sabi 錆び, 寂
Sadame watashibune 定め渡し船
Saga 嵯峨
Sagami 相模
Saiankoku no Tōkyō 最暗黒之東京
saisei 再生
Saitama 埼玉
sajiki 桟敷
saka 坂
Sakai Tadakiyo 酒井忠清 (1624–1681)
Sakai Toshihiko 堺利彦 (1871–1933)
Sakai 堺
Sakamoto 坂本
sake 酒
Sakujō watashibune 作場渡し船
Sakura-chō 桜町
Sakura-no-Baba 桜の馬場
Sakyō 左京
Samisen, see Shamisen
Sanchuan 山川
Sangaku 山岳
Sanjō av. (-ōji, -dōri) 三条 (大路, 通)
Sanjō bōmon dono 三条坊門殿
Sankin kōtai 参勤交代
San-no-maru 三丸
Sanshirō 三四郎
Santō Kyōgen (1761–1816) 山東京伝
San'yabori 山谷堀
Sapporo 札幌
Sarashina 更級 lady (XIth c.)
Saru Genji 猿源氏
sato 里
Satsuma 薩摩
Sawara Shinnō 早良親王 (750–785)
Sawaragi-chō 椹木町
Sei Shōnagon 清少納言 (b.965?–d.1021~1027)
Seiganji 誓願寺
Seikatsu kichi no kōsō 生活基地の構想
seikatsu taikoku 生活大国
Seikatsu toshi 生活都市
seikatsuken 生活圏
Seishin'in 誠心院

Seitaiji 清帯寺
Sekai 世界
Sekigahara, 関ヶ原
Sekino Masar 関野克 (b. 1909)
Sen no Rikyū 千利休 (1522–1591)
Sengoku jidai 戦国時代
Senju 千住
Sensai fukkō kukaku seiri jigyō kuiki 戦災復興区画整理事業区域
Sensai fukkō shi 戦災復興史
Sensaichi fukkō keikaku kihon hōshin 戦災地復興計画基本方針
Sentaku 川澤
Sento 遷都
Sesshū Kamishimo-gun 攝州上下郡
Seta Katsuya 瀬田勝哉
Seto 瀬戸
Settsu 摂津
shakai 社会
shamisen 三味線
sharebon 洒落本
shi nengō 私年号
shi 志
Shiba Yoshimasa 斯波義将 (1350–1410)
Shiba 芝
Shibake 斯波家
Shibuya 渋谷
Shichijō av. (-ōji, -dōri) 七条 (大路, 通)
Shichijō Shinchi 七条新地
shichikyō 七竅
Shiga Shigetaka 志賀重昂 (1863–1927)
Shigaichi keikan kyōtei 市街地景観協定
Shigaichi keikan seibi jōrei 市街地景観整備条例
Shigaika chōsei kuiki 市街化調整区域
Shigyō hachimon (sei) 四行八門 (制)
Shijin sōō 四神相応
Shijō av. (-ōji, -dōri) 四条 (大路, 通)
Shijō-gawara (Shijō-kawara) 四条河原
Shijō-kawara-machi 四条河原町
shikin 而今
Shikinen zōtai 視記念造体
Shiku kaisei jōrei 市区改正条例
Shiku kaisei 市区改正
shima 島
Shimabara 島原, 嶋原
Shimabara no ran 島原乱
Shimodachiuri 下立売
Shimogoryō 下御霊
Shimogyō no kama 下京構え
Shimogyō 下京
Shimogyō-ku 下京区

Shimo-no-chō 下町
Shin Ōhashi 新大橋
Shin Yoshiwara 新吉原
Shinagawa 品川
Shinchi 新地
Shinden zukuri 寝殿造り
Shinden 寝殿
Shinjuku Gyoen 新宿御苑
Shinjuku 新宿
shinkō 信仰
Shinkyō 新京
Shinnyodō 真如堂
shinpo 進歩
shinrin 森林
Shinshōsetsu 新小説
Shinto (see shintō)
Shintō 神道
Shiogama 塩釜
Shioiri 塩入
Shirabyōshi 白拍子
Shirahige bridge 白鬚橋
Shiro no dashi 城の出し
Shirogane 白金
Shirome 白女 (dates unknown)
Shisei to shakaishugi 市政と社会主義
Shiseki meisho tennen kinenbutsu hozon hō 史跡名勝天然保存法
shiseki 史跡
shitaji mado 下地窓
Shitamachi 下町
Shizuka Gozen 静御前 (dates unknown, 12th c.)
Shizuoka Shimizu 静岡清水
shō 生
shōgun tsuka 将軍塚
shōgun 将軍
Shōiken 笑意軒
shoin-zukuri 書院造り
shoin 書院
shōji 障子
shokkata seido 職方制度
Shōkokuji 相国寺
shoshidai 所司代
Shōtei Kinsui 松亭金水 (1797–1862)
shūgaishō 拾芥抄
shuto 首都
soba 蕎麦
Sōgō sekkei seido 総合設計制度
Sōmoku 草木
son 村
sono 苑, 園
Sōrinji 双林寺

sōzō 創造
Sōzokuzei 相続税
Sudachō 須田町
Sudō Tennō (Emperor) 崇道天皇 (750–785)
Sugawara no Michizane 菅原道真 (845–903)
sugi 杉
sugoroku 双六
sukiya tsūro 数寄屋通路
sukiya-zukuri 数寄屋造り
Sumida river, or Sumida gawa 隅田川
Sumida-ku 墨田区
Sumitomo 住友
Sumiya hozonkai 角屋保存会
sumiya 角屋
Sumiyoshi Taisha 住吉大社
Sumpu 駿府
sumu 住む
Suruga 駿河
Surugadai 駿河台
Suzaku av., or Suzaku-ōji 朱雀大路
Suzaku 朱雀
Suzanoo no Mikoto 素戔嗚尊, 須佐之男命
Suzuki Shun'ichi 鈴木俊一 (b. 1910)
ta 田
Tachibana no Hayanari 橘逸勢 (d. 842)
Tago-no-ura 田子の浦
Taian 待庵
Taika 大化
Taimensho 対面所
Taira 平
Takamura Kōtarō 高村光太郎 (1883–1956)
Takase River, or Takasegawa 高瀬川
Takase Shin'yashiki 高瀬新屋敷
Takasebune 高瀬船
Takayama Eika 高山英華 (1910–1999)
Take Motō 武基雄 (b. 1911)
take 岳
Takechō ferry 竹町の渡し
Takehara Kōbee 竹原好兵衛 (dates unknown)
Takeya ferry 竹屋の渡し
Takeya Tetsugorō 竹屋鉄五郎 (dates unknown)
taki 瀧
Takizawa Mayumi 滝沢真弓 (1896–1983)
tami 民
Tamura Akira 田村明 (b. 1926)
Tanba 丹波
Tanba-guchi 丹波口

Tange Kenzō 丹下健三 (b. 1913)
Tango 丹後
Tani Bunchō 谷文晁 (1763–1840)
tani 谷
Tanizaki Junichirō 谷崎潤一 (1886–1965)
tatami 畳
Tatebe Katahiro 建部賢弘 (1664–1739)
Tatekawa 立川
Tatenaosu 建て直す
tayū 太夫
Tayū-chō 太夫町
teikoku 帝国
teisenzu 帝全図
teito 帝都
tenjin 天神
tennen 天然
Tennōji-ku 天王寺区
Tenryū River, or Tenryūgawa 天龍川
tenshu 天守
Tenshukaku 天守閣
tenson 天孫
tento 奠都
Terajima 寺島
Tera-machi 寺町
Tianzhi 田職
Toba no koi-zuka 鳥羽恋塚
tofu 都府
Tōge Sankichi 峠三吉 (1917–1953)
tōge 峠
Tōin Kinkata 洞院公堅 (1291–1360)
Tōin Sanehiro 洞院実煕 (b. 1409)
tokai 都会
Tōkaidō bungen ezu 東海道分間絵図
Tōkaidō bungen nobe ezu 東海道分間延絵図
Tōkei 東京
Tokiwabashi 常盤橋
tokonoma 床の間
toku 徳
Tokubetsu hozen shūkei chiku 特別保全修景地区
Tokubetsu rekishiteki fūdo hozon chiku 特別歴史的風土保存地区
Tokubetsu toshi keikaku hōkōfu 特別都市計画法公布
Tokugawa Hidetada 徳川秀忠 (1578–1632)
Tokugawa Ietsugu 徳川家継 (1709–1716)
Tokugawa Ieyasu 徳川家康 (1542–1616)
Tokugawa Tsunayoshi 徳川綱吉 (1646–1709)

Tokugawa Hidetada 徳川秀忠 (1578–1632)
Tokugawa Iemitsu 徳川家光 (1604–1651)
Tokugawa Ietsuna 徳川家綱 (1641–80)
Tokugawa Ieyasu 徳川家康 (1542–1616)
Tokugawa Mitsukuni 徳川光圀 (1628–1700)
Tokugawa Tadanaga 徳川忠長 (1606–1633)
Tokugawa Yoshikatsu 徳川慶勝 (d. 1883)
Tokugawa Yoshinao 徳川義直 (1600–50)
Tokugawa 徳川
Tokuryoku 徳力
Tokutei gaiku 特定街区
Tokutomi Rōka 徳富蘆花 (1868–1927)
Tōkyō 東京
Tokyo (see Tōkyō)
Tōkyō annai 東京案内
Tōkyō hyakunen kinen 東京百年記念
Tōkyō no Parika 東京のパリ化
Tōkyō ryokuchi keikaku 東京緑地計画
Tōkyō shiku kaisei kyūsekkei 東京市区改正旧設計
Tōkyōshi to shakai shugi 東京市と社会主義
Tōkyōto keikaku kyoku toshi keikaku kachō 東京都計画局都市計画課長
Tōkyō-to 東京都
tomin 都民
Tone river or Tone-gawa 利根川
ton'ya ba 問屋場
ton'ya 問屋
Torifuda 鳥札
torii 鳥居
tōriniwa 通庭
Tosa 土佐
toshi keikaku hō 都市計画法
Toshi kenkyū kai 都市研究会
Toshi kōron 都市公論
toshi no shisō 都市の思想
toshi sōsaku 都市創作
Toshikeikaku Aiichi chihō iinkai 都市計画愛知地方委員会
Toshikeikaku an 大東亜整地祝際都市計画案
Toshikeikaku dōri 都市計画通り
toshizu 都市図
Tōshōgū 東照宮
Tōtōmi 遠江
Toyohashi 豊橋
Toyotomi Hideyoshi 豊富秀吉 (1536–1598)
tsubo niwa 坪庭
Tsuchikabe 土壁

Tsuchimikado av. 土御門大路
tsuga 栂
tsuka 塚
Tsukadajima 佃島
tsuke shoin 付け書院
Tsukishima ferry 月島の渡し
Tsukuba mount 筑波山
Tsukuda ferry 佃の渡し
Tsune (no) gosho 常御所
Tsuta-no-hosomichi 蔦の細道
tsutsumi 堤
Tsuun maru 通運丸
Ubusunagami 産土神
Uchida Yoshifumi 内田祥文 (1913–1946)
Uchida Yoshikazu 内田祥三 (1885–1972)
Ueno 上野
Ue-no-chō 上町
Uesugibon rakuchū rakugai zu byōbu 上杉本洛中洛外図屏風
ujigami 氏神
ukareme 浮女
ukihashi 浮橋
ukiyo-e 浮世絵
Ukyō 右京
Umaya bridge, or Umayabashi 厩橋
ura jakuya 裏借家
ura kimon 裏鬼門
ura nagaya 裏長屋
Urabe Kenkō 卜部兼好 (between 1283? and 1352?)
Urabe no Kaneyoshi (see Urabe Kenkō)
Utsu-no-yama 宇津の山
utsutsumi 現身
wabi 詫び
wafū 和風
waka 和歌
Wakasa 若狭
waki honjin 脇本陣
Wakkanai 稚内
Waseda 早稲田
wasen 和船
Watanabe Shigeru 渡辺滋 (dates unknown)
Watari yagura mon 渡り櫓門
wuchan 物産
Wujun zhi 呉郡志
Xu Yu 許由
Xuanju 選擧
Yada Sōun 矢田挿雲 (1882–1961)
yagura 櫓
yakatabune 屋形船
yakusha 役者
Yakushiji 薬師寺

yama 山
Yamaguchisai 山口際
Yama-no-i-tei 山井亭殿
Yama-no-te 山の手
Yamashina Tokitsugu 山科言継 (1507–1579)
Yamashiro meiseki junkō shi 山城名跡巡行志
Yamashiro meishō shi 山城名勝志
Yamashiro 山城
Yamato av. or Yamato-ōji 大和大路
Yamato 大和
Yamato-e 大和絵
Yanagi Sōetsu 柳宗悦 (1889–1961)
Yanagi-machi 柳町
yange 沿革
Yasaka Jinja 八坂神社
yashiki 屋敷
yashiro 社
Yasui Seiichirō 安井誠一郎
Yatsubashi 八橋
Yebisu 恵比寿
yiwen 藝文
Yodo River, or Yodogawa 淀川
yōga 洋画
Yokohama 横浜
Yokoyama Gennosuke 横山源之助 (1871–1915)

Yōmeimon 陽明門
Yoroi ferry 鎧の渡し
yorozuro 万代
Yosa Buson 與謝蕪村 (1716–1783)
Yoshida hill 吉田山
Yoshida Kenkō 吉田兼好 (1283?–1350?)
Yoshida Tōgo 吉田東伍 (1864–1918)
Yoshiwara 吉原
Yōshūfu shi 雍州府志
Yūami 祐阿弥
yudi 輿圖
Yūjo kabuki 遊女歌舞伎
yūjo 遊女
Yūkaku 遊廓
yūkei 有形
yūkun 遊君
Zaimoku-chō 材木町
Zaji 雑記
zashiki 座敷
zatsu 雑
Zen 善
zenbi 善美
zenkaitai 全解体
zentei 前庭
Zhang Liang 張良
Zhiguan 職官
Zhuangzi 荘子
Zōjōji 増上寺

Index

Adams, Thomas 337
Age of Warring States 41, 43
ageya 77, 80, 82, 83, 95, 97
Aichi 315
aijō 301
Akasaka 110, 181, 215, 231, 236, 302
Akisato Ritō 181
akusho 158
Akutagawa Ryūnosuke 208, 220, 223, 225, 227, 230
Alberti, Battista 303
Ama no ukihashi 210
Amakusa 76
Ama no hashidate 158
Ameyami 163
anniversaries
   Edo 300th anniversary 234, 237
   Edo Tokyo 400th anniversary 234, 243, 249, 250, 251, 252
   Greater Tokyo 500th anniversary 234, 235, 243, 244, 245, 248, 251
   Kyoto 1100th anniversary 3, 23
   Kyoto 1200th anniversary 359
   2600th imperial anniversary 234, 242, 243, 245, 249, 254
   Meiji centennial 243, 245, 246, 247, 248
   Tokyo centennial 234, 245, 247, 248, 252
Andō Hiroshige 138, 144, 146, 188, 221, 389
aobyōshi 140, 142, 146, 148
Aogai no ma 95

Aoshima Yukio 251
Arai Hakuseki 117, 138
architectural freedom 67, 90, 94
architectural heritage 30, 31, 367
Arima Yoriyasu 213
Ariwara no Narihira 209
aruki miko 70
Asada Takashi 327
Asai Ryōi 167
Asakusa 119, 209, 210, 214, 223, 323, 325
Asano Kiyoshi 265
Ashihara Yoshinobu 304
Ashikaga shoguns,
   Ashikaga Yoshiaki 9, 11, 41, 42, 46, 51–64, 74, 385
   Ashikaga Yoshiharu 43, 62
   Ashikaga Yoshiteru 9, 41–47, 49–52, 54, 55, 56, 58, 61–64, 385
asobi 275
asobime 70
Asuka 334
Atake ferry 218, 220, 221
Azuchi 60, 62, 64
Azuma bridge 214, 221, 223

Baishun bōshi hō 82
bakufu 8, 12, 20, 71, 76, 82, 97, 102, 103, 105, 106, 109, 111–121, 124, 125, 130, 178, 181, 184
bakufu dōchū bugyōsho 181
bansho 140, 141, 148
Bellamy, Edward 288, 303

Berlin 287
bijin 188
bijon 310, 333
bikan chiku 348, 352, 363, 373
bikuni 70
Bluntschli, Johann Kaspar 304
bō 5
boat-houses 212, 222
Böckmann, Wilhelm 312
bōka chiku 378
Bōsō hantō 119, 142
Bōsu 227
bridges,
  construction of 217, 220
  crowds on 222
  maintenance of 219
Bueijin-chō 46, 60
Buei-tei 43, 46, 47, 62, 63
bugyō 11
buke shohatto 120
buke yashiki 12, 19
Bunkachō 350
bunkazai 31, 86, 265, 269
Bunkazai hogo hō 31, 348
bunmei kaika 173, 292
bunmeibyō 293
bushi 91
butsu tsugi no ma (butsuji no ma) 88
butsudan 89, 369
byōryō 156

capital
  meaning of, 33, 293–294
  move of 22, 237, 241
capital city 5, 33, 229, 241, 286,
  289–296, 298, 309, 322, 388
cartography, *see* topographical
  representation
castle
  Azuchi castle 385
  compounds, 46
  early modern, 61
  Edo castle 103, 112–113, 117–118,
    119, 124, 131, 134, 136, 138, 141,
    142, 143, 144, 183, 237, 239, 243
  fortifications 44, 56–60
  Fushimi castle 103, 119
  horse riding grounds 50, 58
  medieval 41–42
  Nijō castle 12, 14, 42, 52, 53, 55–63,
    74, 76, 116, 165, 363
castle town, *see jōkamachi*
chabune 213
chadō, or *sadō* 92, 269

Chang'an 5, 6
Changchun 316
chanoyu zashiki 85
Chao Fu 131
chaos (chaotic city) 42, 289, 291, 292,
  295, 299, 304, 342
chashitsu, or tea house 80, 92, 98, 144,
  178, 222, 231, 269, 270
chaya 77, 80, 85, 178
chi 301
Chiba 29
chidorihafu 137
chihōzu 176
chiken 21
Chinese geomancy 5
chiryoku 294, 298
Chitose ferry 216, 218, 221, 222, 223
chō, or block 5, 7, 11, 17, 44, 54, 74, 76,
  77, 83, 105, 146, 158, 163, 164,
  168, 195, 219, 287, 369
chōka shūyō 313
chokibune 212, 213
chōnin 19, 143, 144, 163
Chōshi 222
Chōshū 21
Christaller, Walter 339
Chūdōji 76, 77
Chūgenji 163
Chūō-dōri (av.) 103
Chūsaku keishi chızu 163
city planning, *see* urban planning
clan deity, *see ujigami*
Cocks, Richard 101
collective memory, or urban memory 7,
  14, 29, 32, 153, 154, 159, 165, 167,
  185, 196, 287, 388, 389, 391
conservation, *see hozon*
Copenhagen 100
courtesan 67, 70, 71, 76, 77, 80, 86, 88,
  89, 95, 97, 143

Dai nihon tetsudō senro zenzu 194
daidōgei 71, 75
daigaku 250, 289
Daigokuden 23
Daijōsai 32
daimon 77
daimyō 9, 10, 15–21, 43, 58, 59, 60, 61,
  63, 71, 101, 109, 111, 113, 117,
  118, 120, 122, 129, 130, 131, 133,
  137, 139, 140, 141, 143, 144, 146,
  148, 176, 177, 178, 183, 184, 204,
  237, 302, 388
Dainahegū 263

Index

dainiji chōki keikaku 249
Dairen 316
daraku 289, 296
Datong 317, 325
datsua nyūō 253
daxue (Jap. *daigaku*) 289, 298
dekasegichi 82
Demizu 53, 54
denmasen 213
dentōteki kenzōbutsugun hozon chiku 348, 374
Deshima 101, 108, 117
difangzhi 155
discrimination, *see* social discrimination
Dōchūki 177, 185, 188, 192, 195, 197, 203
dōchūzu 176, 177, 178, 389
Dōgen 276
dōgu 268
dokuritsu jison 297
doma 86, 368
dōmiya daiku 371
Donsu no ma 91
du 33
Duke of Zhou 133

Early modern period 1, 3, 4, 10, 11, 14, 15, 34, 67, 68, 74, 101, 108, 115, 116, 154, 159, 165, 167, 209, 213, 219, 236, 371, 385, 386, 390
earthquakes
  Great Kantō earthquake (1923) 26, 218, 244, 251, 311, 314
  Kobe earthquake (1995) 372, 390
Ebisu 342
Echigoya 12, 20
Edo 1, 2, 4, 7, 9–22, 33, 34, 61, 62, 74, 76, 77, 100–103, 105, 106, 109, 111–124, 129, 130–134, 136–144, 146, 148, 154, 173, 177–180, 183, 184, 202, 203, 208, 210, 213, 217, 219, 220, 227–243, 248–253, 283, 285, 287, 289, 290, 291, 295, 299, 300, 389
Edo,
  as castle town, 17
  commerce in, 17, 20
  defenses of, 16, 19, 122
  founding of, 14, 119
  layout of, 16–17, 19, 121, 130
  popular culture in, 143–148, 291
Edo castle, *see* castle
Edo kai 238
edokko 130, 143, 144, 295

Edozu byōbu 106, 134, 136, 137, 138, 139, 148
eigyō watashibune 215
eisei 295
Eitai bridge 229
Ende, Hermann 312
endō keikan keisei chiku 353, 373
Endō Moritō 164
enoki 178
Enomoto Buyō 238
entertainment 8, 12, 69, 70, 74, 75, 80, 84, 86, 110, 111, 213, 214, 217, 219, 222, 236, 240, 241, 250
eta 75
etsu 156

famous places, *see meisho*
Fan Chengda 156
fangzhi 155, 156
ferries 208, 209, 210, 212–218, 222–227, 230, 231, 389
ferry services,
  regulation of 214, 226
  numbers across Sumida 215–216, 224–225
floods 225
Florence (Firenze) 219
fortresses 9, 11, 41–43, 44, 51, 52, 57, 61–63, 76, 122
Foucault, Michel 172
Frois, Luis 44, 50, 51, 53, 54, 56
fuchi 156
fūchi chiku 347, 357, 363, 373
fūchi chiku seido 373
Fujimi ferry 220, 221
Fujisan 178, 180, 188, 200, 334
Fujiwara family
  Fujiwara no Arisuke 158
  Fujiwara no Fuyutsugu 158
  Fujiwara no Hirotsugu 164
  Fujiwara no Michinaga 168
  Fujiwara Yoshiko 164
Fujiwara capital, or Fujiwarakyō 5, 6
Fukagawa 224, 225, 325
Fukuda Shigeyoshi 313
fukugen 258
Fukuzawa Yukichi 200, 253, 297, 302, 303
Fun'ya no Miyatamaro 164
Funaoka 5
funate 120
funbo 156
furoshiki 383
Furukawa Koshichi 223

407

Index

furyoku 294, 298
Fushimi 12, 21, 58, 97, 103, 111, 124, 164, 353, 357
Fushimi castle, *see* castle
Fusō keika shi 155, 156
fusuma 91
fūzokuga 137, 138

Gakumon no susume 297
gamabune 213
Ganku 91
garyō 86
gatehouses 19, 129, 130, 131, 139, 140, 141, 143, 144, 146
gazetteers, (*see also meisho ki, meisho zue*) 155–156
Geddes, Patrick 334
geisha 77, 88, 95, 213, 222, 239
gekokujō 102
genkan 88
genrōin 313
geographical margins 69
gi nengō 236
Ginza 287, 312, 321, 323, 325, 327
Gion goryō-e 163
Gion shinchi 76, 80–82
Gion-machi 76, 80–82, 163
Gionsha 162
Giorgio Martini, Francesco, di 303
global city 251, 252
globalization 300
godairiki 213
Gofunai bikō 210
Gojō avenue 373
gokaidō 176, 181, 183, 196, 204
Gonchūbō 59
gonin gumi 106
gosanke 113, 118
gosho 32, 49, 50, 57, 63
Gotanda 323
goten 49, 54
Gotō Shinpei 26, 313
goyōtashi 17
Greater East Asian Co-prosperity Sphere 243
green areas, urban parks 290, 311, 312, 315, 316, 319, 321, 323, 327, 330, 338, 358
guji (Jap. *koseki*) 156
Gutschow, Konstanty 259, 268, 272, 338, 342
Gyōtoku 223

hagoita 146

haiku 180, 203
Hakone 121, 199
Hall, John W. 3
Hamachō 218, 221
Hamamatsu 110
Hamburg, 100
hanare zashiki 85, 89
Hangiya Shichirōbee 178
han-kaitai 264
Hanoi 286
hanran 291
Hara Hiroshi 360
Haraobi no jizō 163
hashi, see bridges
hatago 110
Hatchōbori 223
hayabune 222
Hayashi Mata'ichirō 74
Hayashi Shihei 203
Hayashi Yoshinaga 97
Hearn, Lafcadio 270
Hegemann, Werner 334
Heian capital, or Heiankyō 5, 105, 154, 164, 209
Heian-jō machinami zu 15
Heijō capital, or Heijōkyō 5, 6
Heike monogatari 164
Hibiya 105, 146, 287, 312, 327
Higashigawa-chō 163
Higashi-no-tōin 49, 53, 55, 58, 158
Higashiyama hills 163, 164, 353, 357, 359, 363, 374
highways 5, 17, 20, 23, 34, 103, 108–112, 173, 176–178, 183, 184, 192, 196, 215, 230, 339
Himeji 42, 57
hinin 69, 75
hinoki 178, 262, 274, 372
Hiroshige, *see* Andō Hiroshige
Hiroshima 234, 253, 310, 318, 321, 322, 327, 328, 330, 331, 332, 333, 336, 342, 343
Hishikawa Moronobu 138, 178
Hiyori geta 229
hō 6
Hōjō Ujinaga 178
Hokuriku 103
Hokusai 143, 185, 187
Hōnen 162
Honganji 76, 131, 133, 364
Hongō 325, 327
honjin 183
Honkakuji 43, 44
Honkokuji 45, 51, 53, 57, 59

honmaru 122
Hōryūji 265
Howard, Ebenezer 288, 303, 313, 337, 338
hozen (preservation) 347, 348, 350, 358, 373
hozon (conservation) 2, 30, 31, 257–261, 265, 268, 269, 271, 272, 275, 317, 347, 348, 350, 351, 353, 357, 358–365, 373–375, 390
Huang Shigong 131
human buffer zone 105
Hundun Emperor 291
Hyakumanben 162
Hyappongui 221

Ichijō avenue 154
Ichirizuka 17
iemoto 268, 274
Ihara Saikaku 205
iho 264
Ikebe Kiyoshi 327
Ikebukuro 323
Ikeda Mitsumasa 117
Ikkoku no shuto (One nation's capital) 23, 283, 284, 287–293, 298, 299, 301, 304
Ikuta Kizan 301
imado 218, 224
imperial family 163, 166, 235, 239, 243
imperial palace 5, 6, 7, 23, 32, 91, 118, 154, 163, 237, 238, 240, 263, 325, 363
industrialization 26, 173, 208, 283, 285, 299
Inō Tadataka 190
Ippen 162
Ise shrine 260, 262, 264, 272, 273, 274
Ishihara Masao 319
Ishikawa Hideaki 309, 314, 318, 322
Ishikawa Takuboku 227
Ishikawajima 218, 224
issen jōki 223, 230
itajiki 368
Itakura Katsushige 12
Itakura Shigemasa 97
Itakura Shigemune 12, 71, 74
Iwakura mission, or Iwakura shisetsudan 312
Iyo Shinnō 164
Izu 227
Izumi 52, 164, 165
Izumi Shikibu 164, 165
Izumi Shikibu no kofun 164

Jiang Liang 131
jibutsu 289
jiin 156
jikaku 289, 296, 298, 304
jinaichō 3, 77
jing (Jap. *kyō*) 33
Jinmu Tennō (Emperor) 243
jinushi 226
jinushi no kyōyū butsu 226
Jippensha Ikkū 181, 188
jishi menkyo 17
jishisen 11
jiyū minken undō 288, 303
jō 5, 105
jōbōsei 5, 368
jōkamachi (castle towns) 3, 9, 10, 11, 15–17, 34, 42, 43, 61, 74, 103, 183, 386, 387, 388, 390
jōruri 75, 97
jū 257
Jurakudai 11, 14, 61, 64, 74
Jūyō dentoteki kenzōbutsugun hozon chiku 348
jūyō mukei bunkazai 269

kabuki 75, 97, 136, 159, 188, 239
Kachidoki ferry 216, 226
Kadeno-kōji 45, 46, 47, 53, 54, 55, 56, 58, 60, 63, 64, 65
Kadono 4, 5
Kaempfer, Engelbert 19, 20, 100, 101, 102, 106–111, 113, 117, 118, 121, 122, 125
Kagura-oka 168
Kaikō Takeshi 30
kaiku 156
kaitai 274
kaiwai keikan seibi chiku 357, 373
kakegoya 75
kakoi 80, 92
kakoi jorō 80
kakoi no ma 92
Kamakura 16, 33, 119, 348
Kamakura shogunate 70, 118, 119, 368
Kameyama 110
Kamigamo shakemachi 350
Kamigyō 8, 42, 46, 49, 50, 59, 60, 62, 65, 374
Kamigyō no kamae 8
Kamo no Chōmei 257, 264
Kamo river 4, 5, 11, 69, 71, 75, 353, 359, 363, 365
kamuro 80
Kan'in 158

409

Index

Kanagawa 29
Kanazawa 15, 103, 125, 347, 348, 365
kanazōshi 157, 167
Kanda 325
Kanegafuchi Bōseki 224
Kan'eiji 130, 239, 253
Kaneiwa Den'ichi 315
Kang Youwei 288, 299, 303
Kanmu Tennō (Emperor) 164
Kanō Eitoku 138
Kanō painting 137, 138
kanryō 156
Kansai 285
Kantō 15, 16, 17, 111, 119, 129, 213, 285, 313, 314
Kantō earthquake, *see* earthquake
karahafu 122, 131, 137, 141, 148
karamon 131, 133, 140
Karasuma avenue 46, 47, 53, 54, 56
kasetsusei 263
Kasuga gongen reigenki emaki 368
Kasuga no tsubone 50
Kasuga-kōji (av.) 46, 53, 54
Katachi 262
katana gari 103
Katayama Sen 302, 303
Katei no shinfūmi 303
Katō Akihide 103
Katō Hiroyuki 292, 297, 298
Katsura Rikyū (detached imperial villa) 93, 269
Katsushika Hokusai, *see* Hokusai
kawa 156
Kawachi 52
Kawaramachi 82, 154
kawaramono 71
Kawara-no-in 157, 168
Kazusaya 20
kegare 263
Keijūin 44, 62
keikoku keisei 97
keisei 76, 91, 97, 373
keisei bettō 97
Keisei-chō, or Keisei machi 76, 81, 82, 91, 159
keiseiya 77
keishi 11, 156, 163
Keishi junran shū 155
Kenchiku kijun hō 365
Kenkō, *see* Urabe Kenkō
Kensetsu kijun hō 378
kenshi enkaku 155
kenzōbutsu shūkei chiku 353, 373
Kesa Gozen 164

Ki no Tsurayuki 159
Kibi no Makibi 164
kimon 17
Kinai 17
kinenbutsu, *see* monument
kinki shoga 133
kinkō ryokuchi hozen kuiki 358
Kinoshita Mokutarō 227, 228
kirin 131
Kitabatake Chikafusa 102
Kitahara Hakushū 227
Kitano Kami Shinchi 81, 82
Kitano Tenmangū 162, 163
Kiyamachi 154
Kiyomizu dera 351
Kobayashi Kiyochika 208, 221
Kobe earthquake (1995), *see* earthquake
Kōchi 42
Kōda Rohan 23, 214, 221, 283–299, 301, 304
Kofun period 116
Kōhakubai zu byōbu 91
Koki kyūbutsu hozon fukoku 30
Kokua 162
kokudō 195
kokugaku 180
kokuhō 31, 265, 269
Kokuhō hozon hō 31
kokuhō kenzōbutsu 269
kokumin 294
kokutai 294
Komeya-chō 154
Konoe avenue 49, 53, 58
konton 291, 292, 303
konton mushō 291
Kora Tomiko 329
Kose no Kanaoka 158
koseki 155, 302
Koshaji hozon hō 30, 268
kōshi 87, 351, 364, 365, 369
koshigami 270
Kototoi bridge 214
kozashiki 50
kuge 4
kugikakushi 91
Kujō avenue 70
Kujō no yūri 70
kukaku seiri (land readjustment) 28, 313, 314, 315, 316, 317, 319, 321, 322, 325, 333
kumi 107, 371
kumi gashira 107
Kunikida Doppo 301

kunimi 180
kura 8, 368
Kurashiki 348
Kure 329
kurumayose 122
Kusatsu 110
kuse 262
Kushinada Hime 163
Kuwabara Ichio 329
Kuwagata Keisai 185, 204
Kuwagata Shōi 185, 204
Kūya 162, 168
Kyō habutae 155, 157
Kyō habutae oridome 157
Kyō suzume 155, 156, 167
Kyō warabe 155, 156, 157, 159, 162, 163, 164, 165, 168
Kyōbashi ward 226
kyōgen 75
kyōiku chokugo 237
Kyokumokutei 92
Kyokutei Bakin 80
kyōtaku 158
Kyoto 1–4, 7–17, 20–23, 29–34, 41–43, 46, 49, 51–54, 58–63, 67–76, 80, 82, 85, 86, 90, 92, 95, 97, 100, 105, 109–111, 116, 118, 131, 137, 138, 162, 168, 177, 185, 192, 199, 202, 203, 209, 230, 236, 237, 241, 253, 287, 340, 347–367, 375, 378, 379, 382–388
Kyoto,
  as castle town 9
  as modern city 23
  commerce in 7, 12
  cultural heritage in 31–32, 353, 357, 365, 370–371
  defenses of 9
  founding of 2
  layout of 5–9, 11
  population of 7–8, 12
  urban landscape 367, 373–374
Kyoto Hotel 359, 361, 363
Kyoto Mitate association 382
Kyōto shigaichi keikan seibi seido 373
Kyōto shoshidai 4
Kyoto station building 358, 359, 360, 361, 373
Kyoto-shi keikan machizukuri sentâ 384
Kyōto-shi shizen fūkei hozen jōrei 358
kyūeisei 263
Kyūshi 301
Kyushu 75, 97, 162

landscape zones 347, 357, 363
Le Corbusier (Edouard Jeanneret-Gris) 228, 325, 327, 337
Liang Qichao 288, 303
liezhuan 156
London 101, 118, 238, 240, 245, 249, 250, 285
London bridge 219
Louis XIII 112
Louis XIV 112
Lowenthal, David 258

maboroshi 310
machigumi 369
Machi-kōji 46, 53, 59
machishū 369, 371
machiwari 106
machiya 7–9, 14, 26, 31, 85, 86, 90, 92, 350, 357–372, 374, 375, 377–379, 382, 383
machizukuri 300, 342
Maebashi 321
Maeda Gen'i 11
Maejima Hisoka 238
Maeno 110
maps, *see* topographical representations
Marseilles 100
Maruyama Ōkyo 91
Masaoka Shiki 221
Masuda (Shirō) Tokisada 97
matsu (pine tree) 178, 372
Matsubara Nijūsankaidō 302
Matsudaira Nobutsuna 97
Matsudaira Sadanobu 23, 203
Matsudo 222
Matsumoto 42, 57, 178
Matsunaga Hisahide 44, 51
matsuri 8
medieval times 1, 3, 4, 6–8, 41, 42, 52, 62, 68–70, 76, 87, 219, 243, 269, 371
meibutsu 188
Meiji centennial, *see* anniversaries
Meiji era 14, 21, 30, 32, 33, 83, 172–175, 189, 191–194, 195, 196, 199, 200–202, 223, 226, 235, 246, 253, 267, 269, 311, 327, 342, 347, 370
Meiji restoration 82, 237, 240, 245–249, 283, 285, 288, 300
Meiji Tennō (Emperor) 246
meiki 156
Meireki fire (1657) 17, 19, 112, 113, 115, 122, 133, 134, 217, 244

Meirokusha 297
meisho, or famous places 3, 14, 87, 92, 134, 137, 144, 146, 153–159, 162, 164, 165, 167, 177, 180, 181, 185, 199, 203, 204, 389
meishō 31
meisho ki 154–157, 164
Meisho miyakodori 156
meisho zue 92, 154–157, 181
meisho-e 137
memory, *see* collective memory
menoke 110
meshimori onna 110
metsu 257
Mexico 286
Meyami no jizō 163
michi 77, 156, 295
michisuji 77
Mieidō 162, 168
Miho-no-Matsubara 177
Mikawa 15, 65
Mikura-chō 159
Mill, John Stuart 297
Mimeguri shrine 212
Minaguchi 110
Minamiza 97
Minamoto family,
    Minamoto no Tōru 157
    Minamoto no Wataru 165
    Minamoto no Yoritomo 119, 209
    Minamoto no Yoshitsune 70
Minatomachi 3
Minatosaki-machi 76
minka 270, 371
Mino 52, 108
mise 8, 85, 87
misedana 368
miseihin 291
misemono 75
Mishima 181
Mita 80, 325
Mitamura Engyo 15
mitate 144
Mitsui 12, 204
miya 156
miyabi 371
miyage 155
miyako 4, 6, 80, 92, 110
Miyako rinsen meisho zue 87, 89, 92
Miyoshi Yoshitsugu 44
mizu 156, 304
Mizu no Tōkyō 214, 221, 304
mizuzeki (water barrier) 120
mochiie sō 369, 370

modernization 23, 196, 246, 250, 267, 268, 283, 284, 285, 287, 288, 292, 293, 295, 297, 298, 299, 304, 327, 358, 362, 364, 383
Momochitarukan 378
Mongaku, *see* Endō Moritō 165
monuments 3, 7, 23, 29, 30, 115, 116, 133, 146, 153, 165, 166, 167, 241, 258, 259, 274, 286, 329, 334, 359, 360, 362, 385, 388, 389
Mori Kōan 163
Mori Ōgai 302
Moscow 285
mount Fuji, *see* Fujisan
mukei 289
Mukōjima 212, 224, 230
Mumford, Lewis 334
mune 85, 86
muradaka 176
muragata 176
muro 274
Muromachi avenue 8, 46, 47, 50, 51, 52, 55, 60
Muromachi dono 43
Muromachi period 43, 70, 270, 275
Muromachi shogunate 42, 47, 51
Musashi 209
Myōkakuji 43
Myōrenji 383

Nagai Kafū 208, 210, 223, 224, 225, 227, 228, 229, 290, 304
Nagakubo Sekisui 202
Nagaoka 4, 321
nagare 272
Nagareyama 222
Nagasaki 101, 106, 108, 321
nagauta 240
nagayamon 140, 141, 146
Nagoya 15, 29, 120, 314, 315, 319, 321, 322
Naiki-no-i 158
Nakagawa Kiun 159
Nakagyō-ku 154, 163, 164
Nakamikado-kōji 46
Nakamura Masanao 297, 298
Naka-no-chō 74
Nakasendō 181, 202
Nakayama 177
Nakazu ferry 224, 231
namafu cuisine 383
nanban 176
nando 88
Naniwa 158

Index

Nanzenji 43
Nara (capital, city) 5, 164, 199, 286, 334, 348
Nara conference of authenticity 259
nationalism 238, 283, 286, 299
Natsume Sōseki 174, 301
Nawate 156
nengō 235, 236, 237, 246
Nenjūgyōji emaki 368
New York 249
nihinaheya 263
Nihon fūkei ron 205
Nihonbashi 17, 115, 196
nihonga 190
Nijō avenue 74, 154
Nijō castle, *see* castle
Nijō Shinchi 81, 82
Nijō-Horikawa 12
Nijō-yanagi-machi 74
Nijō-yanagi-no-banba 74
nikai zashiki 85
Nikkō 116, 131, 133, 239
ningen kokuhō 269
ni-no-maru 113
Nishi Honganji 131, 133, 164
Nishi Shin'yashiki 75, 77, 97
Nishijin 162, 353, 383
Nishikawa Kōji 2, 350
nishiki-e 189
Nishi-no-tōin 76
Nishioka Tsunekazu 265
Nishiyama Uzō 29, 310, 319, 322, 333, 336, 337, 338, 339
niwa 85, 86
Noh 32, 117, 275, 378
noren 368

ōbori 63
Oda Nobunaga 9, 11, 34, 51, 52, 53, 56, 58, 59, 60, 61, 65, 74, 109, 385, 386
Odawara 16, 17, 119
odoi 11, 71, 75, 76
Ōe no Masafusa 70
ōgumi gashira 106
ōgumi oya 106
Oi river 178
Okabe 110, 242
Okakura Kakuzō (Tenshin) 275
Ōkawa 208, 223, 231
okiya 84, 95
oku mune 86, 90
oku no zashiki 85, 89
Okura ferry 220, 221
Ōmi 20, 43, 52, 60, 62, 65, 103

Ōmori 323
omote jakuya 369
omote mune 90
omoteya 376
omoya 376
Onagi canal 223, 231
Ōnakatomi no Sukechika 158
onari 130, 138
One nation's capital, see Ikkoku no shuto
Ōnin no ran, or Ōnin war 8, 42, 43, 47, 157
onmyōdō 5
Ōokayama 325
Osaka 1, 4, 10, 12, 15–17, 20, 22, 26, 31, 82, 101, 109–111, 120, 213, 219, 230, 247, 287, 319, 321, 386
Ōsakaya 84
osue (reception hall) 50
Ōta Dōkan 119, 243, 244
Ōtani Sachio 327, 331, 343
Ōtemon 113, 122
otona (machi headman) 106, 107, 108
Oumaya ferry 217
Ōwada Takeki 205
Owari 51, 52, 118

pan no kai 227
Paris 15, 67, 112, 113, 115, 118, 121, 204, 238, 240, 245, 249, 250, 285–287, 304, 312, 313
parks, *see* green areas
Peace park (Hiroshima) 322, 327, 331, 332, 333, 342
Perry, Clarence 337
pilgrimage 108, 109, 162, 181, 195, 204, 205
place Dauphine 112, 115
place Vendôme 112
planners, *see* urban planning
pleasure district 67, 71, 75, 76, 77, 81, 86, 92, 159
Ponsonby-Fane, Richard 3
Ponto-chō 68
population growth 100–102
post stations, post towns 108–112
prostitution 68, 69, 70, 71, 74, 75, 76, 77, 80, 81, 82, 111, 159, 222, 387

railways 26, 63, 82, 172–175, 189, 190, 191, 192, 194–200, 204, 205, 220, 239, 316, 317, 339, 360
rakuchū rakugai zu byōbu 12, 49, 59, 60, 71, 137, 138, 154, 185, 368
rangaku 176

413

Rashōmon 5
Reichow, Hans Bernhard 338
rekishiteki ishō kenzōbutsu 357
rekishiteki keiken hozen shūkei 353
rekishiteki keikan hozen shūkei chiku 373
renwu 156
rickshaws 215, 220, 223, 224
ridō (country road) 195
Riegl, Alois 165, 166, 259, 261
risō 298
risshin shusse 284
roji 85, 378
Rokugō bridge 230
Rokuhara 162
Rokuhara-mitsuji 162, 168
Rokujō-misuji 71, 74, 75, 83
Rokujō-no-in 158
Rokujō-yanagi-machi 74
Rome 33
rōnin 75
Rousseau, Jean-Jacques 297
ruins 45, 63, 76, 97, 158, 166, 258, 265, 268, 329, 332
Russo-Japanese War 226, 240, 286
ryōgawa-machi 8
Ryōgoku bridge 212, 217, 219, 220, 221, 222, 223, 225
Ryōsenji 162

sabi 275
Sadame watashibune 214
sadō, *see chadō*
Saga 45, 146
Saga Toriimoto 350
Sagami 209
Saint Augustine 276
St. Petersburg 118
saisei 373
Saitama 29
sajiki 368
Sakai 114, 117, 218
Sakai Tadakiyo 117
Sakai Toshihiko 303
Sakamoto 108, 362
sake 17, 50, 53, 59, 111, 162, 213
Sakujō watashibune 215
Sakura-no-baba 58, 60, 63, 65
Sakura-chō 159
Sakyō 5
samisen 222
sanchuan 156
sangaku 156
Sanjō avenue 154
Sanjō bōmon dono 43, 347

sankin kōtai 16, 109, 129, 176, 285, 295
Sanneizaka 350, 351
san-no-maru 113
Sanshirō 301
Santō Kyōgen 143–144
sanzan 357
Sapporo 223
Sarashina lady 209
Saru genji no sōshi 71
Satsuma 21
Sawara Shinnō 164
Sawaragi-chō 54
Schumacher, Fritz 311
Screens of the capital and its surroundings, *see rakuchū rakugai zu byōbu*
Sei Shōnagon 270, 275
Seiganji 164, 168
Seikatsu kichi no kōsō 336
seikatsu taikoku 251
seikatsu toshi 251
Seishin'in 164
Seitaiji 163
Sekigahara 101, 109, 120, 385
Sekino Masaru 317
Semper, Gottfried 304
Sen no Rikyū 275
Sengoku jidai, *see* Age of the Warring States
Senju 216, 217, 223, 225
Sensai fukkō shi 321
sento 241
Seta Katsuya 46
Settsu 52
sharebon 143
shi nengō 236
Shiba 47, 62, 130, 156
Shiba Yoshimasa 47
Shibuya 323, 325, 341
Shichijō Shinchi 81, 82
shichikyō 291, 292
Shiga Shigetaka 205
shigaichi keikan kyōtei 357
shigaichi keikan seibi jōrei 351
shigaika chōsei kuiki 358
shigyō hachimon sei 105, 368
shijin sōō 5
Shijō avenue 76, 82
Shijō-gawara 12, 75, 159
shikin (instant) 276
shikinen-zōtai 262
shiku kaisei jōrei 313
Shimabara 12, 71, 75, 76, 77, 80, 81, 82, 83, 86, 90, 92, 94, 95, 97, 110, 116, 159, 387
Shimodachiuri 53, 54

414

Shimogoryō 163
Shimogyō 8, 42, 46, 49, 50, 51, 59, 60, 62, 154, 159, 168, 374
Shimogyō no kamae 8
Shin Yoshiwara 77, 143
Shinagawa 21, 111, 119, 325
shinden 368
shinden-zukuri 94, 372
Shinjuku 321, 323, 325, 341
Shinjuku Gyoen 325
shinkō (faith) 298
Shinkyō 317
Shinnyodō 45, 47, 52, 54, 64
shinpo (progress) 289
Shiogama 158
Shioiri 216, 218, 224, 225
shirabyōshi 70
shiro no dashi 52, 61
Shirogane 325
Shirome 70
Shiseki meishō tennen kinenbutsu hozon hō 31
shitaji mado 92
shitamachi 129, 130, 136, 144, 148
Shizuka Gozen 70
shōgun tsuka (zuka) 164, 165
shogunal city 130, 134, 148, 233
Shōiken 269
shoin 91, 92
shoin-zukuri 91, 92, 94, 372
shōji 98, 270
shokkata seido 371
Shōkōbō 57
Shōkokuji 43, 45
Shōwa era 21, 192
Shūgaishō 157, 158, 159, 165, 167, 168
shuto 33, 292, 293, 295, 296
Simmel, Georg 284, 302
Sino-Japanese War 240, 286
Smiles, Samuel 297
soba (noodles) 226
social discrimination 12, 67, 75, 94
sōgō sekkei seido 359
Sōrinji 162
sōzō (zones) 373
sōzokuzei 375
Sudō Tennō (Emperor) 164
Sugawara no Michizane 162, 164
sugoroku 187, 194, 197, 204
Sui dynasty 5
sukiya tsūro 85
sukiya-zukuri 93, 94
Sumida river 19, 209, 212, 213, 217, 222, 223, 227, 230, 323

Sumida-ku 209, 221
Sumiya ageya 82, 83, 86, 87, 90, 91, 92, 93, 94, 95, 97
Sumiya hozon-kai 84, 97
Sumiyoshi Taisha 114
Suruga 15, 119
Surugadai 325
Suzaku avenue 5
Suzuki Shun'ichi 249

Tachibana no Hayanari 164
Tago-no-ura 177
Taian 269
Taika 108
taimensho 44, 50
Taira 162, 168
Takamura Kōtarō 227
Takase canal (river) 154
Takase Shin'yashiki 75
Takasebune 213
Takayama Eika 317, 321, 327, 343
Take Motō 321
Takechō ferry 214, 217
Takehara Kōbee 97
Takeya ferry 208, 210, 213, 214, 215
Takeya Tetsugorō 210
Takizawa Mayumi 319
Tamura Akira 119
Tanba 52, 76, 82
Tang dynasty 5
Tange Kenzō 310, 317, 321, 322, 327
Tango 70
Tani Bunchō 203
Tanizaki Jun'ichirō 227
tatami 91, 270, 369
Tatebe Katahiro 202
Tatekawa canal 222, 223
tatenaosu 264
Taut, Max 329
tayū 71, 77, 80, 84
tea ceremony, *see chadō*
tea-house, *see chashitsu*
teikoku 296
teito 29, 245, 286
tenjin 80, 162
tennen 31
tenshu (kaku) 56–58, 61, 134, 136–139
tenson 264
tento 241
Terajima 210, 218
Thunberg, Charles Peter 213
tianfu 156
Toba no koi-zuka 164
Tōge Sankichi 329

Tōin Kinkata 157, 158
Tōin Sanehiro 157, 158
tokai 285
Tōkaidō 15, 16, 20, 21, 103, 109, 111, 138, 172, 173, 176, 177–189, 192, 196, 202, 204, 205, 360, 389
Tōkaidō bunken nobe ezu 181, 184
tōkei 253
Tokiwabashi 113
tokonoma 91, 92, 275, 369
tokubetsu hozen shūkei chiku 353
tokubetsu rekishiteki fudō hozon chiku 358
Tokugawa period 4, 7, 14, 20–23, 34, 75, 82, 84–86, 91, 93, 103, 111, 114, 116, 129, 133, 134, 138, 139, 153, 154, 157, 167, 172–181, 188–196, 199, 200–205, 208, 213, 214, 216, 226, 236, 253, 269, 270, 275, 323, 369, 371
Tokugawa rule 19, 102, 130, 133, 388
Tokugawa shoguns,
  Tokugawa Hidetada 12, 109, 136
  Tokugawa Iemitsu 109, 130, 133, 134, 136, 137, 139
  Tokugawa Ienobu 117, 138
  Tokugawa Ietsugu 138
  Tokugawa Ietsuna 117
  Tokugawa Ieyasu 12, 15, 17, 33, 61, 62, 63, 65, 74, 101, 105, 109, 117, 119, 120, 129, 130, 237, 290
  Tokugawa Mitsukuni 118
  Tokugawa Tadanaga 136, 137
  Tokugawa Tsunayoshi 117, 124
  Tokugawa Yoshikatsu 118
  Tokugawa Yoshinao 118
tokuryoku (power of virtue) 294, 298
tokutei gaiku 360
Tokutomi Rōka 301
Tokyo 1, 2, 15, 21–33, 82, 119, 141, 148, 192, 196, 199, 202, 208, 214, 215, 218–230, 233–235, 238–254, 283–300, 302, 304, 309, 311–315, 317, 318, 322, 323, 325, 342, 359, 362, 385, 388, 389, 390
Tokyo,
  as capital 236–237, 241–242
  as imperial capital 22, 286, 289
  as modern city 287, 290, 299
  as organism 294–296
  as world city 29, 249, 300
  growth of 29, 285
  foundation of 240
  industrialization of 208, 209, 210, 224–225

planning in 26, 287, 294–296, 312, 314, 316, 322–327
Tōkyō annai 218, 222
Tokyo centennial, *see* anniversary
Tokyo Metropolitan Government 231, 233, 243, 246, 247, 300, 304, 325
Tōkyō no parika 286
Tōkyō ryokuchi keikaku 316
tomin 296
Tone river 119, 120
Tönnies, Ferdinand 288, 303, 304
ton'ya 177, 178, 183, 204
ton'ya ba 183
topographical representation 21, 75, 77, 97, 103, 138, 154, 158, 167, 172, 175, 176, 177, 181, 183–185, 187–192, 194–197, 199, 200–204, 216, 221, 225, 299, 389
Toranomon 144
torifuda 107
torii 115
tōriniwa 86, 88
Tosa 21
Tosa painting 137
Toshi keikaku hō 26, 314, 319, 358
Toshi kenkyū-kai 315
Toshi kōron 315
Toshi sōsaku 315
toshikeikaku dōri 330
toshizu 176
Tōshōgū 131, 133, 136, 239
Tōtōmi 15
town-house, *see machiya*
Toyotomi Hideyoshi 9, 10, 11, 12, 14, 15, 16, 34, 60, 61, 71, 74, 75, 76, 102, 103, 104, 109, 119, 120, 385, 386
transport,
  coastal 213
  river 213, 217, 220, 222
  travel 108–112, 173, 175, 178, 180–181, 187, 188–201
tsubo niwa 88
tsuchikabe 269
Tsuga 372
tsuke shoin 91
Tsukishima ferry 214
Tsukuda ferry 226, 227

Ueno 23, 136, 141, 239, 253, 323, 327
Uesugibon rakuchū rakugai zu byōbu 63
ujigami 8
ukareme 70
ukihashi 209

416

ukiyo-e 19, 129, 130, 138, 143, 144, 148, 177, 178, 181, 185, 188, 191
Umaya bridge 217, 220
Unwin, Raymond 314
Urabe Kenkō 165
Urabe no Kaneyoshi (*see* Urabe Kenkō)
ura jakuya 369, 378
ura nagaya 369
urban landscape 6, 30, 31, 42, 43, 45, 49, 61, 111, 164, 302, 338, 347, 348, 350, 351, 353, 357, 366, 373, 374, 386, 387, 388
urban planning, or city planning 4, 8, 9, 11, 68, 74, 76, 94, 105, 112, 116, 286, 291, 299, 300, 302, 305, 309–316, 319, 321, 322, 325, 330, 331, 332, 334, 336, 337, 338, 342, 343, 347, 348, 368, 373, 377, 386, 390, 391
urbanization 101–104
Usui Kōsaburō 46
Utida Yosifumi 317, 325
Utida Yosikazu 317
utsutsumi 264

vandalism 30
Vienna 285
Vivero y Velasco, Rodrigo, de 101, 121

wabi 275
wafū 94
waka 156
Wakasa 52
Wakkanai 321
Waseda 325
wasen 226
Watanabe Shigeru 330
watari yagura mon 121
Weber, Max 284
wooden structure 378
world city 30, 234, 238, 243, 249, 250, 251, 252, 253, 254, 300
World Heritage (UNESCO) 259, 274
World War II 96, 234, 243, 244, 246, 253, 268, 309, 311, 318, 319, 334, 342, 343, 347, 348, 367, 370–372, 379
wuchan 156
Wujun zhi 156

Xu Yu 131
xuanju 156

Yada Sōun 15
yagura 52, 56, 121
yakatabune 213
yakusha 188
Yakushiji 268
Yamaguchisai 262
Yamano'i-tei 158
Yamashina Tokitsugu 44, 46, 50, 52, 57, 58, 64
Yamashiro meiseki junkō shi 155
yamato-e 137
Yamato-ōji 75
Yanagi Sōetsu 271, 275
yange 156
Yasaka Jinja 162
yashiki 75, 113, 302
Yasui Seiichirō 244
Yazaki Takeo 2, 4, 285
Yebisu 342
yiwen 156
yōga 189
Yokohama 76, 311, 313
Yokoyama Gennosuke 302
Yōmeimon 131, 133
Yosa Buson 91
Yoshida hill 165
Yoshida Kenkō, *see* Urabe Kenkō
Yoshida Tōgo 46, 64
Yoshiwara 76, 77, 212, 222, 387
Yōshūfu shi 155
yudi 156
yūjo 67, 70
yūjo kabuki 136
yūkaku 77, 80, 81, 97
yūkei 289
yūkun 71
Yumoto Fumihiko 45

Zaimoku-chō 154
zashiki 63, 85, 89
zenbi 294, 295
zen-kaitai 264
zentei 86, 88
zhiguan 156
Zhuangzi 291
Zōjōji 136, 239

HARVARD-YENCHING LIBRARY

This book must be returned to the Library on or before the last date stamped below. A fine will be charged for late return. Non-receipt of overdue notices does not exempt the borrower from fines.